Raus

DM 18.—

€ 9,10

DM 18.—

€ 9,10

Secret Southern Africa

Muckleneuk, an old colonial homestead on Durban's Berea which houses three famous Africana collections (see page 148).

Secret Southern Africa

Wonderful places you've probably never seen

AA The Motorist Publications (Pty) Limited Cape Town

First edition © 1994 AA The Motorist Publications (Pty) Limited

ISBN 1-874912-08-4

Secret Southern Africa was edited and designed by AA The Motorist Publications (Pty) Limited, 130 Strand Street, Cape Town 8001

Editor Vincent Leroux
Researcher and indexer Judy Beyer
Picture researcher Rose-Ann Myers
Project co-ordinator Carol Adams
Writers Ted Botha, Katharine Butt, Owen Coetzer, Jill Cooke, Ellen Fitz-Patrick, Jane-Anne Hobbs, Brian Johnson Barker, Peter Joyce, John Kench, Di Paice, Lan Reid, Nicky Schwager, Al Venter, Annelize Visser

The publishers would like to thank the following individuals and organisations for their assistance in obtaining the information for this book:

Beth Peterson, African Images; Air Zimbabwe; Trevor Barrett; Shawn Benjamin; Bredasdorp Shipwreck Museum; Captour; Clanwilliam Information Office; Contour National Nature Conservation and Tourism Board, Ciskei; Trevor Dearlove; Department of Agriculture and Forestry, Venda; Department of Wildlife, National Parks and Tourism, Botswana; Durban Unlimited; Dr Isaac Bailie, Genadendal Museum; George Museum; Grahamstown Publicity Association; Duncan Greaves; Manie Grobler; Knysna Publicity Association; KwaZulu Bureau of Natural Resources; Ladysmith Siege Museum; Lesotho Tourist Board; Harry Locke; Messina Information Bureau; Ministry of Wildlife Conservation and Tourism, Namibia; Mozambique National Touring Company; Natal Parks Board; National Museum, Monuments and Art Gallery, Botswana; National Parks Board; Olifants River and West Coast Tourism; Oudtshoorn Publicity Association; Rita van Wyk, Potchefstroom Museum; Qwa Qwa Tourism and Nature Conservation Corporation; Ted Reilly; Pam McFadden, Talana Museum; Transkei Development Corporation; United Touring Company; University of Natal Campbell Collections; Zimbabwe Tourist Board.

Front cover photograph: Two hikers make their way between the towering walls of Sesriem Canyon, Namibia (see page 276).
Back cover photograph: Rustic accommodation with spectacular bushveld views is available at the Chizarira National Park in Zimbabwe (see page 294).

Wonderful places you've probably never seen

Are you tired of sharing a beach with 10 000 other people, bored with the same old holiday venues and Sunday drives, or fed up with having your walks in the country ruined by an endless paper chase of other people's litter?

If you answer 'yes' to these questions, you're ready for SECRET SOUTHERN AFRICA, an entirely new kind of guide book that concentrates on the off-beat, unusual, quiet and largely unknown parts of southern Africa.

Fortunately, there are still plenty of places of great beauty, tranquillity or interest that have not yet been spoilt. Additionally, there are many secrets hidden within our cities – waiting to be explored at weekends, or even during a lunchtime office break. You may already have heard of one or more of them – or even visited some – but for the most part these pages contain information about wonderful places you've never seen.

SECRET SOUTHERN AFRICA has selected 137 of these, scattered from Cape Agulhas in the southern Cape to Ibo Island in the north of Mozambique, each chosen as a worthwhile destination for exploring, driving, walking, riding or just relaxing.

How the book is organised

The book contains 137 two-page colour spreads, each featuring a 'secret' destination. Included on each of these pages are two special information panels: 'Where to stay' and 'At a glance' – the latter providing useful details, such as how to get there, weather conditions, what to do, special attractions, and where to get further information. (Please note that changes in regional government may affect some of these information entries.)
Where a destination falls within a major city or town, the weather section in the 'At a glance' panel, and the whole 'Where to stay' panel, are omitted.

If you have a particular interest – such as fishing, bird-watching or hiking – you will find a handy chart at the end of the book (page 310) that provides you with an immediate visual overview of all the places at which you can indulge your individual hobby or interest.

HARARE

BULAWAYO

FRANCISTOWN

BEIRA

WINDHOEK

WALVIS BAY

GABORONE

PIETERSBURG

NELSPRUIT

PRETORIA

JOHANNESBURG

MBABANE

MAPUTO

UPINGTON

BLOEMFONTEIN

MASERU

DURBAN

EAST LONDON

PORT ELIZABETH

CAPE TOWN

GEORGE

ATLANTIC
OCEAN

INDIAN
OCEAN

CONTENTS

How to find your 'secret' destination

1 Look at the map on the opposite page (or the list below) and locate the region you need.
2 Turn to the page indicated, where you will find a detailed map and contents list of the region.
3 Select a place on the map or list, and then turn to the page indicated for a full description of this destination.

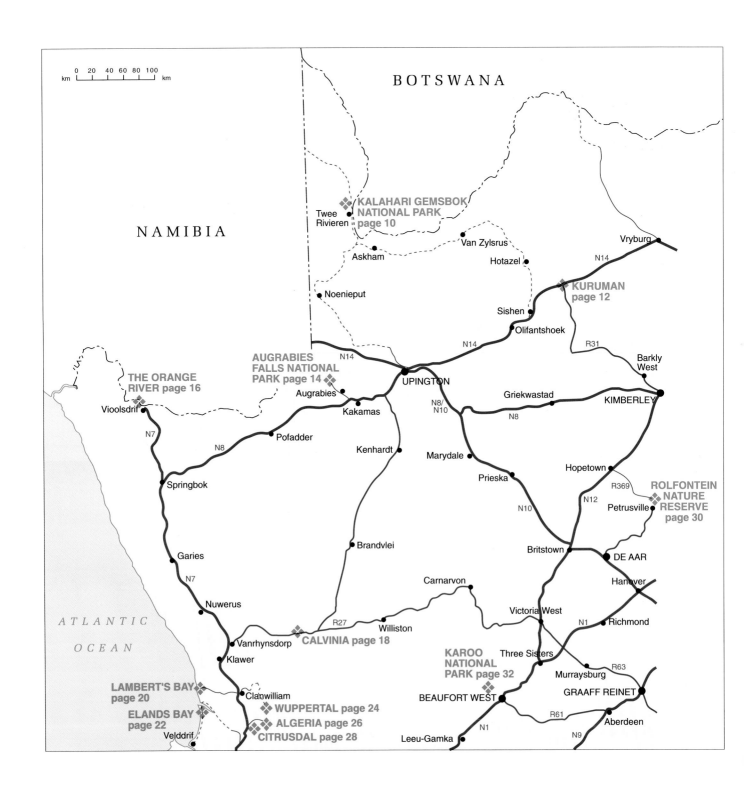

BOTSWANA

NAMIBIA

KALAHARI GEMSBOK
NATIONAL PARK
page 10

Twee
Rivieren

Van Zylsrus

Vryburg

Askham

Hotazel

N14

Noenieput

KURUMAN
page 12

Sishen

Olifantshoek

N14

N14

AUGRABIES
FALLS NATIONAL
PARK page 14

THE ORANGE
RIVER page 16

UPINGTON

Griekwastad

R31

Barkly
West

Augrabies

KIMBERLEY

Vioolsdrif

Kakamas

N8/
N10

N8

N7

Pofadder

Kenhardt

Marydale

Hopetown

ROLFONTEIN
NATURE
RESERVE
page 30

N8

Springbok

Prieska

R369

N12

Petrusville

N10

Garies

Brandvlei

Britstown

DE AAR

N7

Nuwerus

Carnarvon

Hanover

R27

Williston

Victoria West

N1

Richmond

ATLANTIC

CALVINIA page 18

OCEAN

Vanrhynsdorp

Three Sisters

KAROO
NATIONAL
PARK page 32

Murraysburg

R63

Klawer

LAMBERT'S BAY
page 20

Clanwilliam

GRAAFF REINET

ELANDS BAY
page 22

WUPPERTAL page 24

BEAUFORT WEST

ALGERIA page 26

R61

Aberdeen

Velddrif

CITRUSDAL page 28

Leeu-Gamka

N1

N9

NORTHERN/WESTERN CAPE

A million hectares of wildlife wonderland

One of the world's most extensive unspoilt ecosystems supports a timeless, wild paradise – the Kalahari Gemsbok National Park

A lion and a sand dune may seem like an unusual combination, but in this park it's very much the norm.

IN THE VAST UPPER REACHES of the northern Cape, wedged between Namibia and Botswana, lie the warm red dunes of the Kalahari Gemsbok National Park. The largest nature conservation area in southern Africa, the park extends way into Botswana, and is home to large concentrations of predators, antelope and numerous species of smaller wildlife.

Since it was proclaimed in 1931, this park has become known among wildlife enthusiasts, both locally and abroad, as one of the most rewarding reserves to visit. It has succeeded in retaining its unique wilderness aura, thus offering the visitor one of the most pristine experiences of the African bush that he is ever likely to have.

The watercourses of two ancient rivers, the Auob to the west and the Nossob to the east, form the boundaries of the South African portion of the park. The rivers rarely flow, but boreholes punctuate the river beds and provide a basic water supply for the thousands of animals and birds that the area supports. These boreholes not only sustain life in times of prolonged drought, but also fulfil a protective function – predators are less likely to stray beyond the safe boundaries of the park.

The well-graded roads within the park chart the courses of the two river beds, offering visitors a close passage past the waterholes and the large attendant populations of game and bird life.

The park is a mecca for bird lovers, with more than 200 species recorded. The spectacle of bird-filled skies during the rainy season in January and February draws professional photographers from all over the world, and the comfortable caravan set-ups of resident researchers and film crews in the campgrounds testify to the abundance and stability of the game populations.

Sightings of a lion kill or cheetah hunt are common, and the animals, unspoilt by an excess of human attention as in other game parks, have been known to satisfy their curiosity for the two-legged species by staring through the windows of stationary vehicles for hours at a time. In the crispness of an early desert morning this can be an unforgettable experience, and you'll be aware of the privilege of the place and the foresight of those who created such a resource.

One of the pioneer traders to venture into this wild hinterland was Christoffel le Riche. Le Riche was the forebear of the park's first warden, Johannes le Riche – and today it is run by Elias le Riche making it an unbroken chain of family management spanning three generations.

The area was finally protected by proclamation in the early Thirties, but by that time had become

Where to stay

The rest camps are Twee Rivieren (at the entrance to the park), Mata Mata and Nossob. All three camps offer family cottages (two double bedrooms, kitchen and bathroom); self-contained huts (up to four beds, kitchen and bathroom); and ordinary huts (up to four beds with access to a shared kitchen and shared bathroom). Bedding, towels and cooking and eating utensils are provided. Each camp has a camping and caravan site with braai and washing-up facilities and an ablution block. Petrol is available at all the camps. There are small shops selling firewood, tinned groceries, cool drinks, wine, spirits and beer. However, meat, butter and cheese are available only at Twee Rivieren. (This camp has the most modern facilities and the only restaurant and swimming pool.)

Twee Rivieren rest camp.

The early morning rays of the sun fall on a small herd of springbok making its way across the bone-dry bed of the Nossob River.

pathetically depleted of the vast herds that had once roamed the region. Strong measures were introduced to curb poaching, new game were introduced, and gradually the herds began to flourish again.

Today the park has three rest camps for visitors – Twee Rivieren at the entrance gate, Mata Mata to the north west on the Auob riverbed, and Nossob to the north on the Nossob River course.

Twee Rivieren offers sophisticated self-catering bungalows for visitors, a shop, a restaurant and a tranquil camp site. The most welcome facility is the swimming pool, a lifesaver after the long drive on sand roads to the park or a day's game viewing in the palpable heat. The snack bar adjoined to the restaurant provides very inexpensive breakfasts and sells excellent fresh bread.

But the more rustic Mata Mata and Nossob, bordering Namibia and Botswana respectively, are where you should go for a real sense of the place, and to see impressive concentrations of game and bird life. While there are comfortable bungalows at all sites, the camping areas offer excellent basic facilities and there is only the unobtrusive but sturdy electrified fence to separate you from the shifting splendour of the wilderness.

You'll soon settle into a gentle rhythm of early visits to the waterholes to watch the morning's absorbing activities unfold, and then back to camp before noon for a break from the heat and the now soporific animals (very likely to include you). Afternoons are best spent blissfully inert in a cool place before the waterholes are visited again before sunset. The rest camps themselves offer good viewing of smaller game in the cool of the evening – mongoose, the shy honey badger or jackal. And it's very likely you'll see the unmistakable spoor of leopard around the camp in the morning.

The expansive star-lit nights are a treat for city dwellers. But do try to visit the park at full moon. Moonrises are spectacular over this part of the veld, and early dawn is memorable – the glowing orb of the emerging sun balanced with the pale splendour of the moon.

A dusty, double highway – flanked by a solitary, nest-filled tree – threads its way through the rolling hills of the reserve.

The Kalahari Gemsbok National Park at a glance (map page 8)

How to get there: From the south: Approach the park via Upington, which is 825 km from Cape Town via Vanrhynsdorp and Calvinia, or some 950 km via Springbok and Pofadder.

There are several roads leading north between Kakamas and Upington (including the popular route via Lutzputs and Noenieput), but for the least wear and tear it would be best to take the partly tarred route from Upington. The road is not clearly signposted. Take the R360 out of Upington and at the crossroads just north of the town take the road marked Askham (don't take the N14 route to Namibia). After some 88 km of tar, the road forks. At the fork you leave the tar and, keeping right, take the Askham road, which 'rollercoasts' for 50 km over small dunes until another fork is reached. Keep right and after 64 km you'll reach a T-junction. Turn right – back onto the R360 – and continue for 23 km until the road forks. Keep left, on the R360. You will pass the Motel Molopo less than 1 km after the fork, and reach the Twee Rivieren gates 62 km past the motel.

From the north: Travel via Kuruman, which is 540 km from Johannesburg. The tar ends at Hotazel, 61 km beyond Kuruman, and from there the R31 heads west for 263 km. Pass through Vanzylsrus (where there is a hotel) and Askham before joining the R360 near the Motel Molopo. The distance from Johannesburg is 926 km, of which 325 km is dirt road.

Access is not permitted in the area located between the park and Namibia at Mata Mata and Union's End.

There are landing strips for light aircraft at the Twee Rivieren, Nossob and Mata Mata rest camps, but landing permission must be obtained in advance. Cars can be hired by booking in advance through Avis at Twee Rivieren. Phone the park by dialling 0020 and then asking for Gemsbok Park 901.

Weather: Summers are hot and dry, except for possible rainfall in January and February. Winter days are warm but the temperature frequently falls below freezing at night. The park is open all the year round, but the best time for viewing game is from February to May.

What to do: Game and bird viewing. Species commonly seen include lion, cheetah, spotted and brown hyena, gemsbok, red hartebeest, blue wildebeest, eland, steenbok, springbok, black-backed jackal, honey badger, bat-eared fox, ground squirrel and suricate. Lucky visitors may also see leopard, Cape fox and caracal. Giraffe have recently been successfully reintroduced into the park. Eight giraffe brought in from Etosha are housed in a large camp in the dunes north of the Craig Lockhart windmill near Mata Mata. There are more than 200 species of birds.

Special attractions: Predators and raptors, semi-desert landscape photography.

Special precautions: Visitors are advised to take a course of anti-malaria tablets before entering the park. When going for a drive, take water and emergency rations in case you have a breakdown. Stick to the route you have outlined on leaving the rest camp – if you have a problem, the rangers will reach you more quickly.

More information: Contact the National Parks Board at either of the following offices: Pretoria: PO Box 787, Pretoria 0001; tel (012) 3431991. Cape Town: PO Box 7400, Roggebaai 8012; tel (021) 222810.

Oasis at the crossroads of the Kalahari

Once a base for journeys of discovery into the remote interior, the prosperous town of Kuruman rises like a mirage out of the arid plains of the northern Cape

A HUNDRED AND FIFTY YEARS AGO it took an ox-wagon eight days to reach Kuruman from Kimberley, the closest town. Nowadays it's a two-hour drive, yet Kuruman retains its frontier appeal. Established by missionaries, this outpost was once the starting point for some of the great expeditions which opened up the continent. A reason for choosing this godforsaken place was the iridescent Eye – a unique fountainhead where 20 million litres of pure spring water streams daily from a subterranean dolomite cavern with little regard for seasonal fluctuations. Even during times of severe drought the flow, which is the source of the Kuruman River, barely wavers.

The largest freshwater fountain in the southern hemisphere, perhaps in the world, the Eye provides all Kuruman's domestic, industrial and irrigation needs. The area has been developed into an attractive park with rolling lawns, willows and palms.

In 1824, Robert Moffat of the London Missionary Society set up a mission station here and, under his guidance, Kuruman became the best known mission station in Africa, with the Eye becoming known as the 'fountain of Christianity'.

Within a year of his arrival, Moffat had learnt seTswana and began teaching the local population to read and write – he believed in literacy as a foundation of evangelisation. Later he undertook the her-

Rustic materials, such as indigenous wood, thatch and stone, are the keynotes of the Moffat Mission church.

culean task of translating the Bible into seTswana – a task that spanned 40 years. Moffat's early years were difficult and dispiriting. Marauders roamed the countryside, occasionally threatening the station, and the people remained unmoved by the mission teachings. Eventually hard work and dedication paid off and in 1829 his first converts were baptised.

In 1841 the young David Livingstone arrived and Kuruman became his base for exploration to the north. In fact, the majority of his journeys were undertaken while he was attached to this station.

Today the Moffat Mission is the town's main tourist attraction. Wander through Mary's Garden, an overgrown Eden where the stump of the almond tree under which David Livingstone proposed to Moffat's daughter Mary remains. It is surrounded by statuesque old trees – syringa, pear, fig, pomegranate and almond, among others. The Moffats' home, built in 1826, has been restored and is open to the public during office hours.

Open all the time is the stone church built under Moffat's guidance and consecrated in November 1838. Moffat held services in the right wing, while the left wing housed the press for printing the seTswana Bible. The walls are 60 cm thick, and the reed thatch roof is supported by massive beams which were transported 320 km from the western Transvaal by ox-wagon. Capable of seating over a thousand people, the church also has remarkable acoustic qualities. While Livingstone was recuperating after being mauled by a lion in 1845, he married Mary Moffat in this church, and visitors can still see the original register which recorded their union.

The name of the town derives from 'Kudumane', a belligerent Bushman chief who held sway in the area in the 18th century. Today, Kuruman is a thriving place with a steadily increasing population. Mainstays of the local economy are farming and mining: the surrounding hills yield manganese, iron, blue asbestos and various semi-precious stones – and the sparse rainfall and scrubby landscape make it ideal for stock farming. One burgeoning industry is game ranching – Kuruman is fast becoming one of the major hunting areas of South Africa.

Forty-three kilometres south of Kuruman on the Kimberley road is the Wonderwerk Cave. Excavation teams from the McGregor Museum in Kimberley have revealed numerous fascinating artefacts: stone implements and engravings, decorated ostrich eggshells, Bushman hair, pollen dating back about 400 000 years, various animal bones and the 8 000-year-old teeth of a now extinct species of horse.

Millions of litres of pure water bubble forth each day from the Eye – the fountainhead on which Kuruman relies for all of its water needs. Even in times of drought, the flow from this natural spring hardly falters.

Visitors to the cave (by appointment only) can marvel at the Bushman paintings in mixed media – plant roots and blood.

Wildlife is a popular attraction in this wilderness region and a bird sanctuary on the Hotazel road comprises 7 ha of wetlands with over 150 different species of birds. The Billy Duvenhage Nature Reserve (situated just out of town on the road to Sishen) was established in the 1970s when 850 ha were simply enclosed in a game-proof fence, surrounding animals such as grey duiker, steenbok, porcupine and the comical aardvark. Larger animals which had disappeared from the region – ostrich, gemsbok, red hartebeest, eland, springbok, kudu, impala and zebra – were reintroduced with great success. Pride of place goes to the reserve's two white rhinos.

A nice way of rounding off your trip to Kuruman is with a trek along the 11-km hiking trail. Starting at the Eye, the trail passes numerous places of interest. Among the many attractions that can be seen along the way are forts used during the Anglo-Boer War, the Slaughter Tree, a sinkhole and a dolomite cave with seven streams known as the Wonder Hole. The hike finally comes to an end at the Second Eye, another natural spring and the site of a holiday resort.

Built more than 150 years ago, Robert Moffat's church is one of the main tourist attractions of the town of Kuruman.

Kuruman at a glance (map page 8)

How to get there: Kuruman lies in the barren, desolate northern Cape 520 km south west of Johannesburg. Driving from Johannesburg, take the N14 south west from Vryburg and after 138 km you'll reach the town.
Weather: Very hot and dry in summer. In winter the days are mostly mild but it can get very cold with frost at night.
What to do: There is an excellent country club on the outskirts of town where you can play badminton, golf, tennis, bowls and squash at very reasonable rates. Or you can hike, watch game and birds, swim or cycle.
Special attractions: Wonderwerk Cave and the hiking trail.
More information: Write to The Public Relations Officer, PO Box 4, Kuruman 8460; tel (01471) 21095.

Ancient granite gorge on the Orange River

*One of South Africa's natural wonders
lies at the heart of the Augrabies Falls National Park
120 km west of Upington in the northern Cape*

Where to stay

Visitors can choose from a variety of air-conditioned bungalows complete with bedding, towels, soap, eating and cooking utensils and a hot-plate and fridge. There is also an attractive, shady caravan and camping site with excellent facilities including a camp kitchen, ablution block, braai areas and a laundry. The rest camp also has a restaurant, a well-stocked shop and an information centre. Contact the addresses/numbers at the end of the 'Augrabies Falls at a glance' section.

IT HARDLY EVER RAINS in this arid part of the country yet, every minute, 405 million litres of water crashes over the Augrabies Falls. One of the world's six great waterfalls, it produces a heart-stopping spectacle during summer when water sweeps down from highveld storms and the Lesotho highlands. During times of exceptional rainfall, the sheer volume of water plunging over the edge exceeds that of the Victoria Falls.

On its approach to the edge of the plateau, the Orange River quickly accelerates over a succession of rapids and cascades, thrusts forward and arcs elegantly into space before falling 65 m into a massive gorge scoured out of the granite by the water over the millennia.

Several secondary falls make their way independently to the gorge, the most famous of these waterfalls being the spectacularly beautiful Bridal

Veil, which, in times of heaving flooding, becomes part of the main fall.

Visitors can marvel at the river's majesty from the safety of observation points along the edge of the gorge, several with protective fencing. Human nature being what it is, there is always someone willing to risk death for a closer look. In 1979, a Scandinavian tourist ventured beyond the protective fencing and lost his balance. As he fell down the rock face, the friction ripped his clothes from his body (including his belt and underpants), and tore his skin. The force with which he hit the water broke several bones, yet, miraculously, he was able to scramble onto a submerged rock where he was spotted by park workers and rescued. He was one of the lucky ones. Since the park was proclaimed in 1966, over 20 people have been killed – most by falling into the gorge.

In fact, it was another Scandinavian – a Swedish soldier by the name of Hendrik Wikar – who was the first white man to discover the falls in 1775 after deserting in order to escape his gambling debts. He wandered around the Orange River wilderness for nearly four years and, in the journal he kept of his experiences, likened the sound of the falls from a distance to 'the roar of the sea'.

Indeed, the thundering of the main falls is awesome, and the name Augrabies derives from the Hottentot word meaning 'the place of the great noise'. The massive pool into which the main falls tumble is the source of a local legend. Measuring about 92 m across and no-one knows how deep (some experts speculate it might be 130 m), the pool is believed to be the lair of a malevolent water-monkey.

Another legend is that the pool is a repository for a fortune of diamonds which have been washed downriver. In 1934 a severe drought dried up the falls for the first time in recorded history, providing a perfect opportunity to search for diamonds. Fear triumphed over fortune, however, as most locals were too afraid of the 'pool monkey' to investigate. Since then any prospecting has been prevented by the sheer power of the water.

Although the falls are the main attraction and reason for the existence of this park, the 82 415 ha provide numerous other attractions. The scrubby vegetation, typical of semi-desert, features quiver trees, camelthorns, karees and wild olives, and provides a habitat for a number of birds, mammals and reptiles.

Many species have been reintroduced (such as rhino and eland) and you're bound to come across springbok, dassies (there are thousands), baboons,

After plunging over the Augrabies Falls, the waters of the Orange River flow through an impressive, sheer-sided gorge. This is the view from a position called 'Arrow Point'.

One of the vantage points from which visitors to the Augrabies Falls can watch the spectacle of hundreds of millions of litres of water plummeting into the gorge below.

vervet monkeys (who frequently raid the camp site), Cape red-tailed rock lizards, and maybe even a leopard if you're lucky.

Take time to study your surroundings because, as always, the most interesting things are not always immediately apparent. Careful scrutiny might reveal such wonders as the toad grasshopper, which has the squat, warty appearance of an amphibian. There are also porcupines and tortoises, and look out, too, for basking Cape cobras or puffadders coiled on the hot rocks.

Less common predators include the caracal or desert lynx, other smaller species of wildcat, the black-backed jackal, the bat-eared fox and, in the air, you could see fish eagle, the black stork, Ludwig's Bustard and the coyly named rosy-faced lovebird.

The Klipspringer Trail has been designed to take in the park's main attractions on a relatively easy three-day hike. The circuitous route runs next to the southern bank of the Orange and two nights are spent in huts built of local stone. Hikers revel in the spectacular potholed moonscape where the forces of temperature, wind and water have combined to form unique textures and sculptures in the granite. Among the attractions along the route are the Maal-

gate, potholes which have been scoured into the rock by river stones and water over thousands of years. Ararat is a granite rock from which the gorge can be viewed head-on, and at Echo Corner your calls will rebound after a four-second delay. On the final leg of the trail a scramble up the huge granite dome known as Moon Rock will reward hikers with spectacular views over the park.

Augrabies Falls Park at a glance (map page 8)

How to get there: From Upington, take the N8 in a south-westerly direction. About 8 km west of Kakamas there is a turn-off onto the R359, and the park is about 30 km from there. The area is well signposted. Coming from the south, the motorist would take the N7 as far as Springbok, and then the N8 in the direction of Pofadder.

Weather: The climate is one of extremes, with very hot days in summer but very cold nights in winter, in an area of minimal rainfall.

What to do: Hiking, game spotting, swimming.

Special attractions: The Klipspringer Hiking Trail is open from April to October. Book well in advance.

More information: Don't forget anti-malaria tablets or insect repellent. Write to the National Parks Board at PO Box 787, Pretoria 0001; tel (012) 3431991; or at PO Box 7400, Roggebaai 8012; tel (021) 222810.

Go with the flow on the king of rivers

The Orange River cuts through the desert like a shining highway, offering canoeists a unique view of the Richtersveld

THE MORE URBANISED our daily existence, the stronger the call of the wild and the lure of adventure. The average city dweller longs to escape his environment to experience something far removed from the daily grind, and increasing numbers of people are seeking out activities that bring them into contact with nature.

Close on 30 000 South Africans take to the rivers each year, and the Orange River is one of the safest and most scenic. Ranging from tranquil to exhilarating, riding the river is the best way to explore and appreciate this somewhat inaccessible landscape. And the best part is that you need never have been on a canoe or an inflatable raft before.

For most people, the Orange River adventure is a once-in-a-lifetime experience and, as such, one to treasure. Many professional companies take the trouble out of the trip and arrange organised four- to six-day river trails. Unless you're an accomplished and knowledgeable canoeist, it's probably best to join one of these.

The advantages of going on an organised trip are multiple, but do choose a reputable, experienced company. With most professionals, safety is paramount and the guides brook no alcohol on the river or the absence of lifejackets. They are well versed in river lore, safety and rescue as well as being certified in first aid and cardio-pulmonary resuscitation. Many of them are knowledgeable about the plants, animals and bird life encountered along the way. They make an effort to make the journey as enjoyable and educational as possible and, as a bonus, the guides are usually excellent cooks who prepare all your meals over an open fire.

The trip organisers provide all canoes, rafts, lifejackets, medical kit, food and catering equipment (including purified drinking water and ice) and watertight containers for your cameras and other items that you want to keep dry. Some even have back-up vehicles to resupply provisions on about day three or so.

For many, the real challenge is not their fitness level or canoeing skills, but living in close harmony with nature. You wash with a bucket of river water, take very few clothes and, when nature calls, you simply walk out into the wilderness with a small shovel and a loo roll.

Typically, your adventure begins when you arrive at the base camp where you meet your guides and fellow voyagers. After a braai, one of your guides will give an informative lecture and you'll get a rough idea of what the next few days hold in store. After breakfast the following morning you set off downriver. Watches are not worn and there is no official time, so overstressed city dwellers must adapt to a more leisurely pace. You wake to the dawn and the smell of fresh coffee and the clean morning air, and indulge in a farmhouse breakfast. Most of the day is spent on the river with various stopovers along the way to swim, explore or birdwatch. Bird life is concentrated on the river and you'll invariably spot fish eagles, bee-eaters, kingfishers and so on. You might not see many animals, although evidence of their presence abounds, from sounds to spoor and droppings.

Lunch time is usually followed by a siesta or something more strenuous such as a game of volleyball, then it's back on the river. In the evenings,

Shooting the rapids is all part of the fun. However, if you feel apprehensive about doing so, you have the option of landing beforehand and walking the length of the rapids instead.

A party of tired canoeists takes a well-deserved break below a looming mountain backdrop.

A golden dawn to enchant the eye. Spectacular scenery is but one of the attractions of the Orange River adventure.

guides prepare gourmet meals and everyone swaps stories before tucking themselves into sleeping-bags and sleeping under the stars.

Trips are held all year round and temperatures range from 20-40°C – occasionally the sand on the riverbanks is too hot to touch with bare feet. But the dry desert air and the river's moderating influence ensure relative comfort, and you can always plop overboard to cool off. Obviously, every precaution should be taken against the sun, which beats down relentlessly and is also reflected off the river and surrounding rocks.

For the Orange, you can choose either canoes or inflatable rafts. Rafts are generally more stable and restful, suitable for anyone whose priority is relaxation; but for stimulation try a canoe – they're faster, more exciting and more manoeuvrable. On average, you would spend about five hours a day in your craft and in that time cover roughly 12 km in a raft or 30 km in a canoe.

Although the Orange is safe, it's never been called boring. There are long stretches of flat water where you can swim or drift lazily along, and other parts that are generously spiced with exhilarating rapids. If you're not keen on tackling these there is absolutely no pressure to do so. You can walk the route along the bank or join a guide's canoe without any loss of face.

Anyone labouring under the misconception that desert landscape is monotonous is in for a pleasant surprise. Nowhere is the great outdoors greater than in the Namib's exquisite desolation under the vast vault of the African sky, the dry desert air producing a quality of light and colour unmatched in vegetative landscapes. In these unspoilt reaches of the Orange, the green belt which hugs the riverbanks forms a lush contrast with the rugged beauty of the earthy Richtersveld beyond. In some places the painted glory of the desert stretches to infinity over a quivering horizon, while a few kilometres further on you'll be surrounded by sculptured mountains striated with coloured bands, or imprisoned between sheer cliffs which rear up 200 m on either side. In places, strange rock formations enhance the surreal landscape.

As you drift downriver, hypnotised by the rhythmic ripple of your paddles, the profound stillness is occasionally splintered by the haunting cry of the African fish eagle or laughter from another canoe. Converts to this experience describe the journey as being food for the soul. It is while on this trip that many discover the meaning of absolute peace for the very first time.

Orange River at a glance (map page 8)

How to get there: Most well-known companies start the trip from Noordoewer or Vioolsdrif, about six hours north of Cape Town on the N7. At the end of the trip (roughly 80 km west at the confluence of the Orange and Fish rivers) transport is provided back to base camp where the cars are and you stay there overnight before setting off home.
Weather: Hot to sweltering, but cool to chilly at night. A good down sleeping-bag is recommended.
More information: SARA (South African Rivers Association) will provide names of reputable companies, or contact the SA Canoeing Federation. An excellent safety guide is *Don't Drown in the River* by Tony Lightfoot, safety officer of the Transvaal Canoe Union; write to PO Box 41435, Craighall 2024; tel (011) 7891121.

Several well-known companies offer four- to six-day rafting or canoeing trips. Write to them for the latest brochures, prices and kit-lists: Felix Unite, PO Box 96, Kenilworth 7745; tel (021) 7626935/6; River Runners, PO Box 583, Constantia, 7848; tel (021) 7622350; Orange River Adventures, 5 Matapan Road, Rondebosch 7700; tel (021) 6854475.

Grace and charm at the foot of the Hantam Mountains

Established more than 150 years ago, the town of Calvinia in the western Cape is the picturesque hub of one of the country's largest wool-producing areas

Where to stay

There is a caravan park with 44 caravan and tent sites, with laundry facilities and a swimming pool. Write to The Municipality, Private Bag X14, Calvinia 8190; tel (0273) 411011. There are also three hotels: *Calvinia Hotel*, PO Box 441, Calvinia 8190; tel (0273) 411491; *Holden's Commercial Hotel*, PO Box 20, Calvinia 8190; tel (0273) 411020; and the *Hantam Hotel*, PO Box 401, Calvinia 8190; tel (0273) 411512. Also available for holidaymakers is the *Hantam Huis*, a privately owned guesthouse offering accommodation in two separate buildings – the *Dorphuis* and the *Tuinhuis*. Contact Hantam Huis, PO Box 34, Calvinia 8190; tel (0273) 411606.

NAMED AFTER THE RELIGIOUS reformer, John Calvin, the town of Calvinia has an austere ring to it – the sort of place you might half expect to encounter sombre people and dull, utilitarian buildings. However, this could not be further from the truth. The locals are warm and friendly and the town itself has much appeal.

For those with a taste for things past, Calvinia is rich in possibilities for visitors. You can either do a historic walkabout – with the guidance of a detailed leaflet provided by the Tourist Information Office, which is housed in the museum – or be shown around by one of their staff (by appointment). The tour takes you through the rich cultural heritage of the town: the early Trekboers, the Jewish traders who started arriving in the 1850s, and finally the British, in the 1880s.

One of the oldest and most interesting buildings in Calvinia is the recently renovated Hantam House, a townhouse built in 1854 by Field-Cornet A van Wyk in country Cape Dutch style. To finance his urban getaway, he sold off a section of his farm *Hoogekraal* to the wardens of the Dutch Reformed Church.

The building fronts onto Hope Street – the whitewashed plaster walls uneven but sturdy. Inside, the floors have the same irregular authenticity as the walls. In typical Cape Dutch style, there are no passages, with the rooms rather leading one into the other. But whereas Groot Constantia and other well-known restorations gleam with urban polish, Hantam House has a definite country stamp, and is the more charming for it. It has steep end and front gables with half-moon pediments on the spires and a concave-convex gable at the back.

The original glass and cedar woodwork have been preserved, and the dados and borders are believed to have been painted by the Hantam fresco painter, A F Bus. The building houses a coffee shop and a craft shop offering pottery and home-sewn items.

The museum in Church Street is a must for any visitor to the town. It is housed in the old synagogue and includes an astonishingly comprehensive collection of artefacts, many arranged in realistic settings that make the visit a pleasure even for children. Here you can see how soap was made in big black pots, or the workings of an old donkey-driven mill – complete with leather flour bags for the finished product to tumble into.

Among the many curiosities to be found here are a homemade mousetrap, a moustache cup and, strangely enough, black wedding dresses. In keeping with the district's position as a major wool-producing centre, the museum devotes a significant section to an exhibition of sheep and wool farming, past and present. Outside, in a shady garden, there is a Class 24 steam locomotive, built in 1949 and withdrawn from service in 1977.

Another notable building in the town is the Dutch Reformed church, built in 1899. Now a national monument, it is in Neo-Gothic style, with lovely wrought-iron details and a simple bell-tower near the front entrance.

Attractive broekie-lace facades are a feature of many of the homes in Calvinia.

A view of Calvinia from the Akkerendam Nature Reserve with the Hantam Mountains looming up in the background.

If it's the champagne air, unusual flora and wildlife that you are after, you can go hiking in the Hantam. There's a choice of two routes – the one-hour Kareeboom route, and the seven-hour Sterboom route, which traverses the eastern slopes up to the plateau. If you hike with your eyes to the ground, an undreamed of world is revealed: what looks like scrub from the car turns out to be a treasure trove of plants, jostling each other for position against the rocks.

On a larger scale, several antelope species, black-backed jackals, bat-eared foxes and springbok are to be found here. The reserve is a proclaimed bird sanctuary, the Karee Dam being a stopover for migrating birds.

During the flower season, from the end of July to the end of September, the countryside is carpeted in colour. But in order to do the wildflowers justice, you also need to drive from Calvinia to Nieuwoudtville (69 km away on tar) and Loeriesfontein (89 km on gravel). Along the road leading west to Nieuwoudtville are three major areas in which to see the spring flowers: the farms *Matjiesfontein*, *Groot Toring* and *Naresie*, all in the area known as Agter Hantam.

To coincide with the flower season, Calvinia hosts the Hantam Meat Festival during the last weekend in August. For adventuresome gastronomes there are sheep's heads and tails, and a local delicacy called *peertjies* – as well as the more conventional spit roast and braai. Among the various exhibitions and activities on offer is a sheep exposition – highly praised by all of those who know about these things – and dancing to the Klipwerf Boereorkes.

If you're driving up the West Coast, Calvinia and its surrounding *dorpies* (villages) are well worth a detour. But it's also worth making a special trip there if you live in the Cape – it's close enough for a long weekend and far enough away to make you feel that you've truly left the demands of hectic city life behind you.

Calvinia at a glance (map page 8)

How to get there: From Johannesburg take the N1 south to Richmond. After a further 64 km turn north on to the R63 for Carnarvon and Calvinia. From Cape Town take the N7 to Vanrhynsdorp and the R27 east to Calvinia.

Weather: The average summer temperature is 22˚C, but temperatures frequently rise above 30˚C. The average daytime winter temperature is 10˚C, and at night the average is -2˚C but can drop as low as -8˚C with severe frost. The rainy season is usually April to September, but there can be sudden showers in summer.

What to do: Visit the spring flowers from the end of July to September; attend the Hantam Meat Festival on the last weekend in August. Enjoy the flora and fauna in the Akkerendam Nature Reserve, especially the bird life at Karee Dam. Visit the Calvinia Museum in the old synagogue and do a historical walkabout through the restored sections of the town.

Have an excellent cup of coffee at Hantam House and see the Dutch Reformed church, now both national monuments.

Special attractions: Do the one-hour hiking tour across the slopes of the Hantam Mountains in the Akkerendam Nature Reserve; or try the more strenuous seven-hour Sterboom route along the eastern slopes onto the plateau.

Visiting times: The museum is open from Monday to Friday from 8 am to 1 pm, and 2 pm to 5 pm; Saturday from 8 am to noon, and Sunday from 3 pm to 5 pm by appointment only. The church is open on Monday, Tuesday, Thursday and Friday from 8 am to 4 pm and Saturday from 8 am to noon. The nature reserve is open permanently.

More information: Get in touch with the Tourist Information Office at the Calvinia Museum, Private Bag X14, Calvinia 8190; tel (0273) 411712 or 411011.

*The captivating charm of the
Lambert's Bay harbour makes
it a favoured destination for
fishermen and sightseers alike.*

A harboured haven for crayfishing enthusiasts

*Whether you seek action or contemplation, the Cape
West Coast fishing village of Lambert's Bay – 275 km
north of Cape Town – has all you need, on or off the water*

LAMBERT'S BAY has entered South African history books as being the place at which the only naval battle of the Anglo-Boer War took place. As military engagements go, it left much to be desired, consisting of the commando of General JBM Hertzog – during his brief invasion of the Cape – taking pot shots at HMS *Sybille* at anchor in the bay. No one was injured in this somewhat serio-comic episode.

Today the incident is virtually forgotten by even the older members of the town, whose present preoccupations are fish, crayfish and guano. The harbour, needless to say, provides the pivot around which everything in the town revolves – and it's the

best place to head for when you arrive here after a couple of hours' drive from Cape Town.

It's an Impressionist painting of boats and sea; a swirl of colour, heightened by the smells of fish, kelp, tar, and the whiff of guano from the bay. Some 40-odd brightly painted boats make up the fleet, supplying their catch to the cannery overlooking the harbour. The bay also hosts many boats from Cape Town, working the sardine and pilchard shoals in the offshore waters of the Benguela current. A few kilometres offshore is the underwater shelf which supports dense colonies of rock lobsters. During the season, beginning each year on 1 November, swarms of rowing boats, laden with

Lambert's Bay at a glance (map page 8)

How to get there: Lambert's Bay is 275 km from Cape Town, via the N7. This takes you northwards through Piketberg and Citrusdal to Clanwilliam. There, turn left onto the R364 for a further 69 km, passing through Graafwater.
Weather: Fine and healthy, all the year round, though there are some spectacular storms in mid-winter. Since these engulf the entire western Cape region, you'll probably know about them in advance.
What to do: Pretty much anything you can think of in or around a boat can be done at Lambert's Bay. Take your pick from yachts to powerboats, from boardsailing to waterskiing. The tidal pool south of the town is an excellent spot for swimming. Lambert's Bay is on the so-called 'Crayfish Route', which means you can buy or eat crayfish at a number of recognised restaurants and shops. Bird-watching enthusiasts will find much to interest them at the mouth of the Jakkals River at the northern end of the town.
Special attractions: The Sandveld Museum in Church Street has that personal flavour which goes with small museums in small towns. It's open from 9 to 12 am, 2 to 4 pm on weekdays, and from 10 to 11 am on Saturdays. For further information, contact the museum at PO Box 1, Lambert's Bay 8130; tel (026732) 439.
More information: Call the West Coast Tourism Bureau, PO Box 144, Lambert's Bay 8130; tel (026732) 87 or 516.

Bird Island, which is joined to the mainland by a breakwater, is home to a colony of thousands of Cape gannets.

traps and hoopnets, bob out of the harbour, heading for the crayfish beds.

This rich annual harvest is processed by the Lambert's Bay Canning Company. Today, their quota is 42 000 tons of fish, which is turned into fish-oil or fish meal. About 530 tons of crayfish are also handled for export.

Fish and crayfish, however, are not the town's only products. Out in the bay is the accurately, if unimaginatively, named Bird Island. This rocky dot on the marine map is an important breeding ground, supporting some 5 000 pairs of Cape gannets. Here, too, are about 50 breeding pairs of the threatened Jackass penguin, the only such colony between Saldanha Bay and southern Namibia. The island is also a winter station for large flocks of cormorants.

The by-product of the birds, of course, is the guano, rich in phosphorus and a major source of fertilizer. It has been harvested for the past century, and today yields more than 300 tons a year, usually gathered in April. In 1959 the island was joined to the mainland by a breakwater to provide increased shelter for the fishing fleet, and it allows birdwatchers to study the noisy, swarming colonies, especially in the breeding season from September to February. The best time of the day to view the birds is in the early morning or at sunset. In the interests of protection, however, viewing is allowed only from behind a fence.

For those not content simply to stand and watch, however, there is plenty of action: a slipway enables you to launch your yacht, and the sheltered waters of the harbour are ideal for waterskiing. During the crayfish season, you can dive for your own (up to four a day), provided you have a permit. The best time of the year for angling is during the winter months, with galjoen, hottentot and snoek running – the lastmentioned Cape delicacy at their peak in May and June.

Other attractions include a large tidal pool at the southern end of the town. Both the pool and the nearby beaches offer safe swimming. To the north,

the beach stretches away, clean and white. Indeed, it marks the start of the South African west coast proper. While the fishermen in the family take to their rods, the other members can go exploring in the nearby hills or go shell-collecting along the beach. In spring and early summer, the dunes are dotted with flowers, becoming a rich tapestry in the Sandveld hills beyond.

No day trip will be complete without a visit to the Sandveld Museum in Church Street. It features an early horse mill and collections of old guns, clothing and furniture, most of them donated by residents of the area. Here you can trace the development of the bay from the time when it was named after Sir Robert Lambert, commander of the Cape naval station in 1820, to the building of the first canning factory during the Anglo-Boer War (1899-1902).

A visit to an open-air restaurant – described by locals as a Lambert's Bay 'institution' – may well be an ideal way to round off a day trip to the town. From a location close to the sea and, perhaps, within touching distance of ancient rock-formations and cliffs, visitors are invited to tuck into such delicacies as crayfish, snoek, *potjiekos*, home-baked bread, *hanepoot konfyt* (grape jam) and ground coffee, while recounting the day's activities.

Where to stay

The licensed 43-room *Marine Protea Hotel* overlooks the harbour. The address is PO Box 1, Lambert's Bay 8130; tel (026732) 49.

Raston Gasthaus is a very up-market, German-style establishment. It has five double en-suite rooms, a splendid menu, and a private swimming pool. Be warned, though – no children under 16. Contact PO Box 20, Lambert's Bay 8130; tel (026732) 681 for further information.

Private accommodation is also available in the form of various furnished chalets and flats on a daily rental basis. The West Coast Tourism Bureau – tel (026732) 87 or 516 – keeps a list of them plus details.

There is a strategically placed caravan park right on the beach with 250 sites. Contact the Municipality at PO Lambert's Bay 8130; tel (026732) 588.

An elemental favourite of the surfing fraternity

*On the West Coast north of Saldanha,
alongside the cold waters of the Benguela current,
lies Elands Bay – a place of stark and rugged beauty*

An agile surfer cuts a swathe across one of Elands Bay's famous, fast-breaking 'left slides'.

OVER THE YEARS, Elands Bay has become something of a magnet for surfers, who travel up here to take up the challenge of the large, fast-breaking waves generated by storms in the mid-Atlantic. They might be forgiven for seeing little beyond the waves in this lonely stretch of the shore – but there is certainly an elemental appeal about the place, the appreciation of which tends to grow with each subsequent visit.

The small settlement at Elands Bay is concentrated at the juncture of the sea and the sea-end of the Verlorenvlei. It consists of a hotel, a cluster of shops, and a handful of fishing boats congregated around a jetty situated 3 km from the village.

The colours are bleached and everything has a wind-cured look about it. However, for a month or so each year, the hinterland explodes in a kaleidoscope of floral displays: the 'opportunistic' sand-vygies, elandsvy, bittergousblom, beetle daisies, dassiegousblom, and a myriad others, all flowering after about three weeks of rain during early spring.

In the 23-km long Verlorenvlei there is a wonderful variety of bird life (more than 230 species), including many migrants which come to nest here during the European winter.

But it is in the sea itself that the real wealth lies. The upwelling of the Benguela current brings nutrition to the fish shoals, to the crayfish colonies and to the kelp. Up to 3 km offshore, dense underwater forests of seaweed grow, especially the fast-growing *Ecklonia maxima*. Anchored to the sea bed, it pushes up to 12 m in height, its tough, rubbery stem held up at the surface by a gas-filled bulb, with band-like fronds radiating around it. After the winter storms, the beach is littered with tangled fragments of the seaweed, which are soon claimed back by stormy seas.

For the people of this coast, the sea is the great provider, as it has been through the centuries. A record of its legacy is to be found at Baboon Point, where, 80 m above the road, there is a large cave. At the cost of a few minutes' hard, uphill scramble, you can discover the humble remains of an ancient culture.

The walls of the cave are decorated with Bushman paintings, mostly simple outlines of hands, interspersed with various animal forms, including that of the eland after which the bay is named. It is not so much the walls, however, as the floor which has given archaeologists clues to the past. A deep

A room with a view. This cave overlooking the sea at Baboon Point was home to Bushman families for thousands of years.

midden of prehistoric refuse has been carefully excavated, sifted and recorded. The deepest layers of this midden tell a story which goes back more than 15 000 years.

Today the roar of the Atlantic is only a few hundred metres away. But when the cave was first inhabited, the earth was in the grip of an ice age which froze much of the world's sea water. The shore may then have been barely visible, 25 km away, the area in between teeming with game, especially various species of antelope, whose bones dominate the lowest levels of the record. Then, about 11 000 years ago, the thaw began, releasing water from the ice caps. The sea level rose, and the shore gradually advanced to its present position, swamping the grasslands and driving the animals inland.

A fine, dry cave, however, was worth holding on to. Though the buck had gone further inland, the sea would still provide. The hardy Bushmen changed their diet, learning to fish and to catch sea birds. Thus the upper layers of the midden are rich in the bones of marine creatures, of fish, penguins, cormorants, gannets and seals. Here, too, are fragmentary traces of the marine eelgrass, *Zostera*, which was probably used by the Bushmen for bedding.

The cave offered shelter, and the sea gave food. Far from being an uncomfortable or unwelcome environment, Baboon Point was obviously a highly desirable seaside residence.

An unusual feature of Elands Bay is more modern: the Saldanha-Sishen iron-ore railway, built in the Seventies, virtually crosses over the village before disappearing into the 800-m long tunnel situated at Baboon Point. The train, consisting of around 2 km of trucks, trundles through six times daily, its rattling passage disturbing the otherwise tranquil setting.

A gull's eye view of Baboon Point. The village of Elands Bay is situated just to the left of this panorama.

Elands Bay at a glance (map page 8)

How to get there: The very corrugated road from Velddrif, 50 km south of Elands Bay, gives a good impression of the coastline. However, the road through Piketberg, from the east, has the advantage of traversing the scenic Verlorenvlei.
Weather: Hot and dry in summer, with fairly low rainfalls in winter.
What to do: Surfing, fishing (especially crayfish), diving, walking, exploring the dune life and watching the bird colonies.
Special attractions: The magnificent surfing waves and Bushman cave at Baboon Point.
More information: Lambert's Bay Tourist Information Office, PO Box 1, Lambert's Bay, 8130; tel (026732) 635.

Where to stay

The solitary hotel in the village is the *Eland Hotel*, with 16 rooms, PO Box 29, Elands Bay 8110; tel (0265) 640. There is also a camp site – contact the Regional Services Council (West Coast), PO Box 1, Elands Bay 8110; tel (0265) 745 for details. Nearby is the *Verlorenvlei Country Inn*, PO Box 11, Elands Bay 8110; tel (0265) 724.

A rustic fisherman's cottage sits snugly amid surrounding trees at the water's edge of Verlorenvlei. This stretch of water is home to hundreds of different birds, including various migrants from Europe.

A rustic piece of Europe in a hidden valley

*Time stands still in Wuppertal,
a tranquil Cederberg village
whose name is synonymous with
the classic South African veldskoen*

SEVENTY-FOUR KILOMETRES of bone-rattling gravel road lie between Clanwilliam and the isolated settlement of Wuppertal – with a couple of vertiginous mountain passes thrown in to keep drivers alert. As the road crests the top of the Kouberg, the village is suddenly revealed 300 m below, sparkling like an emerald set in the rugged folds of the northern Cederberg.

This picturesque little place has been a Moravian mission station since 1965, although its origins are actually Rhenish. It is wonderfully photogenic, with an unmistakable European influence – more Mediterranean than its Germanic name implies.

Terraced rows of whitewashed, thatched houses cling to the side of a hill which overlooks the orchards. Each house has its own walled garden flanking the steps. These lead up to the stoep, which is shaded by vines from the summer sun's blistering rays. More respite from the heat is provided by the variety of trees: willow, blue gum, palm, beech, oak, syringa, wattle and poplar.

Wuppertal's sheer variety is an assault on the senses: the changing hues and textures of the embracing mountains, the blinding whitewashed houses, and the varied smells borne on warm breezes – such as the aroma of freshly baked bread wafting from the traditional beehive-shaped clay ovens and mingling pleasantly with the spicy fragrance of sun-dried peaches and wild roses.

The name 'Wuppertal' derives from the Wupper River in Germany, from where two Rhineland missionaries, Theobald von Wurmb and Johan Gottlieb Leipoldt (the grandfather of the writer C Louis Leipoldt whose grave lies between Clanwilliam and the Pakhuis Pass), arrived in the Cape in 1829 to spread the Word among the indigenous people. They bought 37 000 morgen of fertile land near the source of the Tra-Tra ('bushy') River and, in 1830, established the first Rhenish missionary farm.

Just how they happened upon this hidden valley in the days when the mountains were virtually trackless and the territory uncharted remains something of a mystery. However, the two missionaries settled down among the seven Khoikhoi families living in the valley and devoted themselves not only to the spiritual upliftment of the people but also to teaching them more secular things. Farming was encouraged and trees, tobacco and other crops were planted – the previously nomadic Khoikhoi were soon to become enthusiastic gardeners. They were taught to read and write, a mill was built and a tannery came into operation. The famous shoemaking industry dates back to those early days when Leipoldt passed on his cobbling skills to the locals.

Shortly after slavery was abolished in 1838, the village's population swelled as many freed slaves arrived from nearby farms. Concerned that they should all become productive members of the thriving community, the conscientious missionaries ensured that the newcomers learnt a useful trade. As a result, they turned out blacksmiths, masons, bricklayers, joiners, thatchers, carpenters, tanners, milliners and shoemakers.

Missionary duties remained the first priority, however, so alcohol was prohibited and witchcraft gradually eradicated. The locals received Christian instruction, sang hymns, prayed and were baptised. The carol-singing festival held every Christmas is a legacy from those times and is something of which the villagers are justly proud.

The elegant mission buildings form the core of the village. The gracious, gabled church was built by the Khoikhoi journeymen under the tutelage of Leipoldt and was consecrated in 1834. The village shop with its high stoep was formerly the mission school and dates back to about 1830; a half-moon stoep is a feature of the First House, one of the original farm buildings. The old smithy as well as several other notable structures are still standing, so it's worthwhile to hire one of the locals as a guide, to ensure that you see all that Wuppertal has to offer the tourist. For instance, starting from behind the church and graveyard, a short walk towards the mountains will bring you to a series of pools and rapids formed in a semi-circle.

Today Wuppertal remains a relatively self-sufficient, autonomous community. Villagers elect their own local government, conduct their own affairs and work their own land. Agriculture is the chief activity of the settlment: tobacco is still produced and Wuppertal's *roltabak* (rolled tobacco) is renowned. The other main products of the area are dried fruit, dried beans and rooibos tea.

Education is still high on the agenda and there are several mission schools. Attendance is compulsory

The houses in Wuppertal, many of them built more than 150 years ago, have a unique charm all of their own.

Wuppertal is virtually enclosed by the rocky mountains of the Cederberg – in fact it is something of a mystery how the village's original founders discovered this isolated valley.

until the end of Standard 7 or the age of 16 is reached, and the community consequently boasts an extremely high literacy rate.

However, like many other rural communities, the inhabitants of Wuppertal have their own unique problems. Along with agriculture, shoemaking was once a thriving enterprise of the village. In fact, in the Thirties and Forties, workers in the tannery and shoe factory would churn out a thousand pairs of handmade, riempie veldskoens a week – without the help of nails or glue. But after a slow decline, the industry eventually slumped in the Sixties, owing to several factors – including antiquated machinery and insufficient funds to replace it; and stiff competition from factory-made shoes.

With insufficient work to support the population, members of the closely knit community had to find weekday work on some of the larger farms in the vicinity of towns such as Ceres, Clanwilliam and Citrusdal, returning home only for the weekend. In addition, many of the young people were forced to leave the village altogether to find work in the towns and cities.

Wuppertal still produces shoes but on a much smaller scale than previously. In fact today, the distinctive, tyre-soled veldskoens from the village enjoy cult status among the cognoscenti.

Although the heyday of shoe manufacture in Wuppertal has passed, it is still an important source of income for many.

Wuppertal at a glance (map page 8)

How to get there: From Clanwilliam (212 km north of Cape Town), take the R364 east through the Pakhuis Pass until the turn-off (40 km from Clanwilliam) to the Biedouw Valley. Follow the road for another 34 km until you reach the village.

Weather: This is a harsh climate of extremes – temperatures soar in summer and plunge in winter.

More information: Captour, PO Box 863, Cape Town 8000; tel (021) 4185214/5 or Clanwilliam Publicity Office, PO Box 5, Clanwilliam 8135; tel (02682) and ask for 554.

Where to stay

No tourist accommodation is available in Wuppertal, although farms in the surrounding areas rent out rooms on a bed-and-breakfast basis, especially during the flower season. Contact Captour, PO Box 863, Cape Town 8000; tel (021) 4185214/5 or the Clanwilliam Publicity Office, PO Box 5, Clanwilliam 8135; tel (02682) and ask for 554. There are 20 camping sites (without facilities) at Khakie Park in the village. Ask at the Moravian Church office for permission to camp; or call (02682) and ask for Wuppertal 4.

Camping in the cradle of the Cederberg

*Nestling in a secluded, peaceful valley
in the Cederberg mountains lies Algeria,
a shady escape two hours' drive from Cape Town
that offers clear air, bracing walks and freshwater swimming*

Where to stay

You can camp or caravan at one of Algeria's 46 camp sites. Permits can be obtained at the office of the Nature Conservator in Algeria, or by writing in advance to the Nature Conservator, Cederberg Wilderness Area, Private Bag X1, Citrusdal 7340; tel (02682) and ask for 3440. Booking is advised, particularly at weekends.

FROM THE TOP of the Nieuwoudt Pass, the long, deep valley of the Rondegat River offers its secrets for the traveller's scrutiny – the distant gurgle of water flowing across rocky river beds and a plantation of pine trees rubbing shoulders with clumps of tall cedars.

Nieuwoudt Pass is the most spectacular entry point to the Cederberg, one of the last great wilderness areas of southern Africa and a paradise for campers and walkers.

A narrow road descends from the top of the pass to Algeria, a neat settlement of cottages, while high above rise some of the better-known rock-strewn crags of the Cederberg: Vensterberg, Protea Peak, Algeria Peak and Uitkyk Peak.

After pausing to admire the view, you're off again – following the narrow road as it twists and turns down the mountainside, with new vistas opening up as the valley ends dramatically at the foot of the Uitkyk Pass.

It is here, between the soaring mountains, that the road finally brings the traveller to Algeria, a shady oasis of green lawns and tinkling water set in some unforgettable scenery. Of the hundreds of thousands of visitors who come to the southwestern Cape every year, only a handful ever find their way to this hidden gem.

The Cederberg has a personality all of its own: a stern, craggy range adorned with some of the most remarkable rock formations to be found anywhere in southern Africa. This remarkable area takes its name from the rare Clanwilliam cedar tree (*Widdringtonia cederbergensis*) which covered the mountains before the arrival of European woodcutters in the area. Today only a few remain among the higher mountain peaks.

The Cederberg has remained remote for two good reasons: first, no tarred road penetrates the wilderness area – but don't let this deter you, the road across the Nieuwoudt Pass is good quality gravel, quite suitable for ordinary saloon cars and caravans. Secondly, there is no hotel accommodation – in these mountains, only camping and caravan sites are available.

If you're wanting your creature comforts, there are good hotels in the nearby towns of Citrusdal and Clanwilliam and you can use your hotel as a base for making daily forays into the wilds. But in order

The rolling lawns of Algeria, the camping and caravanning paradise that lies at the heart of the Cederberg mountains.

Hiking trails in the surrounding mountains take you past a number of fascinating and evocative rock formations.

to enjoy the wonderful tranquillity that Algeria provides, you should at least plan to stay the night – an evening braai under the starry canopy of the Cederberg is an experience that you will doubtlessly cherish forever.

Most of the people who find their way to this mountain hideaway come for the hikes and walks that abound in the wilderness area. Two are suitable even for the more sedentary – to the nearby waterfall at Helsekloof, and a circular route along the Rondegat River to Uitkyk and back. Allow a leisurely three hours for each of these routes – and be prepared for some uphill walking. Signposts point the way to both destinations from the northern bank of the river.

Longer walks and hikes take visitors to the two best known rock formations in the area: the Maltese Cross and the Wolfberg Arch. However, these walks – together with other two- and three-day hikes – require a certain amount of experience and stamina, and should not be undertaken by the inexperienced. Permits for all walks and hikes must be obtained in advance from the Nature Conservator's office at Algeria.

The higher peaks in the range are home to the unique snow protea (*Protea cryophilia*), which is found nowhere else in the world. Look out also for the rocket pincushion (*Leucospermum reflexum*) and the large red disa (*Disa uniflora*) along the banks of mountain streams.

The wooded and open slopes surrounding the Algeria settlement are also home to more than 30 species of mammal, particularly baboon, klipspringer, rhebok, steenbok, duiker, grysbok and the ubiquitous dassie. If you're really lucky you may catch a glimpse of a wild cat, caracal or bat-eared fox. Sightings of leopard and aardwolf have also been recorded.

Bird-watchers can scan the slopes for sunbirds, sugarbirds and Cape canaries. And if you're patient – and determined – you may spot the pair of black eagles (*Aquila verrauxii*) that are known to breed in the area.

One of the high mountain peaks overlooking Algeria glows in the light of the early morning sun.

Algeria at a glance (map page 8)

How to get there: Turn off the N7 21 km north of Citrusdal onto a good gravel road signposted 'Algeria' and drive for about 10 km until you get there.
Weather: Hot, dry summers and cool, damp winters with very cold nights.
What to do: Hiking, walking, bird-watching.
Facilities: There is no shop or restaurant; fires may be lit at the braai spots provided.
Special attractions: Wildlife, freshwater swimming pool.
More information: Write to the Nature Conservator, Cederberg Wilderness Area, Private Bag X1, Citrusdal 7340; tel (02682) and ask for 3440.

A bountiful valley in which the orange is king

*Shaded by the lush foliage of citrus groves
on the banks of the Olifants River is Citrusdal,
a town fragrant with the perfume of fruit blossoms*

A S ONE APPROACHES Citrusdal, the sight of this picturesque town lying peacefully in the fertile valley below is a tonic to the weary motorist. This is the heart of the Cape's successful citrus industry, and a lot more besides.

First stop should be the municipal offices in Church Street where tourist information and bonhomie are dispensed in equal measure. Helpful locals can direct you to some interesting artefacts in and around the town – like the old cannon (now retired to the school grounds) which was fired from the top of Piekenierskloof to inform farmers of the arrival of ships in Cape Town harbour. Ask for directions to Vanmeerhoff Farmstall, where a huge selection of the products and crafts of the area are to be found. And conveniently sited diagonally opposite the municipal offices, the museum is a good place to familiarise yourself with the activities of the town's forefathers.

The first Europeans to discover the area were employees of the Dutch East India Company, Jan Danckaert and Pieter van Meerhoff, who, led by Bushman guides, crossed the mountains into the upper reaches of the Olifants River Valley on

7 December 1660. In the river they caught 'the most beautiful fish in the world', and settled down on the banks for the night. The following morning they saw a massive herd of about 300 grazing elephants moving slowly down the valley. On the spot, Danckaert named the river the Olifants.

Before the Europeans arrived, the area was home to Bushmen and is rich in rock paintings, so much so that some experts believe there are still more waiting to be discovered. The Citrusdal Municipality has a 'rock-art route' leaflet listing those paintings accessible from the town – the most intriguing being Bushman depictions of Europeans in the period dress of 250 years ago.

Farmers have been settled in the valley since 1725. The early orange trees grew so tall that one could ride beneath them on horseback and pluck fruit from the boughs. The oldest orange tree in the country can be seen on the farm Groot Hex River. Still bearing fruit 250 years on, this venerable specimen has been declared a national monument.

The Goede Hoop Co-op opened in 1926 and, today, is South Africa's largest exporter of citrus fruit, handling more than 1 000 tons of oranges a day in peak season. During the picking season visitors can tour the packing sheds, taste freshly squeezed orange juice and, of course, buy oranges.

The orange is so dominant in this town that few realise the area was originally famous for its wine. Napoleon, in exile on St Helena after his defeat at

Rows of hardy orange trees against the backdrop of rocky mountain slopes – a view you'll see in countless places throughout the Citrusdal region.

One of the great attractions of the area are the magnificent displays of wild flowers that make their appearance in spring.

After months of care and attention, a harvest of sun-ripened oranges is finally ready for the market.

Waterloo, insisted that his solitude be sweetened by a good supply of the fortified wines of the Olifants River Valley. These came from the farm *Brakfontein*, where the small cellar in which Napoleon's wine was made still stands.

About 20 km out of town in a lush, leafy kloof, a natural thermal spring gushes to the surface. The spring apparently originates in the Koue Bokkeveld – water sinks down through sandstone to a depth where the surrounding earth is very hot. The resulting build-up of pressure forces this water up until it emerges in the kloof.

Nearby, the Dutch East India Company built a stone homestead (still standing) to accommodate visitors, but over the years the resort fell into a sad state of neglect. An 18th-century commission report stated: 'The baths stand in a cave whose appearance is not calculated to inspire joy, but to awaken

Citrusdal at a glance (map page 8)

How to get there: From Cape Town take the N7 and drive north for about an hour and a half. Just past the top of Piekenierskloof Pass you'll see Citrusdal below you.
Weather: A winter rainfall area with bracing, crisp (and very cold) days when the surrounding mountains are capped with snow. Summers are hot to stifling.
What to do: Hang-gliding, mountaineering, hiking, cycling, angling, canoeing, swimming.
Special attractions: Bushman paintings, The Baths.
More information: Citrusdal Municipality, Private Bag X5, Citrusdal 7340; tel (02662) 81.

melancholy.' Happily, this is no longer so. Over the years The Baths changed hands many times until in 1903 they were bought at an auction on the Grand Parade in Cape Town by a tough Scot, James McGregor. He extended and modernised the resort and today at The Baths his descendants still offer visitors old-fashioned hospitality but with modern conveniences.

The variety of the Citrusdal region, boasting both mountains and water, means an exciting range of attractions. The surrounding peaks and kloofs promise many challenges to climbers, hikers and hang-gliders, and the Olifants River is a favourite among canoeists and anglers. There are thrilling rapids, especially during winter, and the course is varied by islands and narrow channels. Various fish are found in the river, including black bass and yellowfish which can weigh over 11 kg.

In spring, the air in the valley is thick and heavy with the fragrance of orange blossom and this is when the annual Citrus Festival takes place. Usually held over three days in September, the festival is typical of rural shows and, therefore, irresistible to town dwellers. You can watch country pursuits such as horse-riding displays and livestock shows, and enjoy traditional *langarm* dancing. In marquees, trestle tables almost buckle under the weight of wholesome country provender waiting to be washed down with the region's wines. The highlight of the competitive activities is the Citrusdal Cederberg Mountain Bike Marathon, the Cape's mountain bike event of the year.

Where to stay

The Baths have varied accommodation, from self-contained chalets and apartments to rooms with access to communal kitchens and braai areas. Caravans are also welcome. Write to The Baths, Box 133, Citrusdal 7340; tel (02662) 3312.

Piekenierskloof Mountain Resort at the top of the pass offers luxurious accommodation in chalets. Contact them at PO Box 241, Citrusdal 7340; tel (02662) 181. If you'd like to stay in town, try *The Cederberg Hotel,* which has de luxe en suite rooms, PO Box 37, Citrusdal 7340; tel (02662) 82.

Farmers and other locals offer self-contained cottages or bed-and-breakfast lodgings. Contact the Citrusdal Municipality (see other panel for details).

A diverse sanctuary in the Great Karoo

A nature reserve uniquely representative of Karoo ecology lies on the southern shore of the Orange River's P K le Roux Dam in the Cape Province

IF YOU PLACED A PIN directly in the centre of a map of South Africa, you would probably pinpoint the Rolfontein Nature Reserve, roughly midway between Kimberley and Middelburg as the crow flies. Lying along the southern shore of the P K le Roux Dam, Rolfontein is a landscape of contrasts: thickly wooded kloofs, grassy plains and typical Karoo dolerite koppies.

The 15 000-ha reserve was created from the remainder of the farm *Rolfontein* after the completion of the dam. The Cape Department of Nature and Environmental Conservation was entrusted with the land in 1968 and undertook to restore the region's former character and preserve the unique Karoo ecosystem, providing visitors with a park that was both recreational and educational. They erected game fences, built a road network and, with the help of information gleaned from the notes of early travellers, compiled a list of game to be reintroduced.

Over the years the reserve has developed a computerised databank which covers the details of the reserve's wildlife and vegetation. It comprises a grid chart, each square covering an area of four hectares; charts for the three general vegetation areas – riverine, plateau and slope; and charts for each wildlife species. Animal movements are tracked and analysed according to seasons, and the stomach contents of dead animals are examined to establish their diet. The data is constantly revised, updated and expanded, providing a minute study of the area and its inhabitants. A booklet for visitors has also been published, and this includes a spoor identification chart: there's nothing like a fresh animal print to raise the excitement level a few notches.

In this arid and primitive landscape it seems fitting to learn that the earliest human beings in the reserve were early Stone Age people. Numerous flint tools and artefacts have been discovered, some of which are still scattered over the terrain. Archaeologists have established that these people were hunter-gatherers who took shelter in the overhangs and seemed to have quite a varied diet, living off antelope, rodents, reptiles, fish, birds, ostrich eggs, crabs and freshwater molluscs.

Centuries later, it was the Bushmen who occupied these shelters until they were driven out by white settlers, who were also largely responsible for exterminating the region's herds of game and large predators. Formal farming began in 1837 and continued down the years until the farms were expropriated by the government in 1965 to make way for the dam.

Restocking with indigenous game began in the mid-Seventies and today the list includes predators such as cheetah and brown hyaena (to help control the smaller game populations), white rhino, aardvark, aardwolf, bat-eared fox, black wildebeest, red hartebeest, springbok, duiker, warthog, zebra, ostrich, secretary bird, and many others.

The large antelope herds (some 13 species are represented) are a feature of the reserve and the eland population is one of the biggest in southern Africa. Game is carefully managed to prevent overgrazing and soil erosion; so when numbers increase, the animals are either captured and relocated to other reserves or sold.

Nature-lovers will revel in the variety of vegetation found in the reserve's habitats. The densely wooded kloofs and tree-lined watercourses are

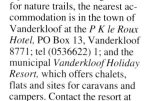

Where to stay

Apart from the overnight huts for nature trails, the nearest accommodation is in the town of Vanderkloof at the *P K le Roux Hotel,* PO Box 13, Vanderkloof 8771; tel (0536622) 1; and the municipal *Vanderkloof Holiday Resort,* which offers chalets, flats and sites for caravans and campers. Contact the resort at PO Box 40, Vanderkloof 8771; tel (0536622) 188.

The Rolfontein Nature Reserve boasts one of the largest eland populations to be found in southern Africa.

The somewhat arid landscape of the reserve makes it easy to spot the many species of wildlife to be found here.

home to sweet thorn (covered with yellow flowers in summer), gnarled, ancient wild olive and evergreen trees such as karee. Such riverine vegetation is particularly favoured by vervet monkeys. The rocky, grassy slopes are where you might spy mountain reedbuck, baboon, caracal, elephant shrew, red hare, porcupine and greywing francolin; and the stacked dolerite boulders are home to rock leguaans, lizards and bats.

There are no fewer than 40 types of grass, including assegaai grass, dropseed grass and rooigras, all of which provide food for the various grazers. Browsers such as kudu and eland prefer the leaves of the trees which they delicately pluck with their lips. Less delicately, eland bulls use their horns to break branches so that they can reach the succulent foliage. Ingeniously, they hook a branch between their horns and twist until it breaks. In this way they are capable of bringing down branches up to three centimetres thick.

On the rocky ridges you'll find kuni, camphor bush, sweet thorn, buffalo thorn, cabbage trees and black thorn – the lastmentioned making a dramatic spectacle in spring when they explode with small white puffballs before the leaves and green seed pods appear. The ridges are the place to look out for

dassies, large groups of which can be seen sunning themselves on smooth, warm rocks. They make their homes in cracks, tunnels or rocky overhangs and are careful never to stray too far from their front doors for fear of their main predators, the black eagle and caracal. They have the curious habit of using the same toilet spot and so, over the generations, huge dung middens are deposited. If you come across one of these, it is a sign that a colony of dassies is not far away.

The dam waters stretch out to infiltrate the reserve's streams, pools and kloofs, and as a result bird life in the region is particularly rich. More than two hundred species have been recorded, including Egyptian geese, spurwinged geese, black duck, yellow-billed duck, martial eagle, fish eagle, hoopoe, pied barbet, turtle dove and so on. The waters also provide homes for other fascinating creatures such as freshwater crabs, various frogs, terrapins, the marsh mongoose and, of course, many species of freshwater fish such as yellowfish, minnow, bream, catfish and carp.

Visitors wishing to hike are provided with maps and allowed to traverse the reserve unhindered. There are two overnight trail huts, each offering basic facilities for eight people.

Rolfontein Nature Reserve at a glance (map page 8)

How to get there: From Cape Town or Johannesburg, take the N1 to Colesberg, from where you turn off northwards onto the R369 to Petrusville. Continue through Petrusville for about 10 km, where you turn right. After 11 km you reach Vanderkloof, the settlement built for workers who constructed the dam. The reserve is signposted from this point.
Weather: Hot, dry summers with occasional rain; mild to cold winters with frost.

What to do: Canoeing and boating are allowed on the P K le Roux Dam and there are various bays and inlets around its edge that are well worth exploring. Angling is permitted in certain areas.
Special attractions: The Pied Barbet Trail.
More information: Write to The Officer-in-Charge, Rolfontein Nature Reserve, PO Box 23, Vanderkloof 8771; tel (0536622) 160.

A scene synonymous with the Karoo – a series of mini mountains, known as koppies, form a stunning backdrop to the flat, arid countryside.

A fascinating realm of stark and timeless beauty

The Karoo National Park near Beaufort West provides a visual record of the geological forces that have been at work in this region for the past 240 million years

FROM THE N1 THE KAROO seems a flat, dry semi-desert that is essentially inhospitable to man – a vast region in which the only sounds to be heard are the sighing of the wind and the occasional bleat of a sheep. Most motorists tend to hurry through this wide expanse, their thoughts preferring not to entertain the fearful possibility of breaking down in the middle of nowhere.

Usually, only those with family and friends living on farms in the Karoo have fallen prey to its special charms. However, the National Parks Board has established a park in the Great Karoo which is a wonderful introduction to the hidden splendours of this region. And of special interest within this park is a superb 400-m Fossil Trail that guides the visitor, step by step, through the mysteries of this region's 240 million-year-old history.

In order for you truly to appreciate this park before going there, it's a good idea to know a bit about the geological history of the area. The Karoo was once flat and marshy, not unlike the Okavango delta of today. Rivers meandered over its face and, in doing so, washed a layer of mud onto the marsh that gradually raised the level of the flood plain.

More rivers flowed over the new plain, depositing a sandy sediment in the mud. More mud washed onto the new plain to form another layer, and so, eventually, over 180 million years, the floor of the Karoo Basin was raised by no less than 2 km.

At this point the earth erupted in volcanic contractions. The neat ironstone now ringing the many koppies in the area was once raging molten rock, forcing its way up through the cracks in the sediment. It cooled, over a few more million years, beneath the earth's surface. Then the weather got to work and more than 2 km of sedimentary rock, interlaced with dolerite, was eroded back down to the level where you find yourself when you embark on the Fossil Trail.

This trail winds below mountain slopes across which erosion has had the peculiar effect of exposing the various historical landscapes, each seemingly being stacked on top of the other. Looking at these graphic slices of ancient worlds, it is easy to imagine the small animals – some of whose fossilised remains are embedded in the rock – scuttling around.

Many of these fossils have been found to be of a particular species that had a big head, barrel-shaped body and short legs – not unlike a dachshund, according to the experts.

But there are also real animals to see, every bit as enchanting as the fossilised 'dachshunds'. For example, there are porcupines and spectacled doormice, vervet monkeys and hairy bats. There are also five different types of tortoises, 11 varieties of geckoes and 18 kinds of snakes, some with names that make one almost curious to encounter them: the spotted harlequin, for example.

Out and about there are larger mammals, such as the Cape mountain zebra and grey rhebok. But the most endearing has to be the bat-eared fox, or *bakoorvos* as it is called in Afrikaans. It stands 30 cm high and has black legs and a black tail tip. This creature's hallmark is, of course, its big ears which help it hear the underground activities of insects, especially termites – its favourite food. Keeping its ear to the ground, the bat-eared fox digs them up with its 2 cm-long front claws.

In a different league are the park's black eagles, with 12 breeding pairs having made their homes in the dolerite krantzes of the Nuweveldberge. For the really fit, there is the strenuous three-day Springbok Hiking Trail which goes to the top of these mountains, taking you right into the nesting grounds of these spectacular predators. Their nests are 4 km apart – only the Matopos in Zimbabwe are so densely populated with black eagles. These nests are

Holiday accommodation in the Karoo National Park is provided by a number of Cape Dutch-style cottages.

not visible from the hiking trail, but the eagles can be seen constantly wheeling in flight above.

As is usual in the great scheme of Nature, something is in continual peril here, and in this case it is the dassies. There are an estimated 28 000 of them in the mountains and they constitute the main food of the black eagles – which also occasionally prey on small antelope and young baboons. Black eagles have also been credited with knocking even largish antelope over precipices, and have even been known to swoop down and harass leopards.

For those not energetic enough to undertake the hiking trail, there is the shorter (11 km) Fonteintjieskloof Trail, and the delightful Bossie Trail of only 800 m. This latter trail takes you on a short loop on which plants are numbered and named. Along the route there is the *bloubos* which is reputed to indicate subterranean water – and which also is said to attract lightning; the *kruisbessie* which indicates good grazing veld; the succulent *dikvoet* whose roots are used for making jam; and an asparagus which was allegedly the first vegetable Jan van Riebeeck ate at the Cape.

It is an added bonsella that such a wonderful natural environment also provides you with such an insight into the area and its conservation. Apart from the various magnificent trails and hikes, there is also a slide and video presentation at the main rest camp at 6 pm every day, as well as permanent environmental education displays at the 'Ou Schuur'. Two scenic game drives take visitors on a 12 km circular route to the Middle Plateau on the Klipspringer Mountain Pass, and a 13 km circular route across the plains through the Lammertjiesleegte. There is also an 80-km four-wheel-drive trail, the first of its kind in the national parks, for which reservations must be made.

Where to stay

There are six-bed cottages, three-bed chalets, and two camping sites within the park. For bookings and more information, contact: Karoo National Park, PO Box 316, Beaufort West 6970; tel (0201) 52828/9.

Karoo National Park at a glance (map page 8)

How to get there: From Cape Town take the N1 towards Beaufort West. The park turn-off 75 km after Leeu-Gamka is clearly marked with a white, thatched building.
Weather: The Karoo is subject to climatic extremes. It is hot in summer, but the weather is unpredictable during the change of season. Winters are bitterly cold.
What to do: Discover the varied natural life of the Karoo. Do the 400 m Fossil Trail and the 800 m Bossie Trail. Visit the Environmental Education Display and attend the slide presentation at the main rest camp. There are also two scenic circular drives – to the Klipspringer Mountain Pass (12 km) or

to Lammertjiesleegte (13 km). Experience the Karoo at close quarters on the unique four-wheel-drive trails. Enjoy excellent Karoo lamb at the restaurant.
Special attractions: Do the 11km Fonteintjieskloof Trail, or the three-day Springbok Hiking Trail, for which a permit must be obtained and a fee paid.
Visiting times: The restaurant is open from 8 am to 10 pm; noon to 2 pm, and 6 pm to 10 pm (Sunday 6 pm to 8 pm). The Environmental Education Display is open from 6 am to 6 pm on weekdays; 9 am to 6 pm on Saturdays, and 10 am to 5 pm on Sundays. The slide presentation occurs daily at 6 pm.

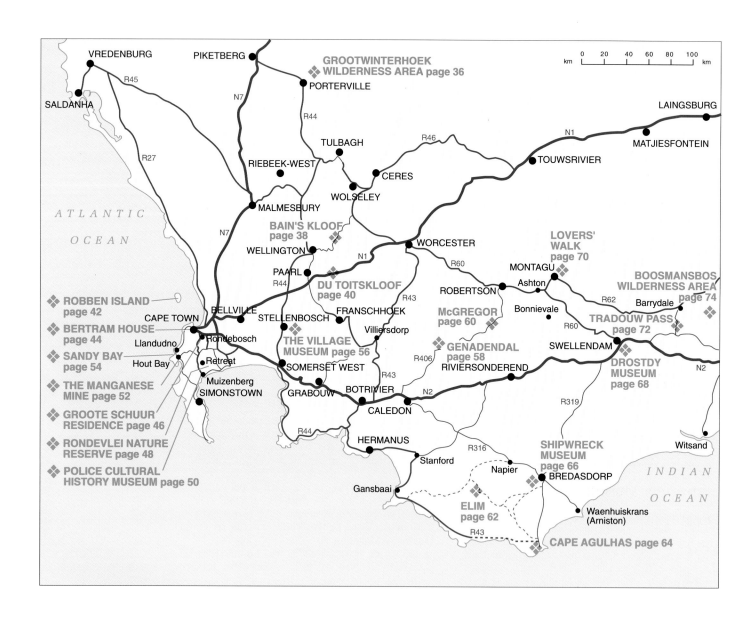

VREDENBURG

PIKETBERG

**GROOTWINTERHOEK
WILDERNESS AREA page 36**

PORTERVILLE

R45

SALDANHA

N7

R44

LAINGSBURG

N1

MATJIESFONTEIN

TULBAGH

R46

TOUWSRIVIER

R27

RIEBEEK-WEST

CERES

WOLSELEY

ATLANTIC

OCEAN

MALMESBURY

**BAIN'S KLOOF
page 38**

WORCESTER

**LOVERS'
WALK
page 70**

N7

WELLINGTON

MONTAGU

Ashton

**BOOSMANSBOS
WILDERNESS AREA
page 74**

N1

R60

PAARL

**DU TOITSKLOOF
page 40**

R43

ROBERTSON

R62

Barrydale

**ROBBEN ISLAND
page 42**

R44

FRANSCHHOEK

**McGREGOR
page 60**

Bonnievale

R60

**TRADOUW PASS
page 72**

**BERTRAM HOUSE
page 44**

CAPE TOWN

BELLVILLE

STELLENBOSCH

Villiersdorp

SWELLENDAM

**DROSTDY
MUSEUM
page 68**

Rondebosch

**THE VILLAGE
MUSEUM page 56**

**GENADENDAL
page 58**

N2

**SANDY BAY
page 54**

Llandudno

R406

RIVIERSONDEREND

**THE MANGANESE
MINE page 52**

Hout Bay

Retreat

SOMERSET WEST

R43

**GROOTE SCHUUR
RESIDENCE page 46**

Muizenberg

SIMONSTOWN

GRABOUW

BOTRIVIER

N2

R319

Witsand

**RONDEVLEI NATURE
RESERVE page 48**

CALEDON

**SHIPWRECK
MUSEUM
page 66**

INDIAN

**POLICE CULTURAL
HISTORY MUSEUM page 50**

R44

HERMANUS

R316

Napier

BREDASDORP

OCEAN

Stanford

Gansbaai

**ELIM
page 62**

Waenhuiskrans
(Arniston)

R43

CAPE AGULHAS page 64

km 0 20 40 60 80 100 km

SOUTHWESTERN CAPE

Portals of paradise
on the path to Die Hel

*Craggy peaks soar above almost 20 000 hectares of
undulating hills, mountain streams and serene valleys
in the Grootwinterhoek Wilderness Area near Porterville*

HIGH UP in the Grootwinterhoek Mountains, a
thundering torrent of water surges through
jagged sentinels of rock and then cascades
into a basin of deep, cool water. Below this elevated
pool, the mountains give way to a valley, beautiful
for its desolation.

Here tiny, sparkling tributaries and rivers traverse
the plateau, feeding the larger Berg and Olifants
rivers in their journey to the sea.

This is the heart of the Grootwinterhoek Wilderness Area – a place originally named Vier-en-twin-
tigriviere Ravine.

*Disas are just one of the many
wildflowers found in this
unspoiled domain.*

The mountain air is cold and crisp, laying a cloak
of sparkling dew on an undulating world of plants
and wildflowers. Incredible rock formations flank
this amphitheatre. To the east, the Grootwinterhoek
Peak pierces the clouds at 2 077 m. Further south,
the Sneeugat and Kleinwinterhoek peaks tower
benevolently above remote footpaths and animal
tracks. In the valley between the peaks, the silence
is broken only by birdsong and the soothing sound
of rushing water.

The Grootwinterhoek Wilderness Area is one of
the better-kept secrets of South Africa's great outdoors: it is a special place for special people – adventurers, hikers and those seeking nature's help to
regenerate over-stressed minds and bodies.

Just a two-and-a-half hour drive from Cape Town
(40 minutes from Porterville) takes you up the
Dasklip Pass to the portals of this forgotten corner
of paradise where more than 90 km of footpaths
await you.

Various walks take you through mountain fynbos
so varied that locals claim there is a fresh flower in
bloom every day of the year.

Leopards roam the craggy mountains in the company of baboons and small antelope such as grysbok and klipspringer. The resident bird life is
prolific and includes black-shouldered kites, black
eagles, ground woodpeckers, Cape sugarbirds,
Victoria's warblers, peregrine falcons, kestrels and
jackal buzzards.

The principal hike is the two-day walk to Die
Hel, during which you camp outdoors and sleep

*Striking rock formations are a feature of this mountainous
area, one of these being Camel Rock.*

Rock pools ideal for swimming in are one of the big attractions of the Grootwinterhoek region.

under the stars. The hike takes you along the Groot-Kliphuis River, crosses the Klein-Kliphuis River, and ascends to an old farmhouse. Here a ranger will direct you to De Tronk, where three unfurnished huts will provide you with shelter for the night.

On the second day, as you descend the rocky heights into Die Hel, the sound of the Vier-en-twintigrivier surging through dark cliffs will lead you to a breathtaking cascade surrounded by rock pools. For the adventurous this is a place to cool off by swimming to the waterfall and being pounded by the cascade.

The real attraction of the Grootwinterhoek is the fact that you don't have to stay on the footpaths that are provided. You can wander off them at any point and find a comfortable spot to lay your sleeping bag down under the stars – a novel experience for the city dweller whose activities are so circumscribed by rules and regulations.

But a word of warning: if you do intend to leave the traditional footpaths, take along a compass and a map.

No more than 24 people, in groups of up to a dozen people each, are issued permits for the area at any one time. In addition, the two-day hike to Die Hel is limited to 12 people each day. Camping or sleeping at Die Hel is prohibited due to a lack of toilet facilities.

The Grootwinterhoek at a glance (map page 34)

How to get there: Three kilometres north of Porterville, on the tarred R365 to Citrusdal, turn right on a good gravel road signposted Cardouw. Drive for 9 km, then turn right again.

The road ascends the Olifants Mountain for 7 km via the Dasklip Pass. At the highest point of the pass there is a turn-off to the private Beaverlac Nature Reserve. After a further 4 km there is a fork. Take the right-hand fork and drive 8 km until you reach a grassy parking area situated at the Groot-winterhoek Forestry Station. Beyond this point only walking is allowed.

Weather: Summers dry and hot; winters very cold (sometimes down to -7°C) and wet (heavy snowfalls and freezing temperatures are common on the peaks).

What to do: Hiking, bird-watching, identifying wildflowers, swimming in mountain pools, and mountaineering.

Special attractions: Two-day trail to Die Hel. Permits available from the Forester, Grootwinterhoek Wilderness Area, PO Box 26, Porterville 6810; tel (02623) 2900. Bushman rock art in caves at Die Hel.

Beaverlac Nature Reserve: A private sanctuary for fynbos and several antelope species (rhebok, klipspringer, grysbok, steenbok and duiker). For permits, telephone the owners at (02623) 2953/2945.

More information: Contact the Forester, Grootwinterhoek Wilderness Area, PO Box 26, Porterville 6810; tel (02623) 2900.

Where to stay

The nearest comfortable accommodation is at Porterville, either at the *Porterville Hotel*, PO Box 4, Porterville 6810; tel (02623) 2178, which has nine rooms at reasonable rates, or nearby, at 11 Church Street, where accommodation and meals are offered at *Die Herberg* guesthouse and restaurant – contact Die Herberg, PO Box 11, Porterville 6810; tel (02623) 2416.

For a night out with a difference, take along a sleeping bag and let the star-filled sky be your roof. There are overhanging rocks and caves you can use for shelter but generally hikers sleep in sleeping bags under the stars.

Pride of the Cape's many spectacular mountain passes

Visitors are drawn to the natural beauty of Bain's Kloof Pass in the western Cape, one of Andrew Geddes Bain's greatest engineering triumphs

Bain's Kloof at a glance (map page 34)

How to get there: From Cape Town, take the N1 towards Paarl. At Klapmuts, take the R44 left to Wellington, and from there get onto the R303, which leads up Bain's Kloof.
Weather: Typical western Cape climate – cold and wet during winter, warm to very hot and dry in summer.
What to do: Hiking, sight-seeing, swimming in rock pools, studying the fauna and flora – a must for nature-lovers.
Special attractions: The drive, Dacre's Pulpit, the rock pools.
More information: Hawekwas Nature Conservation Station, Private Bag X14, Paarl 7622; tel (02211) 611535. The Hiking Trail Office, Foretrust Building, Martin Hammerschlag Way, Cape Town; tel (021) 216290 or 211480.

FOR MANY PEOPLE, Bain's Kloof represents a strange dichotomy: on the one hand there is the spectacular natural beauty of the region, and, on the other, the tragedies that have occurred there over the years.

For example, about halfway up the pass from Wellington, below the soaring peaks of the Sneeuberg and Limietberg, there is a small obelisk, a memorial to Lettie, a child who drowned in a flash flood, and the three teachers who also drowned trying to rescue her. This tragedy occurred a century ago and others have followed.

Nearby are the flattened ruins of Hugo's Rust where, in the late Thirties, a weathy businessman, Mr Jan Hugo, built a gabled mansion for his retirement. But Hugo never lived in his dream home situated above the pass: during a veld fire the house burnt down and he died shortly afterwards. His body lies buried near the ruin, and alongside is the grave of his son, whose remains were brought from North Africa where the younger Hugo died in battle during the Second World War.

Inevitably, the ruin became known as the *spookhuis* ('ghost house') and there have been many reports of strange lights, sounds and spectral appearances in the area – believed by some to be the ghosts of convicts who died while building the pass and who are buried in the vicinity. The burnt-out

ruin of Hugo's house was eventually demolished by the Paarl Town Council in 1978 after the brutal murder of a young Cape Town couple and their dog who were camping nearby. An escaped convict was later arrested in De Doorns and found guilty of the murders. Today, nature has reclaimed the land and indigenous plants proliferate around the remnants of Hugo's home. A poignant reminder of his dreams are the domestic roses you might see entwined in the mountain fynbos.

Yet even this tragic past cannot detract from the splendour of the area. Bain's Kloof is one of the Cape's classic passes and a beauty spot in a league of its own. Naturally, the kloof is named after South Africa's foremost road engineer, Andrew Geddes Bain. This mountain road won him wide acclaim and for many years it was the principal route between the western Cape and the interior.

The route was discovered in 1846 when Bain was riding with the Cape Colonial Secretary, John Montagu, who voiced his desire to find a way through the mountains to connect with Michell's Pass. Bain pointed to the entrance of an unknown kloof and suggested it as a possible route. After exploring the kloof a few weeks later, Bain sent a triumphant message to Montagu: 'The northwest passage has been found.'

The new pass, built by convict labour, was eventually completed in 1853. More than half of its 30-km length had to be blasted out of the mountain with gunpowder, as dynamite hadn't yet been invented. Approaching the pass from Wellington, motorists can see the entrance to what would have been South Africa's first road tunnel. Construction of this tunnel was a headache for Bain and his team: oxen and horses were reluctant to enter the darkness, it was flooded periodically, and the rock was unstable, causing part of the roof to collapse. Eventually, after a landslide blocked the entrance, it was abandoned.

Today, the pass remains as it was built by Bain – except for some additional reinforcements and the fact that the road is tarred. Still in evidence are the dry-stone retaining walls which supported much of the roadway – the introduction and perfecting of which Bain must be credited with.

On the way to the top, the road twists through sandstone and granite massifs and clings precariously to their steep sides. At the summit is a viewsite from where you can take in the glory of the Berg River Valley – a wonderful mosaic of plains, farmland and dams. On a particularly clear day, this enchanting vista stretches all the way to the sparkling sea on the Cape's west coast.

Like a rocky ceiling, the overhanging rocks on Bain's Kloof Pass add to the beauty of one of the western Cape's most famous mountain passes.

The upper reaches of Bain's Kloof Pass provide stunning views of parts of the Boland countryside, including the meandering Wit River.

Where to stay

At Tweede Tol there is a Cape Department of Nature Conservation camping site with ablution facilities. For reservations, contact them at Private Bag X14, Paarl 7622; tel (02211) 611535.

There are a number of one-star hotels in nearby Wellington: *Langham Park Hotel*, PO Box 128, Wellington 7655; tel (02211) 33023; *Commercial Hotel*, PO Box 93, Wellington 7655; tel (02211) 32253; and the *Railway Hotel*, PO Box 502, Wellington 7655; tel (02211) 32065. There is also a caravan park at Wellington – contact the *Pinie Joubert Caravan Park*, PO Box 12, Wellington 7655; tel (02211) 32603.

Slightly further afield, Paarl offers a variety of accommodation, from the simple to the luxurious. Contact the Paarl Publicity Association, PO Box 47, Paarl 7622; tel (02211) 23829/24842.

Through the cusp between the peaks, the road greets the Wit River and descends parallel to the steep river valley. In winter, tall waterfalls and cascades animate the ravine on both sides of the road, and some of them can be admired from various perilous viewsites. As if this were not enough, the pass is further enhanced by several exciting natural formations that Bain incorporated into his road design. The most spectacular is Dacres Pulpit, a massive granite overhang which you cannot help driving under without a sense of vague apprehension. Montagu Rocks and Bell Rocks are other notable landmarks, and at Pilkington Bridge a waterfall gushes down the cliff flanking the road and disappears under the pass.

The beautiful gorge of the Wit River is a wonderland of lush vegetation, large boulders, and waterfalls that plunge into sparkling mountain pools. There can be few more rewarding pleasures than following one of the many trails and cooling off in rock pools along the way. Even the Bain's Kloof baboons are known to be partial to a refreshing dip in the river.

An arduous, two-day hike that can be undertaken in the area is the 36-km Limietberg Trail. It starts from the Hawekwas Nature Conservation Station and reaches Junction Pool after about 14 km – a very welcome sight for those who want to cool off. The overnight hut is only about 5 km further on,

where there is yet another rock pool. Get plenty of rest before the even more challenging second day, which starts with an 11-km walk up to the summit of Pic Blanc. The stupendous views make the slog worthwhile, and from then on it's all downhill for 6 km through the Wolwekloof until you reach the end of the trail at the Tweede Tol camping site.

Day-trippers have a choice of a variety of shorter walks: the Happy Valley Walk is a return trip from Eerste Tol to Junction Pool which takes about an hour and a half; also starting from Eerste Tol is the Bobbejaans River Walk, which takes about five to six hours there and back. The path leads to a beautiful waterfall surrounded by lush greenery and flowers such as gladioli and disas. All these walks require permits, which are available from the Hawekwas Nature Conservation Station.

Tweede Tol is a Cape Department of Nature Conservation camping site which also caters for day visitors who come to enjoy the kloof's famous pools. Campers and picnickers can take advantage of the various walks from Tweede Tol; an inexpensive map is available from the camp manager.

From Tweede Tol the pass flattens out on its descent to the Breede River Valley and the interior. A couple of kilometres beyond Tweede Tol it's worth scanning the peaks for the mountain popularly known as the Sleeping Giant, which often wears a 'handkerchief' of cloud draped over its 'nose'.

A twisting, turning road through precipitous splendours

One of South Africa's most dramatic mountain passes, Du Toitskloof is the main gateway from the western Cape to the Karoo

Where to stay

Both Paarl and Worcester have numerous hotels. In Paarl, accommodation ranges from the sumptuous *Grande Roche*, PO Box 6038, Paarl 7620; tel (02211) 632727, to two caravan parks. These are the *Berg River Resort*, PO Box 552, Suider-Paarl 7624; tel (02211) 631650, and *Boschenmeer*, PO Box 617, Suider-Paarl 7624; tel (02211) 631250.

In Worcester, there is the *Brandwacht Hotel* in High Street, PO Box 192, Worcester 6850; tel (0231) 20150, or the *Nerina Hotel*, PO Box 2104, Pakkersdam, Worcester 6850; tel (0231) 70486.

The Paarl Valley and Worcester Publicity Associations (see other panel for telephone numbers) have lists of guesthouses, and bed-and-breakfast accommodation.

THE N1 HIGHWAY stretching from Cape Town to Johannesburg has many highlights, but one of the most dramatic must be the 27-km long Du Toitskloof Pass between Paarl and Worcester. The Huguenot Toll Tunnel, which was opened in 1988, enables motorists to avoid much of the pass – but if you have time on your hands, driving through Du Toitskloof in its entirety makes for an unforgettable experience.

Generations of hikers and climbers can testify that there is much more to Du Toitskloof than just a road. Numerous trails thread through this mountainous region, and – armed with a good topographical map or guidebook – you will be able to find the signs of the early tracks and wagon roads. Here the Mountain Club of South Africa has three overnight huts for its members.

There are various routes for day hikers or climbers, although many are unsuitable for very small children as most paths are fairly steep in several places. The Krom River offers a hike and scramble of about one and a half hours up to a spectacular pool and waterfall. Hikers can cool off in the crystal depths before enjoying a picnic on the rocks. Bear in mind, though, that the surrounding rock-faces are so high that the sun reaches the main pool only be-

The endlessly twisting road through the Du Toitskloof valley must rank as one of the most scenic drives that the western Cape has to offer.

tween midday and 2 pm in summer. South of the Krom River is the Elands River, a trout fisherman's paradise with waterfalls and pools for swimming. Many of these secluded pools are at the bottom of deep gorges which obtain direct sunshine very briefly, so only the hardy should attempt the icy plunge. Most pools are bracingly cold, but bearable.

Apart from private farms, much of this mountainous area is administered by the Chief Directorate of Nature and Environmental Conservation, which is responsible for maintaining the magnificent disa and lily flowers in the gorges, and the proteas, ericas and other fynbos that proliferate and make such a fine display in spring. Leopards still live in the mountains, and hikers will inevitably come across troops of baboons. Various black eagles and other eagle species have colonised the craggy heights.

But while the pass has resulted in these mountains being easily accessible, their potential dangers should never be underestimated. In winter the climate is unpredictable and no one should take chances or attempt to hike or climb under-equipped. Over the years many inexperienced hikers have been beguiled by the peaceful allure of the mountains – sometimes with tragic consequences.

Du Toitskloof takes its name from Francois du Toit, a Huguenot farmer who was granted the farm *Kleine Bosch* at the foot of the Hawequas mountains in 1692, and who was the first European to cross the nek above his farm. Throughout the 18th century an old Khoikhoi cattle track was the only route through the kloof, until a local farmer built a road that went part of the way. Then, in 1821, an enterprising former soldier, Lieutenant Detlief Schonfeldt, having settled on a farm in Du Toitskloof, decided a mountain road was needed and began lobbying farmers from Franschhoek, Worcester, Paarl and Stellenbosch.

Funds flowed in and Schonfeldt invested heavily in the project himself. After persuading the government to supply tools and explosives, Schonfeldt directed operations at Kleigat, the most problematic section of the pass. After two years' toil, a rough, precarious wagon road was built over a section of the route where, according to one source, 'one false step would plunge the traveller into eternity'. To complete the road, Schonfeldt approached the government for more aid, which was denied. This resulted in his financial ruin, and the project was abandoned.

During the 1870s, the Du Toitskloof mountains were the scene of another commercial enterprise when manganese mining began. The lack of a

suitable road meant that transportation of the ore was a major headache. An aerial cable was erected to carry the ore down to a more accessible slope in buckets, from where it was transported by cableway to Wellington. But the poor quality and low yields of the ore, combined with transportation problems, caused the venture to close down.

The challenge of Du Toitskloof attracted renowned road engineers Andrew Geddes Bain and Charles Michell to survey for a pass, but the magnitude of the job and the enormous expense involved put them off. It was not until the Second World War that the newly formed National Roads Board decided to move the main route to the north from Bain's Kloof to Du Toitskloof. The massive project got underway with the help of more than 500 Italian prisoners of war and the pass was eventually completed with local labour and opened amid great fanfare in 1949.

(Above) The top of the Du Toitskloof Pass provides motorists with magnificent views of the farmlands of the Paarl valley. (Left) The crystal clear waters of the Elands River attract trout fishermen from all over the Cape.

Du Toitskloof at a glance (map page 34)

How to get there: From Cape Town, take the N1 to Paarl. The road bypasses Paarl and the pass is about five minutes' drive further on. Avoid the toll tunnel if you wish to take in all the magnificent sights that the pass has to offer.
Weather: Hot in summer, but winters can be cold and rainy (temperatures can fall below freezing in the higher areas). Mist can make driving, hiking and climbing hazardous.
What to do: Hiking, climbing, fishing, and swimming in the pristine mountain water.

Special attractions: The deep and bracing mountain pools.
More information: Paarl Valley Publicity Association, PO Box 47, Paarl 7620; tel (02211) 23829. Worcester Publicity Association, 75 Church Street, Worcester 6850; tel (0231) 71408. For permits, contact the Government Forester, Directorate of Nature and Environmental Conservation, Private Bag X14, Paarl 7622; tel (02211) 611535. Serious climbers should get in touch with the Mountain Club of SA, 97 Hatfield Street, Cape Town 8001; tel (021) 453412.

Table Bay's doleful 'Island of Exiles'

*Although easily visible from the shores of
Cape Town, Robben Island has maintained
a sad solitude down through the centuries*

SPRINGBOKS JUMP THROUGH THE AIR while near-by, a school of jackass penguins plunge through the surf like black-and-white torpedoes. On the road to the village, at the centre of which is a white, square-towered church, you pass a Second World War cannon and old sailboat cannons – and perhaps see several cars dating back to the Fifties. An unexpected amalgam, indeed – could this really be Robben Island?

Most of us might know where and what Robben Island is – a 574-ha curiosity in the middle of Table Bay – but relatively few of us have ever been there or know what mysteries it contains.

Most of the buildings on the island today date back to the Second World War years, when the island was controlled by the Defence Force. Three 9.2-inch guns still bear testimony to the armaments erected to defend Cape Town, while numerous bunkers from which 6-inch guns have been removed lie empty, their dark interiors just waiting to be explored.

The main centre of the island is a small village that has a post office, bank and a grocery store for the 500 islanders – most of them members of the Department of Correctional Services and their families. Though there is a small hydroponics project on the island, everything else – from milk to building materials – has to be ferried over the 12-km stretch of sea from Cape Town harbour. Is-

landers take one of the 17 trips available per week back and forth from Cape Town harbour in order to do most of their shopping. The island does, however, generate its own electricity and obtains its water from nine boreholes.

What contributes most to the aura of a previous age are the old cars that sputter along the narrow tar roads – including old Anglias and Austins. Over the years, the islanders have tended to choose old jalopies for transportation since there are no serious regulations on the island about the condition of cars, and because vehicles are needed only to cover very short distances.

When the Department of Correctional Services took over the island in 1961, it became a maximum-security prison for political prisoners and a medium-security one for ordinary criminals. The most famous political prisoner on the island was Nelson Mandela, and other well-known names included Walter Sisulu and Namibian leader Herman Toivo ya Toivo.

The last political prisoners were released in 1991, and the Department of Correctional Services presently keeps only about 700 medium-security prisoners on the island.

Much has been done down through the years to restore the island to the ecological haven it used to be centuries ago. As early as 1870, an afforestation programme was started on the island and by 1920 40 000 trees had been planted. In 1991, the island was included in the SA Natural Heritage Programme and its northern extremes were declared a bird sanctuary.

The island now serves as a breeding ground for 28 species of birds, including listed Red Data species such as the Damara tern, the Caspian tern and the jackass penguin. The colony of jackass penguins numbers 5 000 following the release of a number of rehabilitated birds onto the island by the SA National Foundation for the Conservation of Coastal Birds (SANCCOB) in 1982. Other wildlife on the island includes buck, ostrich, rabbit and the non-poisonous mole snake.

Where to stay

At the time of publication there were no accommodation facilities for visitors to Robben Island.

The stone church, designed by Sir Herbert Baker, which was built for the exclusive use of the island's lepers.

Most of the buildings on Robben Island are located at the south-eastern tip. The Cape's west coast can be seen stretching northwards up into the distance.

While the island will most probably turn into a venue for eager, smiling visitors, the melancholic memories of the place may be hard to dispel. The author Lawrence Green described it as 'The Island of Exiles', and this is the role it has played for centuries – a remote and inaccessible place, as one old book put it, for 'lawbreakers, lunatics and lepers'.

The Portuguese were said to have put prisoners here as early as 1525, but no traces of this occurrence have been found. In 1614, ten criminals were sent from Britain to establish a settlement on the island and provide fresh supplies for passing ships. They either died at the hands of Khoikhoi on the mainland or found their way back to England where they were hanged.

However, the island also had other uses. Owing to the antagonism of the indigenous people towards white seafarers, it played a crucial role in providing food. Rabbit and sheep were bred here, and passing sailors also stocked up here with whale oil, and seal meat and skins. The seals, of course, gave the island its name ('robben' being Dutch for seals).

In the early days of the colony, Robben Island proved to be a useful source of building material. Shells from its beaches were burnt for lime and, when the Castle was built, the island supplied the lime and much of the dressed stone used for its construction. Stone from the island was also used to build the Old Town House and many of Cape Town's original steps and tombstones.

Five years after Van Riebeeck's arrival in 1652, the island became the site of the country's very first lighthouse – consisting of a platform on which a fire was kept burning at night when ships of the Dutch East India Company were offshore. The first resident overseer, Pieter van Meerhof, took as his wife a Khoikhoi, Eva, who became the first Christian Khoikhoi in South Africa. She is buried in the church at the Castle.

It was during Van Riebeeck's time that the island first became a true prison. One of the island's most famous prisoners was Harry (or Herrie), a leading trader and chief of the Goringhaikona. He managed to escape to Saldanha in a leaky old boat – one of the island's few successful attempts at escape. The most regal prisoner was the King of Madura who was brought here in 1772 by order of the Dutch East India Company. In his honour, a Muslim memorial was eventually erected on Robben Island in 1969.

From 1845 to 1931 the island also served as both a mental asylum and a home for lepers. At first it was voluntary for lepers to come here, but it later became compulsory. The lepers, unlike the prisoners, were allowed to wander around most of the island till 10 pm. The only building they used which is still standing – the others were all burnt down for health reasons – is a church designed for their use by Sir Herbert Baker in 1896. The main church on the island is a square-towered Cape Gothic structure built in 1841.

There has never been a recorded case of anyone swimming to freedom, yet it could theoretically have been done as the island has become famous as a destination or starting point for long-distance swimmers. The first 13 swimmers set out from the island to Roggebaai in December 1926, a distance of 13,6 km. The only one to succeed – in 9 hours 35 minutes – was 15-year-old Peggy Duncan. A few days later Florrie Berndt swam the distance in 7 hours 25 minutes. Today the records for the 7-km swim to Bloubergstrand are around two hours for women and 1 hour 30 minutes for men.

Because of uncertain winds and fog, the island has been the graveyard of dozens of ships down through the centuries. A recent survey carried out by Navy divers identified at least 22 wreck sites, mostly on the western side.

Robben Island at a glance (map page 34)

How to get there: At present, the only way of seeing the island is to join one of the tours organised by the Department of Correctional Services. These are held on Tuesdays, Wednesdays and Saturdays during the summer months, and when the weather is fine during winter. The tour lasts half a day and consists of a sea trip, lasting 45 minutes, from Cape Town harbour to Robben Island, followed by a guided bus tour of about two hours on the island, and then a sea trip back to Cape Town. Reservations can be made by contacting The Commander, Private Bag, Robben Island 7400; tel (021) 4111006. *More information*: Department of Correctional Services, Private Bag X136, Pretoria 0001; tel (012) 2079111.

A homely monument to a more gracious age

Situated at the top of the Cape Town Gardens, Bertram House reflects the elegant English contribution to life at the Cape in the 19th century

JUST A SHORT WALK from the hurly-burly of Cape Town's city centre, you'll find a uniquely preserved slice of Regency Cape Town – a simple, double-storey home that faithfully mirrors the measured pace and immaculate taste of a bygone age.

Carefully restored and furnished from a variety of sources, Bertram House epitomises the style of a well-to-do British family at the Cape during the early 1800s. Its square solidity is typical of the many houses in late Georgian Cape Town that stood regally alongside the whitewashed, green-shuttered thatched dwellings that were the norm.

Elegance and symmetry were the hallmarks of the Georgian style, yet the house was saved from stuffiness by an informality of spirit, both inside and out. It's not hard to imagine the crinoline-clad ladies of yesteryear tittle-tattling the afternoon away to the satisfying clink of silver teaspoons against the finest of bone china – where the best sweetener of tea was undoubtedly gossip.

The house was probably built by a Yorkshire attorney, John Barker, who named it after his wife Ann Bertram Findlay and registered the property in 1839. In some correspondence of 1836 he writes: 'I am much engaged with bricks and mortar, being my own architect builder ... with my new slate roof, the front of English brick.' Bertram House was declared a national monument in 1962 but the complete restoration took place only in 1983-4.

An interesting feature of Bertram House is its projecting, enclosed porch that shields the entrance from the fierce southeaster – an innovative practical modification from English Georgian adapted for the Cape climate.

The cool, elegant rooms have been restored and furnished meticulously in the period style. Progress through the rooms is soothed along by the muted, soporific ticking and chiming of clocks. Lovers of antiques will be entranced by polished mahogany, walnut and ebony, rich oriental rugs, fine paintings and engravings, and other period paraphernalia.

Downstairs, the interleading drawing rooms are separated by massive panelled doors. These rooms were the heart of the home where most informal life, visiting and recreation took place. Games, needlework and music were daily occupations and the furnishings include card tables, a large square piano and a pedal harp. Any of Jane Austen's Georgian heroines would have been at home here, comfortably seated on a Hepplewhite, and engaged in embroidery and repartee. It was here in the drawing rooms that the family would gather before proceeding to the dining room for dinner.

The main bedroom of the home features a magnificent four-poster bed, beside which stands a baby's cradle.

Dominating the dining room is a polished mahogany table reflecting the shimmering chandelier. The table is set for dinner which, in the early 19th century, was a formal affair, served at about 7 pm. Chinese porcelain and English silver and glass grace the table – the glassware surely no stranger to Constantia's famous wines. After the meal, it was customary for the ladies to rise and retire to the drawing room, leaving the men to rejoin them later after their port and pipes.

These rooms all feature reproduction period wallpaper imported from England which, according to custom and curtailed by expense, was used only in the three best rooms. The rather gloomy wall colours in the other rooms bear testimony to the authenticity of detail. Paint scrapings were taken from each room to determine the original colour scheme and the resulting beige, dark olive green and putty-coloured walls are relieved by the woodwork which is painted fresh white throughout.

The master of the house received visitors in the library, a small but nevertheless imposing room that is as masculine as the morning room next door is feminine. Occasionally used for breakfast, and more often as a morning sitting room, the morning room faces due east, and if you visit the house before noon, the sun streams obligingly through the long sash windows. A somewhat lonely canary in a highly polished brass cage chirps away incessantly in one corner.

Sadly, the kitchen – often the most revealing and interesting part of any house – does not exist: in fact, its original site is unknown. However, there is a small room with a display of furniture and artefacts from the period to give an idea of how it may have looked.

The top of the elegantly curved staircase is lit by a hexagonal skylight. Apart from two bedrooms – one of them furnished with an intimidatingly high four-poster bed – the upstairs section of the house has been devoted to a collection of objects commonly used in daily life at the time. Needlework was considered a suitable pastime for women in that more leisured age and a display includes intricately carved ivory needlecases, glittering cut-steel buttons and a fascinating miniature workbox contained in the shell of a walnut, complete with tiny scissors, needles and a stiletto.

Other interesting exhibits include such vital accessories to 19th-century life as candle snuffers, silver and mother-of-pearl visiting-card cases, a silver letter scale and an inkstand with a 'pounce pot' for drying the ink – everyday utilitarian objects that are

The solid, red-brick exterior of Bertram House. The enclosed porch seen in the front was specially incorporated to shield the entrance from the infamous Cape southeaster.

themselves works of art. There is even an engraved silver matchbox-sized object called a 'vinaigrette', which contained a small sponge soaked in perfume which was used to 'forestall fainting, or ward off unpleasant smells'.

The eclectic jewellery collection varies from a delicate moonstone necklace to a crude bog-oak brooch. There is also a selection of hair jewellery which was popular at the time – earrings, necklaces and so on made from real hair which was woven into intricate and delicate ropes and lattices.

The food and drink collection is one of the most interesting displays and includes indispensables such as a punch strainer, punch and toddy ladles, a tiny silver nutmeg grater, brandy warmers, and a Punch, Judy and Toby condiment set. And would your average 19th-century household have been complete without a pair of silver grape scissors or a silver marrow spoon? Possibly not.

Crystal glassware and fine porcelain grace the large mahogany dining table.

Bertram House at a glance (map page 34)

How to get there: From the centre of town walk towards the mountain all the way to the top of The Avenue – Bertram House will be the last building on your right. Parking is available right in front of Bertram House, access to which is through the Hiddingh Hall Campus from Orange Street (turn down at the Rheede Street traffic lights).
More information: Bertram House, PO Box 645, Cape Town 8000; tel (021) 249381, or the SA Cultural History Museum, PO Box 645, Cape Town 8000; tel (021) 4618280.
Visiting times: The house is open from Tuesday to Saturday from 9.30 am to 4.30 pm. There is a small entrance fee.

A home fit for an imperial king

The official residence of the country's leader is Groote Schuur, the famous home that Sir Herbert Baker designed for Cecil John Rhodes on the slopes of Devil's Peak

AN AIR OF MYSTERY surrounds the area between the old zoo and the Rondebosch Main Road. Although many people are aware that one of South Africa's most remarkable homes stands beyond the sentry-patrolled gates, the barbed wire fencing and thick, obscuring trees, few members of the public have actually been inside it – even though it's possible to do so.

At the mention of Groote Schuur, most people immediately think of the hospital. Yet Groote Schuur is also the house that Cecil John Rhodes had built for himself around a hundred years ago. He bequeathed it to the nation – along with vast tracts of mountainside that stretched all the way to Constantia Nek, Kirstenbosch included. One day, walking across his vast estate, he commented to a friend: 'I love to think that human beings will walk this way long after I am gone.'

Groote Schuur has been the official residence of successive Prime Ministers for nearly a century. What is not widely known is that it is possible for you to visit it by booking onto one of the weekly guided tours that are held when the State President is in residence in Pretoria. There are also occasional open days in aid of charity which are publicised in the press beforehand.

Originally, Groote Schuur (Dutch for 'Big Barn') was built by the Dutch East India Company in about 1657 as part of De Schuur, the company's granary. The original barn was converted into a homestead sometime in the late 18th century and the estate changed hands many times, eventually becoming a summer home to successive British governors.

By the time Rhodes bought it in 1893, Groote Schuur was in a state of neglect. With characteristic singleness of purpose, he immediately set about improving it. By chance he met an untried young English architect who was visiting Cape Town, and commissioned him to restore Groote Schuur. For the architect, Herbert Baker, this was a heaven-sent opportunity to make his name.

Rhodes's brief to Baker was to enlarge the house and restore something of its original Cape Dutch appearance. 'I like teak and whitewash ... I want the big and simple – barbaric if you like,' was Rhodes's quirky instruction to the fledgling architect.

The plan that finally emerged from Baker's drawing board was a charming hybrid of ornate gables, colonnaded verandas, barley-sugar chimneys, whitewashed walls and warm teak woodwork. Groote Schuur was a triumph for Baker who, with this design, actually created a new form of South African vernacular architecture. However, the house that stands today was in fact Baker's second attempt – three years after he had completed his renovation, Groote Schuur burnt down. Baker immediately redesigned it, incorporating a few changes, one of which was to replace the thatched roof with tiles.

Rhodes had agents and minions on the lookout for furniture, books, porcelain, silver and glassware – he had definite ideas and more than enough money to realise them. He particularly wanted items from the Cape, and many of these had to be reimported from Holland. Today, the house and its interior remain almost exclusively as they were in Rhodes's day.

The rooms have a comfortable domesticity, enlivened by evidence of Rhodes's eclectic tastes. The wooden corner posts on one of the staircases are carved in the form of the enigmatic soapstone eagles that were found at the Zimbabwe Ruins; Delft tiles decorate the downstairs skirtings and several of the fireplaces; and some of the fireplaces themselves have Zimbabwe soapstone surrounds and copper hoods.

Among the most interesting items are souvenirs from his travels, including various artefacts from the Zimbabwe Ruins, an exquisitely inlaid Moorish Egyptian travelling writing table, an old Cape stinkwood armoire with secret drawers and an elephant-shaped drinking cup.

There are very few paintings, and in any case, the vast areas of wood panelling don't encourage them. Ranged throughout the house, however, are a series of four rare 17th-century Flemish tapestries, these being allegorical depictions of America, Europe, Africa and Asia respectively. (Australia had not yet been discovered when they were made.)

The front entrance of Groote Schuur. Set into the central gable is a frieze depicting the arrival of Jan van Riebeek at the Cape.

Rhodes's books reflect his wide interests. The study houses a unique collection of obscure Roman and Greek classics. Rhodes commissioned Hatchard's in London to have them translated just for his reading pleasure – a job that took a group of people seven years to complete! Only one copy of each was typed and leather bound, and it remains the only collection of its kind in the world.

The library houses the bulk of the books, most of them dealing with travel and exploration. Ancient Egypt exerted a particularly powerful influence over Rhodes's visionary mind and more than 50 books in his library are devoted to the history, mythology and religion of this ancient civilisation.

When Rhodes was alive, two photographs of falcon statues – representing Ra, the ancient Egyptian sun-god – enjoyed pride of place next to his bed. These images were placed above and below a photograph of one of the soapstone eagles from the Zimbabwe Ruins – the juxtaposition of these images echoing Rhodes's belief that these two civilisations were connected in some way. This triptych of raptor totems has since been moved to a more obscure place in the room – perhaps someone felt uncomfortable with such a prominent place for Rhodes's pagan preoccupations!

The bathroom adjoining Rhodes's bedroom is a highlight. It contains a huge bathtub carved from a single piece of Paarl mountain granite, for which the floor had to be specially reinforced. Water spurts through the mouth of a brass lion, and once the bath is full, it takes a mere five minutes before the water is stone cold again!

Rhodes enjoyed filling his house with people, and during his short residence at Groote Schuur many visitors trooped through the heavy teak front door and took tea or partied on the colonnaded back veranda, his favourite place for entertaining. Among the frequent guests were the Rudyard Kiplings, Lord and Lady Edward Cecil, Baden-Powell, the Duke of Westminster, and the treacherous Princess Radziwill who tried, in vain, to connive a permanent place for herself in Rhodes's bachelor life. She was finally jailed for forging promissory notes from him.

The large bay window of Rhodes's bedroom commands a magnificent view of the slopes of Devil's Peak.

Many of Rhodes's esteemed guests were horrified at his egalitarian habit of throwing open his gates to the Cape Town public every weekend, where they would arrive, children in tow, to picnic happily on the lawns. Rhodes said: 'Some people like to have cows in their park; I like to have people in mine.' Unfortunately it was not a sentiment shared by future leaders of South Africa who occupied the house.

The gardens at Groote Schuur enjoy a matchless setting against the hunched, benevolent presence of Devil's Peak. From the back veranda, shallow steps lead up past the formal terraces to an avenue of stone pines, from where one can gaze down at Baker's handiwork and the spread of urban Cape Town beyond.

The massive rose garden is edged with thick hedges of starry blue plumbago – Rhodes's favourite flower. The incredible esteem in which this controversial man was held is reflected in the fact that for many years after his death – 26 March 1902 – thousands of Capetonians would religiously commemorate the occasion by wearing a sprig of plumbago on their lapels.

Groote Schuur at a glance (map page 34)

How to get there: From the city centre, take the M3 to the southern suburbs and take the Rondebosch off-ramp. The estate lies between the highway and Main Road.
Weather: If you've any choice in the matter, try to avoid the gardens in winter. This part of the Peninsula has one of the highest rainfall levels in the Cape.
Special attractions: Rhodes's bathroom, the furniture throughout the house, the gardens.
More information and guided-tour bookings: Write to The Household Manager, Westbrooke, Rondebosch 7700.

(Above) Cecil John Rhodes.
(Left) The massive bathtub in Rhodes's bathroom – carved out of a single block of granite.

An oasis of peace where only bird cries break the silence

Situated in close proximity to Muizenberg and Zeekoevlei, the Rondevlei Nature Reserve is home to more than 200 bird species during the summer months

One of the hides from which the bird life of Rondevlei may be viewed. The Muizenberg mountain can be seen in the background.

NOT FAR FROM the roar of the powerboats on Zeekoevlei lies a tranquil stretch of water called Rondevlei. This little-known oasis is a natural haven for a wide variety of aquatic bird life and is today one of the country's most important environmental education centres.

When it was established more than 40 years ago, the reserve lay in a rural area with a few farms dotted about. Today, tens of thousands of people live on its borders. Yet, despite the uncomfortably close proximity of suburbia, Rondevlei remains a haven of peace, and home to a large variety of birds, mammals and reptiles.

Armed with binoculars and cameras (no sound equipment is allowed), visitors can wander around the northern shore on a gravel path, from which lead detours into rustic but comfortable hides and look-out towers that are equipped with mounted telescopes. Views from the hides are spectacular, focusing attention on every detail of the vlei as well as taking in the panoramic sweep of the area, such

as the nearby Muizenberg mountains which form a dramatic backdrop to the view.

The 200-ha area consists of a vlei surrounded by low coastal dunes. Apart from the ubiquitous acacia bush – which is gradually being cleared to allow indigenous plant life to re-establish itself – the flora is coastal fynbos and strandveld. Not long ago, just outside the boundary fence, the warden of Rondevlei found a particular protea (*Serruria foeniculaceae*) which had long been assumed to be extinct. This rare protea was subsequently reintroduced into the reserve.

During the winter months, dense beds of grass and reed occupy the shoreline, and only with the receding water level in summer are the mud and sand exposed. In spring, the migratory waders start arriving, and by early summer the bird population is at its most abundant, with a wide variety of species roosting and nesting in the reeds.

The ongoing study programme at Rondevlei includes the daily monitoring and recording of

species and nesting activity, and a set schedule of ringing is undertaken by the Cape Bird Club. Birds ringed here have subsequently been found all over the world, the furthest being a little stint which finally turned up 12 000 km away in the Ural Mountains of Russia.

Since the establishment of the reserve, over 200 bird species have been recorded here, with populations waxing and waning according to climate and environmental changes. They include pelican, flamingo, duck, heron, fish eagle, owl, egret, ibis, Egyptian goose, weaver bird, kingfisher, moorhen, coot and many others – including occasional visits from rare Caspian tern, Arctic tern, house martin, European swallow, little bittern and hoopoe.

Apart from bird-spotting, there are plenty of other creatures that could cross your path. These may include grysbok and steenbok, clawless otter, clawed and long-toed frog, dune mole, water mongoose and forest shrew. Rodents in the area include chestnut tree mice, vlei rats, striped field mice and brown rats – the last-mentioned being unwelcome gate-crashers from the surrounding suburbs. There are also porcupine, Cape hare, four varieties of tortoise and no fewer than 15 varieties of snake. Common are the black water snake, mole snake and the feared boomslang and Cape cobra.

Look out for the hippos that were reintroduced in 1981 amid much fanfare after an absence of almost three centuries. The main purpose of the reinstatement of the hippos was to control the encroaching grass which was responsible for a declining bird population. Since they have settled into the neighbourhood, however, other advantages have become apparent. Channels and paths created by them are serving to contain excess reed growth, and an unexpected bonus is the generous bestowal of hippo droppings: Rondevlei's fish populations and other micro-organisms are the beneficiaries of this largesse, which provides a boost to the nutritional content of the water.

While wallowing in the mud, these new residents inadvertently uncovered hippo bones dating back about 300 years. This supports previous studies which indicate that during the 17th century hippos were fairly common in the vleis of the Cape Flats. In fact, within 18 days of Van Riebeeck landing at the Cape in 1652, one of his men shot and killed a hippo near the present Church Square in central Cape Town. They found the flesh so delicious that hippos were relentlessly hunted to supply passing ships with fresh meat, and by 1700 they were all but extinct in the Peninsula.

The excitement of the hippos' resettlement in 1981, followed by the births of their offspring, turned the Rondevlei hippos into local celebrities. Unfortunately for visitors, hippos are nocturnal and usually laze the day away, reclining in reedbeds or

A large variety of water birds are found at Rondevlei, including the white pelican which is able to soar through the air with seemingly effortless grace.

submerged in deeper water. As a result, they're not often seen, but for those who live in hope there's a clearly marked hippo crossing which bisects the main path and meanders off into dense bush.

The Leonard Gill Field Museum is situated near the entrance to the reserve and includes mounted specimens of birds, reptiles and mammals found in the area and charts of the migratory patterns of birds. There is also information about the work carried out at Rondevlei, including a mock-up that displays the use of mist nets to capture birds for ringing purposes. Invaluable to schools and other organised groups is a small lecture theatre in which audio-visual presentations are given, and a fully equipped resource centre where in-depth studies of the local environment are made.

Even for those without any curiosity about its numerous inhabitants, Rondevlei is an accessible retreat where you can relish a silence that is broken only by bird cries and the distant, muted hum of traffic. Picnickers are welcome as long as their litter accompanies them home, but fires are not allowed. This is a nature reserve, so your pet will not be welcome, and don't even contemplate picking the flowers.

Rondevlei is open every day of the year except Christmas Day from 8 am to 5 pm. There is a small entrance fee and regular visitors can take advantage of an annual season ticket.

Rondevlei Nature Reserve at a glance (map page 34)

How to get there: From the city take the M5 which becomes Prince George Drive; at the intersection with Victoria Road there is a sign for Rondevlei, turn left and follow the road until Fisherman's Walk, turn right and you'll see the entrance ahead of you.
Special attractions: Spotting rare species such as the little bittern or the resident hippos.

Visiting times: The Rondevlei Nature Reserve is open daily from 8 am till 5 pm, except on Christmas Day. A small fee is charged, but regular visitors to the reserve can buy an annual season ticket.
More information: Write to The Warden, Rondevlei Nature Reserve, Fisherman's Walk, Zeekoevlei 7945; tel (021) 7062404.

A look at the long arm of the law a long time ago

*Take a fascinating and chilling walk
through the history of crime and punishment
at the Police Museum on Main Road, Muizenberg*

LOVERS OF CRIME NOVELS will relish the Police Cultural History Museum at Muizenberg. It provides a really atmospheric walk down through South Africa's criminal yesteryears, and even features realistic models enacting particularly dramatic events.

The museum occupies two old buildings: the old police station and the courthouse. Throughout, furniture and equipment are the original police issue, refreshingly unrestored and bearing both the scars and the patina of daily use. Several exhibits have been theatrically mounted as windows to the past – the visitor literally looks through a large plate glass window into a room untouched by the passage of the years.

The first of these is the spartan single quarters that a mounted policeman would have endured until about 1938. The room has a touching homeliness – the highly polished shoes placed neatly underneath the narrow iron bed, the personal items laid out on the table, such as a cutthroat razor and a rather primitive-looking toilet roll. Appropriately situated immediately behind the single quarters are the stables, complete with a model of a horse and a display of essential equestrian equipment.

Different police uniforms make up several of the exhibits in this section: formal police mess dress from a more elegant age worn between 1913 and 1954; the khaki uniform of a policeman during the Second World War, complete with canvas puttees and gas mask; and colonial-style uniforms worn by the 'non-white' mounted police from 1923-38.

Mundane, everyday objects are often the most fascinating, and the display of office equipment includes old pens, inkwells, rounded rulers (so as not to smudge the ink), glue crystals and a paper press. There is also a collection of 'tickey' coins especially produced by the Post Office for police use: in the days before radio, a policeman who wanted to get in touch with the charge office would go to a public phone booth and use one of these police issue coins. They're easily identifiable with a hole in the middle and stamped with the initials GPO and SAP.

Another enlightening display consists of garbage dug up when the garden was being laid out on the site of the old mounted police quarters: decorative old bottles, including a milk bottle, a 'nip' for brandy, and bygone hair-oil and KWV eau de Cologne bottles; spoons, porcelain shards, and an ancient tube of shaving cream – inspiring enough to propel you with your spade out into the garden at home.

Yellow footprints lead you into the second building, which includes the original courthouse and custody cells. More windows to the past, this time a turn-of-the-century charge office and inspector's office eerily set up with lifelike dummies frozen in time. Inside, the scene is so convincing that you feel it's not beyond the bounds of possibility for the characters suddenly to get to work.

Displays detailing several famous murders have been graphically reconstructed with relief models of appropriate scenes. For example, the Batho murder scene features two shadowy figures in the dead of night digging a shallow grave in the sanddunes. Other murders depicted include the once-famous Lindeveldt and Radulfini cases, and the grisly Bain's Kloof killings where John Smith, an escaped prisoner, slaughtered a young couple and their dog who were camping at this well-known beauty spot. Their bodies were discovered near their tent and, when police arrived on the scene, they found a pipe, still warm, belonging to the killer.

Drugs and alcohol share the same display: there are examples of illegal stills, ingenious smuggling

Some of the displays in the Police Museum are delightfully realistic. Here, in an old-world charge office, a pretty member of the public is perhaps reporting the theft of her coach.

The exterior of the Police Museum. Once a police station and courthouse, the building is located a stone's throw from the sea's edge and looks directly out over the wide expanse of False Bay.

methods, piles of dagga and mandrax tablets, and a variety of home-made pipes – including a 'bottle neck', a 'hubbly-bubbly' (water pipe), and two pipes crafted from coconuts.

The only vaguely political content to this museum (apart from the obvious legacy of apartheid) are photographs, shattered windows and scorched memorabilia from the Mowbray and Athlone bomb blasts in the 1980s, and original weapons used in the Bulhoek Uprising of 1921. Apparently at God's behest, sect leader Enoch Mgijima had led his followers, the 'Israelites', to Bulhoek in the eastern Cape, where they squatted illegally to await the end of the world. After several futile efforts to persuade them to leave, hundreds of men under the Commissioner of Police were sent to the area. A fierce battle ensued, at the end of which over 183 of the 500 'Israelites' lay dead or dying.

After inspecting the small, neat and surprisingly cheerful courtroom, follow the ghostly yellow footprints which lead ominously down a steep flight of stairs. Here are the cells where non-white 'awaiting trial' prisoners were held. (Whites were held in Simon's Town and brought through for their hearings.) The gloomy cells are everything you imagine prison cells to be – cold, dark and acrid smelling.

An exhibition of home-made weapons is a special attraction here. Particularly chilling are the zip-guns, all apparently in good working order – they bristle with springs and somehow manage to look far more dangerous than an ordinary manufactured weapon. The museum also has a grim selection of machetes, pangas, assegais, sharpened spikes, barbed fish spears and so on. Even bicycle-chains, it seems, have a new and lethal use when they are looped and attached to the end of a stick, and gardening shears for suburban privets have been taken apart, sharpened and reincarnated as deadly weapons. Long spikes and sword-like weapons seem to be popular, sometimes concealed in colourful walking sticks.

It's almost light relief to visit the cell opposite where there is a reconstruction of waxwork inmates engrossed in a break-out which actually occurred in this very cell, complete with the original scorch-marks and broken ceiling that resulted from the event. The cell also contains a 'punishment bench' with a selection of canes, as well as a rather incongruous drawing-room cushion which was placed over the prisoner's back to protect his kidneys should a lash go astray.

An exhibition case contains old circulars issuing directives for the treatment of prisoners, and some hollow eggshells bear testimony to collusion between the kitchen and the cells – the cook had carefully blown the eggs into which he had inserted matches for the prisoners. The last cell is locked, but visitors can check up on the 'inmate' through the peephole as he stares glassily into space. The cell detail is exact: the game of dice played by the prisoners, their slop-out pails, and the blanket on the floor to sleep on.

All in all, it's quite enough to make anyone contemplating a life of crime reconsider their decision.

The Police Museum at a glance (map page 34)

How to get there: The museum is situated diagonally opposite the Muizenberg railway station on the mountain side of Main Road. The South African and SAP flags are displayed outside.
Visiting times: Open Mondays to Fridays from 8 am to 3.30 pm, Saturdays from 9 am to 1 pm and Sundays from 2 pm to 5 pm. Closed on public holidays. No entrance fee is charged, but there is a donation box.
More information: Police Cultural History Museum, Main Road, Muizenberg 7945; tel (021) 7887035.

A taxidermist's skills have produced a horse so lifelike that you half expect the creature to give a friendly whinny and a shake of its head.

51

An old, abandoned mine overlooking the breakers

Echoing mineshafts and rusting machinery are an evocative reminder of yesteryear on one of the Cape Peninsula's most scenic mountainside walks

HIGH ABOVE FLORA BAY, the craggy face of the mountainside is pockmarked with several large holes – the portals of what remains of an old manganese mine. On the shore a few hundred metres below are the remains of the mine's jetty and, linking the two, like a broken chain, are occasional rusted remnants of the chute used to carry ore down the mountain.

Over the years, the area has been gradually reclaimed by nature. Apart from the occasional explorer and courtesy calls by dassies or baboons, the mine has remained relatively undisturbed for more than 80 years.

Although it's always worth climbing the mountain for the views, wildlife, flowers and general recreation, the remains of the mine are an extra attraction. Be warned, however, that it is extremely dangerous to try to explore it: over the years, portions of its tunnels have collapsed, while rockfalls are an ever-present hazard, especially after heavy rains. There is, however, plenty to see in the immediate vicinity of the diggings.

Soon after setting off along the path you may discover the remains of the controversial chute – consisting of segments of concrete foundation blocks, pieces of rusty old iron pipes and sheeting scattered around. (Most of the larger pieces have been recovered and placed in the Hout Bay Museum.) The path eventually forks and, although both branches will eventually lead you to the mine, the left-hand one is the more direct route to the main horizontal shaft.

About 3 000 tons of sorted ore are stacked in dumps on the site and if you're sharp-eyed (or just lucky), you might discover a relic that has been overlooked. However, anything of interest should be left exactly where you find it, although the museum in the village would no doubt be interested to hear about it.

There are about eight shafts in all – the largest opening is a majestic 15 m in height and about 3 m wide, and the smallest, now extremely difficult to find, had to be negotiated on hands and knees by the miners. Some of the entrances to the mine are heavily overgrown while others have been blocked by rockfalls. A large tree trunk marks the entrance of the longest tunnel – it penetrates the mountainside for a total of 84 m.

Back down in Hout Bay village, the museum has a display relating to the mine. Among the exhibits are a relief model of the area marking the manganese deposits, examples of the rocks found and old photographs of the mine and the jetty. Other relics from the site include a wheelbarrow, pickaxes, hooks, cables and a chainsaw.

The old jetty is not as easy to reach as one would expect. Private and aloof, it is well hidden from the road. Years ago, a sandy beach stretched all the way round from the existing Hout Bay beach to Flora Bay and the jetty would perhaps have been accessible. These days, it's advisable to try to persuade a local to guide you there. The remains of the jetty are easy to spot, the concrete struts marching hopelessly, but nobly, out to sea.

In recent times, mining in the Chapman's Peak area has become a very emotive topic and the debacle in the early 1990s over the mining of kaolin tends to obscure the fact that the region has been mined before, although not with the greatest success. The first mine in the area was on the Silvermine plateau on the other side of Chapman's Peak. The site was given the ironic name after optimistic silver prospectors had sunk a pit there in 1687 and then failed to find even a hint of the metal.

The mine has a number of different entrances, the largest of these being about 15 m in height.

There are conflicting reports about who discovered that the mountainside contained deposits of manganese, but the earliest traceable reference seems to be *The Cape Monthly Magazine* of 1873, which reveals that the discovery was made by someone referred to cryptically as C.B.E. A company was formed to assess the deposits in the 1880s and this eventually led to the establishment of the Hout Bay mine.

The site was originally owned by Jacob Trautmann, a German immigrant who founded Hout Bay's fishing industry. In 1892 Trautmann sold off 22 morgen of land at a pound per morgen. The mountains must have reverberated to Trautmann's reaction when, only months later, the land was discovered to be rich in manganese and changed hands for 120 pounds per morgen. However, events were to come full circle; after the failure of the mine, a younger Trautmann repurchased the property and the family still owns the land today.

When the Hout Bay Manganese Company Ltd was formed, mining started at full throttle. By 1909 the venture was steaming ahead with over 200 turbaned Indian labourers being specially brought to the country to work on the mine. Horizontal shafts were driven into the mountainside and explosives fractured the rock.

Being so close to the sea for the transportation of the ore was a bonus for the company and a jetty was built for loading the manganese onto ships. Rocky outcrops provided foundations for the concrete bases which supported the jetty's struts and girders. But between the mine and the jetty was about a kilometre of rugged, steep mountain. Getting the mined ore down to the jetty and on to the waiting ships posed a problem. The route chosen was seemingly the simplest: straight down the mountain.

A corrugated iron chute (about 750 m long) mounted on silver birch poles was erected, and the manganese was loaded at several stations along its length. The gradient of the slope was about 30° to 45° and there was no method of controlling the velocity of the ore's passage. Not surprisingly, the ore thundered recklessly down the mountainside like a runaway train. The chute was often wrecked and eventually had to be replaced by large iron pipes. But the problem didn't end there – the ore tended to get stuck and block the pipe. A combination of these factors probably gave rise to the legend, often reported as fact, that after dynamiting a blocked pipe to clear it, the liberated ore screamed down the mountain, straight through the hull of a waiting ship, which promptly sank.

Unfortunately, even the most superficial probe exposes this bogus but entertaining tale. First of all, divers have never found evidence of a wreck below the surface; and, secondly, the pipe disgorged the ore onto a levelled area near the jetty. Bags were filled with manganese and then hand-lashed to cocopans which ran on rails along the jetty. If further proof were needed, the rusting remains of the cocopans are still to be seen.

Sadly, the whole operation was doomed to failure. These practical handicaps, together with unfavourable economic conditions abroad and the poor grade of the manganese, conspired to sabotage the venture and in 1911 the Hout Bay mine finally closed down.

(Above) A panoramic view of mountain and sea awaits those who climb up to the entrance of the mine.
(Left) A photograph taken while the mine was operational shows labourers posing on the protea-covered mountainside.

The manganese mine at a glance (map page 34)

How to get there: From Hout Bay, start up Chapman's Peak Drive – beyond the blockhouse a gravel road goes off to the left. Follow this around the hairpin bend on foot. The path to the mine branches off after about 40 m.
More information: Hout Bay Information Bureau/Museum, 4 Andrew's Road, Hout Bay 7800; tel (021) 7903270.

Scenic enclave of the 'bare-it-all brigade'

*Situated just southwest of Llandudno,
the sparkling white beach of Sandy Bay
remains one of the most precious
pearls of the Cape Peninsula*

IN THE SHELTER of a majestic massif with the somewhat undignified name of Karbonkelberg, lies an area of exceptional beauty – one of the last remaining stretches of pristine, natural coastline in the Cape Peninsula.

Set like a jewel amongst this coastal strip of rocky outcrops is the main attraction, Sandy Bay, one of the Peninsula's most inaccessible beaches, making it a favoured venue of naturists down through the years. Apart from its attraction to nudists, the area's unspoilt beauty has made it popular with hikers and conservationists – but unfortunately its commercial potential has resulted in generations of developers itching to get their earthmoving equipment onto it.

Sandy Bay has often been in the local headlines. In less enlightened times, the police would periodically arrest the skinny-dippers, and there has been endless squabbling between conservationists and developers over on-again-off-again plans to turn the area into a playground for the wealthy. The beach is a good ten minutes' walk from the Sandy Bay car park, which is situated at the western end of Llandudno. Along the way is a spring (the only available source of fresh water in the area), small tidal inlets and Hammersteen, a rocky outcrop named after Hammer, an elderly fisherman who was washed from the rocks and drowned. 'Hammer

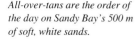

All-over-tans are the order of the day on Sandy Bay's 500 m of soft, white sands.

se spook' (Hammer's ghost) became a legend in the area and is apparently the reason why the spot is still avoided by some superstitious anglers.

Legends of a more urban flavour, however, surround the Sandy Bay nudists. Apocryphal tales of gay abandon draw curious 'first-timers' and many up-country visitors have made special pilgrimages there over the years – the final social mix on the 500 m beach including a disparate blend of naturists, voyeurs, curious tourists and strutting exhibitionists.

Apart from those in pursuit of an unbroken tan, the regulars include families for whom the area is a favourite picnic spot; there are rock pools to explore at low tide and anyone who can bear the numbing chill of the water will doubtlessly enjoy the excellent swimming.

Beyond the boulders bordering the beach, footpaths go off in all directions and hikers enjoy the natural beauty and challenge of the rugged terrain. Some of the paths are marked and one can actually walk all the way around to Hout Bay. However, this is not to be undertaken lightly: in some parts the trail passes perilously close to the sea and can only be attempted at low tide, and in view of the several steep climbs required, it should be avoided by anyone who suffers from even mild vertigo.

For the less ambitious, shorter walks are equally rewarding, particularly if you enjoy the rock shapes, fynbos variety and spectacular views – which include the Twelve Apostles, Little Lion's Head and the sweep of the coast. Following the track, the hiker will discover several caves and shell middens:

Paul's Cave and Shorty's Cave were named after *Strandlopers* who lived there many years ago, and on more than one occasion these caves have proved to be a conveniently remote refuge for criminals – a pair of modern-day cave-dwellers were recently arrested there in connection with a series of burglaries. An abundance of mussel shells was evidence that the fugitives had dined well on local produce!

This wild and unpredictable stretch of coastline is renowned for treacherous, rough seas and killer waves. In 1992 a young woman was swept off the rocks by a freak wave while hiking near Sandy Bay. Her body has never been recovered. The conditions are also responsible for several shipwrecks over the years, the most visible being the remains of the *Romelia* near Llandudno. This Greek-owned vessel, destined for a ships' graveyard in the Far East, broke tow during a gale on the night of 29 July 1977 and landed up on the rocks just off Llandudno.

Further south, the rocky peninsula of Oude Schip was the scene of a shipping disaster back in 1909 when the British steamship, the *Maori*, bound for the Antipodes, was wrecked on the rocks just after midnight on 5 August. The drama stretched over a number of days and, of a crew of 53, only 22 survived the mighty Atlantic rollers that regularly pound the rocks. The Hout Bay Museum has original newspaper pictures of the tragedy among its displays. More recently, in 1987, a Saldanha Bay trawler ran aground near the same spot – luckily, this time, there were no casualties.

Exploring the area, it is easy to understand the passions unleashed by those who want to protect this rugged Eden. The eagles that soar alongside Karbonkelberg's vertical mass are occasionally joined by paragliders who, in fine weather, launch themselves into space and ride the updraughts before landing safely on the beach below. Weather fronts travelling off the ocean strike the western flank of the mountain and its distinctively craggy face has been hewn and wind-scoured into shape by the southeaster. Winds are also responsible for blowing sand over from Hout Bay to replenish the dunes above Sandy Bay as well as the sand on the beach itself.

Botanists and environmentalists have placed a high premium on the area's ecological value, pointing out that the steep slopes of Karbonkelberg sweeping down to the cold waters of the Atlantic Ocean provide a unique environment for a wide variety of plantlife that is unmatched anywhere else on the southern sub-continent. No less than three examples of the Cape floral kingdom are found within this small area: mountain fynbos, coastal *renosterveld* and *strandveld*.

The ecological battle still rages over an area which includes several privately owned plots (such as hotel magnate Sol Kerzner's estate, Klein Leeukoppie) and stretches from the Sandy Bay car park over Little Lion's Head and Karbonkelberg as far as the Oude Schip Peninsula and the Hout Bay Sentinel. Conservationists have formed the Karbonkelberg Nature Reserve Proposal Committee which is lobbying hard for formal conservation status to ensure the proper protection and maintenance of the area.

Sandy Bay is situated on one of the country's most magnificent stretches of coastline. Its beach can be seen just below the sand dunes. Lion's Head is in the far background.

Sandy Bay at a glance (map page 34)

How to get there: From Hout Bay take the M6 (Victoria Road) over the mountain and turn left at Llandudno. Follow the road to the Sandy Bay parking area and then take the footpath. Sandy Bay can also be approached from Bantry Bay – turn right at the Llandudno turn-off.

Weather: Cold, wet and windy in winter (with the odd nice day thrown in); hot in summer, but sometimes windy then, too.

What to do: Swimming, sunbathing (*au naturel* if you prefer), fishing, diving, hiking, bird and wildlife spotting, rock-pool exploring, shell collecting, and paragliding off the mountain.

Special attractions: The naturists, of course!

More information: Captour, PO Box 863, Cape Town 8000; tel (021) 4185214/5. Wildlife Society of South Africa, PO Box 30145, Tokai 7966; tel (021) 7011397/8/9.

Houses of yesteryear recall a golden age

Past centuries come dramatically alive at the Village Museum, a complex of old buildings at the heart of the historic town of Stellenbosch, 55 km from Cape Town

Although Grosvenor House reflects the architectural style between 1800 and 1830, part of it was built in 1782.

A S SOUTH AFRICA'S second oldest town, Stellenbosch has more than its fair share of atmosphere and history. The languid, Continental air of this university town – with its oaklined streets and graceful architecture – invites exploration, and nowhere is the sense of history stronger than in the Village Museum.

This museum was established to provide an insight into the history of Stellenbosch from its founding by Simon van der Stel in 1679, and to follow the course of history down the centuries through the exteriors and interiors of various homes, each one representing the style of a particular period. At present, the museum covers about 5 000 sq m and comprises four residences ranging in time from 1709 to 1850, all of which have been meticulously restored over the years with enormous attention to detail and authenticity.

Before setting off around the Village Museum – which is designed to be explored chronologically – it's best to study the scale model in the entrance building to orientate yourself. Take your cue from the town's relaxed atmosphere and wander through slowly to give your imagination time to adjust to the roll of the centuries.

Passing through an impressively healthy herb and vegetable garden, you first reach the door of Schreuderhuis, the oldest restored and documented townhouse in South Africa. A humble, rustic dwelling, it was built by a German soldier, Sebastian

Schreuder, whom the Dutch East India Company sent to Stellenbosch in 1707. For the next two and a half centuries, generation after generation lived and died within the thick, rough lime-washed walls of the Schreuderhuis. After the Stellenbosch Museum acquired the property in 1972, it took several years to restore it to its original appearance.

Reed ceilings and dung or earth floors were the norm in this sort of dwelling (the floor is now simulated clay) and the house is redolent of the vegetative smell of thatch. The rooms are basically furnished with rare old Cape pieces and the effect – although the home of a poor family – is tranquil and comfortable.

A remarkable contrast is Blettermanhuis around the corner. A typical old Cape house built on an H-plan with six gables, it was the home of Hendrik

Where to stay

There is an extensive range of hotels, guesthouses and camping sites in and around Stellenbosch. For details, contact the Stellenbosch Tourist Information Bureau, PO Box 368, Stellenbosch 7600; tel (021) 8833584/8839633.

The oldest known townhouse in South Africa, Schreuderhuis was one of the few buildings to survive a fire that swept through the area in 1710.

The Village Museum at a glance (map page 34)

How to get there: From the Braak in the centre of town, go up Plein Street, turn right into Ryneveld Street and you'll see the museum entrance on your left.
Visiting times: The Village Museum is open Monday to Saturday from 9.30 am to 5 pm, and on Sundays and religious holidays (excluding Good Friday and Christmas Day) from 2 pm to 5 pm.
More information: Write to The Village Museum, c/o Stellenbosch Museum, Private Bag X5048, Stellenbosch 7600; tel (021) 8872902.

Lodewyk Bletterman, the last landdrost of Stellenbosch appointed by the Dutch East India Company. The house is thought to have been built around 1789 and is furnished to reflect the interior of a weathy Stellenbosch home in the period between 1750 and 1780.

In 1824 Bletterman's widow sold the house for 30 000 guilders (the currency of the Cape at the time) to the landdrost and heemraden and it was converted into offices and a courtroom. The out-building was renovated and served as a school for slaves which opened in 1825. In 1879, the building became the Stellenbosch Police headquarters, and remained so for a century until the Stellenbosch Museum acquired it.

The Storm family portrait hanging in the *voorhuis* (parlour) provides a link with the aristocratic building across the road. The young girl in the portrait is Maria Magdalena Storm, who married Christiaan Ludolph Neethling, the first owner of Grosvenor House. This building is the ancestral home of the Neethling family in South Africa and, together with two Cape Town houses – Martin Melck House and Koopmans de Wet House – is an excellent example of the double-storeyed, patrician townhouse which proliferated at the time. The house reflects the three decades between 1800 and 1830 and has an unmistakable English flavour – a result of the Second British Occupation of the Cape from 1806. Neo-classicism was all the rage, as the facade of Grosvenor House testifies, with its pedimented front door and fluted pilasters supporting an elegant cornice. Inside, the painted ceilings and marbled walls have been faithfully restored to their original appearance. The house is grand and elegant in style, with an enormous hall, a wide staircase, vast doorways and large rooms with high ceilings. Fine paintings, oriental carpets, Cape Regency furniture and English silver abound.

Outside, the garden is equally magnificent. It has been planted to replicate a garden of the period, with old roses, a fenced kitchen garden and formal herb beds. An added bonus is the permanent 'Toys of Yesteryear' exhibition housed in an annexe. A major attraction is the magnificent Uitkyk Miniature House with one-twelfth scale reproductions of some of the furniture and household accessories on display in the houses.

The fourth and final house in the village is Berghhuis. It was built in about the mid-18th century, as a typical single-storey thatched and gabled Cape dwelling. Olof Marthinus Bergh bought the house in 1836 and lived there with his family for over 40 years. It was during their residency that the house underwent a major conversion, with an upper storey and a pitched roof being added. The interior reflects the style of a middle-class family home during the period the Berghs resided here.

This is the only house of the four that has a central passage with rooms leading off it. The atmosphere is somewhat oppressive, due to the gloomy, showy clutter so beloved of the Victorians. Dado rails, heavily embossed wallpaper, dark mahogany furniture, draped *chaise longues* and elaborate ornaments all contribute to the rather cramped effect.

Restoring an old Cape house to its former state is a formidable task. The majority of people have never had the opportunity to view an old Cape house in the process of restoration, but just outside this house there is a room which has been left unplastered so that visitors can see for themselves what an archaeological investigation reveals about original materials and construction.

Berghhuis, a typical mid-18th century dwelling, has embossed wallpaper, dark mahogany furniture and elaborate ornaments.

Historical treasure trove preserved in the 'Vale of Grace'

Almost hidden in a fold of the Riviersonderend Mountains lies a uniquely preserved example of an 18th-century Cape village – the 'national cultural treasure' of Genadendal

EVERY YEAR, thousands of people pass the signpost to Genadendal en route to Greyton, little realising what a unique cultural and historic treasure trove they are missing. The 20 or so buildings that comprise the village centre are considered to be one of the country's most important groupings of 18th- and 19th-century architecture.

Tucked away in the foothills of the Riviersonderend Mountains, the area has changed little over the centuries. William Burchell, who wrote *Travels in the Interior of Southern Africa*, visited Genadendal in April 1811. His first impression still applies today: 'As we approached Genadendal, the mountains assumed a grandeur which the dubious light of evening very much increased. We had not long to contemplate the sublimity of this scene, as night soon drew its dark vale over it. The next morning my curiosity was much gratified on viewing the place by daylight. Its secluded situation, in a pleasant valley surrounded by bold and lofty mountains, perfectly accorded with the purpose for which it was chosen.'

Genadendal was founded in 1738 by Georg Schmidt, a Moravian missionary, who settled in Baviaanskloof (as Genadendal was originally known) among the Khoi and single-handedly set about his mission of converting 'the heathen'.

He planted a pear tree (a descendant of which still thrives today), a vegetable plot and a garden, and built a small dam and water furrow to serve them. Slowly his work began to pay off. The Khoi

started to attend prayers and many from the surrounding areas moved to Baviaanskloof to join Schmidt. But the baptism of his converts offended the powerful Dutch Reformed Church and eventually their opposition, the frustrations of his work, loneliness and isolation wore him down. His return to Europe in 1744 marked the end of missionary work in the Cape for nearly 50 years.

It was only in 1792 that three more Moravian missionaries arrived to carry on Schmidt's work. At Baviaanskloof they found a woman called Magdalena, who turned out to be the only surviving Khoi to have been baptised by Schmidt. Not only that, she had her original New Testament to show them. The missionaries were heartened to find others whose parents had handed down Schmidt's teachings and who still prayed.

Under the influence of the Moravian principles of meekness, simplicity and thrift, the area flourished. Fields were ploughed, crops planted, and Schmidt's dam repaired. In 1797 a mill was erected (reputedly the best in the entire colony at the time); a tannery produced Genadendal leather which became well known, and a major project was the smithy which manufactured the famous Herrnhuter knives – 'the Genadendal knives fetching a higher price among the Boers than those of the same kind imported from Europe', according to Burchell. The town also boasted skilled tailors and cobblers, masons, joiners and carpenters.

The people of Baviaanskloof were also renowned for their beautiful hymn-singing which attracted visitors from all over the colony. 'Nature has certainly not denied to Hottentots a musical ear,' commented Burchell. A church bell (proclaimed a national monument in 1957) was presented to the community by a local farmer and became the focus of village life, calling the faithful to prayer, the children to school, and signalling the time of day to workers in the fields. It was even claimed that it could be heard in Stellenbosch, 60 km away.

Eventually a small chapel was built alongside. After a visit to this chapel in 1796, Lady Anne Barnard wrote: 'I doubt much whether I should have entered St Peter's at Rome ... with a more awed impression of the Deity and his presence than I did in this little church of a few feet square, where the simple disciples of Christianity, dressed in the skins of animals, knew no pride, no hypocrisy.'

Because it was self-supporting – and respected far and wide as a peaceful, industrious, creative community – Baviaanskloof grew into the colony's second largest settlement after Cape Town. In 1806 the Moravian missionaries had to decide on a new

Once a training school, this attractive old building is now the premises of the museum.

name for the community and chose Genadendal, meaning 'Vale of Grace'.

The success of this flourishing community was blighted in more recent times when it fell victim to the iniquities of racial discrimination. With its missionary roots, its industry and training facilities, Genadendal had the potential to develop into a centre of learning – perhaps even another Stellenbosch – but this was prevented by its 'coloured' status. In 1926, the teacher's training college (the first in the country) was closed down by a government which felt that the coloured people had no need of tertiary education and were better employed on the farms in the area. These policies resulted in the impoverishment, degradation and stagnation of the town, and a loss of community pride.

Today, with the slow recognition of the town's historical significance, some of that pride has been restored, along with a portion of the village. The vernacular style is thatched, whitewashed cottages and Cape Dutch buildings, and about 20 structures have national monument status – including the old pioneer's cottage of 1792, the mill of 1798, the school of 1814 and the training school of 1838.

Physically, the village is dominated by the Moravian Church, built in 1891. Distinguished by its side tower crowned with an onion dome, it stands just off the leafy village square. The interior is cool and white and the congregation preserves its heritage of segregating the sexes – men and women enter and occupy different sides of the church.

However, the real heart of the town is its museum which is housed in the old training school. Its very existence is something of a miracle, considering its history. In the 1950s, Genadendal was ravaged by collectors who stripped the town of its antiquities, but despite that the contents of the museum (of which virtually everything originated in Genadendal) were finally declared a National Cultural Treasure in 1991.

Ironically, although the village is a unique part of South Africa's heritage and the museum the only one ever to be given this status, it has no state funding. Ensuring its continued existence is a constant battle, dependent entirely on visitors' donations and private sponsorship.

The village's unique history is well documented in the artefacts, particularly in products from its golden age: elegant copper kettles and old irons, hand-wrought tools from the smithy and examples of the much sought-after Herrnhuter knives, a collection of baths, wooden winnowing shovels, baskets and *mielieblaar* (maize-leaf) hats made on the mission, and locally made furniture and crafts. There are also important documents and photographs, and Magdalena's New Testament has pride of place in a chest made from the timber of the pear tree that Schmidt planted.

Where to stay

Genadendal has no tourist infrastructure but plans are underway to upgrade an existing hostel into bed-and-breakfast accommodation and a conference centre. This will cater for school groups, hikers and so on. For accommodation details, contact the Genadendal Museum, PO Box 137, Genadendal 7234; tel (02822) 8582 or 8115. Greyton, just 6 km down the road, has the *Greyton Hotel*, PO Box 42, Greyton 7233; tel (02822) 9682; *Greyton Lodge*, PO Box 50, Greyton 7233, tel (02822) 9876; *The Post House*, PO Box 42, Greyton 7233; tel (02822) 9995; and about 3 km from the town centre is the municipal camping site, magnificently situated on the banks of the Riviersonderend. Contact the Greyton Municipality, PO Box 4, Greyton 7233; tel (02822) 9718.

Genadendal at a glance (map page 34)

How to get there: Take the N2 from Cape Town and turn left onto the R406 about 3 km before Caledon. Genadendal is about 30 km from the turn-off.
Weather: Winters cold and wet, hot to sizzling in summer.
What to do: Exploring, hiking.
Special attractions: The museum of course, and the new Genadendal hiking trail. This two-day hike starts at the mission in the centre of town and follows a trail over the north side of the mountains. Magnificent views, giant proteas and two natural swimming pools are all part of the experience.

For permits, contact the Department of Nature Conservation, Private Bag 614, Robertson 6705; tel (02353) 621.
More information: Contact the Genadendal Museum, PO Box 137, Genadendal 7234; tel (02822) 8582 or 8115. The Greyton Tourist Information Centre, Dominee Botha Street, Greyton 7233; tel (02822) 9727.
Visiting times: The museum is open Monday to Friday from 9 am to 4.30 pm, and Saturday from 9 am to 1 pm. No entrance fee is charged, but the existence of the museum depends on donations.

Victorian hideaway on the 'road to nowhere'

Tranquillity and relaxation are the keynotes of the quaint village of McGregor, 18 km from Robertson in the Breede River valley

WHITEWASHED COTTAGES set against the shimmering blue backdrop of the Riviersonderend Mountains welcome visitors to McGregor, a village whose remote position far from any major highways has resulted in its remaining one of the best-preserved examples of a mid-19th century village in the Cape Province.

It was the sudden end of the Second World War that kept McGregor's unique architectural heritage intact. At that time Italian prisoners of war were building a new road designed to link McGregor to Greyton, Caledon and Grabouw.

When news that the war was over reached the toiling roadworkers, they happily dropped their shovels for the last time, leaving McGregor to slumber gracefully in relative obscurity along what the locals fondly call 'the road to nowhere'.

Although the road was never finished, you can still cross the Riviersonderend Mountains to Greyton – but only on foot. The end of the road is the start of the Boesmanskloof Trail – an 18 km path that descends deep into the kloof to connect hikers with the Overberg and the southern Cape.

Tranquillity is the main attraction of McGregor. Ask one of the locals what people do here and the answer is usually the same: 'Nothing.' In fact, the very remoteness of the village has brought a varied assortment of city-sick characters to this forgotten corner of the Breede River valley.

Founded in 1861, McGregor was originally named Lady Grey after the wife of the then Governor of the Cape Colony, Sir George Grey. It became the centre of the 'whipstock' industry, supplying the transport riders and wagoners of the mid-19th century with long bamboo sticks specially grown and treated in the village. The name changed in 1903 in honour of the Reverend Andrew McGregor, a Scots minister who established the Dutch Reformed Church in the district.

Little has changed since then. A single tarred road – with the predictable name of Voortrekker Street – runs the length of the village, lined with some of the quaintest Victorian cottages to be found anywhere in the Cape. Look out particularly for the pink iron lacework in front of the Ou Pastorie, and the row of three 1860s thatched cottages that together make up Die Trein, a small self-catering resort where jaded city dwellers can go and unwind to the creak of Oregon pine floorboards and four-poster beds.

Plane trees have been planted on either side of the street – each surrounded by a circle of white-painted rocks that gives a distinct impression of neatness in the clear Boland air.

All of the other streets in McGregor are gravel tracks that form a neat latticework between stoutly built farmsteads that may have once housed the families of local whipstock makers, but today are

The simple but elegant lines of the Ou Pastorie, one of the many interesting Victorian homes to be found in McGregor.

McGregor at a glance (map page 34)

How to get there: Turn off the R60 in Robertson onto a tarred road signposted 'McGregor'. Turn left just after crossing the Breede River.

Weather: Very hot days in summer with cool nights, wettish winters with cold nights.

What to do: Walking, angling, bird-watching, sightseeing.

Special attractions: Boesmanskloof Trail between McGregor and Greyton. Permits must be obtained in advance from The Nature Conservator, Vrolijkheid Nature Reserve, Private Bag X614, Robertson 6705; tel (02353) 621/671.

Rooikat Trail at Vrolijkheid Nature Reserve, signposted 3 km from McGregor on the road to Robertson. Permits must be obtained in advance from The Nature Conservator, Vrolijkheid Nature Reserve, Private Bag X614, Robertson 6705; tel (02353) 621/671.

McGregor Wine Cellar, Private Bag X619, Robertson 6705; tel (02353) 741.

More information: From the McGregor Municipality, PO Box 1, McGregor 6705; tel (02353) 630.

A view of McGregor with the Riviersonderend Mountains seen in the distant background.

Three old historic cottages (Die Trein), situated in the town's sleepy main street, can be rented by visitors.

more likely to be owned by people from Cape Town seeking a weekend retreat. Many of these still have the traditional *bakoonde,* the old baking ovens that are still used to make *volkoringbrood* – nutty, wholewheat bread.

Outside the village, the clear mountain air and fine scenery offer walkers a wide variety of challenges. Best known – and most energetic – is the six-hour mountain hike to the town of Greyton. The local municipality advises a standard of 'reasonable fitness' for those attempting the trail – together with a stout pair of shoes and food for the journey. Water can be found in streams en route – except in exceptionally dry weather, when there may be a problem. If staying in McGregor, you can arrange with the hotel to send transport to Greyton to bring you back by road.

Those with a little less energy, but no shortage of curiosity, can reach a series of waterfalls and deep pools in the Gobos River after about two hours. Keep an eye open for the abundant bird life in the Boesmanskloof, as well as smaller mammals and wildflowers.

An even greater variety of wildlife can be seen at the Vrolijkheid Nature Reserve, including 40 species of mammals and over 180 species of birds. Look out particularly for the endangered honey badger and aardvark – while you cannot fail to spot klipspringer, grey rhebok, duiker, springbok and the shy steenbok. You can either take your car along the 3 km gravel road which provides access to the interior of the 1 800-ha reserve or, alternatively, you can walk.

If you prefer your wildlife on the end of a hook, you can try casting your line into the McGregor Dam just west of the village. Permits, however, must first be obtained from the municipal offices in Voortrekker Street.

Where to stay

Accommodation in McGregor tends to be quaint and comfortable, rather than modern. Top of the list is the *Old Mill House Lodge,* a converted mill at the western end of the town set in a fragrant garden of hydrangeas, bougainvilleas and crane lilies. PO Box 79, McGregor 6708; tel (02353) 841.

Eight kilometres out of town on the gravel road to Boesmanskloof is *Whipstock Farm,* an ideal weekend retreat for families whose children need reminding that there is more to life than television. Here they'll be introduced to the principles of

organic farming – while sampling the fruits thereof at the dining-room table. The farm also offers some bracing walks, including the Whipstock Trail and the Whipstock Kloof Trail (lunch and guide provided for both walks). PO Box 25, McGregor 6708; tel (02353) 733.

If you prefer catering for yourself, *McGregor Country Cottages* offer a fully equipped home from home in thatched *'brandsolder*-ceilinged' (fireproof) cottages that sleep two to eight people. If preferred, you can take your meals in the

adjacent *buitekombuis* (outside kitchen) at the main cottage, complete with wood stove. PO Box 42, McGregor 6708; tel (02353) 816.

Another alternative is to hire one of the three historic, self-contained cottages which constitute *Die Trein* in Voortrekker Street. Each of these picturesque cottages has two bedrooms, a bathroom and a well-equipped kitchen set in spacious grounds with apricot trees and a scenic dam. Contact Die Trein, Voortrekker Street, McGregor 6708; tel (02353) 956.

Picturesque homes in a setting of pastoral simplicity

Among the fertile lowlands of the Cape's south coast, the little mission village of Elim presents a tranquil image of contented self-sufficiency

OVER A CENTURY AGO, the Moravian Brethren decided to try to create their own version of the promised land in a community where the values of faith were enshrined in daily life. Elim, the settlement they founded, has survived little changed, both in spirit and in appearance.

This pastoral settlement can be approached from Bredasdorp, but the most scenic way is along the coastal road through Gansbaai and Baardskeer-dersbos. You drive through rolling pastureland, with mountains in the distance to the north. The farms nearby, irrigated from the Appelkloof River, are used to raise stock and grow fruit, including splendid figs and vegetables.

Finally, you arrive at the lower end of the Elim main street. Here you instinctively slow to a different pace, to an older rhythm of life. A smell of warm dust rises to greet you from a wide street edged with water furrows. On either side there are thatched, whitewashed cottages, their solid walls shadowed by the branches of fig trees. Within the simple design of the cottages there is a lively variety, with the height of the roofs, the shapes of windows and eaves changing from one to the other. In particular, the villagers take a special pride in their thatching. A traditional art, it has been passed down for generations from father to son. In fact, the skill of the Elim thatchers is constantly in demand throughout the region.

The main street is the 'residential area' and culminates at the top end of the village with the gabled and thatched church. Nearby is the original farmstead of *Vogelstruiskraal*, built in 1796 by the Huguenot, Louis du Toit. It was this property that Bishop Hallbeck purchased in 1824 as the starting-point for the mission's work.

Inside, the church is a simple place, filled with light. The walls and the wooden benches are painted white, touched with gold. From the roof hang gilded lamps decorated with flying angels. Women sit on one side of the church, and men on the other. Children, too, have a place of their own. A later addition to the building is the choir balcony, which houses the organ. You can also inspect a fine example of 18th-century German technology in the form of the magnificent old church clock, built in Saxony in 1764 for the church at Herrnhut. Replaced in 1905, it was bought by the Reverend Will, then on leave in Germany, and shipped to Elim, where it was installed in 1914.

You emerge from the cool of the church into the sunshine. The road, shaded by old oaks, cypress and pepper trees, winds past the Pastorie and the mission houses, their gardens dotted with palms, to the communal meeting place and the village store.

Behind the store is a large barn, used for drying wild flowers. In spring the species *Helichrysum* and *Helipterum*, popularly called 'everlastings' or

Where to stay

Elim does not have a hotel but it does have a comfortable guesthouse *Groot Gastehuis*, PO Box 3, Elim 7284; tel (02848) 600.

At nearby Bredasdorp there is the *Standard Hotel* at 31 Long Street, which has 25 rooms (18 with en suite bathrooms) plus an à la carte restaurant and bar. Write to PO Box 47, Bredasdorp 7280; tel (02841) 41140. There is also the *Victoria Hotel* at 10 Church Street, which has 29 rooms (20 with en suite bathrooms). Write to PO Box 11, Bredasdorp 7280; tel (02841) 41159.

Being a mission station, Elim's church building has always played a pivotal role in the affairs of the residents.

sewejaartjies, cover the surrounding countryside. In the old days, all the villagers would turn out to pick the flowers, which were dried and exported as wreaths for graves. At the height of this trade, some 70 000 kg of everlastings were marketed annually. Now the business has declined locally, though some of the Elim girls work on a farm at Phesantshoek, from where the dried flowers are still exported.

Across the way from the store is a very special attraction, in the form of Elim's water mill, the oldest of its kind in the country. As simple and unpretentious as the other buildings, it was erected in 1828 on the site of an earlier structure. In 1881 most of the wooden machinery was replaced by iron, giving it a new lease of life. It fell into disrepair a generation ago, but has now been restored and given national monument status.

Elim at a glance (map page 34)

How to get there: From Cape Town, take the N2, over Sir Lowry's Pass, to Caledon, where you branch off to Bredasdorp. There you take the Agulhas road, before turning right for Elim. Alternatively, you can take the longer but more attractive coastal road to Gansbaai, before turning inland through Baardskeerdersbos.
Weather: As Mediterranean as you could possibly wish for. Cool and damp in winter, with the smell of the sea always in the air, but blessed with long summer days and magical autumn evenings.
What to do: Explore the village, slow down to its pace. Afterwards, you can go on to the nearby coastline, or to Bredasdorp, with its wonderful Shipwreck Museum.
Special attractions: The Moravian Church, with its old clock, the memorial commemorating the liberation of slaves, and the water mill.
More information: Contact the Bredasdorp Publicity Association, PO Box 51, Bredasdorp 7280; tel (02841) 42584; or Mr P Swart, PO Box 20, Elim 7284; tel (02848) 705.

The community of Elim takes great pride in its independent outlook. Unlike similar settlements such as Mamre, Elim continues to operate as a mission station, though no longer in the care of the German fathers. Today, the villagers are responsible for electing their own pastor. The church council is responsible for spiritual matters and the *opsienersraad* (council of wardens) for temporal affairs, but the pastor himself is both head of the church and *voorstander* (mayor) of the village.

Interestingly, the social division in the seating within the church is reflected in the graveyard outside. Men are buried alongside men, women alongside women, children alongside children.

The village of Elim retains the same charming rural atmosphere that it had when it was first established 170 years ago.

The quaint cottages found in Elim are renowned for their individuality and rustic charm.

Cape Agulhas lighthouse – one of the most important navigational beacons on the South African coastline.

An angler's dream, a seafarer's nightmare

Besides being the location of a quaint little fishing village, Cape Agulhas is also the southernmost point on the African continent

A QUESTION THAT OFTEN causes much heated debate is: where do the Atlantic and Indian oceans meet? At Cape Point, near Cape Town, or at the most southerly tip of Africa, Cape Agulhas? The vast difference in the water temperature off Sea Point on the one side of the Peninsula, and off Muizenberg on the other, would seem to indicate that the first answer is correct. Which goes to show how wrong your senses can be!

The geographical truth is that the waters of the Atlantic and Indian meet at Cape Agulhas – at the rocky tip of Africa a kilometre west of the village of Agulhas, to be exact. This quiet fishing resort might not offer the geographic drama of Cape Point – instead of a rocky, narrow peninsula and steep drops

to a churning sea, you find hills of fynbos which gradually slope towards the sea and a lighthouse marking the spot – but international hydrographers agree that this is where the two oceans collide. And what a collision it is!

The meeting of the Indian and Atlantic over the rocky sea bed which characterises the coast off Cape Agulhas causes particularly dangerous conditions for mariners, earning this stretch of coastline the nickname 'Cemetery of Ships'. Since earliest times, mariners rounding the tip of Africa feared this infamous corner, and always endeavoured to stay well away from the coast in order to avoid its vicissitudes. The waves are reputed to be the highest in the world after those off Cape Horn in

South America, and to make matters worse the rocky sea bed doesn't hold an anchor.

The curious sea conditions, however, also give a more positive aspect to Cape Agulhas – especially for anglers. South of the shore lies the Agulhas Bank, one of the richest fishing grounds in the southern hemisphere. The sea bed remains at a constant depth of 120 m for 250 km out to sea and thereafter plunges to 3 600 m. The area is a popular destination for both deep-sea and rock fishermen who come here in the hope of catching yellowtail, kabeljou, leervis, kob and elf.

What has become a haven for fishermen, though, was for centuries a sepulchre for sailors. More than 120 shipwrecks have been identified in the area, ranging from the *Schoonberg* in 1722 to the *Wafra* in 1971. Many of the places you'll pass through in the vicinity of Agulhas received their names from famous wrecks. There's Arniston, the alternative name for Waenhuiskrans, named after a troopship which ran aground in 1815 with the loss of 372 lives; Zoetendalsvlei, named after a Dutch East Indiaman lost in 1673; Northumberland Point, named after an English Indiaman wrecked in 1838; and St Mungo Point, named after a casualty of 1844. The wreck most easily sighted from land is the *Meisho Maru* which ran aground in 1982 and which can be seen by walking or driving a distance of 2 km west of Cape Agulhas.

The physical coastline, in comparison with the treacherous sea, is relatively safe and you can walk along the beach for many kilometres. To the east you will find the 14-km sparkling white beach of Struisbaai, and then Waenhuiskrans (Arniston), named after a cave so huge that a wagon could be turned in it, and further on, the fisherman's village of Kassiesbaai.

The actual village of Agulhas (known officially as L'Agulhas) consists mostly of holiday homes and a caravan park. Adjoining it you'll find the structure for which Agulhas is particularly famous, the second oldest lighthouse in South Africa.

This lighthouse has undergone numerous changes over the years. In the Lighthouse Museum – which now finds its home in the tower and which forms part of the Bredasdorp Shipwreck Museum – one can view the history of lighthouses, this one in particular.

The design of the Cape Agulhas lighthouse was inspired by the Pharos of Alexandria in Egypt – the great light-tower which was considered to be one of

the seven wonders of the ancient world. So important was a lighthouse on this point considered to be that contributions towards its construction were made from as far away as Calcutta, Manilla and St Helena, doubtlessly by companies which would benefit from this safety measure on the sea route they used. The strength of the first light was a mere 4 500 candlepower, which has since been strengthened almost 3 000 times, with the present light boasting a maximum of 12 million candlepower.

In order to give the lighthouse environs more of their original feeling, an indigenous garden has been planted. It hasn't been an easy job to redevelop vegetation which was being threatened by rooikrans and manitoka: the soil is alkaline and the borehole water is rich in chlorides and bicarbonates, both making it difficult to cultivate plants. Furthermore, the area is swept by salt-laden winds.

Despite the precautions taken by the nautical community from early on, Cape Agulhas has always remained a treacherous area for ships. You can see the remnants of several of these ill-fated ships at the fascinating shipwreck museum (see separate entry) in Bredasdorp, 25 km north of Agulhas, a town famous for its surrounding grain farms and merino sheep farming.

The name L'Agulhas derives from the Portuguese word for 'needle'. It has been suggested that the name refers to the fact that, when the early Portuguese navigators reached this point, there was a change in magnetic forces, and the needle of their compasses pointed north without any deviation.

A recent wrecking to have occurred on the Agulhas coastline was that of the Taiwanese fishing vessel, the Meisho Maru.

Where to stay

The immediate area is well served with holiday accommodation. There is the *Arniston Hotel*, Beach Road, Arniston (Waenhuiskrans); tel (02847) 59000; the *Victoria Hotel*, Church Street, Bredasdorp; tel (02841) 41159; the *Standard Hotel*, Long Street, Bredasdorp; tel (02841) 41140; and the *Agulhas Caravan Park*, Main Road, Agulhas; tel (02846) 56015.

At nearby Struisbaai there is the *Struisbaai Hotel*, PO Box 77, Struisbaai 7285; tel (02846) 56625; and further afield there is a camping site with cottages at De Hoop Nature Reserve (see other panel for address).

Cape Agulhas at a glance (map page 34)

How to get there: From Cape Town, take the N2 to Caledon and then the R316 to Bredasdorp. On reaching Bredasdorp, drive through the town and take the Agulhas road.
Weather: Hot, dry summers and wet, cool winters. It can be very windy throughout the year.
What to do: The coastline next to the village of Agulhas is very rocky but there are two tidal pools for swimming. Nearby Struisbaai, with its 14-km white beach, is also a safe place for swimming.

You can take a scenic drive to Elim (see separate entry), which is situated west of the road to Bredasdorp. Elim is a Moravian mission village which, with its fig-treed streets and thatched cottages,

has been described as one of the finest historical streetscapes in the Cape.

From Agulhas, you can take a day's hike westwards along the shoreline to Brandfontein. Alternatively, you can walk eastwards from Agulhas to Waenhuiskrans, a journey of about six hours. On the way, you'll have to cross a river mouth at Die Mond, so make sure you arrive there at low tide.

Contact the Bredasdorp Publicity Association for details of tours of nearby farms and, from April to October, the famous Wool Tour. De Hoop Nature Reserve, north east of Waenhuiskrans, has some beautiful walks and one of the animals you can see here is the endangered Cape mountain quagga.

The reserve has cottages and a camping site and is open from 7 am to 7 pm daily.
Special attractions: The Lighthouse Museum with its fascinating exhibits.
More information: Bredasdorp Publicity Association, PO Box 51, Bredasdorp; tel (02841) 42584; Bredasdorp Museum, PO Box 235, Bredasdorp 7280; tel (02841) 41240; Cape Agulhas Lighthouse Museum, PO Box 124, Struisbaai 7285; tel (02846) 56078; De Hoop Nature Reserve, Private Bag X16, Bredasdorp 7280; tel (02922) 782.
Visiting times: The Lighthouse Museum is open from 9.30 am to 5 pm from Monday to Saturday, and from 9.30 am to 12.30 pm on Sunday.

A fascinating treasure chest of seafaring relics

The tragic history of the Agulhas coastline is dramatically evoked at the Shipwreck Museum, situated in the south-western Cape town of Bredasdorp, 30 km from the coast

THE SOUTHERNMOST COASTLINE of Africa is also one of its most dangerous parts – with an estimated 250 vessels and 2 500 people lost in its waters down through the centuries. No wonder, then, that generations of sailors have referred to this area as the 'ships' graveyard'.

The nearest town to this treacherous stretch of coast is Bredasdorp – a fitting location for the country's foremost collection of artefacts from the ships that have sunk in the waters nearby. Both Bredasdorp and the surrounding Strandveld owe much of their character and history to the ships and wreckage that fate so often washed up on their doorstep.

Having no main transport links, this flat, sometimes bleak wedge of land remained isolated from much of the interior, and the farming community was unavoidably drawn into the tragedies that occurred along the coast: sometimes being involved in actual rescue attempts and often giving shelter to survivors. Inevitably, local traditions were influenced by foreign customs and habits: a number

Carved, colourful figureheads were an attractive feature of many old sailing vessels, and the museum has a number of these salvaged items on display.

of survivors chose to settle in the area and brought valuable skills to it – many being builders, carpenters and cabinet-makers.

The region even has its own special architecture which includes thatched roofs and end gables. As timber was scarce in this barren landscape, window frames, doors, rafters and other items were fashioned out of wood from shipwrecks. But it was inside people's homes that the unique Strandveld character was most apparent: auctions of salvaged goods were held in the aftermath of shipwrecks and oddly contrasting furnishings became a hallmark of the Strandveld style – as can be seen in the Bredasdorp Shipwreck Museum.

The museum is housed in a complex of historical buildings in the centre of town. One of these, the Old Rectory, is thought to have been the original farmhouse of *Langfontein* – the farm on which the town was laid out. A typical example of the sort of rustic dwelling common to the Bredasdorp area in the middle of last century, the Old Rectory has low doorways, thick, irregular walls constructed from mud brick, half-gables and a thatched roof.

Carefully renovated as a replica of a Strandveld house, the rooms are furnished simply, in fact sparsely, with only essential items. The bedroom is dominated by a stinkwood and yellowwood bed that has a straw mattress. Poignant reminders of the region's history include a washstand salvaged from the *Queen of the Thames* and a medicine chest from the *Clan MacGregor*. In the sitting room, a wine cabinet from the captain's cabin of the *Clan MacGregor* can be found, and an original painting of the *Queen of the Thames* hangs above a bar counter from the vessel itself.

The dining room has been opulently furnished in classic Victorian style to contrast deliberately with the spareness of the Strandveld style, and various displays relating to the area are mounted in the exhibition room.

The Strandveld Coach House is behind the Old Rectory and is a meticulously researched, thatched, gabled and cobbled replica built in the 1970s. Within its walls are an old fire engine, horse-drawn carts, hearses and assorted farming equipment.

Situated right next door to the Old Rectory is the old church. A rare example of Cape Dutch Gothic architecture, this interesting hybrid has whitewashed walls, Gothic windows and a steeply pitched roof. The building has gone through many incarnations (including cinema, rollerskating rink and bazaar) since it was built by the Independent Church in 1868, and has now been turned into the Shipwreck Hall.

The slightly gloomy interior of the museum provides an appropriately melancholic atmosphere for the exhibits – most of which are poignant reminders of tragedies at sea.

Atmospherically set up to stimulate the imagination, the interior has been painted dark blue and there is a recorded soundtrack of crashing waves and the lonely cries of seagulls. A series of scale models demonstrates the death throes of a ship until its final disintegration, when it is buried by sand. The bulk of the exhibits are the artefacts and remains from four of the area's biggest wrecks, notably the *Arniston*, the *Birkenhead*, the *Queen of the Thames* and the *Oriental Pioneer*.

Over the years, many spurious accounts have been written about the sinking of the *Birkenhead* paddle steamer off Danger Point. However, what does emerge from the wild tales of heroism is that the famous nautical tradition of 'women and children first' was established then, when the seven women and 13 children were ushered aboard a cutter which reached the shore safely. Owing to a number of blunders, the death toll was far higher than it

might have been. In the end, 454 men perished, with a total of 184 survivors.

Another aspect of the Shipwreck Museum is the Cape Agulhas Lighthouse, 40 km away. By the time the lighthouse became operational in 1849, it was long overdue, as many ships rounding Africa's southernmost tip had already come to grief. The first lamp that was used produced a beam of 4 500 candlepower which was fuelled from oil obtained from the tails of local fat-tailed sheep! A rotating optical system was used from 1914 and an electric light of 12 million candlepower was introduced in 1936.

The still operational lighthouse has been declared a national monument and the lower part converted into a museum under the aegis of the Bredasdorp Shipwreck Museum. Visitors may climb to the top of the tower to take in the view – and catch their breath afterwards in the tearoom.

Where to stay

The two main hotels in Bredasdorp are the *Victoria Hotel*, PO Box 11, Bredasdorp 7280; tel (02841) 41159, and the *Standard Hotel*, PO Box 47, Bredasdorp 7280; tel (02841) 41140, which offer rooms at reasonable rates. For something a bit more luxurious try the new guest house, the *Earl of Clarendon*, PO Box 230, Bredasdorp 7280; tel (02841) 51025.

There is a municipal camping site on your left as you leave town towards Struisbaai. Contact the Municipality, PO Box 51, Bredasdorp 7280; tel (02841) 41135.

Nnumerous bed- and-breakfast facilities are available in private homes and on farms in the area. To find out about these, contact the Bredasdorp Publicity Association, PO Box 51, Bredasdorp 7280; tel (02841) 42584.

Bredasdorp Shipwreck Museum at a glance (map page 34)

How to get there: At Caledon, turn off the N2 onto the R316. Bredasdorp is about 75 km distant, via Napier. You'll find the museum in the centre of town – just head for the tallest building, the NG Church, and the museum complex is close by. The Cape Agulhas Lighthouse is another 40 km away on the R319 beyond Struisbaai.
Weather: Summers are hot and dry, winters wet. It can be extremely windy at various times throughout the year.
What to do: Apart from the museum itself, Wool Route Tours run from May to October and include visits to famous farms and sheep-shearing demonstrations. Contact the Bredasdorp

Publicity Association, PO Box 51, Bredasdorp 7280; tel (02841) 42584.
Visiting times: There is a small entrance fee to the museum, which is open Monday to Thursday from 9 am to 4.45 pm. On Fridays it closes an hour earlier at 3.45 pm and on Saturdays at 12.45 pm. It is open occasionally on a Saturday afternoon. The Cape Agulhas Lighthouse is open from 9 am to 5 pm Mondays to Saturdays and from 9 am to noon on Sundays.
More information: Write to Bredasdorp Shipwreck Museum, PO Box 235, Bredasdorp 7280; tel (02841) 41240.

A turbulent past preserved in a tranquil paradise

In Swellendam's Drostdy Museum, history resides not only in buildings but also in rose gardens and the workmanship of artisans

IF YOU HAD TRAVELLED to Swellendam some 200 years ago, you would probably have stayed overnight at the Drostdy, where your host would have been Johannes Rhenius (the district's first landdrost) or one of his successors. Local craftsmen would have overhauled your wagon after its arduous crossing of the Hottentots Holland and Houwhoek mountain ranges, and the district's farmers would have offered replacements for your draught animals and replenished your supplies.

But Swellendam is no longer as it was then – 'the Colony in the far distant regions' or even the centre of the 'Vrye Republiek' (Free Republic) which rebellious burghers declared briefly in 1795. It is a small town set in what remains a natural paradise at the foot of the Langeberg, and the old Drostdy is now the focal point of its museum complex. It is still a striking example of Cape architecture and filled with numerous items relating to early Swellendam. As with all the national monuments in the town, it is beautifully preserved. But your exploration should not end here. Hold on to your admission ticket, for the Drostdy Museum consists of many historical buildings and the Drostdy itself is merely the best-known of these. Near and beyond it, Swellendam's many secrets unfold.

The Drostdy was built in 1746 to serve as courthouse and residence for the magistrate, and the inevitable consequence of a magistrate's activities was a gaol. You'll find the Old Gaol Buildings, which were considerably altered and enlarged during British governorship, diagonally opposite the Drostdy in Swellengrebel Street. The deputy sheriff lived here, and so eventually would the landdrost's secretary. By then the prison cells were contained in a rear wing added shortly after 1800 and a gaoler's cottage had been built nearby. The cottage later served as the town's post office – a slot in the door is your clue.

Behind the gaol you'll find the Ambagswerf (literally, trades yard). The Ambagswerf testifies to Swellendam's enthusiasm for preserving its history. It was established in the 1970s to pay tribute to the workmanship of artisans of the past. The trades of the coppersmith, leatherworker, wagon-builder and wheelwright have been recreated here, and working

The simple yet charming exterior of the old Drostdy building. Built about 250 years ago, it originally served as both a residence and a courthouse.

A working replica of an old, water-powered flour mill is one of the many exhibits at the Drostdy Museum.

Simple antique furniture and relics of yesteryear can be seen in the old charge office situated within The Drostdy.

replicas of a water mill, horse mill and threshing floor pay tribute to the farming activities of the early settlers.

Now stroll further down Swellengrebel Street, turning left into Hermanus Steyn (the name, incidentally, of the man those burghers installed as their 'president' for 91 days in 1795). At No 4 you'll find Mayville, as fine an example of transitional Cape Dutch/Georgian architecture as you're likely to find. But the charm of Mayville has less to do with architecture than with the rose garden that lies beyond.

In accordance with the wishes of Miss Nita Steyn, who lived in Mayville for many years and bequeathed it to the museum on her death in 1973, the rose garden has been maintained in memory of her and her sister, Nina Barry. Following the design of Gwen Fagan, an expert in this field, a Victorian garden has been established here and the roses so placed that visitors can follow their chronological development from the early 17th century onwards.

The garden consists of two rectangular enclosures linked by a series of arches. Enter the first by turning left through a wide arch that yields a spectacular view of Bourbon roses growing at regular intervals in the central lawn. There is a domed gazebo at the far end covered in beautiful white roses. Noisette roses frame the arches that lead you to the second enclosure, which is divided into eight symmetrical beds planted with a variety of roses. The garden in full bloom in late October is a wonderful sight, so, if possible, try to visit the garden then.

Swellendam is a three-hour drive from Cape Town – a round-trip is easily managed in a day but that shouldn't be your purpose. After all, you still have many historical buildings left to explore and, in addition to the glory of its past, there is the timeless beauty of its surroundings. Just 5 km along the road to Heidelberg you'll find the Bontebok National Park. With nine species of game and almost 200 bird species, it's an excellent opportunity to contemplate national treasures of a different kind.

Where to stay

Swellendam has a caravan park set on the banks of the Cornlands River and within walking distance of the Drostdy Museum. To book a stand or accommodation in one of several well-equipped chalets, contact the Municipality, PO Box 20, Swellendam 6740; tel (0291) 42705.

The town's three hotels are all in Voortrek Street, the main thoroughfare. The *Swellengrebel Hotel*, PO Box 9, Swellendam 6740; tel (0291) 41144, is the most luxurious of these. The others are tʰe *Carlton*, PO Box 33, Swellendam 6740; tel (0291) 41120; and the *Ten Damme*, PO Box 31, Swellendam 6740; tel (0291) 41179.

Drostdy Museum at a glance (map page 34)

How to get there: The town of Swellendam lies just off the N2 highway, about halfway between George (205 km) and Cape Town (227 km), and is on the axis of the R60 to Worcester. There are three exits to Swellendam from the N2. The exit on the Cape Town side leads onto the Ashton road, from where a Swellendam sign guides you to Voortrek Street. The middle exit leads to Station Street; turn right to Voortrek Street. The third exit – at the George end of town – leads directly onto Swellengrebel Street, in which the museum complex is situated.

Weather: Swellendam is hot in summer and its winters are cold. It rains here towards the end of winter and in early spring.

What to do: Explore Swellendam on foot. Nearly all the historical buildings, including those that together constitute the Drostdy Museum, are within walking distance of one another. You could also pay a visit to the Marloth Nature Reserve situated at the foot of the Langeberg, and the Bontebok National Park.

Special attractions: The Ambagswerf and the Victorian rose garden at Mayville are unique.

More information: Write to the Town Clerk, PO Box 20, Swellendam, 6740, or contact Swellendam's Publicity Association, PO Box 396, Swellendam, 6740; tel (0291) 42770.

Visiting times: The rose garden at Mayville is in full bloom towards the end of October. The Drostdy Museum is open to visitors from 9 am to 5 pm from Mondays to Fridays from 10 am to 4 pm on Saturdays, Sundays and public holidays. There is a small admission fee. The Bontebok National Park is open from 8 am to 6 pm from April to September, and from 8 am to 7 pm from October to March.

Situated at one end of Lovers' Walk is the Montagu Springs Holiday Resort.

Where to stay

There are a number of good hotels in and around Montagu. These include the *Avalon Springs Hotel*, PO Box 110, Montagu 6720; tel (0234) 41150; the *Montagu Springs Holiday Resort*, PO Box 277, Montagu 6720; tel (0234) 41050; the *Montagu Hotel*, PO Box 338, Montagu 6720; tel (0234) 41115.

There are also several guest houses, such as the *Mimosa Lodge*, PO Box 323, Montagu 6720; tel (0234) 42351; the *Montagu Rose*, 19 Kohler St, Montagu 6720; tel (0234) 42681; and the *Inn Place Guest House*, PO Box 378, Montagu 6720. There are also a number of self-catering cottages and farmhouses in the area. For more information, contact the Montagu Information Bureau (see address in other panel).

A leisurely riverside walk on the not-too-wild side

Downstream of Montagu's celebrated mineral baths is Lovers' Walk, a scenic two-kilometre ramble through an impressive canyon created by the Keisie River

OVERS' WALK – also known as Badskloof Trail – is a delightful experience. Although you're never far from civilisation, there's always the impression of being in furthest and remotest Africa. This is really a trail in miniature rather than a simple walk, but you don't have to be particularly fit or strong to undertake it. However, it's not entirely suitable for the elderly because of some awkward river crossings, or for the very young – they're likely to get tired, hot and bored.

A good place to start the walk is from the old mill end of Montagu's Barry Street, where the valley of the river is wide and flat. As you set forth, you will be impressed by the dramatically convoluted strata of the nearby hillside – a testimony to a time of tempestuous creation when rock was mud and the earth heaved to create the Cape's distinctive folded mountain system.

The start of Lovers' Walk is suitably romantic, with wide green lawns and tree-shaded benches. Along the way there are overhangs of rock that might perhaps have been home to earlier man and woman. A sign advises caution against falling rocks, and far over to your left is a channel of the jagged river bed – which is normally dry. Beyond this are old, cosy cottages with thatched roofs and well-tended flower pots – but these are soon left behind as you proceed upstream.

You cross the river below the mill, with its house, Eyssenhuis, which was once the home of the miller's family. After this point, the path follows the riverbank, frequently traversing back and forth across the river over rustic bridges. Although the gurgling of the river is clearly audible, the water remains mostly hidden beneath a luxuriant growth of bulrush, or *papkuil*. Rushes of various sorts, especially of the Cyperus family, grow in abundance here and are put to many uses, from plaited ropes to mattresses or *matjiesgoed*.

Shady overhangs along the way invite exploration, and there is one distinctive, free-standing formation called 'The Pulpit'. Dassies live in abundance here and dung beetles can sometimes be observed rolling dassie droppings patiently across the ravine's sandy floor. Black-and-white quills point to a prevalence of porcupines in the area, but the occasional rustling and movements in the scrub and pelargoniums remain, for the most part, mysterious.

As you walk along this trail, you often have the impression of being in a blind canyon as a massive wall of rock looms ahead across your path – but a sudden sharp bend in the river opens up the way each time.

Just downstream of a concrete causeway is a pool deep enough, even in mid-summer, to lie in and cool off. And nearby are a bench and an overhang to provide rest and shelter. Most ravines tend to trap the heat, and the gorge of the Keisie River is no exception. There are a number of good shade trees along the way, mostly keurboom (*Virgilia* species) and the invasive castor-oil plant (*Ricinus* species) of the Euphorbia family. The beans, or seeds, of the castor-oil plant are poisonous, so if there are children walking with you, warn them not to put the seeds in their mouths.

Just about the time you become convinced that you must have taken a wrong turning (even though there aren't any), you follow the river to the right and, in the distance beyond the rock-face, are some buildings that turn out to be the Montagu Springs Holiday Resort. But before you get here, there's another pool, made easily accessible by means of a rudimentary stairway.

When you finally approach the boundary of the resort, look about on the rocks to your right and you will find – situated frighteningly high above your head – a brass plate marking the amazing height reached by the unforgettable floodwaters of 1981. When you then look down below at the river trickling obediently by, the sheer scale of the flood seems incredible.

High up on the left are some inviting caves and overhangs, with a steep and slippery path leading up to them. By this stage, though, only the abnormally energetic or the most remorseless explorer will want to investigate them. For most walkers it's rather time for another dip – this time in one of the resort's pools.

Precipitous rock overhangs and frequent river crossings are a constant feature of this 2-km trail.

Lovers' Walk at a glance (map page 34)

How to get there: In Montagu, drive west along Bath Street (that's in the rough direction of Cape Town), turn right into Barry Street and drive to its end. There's not much parking, so be sure you don't obstruct a driveway. If you want to skip the first, easiest section, turn left into Mill Street just before the end of Barry Street, then right into Tanner Street and continue to the parking area at Eyssenhuis. It's useful to have a vehicle waiting at the other end – that is, at the Montagu Springs Holiday Resort – if you don't want to make the trip on foot in both directions.

Weather: Summer days can be very hot, as can the odd 'bergwind' days in winter. Early morning and late afternoon are probably the most comfortable times to set out. In the afternoons, allow yourself at least two and a half hours of full sunlight. The walk is advertised as being a 40-minute jaunt, but it can easily last two hours if you take an interest in your surroundings and aren't in a hurry.

What to do: Enjoy the scenery, swim and explore.

Special precautions: No dogs are allowed on the trail. Wear a strong pair of shoes and take a shady hat as well as a jacket or jersey. Don't depend on the river for drinking water – you will almost certainly need a drink before you reach the end of the trail. Lovers' Walk is no snakepit, but watch where you put your feet.

More information: Montagu Information Bureau, PO Box 24, Montagu 6720; tel (0234) 41112 or 42471.

The Khoikhoi pathway that challenged the engineers

*The Tradouw Pass between Suurbraak
and Barrydale is a tribute to the determination
of the Cape's early road builders*

Where to stay

The *Barrydale Hotel*, PO
Box 25, Barrydale, 6750;
tel (028) 5721226, is famous
for its good food. The *Anna
Roux Caravan Park* lies at the
Montagu entrance to the town.
Contact it care of the Municipality, PO Box 147, Barrydale;
tel (028) 5721082/3.

*A view of both the new and old
Tradouw Passes. The lower, dust
road seen running alongside the
Buffeljags River is the original,
more hazardous route. It is now
closed to vehicular traffic.*

NEVER MIND the soldiers and statesmen. The
unsung heroes of our past were engineers –
men who blasted tunnels through mountains,
built bridges across rivers, and visualised roads
where there were none. The essential heroism of
these men, battling against seemingly insurmount-
able physical obstacles, can be vividly appreciated
on a drive over the Tradouw Pass through the
Langeberg.

Logic and logistics suggest that you start your
journey at Suurbraak (after stopping in Swellendam
the night before) and head north towards Barrydale,
which has a hotel and a camping site.

Suurbraak and the Tradouw Pass are both
landmarks in the history of the Khoikhoi. The village, in a tranquil valley east of Swellendam, was
founded by the London Missionary Society in 1812,
apparently at the request of a Khoikhoi chief for a
missionary to be sent out to his people. It became a
Dutch Reformed Mission in 1857.

After Swellendam's large number of national
monuments, don't expect too much from Suurbraak. This prettily set village, almost all of which
lies along a single main street, should be appreciated on its own terms. And it is worth considering, while you stroll among the thatched
Suurbraak cottages, that the hardy ancestors of
those now living here routinely crossed the Langeberg on foot, many along the route you're about
to explore.

Indeed, the name Tradouw is derived from the
Khoikhoi words 'tra' (meaning 'women') and
'douw' (meaning 'path' or 'pass'). And as the name
suggests, the road you'll take traces a footpath
favoured by the Khoikhoi women: the men used a
shorter, more difficult route.

Rivers are natural roadbuilders and the Tradouw
Pass follows the deep passage eaten through the
Langeberg by the Buffeljags River. Women's path
or not, the white settlers found it too steep, and the
river too treacherous, for their wagons to pass
through. But the detour via Cogmans Kloof added
several days to the journey, and in the mid-19th
century farmers in the Swellendam district peti-
tioned Parliament to turn Tradouw into a pass that
would connect them with the shipping ports on the
Breede River. Bureaucracy dragged its feet and
there were the usual delays. But by June 1869, engineering genius Thomas Bain was installed at Lis-
more, a farm nearby, and a labour force of convicts
accommodated at Gat Plaats at the southern entrance to the kloof.

Gat Plaats is now a shady picnic spot, and it is
easy to see why this was the chosen setting for the
grand banquet held on 27 October 1873 to open
Southey Pass, named for an erstwhile Colonial Secretary, then the Governor of Griqualand West.
Robert Southey may once have held the position of
Civil Commissioner at Swellendam, but the Khoikhoi claim to the region was older, and proved
stronger. The name Southey Pass did not endure.
And the early history of the pass itself was a series
of disasters.

The river reclaimed it in 1875 and, with it, the
stone bridge across its tributary, the Gats River. A
wooden bridge made of teak, called Letty's Bridge,
replaced it in 1879 and stood steady against the torrent that again washed away the pass in 1902 and in
1906. But modern travellers need not be concerned.
The pass was reconstructed during the 1970s, the
road tarred and the imposing Andries Uys Bridge
built to carry you safely across the treacherous
Gats. The present road is well out of the Buffeljags
River's reach.

Strange rock formations – such as the above cluster of giant, sentinel-like shapes – can be seen along this scenic route through the Langeberg.

Tradouw Pass at a glance (map page 34)

How to get there: Fifteen kilometres after you leave Swellendam in the direction of Heidelberg, turn left off the N2 onto route R324 towards Suurbraak. Some 6 km beyond Suurbraak a road branches sharply to the left, leading to Barrydale via the Tradouw Pass.

Weather: Hot summers, with rain falling towards the end of mild winters.

What to do: Dawdle. After a stroll through Suurbraak, drive slowly over the Tradouw Pass, stopping frequently to enjoy the scenery from the edge of the road. There are braai sites near the water, about half-way along the pass, and again nearer the end, but you must be prepared for a short hike, and take care to put out your fire when you leave.

Special attractions: The old convict station at Gat Plaats is popular for picnics, and there are Bushman paintings further on. The Buffeljags River has some wonderful rock pools for swimming in.

More information: AA Office, PO Box 70, Cape Town, 8000; tel (021) 211550; Municipality, PO Box 147, Barrydale 6750; tel (028) 5721082/3.

Indigenous mountain wilderness in the Langeberg

Both Cape fynbos and Knysna-type forest flourish in the Boosmansbos Wilderness Area, about 40 km north of Witsand on the Cape south coast

MIDWAY BETWEEN Cape Town and Knysna, where the craggy heads of the Langeberg rear up like waves beyond the east-west road, lies a stunning wilderness area of high mountain peaks, deep ravines and broad valleys. Situated only 270 km from Cape Town, Boosmansbos is quite easily accessible for Capetonians who want to strap on their rucksacks and head out there for the weekend.

The name Boosmansbos derives from a hermit who lived in a cave in the area 100 years ago, and made a living of sorts by collecting firewood and wild honey. His solitary life and ill humour earned him the nickname *Bose Man* (evil man) and over the years the adaptation of his name stuck.

Boosmansbos is situated within the Grootvadersbos, which is the most significant remaining pocket of the indigenous forest that once carpeted the area, and is the largest example of this type of forest west of the Knysna/George complex. In fact, this rugged area boasts a spectrum of vegetation ranging from that found in the Knysna forest to the famed mountain fynbos of the Cape.

Beautiful ericas transform the mountain slopes at different times of the year, as does the tall yellowbush which provides a sea of yellow in spring. Another eye-catcher is the distinctive strawberry everlasting which has deep red buds and bright orange stamens set off with silvery leaves, at their most showy from December to March. The area boasts two extremely rare protea species not found

anywhere else – the *Leucadendron radiatum* and the *Spatalla nubicola* of which there are two small groups in the Grootberg, growing at high, misty altitudes. Arm yourself with a good reference book if you're not sure of identifying plants, and you may be lucky.

The indigenous forest has trees such as Outeniqua and yellowwood, stinkwood, wild pomegranate, Cape chestnut, dogwood, Cape holly and South Africa's tallest redwood, which is more than 47 m high with a diameter of 1,2 m.

Wildlife in this mountainous area remains well concealed, but if you're both patient and quiet you may see grysbok, klipspringer, grey rhebok, baboon, honey badger, leopard and caracal. Your best bet at game-spotting is probably late afternoon or early morning as many of the animals in this area are nocturnal. Keen bird-watchers are likely to have better luck with bird life, which includes francolin, Cape bulbul, Cape sugarbird, malachite, black and orange-breasted sunbird, white-necked raven, Narina trogon, Knysna woodpecker and various impressive birds of prey, such as the martial eagle, black eagle, jackal buzzard, rock kestrel, black sparrowhawk, Knysna warbler and olive bush shrike.

There are 74 km of footpaths in this wilderness which cover a variety of terrains, from easy to challenging. Day-trippers can consult the officer-in-charge about the best routes for their purposes, but those with the weekend to spare should try the hike from the Grootvadersbos office to Helderfontein

A pair of hikers make their way past a towering rock formation. Well-established footpaths make this wilderness area an ideal terrain for hiking.

Where to stay

Apart from the forestry huts – which operate on a first-come, first-served basis – there is no accommodation in the wilderness area, so if you don't fancy these or sleeping in the open, bring along a tent. Fires are forbidden, so a camping stove will be useful.

The Bontebok National Park nearby also has caravan and camping facilities.

Nearby Swellendam has a caravan park in the town, prettily set on the banks of the Cornlands River, and within walking distance of the Drostdy Museum. To book a stand or accommodation in one of several well-equipped chalets, contact the Municipality, PO Box 20, Swellendam 6740; tel (0291) 42705.

The town's three hotels are all in Voortrek Street, the main thoroughfare. The *Swellengrebel Hotel*, PO Box 9, Swellendam 6740; tel (0291) 41144, is the most luxurious of these. The others are the *Carlton*, PO Box 33, Swellendam 6740; tel (0291) 41120; and the *Ten Damme*, PO Box 31, Swellendam 6740; tel (0291) 41179. Also available are two cottages and a guest lodge on *Honeywood Farm* outside Heidelberg. Contact the owner at PO Box 17, Heidelberg 6760; tel (02962) 1811.

Huts via Loerklip, with an optional extra day's excursion to Grootberg or deep into the forest of Boosmansbos.

The first day's hike leads through pine plantations, to the rocky promontory known as Loerklip, and then meanders through several lush kloofs while gradually ascending the Dwarsberg. Traversing the slopes, hikers are rewarded with magnificent views of the valley far below: huge vistas, the sparkle of rivers twisting along the valley floor and the village of Barrydale tucked in beneath the northern slopes of the Langeberg.

Overnight accommodation is spartan in accordance with the wilderness ethic, with no facilities except veld toilets. Basic shelter is provided in old forestry rangers' huts. There is, however, a lovely stream which provides crystal-clear drinking water and a few enticing swimming pools, including one with its own waterfall a short way downstream. If you cross the stream and follow the track until it ends, you'll come to a steep slope leading down into the lush Boosmansbos Forest, which contains yellowwood, stinkwood, candlewood and Cape beech trees, among many others.

Hikers heading for the Grootberg should use the Helderfontein Huts as a base camp. For this excursion, retrace your steps of the previous day for one kilometre and follow the path leading to the Klein Witboois River. The track ascends the slopes of the Grootberg and forks after about an hour. The right-hand Kopberg route leads to the top of the highest peak, which features magnificent panoramic views: the Swartberg to the north, patterned farmlands to the south and, 150 km away, Cradock Peak above George.

A different route, via Saagkuilkloof, can be taken from Helderfontein Huts back to Grootvadersbos. Follow the Barend Koen Pad, which was started in 1942 with the intention of reaching the remote kloofs of the Tradouwsberg. The project was abandoned before completion, but the road is still used by hikers and forestry officials. After a few kilometres the road passes Saagkuilkloof, which was named after the many sawpits gouged out by the early woodcutters. Eventually the track descends into the valley, where the shady, grassy banks of the Duiwenhoks River make a perfect picnic stop. From this point the office at Grootvadersbos is under an hour away.

Grootvadersbos (formerly the farm *Melkhoutboom*) was proclaimed a forestry reserve in 1896, and the Boosmansbos Wilderness Area, which oc-

The mountain slopes embraced within Boosmansbos are thickly carpeted with hundreds of varieties of Cape fynbos.

cupies about 14 200 ha of the state forest, was proclaimed in 1978. Grootvadersbos is rich in the earliest recorded history of the country and used to be a familiar stamping ground for the Hessequa Khoikhoi. The nearby Tradouw Pass (see separate entry) was originally a well-marked route taken by Khoikhoi women across the mountains between Swellendam and the Barrydale valley – the men followed a shorter, but more arduous route. In fact the word 'tradouw' is a combination of the Khoikhoi words for women (*tra*) and path (*douw*). In 1873 Thomas Bain built the pass, his task of finding a suitable route made easier by the well-worn footpaths trodden by Khoikhoi women.

Boosmansbos Wilderness Area at a glance (map page 34)

How to get there: From Cape Town, take the N2 east. About 11 km after Swellendam turn left onto the R324. Continue along this road for about 20 km and follow the signs to Grootvadersbos. If you're coming from the Mossel Bay direction, take the R322 from Heidelberg towards Barrydale.
Weather: Generally a comfortable climate, although it can get quite hot in summer, and there is occasionally snow on the mountains in winter. Rain falls in spring and autumn.
What to do: Hiking, game-viewing, bird-watching and swimming in the numerous streams. The Bontebok National Park is not far away, and here you can see the protected bontebok as well as the rare Cape mountain zebra and a variety of other game. Bordering the wilderness area are a number of farms that are managed together as a conservancy with

regard to the protection of the indigenous flora and fauna. Nature trails are currently being planned and accommodation is available.

Nearby Swellendam, with its beautiful, well-preserved architecture in a stunning setting, is well worth a visit. Be sure to visit the Drostdy Museum complex (see separate entry), which includes the old Gaol, the Drostdy, the Mayville Museum and its gardens, and a replica of a water mill.

Witsand and Cape Infanta lie directly to the south of Boosmansbos.
Special attractions: The indigenous forest, the mountains.
More information: Contact The Officer-in-Charge, Grootvadersbos Wilderness Area, PO Box 109, Heidelberg 6760; tel (02962) 22412.

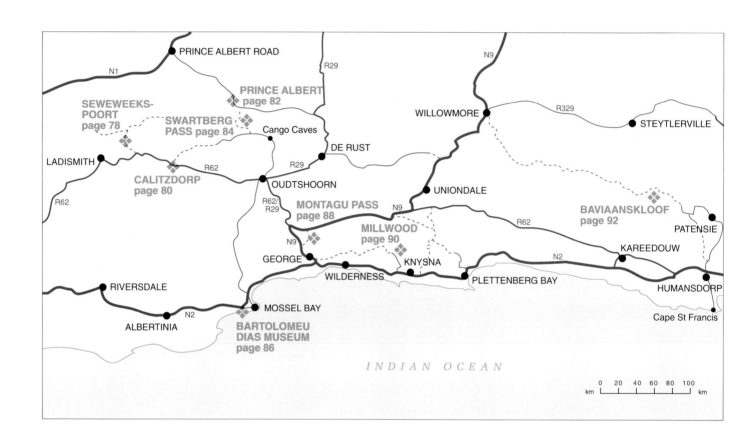

PRINCE ALBERT ROAD

N1

R29

N9

SEWEWEEKS-
POORT
page 78

PRINCE ALBERT
page 82

SWARTBERG
PASS page 84

WILLOWMORE

R329

STEYTLERVILLE

Cango Caves

LADISMITH

DE RUST

CALITZDORP
page 80

R62

R29

OUDTSHOORN

R62

MONTAGU PASS
page 88

UNIONDALE

R62/
R29

N9

MILLWOOD
page 90

BAVIAANSKLOOF
page 92

PATENSIE

R62

N9

KAREEDOUW

GEORGE

KNYSNA

N2

RIVERSDALE

WILDERNESS

PLETTENBERG BAY

HUMANSDORP

N2

ALBERTINIA

MOSSEL BAY

BARTOLOMEU
DIAS MUSEUM
page 86

Cape St Francis

INDIAN OCEAN

0   20   40   60   80   100
km ├──┼──┼──┼──┼──┤ km

SOUTHERN CAPE

An awe-inspiring passage through the Klein Swartberge

Tortured geological formations surround the motorist as he makes his way through Seweweekspoort – the narrow, 15 km-long gorge that connects the Little Karoo with the Great Karoo

Where to stay

There are hotels at Ladismith, Calitzdorp and Laingsburg, while the *Besemfontein Veld Camp* to the north of Seweweekspoort offers accommodation for up to 30 people. (See panel below for address and telephone number.)

SHIMMERING IN THE SUMMER HEAT, the high peaks of the Swartberge run in an almost unbroken line for 200 km from east to west across the southern Cape, a barrier between the relatively fertile lands of the Little Karoo to the south and the drier, more inhospitable scrubland of the Great Karoo to the north.

And yet, like some secret passage through a haunted house, there is a way through the great barrier of the Swartberge: the eerie, echo-filled kloof known as Seweweekspoort.

Through this gorge runs the Seweweekspoort River, a normally placid stream that collects in deep, dark pools between water-smoothed boulders. After heavy rain, however, the river can become a raging torrent, threatening everything in its path – including the road that shares the valley floor.

It is this innocent, gurgling stream that is the real architect of Seweweekspoort, gouging its way through the mountains over millions of years to leave a fantastic collection of weirdly shaped rocks and steep, jagged cliffs. What has happened is that the waters have, over the millennia, stripped away the outer mantle of softer soil to reveal the buckled contours of the Cape folded mountains in all their naked splendour. Here man truly feels an interloper, a fleeting spectator to a drama that is almost as old as the earth itself.

However, man has made good use of this deep slash through the Klein Swartberge, using it since time immemorial as a natural route through the mountains. Just how it came to be called Seweweekspoort, however, remains a mystery. The favourite theory is that it took brandy smugglers seven weeks to negotiate the long route by oxwagon, as they attempted to evade the customs authorities who controlled traffic on the more direct route between Cape Town and the interior. Another has it that the poort was named after one of the founders of the nearby mission station of Zoar, the Reverend Louis Zerwick; over the years *Zerwick se poort* is said to have become Seweweekspoort.

Today, however, the smugglers have long gone, leaving the kloof as a peaceful yet sombre reminder of the awesome power of nature. A narrow gravel

The dust-road approach to Seweweekspoort. In the background are the cloud-capped peaks of the Klein Swartberge.

Seweweekspoort at a glance (map page 76)

How to get there: From the south, take the N2 and then the R323 north from Riversdale to Ladismith. At Ladismith turn east onto the R62; after 21 km turn onto a well-signposted gravel road leading north. The pass begins 5 km from the turn-off. From the north, take the R323 south from Laingsburg on the N1 and follow the signpost left after the Rooinek Pass onto a gravel road. Access is easier from the south, avoiding a long gravel stretch through the Karoo.
Weather: Hot dry summers and mild winters.
Facilities: There are several picnic sites in the kloof, and toilets towards the northern end.
What to do: Walks in the area, identifying flora. The Besemfontein Veld Camp has two hiking trails.
Special attractions: Dramatic cliff scenery, colourful flora, the ruins of the old tollhouse.
More information: Ladismith Municipality, PO Box 30, Ladismith 6885; tel (02942) 20. For more information about the Besemfontein Veld Camp, write to Private Bag X216, Ladismith 6885; tel (02942) 325.

The pincushions seen in the foreground are just one of the many plant species found amidst the rocky terrain.

road runs along the valley floor, curving between the rocks that rise towards the distant blue of the sky above.

Whether approaching the pass from the north or south, your first impression is the same: disbelief. Surely the mapmakers have made some mistake, how could there possibly be a way through that seemingly impenetrable wall of mountains? Then, just as the road seems to end against a twisted wall of rock, the gap opens up, and the road snakes tantalisingly into the mountains between orange-red buttresses of heaped sandstone. Here a secret world of wonders opens up, dominated by the highest peak in the Swartberge and the southern Cape, the 2 325-m Seweweekspoort Peak.

There is nothing difficult or dangerous about the 15 km drive through Seweweekspoort, for this is a pass through the mountains, not over them. The steepest gradient is an easy 1:14 as the road climbs gently from the broad valley of the Little Karoo towards the higher elevation of its altogether grander cousin, the Great Karoo.

The well-watered valley floor is home to a wide variety of flora, contrasting starkly with the more barren walls of the poort, where aloes, nerinas and a variety of daisies cling to convenient terraces for support. Most precious of all is the rare *Protea aristata*, first discovered in 1928 and then lost to botanists for 25 years until a clump was found growing alongside the road in Seweweekspoort. Since then, several others have taken root higher up on the rocks.

The present road was opened in 1860 after two years of work by road engineer A G de Smidt and a gang of convicts. Work continued however, until 1862. Near the northern entrance stand the ruins of an old tollhouse, reputedly haunted by the ghost of a long-forgotten toll-keeper swinging his lamp in a bid to stop passing vehicles.

Clusters of hardy aloes are a common sight in the drier reaches of Seweweekspoort.

A charming destination for wine enthusiasts

The friendly atmosphere of a country town and good full-bodied wines are just some of the attractions of the often by-passed Calitzdorp area

SOMEWHAT NEGLECTED by the tourist, but well worth visiting, is the small town of Calitzdorp situated in the lovely Gamka River valley. It is notable for its old-fashioned charm, its friendly and hospitable residents, and especially for its large Renaissance-Byzantine style church that is capable of accommodating a congregation of over 1 500 – the stinkwood and yellowwood vestry table is more than 5 m long.

Calitzdorp is also well known for its fine wines and the area boasts its own wine route – a network of three venues that invite you to sample their excellent, full-bodied, rather fruity vintages (the grapes of the region have a high sugar content), their fortified wines, and also the delicious, honey-sweet dried fruit produced in the area.

The local co-operative, which is supplied by a hundred or so farms scattered over an area that stretches from the Swartberg to the sea, specialises in rich dessert wines, among them Hanepoot and Muskadel. There are tasting facilities and cellar tours, and wines are on sale to the public.

On the edge of town are the highly regarded *Boplaas* cellars, the first in the country to distil an estate brandy. Here, too, sweet, heavy wines are to be found, but *Boplaas's* flagship products are its ports (which have won many awards), made in the true Portuguese fashion. The tasting room is open from Monday to Saturday; and in high summer

(5 December to 10 January), and for two weeks over Easter, visitors can enjoy home-cooked farm lunches in the restaurant. The estate also makes and sells dried-fruit rolls – six different kinds – together with a variety of jams and chutneys.

Nearby is *Die Krans*, the oldest cellars in the Little Karoo and similar to *Boplaas* in its guest amenities and wine types – though the estate is broadening its range, venturing into such grape varieties as Cabernet and Chardonnay, which are grown on the higher slopes of the mountains. Adding interest to your visit is *Die Krans's* 20-minute self-guided 'vineyard route', whose path meanders among the serried ranks of vines and along which there are signs identifying the different cultivars.

The *Die Krans* wine estate donates part of the profits from one of its labels – a white Jerepigo – to the upkeep of the Gamka Mountain Reserve, a rugged, ravine-sliced, 9 500-ha expanse of countryside to the southeast of Calitzdorp. The reserve was proclaimed in 1970 to protect the threatened (and at one time very nearly extinct) Cape mountain zebra, but is now better known perhaps for its rare and often beautiful plants, among them succulents, ericas and proteas.

In 1987 the reserve achieved botanical prominence with the discovery of an entirely new protea species *Mimites chrysanthus* which, as far as is known, grows here and nowhere else.

Clusters of cypress trees provide a natural counterpoint to the attractive spire of Calitzdorp's church.

Where to stay

The *Queen's Hotel*, with 10 rooms, six en suite, is in Queen's Street. Write to PO Box 11, Calitzdorp 6660; tel (04437) 33332. For a more informal stay, you could try the *Welgevonden*, PO Box 15, Calitzdorp 6660; tel (04437) 33642. This is a comfortable four-roomed guesthouse that offers bed and breakfast at reasonable rates, with dinner provided on request. Some of the attractions of this charming place are its reed ceilings, patchwork furnishings and large, shady garden.

Also welcoming is *Die Dorpshuis* in Van Riebeeck Street, which offers spacious rooms (with TV and private bathroom) and a pleasant coffee shop. To make reservations, write to PO Box 264, Calitzdorp; tel (04437) 33453. Alternatively, you might prefer a farm holiday at *Groenfontein*, at the foot of the Swartberg, 20 km from Calitzdorp. The address is PO Box 30, Calitzdorp 6660; tel (04437) 33762.

And then there's the renowned *Calitzdorp Spa* on the south bank of the Olifants River. It has 40 fully furnished, self-catering, four- and six-bed chalets, restaurant, cafe, shop and, of course, mineral-rich waters which bubble up from the ground into four therapeutic swimming pools at a warm and constant 50° C. There's also a terraced camping area served by four ablution blocks. For details, contact Calitzdorp Spa, PO Box 127, Oudtshoorn 6620; tel (04437) 33371.

Around 90 different kinds of bird have been identified within the reserve's boundaries, including the booted and the black eagles and the pale chanting goshawk – the only African bird of prey that is polyandrous (two males sharing a female).

The Gamka Mountain Reserve has limited tourist facilities, but hikers and walkers are made very welcome. Established trails include a short 20-minute excursion; a six-hour, 15-km ramble along a deep kloof; and, for the more energetic, a two-day, 26-km guided hike (minimum six adults, maximum 10), which must be booked in advance.

Calitzdorp serves as a convenient base from which to explore the general region – some of the most rewarding drives being those that lead over the splendidly scenic Little Karoo mountain ranges.

North of the road that connects the town with Ladismith (the R62) is the Seven Weeks Poort (or Seweweekspoort). Towering above this pass is the 2 326-m Seweweekspoort Mountain, the highest in the range. There are several charming picnic spots along the way, all with magnificent vistas. Turn left at the bottom and carry on to the junction with the R323, which will lead you to the N1 highway at Laingsburg – 27 km from which is the enchanting little Victorian village of Matjiesfontein. From here, make your way back via the R323 through Ladismith (the Towerkop cheese factory here welcomes visitors) and the R62 to Calitzdorp to complete a most pleasant 230-km trip.

Calitzdorp at a glance (map page 76)

How to get there: The town is on the R62, 52 km west of Oudtshoorn. From Cape Town, take the N1 highway to Worcester and then follow the R60 east to Ashton, turn north through the scenic Cogmans Kloof to Montagu and continue eastwards on the R62 through Barrydale and Ladismith. Alternatively, drive to Barrydale via the N2 highway past Swellendam, turning off on the R324 to negotiate the Tradouw Pass.
Weather: Rain falls throughout the year, but averages a low 150 mm. Summers are hot; winters cool to cold, and very cold on the mountains above, where snow occasionally mantles the higher peaks.
What to do: Sightseeing in town and vicinity; hiking; scenic drives to and over the mountains.
Special attractions: Among the area's nature reserves are the Gamka Mountain Nature Reserve. For information and permits contact the Officer-in-Charge, Private Bag X21, Oudtshoorn 6620; tel (04437) 33367. On the slopes of the Swartberg, to the north of Calitzdorp, is the Gamkapoort Nature Reserve, which has an impressive dam, a magnificent gorge below it, and wonderful mountain scenery all around. For information and permits contact the Officer-in-Charge, Gamkapoort Nature Reserve, PO Box 139, Prince Albert 6930; tel (04436) 905.

If you have a soft spot for train travel, there's the Ostrich Express which runs between Oudtshoorn and Calitzdorp and back again. An overnight stop is made at Calitzdorp, where passengers are wined and dined before spending the night on the train. For more information, contact Ostrich Express, PO Box 59, Oudtshoorn 6620; tel (0443) 223540.

The Swartberg Mountains, looming up just to the north of Calitzdorp, have much to offer the hiker and outdoor enthusiast.

Whitewashed gables and a forgotten goldrush

Don't whizz past the road sign to Prince Albert on the southern fringe of the Great Karoo – it's a small village with great charm at the foot of a mighty mountain

THERE ARE TWO KINDS of people who drive through the Karoo – those who race on to their destination and leave it behind them as soon as they can, and those who linger in its vast open space and serene silence. For those who take the time to explore the villages and scenery that lie beyond the Cape Town/Johannesburg highway, the Karoo's special magic unfolds.

Prince Albert lies at the foot of the mighty Swartberg range, 45 km from the highway and about 72 km from Oudtshoorn via the breathtaking Swartberg Pass. It is an enchanting little oasis watered by the mountain streams of the Swartberg range. Here the peaceful atmosphere of the 19th century lingers on, preserved along with the town's varied architecture.

Prince Albert, as you will discover if you visit the Fransie Pienaar Museum at 16 Church Street, began in 1762 as a farm called *Kweekvallei*, owned by one Zacharias de Beer. His son Samuel sold the farm to two brothers and like modern-day developers, they subdivided it into plots. A village began to develop around 1842. It was initially known as Albertsberg, but renamed Prince Albert to honour Queen Victoria's consort.

For a fleeting moment in its history, Prince Albert seemed set for a glittering future of wealth and splendour. The discovery of gold in the northern outlying areas in 1890 brought prospectors from far afield, with their spades, pans and great expectations. But the easily won gold was soon worked out and, as the fortune-hunters drifted away, peace returned to Prince Albert.

Relics of the goldrush are displayed in the museum, along with a collection of family Bibles, Cape furniture, firearms and farm implements. The most bizarre exhibit is a coffin, just 30 cm long, complete with brass fittings. It was found, firmly sealed, in the loft of a former local cabinet-maker and remains unopened to this day.

Three distinct forms of architecture coexist in Prince Albert – the flat-roofed buildings typical of the Karoo, the intricate lattice work of Victorian originals, and the traditional gabled houses characteristic of the Cape. Among the large number of whitewashed gables that have survived are a number of so-called Prince Albert gables. These are *holbol* (convex-concave) gables, sometimes supported on short pilasters and with characteristic horizontal mouldings. Once you've learnt to recognise them, it's fun picking them out as you stroll through the village. Look out for Prince Albert gables at 5 Deurdrift Street, 8 and 12 De Beer Street and 1, 5 and 23 Church Street.

The local museum (below and right) was established in 1972 and named after Mrs Fransie Pienaar who donated a number of antiques towards the project.

The impressive-looking Dutch Reformed Church was built in 1865. A 'sandbag' fort was set up in its grounds during the Anglo-Boer War.

The handsome Dutch Reformed Church is (where else?) in Church Street, facing Pastorie Street, and at 29 Christina de Wit Street you'll find the home of the miller – an important person in a town whose old water mill is its best-known landmark.

The grinding of wheat forms an interesting chapter in the history of South Africa. The first settlers at the Cape, coming as they did from the Netherlands, made use of windmills. But as the settlement expanded into the interior, water mills – and in the absence of water, horse mills – were set up at strategic points. The mills played an important part in the life of the community and most of the places where they were erected are known. Unfortunately, few water mills survive and the one at Prince Albert is therefore of considerable historical and cultural importance.

The Prince Albert Mill on the outskirts of the village, on the road to the Swartberg Pass, was erected in about 1850 by Mr H J Botes. He built the little building that houses the mill as well as a water wheel 2,4 m in diameter and then constructed a furrow to lead the water from a mountain stream. The mill was taken over from Mr Botes by a Mr N Alberts in 1865. In due course it passed from him to his son, and eventually to his grandson, who sold it in 1978 to the Theron family, the present owners.

The operation of the mill was therefore a family business in which the owner periodically renewed the water wheel and ground new grindstones from sandstone brought from the district of George. The capacity of the mill was about one bag of wheat per hour, and Prince Albert's older residents claim that bread made with this flour had a special taste and texture.

In 1963 the old mill was threatened by modern development. The road on which it lies had to be widened and it was found that the mill encroached on the road reserve. Fortunately it had been proclaimed a national monument and, with the sympathetic collaboration of the authorities, a solution was found that left the historic mill untouched.

We'll never know just how many historical sites have been lost in the modern quest to find the shortest route between points A and B. But there are still many secrets to be uncovered by those prepared to take the long way round. Prince Albert lies along such a detour, but this pretty village offers much to compensate you for your trouble. Its ostrich biltong is famous, as is the delicious dried fruit. And there is always an ice-cold glass of ginger beer to wash the Karoo dust from your throat. Homemade and complete with raisins, Prince Albert's ginger beer alone is said to be worth the drive.

Where to stay

The *Swartberg Hotel* in Church Street is a small hotel furnished with some of the town's original antiques. Rondavels set in the beautiful garden that surrounds the hotel offer self-catering accommodation. Contact them at PO Box 6, Prince Albert 6930; tel (04436) 332.

Prince Albert at a glance (map page 76)

How to get there: There are two turn-offs to Prince Albert from the highway between Cape Town and Johannesburg – the R328 turns off 39 km south of Leeu Gamka, the R353 is 30 km on.

Weather: In mid-summer the Karoo is so hot that the tarmac softens at the side of the road. In winter the nights are icy but the days warm and clear.

What to do: Linger in Prince Albert en route between the N1 and the Cango Caves near Oudtshoorn. Explore the town and the Swartberg Pass beyond.

Special attractions: The Prince Albert Mill is one the few remaining water mills in the country; the Fransie Pienaar Museum is well worth a visit.

Visiting times: If the mill is locked, you can ask for a key at a reasonable hour from the owners; they live in a house on the property.

Other information: Contact the Town Clerk, PO Box 25, Prince Albert 6930; tel (04436) 962, or the Information Officer, Fransie Pienaar Museum, Prince Albert 6930; tel (04436) 366.

A hair-raising drive through hairpin bends

Linking the Little Karoo and the Great Karoo, the 24-km Swartberg Pass climbs a spectacular 1 585 m during its northward ascent

WHEN MOTORISTS SPEAK about the Swartberg Pass they do so in the same exhilarated tones as do surfers recounting a particularly exciting wave: no matter how many passes you have driven over, ascending and descending back and forth across this mountain terrain for the first time is bound to be an unforgettable experience.

Being one of the most formidable passes in southern Africa, however, the Swartberg requires a steady hand on the steering wheel and a cool nerve. A notice at either end of the pass warns that 'caravans and horse-drawn vehicles' are not permitted – and it's not hard to see why. There are some truly awesome gradients, particularly on the southern slopes, as well as several tight hairpin bends.

The rewards, however, are handsome indeed. In typical Swartberg fashion, the mountains yield up their wonders in large measures: huge buttresses of buckled, orange-red rock contrast with the placid waters of hidden, riverside picnic spots that are surrounded by some of the rarest wildflowers in southern Africa.

The Swartberg Pass links the 'capital' of the Little Karoo, Oudtshoorn, with the picturesque village of Prince Albert and the Great Karoo beyond, and is undoubtedly the best way to see the rugged grandeur of the Groot Swartberg range. Few roads in the country offer such outstanding views, and a feeling of getting close to some truly awe-inspiring works of nature – not to mention the works of man. The Swartberg Pass was built long before the advent of the bulldozer and the steamroller, and its construction was a singular challenge to the skills of the engineer who designed it.

The roadbuilder in this particular case was the veteran of a dozen other Cape passes, Thomas Bain, son of his equally famous roadbuilding father, Scots-born Andrew Geddes Bain, whose keen eye and unyielding determination led to so much of the southwestern and southern Cape being opened up.

Asked in 1875 to survey a possible pass, Bain reported positively, and a local contractor agreed to build the road in 18 months. Thirteen months later, the road ground to a standstill after only 6 km – the contractor bankrupted by the unexpected amount of work required on the project.

The Cape Government called on Bain to come to the rescue, offering the services of hundreds of convicts from the jail at Knysna. After four years of toil in baking heat, freezing snow and driving rain, the job was done, and on 10 January 1888 the pass was finally opened.

Since then the road has hardly changed – lifting skywards from the floor of the Little Karoo in an almost unbroken ascent for over 1 000 m, passing the ruins of the old Halfway House Inn before reaching the summit of the pass at 1 585 m above sea level.

Where to stay

There are several hotels and camp sites in and around Oudtshoorn, and a hotel at Prince Albert. Camping is not allowed on the pass. For excellent bed-and-breakfast accommodation, contact the Klein Karoo Marketing Association, PO Box 1234, Oudtshoorn 6620; tel (0443) 226643 or 225007.

Swartberg Pass at a glance (map page 76)

How to get there: From Cape Town, take the N2 east and the R328 north to Oudtshoorn. Continue north along Baron von Reede Street (which becomes the R328) towards Schoemanspoort and the Cango Caves. The pass starts approximately 46 km north of Oudtshoorn. If you're travelling from Johannesburg, drive south along the N1 until you reach Prince Albert Road. Turn left onto the R328. The pass starts about 45 km along the R328, south of Prince Albert.
Weather: Hot summers, icy winters – often with snow.
What to do: Hiking, picnicking, and fishing and swimming in river pools.

Special attractions: Spectacular views and the opportunity to see rare wildflowers. More than 600 plant species have been identified on the pass, and wildlife includes mountain and grey rhebok, klipspringers, duikers and grysbok.
Facilities: There are two tree-shaded picnic sites alongside the road, one on either side of the summit.
More information: The Tourist Bureau, PO Box 255, Oudtshoorn 6620; tel (0443) 222221. For more information about the Swartberg Hiking Trails contact the State Forester, Private Bag X658, Oudtshoorn 6620; tel (0443) 291739 or 291829.

Various points on the pass offer magnificent scenic views of Karoo farmlands far below.

(Above) Just what a feat of engineering the Swartberg Pass represents is clearly evident in this aerial photograph. (Below) In places, the pass is a seemingly endless succession of hairpin bends.

Several viewsites have been built alongside the road, offering endless vistas of the farmland far below and the distant Outeniqua Mountains.

Cradled for a moment between the high peaks of the Oliewenberg (1 857 m) to the east and the impressive dome of the Kangoberg (2 024 m) to the west, the road twists sharply to the right before plunging down into the tumbled kloofs of the Swartberg Mountains. This section is much longer than the ascent, lifting over a mountain ridge before a spectacular plunge through a series of ever-tightening hairpin bends to the cool depths of a pelargonium-choked kloof. This kloof is dominated by a great pinnacle of folded, blood-red rock known appropriately as the Cathedral.

Finally, with a last twist through the narrow opening of the kloof, the road shakes free of the Swartberg Mountains to run straight and wide into the Great Karoo beyond.

A few kilometres past the summit of the pass, a four-wheel-drive track leads left for 57 km to a lonely settlement known as Die Hel, following the backbone of the Swartberg Mountains before falling between the narrow walls of the Gamkaskloof. It is inadvisable to do this drive in a normal saloon car.

Warning: The Swartberg Pass is closed to caravans and trailers. During winter, enquire locally in case the road has been closed because of snow or heavy rain.

On display in the Maritime Museum is an exact replica of the caravel in which Bartolomeu Dias made his epic voyage from Portugal.

Museum among the milkwoods at 'Aguada de Sâo Bras'

A fascinating glimpse into the world of the early navigators is provided at the Bartolomeu Dias Museum complex in Mossel Bay

THERE'S FAR MORE than just offshore drilling at Mossel Bay, where the subcontinent's European links were forged over five centuries ago. The Bartolomeu Dias Museum complex was developed over a number of years to celebrate the area's rich historical legacy, and finally culminated in the quincentenary festivities in 1988. There are several high points on this particular voyage of discovery, so ensure that you have at least a few hours to spare.

In his relentless quest to find a sea-route around the tip of Africa to India, Bartolomeu Dias was the first white man to set foot on the subcontinent in 1488. En route from Portugal with two caravels, Dias landed in a protected cove on the festival day of St Blaise. He discovered a freshwater spring and named the bay in the saint's honour. So *Aguada de Sâo Bras* (Watering Place of St Blaise) was the lyrical name first given to Mossel Bay. Its present name was bestowed on it in 1601 by the Dutch

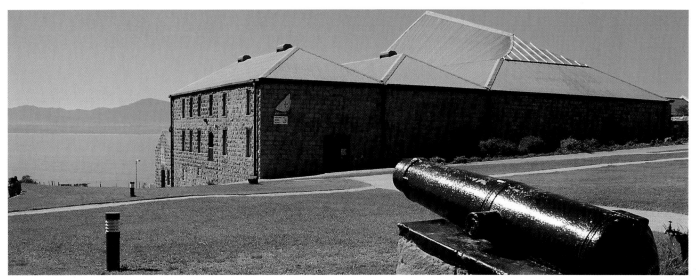

explorer Paulus van Caerden, who found only mussels to quell his hunger pangs.

Almost 10 years after Dias landed, his successor, Vasco da Gama also landed here and carried out what locals are proud to describe as the first commercial transaction with the Khoikhoi. According to some sources, Da Gama traded bells and bracelets for a bull, but other sources insist it was the sailors' distinctive red caps that the Khoikhoi so coveted. For many years Mossel Bay was the principal landing spot for explorers rounding Africa, because here they could stock up with fresh water and meat.

The information centre and reception area for the museum complex is situated in the Granary, a replica of the granary built in 1786 by the Dutch East India Company. The present building was erected on the remains of the original foundations according to the specifications found in the Cape Archives. However, for a crash course on the district's cultural heritage, it might be better to begin your tour at the Local History Museum in Market Street.

This consists of two buildings: the main one was erected in 1879 and its stolid, phlegmatic demeanour testifies to the work of British stonemasons who were responsible for much of the stonework around Mossel Bay. The annexe, a small, white building typical of the Karoo, dates back to 1858, when it was the town's first municipal and community centre. Shops from the town's early days have been reconstructed here, and the good old Union Castle mailship days are nostalgically recalled with photographs and memorabilia.

Bartolomeu Dias Museum at a glance (map page 76)

How to get there: The museum complex is easy to find – simply follow the signs at the main traffic lights.
Weather: Known as 'Karoo by the Sea', Mossel Bay revels in a moderate climate – it's never too hot and never too cold.
Special attractions: Visitors can watch the whales and dolphins at play in the nearby yacht club basin.
More information: The Information Centre, Bartolomeu Dias Museum, Private Bag X1, Mossel Bay, 6500; tel (0444) 911067.
Opening times: Mondays to Friday 9 am to 1 pm and 2 pm to 5 pm (open all day during school holidays); Saturday from 10 am to 1 pm and Sunday from 2 pm to 5 pm.

The Maritime Museum has been adapted to house a full-sized replica of Dias's caravel. Visitors can climb on board (by appointment), explore and marvel. All sorts of maritime paraphernalia are on display, covering the mixed fortunes of not only the Portuguese explorers but also the Dutch and British navigators whose history clings to these south-eastern shores.

There are also early maps, including a copy of the Martellus map (the first ever of the Mossel Bay area), artefacts from shipwrecks found along the coast, and spices, coins and precious stones from those heady trading days.

Another 'first' claimed by the Mossel Bay community is the first post office in southern Africa. In 1500 a ship's commander, Pedro d'Ataide, left a letter containing an account of his voyage in a navigator's boot which he hung in a milkwood tree. The message was discovered about a year later by Da Nova, who left a letter of his own there. For many years thereafter, mariners left messages inscribed into large stones around the base of the tree. And so it became known as the Post Office Tree. This magnificent milkwood tree with its enormous, gnarled branches, is now a national monument.

The Shirley Building next to the Post Office Tree houses the Shell Museum, and conchologists will delight in this vast collection. From here it's a short walk to Dias's perennial spring, which, these days, flows into a small, scenic dam. The surrounding nature reserve is an integral part of the museum complex, and much effort has been made to preserve the plant life peculiar to the region and to reintroduce those species that have disappeared. Contour paths take visitors through milkwood, aloes and wild olive groves in an area bright with indigenous coastal fynbos. From these paths there are striking views of the bay and a *padrão* or stone cross marks the spot experts believe was the landing site of Bartolomeu Dias over 500 years ago.

Your final port of call should be Munrohoek Cottages, some of the district's oldest houses, which were built by one Alexander Munro in the 1830s. Housed in one of these old cottages is a gallery which features locally made arts and crafts, and you can round off your journey in the tearoom with a welcome pot of tea and scones.

The Maritime Museum building was originally erected in 1901 as a sawmill and grain mill.

Where to stay

Mossel Bay has varied and ample accommodation, ranging from smart hotels to bed-and-breakfast in local houses and on farms. Contact the Information Centre for a list. Closest to the museum complex is the *Post Office Tree Guest House*, PO Box 349, Mossel Bay 6500, which has 12 en-suite rooms; tel (0444) 913738.

There are three municipal caravan and camping sites at Mossel Bay – contact the municipality at PO Box 25, Mossel Bay 6500; tel (0444) 912215.

Up and over the Outeniquas on a winding ribbon of road

Montagu Pass, one of the country's oldest and most beautiful passes, takes the traveller from George, across the mountains, to the Little Karoo

TUNNELS OF GREEN FOLIAGE, old indigenous trees, cool streams, wonderful views of sea and plateau, and a fascinating sense of history. These are the rewards that await the traveller who forsakes the Outeniqua Pass between George and Oudtshoorn in favour of the older, and gentler, Montagu Pass nearby. Despite its narrow roadway and the occasional blind corner, Montagu Pass is one of the most rewarding of all the country's mountain passes. There is even, so modern travellers assert, a resident leopard.

Leave George on the R29 for Oudtshoorn, taking the Witfontein Road and following the signs for the pass by turning off through part of the Witfontein forestry plantation on the outskirts of the town. Within a few kilometres, and still on only the gentlest of gradients, you reach the old tollhouse, snug and solidly built of local stone. It once had a thatched roof, but that was lost in a fire more than a century ago.

Here the tollkeeper pushed aside the white-painted bar across the road for travellers who had paid the set tariffs – in 1867 they were the equivalent of two cents for each wheel of a vehicle, one cent for each animal drawing a vehicle, half a cent for each sheep, pig or goat and two cents for other animals that were not in harness. An early tollkeeper, who made leather velskoens for passers-by, saw his little home industry expand to fill a full-scale factory, while another incumbent was Charles Searle, who went on to found the nearby town of Great Brak River.

The steeper gradients are encountered beyond the bridge across the Keur River, only a kilometre or two beyond the tollhouse. There is space to park here, and to enjoy the quiet of this sylvan scene of rustic stone bridge and rippling stream. In summer it is cool and green, a favourite place of those who know it and who live within reach. Here, in a solemn ceremony widely reported in the local newspapers in 1848, Mrs Bergh, wife of the former local magistrate, broke a bottle of wine on the parapet of the bridge and declared to the assembled crowd 'I christen this splendid road Montagu Pass.' The road is still much as it was then, although here and there the vegetation has changed, with indigenous trees having been replaced with exotic pine and acacia.

Soon after the Keur River bridge comes *Die Noute* ('The Narrows'), where the cliffs tower above the roadway. Here, as in other places along the road, can be seen the inward set of the lowest course of stones of the dry-packed wall. This course caught the rims of wagon wheels and prevented the bulky hubs from crashing into the stonework.

Past *Die Noute*, a massive boulder of the same sandstone lies just off the road, beyond the wall, and locals call it the *Moertjiesklip*, which, used in this sense, really has no polite English equivalent, although the reference is to its great size.

There are several versions of the story of its origin. According to one, the name dates back to the building of the pass, of which much of the work was carried out by convicts. Several convicts were

Montagu Pass winds its way past a railway bridge, towards a verdant mountainside. Shortly after the pass was opened in 1847 English novelist Anthony Trollope described it as being 'equal to some of the mountain roads through the Pyrenees'.

An unusual view of the winding Montagu Pass from a view site on the nearby Outeniqua Pass.

working, chained together, when their labours dislodged this same boulder from a position above the roadway. They heard it stir, saw it move and realised the danger that they were in. They ran, but in different directions and, being chained together – so the story goes – made no progress at all, and were crushed to death by the great boulder's fall. Their ghosts are still said to haunt the spot on the anniversary of the fateful day.

Only a signpost a kilometre further tells you of the Old Smithy – once a substantial building that has been illegally carried away, stone by stone over the years, to private gardens. Name boards announcing *Regoptrek* ('Vertical Haul') and *Grogdraai* ('Grog Bend') explain themselves, as does *Stink-houtdraai* ('Stinkwood Bend'), where the railway viaduct (built about 1910) crosses the roadway, and a few of the stinkwood trees remain.

At the summit of the pass is a disused silica quarry and just beyond the summit, on the right, is a building that was once the North Station Hotel (it was previously one of the main convict stations). In the days of horse-drawn transport, many George newlyweds spent their honeymoon here. Not far away, the older Cradock Kloof road joins the Montagu Pass, and the ruts gouged by the brake-locked wheels of countless wagons are still to be seen`in the rock. Northward, the road winds its way to the village of Herold – and beyond that, it can be traced though farmland for many kilometres.

Montagu Pass at a glance (map page 76)

How to get there: From Oudtshoorn and the Langkloof turn south from the R62 onto the gravel road signposted 'Herold' and 'George via Montagu Pass', about 9km east of the junction with the R29. From George, follow the signs for 'Oudtshoorn' and turn right for 'Witfontein' and 'Montagu Pass' on the outskirts of George.

The road is usually well maintained and has easy gradients, the steepest being 1:6, but some blind corners and the narrowness of the roadway demand careful driving, especially when the surface is wet. The length of the pass, from Witfontein to Herold, is some 10 km. An excellent overall view of the road can be obtained from the 'Historic Passes View Site' on the Outeniqua Pass above George.

Weather: The pass is located in a region in which rainfall is well distributed throughout the year, with March the wettest month and July the driest. The pass is usually invitingly cool, even when the hot berg winds sweep over the area during late summer and autumn.

What to do: Hiking, taking in the views, bird-spotting, identifying flowers and trees. Park where it is safe and enjoy a close study of road-making as it was practised early last century. The dry-packed stonework and drainage system are particularly impressive.

Special attractions: A feeling of closeness to nature in remote places little changed by the passage of time. Places where you can picnic include (from south to north) Tollhouse, Keur River Bridge, Old Smithy, *Stinkhoutdraai* and the summit.

More information: The Curator, George Museum, Private Bag 6586, George 6530; tel (0441) 735343 or 740354.

Forgotten dreams of gold among the yellowwoods

Amidst the tranquillity of Knysna's tree-cloaked mountains, only tantalising traces remain of the gold-miners of Millwood

IT SEEMS AMAZING that men should have detected the presence of gold in the high evergreen forests of Knysna. But they did, and the estimated 700 fortune-hunters who flocked to the area dug and panned frenetically here until the thin, golden veins of the area ran out. Then they left for the Witwatersrand, leaving the scattered remains of a ghost town among the forests of Millwood.

The very first nugget was found in 1876 in the bed of the Millwood stretch of the Karatara River – in fact, you can still probably find tiny traces of alluvial gold if you know how to use a prospector's pan and have the required licence.

The excavations of the early miners – most of whom seemed somewhat half-hearted in appearance – are still to be found alongside the path that leads from the picnic site at Jubilee Creek and passes through fairly dense shrub and forest. Nearby is Forest Creek, scene of some of the area's richest alluvial strikes, while the sombre name of Poverty Flats speaks for itself.

As you drive to Millwood, your approach is along the old wagon route once called Knysna Road. Beyond the site of Monk's Store (also known as Materolli) the road divides, the section bending to the left becoming the main road of Millwood town. Not much remains – the location of what were once the main streets of the town is identified by wooden posts and boards, and the only foundation stones to be found are those of the front stoep of the Millwood Hotel. Few foundations were in fact dug here – most of the buildings, including

hotels, were tents or structures of corrugated iron on a wooden framework.

Perhaps the most permanent and touching reminders of fleeting domesticity are the garden flowers still to be found among the weeds and forest growth, and a few gnarled and straggling fruit trees, including figs, vines and even the occasional orange.

It's interesting to reflect, while wandering around here, that this beautiful place could, if the gold deposits had been richer, have become another noisy, crowded Witwatersrand. Fortunately for posterity, the gold was quickly exhausted and the Millwood diggers started making their exodus to the Reef after the yellow metal was discovered there in 1882.

The old cemetery is worth a visit, if only to honour the memory of past pioneers. It has little enough information to impart about individuals – of the 100 or so people who were buried here during the town's boom period, only two were given inscribed gravestones. Periodically, the area around the cemetery is cleared of growth, but at other times you may have to scramble through bushes and prickly creepers.

A major working that, more than 100 years later, is still quite easy to find is the lower tunnel of the Australian Bendigo Syndicate, just down the slope from the recovery plant – a position still marked by the boiler of a stationary steam engine. All digging at Millwood was done by hand, which makes the dimensions of this tunnel – it is about 160 m long –

Where to stay

Knysna offers a variety of accommodation ranging from hotels and guesthouses to bed-and-breakfast, self-catering and caravanning facilities. For information concerning accommodation, contact the Knysna Publicity Association (see other panel for address).

A boardwalk offers visitors a comfortable route into one of the tunnels of the Millwood mine.

This old boiler, standing abandoned amidst the forest vegetation, marks the entrance to the old Bendigo Gold Mine at Millwood.

particularly impressive. The first few metres of the tunnel are usually wet and muddy but, once you are well inside, the floor is fairly dry. But beware, the long and dark excavation is now the home of an immense flock of bats that whirls about to the needless alarm of many visitors.

Uphill from the recovery plant there are more workings, as well as a storage dam, all being part of the Bendigo Mine complex. These workings, which include deep, very low shafts that are often flooded, are less safe to explore than the main tunnel further down the hill.

In the bush are more relics – from steam-powered machinery to the tumbled walls of a remote cottage. Some of them are on or close to paths and are signposted, while others are still covered by the dense foliage. The entire area of Millwood has yet to be explored, however, and its detailed story remains still to be written.

For a more sedate examination of Knysna's gold mining past, you can visit the Millwood House Museum in Queen's Road, Knysna.

You can explore tunnels that are signposted in the old Millwood complex. However, beware of mud and bats.

Millwood at a glance (map page 76)

How to get there: Turn north from the N2 two kilometres west of the bridge across the Knysna Lagoon onto the road for Rheenendal. After passing through Rheenendal, turn right onto the Bibby's Hoek road, on which you will pass the Goudveld Forestry Station. Follow the signs for Jubilee Creek, and then follow the signs for Millwood, both sites being well worth a visit. Once past the forestry station, you are on forest roads, used not only by visitors but by vehicles going about the business of forestry. Most of these are very large and, fortunately, slow moving, but they may require you to move your own vehicle out of the way. Although speeds are not monitored, a limit of 40 km/h is reasonable. Beware, the roads are muddy and slippery when wet.
Weather: The area has a year-round rainfall, but all seasons have many delightfully clear, sunny days. Sunless winter days in the forest can be uncomfortably cold. For exploring the workings, the best time to go is after a prolonged dry spell, but bear in mind that this is when the risk of fire in the forest is at its greatest. Take a strong pair of waterproof shoes, a reliable torch and warm clothing.

Special precautions: If you are not particularly careful, it's easy to lose your way in the forest – especially as it gets darker in the late afternoon. Consequently, it would be a sensible idea to let somebody know what time you intend returning from Millwood.
What to do: A visit to the Millwood mining site offers a rare opportunity to explore not only indigenous forests and plantations but an important site of early mining development. Enjoy the restfulness of a tranquil picnic site or follow the black-and-yellow emblem of crossed pick and spade that marks the Millwood Mining Walk. This is an easy trail of 5,6 km that can be walked comfortably in two hours and includes the village and much of the goldfield.
More information: Regional Office of the Department of Forestry, Private Bag X12, Knysna 6570; tel (0445) 23037. Millwood House Museum, Queen Street, Knysna 6570; tel (0445) 22133. Knysna Publicity Association, PO Box 87, Knysna; tel (0445) 21610. The Secretary, Millwood Goldfield Society, c/o Knysna Municipality, PO Box 21, Knysna 6570; tel (0445) 22133.

A long day's journey through the kloof of the baboons

The dirt road between Andrieskraal and Willowmore at the edge of the Karoo is for intrepid travellers only, but the spectacular beauty of the Baviaanskloof amply rewards you for the hot and dusty drive

FILL YOUR TANK WITH PETROL, and make sure there's an experienced driver at the wheel. You are about to discover one of the most spectacular ravines in South Africa – but the road through the Baviaanskloof is not for novices, and there are no filling stations along the way. Set aside at least one day since this is scenery you'll want to absorb at leisure.

The most popular approach to the Baviaanskloof is from the east, so you will probably buy your supplies in Port Elizabeth. But it is worth forgetting an item or two, if only for an excuse to linger in one of the delightful little villages on your way. You might stop at Loerie, a quiet settlement in the foothills of the Elands Mountains where the Knysna loerie lives, and, if you started out early enough in the day, detour beyond it to the Loerie Dam or the Otterford State Forest.

You could also stop and stretch your legs at Hankey, a mission station dating back to 1822, which is now a centre for citrus fruit, tobacco and vegetable farming. A sign on your left, as you're about to enter the town, invites you to 'Enjoy view'. Magnificent views of the town and surrounding farmlands will greet you if you stop, while the Yellowwoods camp site at the far end of the town offers an opportunity to share your picnic with malachite kingfishers, rednecked francolins and other rare and beautiful birds.

A short distance beyond Hankey, a signpost to the left indicates the road to the historical Philip Tunnel, excavated in the 1840s for the purpose of irrigation. Excavation by the missionaries and their Khoikhoi charges was undertaken simultaneously from both sides of the ridge and took almost a year. When the tunnellers eventually broke through the ridge, the two tunnels coincided perfectly. A feat of engineering, or an act of faith? That's food for thought as you walk up towards the Bergvenster (mountain window), a geological curiosity from where you'll catch the first glimpse of the magnificent Baviaanskloof mountains.

After Hankey, the road descends into the Gamtoos valley and in springtime is fringed with wild flowers which yield to poinsettia and bougainvillea as you enter Patensie. This is where the local oranges are packed for export, and where the branch line of the Apple Express via Hankey ends. Your adventure is about to begin, because about 20 km after Patensie the road joins the R332 beyond Andrieskraal, peters out, turns to gravel and enters the Grootrivierpoort. The first steep pass peaks at Combrinck se Berg (near the remains of a cableway built years ago by the resourceful people of this region to transport local produce across the kloof) then turns south and winds steeply downhill.

The road across the valley now follows the course of the Bukkraal River past the settlements of Kleinrivier and Kruisrivier to the Baviaanskloof River, where you will enter the kloof that you've come so far to see. Cape Nature Conservation and the Southern African Nature Foundation have recently embarked on an ambitious project to protect the rugged beauty and rich wildlife of the Baviaanskloof. When this project is completed, this wilderness area will comprise over 200 000 ha and have the highest protection afforded by present nature conservation legislation.

As the name Baviaanskloof suggests, this is baboon country (*baviaan* is Dutch for baboon). They were once so prolific in this area that around the turn of the century one Pieter Strijdom (whose son became a prime minister of the Union) had what he thought was a splendid and possibly lucrative idea to reduce their population: a factory specialising in the manufacture of shoes, luggage and garments from baboon hide. Happily for the baboons, the fashion didn't catch on.

Very soon after you embark on the 7-km climb up the kloof you'll discover why this beautiful pass has remained a secret for so long. The road twists precariously up the mountain, its sides plunging

Where to stay

There is no accommodation along the 168 km between Andrieskraal and Willowmore, but at Geelhoutbosch in the Willowmore district there are five fully equipped, six-bedded bungalows controlled by Cape Nature Conservation. Braai wood can be bought here, but you should bring your own food. Bedding is provided. For further information and permit details, contact the Reserve Manager, Cape Nature Conservation, PO Box 218, Patensie 6335; tel (04232) 30270.

A blaze of winter colour is provided by this landscape of aloes. A wide variety of hardy, drought-resistant plants thrive in the Baviaanskloof area.

A river, turgid with heavy winter rains, flows close to the edge of the dust road. The Baviaanskloof drive takes you through breathtaking gorges and enchanting scenery.

steeply, and the gravel is loose and dangerous at times. But an experienced and, above all, patient driver should take you safely to the top, and the exhilarating scenery more than compensates you for your effort. There are cool streams and deeply chiselled gorges, the mountainside clad in red-hot pokers, agapanthus and pelargoniums, and a chorus of birdsong. From Geelhoutbosch onwards, your journey takes you through the real Baviaanskloof – all along the river and past several farming communities on the way.

As you head towards the farm *Verlorenrivier,* sparser vegetation prepares you for your arrival at the edge of the Karoo. The Nuwekloof Pass is the final mountain pass on your route; on its slopes you'll see the rare Willowmore cedar. Soon you will reach Willowmore itself, the Karoo town that marks the end of the Baviaanskloof trip.

After travelling for 168 km on gravel, you'll probably be quite relieved finally to see tar. But the sheer effort of your journey will doubtlessly enhance your sense of discovery.

The Baviaanskloof at a glance (map page 76)

How to get there: From Port Elizabeth travel on the N2 towards Cape Town and after about 40 km turn onto the R331 to Hankey. Continue for about 56 km, past Loerie, Hankey and Patensie, until the road joins the R332 from Humansdorp and the tarred road peters out.

Weather: It's very hot in summer and heavy winter rains can wash away parts of the dust road, leaving you stranded. The best time of year to visit the area is therefore autumn or spring.

What to do: Drive carefully and stop frequently to enjoy some of the most magnificent scenery in South Africa.

Special attractions: Philip Tunnel and the Bergvenster outside Hankey, the old cableway near Combrinck se Berg and the rare Willowmore cedar found on the slopes of the Nuwekloof Pass.

More information: Gamtoos Agricultural Route, PO Box 206, Patensie 6335; tel (04232) 30437; or Cape Nature Conservation, Private Bag X1126, Port Elizabeth 6000; tel (041) 3902179.

LESOTHO

N1 COLESBERG

N9

BURGERSDORP
page 96

R391

MIDDELBURG

N10

Aliwal
North

R58

Lady Grey

R58

Barkly East

R396

RHODES
page 130

R56

NAUDÉSNEK
page 130

N2

Maclear

R61

Lusikisiki

PORT
GROSVENOR
page 128

Port St Johns

R56

Elliot

R61

Engcobo

UMTATA

R61

MOUNTAIN
ZEBRA
NATIONAL
PARK
page 98

CRADOCK

R61

QUEENSTOWN

N6

R67

Idutywa

COFFEE BAY
page 126

Cathcart

Butterworth

SOMERSET
EAST page 100

R63

Seymour

Cookhouse

ADELAIDE
page 102

HOGSBACK
page 116

Fort Beaufort

Alice

R345

STUTTERHEIM

KEISKAMMAHOEK page 118

AMATOLA HIKING
TRAIL page 120

MAZEPPA BAY
page 124

KING WILLIAMSTOWN

N10

FORTS
ROUTE
page 110

BISHO

KAFFRARIAN
MUSEUM page 122

EAST LONDON

R75

GRAHAMSTOWN

Peddie

INDIAN OCEAN

THE OBSERVATORY
MUSEUM page 108

R67

BATHURST
page 112

WATERS MEETING
NATURE RESERVE
page 114

UITENHAGE
page 104

N2

Alexandria

PORT ALFRED

Loerie

PORT ELIZABETH

APPLE
EXPRESS
page 106

0 20 40 60 80 100
km   km

EASTERN CAPE/TRANSKEI

A Karoo oasis that influenced the country

*The Merino sheep-farming town of Burgersdorp
in the northeastern Cape has been a pivotal point
in Afrikaner history, culture and religion*

MANY TOWNS IN SOUTH AFRICA are named after one person, but Burgersdorp was aptly named after many people: all its inhabitants, in fact. 'Town of citizens' is what Burgersdorp means, and that is exactly how it was started – on the initiative of 300 Afrikaner families.

The oldest town in the northeastern Cape, Burgersdorp was founded on the farm *Klipfontein* in 1846. The inhabitants became the envy of other Karoo towns because, being sheltered in a valley below the Stormberg Mountains, they enjoyed a somewhat milder climate and had access to their own water from the Stormberg Spruit.

The migrant families who first came here were granted permission by the Dutch Reformed presbytery in Graaff-Reinet to establish a parish of their own. Their new town, to the locals' chagrin, was initially to be named in honour of the governor, Sir Peregrine Maitland, but he declined because Britain couldn't decide whether or not to make the town a municipality. In the end, they didn't, and the 'burgers' held sway instead.

The town's most imposing symbol is its Dutch Reformed Church. Started in 1912, it is a splendid building of dressed sandstone, which boasts a huge steeple and clock tower, and a large silver dome and cupola. Looking at the imposing, physical solidity of the building, you wouldn't think that 50 years earlier the Dutch Reformed Church had been threatened by a breakaway church, which would also become an important part of the life of Burgersdorp and of the Afrikaner.

In 1860, parishioners who had left the Dutch Reformed Church helped start a new denomination, the Gereformeerde Kerk ('Reformed Church'). They invited the Reverend Dirk Postma, from Rustenburg, to start a congregation. Nine years later Postma established a seminary too. Housed in an outbuilding behind the parsonage in Piet Retief Street, this became the Theological Seminary of the Reformed Church in South Africa. The first lecturer of the initial five students was Jan Lion-Cachet, whose belongings are today on view in the old seminary, which has been turned into a museum.

In 1905 the seminary was moved to Potchefstroom, where it later became the Potchefstroom University for Christian Higher Education. Postma, a vehement proponent of Christian National Education – which would one day be taught in most South African schools – became one of its first rectors. Even though the seminary was moved, however, Burgersdorp has remained a stronghold of the Reformed Church, its members often being referred to as 'Doppers'.

(Bottom left) The original, damaged statue of the Taalmonument stands alongside a later replica. On the right is a memorial to the townsfolk killed during the Anglo-Boer War. (Bottom right) The highly decorative and unusual drinking fountain erected to celebrate the 1897 Diamond Jubilee of Queen Victoria.

The Afrikaans language also received an important boost from Burgersdorp. When the Cape Colony was granted self-government in 1854, the constitution only provided for English as a medium of communication. Despite numerous requests, MPs were not allowed to address the Cape Parliament in any other language. Burgersdorp became the centre of a strong movement to have Dutch recognised as an official language.

Important congresses of the Afrikanerbond were held in the town. In 1882, after 25 years of demanding that their language be recognised, they achieved this aim. To commemorate their victory, it was decided to erect a *Taalmonument* (language monument). Money was collected from around the country and the monument was unveiled in 1893.

The statue depicts a woman pointing her finger at a tablet held in her other hand. The main inscription reads, *De Overwinning de Hollandsche Taal* ('The Triumph of the Dutch Language'). It was badly damaged during the Anglo-Boer War, after which Lord Milner had it removed. A replica was made and erected in 1907, but the original – missing its head and one arm – suddenly turned up in a King William's Town workyard in 1939. Now the two statues stand side by side in Burger Square.

Nearby is a memorial to the townsfolk who died during the Anglo-Boer War, a monument unveiled in 1908 by the Afrikaner hero, General Koos de la Rey. The Anglo-Boer War battle that took place near Burgersdorp, in late 1899, was the Battle of Stormberg. Along with two other battles that took place at the same time and in which the British suffered defeat – Colenso and Magersfontein – Stormberg contributed to what became known as 'Black Week'. In the Battle of Stormberg, a commando of 400 Boers fought a much larger British force and subsequently took possession of Burgersdorp. Four months later, however, the town – important for being on the East London-Bloemfontein railway line – was re-occupied by the British and many of the rebels were incarcerated in the Old Jail, built in 1861.

Overlooking the town from the north, you will notice a blockhouse called *Brandwag* (sentinel) – one in a line of forts that Lord Kitchener had built across the Cape frontier towards the end of the war. It's similar in style to those at Wellington and Laingsburg – together they formed part of a line of forts that extended from Queenstown, via Molteno and Burgersdorp, to Bethulie.

Despite its importance in Afrikaner history, the town also contains a remarkable piece of sculpture dedicated to their erstwhile foe, Queen Victoria. It

consists of a very ornate drinking fountain that was erected on the corner of Kerk and Chase streets in 1897 to celebrate her Diamond Jubilee. Surmounted by a crown, this spectacular work of art has a lacework dome supported by eight columns, and the fountain itself consists of a stork poised over an urn from which water flows. Salamanders crawl up the central column and other storks and doves peep out from the canopy.

Over the years, Burgersdorp has developed into a typical Karoo *dorp*, earning its living largely off the farming of Merino sheep, which thrive on the sparse but rich vegetation of the semi-arid countryside. For a taste of farm life, without actually visiting a farm, you can visit De Bruin House in town – it's a typical Karoo *tuishuis* (homestead), complete with its original dung floor.

Unlike most other Karoo towns, Burgersdorp has the advantage of lying in the shelter of a valley. The surrounding Stormberg Mountains can be seen in the background.

Where to stay

The Jubilee Hotel, PO Box 65, Burgersdorp 5520; tel (0553) 31840; and the *Goedehoop*, a guest farm 40 km from town, where you can enjoy walks or bird-watching, or simply savour the life style of a typical Karoo farm. Contact them at PO Box 228, Burgersdorp 5520; tel (0553) 31433.

Some 20 km from Burgersdorp is the *Oatlands Holiday Farm*, which offers some excellent hikes. Contact the farm at PO Box 263, Burgersdorp 5520; tel (055312) 73304. Also situated about the same distance from town is *Wasbank*, another farm offering holiday accommodation. Contact them at PO Box 253, Burgersdorp 5520; tel (055312) 74821.

Burgersdorp at a glance (map page 94)

How to get there: From Cape Town and Johannesburg take the N1 to Colesberg. Turn east onto the R58. Colesburg lies some 140 km along the R58.

Weather: Summers can get extremely hot – up to 38°C in the semi-arid terrain – but the best months to visit are November to April.

What to do: The rugged 425-ha Die Berg Nature Reserve is located a short distance outside town. Once you have entered the reserve, you have to go on foot. And remember: it's a steep climb. Permits are free and are available at the municipality. The De Bruin Dam, 8 km on the Jamestown

road, has facilities for camping, boating and fishing. A nature trail has also been laid out nearby. The Brandwag blockhouse can be found just outside town, on the road to Aliwal North. Although there are Bushman paintings in the vicinity, they are all on private farms. Contact the municipality to find out if any tours can be be arranged.

Special attractions: The Stormberg Cheese Factory is renowned, and visits can be organised. Contact the factory at PO Box 115, Burgersdorp 5520; tel (0553) 30456.

More information: The Burgersdorp Municipality, PO Box 13, Burgersdorp, 5520; tel (0553) 31777.

A safe and scenic haven for an endangered species

West of Cradock in the wide open spaces of the Karoo is the Mountain Zebra National Park, one of South Africa's least-known but most rewarding national parks

Where to stay

The accommodation on offer in the rest camp is clean and comfortable. There is a choice of 20 two-bedroom chalets, fully equipped and complete with double glazing, insulation and fireplaces for the cold winter nights. Alternatively, there are also 20 caravan and camping sites with ablution and laundry facilities.

There is a shop where you can get bread, milk, meat, alcohol, films, firewood, curios and non-perishable food; a restaurant which offers light snacks as well as an à la carte menu; and a petrol station.

If you're looking for an old-world experience to go with the scenic splendour, stay at the *Doornhoek Guest House,* which has three bedrooms, each with its own bathroom, a fully equipped kitchen and living room, all beautifully furnished with antiques. To book, contact the National Parks Board offices in Pretoria or Cape Town (see other panel for addresses).

THE CAPE MOUNTAIN ZEBRA is one of the world's rarest mammals, and the star attraction of the Mountain Zebra National Park. Although the park was established purely for the protection of the near extinct *Equus zebra,* it is surely the diamond of South Africa's national parks: a spectacular mountainous wilderness unchanged for eons.

Magnificently situated on the northern slopes of the Bankberg in the high plateaux of the Karoo (1 300 m above sea level with the 1 957 m-high Spitskop as the highest peak), the park lies about 25 km from Cradock, the nearest town, with historic Graaff-Reinet about 80 km west as the crow flies.

Bracing champagne air, beautiful vistas, profound silence and wide open spaces are all on offer and, in addition, visitors are rewarded with a very personal wilderness experience. Here they can move through the environment unchallenged by dangerous big game, yet enjoy a fascinating variety of wildlife in its natural habitat. The Karoo's unique environment has been described as an open-air laboratory where both layman and scientist can study, at close quarters, the various life forms that have adapted themselves to the harsh and arid conditions.

The lovely Cape mountain zebra once roamed freely in the Cape's mountains, but by the time the park was established in 1937 they had been all but wiped out by hunters. A particularly obtuse

A Cape mountain zebra mother and foal – members of one of earth's rarest animal species.

politician then described them as 'donkeys in football jerseys'. Thankfully, more sensible people realised the tragedy of exterminating these unique creatures, and the farm *Babylons Toren* was bought by the National Parks Board, who used it as a core for the establishment of the 6 536-ha park.

This species is the rarest, smallest and most beautiful of the zebras: only 1,2 m high with stunning geometric stripes completely different to those on any other zebra species. In fact, each of the zebras is unique and identifiable by its stripe pattern, and this rare population is documented and studied by means of a stock book. Their numbers have climbed from 25 in 1964 to over 200 today. In addition, an equal number have been relocated to other parks in the Cape to recolonise their ancestors' stamping grounds.

Many other indigenous creatures also have their home here, and visitors should head for the good grazing of the Rooiplaat plateau as this is where the antelope tend to converge. You're likely to see kudu, springbok, wildebeest, eland, blesbok, steenbok, red hartebeest, grey rhebok, mountain reedbuck, klipspringer and duiker. Various predators prowl the area: cats such as the caracal, the small but vicious black-footed cat and the African wild cat; aardwolf, Cape fox, bat-eared fox and black-backed jackal are also found.

You can also look out for many other animals, including four different mongoose species – most prominently the red mongoose which lives in large colonies and can be seen on the open plains. There are also suricate, various small rodents, dassies, hares, baboons and over 200 species of birds, including ostriches and the rare booted eagle, black eagle, Cape eagle owl, chanting goshawk, African spoonbill and blue crane.

A particularly fascinating inhabitant of the park is the long-horn beetle, recognisable by its impressive antlers and distinctive colouring. Should you be fortunate enough to find one, you'll be admiring a true warrior. As soon as the larvae of these beetles hatch, they begin to eat each other, and this cannibalistic feeding frenzy ends only when they are too few and far apart to meet.

The unique Karoo vegetation includes sweet thorn, karee, Karoo aster, globe karoo, the wonderfully named *koggelmandervoetkaroo* and *witmuistepelkaroo,* aloes, kiepersol trees, groves of wild olives in the high ravines, white stinkwood, camphor bush and glossy currant. If you're lucky enough to time your visit after good rains have fallen, the rolling landscape of the park turns indigo with blue tulips.

A particular attraction is the hiking trail which takes in the park's most beautiful and dramatic scenery, and is by far the best way to experience the park. The trail is criss-crossed with game tracks and there are Bushman paintings to be discovered. The 31-km trail takes three days and two nights to complete, and leaves from and arrives back at the rest camp. Overnight accommodation is provided in picturesque stone huts. It takes about five to six hours to complete the 11 km on the first day's hike, a trail which leads up and down through the lush gorges of the Fonteinkloof and Grootkloof streams. The first night is spent at Olienhut, where there is accommodation for 12 people (six per room) as well as shower and toilet facilities and a fireplace. Basic cooking utensils and firewood are provided. The following day you retrace your steps, then climb to the summit of the Bankberg, from where you can see Kompasberg. It takes seven or eight hours to complete the 12 km to the welcome sight of

Kareehut, equally well equipped. The final leg back to the rest camp is an easy 8-km stroll.

If, however, this all seems a bit much, there are alternatives. A number of shorter walks have been laid out which can be accomplished in anything from 15 minutes to five hours. It is also possible to take in the trail on horseback; there are about 37 km of good gravel roads that travel through a variety of scenery; and, for something different, a four-wheel-drive trail has recently been established.

The park boasts a national monument in the form of *Doornhoek*, an old farmstead overlooking a dam which served as the set for the TV series *Story of an African Farm*. Dating back to 1836, the farmhouse has been meticulously restored and features yellow-wood ceilings, oregon pine floors, copper door handles and stained glass windows. Beautifully furnished with pieces dating from the era, *Doornhoek* also has modern conveniences and can be hired as a guest house for a maximum of six people.

Their future secure, a herd of Cape mountain zebra graze in the confines of the Mountain Zebra National Park, near Cradock in the eastern Cape.

Mountain Zebra National Park at a glance (map page 94)

How to get there: From Johannesburg, take the N1 south as far as Colesberg, then the N9 to Middelburg. Just south of Middelburg, turn left onto the N10 and continue for about 95 km until, about 6 km before Cradock, you turn right onto the Graaff-Reinet road. After about 5 km, take the road to your left and from here the way is well signposted. From Cape Town or Durban, take the N2 as far as the N10 turn-off between Grahamstown and Port Elizabeth (about 80 km east of Port Elizabeth and 74 km west of Grahamstown). Drive through Cradock and continue as above.

Weather: As in many arid areas of the world, the Karoo climate is one of extremes, although the altitude of the Mountain Zebra National Park makes it a little less so. Summers

are generally warm to very hot (the temperature sometimes soars to a sweltering 40˚C). There is occasional rainfall in winter and early spring. Winters are generally pleasant and sunny, but it can become very cold at night (the temperature has been known to fall to below -10˚C), and snow falls on the higher mountain peaks.

What to do: Hiking, horseriding, swimming (there is a pool in the rest camp) and exploring.

Special attractions: The animals, the silence, the grandeur, the unique environment.

More information: Write to the National Parks Board, PO Box 787, Pretoria 0001; tel (012) 441191; or PO Box 7400, Roggebaai 8012; tel (021) 4195365.

A tranquil town packed with architectural delights

Recapture the unhurried pace of bygone years at the eastern Cape town of Somerset East – an equally charming twin to nearby Graaff-Reinet

Where to stay

Somerset Hotel, PO Box 20, Somerset East 5850; tel (0424) 32047. *Middleton Hotel*, PO Box 9, Middleton 5180; tel (0424) 71250. At the Walter Battiss Gallery is the Fook Nook, a flat which may be rented by art-lovers. Contact the Somerset East Museum (address in other panel) for more details.

For the names of various lodges and farms offering accommodation, including the *Besterhoek Lodge,* contact the Somerset East Publicity Association (address in other panel).

IN THE VAST STARKNESS of the Karoo, towns and farms stand out like welcome oases, their trees and carefully tended gardens offering a cool respite from the dry heat. A town which deserves this description more than any other is Somerset East, which lies serenely at the foot of the lushly wooded Bosberg range.

It was this very lushness, in fact, which attracted the man whose name it bears today, the most controversial of all the governors at the Cape, Lord Charles Somerset. But the story of Somerset East goes back even further than the early 1800s, when he arrived.

It was in 1775 that a group of Dutch farmers were given permission to settle in this fertile area some 200 km inland from Algoa Bay. The site had deep soil, plenty of water from the Little Fish River (a tributary of the Great Fish) and so many streams flowed down the mountains that 16 waterfalls could be seen from the site they chose for their village.

One of the very first farmers who moved here to grow tobacco was Louis Trichardt, who would eventually become a famous Voortrekker leader. Some people say that the Trichardts lived in the Cape Dutch house at 9 Paulet Street, arguably one of the most historically prized buildings in the town. However, it is much more likely that the building was erected at a later date. It was probably built as a home, but it subsequently became the premises for the drostdy and, even later, for the Dutch Reformed Church.

The Afrikaner farmers' dream of creating an oasis of their own in the cool shadows of the Bosberg was interrupted in 1814, however, when Lord Somerset expropriated the land. A year later he established a farm to improve stock breeding and, more importantly, to supply vegetables and fodder to troops and the Albany settlers.

Ten years later the town of Somerset was proclaimed. The East part of Somerset East's name was added only after another three decades, probably in order to differentiate between itself and Somerset West, which lies near Cape Town. During his term of office, which ran from 1814 until 1826, Lord Somerset oversaw certain important events, most notably the arrival of the 1820 Settlers and the implementation of Britain's first policy towards the Xhosas on the eastern frontier.

Controversial, and even disliked, though he was, Somerset and his family gave numerous names to the town. Wander through the shady streets today and you will find Charles Street (named after Somerset himself), Worcester Street (after his brother, the Marquis of Worcester), Beaufort Street (after his father), Paulet Street (after Somerset's second wife, Lady Mary Paulet), Frances Street (after his daughter-in-law Frances Heathcote), and Henry Street (after his son).

The town resonates with history, dominated as it is by at least 13 national monuments, and many other buildings which are old enough to qualify for that status. The best place to view them is in Paulet Street. At No 107 you will find Mill House, a privately owned home that is one of the oldest dwellings in the area. Further down the road, there's the Hope Church, belonging to the Congregational Church of Somerset East. The church was created specifically for the coloured community and erected on an erf owned by Dorothy Evans, the widow of the Rev John Evans, who had served in Cradock.

One of the very first buildings, built in 1815 as an officers' mess, stands at No 45 Paulet Street. This became the home of one of South Africa's most famous artists and champions of artistic freedom, Walter Battiss. (He was also an amateur archaeologist, a teacher and a professor.)

Once an officer's mess, this building in Paulet Street eventually became the home of the famous South African artist, Walter Battiss.

Battiss's great-grandfather, John Hartley Battiss, was a Royal Engineer who built forts for Lord Somerset. It was in his grandfather's house, at No 4 Bathurst Street, that Battiss was born in 1906. The family moved house several times and finally rented the house in Paulet Street, turning it into the Battiss Private Hotel. During the First World War, however, they closed down the business and moved to Koffiefontein.

The building now houses a permanent collection of works by the artist, widely regarded as the first white artist in South Africa to be strongly influenced by African art, showing a strong attraction to Bushman rock painting. Though the old-worldly setting initially seems at odds with the artist's flamboyant work, together they comfortably marry the old and the new. Here you can see his soft watercolours and works inspired by Fook, the concept Battiss created with Norman Catherine about an imaginary place for people with a keen imagination and the talent to exhibit the playful side of their character.

The building still boasts a beautiful fanlight and railings, while several of the fireplaces have the royal coat of arms built into them. Yellowwood from the Bosberg provided wood and beams for some partitions on the first floor.

One of the most interesting places to visit in Somerset East is the town's museum, which was originally built as a Wesleyan chapel and consecrated in 1828. In 1835 the house was occupied by the Dutch Reformed Church as a parsonage, which is what it remained for more than a century. It passed into private hands and in 1971 became a museum.

Still known as the Old Pastorie, this double-storeyed Georgian house was extensively restored in the 1980s. Surrounded by a magnificent country garden with over 700 rose bushes, the museum depicts the area's history back to 1770. The interior combines English Georgian elements with traditional Cape features, such as beamed ceilings and *muurkaste* (built-in cupboards), the yellowwood also having come from the Bosberg. The house is furnished with late-19th century pieces. On the second floor there are historical documents, maps and photos. The porcelain collection, textiles and furniture on display belonged to the Hofmeyrs, one of the families who served the Dutch Reformed Church and lived in the house for 90 years.

(Left) The Bosberg Nature Reserve outside Somerset East has a scenic 15 km circular hiking trail.
(Right) The Old Pastorie, one of the town's most famous buildings, houses a museum devoted to the history of the area.

Somerset East at a glance (map page 94)

How to get there: Follow the N2 to Port Elizabeth and some 50 km east of the city turn north onto the R10 for Cookhouse. At Cookhouse, turn west onto the R63 – Somerset East is 25 km along this road.
Weather: Moderate to hot summers and mild winters.
What to do: The Somerset East Museum is open from 8 am to 5 pm daily, and from 10 am to noon on Saturday. Besides its exhibits, it is well known for the sale of fresh produce and flowers. Outside the museum you'll find a rare Victorian postbox, and all mail posted there receives a special museum stamp. The Battiss Gallery is open from 10 am to noon daily. Temporary exhibitions of the works of

eastern Cape artists are held regularly. Every July, Somerset East holds the country's only Biltong Festival, where you can buy game biltong at cost price.

Outside town lies the Bosberg Nature Reserve and Hiking Trail. The 2 050-ha reserve rises to 1 630 m above sea level, and hikers pass through a variety of vegetation types, including indigenous forest rich in stinkwood, yellowwood and wild olive. The 15-km circular trail along a bridle path goes by way of an overnight hut perched on stilts, from where you can enjoy spectacular views over the Bestershoek Valley. At Bestershoek itself, a bird lookout hut has been erected under the auspices of a local bird-lover who has identified at

least 240 birds in the area. The Besterhoek Lodge, a fully appointed cottage situated within the reserve, sleeps six people.

The 85m-high Glen Avon Falls can be reached from the farm Glen Avon. For those who choose to drive instead of walk, don't miss Auret Drive, which runs along the slopes of the mountain. Further from town are the scenic drives over Bruintjieshoogte Pass to Pearston, Swaershoek Pass to Cradock and Daggaboersnek to Cradock.
More information: Contact the Somerset East Publicity Association which is situated at the Somerset East Museum, PO Box 151, Somerset East 5850; tel (0424) 32079.

Monument to peace in a frontier town

The Great Fish River Valley has seen many bitter wars, but at Adelaide, 37 km west of Fort Beaufort, a military post has grown into a peaceful town

YOU'RE IN SCOTTISH settler country when you've reached Adelaide, on the banks of the Koonap River. It is here, where the rugged Winterberg range defines the northern limits of the Great Fish River valley, that poet-philanthropist Thomas Pringle brought his Scottish party of 1820 settlers. The new arrivals soon discovered that theirs was by no means the only claim to this promised land. It had to be won, in a series of bitter frontier wars; and, like so many of the sleepy small towns in this region, Adelaide was once a fiercely defended military post.

A town grew gradually around Fort Adelaide, so named in honour of Adelaide, Queen Consort of England's William IV. It achieved municipal status in 1896 and today it is a centre for the wool, mohair, citrus and grain industries that flourish here. In contrast with Fort Beaufort, some 37 km to the east – where a museum in the former officers' mess houses some intriguing militaria – Adelaide has largely shed its military origins in favour of preserving its religious and cultural heritage. The orderly clutter of a prosperous Victorian household has been recreated in the old Dutch Reformed parsonage, built in the 1850s and now housing the Our Heritage Museum. ('Victorian' in this context refers to the period, not the style.) Styles vary from room to room, from the *riempiesbank* (thong-seated bench) in the *voorhuis* (front room parlour) to a frontier bedroom with furniture of yellowwood and

stinkwood and a kaross sewn from jackal pelts, to the brass bedstead decorated with mother-of-pearl in its Victorian counterpart.

Two magnificent chandeliers, an 1898 Edison gramophone and two beautifully inlaid 18th-century chairs are the *pièces de resistance* in the study, which has been furnished as it would have looked in the days of *dominee* (parson) George Stegmann. It was, after all, Stegmann who motivated and supervised the construction of this building. Indeed, he'd made the construction of a worthy Dutch Reformed church and parsonage at Adelaide the condition for accepting an appointment here.

Visitors to the parsonage and the beautiful church with its impressive square tower (on which British soldiers mounted a cannon during the Anglo-Boer War), will conclude that the *dominee* must have felt a nice sense of accomplishment. Dignified and pleasing on its own, the double-storeyed dwelling stands on a plot of about 3 ha on the banks of the Koonap River in a large garden of rose bushes (there are about 700), shrubs and indigenous trees. In the springtime, it seems to be one vast bed of roses blooming around a children's playground – a handy diversion for little ones while you take in a little cultural history, though they'll be equally fascinated with the display of 19th-century toys in the parsonage nursery.

Our Heritage Museum was opened in 1967 – the building having served as a parsonage for more than

Where to stay

Adelaide has two hotels, both on Market Square. They are the *Commercial Hotel*, PO Box 1, Adelaide 5760; tel (046) 6840155, and *Midgleys Hotel*, PO Box 17, Adelaide 5760; tel (046) 6841058.

The foothills of the Winterberg range near Adelaide are a prime area for sheep farming.

The building housing Our Heritage Museum was constructed in 1858 to serve as a parsonage for the Dutch Reformed Church. Its main exhibit is a glass collection of more than 1 000 pieces.

a century – and proclaimed a national monument in 1975. In addition to its imaginative lifestyle displays and beautiful antique furniture, the museum houses an outstanding collection of glass, china and silver. This includes German, Viennese, English and French Lalique glass and a large Wedgwood collection complemented by Dresden, French and English porcelain. No expert knowledge is necessary to appreciate the superb artistry of these exhibits. But another item on display does deserve a little introduction.

The portrayal of late 19th-century life spills over into the outbuildings, where carts, carriages, wagons and tools are displayed in the coach-house and a dairy and laundry recreated below yellow-wood ceilings and beams. So your visit to the museum should not be confined to the parsonage, nor should your visit to the region begin and end in Adelaide. To the north you'll find the beautiful Mankazana Valley and in the surrounding farmlands there are some fine examples of settler fortified houses dating back to frontier war days.

It's impossible to visit this region without being reminded of how hard people fought for it. However, you will also find several moving reminders of reconciliation. For instance, there's a tombstone in Adelaide in memory of four-year-old Ebenezer Davidson, who was abducted and murdered outside the Glenn Thorn Church (his body was later found on nearby Governor's Kop). Two men were arrested and investigations revealed that the boy had been killed because of a mistaken belief that he was the son of a man against whom the murderers harboured a grudge. At the trial of the two accused (both of whom were found guilty), the court heeded a plea by Ebenezer's father, the Rev Peter Davidson, that their lives be spared so that no other family need mourn. And there is the Dutch Reformed Church itself, inaugurated by *dominee* Stegmann as a monument to peace.

Adelaide at a glance (map page 94)

How to get there: About 6 km east of Grahamstown, the N2 is joined by route R67. Follow this road north to Fort Beaufort, and then the R63 west to Adelaide.
Weather: Settler Country is hot and dry.
What to do: Explore Adelaide on foot, but don't ignore the surrounding farmlands, which are rich in history and scenery.
Special attractions: In the old parsonage with its rose garden setting, visit Our Heritage Museum, 29 Queen Street, Adelaide, 5760; tel (046) 6840290.
Visiting times: Monday to Friday, 8 am to 12.30 pm and 2 pm to 5 pm; Saturday 8 am to 12 noon. The museum is open on public holidays from 10 am till noon, but closed on religious holidays and New Year's Day.
More information: Contact the Adelaide Publicity Association, Private Bag X350, Adelaide 5760; tel (046) 6840034.

In winter, temperatures in the vicinity of Adelaide plummet and the nearby Winterberg range is often covered in a thick blanket of snow.

A town built on wheels

*Just 30 minutes along the freeway from the 'Friendly City'
you'll find Uitenhage – a town full of charm and surprises,
being much, much more than Port Elizabeth's industrial backyard*

Jack, the legendary baboon that operated the Uitenhage train signals on behalf of his crippled master.

YOU DON'T EXPECT to find an aviary in the heart of an industrial town, crystal water gushing from perennial springs, or oaks and jacarandas lining its streets. But this is Uitenhage, where the gardens are magnificent, the bird life plentiful and industry flourishes alongside history on the banks of the Swartkops River.

Uitenhage, now a motor manufacturing centre, is the eastern Cape's oldest town. Its origins go back to 1804 when persistent clashes between the Xhosa and white settlers made it necessary to create a new magisterial district. It was called the Eastern Cape District – later named Uitenhage after J A Uitenhage de Mist, the Commissioner General of the Cape at the time of the district's establishment. A farm known as *Rietvallei*, situated on the banks of the Swartkops River, was chosen as the site of the new drostdy and it became the nucleus of today's town of Uitenhage.

One of the town's most significant founding fathers was American-born General Cuyler who came to Uitenhage via a distinguished career in the British Army and never left. He was landdrost of Uitenhage for more than two decades, retiring in 1827 to Cuyler Manor, an elegant Cape Dutch homestead 5 km outside the town. Like the old drostdy, which had been Cuyler's official residence, this is now a museum. It is furnished with pieces from the early 19th century, among which is a table made of mahogany from the Dutch vessel *Amsterdam* that ran aground near the Swartkops River mouth in 1817.

De Mist had by then returned to Holland, never to see the town that bears his name, but he heard of the *Amsterdam*'s misfortune and how the kind people of Uitenhage had rallied to assist the shipwrecked crew. To demonstrate his appreciation, he sent them a valuable gift – a massive Bible bound in leather-covered oak with great silver clasps. The De Mist Bible now holds pride of place in the Old Drostdy Africana Museum.

If you think that one museum is pretty much like another, Uitenhage will surprise you yet again. Behind its graceful gabled facade in Caledon Street, you'll find – in addition to displays of local history – the Volkswagen Collection of cars. It's a must for Beetlemaniacs, as various models show how this popular people's car evolved.

But when people call Uitenhage a 'town built on wheels', it's not just steel and rubber they're thinking of. In Market Street you'll find the old Uitenhage Railway Station, a delightful architectural folly whose steeply pitched roof, Gothic trappings and frilled woodwork lend it the character of a favourite doll's house. It is said to be the oldest railway station in South Africa, built in 1875, the year of the opening of the railway from Port Elizabeth. And it says something of the people of Uitenhage that their station sat firmly astride the path of the rails, as if to say that here the journey was complete. Such defiance meant, inevitably, that the station would have to be replaced. The Dolls' House, as locals fondly call it, had its most perilous moment in 1957, when a progressive Uitenhage MP presented it to parliament as 'an old antiquated, obsolete building...not only an eyesore...but definitely a disgrace.'

But fortunately nostalgia prevailed over progress. The new station was located elsewhere and the Dolls' House remains as a steam-transport museum

Built more than 150 years ago for one of Uitenhage's founders, Cuyler Manor is now one of the town's principal museums.

The cute design of the old Uitenhage Railway Station has resulted in it being fondly referred to as The Dolls' House.

where you can step into various compartments of Victoriana by entering the luggage office, ticket office, tearoom and even the station master's living quarters up a flight of narrow wooden stairs. The old railway workshops in the heart of the town, consisting of magnificent Victorian red-brick buildings, are currently being restored to house a variety of small businesses and recreational facilities.

Every town has its legend and Uitenhage is no exception. Uitenhage's legend is a baboon called Jack who in the late 1880s operated the signals on behalf of his handicapped owner, signalman James Wide. After he'd lost both legs in an accident, Wide bought Jack at the market-place to help push him between his home and the signal house on the trolley he'd devised. Jack soon graduated from this simple task to trainee signalman and eventually operated the signals on his own. Word of his accomplishments, spread by astonished passengers, brought Uitenhage worldwide fame, and photographs of this astonished pair are on display in the museum. So are a scrupulously maintained 1916 locomotive, a mainline coach and an old suburban

coach, and an 1897 Cape Government Railway locomotive, all at rest in this railway cul-de-sac.

What you won't find here are Little Bess and Pioneer, the first two little steam engines imported and brought here. But you *will* find a working reincarnation of Little Bess at Willow Dam nearby – for children of all ages she offers a thrilling ride. Magennis Park off Church Street has an aviary and fountains, and Cannon Hill has a cactus garden of some repute plus a lookout tower that commemorates the coronation of King George V which gives a 360° view of the town. And some 8 km out of town, on the Graaff-Reinet road, there's the resort and nature reserve known locally as the Springs, named for that artesian fountainhead from which millions of litres of crystal-clear water bubble up from the ground.

The Groendal Wilderness Area is within reach, and so is the well-known 16 km Blindekloof walk – all reminders that Uitenhage has room for industry and history, and for bird life and beauty, too. Hikers must obtain a permit from the Chief Forester, PO Box 445, Uitenhage 6230; tel (041) 9925418.

Where to stay

You'll find hotel accommodation at the *Crown Hotel*, 142 Caledon Street, Uitenhage 6230; tel (041) 9924417; *Rose and Shamrock Hotel*, PO Box 180, Uitenhage 6230; tel (041) 9921351; *Waterford Hotel*, 127 Durban Street, Uitenhage; tel (041) 9228016.

Uitenhage welcomes campers at *Springs Caravan Park* some 12 km north of the town. It has a swimming pool, a picnic area, camping sites, rondavels and fully equipped chalets.

Uitenhage at a glance (map page 94)

How to get there: Uitenhage lies 34 km northwest of Port Elizabeth on the R75.
Weather: Hot and humid summers, mild winters. Hikers should beware of heat exhaustion in summer. To see the magnificent aloes at their best in the Springs Nature Reserve, visit Uitenhage in the winter.
What to do: Discover Uitenhage's secrets – its past, its parks and its beautiful countryside.
Special attractions: The Drostdy, Cuyler Manor and the Old Railway Museum together constitute the Uitenhage Historical Museum, PO Box 225, Uitenhage 6230; tel (041) 9922063.

Visiting times: All three museums are open from 10 am to 1 pm and 2 pm to 5 pm on weekdays. Cuyler Manor is also open on Sundays from 2 pm to 5 pm. All the museums are closed on public holidays.
More information: The Town Clerk, PO Box 45, Uitenhage 6230; tel (041) 9926011; SA Tourism Board, Satour House, 23 Donkin Street, Port Elizabeth 6001; tel (041) 557761. The indoor sports centre, situated next to the municipal swimming pool in High Street, serves as an information centre for Uitenhage. It is open from 7 am to 4.30 pm on weekdays, with assistance also frequently being available up to 10 pm on weekdays and weekends; tel (041) 9924258 or 9926011.

Full steam ahead through breathtaking scenery

Catch the Apple Express from Port Elizabeth to the Gamtoos town of Loerie – it's a thrilling ride along one of the world's last narrow-gauge railway lines

THERE ARE TWO WAYS to explore the rugged landscape that lies inland of Port Elizabeth, and two ways to cross the Van Stadens River gorge. You can travel by car and cross the Van Stadens River via a four-lane concrete-arch bridge – or you can sit back and relax on the Apple Express.

Humewood Road Station, just outside the city centre, is the terminus for this fascinating little train. The track between here and the town of Avontuur, 285 km away in the Langkloof, is one of the few narrow-gauge railway lines left in the world. The diminutive steam engines, collectively known as the Apple Express, have been puffing their steady way along it since 1906. It's a working train, used to haul fruit from the Langkloof orchards to the harbour in Port Elizabeth, but at scheduled times throughout the year it offers day-long tourist excursions as far as Loerie in the Gamtoos valley, a three-hour ride away.

From Port Elizabeth it passes through the thick bush on the plain between mountain and sea, and crosses the gorge of the Van Stadens River on a 71-m high steel-girder bridge. The precipitous sides of this deep and dramatic gorge were a major road obstacle for many years. The first proper road across it was completed in 1867, but floods repeatedly destroyed the river crossing however often it was rebuilt.

A better road and bridge were constructed in the 1880s, but the descent on both sides remained dangerously steep until the late 1960s, when local authorities, perhaps mindful of the fact that some of the most inspired early roads in this country were the work of Italian prisoners of war, hired an Italian firm of civil engineers. In October 1971, a spectacular modern bridge was opened which spans the gorge so smoothly that many travellers speed over it without realising that they've just crossed one of the greatest bridges in the world.

The railway bridge is even more remarkable – it's the highest of its kind in the world. And for hiking enthusiasts, a ride aboard the Apple Express is a novel way to reach the beautiful Van Stadens Wild Flower Reserve and Bird Sanctuary, which conserves over 150 ha of wildflower and forest country on the eastern side of the gorge. A return ticket to Van Stadens gives the hiker three hours of inspiring trailing, while cyclists can purchase tickets to or from Van Stadens and cycle in the opposite direction; cycles are transported at a nominal fee.

From here the Apple Express steams through a green, rolling countryside of hills and indigenous forests presided over by the massive Groot Winterhoek range. And at Loerie station, the braai fires are burning even as you ascend the steep pass into the valley of the Gamtoos. Passengers on the Express should remember to bring their own meat if they want to participate in this unusual picnic. A tuckshop on board sells refreshments on the way.

From Loerie, the sightseeing excursion returns to Port Elizabeth, but the line continues beyond Loerie past a small junction where one branch swings north to Patensie and on to the Langkloof via Humansdorp. In spring and summer, the kloof is ablaze with wildflowers and covered in orchards, and the air is filled with the smell of spring blossom or the fragrance of ripe fruit during the picking season. You're road-bound, now, as the Apple Express has reverted to its worker status and will chug on to its final destination, to be loaded up with the harvest of the Langkloof for Port Elizabeth.

At the time of writing, the Apple Express was available to day-trippers only on Saturdays from June to January, and on the first Saturday of every month for the rest of the year. It departs from Humewood Road Station in Port Elizabeth at 8 am and returns at 4 pm. Passengers are also carried on Thursdays, but no refreshments are available. Spoornet have indicated that the Apple Express will soon extend its service to tourists. For further details, contact the Port Elizabeth Publicity Association or the station – see facing page for addressess and telephone numbers.

One of the gleaming Apple Express steam engines that make their way back and forth along the route.

One of the literal high points of the journey is crossing the 71-m high steel-girder bridge over the Van Stadens River gorge.

The Apple Express at a glance (map page 94)

How to get there: The Apple Express departs from Humewood Road Station.

Weather: Hot summers and mild winters.

What to do: Catch the Apple Express in Port Elizabeth for a day-trip to Loerie and back; explore the Langkloof by car. Or buy a return ticket to Van Stadens and hike through the Van Stadens Wildflower Reserve and Bird Sanctuary, making sure you don't miss the return journey three hours later.

Special attractions: Crossing the deep and dangerous Van Stadens River gorge is always an adventure. The road bridge is one of the world's finest; the narrow-gauge rail bridge the world's highest.

Operating times: At the time of going to press, the Apple Express carried tourists on Saturdays only, from June to January. Spoornet in Port Elizabeth have details of the Apple Express's extended activities. Contact Spoornet at tel (041) 5072360, or book at your nearest railway station.

More information: Contact the Port Elizabeth Publicity Association, PO Box 357, Port Elizabeth 6001; tel (041) 521315.

Where to stay

Not for nothing is Port Elizabeth known as the Friendly City. In defiance of its windy reputation, this harbour city welcomes visitors, and a wide range of accommodation is available. For details, contact the Port Elizabeth Publicity Association, Market Square, Port Elizabeth, 6001; tel (041) 521315.

Step into the clockwork mind of a Victorian eccentric

In his house – now the Observatory Museum in Grahamstown – Henry Galpin created a memorial to himself, combining a study of the stars with the lure of his celebrated 'camera obscura'

BY MERELY STANDING OUTSIDE the Observatory Museum in Bathurst Street you realise that you are in for a novel experience. Above an elegant, two-storey Georgian facade, three curious towers rise, each with its own design. The impression is less of a house than of a stage magician's box of tricks.

This unusual museum began as the home and business premises of an eccentric English immigrant in the last century, Henry Carter Galpin. Although he was a jeweller and watchmaker by trade, his passion was for optics and astronomy. His restored house is a celebration not only of one man, but of the spirit of an age.

It is worth observing the three towers in detail, before you enter the house. The one at the left, looking vaguely like a factory chimney with railings round the top, contains a spiral staircase leading to the elaborate square tower alongside. This structure is Galpin's famous camera obscura. Separate from the others, at the right end of the building, is the clock tower. Having checked the time by

the position of the sun in his observatory, Galpin would set the clock on the tower. In their turn, the people of the town would adjust their clocks and watches to the time on the tower.

Galpin was born in England in 1820 and trained as an architect and civil engineer. Ill health forced him to abandon engineering, and instead he took up clockmaking and jewellery manufacture. As his health remained uncertain, he emigrated to the Cape, arriving towards the end of 1848. In Cape Town he met and married Georgina Marie Luck, then moved to Grahamstown in 1850.

There he set up in business in his new house, which developed into the first multi-storeyed building in the eastern Cape. Apart from his shop on the ground floor, two storeys were added to accommodate his growing family of seven sons. The back section features three tiers of decorative wooden verandas, with a Victorian kitchen in the London-style basement.

All this represented Galpin's terrestrial concerns. But his larger interests were celestial and optical. From the landing of the second floor, you squeeze through a doorway some 45 cm wide at the base of the spiral staircase tower. Finally, you step out onto the balcony of the camera obscura. While its original use as an observatory had practical value, it was its transformation into a magic picture show in the early 1880s that caught the public fancy. Indeed, its popularity became such that Galpin was obliged to charge a shilling admission to limit the numbers.

In principle the camera obscura, meaning simply dark room, is the same as a photographic camera. You step through the door into a small chamber, in the centre of which is a concave, circular table. Here, in effect, you are inside a camera, between the 'lens' and the 'film'. Your guide closes the door

The rear view of the Observatory Museum is decorated with iron-bedecked balconies.

The main bedroom in Henry Galpin's old house is beautifully furnished with Victoriana.

behind you, shutting out the light. He then pulls a rope which adjusts the angle of a mirror in a rotating turret. A moving image in miniature of part of the surrounding streetscape is reflected on a special glass. Another pull of the rope brings a further segment of the panorama into view. Slowly, full colour pictures of the city pass in front of you until the whole circuit has been completed.

In Galpin's day, of course, it would have been a vista of Victorian Grahamstown, with its horses and ox-wagons, its crinolined women and blanketed Xhosas. Much has changed since those days. The elegant costumes of yesteryear have gone and the carriages have been replaced by motor cars. Across the street, peering up at this strange building, are today's tourists, clutching their own handsized cameras. Time has passed, but Galpin's camera obscura still retains its magic.

The Observatory Museum at a glance (map page 94)

How to get there: The museum is situated in Bathurst Street, off High Street, Grahamstown.
What to do: Go around the Observatory Museum, then explore the settler city of Grahamstown, with its evocative 19th-century architecture. Places of interest include three other museums and the 1820 Settlers Monument.
Visiting times: Monday to Friday from 9.30 am to 1 pm, and from 2 pm to 5 pm; and on Saturday from 9 am to 1 pm. The museum charges a small admission fee.
More information: Call the museum, c/o Albany Museum, Somerset St, Grahamstown 6140; tel (0461) 22312.

Where to stay

There are two hotels within easy walking distance of the museum. They are:

The *Crillion Hotel* on the corner of Bathurst Street and High Street. It has 24 rooms, an à la carte restaurant and a bar. PO Box 68, Grahamstown 6140; tel (0461) 311555.

The *Grand Hotel* in High Street, just around the corner from the museum. It was once the home of an 1820 settler, and has been in operation for over 100 years. The 'Grand' has two restaurants, a coffee bar, a cocktail bar, and a wine cellar. PO Box 23, Grahamstown 6140; tel (0461) 27012.

The camera obscura in operation. The streets and buildings of Grahamstown can be seen reflected in the concave glass.

109

Old stone fortresses with many a tale to tell

Take an evocative drive to the various forts that were built to guard and protect the Cape's eastern frontier about 150 years ago

THERE'S SOMETHING ABOUT FORTS that seldom occurs to the average tourist: they were built to guard the surrounding countryside and, almost without exception, they also command magnificent views. This fact alone, especially in the hilly landscape of the old eastern Cape frontier, makes a visit to these silent bastions well worth your while.

Most of the forts were built between 1837 and 1846 as secure bases for soldiers of the British Army, as well as for a locally raised 'Hottentot Corps', whose unenviable task it was to patrol the frontier between white settler-agriculturalists and Xhosa pastoralists. Forts were erected at prominent sites, and a great many of the more substantial structures still remain. Few were actually attacked or besieged, the Xhosa preferring to bypass them and lure the soldiers to battle in the bush.

At the heart of the defensive system is Fort Selwyn on Gunfire Hill, built in 1836 with an unimpaired view of Grahamstown. In plan, the fort is an asymmetrical star of seven points, a design that effectively increases the length of the defended perimeter without increasing the enclosed area. This

enables a greater number of riflemen and gunners to man the walls against attack, and to provide one another with covering fire. The sloping stone walls have an average thickness of just under a metre, and a maximum outside height of 1,8 m. The fort was formerly surrounded by a ditch, which was intended to create an additional obstacle for attackers who, in the event, never arrived. But if they had come, and if the defenders had been beaten back from the walls, there remained the barrack room, with its loop-holed shutters, for the 'last stand' – so often the lot of the red-coated soldiers in far-flung parts of the Empire.

Contact between outposts was vital and was maintained by semaphore signals, the restored signal arms of Fort Selwyn being able to show exactly how it was done. Lying 16 km roughly east from Fort Selwyn, and in line of sight, is Governor's Kop, its summit surmounted by stone-built Collingham Tower. It lies just to the north of the N2 national road to East London, and was once the relay station for signals between important lines of forts. The northerly line ended at Fort Beaufort, while that to the east passed through Fraser's Camp, Piet Appel's Tower and Fort Peddie, with a southerly branch leading from Fraser's Camp through Cawood's Post to Bathurst. Each tower was in sight of those on either side, and each was equipped with semaphore arms to convey messages 'down the line'. Unfortunately, the signalling system failed to take account of the frequent mists that seriously reduced visibility, and a contemporary local wit lampooned it as 'a signal failure'.

The signal towers have lost their roofs to more than a century of neglect, but, in most cases, the stonework stands firm and solid. They follow a similar design, with Fraser's Camp tower probably the most complete and readily accessible. It is about 30 m high, and the only entrance – on the first floor – was reached by a ladder that the garrison would draw inside after them. An internal staircase led to the flat roof of the tower where the semaphore arms were mounted, and narrow slits in the walls enabled the defenders to cover the approaches. The barracks lie somewhat to the east.

It was at Fraser's Camp one night that a rebel soldier fired his musket into one of the rifle slits, killing Ensign Thomas Crowe of the Cape Mounted Riflemen. The rebels were caught, tried, and executed by firing squad below Fort Selwyn, and their unmarked graves are lost somewhere in what is now the 1820 Wildflower Reserve. Tom Crowe's grave, with a lengthy inscription, is in the old cemetery in Grahamstown. It's worth noting that his young

The Old Provost, or military prison, situated below Fort Selwyn. The Fraser's Camp mutineers were the first prisoners to be held here.

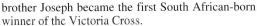

(Left) During the 1830s, towers such as this one at Fraser's Camp were built to relay semaphore messages between a series of forts that dotted the eastern Cape countryside. (Right) The Martello tower at Fort Beaufort is the only one of its type to have been built inland.

brother Joseph became the first South African-born winner of the Victoria Cross.

Fort Peddie is situated within the bustling town of Peddie that gradually grew around it. It was from the fort's cavalry barracks, with their gaping door-ways and sagging roofs, that the 7th Dragoon Guards rode out to slaughter their foe in a devastating charge on the flats near the Gwanga River, just past the outpost at Breakfast Vlei. In a later incident, the commander of Fort Peddie, Major Henry Eardley Wilmot, was shot in the back by one of his own men – accidentally, it was said officially. He lies buried in an old neglected civilian cemetery near the walls of his fort – a long way from Berkswell Hall, his stately Warwickshire home.

Overgrown and lonely are the distant ruins of Fort Armstrong, taken by rebels and then shattered by the gunfire of the very men who had built it. Only the tower is reasonably intact, situated close by the Kat River. These lazy waters once formed a boundary of the Kat River Settlement where hopeful men and women toiled – and ultimately lost everything.

Dick King, riding from Port Natal to Grahamstown in 1842 to call for British reinforcements against Boer besiegers, struggled through nearby Trompetter's Drift on the Great Fish River, situated on the old route between Grahamstown and Fort Peddie. A squat gun tower and perimeter walls still loom over the water and, further upstream, Fort Brown overlooks another crossing place.

It was along a tributary of the Great Fish River, the Koonap, that soldiers at Koonap Post, on one rainy January day in 1844, watched helplessly as Sergeant Mullins of the 91st Regiment was swept away on the flood and drowned. Poor Mullins had been hurrying back to Fort Beaufort to be married to a young woman called Mary Ann. Frontier life was hard, and many lives were short, so Mary Ann dried her tears and was subsequently married to Troop Sergeant-Major Moffat, who was soon to be discharged from the army after losing an arm to a well-thrown assegaai.

You'll find something of a novelty at Fort Beaufort, which is a museum today: it boasts the only Martello tower in the world that was not built as a seaward defence fort. The view from the top is as fine as ever, but the redcoats are long gone, and that distant movement is no more than a bush stirring in the wind, or a cow contentedly grazing.

Forts Route at a glance (map page 94)

How to get there: There's a spread of places to be seen, and they can best be visited on a circular day drive using Grahamstown, Fort Beaufort, Alice, King William's Town or Peddie as your base. On the N2 between Grahamstown and Peddie are Governor's Kop and Fraser's Camp, with a short excursion up a gravel road to Trompetter's Drift. Fort Brown is alongside the R67 between Grahamstown and Fort Beaufort and, further north, near Katberg, lies Fort Armstrong. A suggested return route to Grahamstown from Fort Beaufort is via Seymour, Alice and Peddie. The forts can also be very conveniently explored from Hogsback.
Weather: Rainfall is distributed fairly evenly during the year and the climate is usually temperate. Despite faint sea breezes, summers can be very hot; winters are very cold.

Special precautions: Keep an eye open for livestock straying onto roads, especially in the more rural districts when you are driving on gravel. Michel's Pass (also known as New Katberg Pass) between Hogsback and Seymour is untarred, very narrow and very steep, and is best avoided in wet weather. Hogsback Pass, between Hogsback and Alice, is a safer route.
What to do: Enjoy the scenery that you'll encounter at and between the old forts. Soak up the history of the places and give some thought not only to those so prominently commemorated but to their valiant enemies.
More information: Grahamstown Publicity Association, Church Square, Grahamstown 6140; tel (0461) 23241. Fort Beaufort Museum, Durban Street, Fort Beaufort 5720; tel (0435) 31555.

Where to stay

There is a wide range of accommodation in Grahamstown, and there are hotels in Fort Beaufort, Alice and Peddie, and at Hogsback.

Historic English village in settler country

On the road between Port Alfred and Grahamstown lies the rural hamlet of Bathurst, where the dreams and enterprises of many 1820 Settlers flourished and grew

Where to stay

Pig and Whistle Hotel, PO Box 123, Bathurst 6166; tel (0464) 250673; or the *Medolino Caravan Park*, PO Box 20, Kowie West, Port Alfred 6171; tel (0464) 41651.

The stone survey beacon from which early settlers were shown their allotments of land. Surrounding the structure is a stone-wall toposcope.

AN ESSENTIAL ENGLISHNESS clings to the old buildings in the village of Bathurst, and no wonder. Founded in 1820, it served as the first administrative centre for the 1820 Settlers before Grahamstown took over as the eastern Cape's capital.

Picturesque, rustic and reminiscent of England's Cotswolds, Bathurst is one of South Africa's smallest municipalities. The town's attractiveness owes much to the early settlers who were, of course, responsible for most of the gracious old buildings. The village also boasts some magnificent old oak trees which line the streets and dominate the gardens. One notable specimen situated not far from the Pig and Whistle has an astonishing spread of about 120 m.

The very oldest building in the town actually existed before the arrival of the settlers: the military built the Old Powder Magazine, a stone structure with a domed roof. For drama and history, however, nothing beats St John's Church. One of the most beautiful of Bathurst's old buildings, St John's is a national monument, a beautiful stone edifice that bears the distinction of being the oldest unaltered Anglican church in South Africa. The foundation stone was laid in 1832 and the church was finally completed in December 1837 and opened with a sermon on New Year's Day 1838.

During the turbulent frontier wars the outer walls of the building were fortified and this church became a fortress in the war-wracked countryside. Sitting inside the cool interior it's hard to imagine those turbulent times when women and children loaded guns while the men held off Xhosa warriors until relief arrived from Grahamstown.

St John's is unique in having two pulpits, both built by the same craftsman and dating back to the early years of the church. Another notable feature is a piece of Queen Elizabeth's coronation carpet from Westminster Abbey that was presented to the church and is proudly displayed in the vestibule.

The Wesleyan Church, a couple of years older than St John's, is another national monument that withstood various sieges during the frontier wars. It contains the family Bible of the settler, Jeremiah Goldswain (famed for his diaries, phrased in the quaint English of his era), who was the one-time proprietor of the Pig and Whistle Country Inn.

This inn (formerly known as the Bathurst Inn) was built in 1831 by Thomas Hartley, a blacksmith from Nottingham. Jeremiah Goldswain took it over in 1852 and added accommodation where a forge had been. The inn survived down the years, enduring fires and looting during the frontier wars, and remains a popular watering hole to this day. Its present name, the Pig and Whistle, was apparently affectionately bestowed by men from the nearby airschool who used to patronise the inn during the Second World War.

Hartley and Goldswain's names are linked again in Morley House, another gracious stone dwelling which Hartley built in 1828 and in which Goldswain once lived. Another famous occupant was big-game hunter Henry Hartley. Today Morley House is, appropriately enough, an antique and bric-a-brac shop.

On the outskirts of Bathurst is yet another doughty survivor of the frontier wars. Battle-scarred but still standing, Lombard's Post is a fortified stone farmhouse dating back to 1835.

Thanks to Samuel Bradshaw, a settler from Gloucestershire who built a water-driven wool mill here in 1821, Bathurst was the embryo from which South Africa's enormous wool industry grew. Four years later, a coarse woollen cloth was being made from wool from settlers' sheep, and so it also has the distinction of being the country's oldest textile factory. The mill was later converted into a grain mill and the original grindstone can still be seen. Bradshaw's Mill has been restored as a working museum and operates with a reconstructed water wheel.

Today Bathurst is an agricultural centre: the Bathurst Agricultural Show is the town's annual event held each Easter. The Bathurst Agricultural Museum is one of the finest of its kind in the

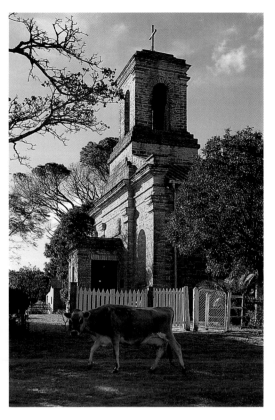

country, containing a unique collection of over 2 000 historical agricultural implements.

As their logo, the museum uses a silhouette of a plough made in 1821 by settlers known as the Bowker brothers for use on their farm *Tharfield*. However, this unique plough is not on display here: if you should have a burning desire to see it, you'll have to visit the Settlers Museum in Grahamstown. Nevertheless, many other items constructed by Bathurst settlers are on display, and the collection includes many other ploughs, tractors (in running order), carts, yokes, wagons, *remskoene* (brake shoes), butter churns, even ostrich egg incubators. Also on display are various items that were in daily use in settlers' homes, such as sewing machines and kitchen utensils.

One of the main attractions of the village is the circular toposcope that is built around the stone beacon from which many 1820 Settlers were shown their allotments of land. Embedded in the toposcope are 57 bronze plaques recording details of each settler party. Many descendents of the 1820 Settlers make the pilgrimage here to trace their roots in

Africa. The toposcope was the idea of historian Ted Morse Jones and was built in 1968 around the hilltop beacon, which is a national monument. From here there is a panoramic view of settler country stretching from the Great Fish River to the coast.

Another first for Bathurst is that it was from here that South African pineapple production really took off – from the toposcope the area's flourishing pineapple fields can be admired. Although pineapples were brought to the Cape from Java by the Dutch in 1660, and grown two centuries later in Natal, they were still very rare. But in 1865 a Grahamstown barber called Lindsay Green gave Charles Purden 35 Natal pineapple tops or crowns for experimental planting on his farm *Thorndon* near Bathurst. Conditions appeared to be ideal for the fruit and the experiment was a resounding success. The first crop of pineapples produced was sold on the Grahamstown market for about 75 pence each, an enormous amount in those days. By 1904, the region's pineapples were being exported to England and today South Africa is the eighth largest producer of pineapples in the world.

(Left and right) The exterior and interior of St John's Church. This historic building acted as a settler fortress during times of war.

Bathurst at a glance (map page 94)

How to get there: Bathurst lies between Port Alfred and Grahamstown on the R67. Travellers from Cape Town and Durban would take the N2 to Grahamstown and take the R67 from there. From Johannesburg take the N1 to Colesberg. Just outside Colesberg the N9 leads to Middelburg, from where you turn left onto the N10. This road will take you all the way through Cradock and Cookhouse until it finally joins the N2. Take the N2 east to Grahamstown.

Weather: Bathurst is hot in summer and warm to mild in winter, although it can get cold at night.
What to do: Explore and sightsee. This is also excellent cycling territory and the countryside is best appreciated from a bike.
Special attractions: The unique atmosphere of old England, especially in the Pig and Whistle. Summerhill Park, a settler farm just outside Bathurst, has been developed into a tourist attraction. It includes displays relating to the pineapple industry,

a mini-farm and a Xhosa village. There is the Waters Meeting Nature Reserve on the Kowie River (see separate entry); this includes the famous Horseshoe Bend on the Kowie River as well as picnic sites at the Ebb and Flow – the highest point to which the salt tide pushes upriver.
More information: Town Clerk, PO Box 128, Bathurst 6166; tel (0464) 250639. Grahamstown Publicity Association and Information Bureau, 63 High Street, Grahamstown 6140; tel (0461) 23241.

A tranquil riverine retreat
for canoeists and bird-watchers

*About 30 km upstream from the mouth of the Kowie River and the
holiday resort of Port Alfred is the Waters Meeting Nature Reserve,
an idyllic stretch of river with picnic and camping sites*

THE FIRST VIEW that you get of the Waters Meeting Nature Reserve is shortly after taking the gravel road heading south from the village of Bathurst. After driving for 5 km through farmlands, you suddenly find yourself at the edge of the Kowie River ravine, a point that commands a breathtaking view over the river, meandering in lazy loops across the bush-filled plain below you.

There's even a wooden platform jutting out over the edge of a cliff to enable you to enjoy this splendid panorama even more. Far below you, in the nature reserve itself, a wooden jetty can be seen on the river. This jetty marks the end of South Africa's only canoe trail.

As you stand admiring the scenery, you'll soon become aware of the rich variety of flora; many of the trees in the vicinity have been numbered as an aid to identification. And if you wait patiently, you might even see the pair of fish eagles that have staked out the reserve as their personal domain.

About 100 m further along the road you'll come to the entrance to the unusually named Waters Meeting Nature Reserve. After paying a small entrance fee, follow the road along its steep, winding descent for about 2 km. Eventually you'll arrive at Ebb and Flow, an extensive picnic site situated at the bottom of the ravine.

Here, each site is provided with tables, benches, a braai site and a supply of firewood. Fresh running water and toilet facilities are also provided. Because the reserve is so little known, don't be surprised to find, even at the height of the holiday season, that you have the whole picnic spot to yourself!

Directly below the picnic area is a causeway that marks the point where the salt-water tides of the river meet the fresh water flowing down from inland areas. If the tide is high, you'll have salt water on one side and fresh on the other, hence the name of the reserve, Waters Meeting. This causeway is a historic spot because, for several decades during the last century, it was the only point at which farmers could ford the river without the risk of getting wagon cargoes soaked.

You can follow the road these pioneer farmers once used – it wanders for several kilometres along the right-hand bank of the river, eventually disappearing into cultivated farmlands. This is a worthwhile walk for the bird-watcher as the bush in the area is rich in wildlife, and in early summer there is a profusion of brightly coloured butterflies.

Alternatively, you could paddle down the river, starting at the causeway (if the tide is high). By booking onto the unique Kowie Canoe Trail, you will be given a canoe, double paddles, the use of the rest hut, fresh water and braai wood, and a permit to sleep in the forest. Should you prefer to use your own canoe, you pay the same as if you were using the canoe provided.

The canoe trip is highly recommended, because being a noiseless form of transport, a canoe allows a close approach to wildlife along the riverbanks. You can expect to see birds nesting on overhanging branches, giant water leguaans basking in the sun, brilliantly coloured kingfishers diving into the water, or fish eagles and ospreys patrolling the river in search of an unwary fish.

If you follow the several meanders of the river for about 3 km, you'll eventually come to the wooden jetty you spotted from the lookout point high up on the cliff above you. Stop here for a rest or take a walk through the forest. Alternatively, try a bit of angling – this is an excellent fishing spot.

Set into the forest nearby is a four-roomed rest hut with bunks for eight, tables and benches, a braai area and fresh running water. If you listen carefully you may hear some of the sounds of the forest – the persistent tap-tapping of a Knysna woodpecker, or the melancholic call of a nerina trogon. It is worth getting a glimpse of these uncommon birds, because the woodpecker's habit of scrabbling over the bark of trees is highly comical, and the metallic green and brilliant red of the somewhat shy trogon is most unusual for our indigenous birds. Don't be deceived by what may sound like a wooden barrel

The tranquil Waters Meeting picnic spot, beside the causeway where the Kowie River's salt and fresh waters meet.

The hiking trail follows the old pioneers' road through rich riverside forest – the haunt of bushbuck , eagles and the shy narina trogon.

being sawn in half – this is the call of the Knysna loerie. It may reward you by flying across a forest clearing, displaying its blood-red wing feathers and moss-green crest.

Should you decide to stay overnight in the hut, there are a few nocturnal sounds you should be prepared for. Late at night you might be startled by a very loud snort coming from the depths of the forest. This will be followed some ten seconds later by more snorts, with a diminishing interval between each, until they all blend into a rasping, squealing racket that sounds like the cry of some poor creature being torn apart by a predator. Don't be alarmed – this dreadful serenade comes from an animal little bigger than a large guinea pig, the bush dassie. It is almost identical to the common rock dassie, but is strictly nocturnal in habit.

Even if you have not made the canoe trip, you can still sample the delights of this pristine forest by taking the hiking trail (book in advance). This starts some 300 m above the causeway, and is signposted on the road you originally came down. One section of the trail crosses a stile and heads northwest, providing a 2 km walk through a forested area to the wall of a newly built dam – the main water supply for Port Alfred.

The section of trail heading east is recommended, as this brings you through an example of Kowie Bush at its impenetrable worst. Do not attempt to leave the trail, because you won't get very far – the thorns of the *droog-my-keel* bush, the bee-sting bush and the cat's claw creeper present a formidable barrier! Further down the trail the bush opens up into tall riverine forest. Walk quietly here and you'll be rewarded by the sight of several buck species: bushbuck mostly, but also steenbok and red duiker. If you're fortunate, you'll also see Africa's smallest antelope – the blue duiker. This shy little creature, which locals call a bluebuck, is no bigger than a Maltese poodle!

The trail eventually reaches the riverbank and follows this until, after about 2 km, you come to the canoe jetty mentioned earlier. En route you'll be struck by the changing composition of the forest: first the Karoo *boerboon* trees with their gnarled branches and the deep magenta blooms that pop out at intervals from bare stems. Then come the forest *boerboons*, more upright in appearance but easily identified by their large pods and the broadbean-like seeds.

The trail follows the left bank of the river for about 5 km until it reaches the southern boundary of the reserve. It's worth taking this route as you'll see a variety of wildlife on the riverbank: many species of waders when the tide is low, weavers nesting in the reeds, hadedas with their twiggy platform nests on overhanging branches – and perhaps a giant mountain tortoise crossing your path.

Where to stay

Caravanners and campers can stay overnight at the camping site, and canoeists can put up in the four-roomed rest hut at the end of the Kowie Canoe Trail.

Hotel accommodation is available at several comfortable hotels in Port Alfred, 11 km south of Bathurst. They are: *The Halyards* (on the Royal Alfred Marina), PO Box 208, Port Alfred 6170; tel (0464) 42410; the *Hotel Kowie Grand*, PO Box 1, Kowie West 6171; tel (0464) 41150; and the *Hotel Victoria*, PO Box 2, Port Alfred 6170; tel (0464) 41133.

A number of beach cottages, cabanas, holiday flats and chalets, caravan parks and bed-and-breakfast facilities offer a variety of accommodation in the area. Contact the Port Alfred Publicity Officer for details (see address in other panel).

Waters Meeting Nature Reserve at a glance (map page 94)

How to get there: Take the Grahamstown road from Port Alfred and you'll reach Bathurst after about 12 km. At the *Pig 'n Whistle Hotel*, where the main road in the village takes a right-angled turn up a hill, take a gravel road (poorly signposted) to the left. This heads south at first, but turns southwest after half a kilometre. Various unmarked farm roads lead off at intervals, but ignore these; keep heading west for about 6 km until you reach the Horseshoe Bend lookout point. About 100 m

beyond this is the gate to the Nature Reserve, and 2 km further on is the picnic spot and the start of the hiking trail.
Weather: Lying halfway as it does between the summer and winter rainfall regions, the Bathurst district enjoys the benefit of both climates. Summers have the occasional shower and are seldom excessively hot and humid. During winter the nights can be cold and crisp on occasion, but the days are usually mild and pleasant.

What to do: Go picnicking in serene surroundings beside an old river crossing, go canoeing down the river (booking is essential), or hike along a quiet forest trail to a secluded fishing spot on the river. Nearby Bathurst has many interesting reminders of the 1820 Settlers, as well as a tour of a showcase pineapple farm at Summerhill Park, just outside the village.
Special attractions: The country's one and only canoe trail.

Primeval splendours in the heart of the Amatole Mountains

*Poised on the eastern rim of a dramatic escarpment,
half hidden among ancient indigenous forests,
the old-world village of Hogsback is a hiker's paradise*

IF EVER A PLACE was made for people who like their 'getting away from it all' to be as restful as possible, the village of Hogsback certainly is. The handful of hotels along the main street are warm, hospitable and well endowed with home comforts, but the real magic of the place lies in the beautiful forests situated around the village and on the surrounding hills.

If you enjoy hiking, this is one area you shouldn't miss – especially the routes along the 1 820 m-high Hogsback Mountain, rising over the area to the east.

Looming up out of a vast spread of indigenous forest, this range is reputed to resemble exactly the backs of the wild pigs which root in the woods by night, and the general consensus is that this is how it got its name.

Where to stay

The following are all situated on the main road through Hogsback village, and are well signposted:

The *Hogsback Inn* has 32 rooms, plus an en suite annexe. The hotel occupies the site of the first building in Hogsback, put up in 1850. Attractions include a swimming pool, tennis court, games room, bowls and horse-riding. Contact PO Box 63, Hogsback 5721; tel (045642) and ask for Hogsback 6.

Hogsback Mountain Lodge – otherwise known as *Arminel*. This licensed holiday resort has 24 thatched-cottage bedroom suites, all with a magnificent view of the Hogsback range. There is also a swimming pool and a tennis court. Contact PO Box 67, Hogsback 5721; tel (045642) and ask for Hogsback 5.

King's Lodge has 23 bedrooms in a chalet complex. Swimming and bowls are available. Write to PO Hogsback 5721; tel (045642) and ask for Hogsback 24.

The *Amatola Guest House* has seven rooms, one of which is a self-catering rondavel. Write to PO Box 45, Hogsback 5721; tel (045642) and ask for Hogsback 59.

A number of private mountain cottages and chalets in the area are available to rent. Enquire at the hotels for more information.

Many of the walks in the area have as a final destination a waterfall – such as this one, called The 39 Steps.

The earliest written reference to the name was found in the journal of the famous painter Thomas Baines, who passed the 'Hogs Back' while on his travels to the interior in 1848. The view from above the village is breathtaking and includes, besides the Hogsback, the highest peak in the area, the 1 954 m Gaika's Kop.

Back in the 1850s, this was frontier country. To the local Xhosas, it was *Qabimbola*, 'where they paint the clay', after the clay deposits used in the ritual painting of faces. To British troops stationed here, it was probably mostly a headache and a number of forts were built to guard the border, a necessity in view of the constant friction, especially over cattle rustling. One of these was Fort Michel, named after Colonel Michel of the Warwickshire regiment, who was at one time in charge of troops in the area.

The conflict continued further to the north, leaving the Tyumie Valley at peace. By this time, Hogsback had become known as a convenient stopover on the road to the interior – where cattle could graze and weary travellers rest.

A small settlement started to grow. One of the early settlers was a gardener from Britain whose legacy survives in the local gardens and even in the forests nearby, which are dotted with European flowers, bushes and trees. They include rhododendrons, azaleas and, on a Wordsworthian note, a quite considerable population of daffodils. Many European fruits and berries also thrive happily at this altitude.

By the turn of the century, local farmers and townsfolk from further afield, lured by the quaint 'Englishness' of the village, began to build their holiday homes here, and its charms became more widely known.

But it is the older African forests that provide the real atmosphere at Hogsback. To enter them is to penetrate a truly mystical world. In the old days, getting lost did not require very much effort. Today, the Hogsback Inn, in co-operation with the Department of Forestry, has marked out a network of walks and climbs. The paths are defined by a hog emblem, in red, green or yellow, depending on the route. Many of the trees are numbered as an aid to identification.

From your hotel or guesthouse, you can begin with a gentle stroll down Oak Avenue. This double row of century-old trees is used as a natural cathedral at Christmas and Easter. Open-air services are conducted here, the congregants seating themselves on logs beside the road. Nearby is the Arboretum, a 'living museum' of trees, both European

Gentle mountain slopes and a rich variety of vegetation make Hogsback a haven for hikers.

and African, including a real European holly tree sporting clusters of bright red berries.

Having got your breath and become used to the altitude, you can begin to explore deeper into the Tyumie Forest. 'Tree key' in hand, you can pick out all the species, from the Outeniqua yellowwoods, to the giant lemonwood, stinkwood, ironwood, and sneezewood. Other indigenous trees to look out for are Cape chestnut, assegai, camdeboo, knobwood and red pear.

The forest floor is a tangled counterpoint of roots and there are groves of tall ferns, from which you will be observed by the many small inhabitants that populate the forest, especially the reclusive samango monkey. The samangoes swing from tree to tree, examining the less agile primates as they limber up their city muscles.

Most of the walks have a pool or waterfall as a final destination, and it is one of the pleasures of this kind of exploration to hear the sound of the falls approaching. Among them are the Madonna and Child, Swallowtail, The 39 Steps, Bridal Veil and the Kettlespout, where the water shoots forth from the top of a cliff.

Finally, you emerge above the tree-line to tackle the mountains. Pick a fine, clear day before you attempt the higher reaches of the Hogsback. In ascending order of challenge are Tor Doone, directly behind the village; the main Hogsback peak; and – a full day's expedition – Gaika's Kop. They are hard work, all of them. But your reward is assured, both in the incomparable views of the landscape spread out below and in the welcome at the hotel fireside as the sun goes down.

Hogsback at a glance (map page 94)

How to get there: There are two approaches, the first being from the Ciskei. Drive a few kilometres along the R63 from Alice, going towards King William's Town, then turn left up the R345, for a further 30 km. This way has the advantage of spectacular views in the last few kilometres, as you rise steeply up the thickly wooded valley of the Tyumie River. Alternatively, you can make your approach from above, also on the R345, from Cathcart, a distance of 51 km.

Weather: This is mountain territory, but the weather is generally reliable, despite a healthy annual 1 000 mm of rain, mostly in summer. Winter is wonderfully clear and bracing, with the peaks often

covered in snow in July and August. So be warned, though: winter nights can be very cold. Surprisingly, given its altitude of about 1 200 m above sea level, there is in fact very little wind in and around the village area.

What to do: The Hogsback hotels offer facilities for tennis, swimming and bowls. But it is the surrounding countryside which provides the main allure, with splendid walks and climbs. Permits for the forest walks may be obtained from the Hogsback Forestry Station, PO Box 52, Hogsback 5721; tel (045642) and ask for Hogsback 55.

Special attractions: In the village are craft shops, as well as a quaint little rondavel library in Redcoat

Lane, open a couple of hours a week. There are also a supermarket and a post office. Nearby, in the forest, is the Arboretum, a garden of cultivated trees from around the world, including a stand of the largest Californian redwoods in southern Africa. A short drive away are the tiny church of St Patrick on the Hill, and Fort Michel near Tor Doone.

More information: At present, there is no general information service in Hogsback. However, the main walks in the area are described and marked in *Exploring Hogsback*, or, as it is more affectionately known, *The Piggy Book*, named for the hog sign that marks all the walks. This booklet is available at the hotels and shops in the area.

Land of warrior-chiefs and bitter battles

Piece together the events of the Seventh Frontier War from clues found near Keiskammahoek, a pretty mountain village near Stutterheim

KEISKAMMAHOEK IS ONE of the most picturesque towns in the eastern Cape region – an area that still bears the scars of the struggle between settlers and indigenous peoples in the battle for land.

As you explore the area between Alice and Keiskammahoek, you'll find ample evidence of the long-drawn-out battle between the Xhosa and the Cape government that lasted almost 100 years. And since this is Xhosa territory, in a historical as much as a contemporary sense, it is appropriate that your visit focuses less on the legacy of the colonists than on that of their Xhosa adversaries.

All in all, nine frontier skirmishes occurred between 1779 and 1878, and this scenic part of the Amatola mountain range was the battlefield for the seventh of these, known as the War of the Axe.

The reason for this appellation was that in March 1846, a British patrol that was sent to arrest a Xhosa man suspected of stealing an axe was ambushed and its members killed. A colonial force under Lieutenant-Colonel John Hare subsequently retaliated, and the Xhosa people fought back. A bitter war ensued that would last for over 18 months, until the last chief surrendered at Keiskammahoek in December 1847.

Several military forts were built at the end of this war, to oversee the uneasy peace. The largest of these, Fort Hare, has since lent its name to the university on the outskirts of Alice, a town on the left bank of the Tyume River, about 23 km east of Fort Beaufort. The modern campus lies on a grassy slope overlooking the town and in its grounds a double-storey, redbrick tower and a few bastions are all that remain of Fort Hare. But its recent history has not been without glory, for among those who have attended the university have been Zimbabwean Prime Minister Robert Mugabe, Nelson Mandela and Oliver Tambo.

From Alice, head east towards King William's Town, and about 3 km beyond Middledrift turn left towards Keiskammahoek. About 6 km from the turn-off, you'll pass the old Burnshill Mission Station. This is where Colonel Hare's First Division was defeated at the start of the Seventh Frontier War, but near it, within walking distance, you'll find a memorial to an earlier era in this region's history – the grave of Paramount Chief Ngqika who died here in 1829.

Ngqika's claim to the chieftainship was shaky from the start and he tried to reinforce his position by courting the favour of the colonists. He won the

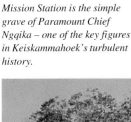

Situated close to the Burnshill Mission Station is the simple grave of Paramount Chief Ngqika – one of the key figures in Keiskammahoek's turbulent history.

Many of the slopes of the Amatola Mountains are thickly wooded, offering plenty of shade for hikers during the summer months.

Where to stay

There is a hotel at Keiskam-mahoek appropriately named the *Keiskamma Hotel*. Write to PO Box 119, Keiskammahoek, Ciskei; tel (040242) ask for 28.

support of Governor Lord Charles Somerset whose partisanship infuriated other Xhosa chiefs and was one of the causes of the Xhosa War of 1819. Ngqika's son Sandile was of a different political persuasion – indeed, it was his refusal to co-operate with the colonial government that precipitated the War of the Axe.

From Burnshill the road follows the direction of the Keiskamma River and brings you to the heart of the Amatola Mountains and the pretty town of Keiskammahoek. Not surprisingly, it began life as a frontier post established in the wake of the Seventh Frontier War, and the remains of the stone-built Keiskammahoek Post are an impressive sight. There is a Frontier War Memorial on the fringe of the town, an assortment of old buildings, a large, modern hospital near the eastern entrance, and a flourishing factory producing fine articles from yellowwood that can be admired (and purchased) in a showroom on the premises.

About 19 km outside Keiskammahoek, on the road leading northeast towards Stutterheim, a road branches southwards to the Evelyn Valley. Here, at the foot of Mount Kemp, lies the grave of Sandile, Ngqika's son. His intransigence started the Seventh Frontier War, his surrender marked its end. An oath of allegiance to the British Queen won him his freedom, but his allegiance to his people proved stronger and the Ninth Frontier War eventually claimed his life.

But enough of history. The Amatola Mountains may have seen many bloody battles and the rise and fall of great warrior-chiefs, but to the modern visitor it offers much more – excellent opportunities for trout-fishing, for example. Or you can simply enjoy the captivating views and decide for yourself if this was a place worth fighting for.

One of the most well-known landmarks in Keiskammahoek is Ballantine's Mill, built by a Scottish settler at the end of the last century. It subsequently became the site of one of the country's largest wagon building factories.

Keiskammahoek at a glance (map page 94)

How to get there: From Fort Beaufort (82 km north of Grahamstown) travel eastwards in the direction of King William's Town, passing Alice on your way, and 6 km after Middledrift turn left towards Stutterheim.
Weather: Warm, wet summers and cool, crisp winters with cold nights. Snowfalls may occur, but generally do not last for very long.
What to do: Piece together the events of the Seventh Frontier

War between Fort Hare at Alice and Sandile's grave near Stutterheim.
Special attractions: The yellowwood factory in Keiskammahoek has many fine items on display in a showroom on the premises.
More information: Contact Contour (the National Nature Conservation and Tourism Board) at PO Box 186, Bisho, Ciskei; tel (0401) 952115.

A strenuous hike through spectacular landscapes

Mysterious forests, towering mountains, grassy plateaux: these are the keynotes of the magnificent Amatola Trail

THE WORLD IS WAKING UP to the magnificence of South Africa's hiking trails, and they don't come much more spectacular than the Amatola Trail. The trail leads through an area of deep, enchanted forests, silver waterfalls, challenging valleys and mountains, and a region which is also rich in history, both Xhosa and settler.

But before you start airing your sleeping bag, be under no illusions: the Amatola Trail is not for everyone. It takes six days to complete the 105-km walk, with the average day's hike being 17,5 km through challenging terrain. Only fit and experienced hikers should therefore attempt it. But all is not lost if you don't shape up: it is possible for the less able-bodied and adventurous to tackle the route in sections. Each overnight hut can be a starting point and there are various exit points for those who've had enough.

Most of the trail leads deep into indigenous forest, where the tree canopy is about 25 m high and so dense that in many places no sunlight ever reaches the ground. This is everything a forest should be: massive moss-padded trees, trailing lianas, clumps of ferns, flowers, lichen, mushrooms and toadstools. It's a glorious, almost subterranean experience, to move silently through the green depths on a springy carpet of dead leaves.

Now and then the path passes beneath a pool of light that has managed to penetrate the leafy canopy, and in other places the forest is lit by the silver flash of a waterfall. The forest's mystery is enhanced with the sounds of creatures unseen – birds and insects calling, frogs croaking, something

rustling – and sometimes you might even see casts left behind by the eastern Cape's famous giant earthworms.

The variety of wildlife you might see on the Amatola Trail is huge, yet this area used to be home to lion, elephant, buffalo, black and white rhino and leopard. Plans are afoot to reintroduce some of these species, but in the meanwhile lucky hikers may see bushpigs, bushbuck, duikers, dassies, porcupines, hedgehogs, striped polecats and weasels, samango and vervet monkeys, baboons, bats, numerous frogs and toads, and many harmless snakes as well as some not-so-harmless ones such as the boomslang, rinkhals, Cape cobra, puffadder and rhombic night adder. If, at night, the air is suddenly split with a bloodcurdling scream, try not to panic. The culprit is undoubtedly the nocturnal tree dassie: often heard, seldom seen.

An enormous variety of birds occupies the forests, including hadedas, ducks, Cape parrots, forest buzzards, Knysna loeries, wood owls and giant kingfishers. A different variety of birds exists out on the scrub and macchia grassland, such as Cape canaries, yellow-billed kites, spotted eagle owls, jackal buzzard and black-shouldered kites.

The trail starts off deceptively easily at Maden Dam, and the day's hike is a leisurely stroll through indigenous forests, pine plantations and along plateaux. The first night is spent at the old Evelyn Valley Forest Station, which has been converted into an overnight hiking hut with accommodation for 30 hikers. It enjoys an incredible view over the forest canopy towards the sea, and flocks of Cape parrots setting out on an evening or early-morning forage are a common sight. Put your feet up and have a good rest, because day two of the trail, from Evelyn Valley to Dontsa Forest, is the longest and most challenging of the six days.

You'll need an early start and as this is the only part of the trail where water is in short supply, don't miss a chance to fill your bottle. A hard day's walk takes you through the magnificent Abafazi Forest; you'll cross sparkling streams, emerge into open grassland, dive back into forest until the path eventually leads up to Dontsa Forest Station where the log cabin, perched on an outcrop among tall pines, is a welcome sight. Weary as you may be, be sure to follow the short paths nearby. These lead to pleasant rock pools and waterfalls where you can cool your aching limbs.

Still more forest awaits you the following day, when the trail leads back into the cool green depths. Along the way a magnificent waterfall drapes itself sensuously across the rocks like a supple length of

A hiker traverses a lush slope on one of the easier sections of the Amatola Trail. Most of the trail leads through dense forest and tough, mountainous terrain.

The Amatola Trail is criss-crossed throughout its 105 km length by tinkling streams – ideal places for hikers to stop and soothe their weary limbs.

satin, and appears to emit its own strange light. More waterfalls await until the path climbs towards a plateau of macchia grassland and dazzling wild flowers. From here you can see Sandile and Cata dams, and rural countryside below with villages dotted about the valley. Hikers follow a precarious mountain path towards the Cata River and pass through still more forest, waterfalls, pine and grassland until reaching the overnight spot which lies in a huge amphitheatre beneath Geju Peak. Accommodation is provided in traditionally styled (albeit slightly modified) Xhosa huts with dung floors. Beds with mattresses are provided and for the hardy there is also a bush shower, filled by bucket.

The summit of Geju Peak is where you're headed for on day four. From here, you are rewarded with views of more rural villages, Gaika's Kop, Elandsberg, Hangklip at Queenstown and the Keiskamma River Basin reaching all the way down to the Indian Ocean. The trail then descends to the Mnyameni ('dark place') Valley through a verdant kloof, passing by numerous exquisite waterfalls. The steep descent is quite hair-raising in places, with sheer drops and the ever-present possibility of plunging headlong into the abyss, especially as the stunning beauty of the surroundings is so distract-

ing. Eventually, however, you reach the thatched hiker's lodge which is magnificently sited next to the river in a steep valley between the Hogsback Peaks and Geju Peak.

The penultimate day of the trail passes through indigenous forest on the way to a spectacular contour path which hugs the ridge behind the highest of the Hogsback Peaks, where you might spot falcons and other birds of prey. Back in a lush kloof, numerous exquisite rock pools line the way, and it's well worthwhile giving in to the temptation of diving in. The day's walk terminates in the heart of the lush Zingcuka Forest where samango monkeys, loeries, bushbuck and duikers live. The Zingcuka Hut on the last night is, appropriately, the most luxurious, with electricity and a hot shower.

The final leg of the Amatola Trail leads through more lush indigenous forest with yet another wonderful waterfall, but, by this time, you can be forgiven for being immune to its beauty. The climb to the top of the Hogsback ridge is rewarded with a view of the Hogsback resort, forest reserve and Tyumie River Basin. This challenging trail ends on the sixth day at the Tyumie River/Wolfridge Road, where you'll doubtless feel a heroic glow of achievement, having conquered the Amatola.

Where to stay

The trail lodges along the route provide basic accommodation for 16-30 people, with beds and mattresses, a tap and a toilet. There is usually plenty of firewood and huge cast-iron cooking pots are provided at most lodges.

Amatola Hiking Trail at a glance (map page 94)

How to get there: From Johannesburg, take the N1 as far as Bloemfontein, and then head south on the N6 and the R30, passing Aliwal North, Queenstown and Stutterheim, to King William's Town. From there, take the R63 west for about 24 km and turn right onto the Keiskammahoek Road. The area is well signposted. From Cape Town and Durban, take the N2 (east from Cape Town, south from Durban) to King William's Town, and follow directions above.
Weather: Warm in summer with a high rainfall and mountain mists. The temperature drops sharply at night, and in the winter months snow may fall on the surrounding mountains.

What to do: There won't be much time to do anything other than hike, but it is possible to fish for trout (permits are required) and, if it's not too cold, you can swim in sparkling pools along the way. Keep all your wits about you while wildlife-spotting: there's a unique variety, from tiny insects to buck.
Special attractions: The large areas of indigenous forest and many waterfalls.
More information: Write to Contour (the national nature conservation and tourism board), PO Box 186, Bisho, Ciskei; tel (0401) 952115. Book well in advance.

More than just a mausoleum for Huberta the Hippo

Considerably more than a last resting place for its most famous exhibit, the Kaffrarian Museum in King William's Town provides a vivid record of a hardy pioneer community

S HE WAS A FOUR-LEGGED TOURIST, whose travels began in Zululand. In November 1928, contrary to hippopotamus habit, she took up a wandering life. Her fame spread quickly, especially after she dropped in on a party at the Durban Country Club. Over the next three years, Huberta continued to wander south, steadily munching her way through the cane fields.

Altogether she walked a distance of 1 600 km, during which she became a national heroine. Alas, her odyssey came to an end in April 1931, when she was shot while wallowing in the Keiskamma River. Her hide was retrieved and sent to England for taxidermy and mounting. Now, six decades later, she stands, glassy-eyed and perhaps a shade reproachful, on her podium in the Kaffrarian Museum in King William's Town.

There is no doubt that Huberta is the star of the show, but the arrangement of the displays artfully contrives that you will see many other things on the way to her, beginning with the building itself. For the Kaffrarian Museum, built in 1898, is a museum piece in its own right. It has all the elaborate elegance, the desire to impress – even in the far-flung corners of the colonies – that was typical of so many British buildings erected during the last century. Standing prominently on the corner of Albert and Alexandra roads, it is a memorial to the town, its pioneers, soldiers, missionaries, and the Xhosa people of the Ciskei.

The original entrance was in Albert Road, but is now in Alexandra Road. Inside, you find yourself in

an atmosphere redolent of early King William's Town, in the days when it was the capital of the Province of British Kaffraria.

The first rooms show the solid Victorian society of the town, with items ranging from elaborate period costume – 'Sunday best' – to practical reminders of a hard-working frontier community. In particular, it was a centre of wagon and carriage manufacture, and there are displays both of the vehicles and of the wainwrights' tools. Other industries are recalled in collections of farming implements and handmade hats. Here, too, is a fine reconstruction of a 19th-century shop, selling everything from a needle to a pick.

It is a picture of self-sufficiency, often branching out into ingenious eccentricity, as is witnessed by Mr Kidson's home-made 'kick-gate', which closed on a spring behind the visitor. Other images of frontier inventiveness are found in the displays of the German farmers, who settled in the area in the mid-1850s.

A military base, manned by the Cape Mounted Rifles, was an important part of the military and social history of the area. They were responsible for patrolling the frontier, and their history finds an echo in the evocative collections of uniforms, medals, accoutrements and arms, musical instruments, documents and paintings, associated with the Frontier Wars.

But the heart of the collection is its natural history section, at the rear of the museum. Here are wonderful dioramas, creating a memory, tinged

Where to stay

The *Grosvenor Hotel*, the town's main hotel, is situated in Taylor Street, a block from the museum. It has 15 rooms, all with en-suite bathrooms. For details, write to PO Box 61, King William's Town 5600; or tel (0433) 22311.

Huberta the Hippo – her body preserved for posterity and her exploits described alongside.

The strikingly unusual architecture of the Kaffrarian Museum is every bit as interesting as the many exhibits within the building.

with melancholy, of a lost Africa, of a time, barely a hundred years ago, when the veld teemed with game – springbok, kudu, eland, hyaena, zebra, lion and elephant. And of course, Huberta herself, boldly labelled, complete with a graphic description of her adventures.

Nor is the museum's collection limited to the large and impressive. On the first floor is the Pym Gallery, which features the smaller vertebrates, as well as birds, insects, snakes and snails, down back through the chain of evolution to shells, rocks, minerals and fossils.

Despite the wealth and variety of what you see, it is only a fraction of the whole. About 200 items are on display, the bulk being held in storage or for study. Altogether, the museum comprises a staggering 40 000 specimens, constituting one of the biggest mammal collections in southern Africa and the fourth largest in the southern hemisphere. It was largely the work of one man, Captain Guy Shortridge, the second director of the museum. Appointed in 1921, he undertook collecting expeditions, ranging from Namaqualand to present-day Malawi, accumulating an invaluable record of a fast-fading Africa.

Around Shortridge's core collection, other branches have grown, including the Victorian exhibits. In the early 1980s the adjacent post office building in Alexandra Road was acquired as an annexe to the museum. It is here, a few steps away, that you will find a record of the ethnic traditions and cultures of the Xhosa and Khoisan people. The displays include stone implements as well as weapons. A domestic note is provided by Xhosa dolls dressed in red blankets and beads, made in the 1930s. An intriguing modern contrast is seen in two large wire, felt, cardboard and plastic cars, of dazzling ingenuity, made by a local township artist, on show at the entrance.

The complex also includes the South African Missionary Museum, around the corner in the old Wesleyan Church in Berkeley Street. Established in 1971, it features an array of missionary printing presses, among them the Chumie press, on which the first Xhosa texts of the Bible were printed in 1823, and the Albion press, on which the Reverend John Appleyard produced the first complete Xhosa version of the Bible.

Taken all together, the three sections of the museum create a wonderful historical kaleidoscope.

Kaffrarian Museum at a glance (map page 94)

How to get there: The Kaffrarian Museum is situated on the corner of Albert and Alexandra roads in King William's Town. The Missionary Museum is just a short walk away at 27 Berkeley Street.
What to do: Besides the museum, various other points of interest are the original town hall, the 19th-century hospital and the ruins of Fort Murray, outside the town.

Special attractions: Obviously, Huberta the Hippo. Aside from the permanent displays, the museum mounts temporary exhibitions on a wide range of topics. There is a small but well-stocked gift shop just inside the door to the main building.
Visiting times: Mondays to Fridays, 9 am to 1 pm, and from 1.45 pm to 4.30 pm; on Saturdays from 10 am to 12.30 pm; and on Sundays from 2 pm to 4.30 pm. It is closed on Christmas Day. There is a small

admission fee for adults; children enter free. The Missionary Museum is open at the same times from Monday to Friday, but is closed on Saturdays, Sundays and all public holidays. Admission is free for both adults and children.
More information: Call the Kaffrarian Museum, PO Box 1434, King William's Town 5600; tel (0433) 24506. (Same address and telephone number for Missionary Museum.)

Last of the great coastal fishing spots

Mazeppa Bay, situated at the southern end of the Wild Coast, is about as unspoiled a seaside resort as you are likely to find on the southern African coastline

Where to stay

The only hotel here is the *Mazeppa Bay Hotel*, Private Bag 3014, Butterworth; tel (0474) 3278. It offers comfortable accommodation in a complex consisting of double rooms, family rooms and thatched rondavels. There is also a camp site, without facilities, owned by the Transkei Nature Conservation Division of the Department of Agriculture and Forestry. Permits to use the camp site must be obtained (see address in other panel).

To CLAIM THAT ONE PART of the 250-km Wild Coast is more beautiful than another is like trying to describe the difference between a place which is stunning and another one which is breathtaking. People who take the risk of doing so, however, pinpoint one particular destination on the coast of the Transkei – Mazeppa Bay.

Named after a trading vessel (reputedly a gunrunner) which frequently called in here during the 1830s, Mazeppa Bay is most famous for its superb fishing. It was, in fact, fishermen who built many of the cottages and shacks which now pepper the area. So prolific are the fish here that there's a saying: 'If you don't catch a fish at Mazeppa, you'll never catch one.'

Favourite angling spots include The Island, Shark Point and Boiling Pot. Qora Mouth, slightly to the north of Mazeppa, is also a popular fishing venue, particularly in the winter months when the kabeljou escape the cold waters of the Cape.

During the summer months, the catches include big reef fish, such as the musselcracker, and during autumn the annual sardine runs attract large numbers of game fish. Galjoen is a perennial, while you also find barracuda, bronze bream, blacktail, kob, yellowtail, shad, garrick, mackerel and queenfish. In the waters of the Qora River you can also catch leervis and bonito.

The fish for which Mazeppa is famous, or rather, infamous, is the shark. Hammerheads, dusky greys and ragged-tooths have all been caught here. The biggest, weighing 791 kg, was a Great White. Since then, however, the Great White has been declared an endangered species and hunting it is a punishable offence.

Mazeppa has some of the finest beaches on the Transkei coastline. The most popular is First Beach, situated close to the hotel. From here you reach Mazeppa's renowned island by taking a breathtaking walk across a 100 m-high suspension bridge.

The other two main beaches, Shelly Beach and Second Beach, lie on the south side of the lagoon and are ideal for walks and shell collecting. Dense groves of wild date palms fringe these beautiful beaches and have been an invaluable resource for the locals. The sap of the date is tapped to make a strong alcoholic drink, while the fruit is tasty and nutritious; the shredded fronds are used to make mats and the strong midribs are used for brooms.

Besides fishing, another activity which draws people to Mazeppa in particular, and to the Wild Coast in general, is hiking. The Wild Coast Hiking Trail runs the full length of the Transkei coast and can be walked in about two weeks. Otherwise, it can be taken in sections – Umtamvuna to Msikaba, Msikaba to Agate Terrace, Silaka to Coffee Bay,

Access to The Island – one of Mazeppa Bay's best angling venues – is by means of a suspension bridge.

Coffee Bay to Mbashe and Nqabara to Kei River. The last of these is a six-day hike, in the middle of which is Mazeppa.

Marked with white footprints, the Wild Coast Hiking Trail has a number of hikers' huts equipped with bunks, toilets, cooking pots and running water. Many estuaries must be crossed during the course of the trail and hikers should be extremely careful when doing so. (If a crossing on the trail seems hazardous, explore upstream to find a safer one.) There is a rewarding hike from Mazeppa to nearby Manubi Forest, which consists of 1 360 ha of indigenous trees and shrubs, and, 6 km north, to Qora Mouth, where a rowing boat is available to ferry you across the river.

(Above) Sunrise at Mazeppa Bay.
(Left) A pair of goats adds a distinctly rural touch to this seaside scene .

Mazeppa Bay at a glance (map page 94)

How to get there: Take the N2 north from Butterworth. About 200 m after crossing the Gcuwa River, on the outskirts of town, turn right to Centane/Kentani. Drive through Tutura and at Centane take the road to Mazeppa and Nxaxo Mouth. Cross the Kobonqaba River and descend Cat's Pass – from where you can see the valley of the Qora River. After travelling 48 km from Centane, you'll reach Mazeppa. Motorists are warned that many of the Transkei roads off the N2 are in dubious condition. Enquire locally about the condition of roads, particularly those leading to the coast. As an additional precaution, carry an extra spare tyre or tyre repair kit.
Weather: Mild and moderately humid, with rain in summer. Winters tend to be dry.
What to do: Surfing, hiking and – of course – fishing. Angling is particularly good at Shark Point and Boiling Pot, and 6 km to the north at Qora Mouth.

Swimming is good, with the water usually pleasant and

clear. Mazeppa is excellent for beachcombing, the coast still being littered with pieces from shipwrecks. Few wrecks can still be seen from the coast, and the *Jacaranda*, a light coaster wrecked off the mouth of the Kobonqaba River in 1971, is the only one that remains virtually intact. Most sandy beaches will reveal cowries, cones and murex shells. The rock pools offer a rich world of marine life.
Special precautions: Never swim in murky or muddy water around the river mouths after floods – these are favourite conditions for sharks.
More information: The Transkei Nature Conservation Division, Department of Agriculture and Forestry, Private Bag X5002, Umtata; tel (0471) 24322 or 312711/2. The Department of Industry, Commerce and Tourism, Private Bag X5029, Umtata; tel (0471) 26685. Wild Coast Holiday Hotels Central Booking Office, Private Bag X5028, Umtata; tel (0471) 25344/5/6.

A tranquil, rugged bay steeped in history

The slow tempo of past centuries pervades Coffee Bay, a sleepy little Transkei coastal resort situated 100 km from Umtata

Where to stay

The *Ocean View Hotel* at Coffee Bay has recently been refurbished by the Transkei Development Corporation, bringing it into line with what is required of a good family hotel. Reservations can be made at the Central Booking Office in Umtata on (0471) 25344/5/6 or by writing to the hotel at PO Box 189, Lusikisiki, Transkei; tel (0475) 441282.

The *Hole in the Wall Hotel and Holiday Village* has 22 comfortable en suite rooms and a range of family chalets in the form of thatched cottages. It has a swimming pool and an outdoor 10-pin bowling alley. For bookings, contact their Durban office at (031) 258263 or Umtata (0471) 370252 or 25344/5/6. Alternatively, write to: Hole in the Wall Hotel and Holiday Village, PO Box 17179, Congella 4013, or Private Bag X558, Mqanduli, Transkei.

COFFEE BAY IS REPUTED to have been named as a result of a cargo ship carrying coffee beans being wrecked at the mouth of the lagoon in the middle of the 19th century. According to local lore, the beans were washed up on the shore, took root, and subsequently grew into coffee trees – but there is no sign of them today. The only coffee you're likely to find is that served by the waiters at the local hotel.

One of the big advantages that Coffee Bay has over many of the other small coastal resorts in the Transkei is that it is accessible by tarred road from the N2 – and quite a good one at that. It's a place for holiday-makers who want a quiet, out-of-the-way place to put up their feet. Among its many attractions are excellent fishing and spectacular walks through coastal bush that is inhabited by a plethora of bird life.

One of the best vantage points of the area is Maphuzi Point ('the Place of Pumpkins'), which can be reached by strolling up a badly rutted track behind the Ocean View Hotel. Initially it's a steep walk, and in one place there is a huge donga across the road. But once you're there, the view is unsurpassed anywhere else in the Transkei – and that takes some doing! A few kilometres up the coast lies Mtata River Mouth. A gravel road leads there, descending down a valley and over a newly constructed bridge.

One of Coffee Bay's main virtues is that it is an excellent base from which to explore other nearby parts. It's less than an hour's drive from Umtata, and only 15 minutes from that marvellous geological freak – Hole in the Wall.

To visit Hole in the Wall, drive right past the Hole in the Wall Hotel and the neat holiday shacks at the top of the hill. Below you, like a weathered old battleship, is the rocky island that gives the place its name. If it's 'working' – with the sea crashing through the hole in the middle – it is an experience not to be forgotten. *EseKhaleni* ('the Place of the Sound') is what the locals call it, and you hear why it's called this if you follow any one of a series of paths that wind down through the grass and forest to the shore.

The Mpako River joins the sea to the south, and it is generally fairly safe to bathe there at low tide. The pathway meanders through a tropical, bird-filled forest – the only other people you're likely to meet are anglers trying their luck.

Much as you may want to, don't be tempted to climb Hole in the Wall. One chap did, and was stuck on top for four days until a rescue team arrived from Umtata to bring him down. You can also

Hole in the Wall – a rocky island just off the beach through which the endless crashing of the surf has carved a tunnel.

Built on the banks of the Mtata River, the little resort of Coffee Bay is a perfect place for 'getting away from it all'.

walk to Hole in the Wall from the Hole in the Wall Hotel, doing so along the seashore and up over a series of hillocks. The lunches at this hotel are usually excellent – in fact, good food is one of the strong points of Transkei hotels and holiday resorts, particularly at the weekend when huge seafood buffets are laid on.

The Coffee Bay area has quite a bit of historic interest. Dick King rode this way (there is a memorial to the ride just outside the village of Mancam),

Cecil Rhodes passed by when he was Cape Prime Minister, and the 27th Regiment of Foot camped here on their way to fight the Battle of Congella in Port Natal before it became Durban. The regiment later became the famous 24th South Wales Borderers who were massacred at the Battle of Isandhlwana in 1879 during the Anglo-Zulu War. In fact, in the middle of the last century, the whole area seethed with military action as Pondo and Tembo leaders fought British domination.

Coffee Bay at a glance (map page 94)

How to get there: From Umtata, take the N2 south. At Viedgesville, 20 km away, turn left off the N2; 14 km later you will enter the picturesque village of Mqanduli, where the locals have a small market. Take the signposted road to Coffee Bay. You will pass the hamlet of Ngqungu and Mancam. The Dick King memorial is near here. Coffee Bay is some 70 km from Viedgesville. The Hole in the Wall turn-off is 16 km from Coffee Bay, signposted, at the Ncwanguba trading store.

The road to Maphuzi Hill and the golf course is some 2 km from the Ocean View Hotel, turning sharp right, and up a rutted track. Once on top of the hill, you will see a track that meanders past the golf course to the cliff edge.

To get to Mtata River Mouth, turn right 3,5 km from the Ocean View Hotel on a gravel road that crosses the Mtata River bridge. This road joins the Mtata River Mouth road at

a distance of some 14 km. Turn right and drive for another 14 km to the river mouth.

Weather: Mild and moderately humid with rain in summer. The winters are dry.

What to do: Hiking, birdwatching, fishing and swimming.

Special attractions: At Coffee Bay, a walk, or a drive, to Maphuzi Point for perhaps the most spectacular view in the Transkei. Also, a drive or a walk to Hole in the Wall. The walk is along the beachfront from the hotel, up over a series of hillocks to the magnificent vista of the rock.

More information: Contact the Wild Coast Hotels Central Booking Office at Private Bag X5029, Umtata, Transkei; tel (0471) 25344/5/6. For permission to camp on the Mtata River banks, contact the Transkei Nature Conservation Division, Private Bag X5002, Umtata, Transkei; tel (0471) 24322 or 312711/2.

A rocky graveyard of fortune-hunters' dreams

At Port Grosvenor, situated towards the northern end of the Wild Coast, the might of the sea has foiled all of man's attempts to raise a lost treasure

THE TRANSKEI HAS SOME of the most beautiful expanses of unspoilt beach in southern Africa, but it also has some very rocky and treacherous stretches of coastline which have contributed to the sinking of scores of vessels down through the centuries.

One of the most famous of these shipwrecks is the *Grosvenor*, which sank at Lambasi Bay during the stormy night of 4 August 1782. Port Grosvenor was named after the wrecked ship and, as the name would suggest, this little bay – into which the Lambasi River flows – was originally intended to be a port. However, because the Pondo chief at the time (1885) had given trading rights to two rival traders, neither of whom would allow the other to trade, the port was never used. Today, Port Grosvenor is a sparsely populated strip of coastline with no public facilities. But the saga of that fateful night more than two centuries ago continues to attract curious visitors to this lonely spot.

When the *Grosvenor* ran aground, only 14 of the people on board the ship drowned, but of the 138 survivors, only six finally reached the distant Algoa Bay six months later. A government search party found 12 more survivors, but the fate of the rest remains a mystery to this day. Probably they died of starvation or disease, or were killed by tribesmen.

It was only a century after the wreck of this English ship that feverish speculation arose regarding the *Grosvenor*'s cargo. The first report that she had been carrying fabulous treasure appeared in the 'Natal Mercantile Advertiser' of 1880. The *Grosvenor*'s log and papers were lost, but the ship's bills of lading showed that she carried a cargo of bullion, and from somewhere came the theory that she was also carrying the Peacock Throne of Persia, the prized possession of Shah Jehan, the warrior king who built the fabulous Taj Mahal in India.

Things really took off in 1882, when about 150 gold and silver coins were found washed up on the beach at Lambasi Bay. This discovery marked the start of a number of fortune hunts which collectively spent a small fortune on a fascinating series of salvage schemes. None of these costly attempts produced more than a few bits and pieces and eight ships' cannons!

One attempt, in 1907, ended in tragedy when a diver drowned after his air hose was severed by a sharp rock. In 1921, an ingenious Johannesburg mining engineer tried to tunnel under the sea bed by solidifying the surrounding sand with liquid cement. At one stage a black mamba made the tunnel its home and delayed work for days. Ultimately, the scheme failed, and the remains of this ill-fated attempt can still be seen today.

In 1938 another salvage attempt was made – this time the plan was to build a breakwater around the site of the wreck. However, as fast as the breakwater was built, the sea smashed it to pieces. The next fortune-hunter to come along decided that the best method was to lift the wreck piece by piece by means of a crane. However, when a suitable crane

(Bottom left) The undersea tunnel built by a Johannesburg mining engineer in his attempt to find the Grosvenor's *fabled treasure.*
(Bottom right) An abandoned rusted piece of equipment stands as mute testimony to one of the failed salvage attempts.

The lonely stretch of Transkeian coastline on which an English vessel, the Grosvenor, *sank more than 200 years ago.*

was finally delivered at Durban Docks, there was not enough money to pay for it. After attempts at buying another crane failed, the plan collapsed.

The final attempt came in 1952 when some salvagers, unsure at this stage exactly where the wreck lay, tried to blast the sand and rubble away from the probable site. However, bad weather, treacherous currents and sharp rocks made the operation so risky that it, too, was eventually abandoned.

For the past 30 years or so, the wreck site has remained undisturbed by any further salvage attempts. Today, as you walk along this lonely stretch of shore, the rusting and eroding remains of the various salvage attempts are the only reminder of an old conviction that there's treasure to be found 'below them waves'.

Where to stay

The nearest accommodation is to the south of Port Grosvenor at the *Embotyi River Bungalows*, PO Box 189, Lusikisiki; tel (0475) 441282, which offers full board. Further south, there is accommodation at Port St Johns. Overlooking the bay and golf course at Port St Johns is the *Protea Cape Hermes Hotel*, PO Box 10, Port St Johns; tel (0475) 441234. There is also the *Second Beach Holiday Resort*, PO Box 18, Port St Johns; tel (0475) 441245, which is situated on the edge of a lagoon, and the *Coastal Needles Hotel*, PO Box 9, Port St Johns; tel (0475) 441031.

Some 6 km south of Port St Johns is the upmarket *Umngazi River Bungalows*, PO Box 75, Port St Johns; tel (04752) 747. Bookings for all the resorts may also be made by contacting Central Reservations, PO Box 103, Umtata; tel (0471) 25344/5/6.

Port Grosvenor at a glance (map page 94)

How to get there: A four-wheel-drive vehicle is a virtual must for the journey to Port Grosvenor. If you want to risk it in an ordinary car, be sure to enquire beforehand at the Lusikisiki garage, police station or magistrate's court as to whether the road is safe to travel on. Recent rains can make it impassable to an ordinary vehicle.

At the entrance to Lusikisiki, on the road from Port St Johns, look for a faded green sign that points to the Magwa Tea Company, on your right. Ignore all roads turning left, and pass signs to the Magwa Falls (if you have the time on the way back, a 5 km diversion brings you to these spectacular falls). Watch for a fork at 7 km and bear right. There is a badly repaired, almost illegible signpost with Lusikisiki on it and some letters that read: 'De..orit'. The track to Port Grosvenor is precisely 25 km from this signpost. Set your odometer here and proceed. You will pass the village of Ndindini, go through a small but beautiful pass, and then past the Ntlavukazi general store. Keep going. At around 25 km, keep an eye open on the right, where you will find the begin-

ning of a roughish track through the grass. Take this route and, as you do so, you'll notice that you are approaching the sea. If the road is muddy, some smart negotiation is necessary. Try to stay off the verges as the grass hides rocks. This track will take you the 7 km down to the sea.

Weather: Mild and moderately humid in summer with rain; dry winters.

What to do: Walk along the coast with nothing but the crashing sea and calls of the seabirds to disturb the silence.

Special attractions:The beauty and solitude of the wild, unspoilt coastline and the possibility (albeit rather a remote one!) of finding something valuable washed up on the shoreline.

More information: Contact the Department of Agriculture and Forestry, Private Bag X5002, Umtata; tel (0471) 312711/2, or visit them at the Botha Sigcau Building in central Umtata. Alternatively, contact the Transkei Development Corporation, Private Bag X5028, Umtata; tel (0471) 25344/5/6.

Pretty farms and smallholdings cover the rolling hills that surround the village of Rhodes.

Take the country's highest road to the hamlet of Rhodes

From the elevated heights of Naudésnek, travellers can enjoy spectacular views of the craggy peaks of the southern Drakensberg range

YOU'RE LITERALLY ON TOP OF THE WORLD when you've reached the dizzy summit of Naudésnek in the southern Drakensberg. This 100-km stretch of gravel road between the small villages of Maclear and Rhodes is the highest road in South Africa, reaching 2 920 m where it peaks. It's a delightful journey, especially if you undertake it from the east where its great scenic beauty finally culminates in the unique charm of Rhodes. You can also approach it from the west with Barkly East as your starting point and Maclear your destination.

The winding route of South Africa's highest stretch of road commands spectacular views along the way.

The pass was named after the brothers Stefanus and Gabriel Naudé, cattle farmers who, around 1896, let their horses instinctively pick out a route across the mountains. With picks and shovels and a horse-drawn cart, the intrepid brothers followed, hoping to find an access route to the cattle markets in the valley beyond.

The present road – completed in 1911 – owes much to the resourceful Naudé brothers and their fine horses, but its purpose was somewhat different from that of their road. It was intended as a military highway linking Maclear with Lundeans Nek and built to facilitate the pursuit of cattle rustlers and the movement of troops around Lesotho's southern border.

Today it is a scenic road that offers almost aerial views of the hills and valleys. It is, however, treacherous in winter, sometimes being closed by snowfalls, and the gravel surface requiring extremely cautious driving in wet conditions.

When you set out eastwards from Maclear, the gravel road leads up the beautiful green valley of the Pot River. Indeed, the Pot River Pass is a continuation of Naudésnek, a mostly uphill drive that will make the ascent of the nek seem much longer and the descent (just 19 km from the summit) much steeper. At the foot of the pass there is a pleasant picnic site near a memorial to the Naudés; Rhodes is just 12 km from here.

The village of Rhodes, situated on the banks of the willow-fringed Bell River, was established in 1893 as a church centre on the farm *Tintern*, and originally named Rossville after the local Dutch Reformed minister, David Ross. The Reverend Ross devoted his entire life to serving this region, but such is the seductive power of fame that, when Cecil Rhodes sent the village a gift of stone pine trees, the locals promptly renamed the town after him. These stone pines still spread their shade over the town's main street, which otherwise consists of

little more than a few quaint corrugated iron cottages and several earth-walled shacks.

The village houses few permanent families now, but remains popular with visiting artists, hikers and fly-fishermen and, of course, the ski-enthusiasts who flock here when the snow on the slopes of nearby 3 001 m-high Ben Macdhui is metres deep. These seasonal visitors evoke a time when Rhodes was a popular horse-racing venue, and bookies from Durban, wagonloads of liquor from East London, visiting wool buyers and local cowboys converged on – and sometimes came to blows in – the bar of the Horseshoe Hotel. Dice, billiards, card games and fist fights provided the entertainment, punctuated by frequent toasts to Wydeman, the strongest of the oxen which drew the liquor wagons and whose polished horns were mounted here when he finally laid down his load.

To present-day visitors, Rhodes offers serenity, crisp mountain air and a peaceful countryside. It's a mandatory stop – whether you've come to try out the ski slopes or merely to look for links with the past, whether you're planning to stay or just to catch your breath after the wild beauty of Naudésnek.

Naudésnek and Rhodes at a glance (map page 94)

How to get there: From Maclear, off the R56, the R396 branches westwards to Rhodes via Naudésnek. To reach Maclear, from the N1, take the R58 eastwards from Colesberg to Aliwal North and Elliot. The road joins the R56 at Elliot. Follow it eastwards to Maclear.
Weather: Rhodes is noted for its cold, bracing climate.
What to do: Cross the southern Drakensberg at Naudésnek and plan to stay overnight in Rhodes.
More information: Contact the Information Office, Maclear Municipality, PO Box 1, Maclear 5480; tel (045322) 25; or The Municipality, Private Bag X15, Barkley East 5580; tel (04542) 73/123.

Where to stay

The *Rhodes Hotel*, formerly the Horseshoe Hotel, is now more than 100 years old and Wydeman's horns still hang in the bar. Annexed to the hotel, are four houses for rent. A municipal camping site offers very basic facilities for adventurers with vehicles powerful enough to tow a caravan over the Drakensberg. For more information on any of these, write to Rhodes Hotel, PO Box 21, Rhodes 5582; tel (04542) ask for 21.

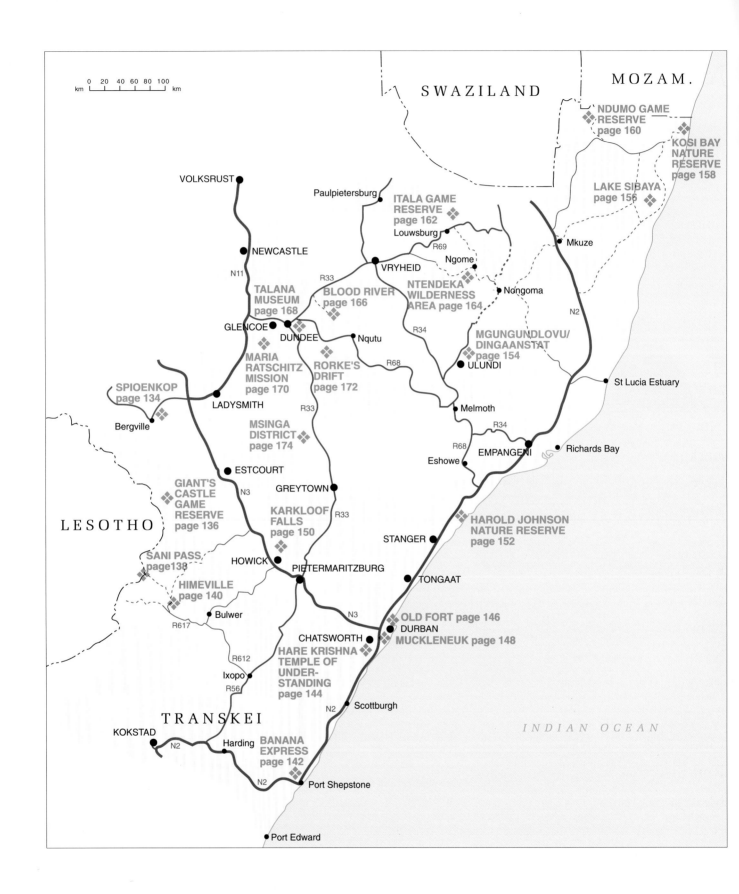

SWAZILAND

MOZAM.

NDUMO GAME
RESERVE
page 160

KOSI BAY
NATURE
RESERVE
page 158

LAKE SIBAYA
page 156

VOLKSRUST

Paulpietersburg

ITALA GAME
RESERVE
page 162

Louwsburg

R69

Mkuze

NEWCASTLE

N11

VRYHEID

Ngome

Nongoma

N2

TALANA
MUSEUM
page 168

R33

BLOOD RIVER
page 166

NTENDEKA
WILDERNESS
AREA page 164

GLENCOE

DUNDEE

Nqutu

R34

MGUNGUNDLOVU/
DINGAANSTAT
page 154

MARIA
RATSCHITZ
MISSION
page 170

RORKE'S
DRIFT
page 172

R68

ULUNDI

St Lucia Estuary

SPIOENKOP
page 134

LADYSMITH

R33

Melmoth

R34

Bergville

MSINGA
DISTRICT
page 174

R68

EMPANGENI

Richards Bay

Eshowe

ESTCOURT

GIANT'S
CASTLE
GAME
RESERVE
page 136

N3

GREYTOWN

KARKLOOF
FALLS
page 150

R33

LESOTHO

HAROLD JOHNSON
NATURE RESERVE
page 152

STANGER

SANI PASS
page 138

HOWICK

PIETERMARITZBURG

Tongaat

HIMEVILLE
page 140

Bulwer

R617

N3

OLD FORT page 146

DURBAN

MUCKLENEUK page 148

CHATSWORTH

R612

HARE KRISHNA
TEMPLE OF
UNDER-
STANDING
page 144

Ixopo

R56

Scottburgh

N2

TRANSKEI

INDIAN OCEAN

KOKSTAD

N2

Harding

BANANA
EXPRESS
page 142

N2

Port Shepstone

Port Edward

NATAL

A hilltop drenched in the blood of an epic battle

A tranquil sense of solitude greets the visitor to Spioenkop, 30 km south of Ladysmith, the site of one of the most fearsome events of the Anglo-Boer War

RECALLING THE BATTLE OF SPIOENKOP, the Boer commando, Denys Reitz, wrote, 'There cannot have been many battlefields where there was such an accumulation of horrors within so small a compass.' Almost a century later, it is hard to imagine that it was on this quiet, sunlit hill that Boer and Brit fought one another in the bloodiest battle of the Anglo-Boer War.

From the top of the battlefield, or viewing it from the tranquillity of the nearby dam and game park, it is hard to imagine the hideousness of that night and day almost a century ago. Lest we forget, however, the summit is a memorial comprising numerous monuments and graves, the most poignant being a long, low curved trench under which lie an estimated 600 British soldiers who were buried where they fell in the trench – a mass grave they in effect dug for themselves.

At the turn of the century the Boers had occupied much of Natal and were ranged along the Tugela in preparation for an onslaught into the Natal heartland. They whipped the British on several fronts, the most humiliating British defeat being the Battle of Colenso where the toll of over a thousand British casualties to only eight Boers was a severe blow to British national pride.

In January 1900, the commander of the British forces, General Sir Redvers Buller (who had done little to distinguish himself since being sent to rout the invading Boers) crossed the Tugela and, together with General Sir Charles Warren, planned a two-pronged attack to outflank the Boers and advance on Ladysmith – which, although held by the British, was besieged by the Boers. Boer forces in the area numbered only five or six hundred men, so the armies had to advance without delay if they were to succeed. However, Warren procrastinated for several days, during which time the Boers reinforced their numbers.

Buller eventually lost patience and gave Warren an ultimatum – move on Ladysmith or retreat across the Tugela. Warren's decision was to take and hold Spioenkop, the commanding hill which seemed to be the key to relieving Ladysmith. On the night of 23 January 1900 he sent about 1 700 men to storm Spioenkop under cover of darkness. The men began the long climb up the southwestern ridge of Spioenkop in a steady drizzle. When they reached an open slope below the summit five hours later, they were ordered to fix their bayonets. Just metres away in the darkness a slumbering Boer party of men were woken to the chilling clatter of hundreds of bayonets fixing into their sockets. Firing wildly, all but one of the Boers escaped into the darkness.

At 2 am both Boer and British camps 400 m below heard the troops cheer as they crested the summit. But the British triumph was misplaced. One advantage the Boers had was their familiarity with the area's topography and terrain. Warren had ordered the attack on Spioenkop without any prior reconnaissance – and did not realise that, viewed from the north, Spioenkop was not the bastion it appeared to be from the south. The Boers moved seven pieces of artillery onto the surrounding hills and prepared for battle.

On the summit of Spioenkop the British began to dig a trench but soon struck rock below the surface and could manage only a shallow ditch less than half a metre deep. At dawn a thick mist shrouded the summit and when it began to lift at around 7 am, the full horror of their situation became clear – the summit was totally exposed to the surrounding hills.

An hour later, when the mist finally lifted, Boer forces engaged the British in ferocious hand-to-hand battle. This was followed in the afternoon by a

The summit of Spioenkop, on which British soldiers died in their hundreds under a relentless barrage of Boer shells.

Crosses of various shapes and sizes mark the graves of the English troops who met their end at the Battle of Spioenkop.

relentless shelling of British reinforcements arriving on the scene. Boer shells rained down with deadly accuracy, sometimes at a rate of seven a minute, turning the summit into a hell of splintering rock, flying metal and shattered bodies. Winston Churchill, as a war correspondent witnessing the battle, wrote: 'Many of the wounds were of a horrible nature. The splinters and fragments of the shells had torn and mutilated in the most ghastly manner.'

The British finally succeeded in breaching the Boer lines by evening, and to secure the hill they had only to bring in more reinforcements. However, a combination of official incompetence and poor communication produced an order for a British withdrawal from the summit. Ironically, the Boers simultaneously retreated down their side of the hill, believing they had lost the battle.

By the following morning the British had withdrawn to the banks of the Tugela. When several Boers cautiously climbed the northern slope of Spioenkop looking for wounded comrades, they found to their utter amazement that, apart from those killed or wounded, the summit was deserted. The British had gone.

Today visitors can explore the battlefield and follow the events with the aid of a self-guided trail map available from the Natal Parks Board office or from the attendant at the battlefield. Following the ridge to the summit is a tough walk of about three hours, but there is an easier way via a paved road that winds all the way to the top.

The historical weight of the Anglo-Boer War almost crushes any other claims from the past, yet it was from the crest of this hill that the Voortrekkers were believed to have had their first panoramic sighting of Natal. The Spioenkop Dam was built in the 1960s, swallowing several kilometres of the Tugela and some historical sites such as Trichardt's Drift, where Buller's troops had crossed prior to the fateful battle. The area falls under the aegis of the Natal Parks Board and, apart from the Spioenkop Dam, remains much the same as it was at the turn of the century.

The dam is ideal for watersports and there are numerous slipways for powerboats, although there are no boats for hire. Waterskiing, canoeing and sailing are popular activities, as is angling, and fishermen are welcome to try to land carp, bass, bluegill and tilapia.

Game is plentiful, and you can arrange walks or tours through the park to view the wildlife, which includes the white rhino.

Where to stay

The Spioenkop Reserve has fully equipped chalets and camp sites with water and electricity. There is also the rustic *Ntenjwa Bush Camp*, 14 km from the main camp along the dam, which can accommodate eight people only. Bring your own swimming towels, food, drink and braaiwood. To book accommodation, contact the Natal Parks Board Central Booking Office in Pietermaritzburg (see other panel for address).

Spioenkop at a glance (map page 132)

How to get there: Spioenkop Resort: From Johannesburg, take the N3 towards Durban. After the Tugela toll post take the first turn-off, signposted to Ladysmith and Bergville. Turn left, and after about 4 km turn right onto the Winterton road. The entrance to the resort is about 21 km down the road. Spioenkop Battlefield: Directions as above until the turn-off from the N3 – turn right, cross over the toll road, and carry on exactly 3 km. Turn left onto a dirt road (marked 'Spioenkop Battlesite') and proceed about 10 km. Drive up the paved road and dirt track to the battlefield parking site. There is a nominal charge per head.

Weather: Hot in summer, mild to cold in winter.
What to do: Sailing, waterskiing, fishing, swimming.
The main camp at the Spioenkop Resort has tennis and volleyball courts (bring your own racquets and balls) and a large swimming pool.
Special attractions: The Spioenkop battlefield area and the museum. Conducted tours of the battlefield can be organised through the Curator, Siege Museum, Ladysmith; tel (0361) 32231.
More information: Natal Parks Board, PO Box 1750, Pietermaritzburg 3200; tel (0331) 471981

Rugged wilderness in the 'dragon mountains'

Majestic mountains, unspoilt terrain, rare wildlife and primitive art are all to be found at Giant's Castle Game Reserve, only three hours and a world away from two major cities

GIANT'S CASTLE GAME RESERVE is set in one of the most breathtaking parts of the dramatic Drakensberg range – on a grassy plateau at the base of a 3 000 m-high, 25 km-long basalt wall which looms up behind the hutted camp.

The Zulu name for the Drakensberg is *Quathlamba*, roughly translated as 'barrier of upward-pointing spears', a particularly appropriate name for the mighty sequence of angular, unforgiving peaks. From the reserve, many of the Drakensberg's famous features can be seen: Cathkin Peak, Champagne Castle and the distinctive Thumb. Giant's Castle itself is one of the Drakensberg's most impressive landmarks, its forbidding mass having provoked superstition and legend. Known as *iNtabayikonjwa*, according to the local lore, it is not advisable to point directly at the mountain, which apparently retaliates by producing bad weather – a reference, perhaps, to the sudden violent thunderstorms the Berg is renowned for.

Nearly 35 000 ha in extent, Giant's Castle was originally proclaimed a reserve in 1903. The reason for its establishment was to protect the eland, of which only 200 had survived the ruthless decimation by white hunters. Today, South Africa's rarest antelope species thrives here, and the once endangered eland now number about 700 within the reserve, with about 1 100 roaming elsewhere in the Drakensberg.

The region also boasts mountain reedbuck, oribi, grey rhebuck, blesbok, bushbuck, grey duiker, red hartebeest, baboon, jackal, porcupine and mongoose as well as bats, otters, hares, mice, rats, shrews and moles – not to mention a variety of rep-

tiles from chameleons to snakes. Cats such as serval, caracal, African wildcat and, it is speculated, leopard also live deep in the mountains, but are seldom seen.

For bird enthusiasts, Giant's Castle is a treat, with over 140 species having been recorded. These include stork, ibis, duck, secretary bird, black eagle, buzzard, falcon, Cape vulture, owl, kite, kingfisher, hoopoe, swift, and crane. On the grasslands, look out for the long-tailed widow bird whose sweeping tail feathers were prized by Zulu warriors of a particular rank as a part of their headdress.

Ornithologically, however, the biggest drawcard of this reserve is the threatened bearded vulture or lammergeyer. Lammergeyers tend to build their nests high up on inaccessible ledges and crags, so a special hide has been constructed to give visitors a close-up, uninterrupted view of these huge birds feeding on bones and meat that have been specially provided. This practice of providing bones arose to prevent vultures from feeding on poisoned sheep carcasses that farmers bait to kill jackals. (Note that prior booking of the hide is necessary.)

Lucky visitors will witness a habit peculiar to the lammergeyer. As a result of its particularly weak beak, the vulture drops bones from a height on to the rocks below so that they shatter and it can feast on the marrow.

The Boesmans and Little Tugela rivers originate in the Giant's Castle Game Reserve, so the whole region is well-watered and yields a healthy variety of vegetation, from bright patches of lichen which spatter the boulders with colour to patches of forest in kloofs and protected valleys. But the vast majority of the region is covered with grassland which, paradoxically, is dependent on fire to maintain its best condition. Fire, considered a natural and even necessary occurrence here, is often started by lightning, or in the event of rock falls, friction from the rocks that causes sparks which ignite the dry grass. Without fire, the condition of the grass and other vegetation deteriorates, producing scrub and small woody plants. In this way, fire stimulates the growth of many species, especially wildflowers.

According to experts, the Bushmen living in the area used to burn the grasslands to stimulate new growth and attract game to the area, and subsequently both black and white farmers used the same technique to provide their livestock with succulent winter grazing.

Experiments are conducted continually to determine the most effective burning pattern, and areas deliberately protected from fire are also set aside so that the results can be studied.

There are over 800 species of flowering plants in the reserve, including ericas, orchids, lilies, irises, proteas and bottlebrush, all best viewed in the spring when they are at their most flamboyant.

The Giant's Castle area is renowned for having the richest collection of Bushman paintings in South Africa. Thousands are found at more than 50 different sites – caves, overhangs and rock shelters – providing pictorial evidence of their life style, rituals and spiritual beliefs, as well as of the animals that were once endemic to the region.

The fact that so many paintings exist, coupled with the vastness of the landscape, points to the likelihood that still more are yet to be found. Of

The Injasuti Hutted Camp nestles in the shadow of Cathkin Peak (left) and Monk's Cowl and Champagne Castle (right).

Dawn in Giant's Castle Game Reserve – and the world awakes to an explosion of colour.

those that have been discovered, the only caves open to the public are Main Cave and Battle Cave.

There is also an excavated hearth, the strata clearly indicative of the passing ages, and a showcase containing artefacts such as tools, weapons and clothing. An audio commentary is available on Bushman history and customs, as well as descriptions of the surrounding paintings and interpretive displays. Battle Cave, situated some way away near Injasuti, has, as its name implies, paintings depicting battles between rival Bushman groups.

Within the reserve, cars are permitted only on the access roads to the camps, so moving around is limited to either walking or horse-riding – both exhilarating options, given the beauty and grandeur of the surroundings. There are many walks and trails to choose from, covering a wide area and most habitats. Day-trippers can pack their sandwiches and head for the hills, ever mindful not to stray from the footpaths and that fires should be lit only

at authorised sites. In summer you can cool off in the beautiful mountain pools and streams. After heavy rains, be careful of whirlpools and loose boulders. Thunderstorms develop with frightening suddenness in the mountains, and both hikers and riders should be prepared for them.

For the fit and adventurous who relish the challenge of longer trails, there are three mountain huts available, but bookings and arrangements should be made well in advance.

For casual horse-rides, no riding experience is necessary and these set out from Hillside every morning in the company of a guide. More adventurous riders can arrange two- to four-day pony trails covering the remote wilderness in the northern part of the reserve. All your requirements (excluding food) are taken care of, and the nights are spent in a series of caves. Only experienced riders should go on these trails, which have a minimum age limit of 12 years.

Where to stay

Giant's Castle Camp has a lodge, four self-contained cottages and various bungalows with bathrooms. There is a fully equipped communal cooking area with cooks available to prepare the food you bring. *Hillside* is situated about 32 km from the main camp and is a caravan and camping site with hot and cold ablution facilities. There is also an eight-bed, fully equipped hut where visitors must provide their own linen. There are more self-contained bungalows and a small camping site at *Injasuti*, in the northern section of Giant's Castle Game Reserve. Accommodation is also available in two caves, each sleeping eight people. (See other panel for addresses.)

Giant's Castle Game Reserve at a glance (map page 132)

How to get there: From Johannesburg or Durban, take the N3 to either Estcourt or Mooi River; from these towns the way to the reserve is clearly signposted.
Weather: Warm to hot in summer with rain, although the nights can be cool. Winters are crisp and dry and can be extremely cold, with frost and snow.
What to do: Hiking, bird- and game-spotting, swimming, riding and angling (the Injasuti River provides good rainbow-trout fishing, but anglers will need a licence). Giant's Castle is excellent climbing country for experienced mountaineers.

Special attractions: The Bushman galleries, the vulture hide.
More information: Write to The Reservations Officer, Natal Parks Board, PO Box 1750, Pietermaritzburg 3200; tel (0331) 471981 or The Officer-in-Charge, Giant's Castle Camp, Private Bag X7055, Estcourt 3310; tel (0363) 24718.

For information on Hillside, write to The Officer-in-Charge, Hillside Camp Site, PO Box 288, Estcourt 3310; tel (0363) 24435. For information on Injasuti, write to The Camp Superintendent, Injasuti Camp, Private Bag X7010, Estcourt 3310; tel 0020 and ask for Loskop 1311.

Spectacular gateway to the 'Mile-High Kingdom'

The Sani Pass, linking Natal with Lesotho, ranks as one of the most rugged and exciting drives in southern Africa

THERE ARE FEW mountain passes as famous in name or spectacle as the Sani. South Africa's own Khyber Pass, the Sani epitomises the ruggedness and beauty of the terrain along the border with Lesotho. It is one of the highest passes in the world – driving over it is an experience as rarified as the air you breathe when you finally reach the summit.

One of the traditional passes from Natal into the 'Mile-High Kingdom' of Lesotho, the Sani makes up part of the road linking Himeville to the remote settlement of Mokhotlong in north-east Lesotho. It cuts through the Natal Drakensberg Park, which, at 262 000 ha, is the largest single proclaimed conservation area in Natal.

Though the entire road is about 93 km long, the pass itself stretches only about 25 km, beginning just past the Sani Pass Hotel and ending at the Lesotho border. Over this short distance, however, the road climbs more than 1 000 m, to a height of about 2 874 m. The route takes a four-wheel-drive vehicle some three hours to complete. So don't be fooled by the gentle start, because the gradient is as steep as 1:2.5 in places, and the road soon becomes as gruelling as any you're ever likely to travel. The Sani Pass follows the upper valley of the Mkomazana River, winds around excruciating hairpin bends, and skirts the edge of the escarpment.

Named after the San people (Bushmen), who were among the first hunters in the Drakensberg and the first to make use of this route, the pass could, it is claimed, have been named after Chief Rafolatsani, also known as Tsani, who once lived on Sani Top. Either way, it remains almost as primitive as it was centuries ago. Along the narrow track that climbs up the mountain beside the Mkomazana, Sotho riders still escort mule-trains taking wool, mohair and peas one way, meal and other goods back home. No matter how advanced four-wheel-drive vehicles become, many people still regard the hardy, sure-footed Basuto pony as the safest means of transport on this treacherous part of the Drakensberg.

Originally developed as a bridle path in 1913 by a trader named James Lamont, the pass was opened to a regular jeep service in 1949, carrying passengers and supplies. Over the years, several daring attempts have been made to cross the pass in vehicles less rugged than a four-wheel drive. Between 1956 and 1964, people managed to negotiate the pass with a small German car, a motorcycle, a motor scooter and even with a caravan attached to a four-wheel drive. With all these outrageous attempts it was almost obvious that, when the Sports Car Club began the Roof of Africa Rally in 1966, the organisers should include the Sani as part of the route. While four-wheel drives are the recommended form of transport, it is possible to drive a saloon car up to the South African border post and from there to take a two-hour walk to the summit, about 6 km in distance and 1 000 m in elevation away. Only the very fit should attempt this, though.

The mountains on all sides provide countless walks and hikes and at the Lesotho border you can find refreshments and accommodation at the highest pub in southern Africa. Called the Sani Top Chalet, it attracts skiers in winter, even though the snow is short-lived. Its fame stems from the fact that it is the highest licensed hotel in southern Africa, albeit offering only six bedrooms and a kitchen where you have to do your own cooking. The highest peak on the subcontinent, Ntabana Ntlenyana (3 482 m), which means 'Little Mountain – Something Just a Little Beautiful', is located 16 km from the chalet.

If you stand on the summit of Sani Pass, you can look south and see Hodgson's Peaks, named after

The view from the very top of Sani Pass. One sharp bend after another makes this drive a somewhat tiring and hazardous experience.

The drive up Sani Pass represents a gradual transition from the gentle, lower slopes of the Drakensberg Range, right up to its precipitous peaks.

Where to stay

Sani Top Chalet, c/o Himeville Hotel, PO Himeville 4585; tel (033722) 5. *Sani Pass Hotel*, PO Box 44, Himeville 4585; tel (033722) 29/30. *Himeville Arms Hotel*, PO Himeville 4585; tel (033722) 5. *Underberg Hotel,* PO Underberg 4590; tel (033) 7011412.

There is also *Loteni Hutted Camp*, Natal Drakensberg Park, PO Box 14, Himeville 4585; tel (033722) 1540 or Natal Parks Board, PO Box 662, Pietermaritzburg 3200; tel (0331) 471981. Loteni offers bungalows with refrigerators and ablution facilities, and two kitchen blocks staffed by experienced cooks serve the camp.

There are camping facilities in the Himeville Nature Reserve, PO Box 115, Himeville 4585; tel (033722) 36.

Thomas Hodgson, who, on a punitive raid against the Bushmen, was accidentally shot by one of his comrades and died at Giant's Cup. He was buried on the slopes of the peaks now named after him.

The area around Sani Pass is rich in rock paintings. From the Sani Pass Hotel, two paths lead to painted rock shelters. The shorter walk, along the Gxa-Lingene River to the Good Hope Caves, takes about an hour. Although very little art remains because of poor rock-face and vandalism, it is a good place to see the remnants of Bushman habitation. Archaeological research here has revealed that a Later Stone Age people lived here as far back as 7 600 years ago.

In the second cave, more paintings are visible, including a horse and rider, a buck, several other animals, and a figure with a bow and quiver. A third site, which also offers fairly clear paintings, is situated on Ikanti Mountain, roughly two hours' walk from the hotel.

Sani Pass at a glance (map page 132)

How to get there: From Pietermaritzburg, take the road through Bulwer, Underberg and Himeville to the Sani Pass Hotel, situated in a valley of the Drakensberg foothills. On the Himeville side of the hotel, you'll find Giant's Cup Motors, the base of the transport company which offers a daily service up the mountain if there are enough passengers. Make sure about what vehicles are allowed up the pass before tackling the ascent. Saloon cars are allowed as far as the South African border post, after which only four-wheel-drive vehicles are allowed on the very steep, zigzag section of the pass.
Things to do: There are lots of walks and hikes along the mountains, cliffs and rivers. Many of the walks are in the Natal Drakensberg Park, which is administered by the Natal Parks Board. A nominal entrance fee is required.
Weather: Summers fine and hot. In winter it gets so cold that a dam near Sani Top freezes over and can even be used for ice-skating.

More information: Natal Parks Board, PO Box 662, Pietermaritzburg 3200; tel (0331) 471961; Natal Parks Board, PO Box 116, Himeville 4585; tel (033722) 1540; Lesotho Tourist Board, 2nd Floor, Maseru Sun Cabanas, PO Box 1378, Maseru 100; tel (09266) 323760/322896. For Sani Top Chalet write to c/o Himeville Hotel, PO Himeville 4585; tel (033722) 5. For transport information write to Mokhotlong Mountain Transport, PO Box 12, Himeville 4585; tel (033722) 1302.

Tranquil settler village amid the mountains

Clear streams, invigorating mountain air, rest and recreation await you in the Drakensberg hamlet of Himeville

PICTURESQUE HIMEVILLE is no secret to that hardy breed of anglers who flock here between September and May to fish the country's best trout waters.

Lying in the rolling grasslands of the Drakensberg foothills at the entrance to the imposing Sani Pass, the village is delightfully pretty with colourful gardens framing the main street. There is a supermarket, a tearoom, a craft shop and an attractive hotel. The Himeville Arms Hotel is a cosy country inn, dating back to 1906, where anglers congregate in the pub after a hard day's fishing and tell tall trout tales.

At the heart of the town is a fort built out of the local sandstone by Scottish stonemasons in 1893. It is now a national monument housing a fascinating museum. Many exhibits are of a military nature, although Himeville has managed to remain fairly aloof in disputes, mainly due to the inhospitability of the area – especially in winter.

Among the displays are a Zulu room, a Bushman room and a wildlife room; and, of course, trout fishing features prominently. The old prison warder's house has been furnished as a typical settler house; an ox-wagon and various farming and agricultural implements from the early days of white settlement (the mid-1880s) are found in the central courtyard.

Most visitors come to Himeville for the great outdoors. The surrounding countryside offers memorable trails on horseback or on foot through the undulating grassland thick with sugarbush, wild bottlebrush and proteas. This is spectacular climbing country – Hodgson's Peaks overlook the village and just over the border, in Lesotho, at 3 482 m, is southern Africa's highest peak, Thabantshonyana.

Freshwater angling is a major tourist attraction in the area surrounding the picturesque village of Himeville.

With over 200 km of rivers in the area there are some fairly safe stretches for canoeing and tubing. (If you've come unprepared, tubes can be bought at the Underberg Garage.)

In a grassy valley about 2 km from the village is the Himeville Nature Reserve. Extending for about 105 ha, the reserve boasts two trout-filled lakes that are a favourite with fishermen. Besides proper trout-fishing tackle, anglers are required to kit themselves out with a provincial licence and an angling permit, both of which are available from the reserve office. Non-anglers should not feel left out: rowing boats can be hired in order to view the various waterfowl; other wildlife found in the reserve are mainly highland antelope such as reedbuck, duiker, wildebeest and blesbok.

Another nature reserve nearby is the brainchild of a local farming couple, Kenneth and Mona Lund. Avid tree lovers, they began growing exotics and planted poplar, elderberry, ash, maple, oak, plane, alder, birch, cypresses, cherry, tulip trees, crab apples and more. In the centre of the reserve a lake reflects the beautiful foliage and creates a dramatic spectacle in autumn.

The Himeville district is well known as the starting point for visiting some of the Drakensberg's most notable rock-art sites. From the Cobham Forest Station you can join a trail which, after about 20 minutes, reaches Cobham Cave – a large cavern with eland painted on the ceiling. Another hour's walk and you'll come to Bathplug Cave, so named because water flows into a hole in the cave floor. Here Bushman artists painted hundreds of stick figures in a frenzy of expression – gesticulating, running, leaping.

But the real treat is Mpongweni Shelter, which has the finest gallery of rock paintings in the Drakensberg. This cave, which has been declared a national monument, is reached after a strenuous three-hour walk. Its inaccessibility is part of the attraction as much of the work is still in pristine condition, unviolated by vandals. This is one of the last Bushman sites, from the so-called 'horse period' of about 1850. Horses there are many: some red, some black, some with riders. Men are featured engaged in dance and various manly pursuits – such as spearing fish from canoes – and wearing animal heads and skins. The women, who all sport the prominent buttocks and heavy thighs associated with health and prosperity, are depicted carrying babies and clapping rhythmically for dances. A detailed painting of a cattle raid is particularly apt as this shelter is on the route along which the cattle were driven across the mountains.

Himeville at a glance (map page 132)

How to get there: Himeville lies some 200 km west of Durban. Follow the N3 to Howick and turn onto the R617 towards Bulwer and Underberg.
Weather: Himeville often has all four seasons in the space of one day! Summers can be hot (but always cool in the evening) and winters are very cold, often with snow.
What to do: Angling, canoeing, tubing, hiking, and there are also facilities for bowls, tennis, golf and horse-riding.
Special attractions: The museum and rock art.
More information: Southern Drakensberg Publicity Association, PO Box 300, Underberg 4590; tel (033701) 1096.
Visiting times: The museum is open on Wednesday and Friday from 10 am to 12 noon and at weekends from 9.30 am to 12 noon.

Where to stay

The *Himeville Arms Hotel* has 12 en-suite guest cottages in the gardens. Write to Himeville Arms Hotel, PO Himeville 4585; tel (033722) 5. The *Himeville Nature Reserve* has 10 camp sites, an ablution block with hot and cold running water, and braai areas. Contact the Officer-in-Charge, Himeville Nature Reserve, PO Himeville 4585; tel (033722) 36.

Shake, rattle and roll your way through the plantations

You can take a wonderful ride back into the golden age of steam travel on the Banana Express along Natal's South Coast

THE SIGHTS, SOUNDS AND SMELLS of steam trains strike a nostalgic chord in everyone, whether or not these were part of their past. Travelling in one of the Banana Express's original coaches dating back to 1907, it becomes clear why this form of transport has been so eulogised. A steam train seems almost alive as it puffs and struggles on the uphills and clatters freely on the downhill gradients.

The place to catch the Banana Express is at the Beach Terminus in Port Shepstone, known to everyone as the Banana Express Station. There are two journeys: a one-and-a-half hour return to Izotsha on Thursdays and Sundays (also Mondays, Tuesdays and Fridays during school holidays), and a longer six-and-a-half hour trip to Paddock and back on Wednesdays and Saturdays.

On the way to Izotsha the train hugs the coast for 7 km and passengers are treated to unparalleled views of the Indian Ocean and several inviting, secluded beaches. Swinging inland, the view is no less rewarding as the train winds steadily up through the sugar-cane and banana plantations. The Banana Express stops at Izotsha for 20 minutes while the steam engine is filled with water. This is an ideal opportunity for children to be invited into the cab to blow the whistle and have their photographs taken before the return journey.

Although Paddock is only 20 km from Port Shepstone as the crow flies, the Banana Express

The 'Red Dragon' is the name given to the main engine used on the route. In railway enthusiast terminology, it is known as a Class NGG16A No '141'.

twists and turns for 39 km on a far more memorable journey than any crow has ever experienced. The ride is the same as far as Izotsha, but after that the train climbs through typical Zulu country – undulating grasslands studded with traditional huts, rolling sugar-cane, pawpaw, pineapple and banana plantations and indigenous forest – to Paddock, 550 m above sea level. Paddock Station dates back to the turn of the century and is a national monument with plenty of memorabilia for railway buffs.

There is a period museum in the old station-master's house, full of mysterious and interesting paraphernalia and lacking only period people for complete authenticity. After exploring, visitors can enjoy a braai in the gardens before the return journey. But this need not be a simple there-and-back excursion, however unique. With the Oribi Gorge so tantalisingly close, the Banana Express offers train travellers two other options.

With the Baboon View Trail option, passengers travel to Plains Station (10 minutes before Paddock) and are escorted to the Oribi Nature Reserve by a ranger. After a short lecture on the history and wildlife of the area, visitors are taken on a 45-minute hike along the Baboon View Trail. Meanwhile, back at the *boma*, a succulent braai is prepared and hungry hikers can relax and eat before returning to Port Shepstone by rail.

Another option is known as Oribi Viewsites, where you are taken by motor coach to such notable Oribi venues as Baboon's Castle with its panoramic views, or Overhanging Rock. Visitors can travel out by coach and take the train back after the braai at Paddock Station, or the other way round.

The Banana Express staff are justly proud of its history. For most of this century the narrow-gauge

The departure point for the Banana Express is Port Shepstone's Beach Terminus.

Where to stay

Port Shepstone is a well-established holiday resort with a large variety of accommodation. Contact the South Coast Publicity Association, PO Box 25, Margate 4275; tel (03931) 22322.

line between Port Shepstone and Harding was faithfully served by Garratt steam locomotives transporting goods and passengers back and forth.

In 1986 the locomotives and coaches were almost consigned to the scrapyard in the name of progress. The railway authorities closed the line after decreeing it unprofitable and pronouncing that the steam era had finally come to an end. A considerable number of people disagreed, however. The Alfred County Railway Committee was formed to save the Banana Express and a fund-raising drive steamed ahead – the public was lobbied and petitions were signed. Farmers and business people wanted the train for freight and almost everyone wanted it for pleasure. Resolve and initiative paid off and the result was that the Port Shepstone & Alfred County Railway became the first privatised train service in the country.

Today, as before, the Banana Express is the tourist branch of the railway. The freight service

still runs between Port Shepstone and Harding, hauling timber to the coast and livestock, cement and fertiliser inland. At Paddock Station visitors have the opportunity to witness the trusty Garratt locomotives doing their thing when the steam engine meets the diesel freight train from Harding and wagons are exchanged. These specially designed Garratts are the most powerful steam locomotives ever to run on track this narrow (only 610 mm) and have attracted the attention of railway enthusiasts worldwide.

A ride on the Banana Express is guaranteed to provide an exciting and memorable day's outing for any child or adult.

Banana Express at a glance (map page 132)

How to get there: Coming into Port Shepstone on the N2 from Durban, pass through two sets of traffic lights. Just before the third set, take the slip road off to your left and turn immediately left.
Weather: Hot in summer, mild to warm in winter.
Special attractions: The original carriages and locomotives.
What to do: Sit back and relax!
More information: Banana Express, PO Box 572, Port Shepstone 4240; tel (03931) 76443.
Operating times: The Banana Express leaves for Paddock on Wednesdays and Saturdays at 10 am throughout the year. The excursion to Izotsha leaves on Thursdays at 10 am and Sundays at 11.30 am throughout the year and on Mondays, Tuesdays and Fridays at 10 am during school holidays.

An exotic temple to enchant the soul

The Hare Krishna Temple of Understanding in Chatsworth, southwest of Durban, is a masterpiece of devotional architecture, blending ancient Eastern culture with modern Western technology

AKE OFF YOUR SHOES and walk across the pale pink and white Portuguese marble floor into the Sri-Sri Radha-Radhanath Temple of Understanding in Chatsworth near Durban. This is a moment you're not likely to forget. A temple of the Krishna Consciousness Movement, it is a unique combination of traditional, contemporary and futuristic architecture, in which every feature has symbolic significance and every line and measurement complies with scriptural injunctions.

The public's knowledge of Krishna Consciousness is probably limited to the sight of chanting, orange-robed, shaven-headed devotees proclaiming their faith in city streets. And no wonder. It took four centuries for this Indian religious movement to reach the West, and it has existed in South Africa only since 1975. Outside the movement, most people are unfamiliar with the ancient Vedic scriptures on which it is based – the Bhagavad Gita, Sri Isopanisad and Srimad Bhagavatam – or with the deity Krishna (also known as Hare, Rama, Vishnu or Ishvara), who is central to the movement's philosophy. But if you want to understand more about this fascinating religion, or if you simply want to enjoy an exotic spectacle unique in the southern hemisphere, there is no better place to start than the Temple of Understanding.

The temple was built in the early 1980s in accordance with the wishes of A C Bhaktivedanta Swami Prabhupada, the movement's spiritual leader

in the West who had visited South Africa shortly before his death in 1978. It was designed by Austrian architect Hannes Raudner, a Krishna devotee also known as Rajaram Das. Because the Vedic scriptures stipulate that symbolism is the proper language of the architect, Rajaram Das made every effort to reflect the character and approach of Swami Prabhupada in the temple's structure and atmosphere. Every aspect of the construction – from the leaves, fruit and gemstones buried in the foundation to the castings decorating its three towers – is richly symbolic.

Seen from the air, the building with its surrounding garden, walkways and moat resembles a huge lotus flower – the Hindu symbol of transcendence and spiritual awakening. The design itself is based on a traditional formula – a geometric layout with symbolic and philosophical meaning. Among the basic symbols you will recognise are circles, triangles, squares and octagons. The octagon is regarded by devotees of the Hare Krishna movement as a symbol of Krishna or Vishnu.

The million-litre moat and circular walkways around the building represent the endless cycle of life and death, as contained in the philosophy of reincarnation. A bridge spans the moat at the western entrance to the temple chamber: the person walking over it symbolically transcends the cycle of earthly existence.

The octagonal temple chamber is richly adorned, yet it seems to generate an atmosphere of peace and calm. Specially laminated glass windows in the walls, which are covered with Japanese oak panels, beading and mirrors, offer a 360° view of the gardens and moat. Portuguese marble was used for the altar and the floor. The central design in the middle of the chamber is a star with the eight points of the compass, this being executed in a variety of different coloured marbles.

The roof has eight panels, each 3 m high, which depict Krishna's various activities and manifestations. Reproductions of original paintings by artists of the International Society for Krishna Consciousness (ISKCON) were made using a computer and laser beams. They are expected to last at least three hundred years. A further 35 smaller panels illustrating Krishna's pastimes on earth are alternated with Japanese mirrors. An original painting depicting Krishna and his consort Radha in the spiritual world adorns the skylight.

The temple is lit with Italian crystal chandeliers and smaller wall-lamps in the shape of lotus flowers. A total of 550 light bulbs, reflected in 330 square metres of mirror, creates an overwhelming

A number of unique and unusual design features put the Temple of Understanding in an architectural league of its own.

Eight spectacular painted panels on the roof of the temple – three of which can be seen above – depict various aspects of the god Krishna. The central shrine seen at floor level contains figures of Krishna and his female consort, Radharani.

spectacle. A constant temperature is maintained in the temple chamber.

Lord Krishna and Radharani, the queen of devotion, are worshipped in the temple in the deity forms of Sri-Sri Radha-Radhanath, and their two colourful figures stand upon an elaborate altar at one end of the vast room. They are bathed and freshly dressed, decorated and garlanded every day. Food is presented to them by devotees six times a day, followed by a ceremony when lamps, flowers, incense and fans are offered to the accompaniment of chanting.

The opulence of the Temple of Understanding suggests enormous wealth, but sheer ingenuity kept the cost of building this fantastic architectural creation to just R3 million – a fraction of the sum that most office blocks cost to build. To save funds, the ISKCON construction company was established and the temple built almost entirely by followers of Krishna.

A major saving was made by the bold decision not to use a crane. Decorative work, such as the castings on top of the dome, were hoisted up by a scaffolding system. It was a complicated and risky operation to position the heavy concrete blocks, some of which weighed between 1 and 1,7 tons. Not surprisingly, prayers and chanting accompanied the entire process.

Another task undertaken by the devotees and completed within an incredible three weeks was the manufacture of 35 000 stainless steel roof-tiles. The building took four years to complete.

The main objective of the Temple of Understanding is the spiritual upliftment of the community. But it is also an awe-inspiring spectacle that should be on the itinerary of every tourist in South Africa. Visitors are welcomed along with the faithful, and guides are available to explain the symbolism. Tours are free and include the temple chamber, inner sanctuary, surrounding moat and gardens. There is also an exotic gift shop and a vegetarian restaurant on the premises.

The Temple of Understanding at a glance (map page 132)

How to get there: Take the Chatsworth-Mobeni turn-off from the N2 south, and drive inland on the Higginson Highway (M1), then turn left to the Chatsworth Centre.
Weather: Durban weather is hot and humid in summer, warm in winter.
What to do: Explore the temple and surrounding grounds. It is a good idea to join a guided tour to appreciate the symbolic meaning with which every detail is invested. And don't forget: shoes off when on sacred ground.

Special attractions: Devotees worship at the effigies of Lord Krishna and Radharani six times a day, offering food, flowers, lamps, incense and fans. It's a fascinating glimpse into an exotic world.
Visiting times: The temple welcomes visitors between 7am and 8.30pm daily.
Other information: PRO for the Temple of Understanding is Anuradha Das. Contact her at PO Box 56003, Chatsworth 4030; tel (031) 435815 or 433367.

The entrance to St Peter in Chains. Inside this small chapel, memorial plaques pay tribute to fighting men who have died in the service of their country.

The entrance to St Peter in Chains. Inside this small chapel, memorial plaques pay tribute to fighting men who have died in the service of their country.

A garden of remembrance for the souls of the brave

Here, in a quiet corner of Durban, among flowers and cycads and the calls of turtledoves, is the Old Fort – once a place of siege, now a memorial to soldiers of many wars

One of the many interesting military relics to be seen at the Old Fort is a cannon recovered from the Grosvenor, *a British vessel that was wrecked on the Wild Coast in 1782.*

THE ATMOSPHERE is hushed, but poignant. After the sub-tropical warmth of the gardens outside, the air inside is cool and limpid, smelling of wood and polished brass. Around the walls of the building, interspersed with the flags of many regiments, are memorial plaques to men who sacrificed their lives on land, sea, and in the air, across the span of a hundred years.

This is the chapel of St Peter in Chains, and it is one of the many memorials contained in the quiet precinct of Durban's Old Fort. Indeed, much of the story of this historic site can be gleaned from the variety of plaques you find on arrival. The first is found beside the main gate. Done in ceramic tiles, it provides a bald description of the origin of the fort:

'Within this area was situated the camp in which a small British force under Captain T. Charlton Smith of the 27th Regiment (Royal Inniskilling Fusiliers) was beleaguered by the emigrant Boers under Commandant Andries Pretorius in 1842. To secure relief for the garrison, Dick King rode 600 miles to Grahamstown. From 1842 to 1897 it was occupied by various regiments and detachments of the British Army.'

That is admirably succinct and historic. But where, you may wonder, is the throb and stir of battle, and the thunder of the guns? Walk through the lych gate into the grounds and you begin to sense the distant tremors of past action. A little way into the gardens is a model of the original fort, a diorama of the scene as it was when, early in May 1842,

Captain Thomas Charlton Smith and his soldiers made their camp here.

The diorama shows the circle of wagons he used to create a laager, enclosing an area of some 2,2 ha. Behind this crude but effective barricade, the British troops endured 26 days of intermittent bombardment from Andries Pretorius and his Boer soldiers. It ended on 24 June with the arrival – thanks to the efforts of Dick King – of HMS *Conch*, followed two days later by HMS *Southampton*. The soldiers who died in the siege were buried in the cemetery nearby.

Natal remained in the hands of the British, a loyal outpost of the Empire. The Old Fort grew in size, with a barracks and an ammunition magazine being added in 1843. However, in 1897 it was finally closed down.

Nevertheless, the building remained in the hands of the Royal Durban Light Infantry, and it is to one of their officers, Brigadier-General G Molyneux, that we owe its preservation. Today you can witness the fruits of his initiative as you wander to the chapel around the flagstoned pathway that skirts what was once the parade ground. Converted from the powder magazine in 1926, the chapel is not only a memorial to many soldiers but a favourite place for Durban weddings. Nearby are the original barracks, now converted into a row of cottages for military pensioners.

The heart of the fort, however, is the Garden of Remembrance. Here, you can sit on an oak seat made from the timbers of HMS *Southampton*, one of the ships which relieved the beleaguered garrison. Nearby is the ship's bell of the cruiser HMS *Durban* which ended a long and honourable career in 1944 as one of the vessels sunk to form Mulberry Harbour for the allied landings in Normandy. There is a plaque to John Ross who, with a Zulu escort, walked all the way from the fort to Delagoa Bay and back to obtain medicines for his fellow castaways. Another accompanies two old field guns, fired at the coronation of the Zulu King Cetshwayo. A darker note is sounded by the memorial to the 400 officers and men who went down with HMS *Natal* when it blew up at its moorings in Scotland on New Year's Eve, 1915.

If these are the public tributes, the more private details of the soldier's life are to be found nearby, in Warriors' Gate – a museum and shrine to the men of many wars. It is also the headquarters of the ex-soldiers' organisation, the Memorable Order of Tin Hats (the 'Moths') which was founded in Durban in 1927. Vaguely Norman in style, the museum was built in 1934, and vested in the Historical Monuments Commission the following year. Here

The imposing, Norman-style building known as Warrior's Gate. In addition to housing an evocative collection of military memorabilia, it is also the headquarters of the 'Moths'.

you can ponder the personal mementos of the men who fought, their uniforms and medals, their photographs, their regimental newspapers, recording the long trail of tragedy and triumph from Delville Wood, the Somme and Gallipoli, to Italy, North Africa and Normandy.

The cannon's roar has long faded from the Old Fort, and the dust of battle settled. The memorials are set among lovingly tended gardens. Here are palms, jacarandas and gum trees growing close to, and distributed among, a magnificent collection of cycads – ancient tropical gymnosperms which flourish in this lush climate. If the past has its multitude of ghosts, the mood of the present is one of reconciliation, of timeless tranquillity.

Old Fort at a glance (map page 132)

How to get there: On the north side of Durban, the Old Fort is situated on the corner of Old Fort Road and NMR Avenue, next to the Kingsmead Cricket Ground. The main entrance is on Old Fort Road.
What to do: Durban Unlimited runs a 'Feel of Durban Walkabout', which includes the Old Fort and Warriors' Gate. This takes place on Mondays, Wednesdays and Fridays, from 9.45 am to noon.
Special attractions: The chapel of St Peter in Chains, the Garden of Remembrance, the display of cycads, and tropical

trees and flowers. Also, the collection of military memorabilia in Warriors' Gate.
More information: For information on the Old Fort area, contact Durban Unlimited, PO Box 1044, Durban 4000; tel (031) 3044934 or 322595/322608.

Open on weekdays and Sundays, from 6 am to 6 pm. The site also includes the military museum, Warriors' Gate, which is open from 10 am to noon, and from 1 pm to 4 pm on weekdays and Sundays. Both are closed on Saturdays and public holidays.

Sugar baron Sir Marshall Campbell named his dream house Muckleneuk – after the first sugar mill that he managed in Natal.

A grand old home filled with historic treasures

Three famous Africana collections are housed in Muckleneuk, a beautiful colonial homestead situated on the Berea, a few kilometres from the Durban city centre

MUCKLENEUK IS ONE of Durban's architectural treasures. Set within glorious gardens, and shaded by huge old trees, this beautiful double-storey residence commands panoramic views of the city of Durban and the blue Indian Ocean beyond. The house was left by William Campbell to the City of Durban, and the Campbell family collections, which were bequeathed to the University of Natal, are permanently housed here.

Muckleneuk was built in 1914 for Sir Marshall Campbell – a sugar baron and senator after whom nearby KwaMashu was named. After completion of his lovely neo-Cape Dutch-style home, Sir Marshall Campbell gave the challenging job of landscaping the large garden to his daughter Margaret – known to all as Killie.

A dedicated gardener, Dr Killie Campbell achieved fame in horticultural circles for the new species of bougainvillea that she and her gardener William Poulton were responsible for hybridising. (Bougainvilleas, which flourish in Natal's hot, humid climate, were introduced to South Africa from the Indian Ocean island of Mauritius.) The species she created include 'Natalia', with its delicate, dusty pink flowers, and 'Killie', which blossoms in a multi-coloured array of bronze, cerise and mauve flowers. These and many other species of bougainvillea are to be found growing throughout the garden.

Not only was Dr Campbell a keen horticulturalist, she also made her mark as a philanthropist, an amateur nurse, a sportswoman and an amateur historian. Her keen interest in the past led to her becoming an avid collector of memorabilia relating to the Nguni peoples and to the early settlement of whites in Natal.

A woman of enormous energy and enthusiasm, Dr Campbell was one of Durban's best-loved characters. Born in 1881, she died in 1965 at the age of 84, leaving behind her a prodigious collection of important Africana consisting of many rare and unique items, including over 40 000 books and rare manuscripts which she bequeathed to the University of Natal.

The Killie Campbell Africana Library, housed in Muckleneuk's new wing, is the result of a life devoted to collecting rare books, pictures, maps and unpublished manuscripts about Africa from all over the world. Dr Campbell's love for Africana started in the dusty book and antique shops of London. As a young woman, she travelled every year to England and there, in these shops, she would spend her entire allowance on Africana – much to the chagrin of her mother, who would rather her daughter had bought clothes! This passion gradually overtook the other interests of her life and she devoted most of her time to assembling her library – recording, collecting and preserving items reflecting South African history.

Since 1965, the University of Natal has not only taken over the responsibility of maintaining the Muckleneuk homestead, but has continued to acquire items for the library, particularly in the fields in which Dr Campbell specialised. Muckleneuk now houses the three famous Campbell collections: the Killie Campbell Africana Library, the Mashu Museum of Ethnology, and the William Campbell Furniture Museum (named after Killie's brother).

The Mashu Museum of Ethnology contains collections of weapons, ornaments, carvings, utensils, tools, beadwork and other examples of black culture in southern Africa. Also found here is the extensive collection of Barbara Tyrrell paintings – over 250 in all – which form a unique record of the customs, rituals, ceremonies and social dress of the African and Bushman people of southern Africa.

The William Campbell Furniture Museum features a large selection of furniture brought to Natal by the early English settlers, as well as notable pieces that were made in the Cape. In the picture collection there are also paintings, engravings, drawings and etchings by 19th-century Africana artists and contemporary black artists with Natal/KwaZulu connections.

Muckleneuk is still furnished much as it was when the Campbells lived there. The stately entrance hall, majestic staircase and long gleaming corridors provide the perfect setting for sumptuous carpets, colourful paintings, and handsome pieces of furniture.

Paintings, antique furniture and rare carpets – part of the treasure chest of Africana housed in Muckleneuk.

Recently, the University's Campbell Collections and its Oral Documentation and Research Centre were merged to form the Campbell Collections and Centre for Oral Studies. The centre now focuses on research, teaching and documentation.

Dr Campbell's father, Marshall, came out to South Africa in 1850 at the age of two, with his parents William and Agnes Campbell. Of Scottish/Irish descent, the family quickly adapted to colonial life in South Africa. Many members of the Campbell family have distinguished themselves down through the years. They include Roy Campbell, one of the country's most celebrated poets; his sister Ethel Campbell, the noted Durban historian; Dr George Campbell, a one-time chancellor of the University of Natal; and Killie's brother, William ('Wac') Campbell who, like his father, was managing director of the sugar company, Natal Estates Limited. Each, in their own way, contributed to the heritage of South Africa, a vital part of which Dr Campbell preserved so lovingly at Muckleneuk.

On her death on 27 September 1965, Killie Campbell's ashes were scattered, in accordance with her wishes, beneath an *umkhuhlu* tree in the garden of Muckleneuk.

Muckleneuk at a glance (map page 132)

How to get there: From central Durban, take the Berea Road and turn right into Essenwood Road. Travel north past the Musgrave Centre (on your right) and into Marriott Road. Muckleneuk is on the corner of Marriott and Essenwood roads, at 220 Marriott Road.

Special attractions: Among the many interesting items in the Mashu Museum of Ethnology is an ivory bangle reputed to have belonged to Shaka, and a stool carved by Dinizulu with a small knife from a single block of wood while he was held prisoner on St Helena. The William Campbell Furniture Museum has a notable collection of 18th- and 19th-century pieces, including *rusbanke* (couches) and armoires. Among

the many treasures in the Killie Campbell Africana Library are early missionary imprints, letters, diaries, paintings and photographs.

More information: Contact Durban Unlimited, PO Box 1044, Durban 4000; tel (031) 3044934.

Visiting times: The Killie Campbell Library is open from 8.30 am to 4.30 pm on weekdays and from 9 am to noon on most Saturdays. An appointment must be made to visit the museums – a rule which ensures that groups are kept to a reasonable size. (Tel (031) 295066 for bookings.) Guided tours last approximately an hour and are presented to suit the special interests of visitors.

Hidden cascades in Natal's misty midlands

A series of little-known waterfalls,
such as Karkloof Falls, glisten like jewels
in the lush Natal green belt close to Howick

Where to stay

The best base for the falls area is Howick, where you'll find the *Howick Falls Hotel*, PO Box 22, Howick 3290; tel (0332) 302809. and the *Old Halliwell Country Inn*, PO Box 201, Howick 3290; tel (0332) 302602. For camping and caravanning, try the *Howick Caravan Park* – contact the Municipality at PO Box 5, Howick 3290; tel (0332) 306124.

TO ESCAPE THE HEAT and humidity of the coast, Natalians head inland to the misty, fertile midlands. Here, most visitors expend their sightseeing energy on the Howick Falls – reputedly the most photographed in South Africa. Yet this area is home to several other picturesque, lesser-known falls, each unique, and all within easy reach of each other.

The most interesting of these, the Karkloof Falls, are situated 18 km east of Howick in the remote Karkloof Valley. Here the Karkloof River prefaces its descent to the valley floor with a seductive cascade before the main event, a graceful, vertical dive of 105 m.

Despite their beauty, the falls are not without potential peril. At least one life has been claimed among the jagged rocks at the bottom of the sheer drop where the water boils and churns. Back in 1938, three teenagers, full of the confidence of youth, set about climbing the adjacent rock-face to the top of the falls. They had almost succeeded when one boy gripped a loose rock, lost his balance and plunged to his death.

The beautiful, thickly wooded Karkloof Valley was once the main wagon route between Natal and the Transvaal. In fact, the name Karkloof is said to have originated in the middle of the last century

Set amongst plantations of pine, Woodhouse Falls are the smallest of the falls in the area.

when a laden ox-wagon overturned and was abandoned, becoming a familiar landmark to other travellers over the years.

The Karkloof district was put firmly on the sporting map by the skill and ingenuity of the legendary Shaw family, who dominated the activities of the local polo club, using sticks and balls hewn from indigenous yellowwood trees. According to local lore, young Campbell Shaw developed an almost telepathic bond with his horse to the extent that he was able to power through the chukkas without the aid of a bridle.

In the rugged Karkloof Mountains is the 223-ha Karkloof Nature Reserve, which was established in 1980. Bushpig, various antelope such as bushbuck and blue duiker, and even leopard, stalk the rocky ledges and crags. Bird life is also abundant and the crowned, black and martial eagle breed here – they're a familiar sight soaring above the ravines. For those interested in trees, the reserve boasts indigenous forests which include yellowwood and rare black stinkwood trees.

The entire region situated around the Karkloof Falls, including the various timber plantations, is owned and maintained by Sappi. They have created well laid-out walking trails and beautiful picnic and braai spots on the banks of the river, above the falls, where it is quite safe to swim. The area is, however, closed during the dry winter months because of the fire hazard, and also year-round during the week owing to logging activities.

A special viewsite affords the visitor a spectacular view of the Karkloof Falls and the surrounding countryside.

If you wish to take your exploration a bit further, head for the nearby Woodhouse Falls, named after the unfortunate farmer who lost his life here. Back around 1880, William Woodhouse was attempting to cross the river on horseback just above the falls. His horse lost its footing and Woodhouse was thrown off and swept over the falls. The horse managed to reach the bank safely, but Woodhouse's body was found in the pool at the foot of the falls. At only 10 m high the falls don't appear to be particularly lethal, but the volume of water going over, particularly in the rainy season, is not to be underestimated.

A few kilometres away, the lovely Cascade Falls on the Gobongo River are as frothy and lacy as a wedding gown. The tiered waterfalls flow into an irresistibly inviting sunlit pool where swimming is a pleasure: in places it's possible to sit directly underneath the falls and benefit from a gentle massage of river water.

Carry on down the Gobongo and eventually you'll reach the equally beautiful Shelter Falls, which are 37 m high and framed by lush vegetation. These falls are best approached along the path which traverses a shady, green ravine and eventually emerges at the bottom of the falls where visitors can experience the heady exhilaration of gazing upwards at thousands of litres of water crashing down mere metres away.

This verdant territory abounds in local myths and legends, particularly concerning those unlucky enough to have ended up at the bottom of the various falls. But one of the more uplifting legends of the area concerns one John Goodman Household, an enterprising youth who lived in the region of the Karkloof Falls in the 1870s.

Fascinated by the variety of birds riding the thermal draughts over the valleys, he longed to imitate them. One day he shot a vulture and studied it carefully, noting relevant details such as weight in proportion to wingspan. Then he set about making his own wings, using steel rods, bamboo poles, treated silk and paper, and suspended a swing seat for himself in the middle.

His initial experiment failed, but undaunted, he built more wings. He roped in his brother and several farmhands to help and, to save face with neighbours lest he fail, Household took the precaution of trying his maiden flight under cover of darkness, albeit on a brightly moonlit night. They carried the craft to a ravine and launched it with Household bravely in the swing seat.

Apparently the craft soared like an eagle out over the valley, climbed over 100 m and travelled across the valley for more than a kilometre before crashlanding. Household broke his leg on impact and was forbidden by his parents to fly again, so the remains of his craft were eventually thrown away. Nevertheless, this brave attempt is possibly Africa's earliest recorded flight.

Apart from the obvious attractions of the falls, the rivers offer a variety of recreation from swimming to tubing and canoeing, but visitors are warned to remain ever mindful of the potential dangers. Angling is also popular, and the rivers contain trout (especially between August and May), Natal scaly, barbel, carp, bass, bluegills and monstrous eels, some more than two metres long. There are numerous walks and trails or, if you prefer, pack your mountain bike.

Karkloof at a glance (map page 132)

How to get there: Howick lies just off the N3 about 30 km northwest of Pietermaritzburg. Follow signs from Howick to the Karkloof Valley.
Weather: Mild to hot in summer, cool to cold in winter.
What to do: Hiking, angling, swimming and canoeing.
More information: Natal Parks Board, PO Box 662, Pietermaritzburg 3200; tel (0331) 471961; Pietermaritzburg Publicity Association, PO Box 25, Pietermaritzburg 3200; tel (0331) 20571.

The banks of the river just above the Karkloof Falls have a number of attractive, well-maintained picnic sites.

Remnants of the Anglo-Zulu conflict in a scenic reserve

*Spread across the banks of the Tugela River
just off the N2 highway, the Harold Johnson Nature Reserve
was once the site of an important British military camp*

THE HAROLD JOHNSON NATURE RESERVE is one of a chain of reserves that preserve and protect Natal's indigenous floral habitats. Open throughout the year from dawn till dusk, the 104-ha reserve consists of scrubland, valley bushveld, and coastal vegetation with indigenous inhabitants such as blue, red and grey duiker, bushbuck, bushpig, impala, zebra, crocodile, and a rich variety of bird life and butterflies.

Ideal for day-trippers, facilities include a picnic and braai area where firewood can be bought from the ranger. Limited camping facilities are available, but only to those who book well in advance. Visitors can take themselves on various self-guided trails including the 9-km Bushbuck Trail; but the highlight is the fascinating Remedies and Rituals Trail. At under 2 km, the trail is not exactly an arduous physical challenge, but rather an absorbing educational meander that can be comfortably completed in an hour. The trail has been planned to introduce visitors to those plants which were important medically or spiritually (or both) to the early inhabitants of this region, both the white settlers and the Zulu.

There are direction markers along the route; the various trees and plants are identified and their uses described. For example, both Zulus and settlers prized the buffalo thorn tree (*Ziziphus mucronata*): the settlers roasted and ground the stones of the berry and used it as a substitute for coffee; and for the Zulu the branches of the tree were a vital element in the burial of chiefs. The bark extract from the tree fuchsia (*Halleria lucida*) was used by Zulu medicine men to induce vomiting and is apparently still in use, especially after an alcoholic binge! The flowering of the red-leafed bush willow or ghost tree (*Combretum kraussi*) was regarded as a herald of spring and a signal to the Zulu to begin ploughing and planting; the bark from the lavender tree (*Heteropyxis natalensis*) is reputed to be both an aphrodisiac and a cure for impotency; and both white settlers and Zulus used an infusion of coastal silver leaf (*Brachylaena discolor*) to treat diabetes and renal conditions.

Within the reserve are two historical monuments dating back to the Anglo-Zulu wars. On a hill overlooking the Tugela is the site of Fort Pearson. The unrest resulting from the power struggle for succession where Cetshwayo defeated and killed his brother Mbulazi caused a nervous Natal Government to build seven forts along the banks of the Tugela to protect their northern border. One of these, Fort Williamson, was replaced by Fort Pearson, which was built at the pont crossing a kilometre upriver in 1878. It was from Fort Pearson that the British marched into Zululand at the start of the Anglo-Zulu War.

Today, little remains of Fort Pearson apart from the outer trenches. There is a small picnic area, a stone cairn, various plaques and some naval graves

Where to stay

There is an abundance of accommodation of every variety on Natal's north coast, although you need to book well in advance during the season. Contact the Durban Publicity Association. Anyone wishing to camp at the Harold Johnson Nature Reserve should contact the Officer-in-Charge. (See other panel for addresses.)

The old, gnarled Ultimatum Tree – in the shade of which began the final countdown to the Anglo-Zulu War of 1879.

A somewhat empty Tugela River winds its way through the Harold Johnson Nature Reserve. Fort Pearson was situated on the hills seen in the background.

(during the war the fort was occupied by men from the Royal Navy). It stretches the imagination to stand on the lonely hill in a deserted landscape and consider that up to 5 000 men were accommodated here at various times during the war. There is a magnificent view of both the Tugela and across to the opposite bank, where Fort Tenedos was built in 1879 to guard the pont crossing on the other side. More war graves from the period lie about a kilometre to the south.

Immediately below Fort Pearson at the old pont site on the right bank of the Tugela is another national monument, the Ultimatum Tree. It was in the shade of this sycamore fig on 11 December 1878 that representatives of the British Governor, Sir Bartle Frere, met a Zulu delegation and presented them with an ultimatum.

At this time, the differences between the British Government and the Zulus had reached flashpoint. There was the issue of the border dispute between Zululand and the Transvaal, but the real bone of contention was the Zulus' military might.

Among other things, the British demanded that the Zulus abandon their traditional military system, that they pay compensation for the molesting of two white men, that missionaries be allowed to return to Zululand and that a British resident be appointed to live with their king Cetshwayo, to supervise relationships between themselves and the Zulus.

The Zulus were given 30 days in which to reply. When the time was up they asked for an extension, which the British took as a rejection of the ultimatum. So on 12 January 1879 the British invaded Zululand from Fort Pearson and the Zulu War of 1879 began.

A photograph of the actual delivery of the ultimatum and the two delegations under the tree can be seen in the Durban Museum. A steep path from the marker at Fort Pearson will lead you to the Ultimatum Tree, or it can be approached by road. The area surrounding the tree is fenced off, but you can still enter it, read the plaque, gaze across the Tugela and absorb the historical atmosphere.

Harold Johnson Nature Reserve at a glance (map page 132)

How to get there: From Durban, take the N2 to the north. The reserve is about an hour from Durban, 24 km from Stanger. Five kilometres south of the John Ross bridge, there's a turn-off to the right leading down to the south bank of the Tugela. The area is well signposted.
Weather: Hot and humid in summer, mild to warm in winter.
What to do: Exploring, hiking, game and bird-spotting.
Special attraction: The Remedies and Rituals Trail.
More information: Harold Johnson Nature Reserve, PO Box 148, Darnall 4480; tel (0324) 61574. Natal Parks Board, PO Box 662, Pietermaritzburg 3200; tel (0331) 471961. Durban Unlimited, PO Box 1044, Durban 4000; tel (031) 3044934.

'Here rests a brave British soldier' is the wording on these tombstones situated near the Ultimatum Tree. This simple but poignant inscription was used when the body of a soldier could not be identified.

'The secret conclave of the elephant'

Mgungundlovu, situated just south of the White Umfolozi River in northern Natal and once the royal capital of Dingane, offers a fascinating glimpse into the mind of this Zulu king

THE RECONSTRUCTION of Mgungundlovu is a work in progress, but that does not mean you should postpone your visit until the historians and archaeologists have packed up their tools and left. The process by which the royal capital of Dingane is being raised, quite literally, from its ashes, is fascinating. Guides are on hand to fill in the gaps left by time, and if you visit the museum during winter, you will find archaeologists at work, sifting the terrain for clues to information not found in history books.

A tour of Mgungundlovu will take you past completed huts, and many more under reconstruction, thus providing you with an opportunity to study both hut-building techniques and the social life of the Zulu. Finally, your walk will culminate at the grave of Voortrekker leader Piet Retief, whose death here was a significant and controversial chapter in the history of the country.

The events leading up to the killing were briefly as follows: After the Voortrekkers had entered Natal from the Orange Free State in November 1837, their leader Piet Retief paid a visit to Dingane, king of the Zulus, to obtain land for settlement. He received a hearty welcome and an apparent indication that Dingane would grant the land on condition that Retief recovered stolen cattle from hostile chief Sekonyela and gave him 11 rifles. Retief returned the cattle, but failed to provide the rifles.

On the morning of 6 February 1838, Retief and his men entered Mgungundlovu leaving their guns outside. The meeting proceeded smoothly until at a sudden shout of *'Babulaleni abathakathi!'* ('Kill the wizards!') from Dingane, warriors overpowered the visitors and dragged them to KwaMatiwane where they were killed. The remains of the Retief party were later found by trekkers who claimed that a land deed, signed by Dingane, was among the possessions (many historians doubt this ever existed – certainly none exists today).

Hindsight has revealed that, from the start, Dingane viewed the Trekkers as a threat that had to be eliminated. His carefully planned deception gives a fascinating glimpse into the mind of the Zulu king; the royal capital Mgungundlovo, reconstructed with the help of archaeological and conventional research, gives more.

Dingane was a notable character, charming, intelligent, shrewd and artistic. He was tall and muscular and obsessed with personal cleanliness. He had a sense of grandeur and a style unique among rulers of the day. He spent most of his time in the *isigodlo* (royal area) being entertained by his mistresses with song and dance. Their dress, for different occasions, he designed himself and many of the songs were composed by him.

He was not like Shaka, a warrior-king. Indeed, his people considered him a liberator, who had killed Shaka in order to free Zululand from the heel

Where to stay

There is accommodation for limited numbers of visitors at *Babanango Valley Lodge*, PO Box 10, Babanango, 3950; tel (03872) 1303.

The site of Dingane's capital, built on flat terrain to enable the king's guards to spot the arrival of potential enemies.

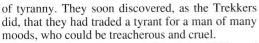

(Left) A monument to the murdered Voortrekker leader, Piet Retief.
(Right) An artist's impression of the arrival of Piet Retief at Dingane's headquarters.

of tyranny. They soon discovered, as the Trekkers did, that they had traded a tyrant for a man of many moods, who could be treacherous and cruel.

Mgungundlovu was established in 1829 and finally burnt down on the order of Dingane soon after the Battle of Blood River. Its name is derived from the Zulu phrase *ungungu we ndlovu*, which means 'the secret conclave of the elephant'. Its function was that of military settlement and Dingane's royal capital.

More or less oval in shape, it consisted of some 1 700 huts that could house up to 7 000 residents. Standing six to eight deep, the huts formed a huge circle around an open arena known as the large cattle kraal, a space also used for military parades and gatherings. The circle of huts was enclosed both inside and out by a strong palisade.

From the main entrance on the northern side, the huts of the warriors stretched around the circle to the royal enclosure directly opposite and about 600 m distant. The king, his mistresses and female attendants resided here. Dingane never officially married, but surrounded himself with at least 500 women who were divided into two groups. The white *isogodlo* was the largest group and consisted mainly of girls presented to the king by his important subjects.

The black *isogodlo* comprised about 100 privileged women selected at the annual *umkhosi* ('rites of the first fruits') and included the *Bheje* – a smaller group favoured by the king as his mistresses, some of whom lived in a small, private settlement behind the main complex.

The huts of the black *isogodlo* were divided into compartments, and within one of these stood the king's private hut. Archaeological excavations have revealed that this hut, with a diameter of approximately 10 m, was probably the largest hut ever built in the traditional Zulu manner. It was supported by 22 posts entirely covered in glass beads, of which the molten remains have been recovered.

Coppersmithing appears to have thrived at Mgungundlovu and the remains of crucible shards, slag and spilt copper found at KwaMbecini west of the main complex suggest that this was the coppersmithing site. Oral tradition claims that Kwa-Nkata, just outside the complex near the main entrance, was Dingane's execution ground, but historians believe it was located on a ridge northeast of the settlement known as KwaMatiwane. This is where the skeletal remains of the murdered Voortrekkers were found, and the controversial land treaty reputedly retrieved from a leather bag near the remains of Retief.

Visitors to the Mgungundlovu Museum (formerly known as Dingaanstat) have to be accompanied by an official guide. Try to avoid walking on the exposed hut floors or excavation areas; and as far as picking up artefacts is concerned, the rule here is definitely 'hands off'!

Mgungundlovu at a glance (map page 132)

How to get there: If you're travelling southwards from the Transvaal, Mgungundlovu lies approximately one hour's drive south of Vryheid, off the R34. If you are travelling from Durban, drive northwards along the N2, and take the turn off onto the R68 to Eshowe. At Melmoth the R68 branches west and the R34 continues northwards, passing Mgungundlovu (signposted 'Dingaanstat') en route for Vryheid.

Weather: Summers are generally hot and humid, while winters are mild.
What to do: Explore Mgungundlovu on a guided tour.
Special attractions: A section of the royal enclosure, which has been reconstructed as authentically as possible.
Visiting times: The museum is open from 8 am to 5 pm daily.
More information: Contact Mgungundlovu Museum, Private Bag X831, Melmoth 3835; tel (03545) 2254.

Unspoiled serenity of a sub-tropical lake

At the heart of the KwaZulu region known as Maputaland is Lake Sibaya – the country's largest natural freshwater lake and one of the few remaining untouched wilderness areas in southern Africa

LAKE SIBAYA LIES LIKE A PEARL in a string of lakes that stretches from Kosi Bay in the north to Lake St Lucia in the south. Five thousand years ago it was a sea estuary – but today it is separated from the Indian Ocean by a ridge of forested dunes.

The lake's unspoilt shores consist of a labyrinth of inlets, small coves and waterways. Covering some 77 sq km, the blue, placid depths of the lake reach down to 40 m in some places. Interestingly, there are still about ten species of marine fish living in the lake which have adapted themselves to fresh water. These include the Mozambiquan tilapia, which, due to a lack of suitable nutrients, does not achieve a weight of more than 1,5 kg.

Fishing is possible here and, although private vessels are not allowed, boats can be hired at a reasonable rate for exploring, sightseeing and fishing. Swimming is prohibited, due to the presence of a thriving population of hippo and Nile crocodile, both of which are vital to the lake's ecosystem.

The crocs are responsible for keeping the catfish population under control, and hippos transfer nutrients from shore to lake by eating land vegetation and then thoughtfully relieving themselves in the water. They also keep channels open, control the growth of reeds and churn up the sediment at the bottom of the lake.

Dominating the neighbourhood, however, is a huge variety of birds (280 species have been recorded) for which this lake is justly famous. Sibaya is home to one of the largest known colonies of fish eagle and there are no fewer than three types of kingfisher – pied, giant and malachite – as well as cormorants, flamingos, pelican, and herons, to mention but a few.

Bird-watching can be done by boat or from the comfort of the excellent hides overlooking seasonal pans. To explore on foot, there is a 3-km trail which takes in the shore and forest. On this trail you might be lucky enough to see some of the other animals of the region, including white-tailed mongooses, side-striped jackals, civets, water leguaans, reedbuck and the forest cobras.

Overlooking the lake, sheltered beneath the protective embrace of shady umdoni trees, is Baya Camp: rustic, picturesque and specially designed to blend with the wilderness. Sited about 150 m from the shoreline, the camp consists of seven very comfortable thatched bungalows, each with a hand basin and cold running water. Bedding is supplied by the camp and each bungalow has battery-powered electric lights, although there are no plug sockets.

The excellent ablution facilities have hot and cold water, with the hot water dependent on both boilers and solar power. Timber boardwalks link the bungalows, ablution facilities, sundeck and communal *boma* where cooking, eating and socialising goes on. There's a communal kitchen equipped with

Where to stay

Baya Camp has three four-bed and four two-bed bungalows. Book well ahead, though the camp will not accept bookings made more than six months in advance. Bring your own food; there is a small store with basic supplies 4 km away, otherwise the nearest place for food and petrol is Mbazwana, some 18 km away. Firewood can be purchased at the camp.

The flamingo is one of 280 species of birds that have been recorded in the Lake Sibaya area.

An aerial view of the coastline of northern Natal, with Lake Sibaya stretching far inland.

fridge and freezer, and even experienced cooks who'll prepare your food on request.

Administered by the KwaZulu Bureau of Natural Resources, Lake Sibaya has been earmarked to become a Tribal Game Reserve. Local inhabitants will co-manage the reserve, using the environment as they have always done. This new, holistic approach to conservation is considered by experts to be the answer for Africa and will accommodate the ever-increasing number of 'ecotourists', to use the current buzzword. In terms of this new policy, reserves will be Africanised – in other words, rural development, conservation and tourism will go hand in hand in these areas.

Until recently, this pristine environment wasn't easily accessible to visitors, roads being virtually nonexistent. But with the surge of interest in conservation and ecology, unspoilt wilderness areas such as this have become highly sought after. Roads are still not the strong feature here, particularly after rains; even though four-wheel-drive vehicles are not a necessity, they do make life a lot easier.

A four-wheel-drive vehicle is a must, however, if you want to reach the sea from Sibaya, even though it's not far away. Permits to visit Nine Mile Beach are available to camp residents, and you can pack a picnic and spend a day enjoying the spotless, sparkling sand and sea. Sheltered rock pools are teeming with marine life, and the presence of sharks (and the absence of nets) in the sea means that it's probably advisable to confine your swimming and snorkelling to these beautiful pools.

Lake Sibaya at a glance (map page 132)

How to get there: From Johannesburg take the N3 southwards, turning off onto the R23 shortly after Heidelberg. Continue along the R23, joining the N11 at Volksrust, until you get to the R34 (38 km after Volksrust). Turn left and continue to Vryheid. From Vryheid the R69 leads to the N2, from where you follow the Sodwana signs to Mbazwana. At Mbazwana, turn left to the forestry office. From Mbazwana it is 16 km to Baya Camp and the road is well signposted.

From Durban take the N2 north. About 12 km after Hluhluwe, take the lower Mkuze road and follow the Sodwana signposts to Mbazwana. Follow the signs to Baya Camp.

Weather: Hot and humid in summer with rain. Mild in winter.
What to do: Relaxing, boating, walking, bird-watching at the lake. Swimming, snorkelling and beachcombing at Nine Mile Beach, and Baya Camp also has a small swimming pool.
Special precautions: Take the necessary precautions against bilharzia and malaria.
Special attractions: The untouched wilderness and serenity of the lake; the fish eagles.
More information: Write to The Reservation Office, KwaZulu Bureau of Natural Resources, Private Bag X9024, Pietermaritzburg 3201; tel (0331) 946696/7/8.

A primal paradise carpeted with 'sands of gold'

The sub-tropical lake system of Kosi Bay, situated near South Africa's border with Mozambique, is one of the last untouched regions of southern Africa

IN THE NORTHEASTERN CORNER of Maputoland, a narrow isthmus of forest-fringed sand shears off into the ocean to reveal the mouth of a huge inland expanse of water known as the Kosi Lakes.

The Portuguese explorer Manuel de Mesquita Perestrello, who weighed anchor here centuries ago, was so inspired by the beauty of this natural mouth that he called it Rio de la Madãos do Oro – 'the river of the sands of gold'.

During the day, the beaches do indeed have the radiance of gold, and at night – as if affirming their daytime lustre – the sand emanates a gentle phosphorescence that illuminates the sea around it.

Kosi Bay ranks as one of South Africa's truly wild places. Washed by a warm sea, its sub-tropical shores have surrendered 18 km of their hinterland to a network of lakes whose beauty is enough to take one's breath away.

A confused British seaman, Captain W F Owen, thought the estuary marked the point where the Mkuze River flowed into the sea. He not only misplaced the Mkuze (which flows into the St Lucia Estuary) but he also got the spelling wrong, calling it the Kosi River. But the name remains.

The Kosi Bay Nature Reserve is made up of a series of four lakes: Makhawulani, Mpungwini, Nhlange and Amanzimnyama. The largest is Nhlange ('the place of reeds'), which forms a superb natural harbour 8 km long, 5 km wide and 50 m deep, surrounded by a magnificent wilderness of forest and bush. The fringes of Amanzimnyama

For the local fishermen, the favoured means of transport through the maze of waterways is a canoe made from a number of individual wooden poles.

('black waters') have particularly large populations of crocodile and hippo.

Here dense swamp forests and giant Kosi palms (*Raphia australis*) line the lake shore, while water lilies and other freshwater plants flourish in the placid waters.

The mangrove swamps in the area are a very important ecological link in the northern Natal coastline, serving as a nursery area for marine invertebrates and fish.

A tidal estuary, fed by the inlet called uKhalwe ('the distant one') and known as eNkhovukeni ('up and down'), completes the network of lakes.

The inflow of vast quantities of warm water from the sea brings with it an ever-changing, teeming population of sealife large and small. Sea pike, grunter, bream and a variety of other fish make their way into the lake-chain, seeking out a level of salinity that will suit them.

It's not only the fish that flourish in this wonderful waterland. The complex also supports thousands of plants and insects, numerous animals and more than 250 species of birds. In fact, all that seems to be missing in this primeval landscape of mangroves, rare orchids, raffia palms, cycads and swamp fig trees is a dinosaur or two!

Geologists believe that the lakes were formed as a result of a dramatic drop in the levels of the world's oceans: the receding sea left behind the narrow, lakeside peninsulas that characterise the region today.

The Kosi Bay Nature Reserve is run by the Kwa-Zulu authorities and covers 11 000 ha of land. Its main camp lies along the banks of Lake Nhlange, and offers three thatched lodges and 15 camp sites, with hot- and cold-water showers.

The natural vegetation of the Kosi Bay lake system is rich and varied and includes dense thickets of raffia palms, as seen here.

At Bhanga Nek, the Turtle Survey Team of the Natal Parks Board and the KwaZulu Bureau of Natural Resources has been working hard to restore dwindling populations of leatherback and logger-head turtles.

Kosi Bay is an angler's paradise, popular for its excellent catches of queenfish, grunter and bar-racuda, which occasionally enter the lakes from the sea. The Kosi Bay Estuary has a beautiful, densely populated reef where you can snorkel in the warm, crystal-clear waters.

If you're not a fisherman you can always watch the Zulus use a *thonga* fish trap (a structure of poles that channels fish into a small enclosure in which they are then speared) – a very effective way of catching fish. Swimming in the lakes is not recom-mended because of the danger of crocodiles and hippos. Furthermore, bilharzia occurs in Lake Am-anzimnyama.

Bird-watching is excellent and species you're likely to see include flufftail, palm-nut vulture, fish eagle, white-backed night heron and crab plover.

The network of lakes teems with fish, which local fishermen are adept at catching – the skilfully constructed fish trap being one of the preferred methods.

Kosi Bay at a glance (map page 132)

How to get there: The easiest way to get to Kosi Bay is via Jozini Dam, from the N2. Bear left in Jozini, as though heading towards the Ndumo Game Reserve. Drive past the Ndumo turn-off to Kwangwanase. Continue straight ahead through the town of Kwangwanase itself (the last stop for petrol and supplies) and turn right at the signposted turn-off at the Star of the Sea mission. From here, 14 km of good sand road takes you to the camp at Lake Nhlange. The road from the camp site to the river mouth is 18 km of bad sand road that is suitable only for four-wheel-drive vehicles. Only five vehicle permits are issued each day for visits to the mouth.

Weather: Hot, humid summers and mild winters.
What to do: Fishing, skindiving, bird-watching, boating and hiking.
Special attractions: A major attraction at Kosi Bay is the four-day Kosi Trail which takes in the mangroves, marshes, swamp forests, raffia palms and the grasslands surrounding the lakes.
Special precautions: Take anti-malaria tablets before and during your stay.
More information: Write to the KwaZulu Bureau of Natural Resources, 367 Loop Street, Pietermaritzburg 3201; tel (0331) 946696/7/8.

Where to stay

The camp at Lake Nhlange has two-, four- and six-bed thatched luxury lodges, and a camp site. Take your own food and drink; the nearest shop is at Kwang-wanase about 40 km away. All reservations and enquiries should be addressed to Central Reser-vations, KwaZulu Bureau of Natural Resources, Private Bag X9024, Pietermaritzburg 3200; tel (0331) 946696/7/8.

A primal, sub-tropical Eden of interlacing waterways

Crocodiles, hippos and a wonderful variety of birds are found in abundance at Ndumo, a small game reserve situated 470 km north east of Durban

NDUMO GAME RESERVE could be described as a pocked-sized Okavango. Lying on the Pongola flood plain on the Mozambique border, this 10 000-ha reserve comprises a delicate lattice-work of pans and mysterious forests.

The reserve was established in 1924 in order to protect hippo and now protects the highest population density in the region. There are also plenty of crocodiles as well as a variety of mammals, such as impala, nyala, bushbuck, grey and red duiker, white and black rhino, buffalo, zebra and giraffe.

The reserve boasts more than 400 species of birds, almost as many as in the Kruger National Park (which is 190 times larger). This huge and diverse avian population is centred on the 4 km long Nyamithi Pan and the 6 km long Banzi Pan, and includes such aquatic species as white pelican, black heron, hamerkop, pygmy goose, water dik-kop, jacana and Pel's fishing owl.

Other birds to watch for are the pink-throated twinspot, green-capped eremomela, the yellow-spotted nicator, the broad-billed roller, the brown-headed parrot and southern banded snake-eagle. Fish eagles are ever-present and easily seen, and you'll spot them during game drives, perched high up on trees lining the pans.

One reason for the abundant bird life is that the seasonal ebb of the pans (which are fed by the Pongola River) exposes extensive beds of aquatic vegetation, which are a source of food for thousands of birds.

Driving within Ndumo during summer can be quite an adventure, as heavy rains can make the potholed roads slippery and difficult to negotiate. Although Ndumo enjoys a moderately dry, sub-tropical climate with 30 per cent less rain than at the coast, flooding often occurs in summer, catching inexperienced visitors off guard.

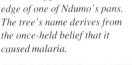

A cluster of fever trees lines the edge of one of Ndumo's pans. The tree's name derives from the once-held belief that it caused malaria.

A reed cormorant – one of the most common bird species found within the reserve.

Depending on demand, morning and afternoon tours in sun-canopied Land Rovers are conducted around the pans – these can be arranged with the camp superintendent. Other areas are open to normal motoring, and a self-guided auto trail brochure is available. You may take a day walk, but you must be accompanied by a game guard.

The special auto trail takes you through dense mahemane bush, open thornveld and groves of fever trees, punctuated by smaller groves of palm trees, and colourful displays of wild orchid and impala lily. (One of the best-known hunters in Africa during the last century, Frederick Courtenay Selous, who hunted in this area in 1896, described the mahemane bush as the thickest he had encountered in his wanderings through Africa.) A lookout tower along the trail gives you panoramic views of the reserve, with a distant view of Mozambique.

Although originally established by the Natal Parks Board, Ndumo is now administered by the KwaZulu Bureau of Natural Resources.

Ndumo at a glance (map page 132)

How to get there: To get to Ndumo from Durban, turn right off the N2 at the Jozini turn-off. Continue through Jozini village and bear left along the dam wall. Turn left at the Ndumo sign – the tar road becomes a sand one which leads to the reserve 14 km on. A highlight of the drive to the reserve is the magnificent view over Maputoland from the top of the Lebombo Mountains.
Weather: Very hot summers and mild winters.
What to do: Bird-watching and game viewing.
Special attractions: Large numbers of hippos, crocodiles and birds.
More information: KwaZulu Bureau of Natural Resources, 367 Loop Street, Pietermaritzburg 3200; tel (0331) 946696/7/8.

The roots of the sycamore fig often assume strange and evocative forms.

Where to stay

There is no caravan or camping site at Ndumo, but there are comfortable three-bed huts, or 'squaredavels', set among giant marula trees. Each hut is fitted with a gas-powered refrigerator, and a communal kitchen is available. A chef is always on hand to cook a meal for you. Bedding, cutlery and crockery are provided, but you must provide your own food. There is electricity.

To book, write to the Central Reservations Officer, Kwa-Zulu Bureau of Natural Resources, Private Bag X9024, Pietermaritzburg 3200; tel (0331) 946696/7/8.

Perched on the head of a hippo, a yellow-billed egret gives itself an early morning preening.

A game paradise saved from oblivion

*Once faced with virtual extinction, hundreds of wildlife species
in northern Natal are now protected at Itala,
a game reserve which ranks among the country's finest*

Where to stay

Accommodation is provided at various camps within the reserve. For reservations for Ntshondwe rest camp, Ntshondwe Lodge, the bush camps and wilderness trails, contact The Reservations Officer, Natal Parks Board, PO Box 1750, Pietermaritzburg 3200; tel (0331) 471981. Enquiries may also be made direct: telephone Itala reception (0388) 75105. To reserve a camp site, contact The Warden, Itala Game Reserve, PO Box 42, Louwsburg 3150; tel (0388) 75239. For queries concerning the conference centre, contact the Conference Organiser, Itala Game Reserve, PO Box 98, Louwsburg 3150; tel (0388) 75106.

Even if this pair of ibises was not present, the white droppings would give away the presence of their nest.

FOR MORE THAN HALF A CENTURY the broad spaces south of the Pongola River lay fallow, neglected by the environmentalists, its wildlife depleted, its vegetation infested with alien flora. Then, in 1972, the authorities proclaimed the area a formal game reserve – and so began one of the more inspiring stories in the annals of conservation.

Itala covers some 30 000 ha of varied countryside northeast of the northern Natal town of Vryheid. Before the arrival of the late 19th-century Boer settlers the area was rich in game, but the hunter's rifle and the great rinderpest epidemic of 1896 made crippling inroads into the vast herds of wild animals. More game – a great deal more – disappeared in the years after 1919, when a protracted, misguided and, in the event, near-disastrous campaign was launched to eradicate the disease-bearing tsetse fly that plagued the surrounding ranchlands. Tens of thousands of wild animals were slaughtered before, finally, in the early 1950s, extermination was abandoned in favour of chemical control.

By the time the Natal Parks Board (NPB) took control of Itala in 1973, tenant farmers had been in occupation for some years, soil erosion and overgrazing had damaged the land, and very little game remained. Indeed, a total of 25 mammal species had become locally extinct.

The situation was serious but, happily, not irreversible, and the NPB resolved to restore Itala to its original pristine character, to bring back the game, to transform what was, at the time, a Cinderella among reserves into one of the country's most important game conservation areas.

The NPB's rescue operation has been hugely successful. Damaged veld was allowed to recover and farming land was reclaimed. Records from the long-defunct Pongola reserve, not far from Itala, were examined to establish what wildlife populations the region had sustained in the old days and a stocking programme launched that has seen the reintroduction of 20 large species, among them elephant and buffalo, white and black rhino, giraffe, kudu, tsessebe, eland, cheetah and brown hyaena.

Today the reserve is home to 80 different types of mammal, including one of the country's largest populations of klipspringer; to more than 320 bird species – among them such notables as bald ibis, bat-hawk, martial eagle, goliath heron, Cape eagle-owl and brown-necked parrot – and to nearly 100 varieties of amphibian and reptile.

The reserve – about a quarter of which comprises open bushveld, the remainder mainly steep, densely covered valleys – is home to all the major game species except lion. For visitors, there are well-maintained gravel roads that lead through the most promising wildlife areas to observation points and picnic sites. An informative self-drive guide booklet is available at Ntshondwe camp.

For those who want a longer, closer look at the wilderness, the Natal Parks Board lays on conducted three-day trails during the winter months (March to October). These run from Friday to Monday and are limited to parties of eight; hikers spend their nights in the tented base camp (the conditions, though, are anything but primitive: among the amenities are flush toilets) and make daily excursions into the veld. Your hosts provide all the camping gear, including sleeping-bags, but bring your own food (and drink). Budget for a consumption rate of around a kilogram a day per person; provisions are usually pooled, and the cooking chores shared.

Itala's pride is its new rest camp, a place wholly in keeping with its superb surrounds and named Ntshondwe after the great cliffs that rise above it. The vistas take in the escarpment and the magical valley below; thatched buildings hug a boulder-strewn hillside graced by giant euphorbias and, in winter, by the brilliant colours of the erythrina blossom. Accommodation consists of 39 self-contained one-, two- or three-bedroomed cottages and chalets, each with its own fully equipped kitchen, though for those who don't feel like fending for themselves, there's also a licensed à la carte restaurant and take-away, and a coffee shop in situ.

Among other visitor amenities are a cocktail bar, a curio shop, a mini-market, two open *boma* areas for sociable gatherings and a lovely little rock pool that beckons you during the heat of a summer's day

Ntshondwe rest camp blends in so well with the landscape that it seems it could almost have grown out of the ground!

– all of which are part of the central complex, sited close to a water hole that attracts crocodiles and a splendid array of birds. Close by is the modern conference centre, which has a 90-seat auditorium and two smaller halls, breakaway rooms and bedroom units, and a small, rustic camping ground with basic services (communal kitchen, cold-water showers). There are no facilities for caravans.

Farther up the hill you'll find Ntshondwe Lodge, a luxurious three-bedroomed guesthouse with its own swimming pool, sun deck and barbecue area. The lodge provides complete privacy, and the views across the valley are breathtaking.

Very different, but in their own way just as attractive, are Itala's three bush camps, idyllic retreats sited well away from the main tourist routes. Each

has a distinctive character: Thalu is a reed, timber and thatch two-bedroomed cottage that nestles snugly in the bend of a river; Mbizo, overlooking the rapids and pools of the Mbizo watercourse, accommodates eight people in its two huts; Mhlangeni is quite enchanting: its two five-bed units, linked by an inviting sundeck, are set on a rocky knoll above the Nseme stream, near the upper reaches of the Pongola River.

All three camps at Itala offer solitude, tranquillity, and an authentic African bush experience. At each, a game guard takes you on day walks through the veld; in the evening you sit around the open fire, beneath the stars, to talk of the wilderness you've explored, and to listen to the many sounds of the African night.

Itala at a glance (map page 132)

How to get there: The reserve is situated near Louwsburg in northern Natal. By road from Durban: take the route through Eshowe and Melmoth to Vryheid and then the tarred road to Louwsburg via Hlobane. From the Transvaal: via Piet Retief and Paulpietersburg. From Natal north coast: take the main route to Pongola; turn left to Magudu and then right onto the Louwsburg/Vryheid road. The nearest general supplies outlet is at Louwsburg, 5 km from the reserve gate and 25 km from the field office. Petrol may be bought at the main gate. By air: Itala has its own 1 200-m tarred airstrip. Make landing arrangements in advance with the reserve office; tel: (0388) 75105. On arrival, visitors destined for Ntshondwe should report to camp reception before 4.30 pm (after which the office will be closed).

Visitors who have booked into either the Thalu or the Mbizo bush camp or the camping ground should report at the field office, also before 4.30 pm.

Those who have reserved accommodation at Mhlangeni bush camp may drive directly to the camp, turning right immediately after entering Itala. Hikers are advised to arrive by noon on the Friday, which will give them plenty of time to settle in before dark. They will be met by the Trails Ranger at Ntshondwe.

Weather: Typical of other bushveld areas: summer days are hot, with clouds building up from around noon to produce heavy late-afternoon downpours. Winter days are clear-skied and mild to warm, the nights chilly and occasionally cold. Take warm clothing if you visit the reserve between May and August.

What to do: Take your choice of game-viewing and bird-spotting, walks and hikes, or relaxing around camp.

Special attractions: Scenic variety within the reserve. The general region offers some rewarding day drives: to the south and southwest are the great battlefields (and much else of historical and cultural interest) of Zululand; to the east the splendid game parks and reserves of the coastal belt (Umfolozi, Hluhluwe, Mkuzi, Ndumo and the St Lucia complex among them).

Special precautions: Itala is a malarial area so be sure to take a course of anti-malaria tablets. (Start taking the tablets prior to your departure).

More information: Contact the Natal Parks Board, PO Box 1750, Pietermaritzburg 3200; tel (0331) 471981.

The imposing form of Ntendeka Cliff after which the wilderness area has been named.

Ancient Zulu refuge in the 'place of precipitous heights'

Rare plants and animals make their home in Natal's Ntendeka, a wilderness area within the indigenous Ngome forest

Where to stay

No camping is allowed in the wilderness area, but there is a camp site on the Ntendeka boundary (tents only, no caravans) with toilet, hot-water shower and braai facilities (including braaiwood). Alternatively, the nearby town of Vryheid has a range of accommodation at reasonable prices.

SOUTH AFRICA'S smallest and arguably most beautiful wilderness area is Ntendeka, consisting of 5 250 ha of undulating grasslands, verdant forests and dramatic cliffs with breathtaking waterfalls. Rivers and streams have formed deep valleys and the varied topography has resulted in great variations of temperature, rainfall and vegetation in this relatively small area.

Lying within the Ngome State Forest, Ntendeka remains romantically isolated. Yet, being so small, it is one of southern Africa's more accessible wilderness areas and can easily be explored on foot from one end to another. Over 45 km of footpaths exist, most passing deep beneath the forest canopy on a soft carpet of leaves. Some well-trodden routes were established by the area's earliest inhabitants, such as the Zulu Highway, a traditional route leading from the plains to the highlands. This ancient way starts from the police station on the northern boundary and leads hikers past an *isiVavine* or stone

cairn, where it is customary for passers-by to add another stone for good luck.

Woodcutters discovered the potential of this forest way back in 1876. Scores of them moved into the forest and it was heavily exploited for over 20 years until the outbreak of the Anglo-Boer War. During this period many of the forest's biggest trees (particularly yellowwoods) were felled. Evidence of the woodcutters' saw pits can still be seen, giving some indication of the size of the trees they worked. A stone oven near the western boundary of the wilderness area is another relic from this period.

Despite the ravages of over 20 years of uncontrolled logging, the area has been protected since 1905, and remains a majestic, lush, high-canopy forest, with a rare combination of both coastal and inland tropical forest that is not found in any other conservation area in Natal. The vegetation is thick and richly textured, from delicate, lacy fern fronds to the giant-leaved *Streptocarpus*.

More than 180 species of trees and shrubs have been recorded here, and rare species include the bastard stinkwood, the Natal hard pear, green witch hazel and the terblanz beech which is also found in Tanzania and Madagascar. Both terrestrial and tree orchids thrive in the green heart of the forest, and in season, Ngome lilies and clivias create a showy display. The tallest, most prolific trees are the forest waterwood, some growing as tall as 30 m. Other common trees are the bushwillow, silver oak, tree fuchsia and knobwood.

One of Ntendeka's most intriguing specimens is the strangler fig, and an excellent example can be seen at the Ntendeka camp site. Birds or animals drop seeds into trees, which usually germinate in the forks of branches. Long aerial roots snake around the tree towards the ground, where they establish themselves in the earth. The stem then becomes thicker and stronger, locking the host tree in a fatal embrace.

East of Ntendeka Cliff is an exquisite waterfall, looking fragile and sheer against the hard, horizontal slabs of rock. There are numerous other lovely cascades, streams and fresh, clear pools, many of them bounded by smooth boulders, softened by moss and framed with lacy greenery.

Out in the open grasslands umbrella-shaped tree ferns seem to march along the watercourses, and in the spring, delicate wildflowers – including coral candelabras, watsonias and white ericas – speckle the landscape among the grass.

A variety of animals live unobtrusively in the wilderness area, including baboon, samango monkey, vervet monkey, grey, blue and red duiker, bushbuck, bushpig, dassies, porcupine, caracal, and many other smaller creatures such as snakes, beetles, butterflies and frogs.

Bird life is more prolific, with nearly 200 species having been recorded in the Ntendeka area – including some endangered birds such as white stork, martial eagle, house martin and blue swallow. You might also see the comical bald ibis, secretary bird, purple-crested loerie, crowned eagle and trumpeter hornbill.

Remember that loud conversation and laughter are bound to sabotage your chances of seeing any wildlife. Shy forest creatures will leave their hiding places only if a tranquil atmosphere prevails. The best course of action for seeing the resident animals in their natural habitat is to settle down quietly and patiently in a forest clearing, keep your eyes and ears open and attune your senses to the surroundings. You may be well rewarded.

A waterfall crashes down a tree-lined ravine. There are several breathtaking waterfalls in the Ntendeka Wilderness Area.

Ntendeka Wilderness Area at a glance (map page 132)

How to get there: From Johannesburg, take the N3 south until about 5 km past Heidelberg where you take the R23 past Standerton to Volksrust. Turn south onto the N11. Just before reaching Newcastle, take the R34 east, continue past Utrecht and on to Vryheid. From there, take the R69 for about 20 km, then turn right at the Nongoma Road (R618), and carry on for a distance of about 50 km until you see the Ngome Forest Station sign. The forest station is situated about 600 m to the right.

From Durban, take the N2 north until the R618 turn-off at Mtubatuba. Continue on this road past Nongoma until you see the sign for the Ngome Forest Station.

Weather: Summers are hot to warm, with rain and mist; winters are mild, with occasional snow on the plateau and periodic berg winds.

What to do: Hiking, wildlife-spotting, flora-identifying and everything else you associate with the wilderness. You may drink the running water and swim in the pools, but any use of soap or detergents is prohibited.

Special attractions: Ntendeka Cliff and the exquisite waterfall on the eastern side, the giant-leaved plant and fern species.

More information: Write to The State Forester, Ngome State Forest, Private Bag X9306, Vryheid 3100; tel (0386) 71883.

No less than 64 bronze ox-wagons mark the heart of the Blood River battlesite – silent testimony to one of the most pivotal military events in South Africa's turbulent history.

The place of a covenant forged in blood

The reconstructed battlesite at Blood River, situated near Dundee in northern Natal, dramatically illustrates a victory for fire power and military strategy in one of the most famous battles in South African history

Where to stay

Dundee is the centre nearest to Blood River, and indeed of the Battlefields Route. Its accommodation includes: *El Mpati Hotel*, PO Box 15, Dundee 3000; tel (0341) 21155; the *Royal Hotel*, PO Box 31, Dundee 3000; tel (0341) 22147; the *Dundee Municipal Caravan Park*, Private Bag 2024, Dundee 3000; tel (0341) 22607.

THE CAPE HAS ITS WINE ROUTE: Natal has a Battlefields Route. Some of the fiercest battles of the Great Trek and three major wars were fought on this province's lush hills and plains.

From Dundee, about half-an-hour's drive in the direction of Vryheid brings you to the Battleground of Blood River, one of the best-known and most emotionally regarded military clashes in the history of South Africa.

Today the battlesite is a remarkable monument consisting of 64 replica Voortrekker wagons cast in bronze and situated just as they were on the day of the famous battle. Also on display are replicas of the three cannons that proved so decisive in halting repeated Zulu charges against the laager. For the curious visitor – or ardent historian – the reconstructed battlefield brings to life a bloody but fascinating chapter in South Africa's annals.

If you have already visited the museum at Mgungundlovu (see separate entry), you'll know the background to Blood River. It was, in essence, an act of retribution to avenge the massacre of Piet Retief and his followers at Mgungundlovu. The Boers' victory at Blood River ensured the survival of the Trekkers in Natal and paved the way for the establishment of the Republic of Natalia.

November 1838 had been a bleak month for the Voortrekkers in Natal. Their bid to settle in

Zululand had ended in death, disaster and dissension. Unable to choose a leader after the death of Retief, the Voortrekkers called on a dynamic farmer from Graaff-Reinet to lead them to victory. Andries Pretorius joined the Trekkers on 22 November and within a week had organised a commando of 468 men with whom he set off for a final reckoning with the Zulu king, Dingane.

Pretorius was a brilliant military tactician and a natural leader. Though his commando would be outnumbered at a ratio of more than 20 to one, fire power gave them the edge over an enemy armed with *knobkieries* (clubs) and spears. A fortified laager, strategically placed to concentrate the Boers' fire power, would secure the advantage. But his masterstroke was the way in which he forged and fortified the spirit of his men prior to the battle. This he did by means of a special religious 'covenant' made on 9 December and repeated every evening before the day of the battle. What this covenant amounted to was that, if God would grant the Voortrekkers a victory over the Zulus, they would build a church in His honour, and they and their descendants would commemorate the day of victory every year from then on.

The Day of the Covenant is still celebrated on 16 December by a large number of people who see the victory as a miracle which must be attributed to divine intervention. Though modern historians take issue with that view and philosophers question the very concept, it is reasonable to assume that, if such a covenant existed (and there are researchers who claim it did not), it did much to strengthen the morale of the undisciplined and disheartened men under Pretorius's command.

To visitors at the monument at Blood River, with its full-scale reconstruction of the laager, Pretorius's strategic brilliance is immediately evident. At this site, the Ncome Spruit forms a right angle with a deep donga, two natural features that protected the laager on two sides. By digging in here, Pretorius would eventually force the Zulus to launch their main attack from an open, treeless plain in the northwest.

The laager, traditionally a rectangular shape, was adapted to these circumstances. Only the wall of wagons that ran parallel with the donga (situated about 20 m from it) was completely straight. The rest of the wagons were arranged in a wide crescent from one end of this wall to the other; in reality the laager resembled a capital 'D'.

Wagons were drawn up close to one another with the shaft of one tied firmly to the deck of the one in front, and wheels were joined with trek-chains. A large gateway in the middle of the crescent provided last-minute access for the Voortrekkers' oxen and horses, and an exit for a mounted commando, while two small cannons were mounted in smaller openings at the northeastern and northwestern corners.

Weather conditions favoured the Voortrekkers. The night of 15 December was moonless and the starlight was obscured by thick mist. The Zulu commanders had planned to attack under cover of the night, but in the pitch darkness they lost their way and reached the laager only towards the morning of the sixteenth. When light dawned, the Trekkers were shocked to discover that they were completely

The drama of the Battle of Blood River is faithfully captured in this painting by W H Coetzer, which hangs in the Voortrekker Museum in Pietermaritzburg.

surrounded by a dense mass of Zulu warriors, still being augmented by the arrival of new regiments.

But the strength of the position and, paradoxically their vast numbers, told against the Zulus. It was simply too large an army to be deployed in such confined space. Though they rose as one man and charged, there was no room to hurl an *assegai* or a *knobkierie*, and warriors were trampled to death in the charge. The defenders could hardly miss as they fired volley after volley into the approaching mass. When Pretorius sensed the attacks were weakening, the gateway was opened to allow the mounted men to pour out in a counter-attack. The Zulu regiments lost the cohesion that was their most effective tactic and retreat soon turned into headlong flight.

Of the 12 000 warriors despatched by Dingane, 3 000 lay dead by midday, while Trekker losses were limited to three wounded. The casualties are instructive. To those who uphold the covenant, they seem nothing short of miraculous. But to military historians, they dramatically illustrate the disparity between the power of firearms operated from a defensive position and stabbing-spears wielded in the open.

Whatever emotional and spiritual significance descendants have chosen to attach to the victory at Blood River, the overwhelming impression on a visit to the site is this: courage on both sides must have been great indeed.

Blood River at a glance (map page 132)

How to get there: From Dundee, head north for Vryheid. After about 21 km, take the turn-off to your right; you'll reach the site after about 19 km.
Weather: Hot, humid summers and crisp, clear winters are characteristic of this part of Natal.
What to do: The laager has been reconstructed on the original battlefield. Its position in an angle formed by a donga and the Ncome Spruit is significant, as the strategic location of the laager is considered crucial to the victory.
Special attractions: The full-scale reconstruction of 64 ox-wagons, all cast in bronze, as

well as replicas of the various cannons deployed in the battle, make this a most remarkable war monument.
Visiting times: The museum is open daily. From Dundee, allow about two to three hours for the excursion.
More information: Contact the Dundee Publicity Association, Private Bag X2024, Dundee 3000; tel (0342) 22654; the Information Bureau, Vryheid, PO Box 57, Vryheid 3100; tel (0381) 2137; the Pietermaritzburg Publicity Association, PO Box 25, Pietermaritzburg 3200; tel (0331) 451348/9.

Original flashpoint of the Anglo-Boer War

If the country's mining or military past interests you, you'll be fascinated by the Talana Museum complex, situated a few kilometres outside Dundee

The Consol Glass Collection forms one of many fascinating exhibits at the Talana Museum.

MORE OF AN EXPERIENCE than simply a collection of artefacts, the Talana Museum, situated on a battlefield, is the only museum of its kind in South Africa. The scope of its displays is breathtaking – from military uniforms and coal miners' helmets to pieces of glass five millennia old. It's a happy coincidence that the word Talana is Zulu for 'the storage shelf for the chief's precious possessions'.

The rich and varied history of Talana began with the Smith family from Scotland. Tom Smith, a builder who immigrated from the district of Dundee, bought 1 500 ha from a Voortrekker and built a two-roomed cottage on the slopes of Talana Hill. The cottage is one of nine buildings preserved on the 10-ha property today.

In 1864 Tom was joined by his brother Peter and his family. While Tom made bricks from clay he dug from the nearby Steenkoolstroom and built houses, Peter farmed and mined coal from the hill. The Dundee Brick & Tile Company became famous for Tom's red face-bricks, a style that was chosen by the Rand magnates when they built their gracious homes in Dundee.

Before Dundee was started, however, the Smith brothers sent their products to market in Pieter-maritzburg. Though the journey by ox-wagon was long and arduous, they both prospered.

A tent town flourished on part of their farm, although its growth was due largely to the fact that troops recalled from Zululand after the Battle of Isandhlwana built and occupied a fort nearby. It attracted traders and missionaries, among others, but when the soldiers left in 1879, the village was threatened with total evacuation. To avert this, Peter wisely donated 500 ha of his farm for the foundation of a town to be named after his birthplace in Scotland – Dundee.

Coal mining boomed in the 1880s and by 1896, no fewer than 13 coal mines operated in and around Dundee. The first organised coal company, the Dundee Coal Company, was floated on the London Stock Exchange in 1889 and Dundee subsequently became the centre of the coal mining industry in Natal. Because numerous highways and byways from the Rand to the coast and from north to south crossed in Dundee, it became known as the Meeting Place of the Seven Roads.

Besides the business of coal and bricks, though, there was something else for which Talana would soon hit world headlines: the Anglo-Boer War. It was here that the very first battle of that war took

The cemetery at Talana Hill, where the first British casualties of the Anglo-Boer War were buried.

place. On the dawn of 20 October 1899, nine days after the end of a Boer ultimatum to the British, commandos attacked the 4 000-strong force at Talana. While the battle was seen as a British victory, they lost 250 men, including their commander, General Sir William Penn-Symons. The Boers lost 145 men, but their spirits were unbroken, and they soon started bombarding Dundee.

Two British forts and the old gun emplacements of both sides are reminders of the battle that raged at Talana. Some British soldiers are buried in the cemetery, along with members of the Smith family. Look out for the grave of Dr Prideaux Selby, first doctor and Justice of the Peace to the Voortrekkers of the Biggarsberg. Headstones of other pioneers, which were rescued from various parts of the district, have also been erected. Talana, it's interesting to note, is the only museum to have a cemetery as part of its exhibits.

The indoor part of Talana, however, is where the real adventure begins. The history of the Zulus, Boers and British in the area can be viewed in the gracious Talana House. Built by Peter Smith's son, Thomas Patterson Smith, in 1896, Talana House boasts displays not only of the Anglo-Boer War but also of the life of early inhabitants of the Biggarsberg who lived in caves and rock shelters; the rise of the Zulu kingdom; and the ensuing conflict between Zulu and Voortrekker, culminating in the Battle of Blood River.

Enlarged in 1904, the house became a venue for sumptuous parties. The family entertained famous guests, including Princess Alice, the Countess of Connaught, Jan Smuts, Louis Botha and Sir Redvers Buller. And, being true Scotsmen, the Smiths always made sure that their guests had enough whisky, which they distilled themselves.

Near the main house, Tom Smith's original cottage has been restored and refurnished to its former simplicity, if not glory. So has Peter's workshop, which now houses a display of blacksmithing and carpentry tools. Smaller building exhibits include a cooling room, where they stored food, and a stone milkshed, built in 1924. There is also a small cottage, called Miner's Rest and which is typical of the home in which mine employees stayed in the early part of the century.

Seeing that the Smiths and Dundee played such a major role in the development of the vital coal industry, it's small wonder that the Chamber of Mines chose to situate its national museum at Talana – and this is definitely a museum with a difference. Even though it's been constructed above ground, everything has been done to recreate the feeling of being hundreds of metres beneath the earth's surface. A tunnel with wall faces resembling coal has been constructed, and the museum covers the history of coal mining, from the development of the fossil itself through to the headgear worn by miners.

But perhaps the most eye-catching exhibit at Talana is one that had less to do with the Smiths than with the town they founded. The Consol display, depicting the history of glass, commemorates Dundee's association with the glass industry, established here because of the availability of silica sand and coal. Some of the 580 pieces in the display date back to 3 000 BC, although most of them are between 120 and 200 years old, with the majority of the items having been collected in South Africa.

Henderson Hall is one of 11 buildings on the site of the Talana Museum. The hall houses industrial displays of coal, glass and bricks.

Talana Museum at a glance (map page 132)

How to get there: Follow the R33 leading northwest out of Dundee to Vryheid for 3 km.
Weather: Very hot and humid in summer, but any time of the year is good for a visit.
What to do: The museum is open from 8 am to 4 pm on weekdays, and 2 pm to 4 pm on weekends and holidays. The museum grounds, which include an old plantation of gum trees under which British soldiers once took cover, are perfect for walks and picnics. There are trails up to

the old forts, the gun emplacements and the cairn which marks the spot where General Sir William Penn-Symons was mortally wounded. In the vicinity of Dundee are also the battlegrounds of Blood River, Isandhlwana, Rorke's Drift and Elandslaagte, all of which are marked by a cannon on roadsigns.
More information: Talana Museum, Private Bag X2024, Dundee 3000; tel (0341) 22654. Dundee Publicity Association, PO Box 76, Dundee 3000; tel (0341) 22677.

The legacy of monks and a girl called Maria

*A beautiful church and several fine buildings
are a proud reminder of the once thriving
Maria Ratschitz Mission near Dundee in northern Natal*

I**N THE LATTER HALF** of the 19th century, a young girl called Maria drowned in the Bohemian village of Ratschitz thousands of kilometres away from Natal. A half-hour's drive from the Natal town of Dundee brings present-day travellers to a beautiful church on an abandoned mission. Its name is Maria Ratschitz. What is the connection?

The Maria Ratschitz Mission was established in 1886 by two Trappist monks from the Mariannhill mission. Trappists are known to observe silence and a lifestyle characterised by austerity, and these brave monks – who made their home in a simple wattle and daub cottage, framed by two huge yellowwood trees – were no exception.

But the two monks were not above indulging in a little nostalgia for their European roots. The site they had chosen, situated on a green hillside lying at the foot of the Hlatikulu mountain, reminded them of their Bohemian home.

Funds for their mission were provided by the parents of the tragically lost Maria, and the monks did their benefactors proud. They worked hard to create a model farm with superb vineyards and a fine Friesian herd, and to instill sound farming principles in the local people. They offered instruction in the skills of wagon-building, blacksmithing, wine-making and cooperage, building, carpentry and shoemaking, provided medical care and nurtured good relationships with surrounding farmers.

Their finest legacy is a splendid church, built soon after the Anglo-Boer War with funds sent from Bohemia. Its building was overseen by the renowned Abbe Pfanner of Mariannhill, and the sturdy church features a tall, elegant bell-tower, a

Where to stay

The *El Mpati Hotel*, PO Box 15, Dundee 3000; tel (0341) 21155, offers comfortable accommodation, while next door the *Royal Hotel*, PO Box 31, Dundee 3000, welcomes visitors in a country style; tel (0341) 22147.

Dundee has a municipal caravan park with two fully equipped rondavels for rent. Contact the Municipality, Private Bag X2024, Dundee 3000; tel (0341) 22121. There are also a number of lodges, self-catering cottages and bed-and-breakfast establishments in the area.

Accommodation closest to the Maria Ratschitz Mission is at *Balbrogie Guest Farm*, off the main road between Ladysmith and Newcastle. Contact them at Private Bag X70141, Wasbank 2920; tel (0345) 352.

A very imposing bell-tower is just one of the features of the Maria Ratschitz Mission church which make it one of Natal's most impressive religious buildings.

high altar and pulpit, skillfully painted murals and magnificent stained-glass windows. It is certainly one of the most beautiful churches in Natal and its loveliness makes the subsequent history and demise of the mission seem all the more tragic.

After a thriving half-century, the community that had grown up around the Maria Ratschitz Mission became a victim of the apartheid policy adopted by the South African Government since 1948. Zoning under the Group Areas Act declared the mission a so-called 'black spot' and its people were marked for forced removal. In the 1960s, the community was relocated to Lime Hill. The church moved its personal and financial resources elsewhere, and only a handful of families were allowed to remain in the area, to serve as labour for nearby farms.

The Dominicans, who had been running the mission since the First World War, withdrew and English Franciscans took their place. But the mission was already doomed, and all subsequent attempts to revive it have so far met with failure. Since the 1960s, the Maria Ratschitz has seen sporadic bursts of activity, most notably when Neil and Creina Alcock introduced an arts and crafts scheme in the 1970s. Their project became, like the original mission, a victim of South Africa's rather violent history.

Though the mission remains a sanctuary to some, nearly every reference to it in visitors' guides to Natal begins with the word 'abandoned'. It's a word that inspires mixed feelings in the hikers who visit the area. Several hiking trails lead from the mission into the surrounding hills and nothing disturbs the tranquil loveliness of the scenery. A popular route is the Monk's Trail, a relatively easy two-day hike that starts at Balbrogie Guest Farm nearby, climbs the Hlatikulu Mountain behind the mission station and culminates on the second night at the old monks' dormitory, one of several fine buildings that remain in the area.

The Maria Ratschitz Mission lies about 36 km outside Dundee, the geographical and administrative centre of northern Natal, a service centre for the farms of the area, and one-time frontier mining boom town. To visitors, it is a convenient staging post for visiting four of South Africa's most famous battlefields – Blood River, Isandhlwana, Rorke's Drift and Talana.

But it would be a mistake to overlook the unique charms of Dundee itself. It has the only glass museum in South Africa, the only display celebrating the history of the humble brick, and, in the Moth shellhole and museum, the most comprehensive collection of military memorabilia. Finally, on a lighter note, the Dundee Golf Course is said to be northern Natal's finest.

One of the impressive stained-glass windows that grace the interior of the church.

The Maria Ratschitz Mission at a glance (map page 132)

How to get there: From Dundee take the R602 leading south-west towards Ladysmith. After 20 km you'll reach a four-way intersection; turn right onto a dirt road signposted Newcastle/Collings Pass. After about 10 km a small sign indicates the Maria Ratschitz turn-off to your right. This road is in a poor condition.
Weather: The climate is moderate with warm, often sultry summers and crisp, chilly winters.
What to do: Visit one of Natal's most beautiful churches

on the deserted mission, but don't ignore the many charms of nearby Dundee.
Special attractions: Embark on the Monk's Trail, a two-day hike that culminates at the old monks' dormitory. It is one of several hiking trails in the area.
More information: Contact the Dundee Publicity Association, PO Box 76, Dundee, 3000; tel (0341) 23304. For details of the Monk's Hiking Trails and others in the area, tel (0245) 352.

A place of heroism and a wellspring of art

Rorke's Drift, situated 46 km southeast of Dundee, is the site of one of the most famous battles of the Anglo-Zulu War

WHEN A SWEDISH MISSIONARY established a mission station near Rorke's Drift in 1876, little did he know that three years later this humble site would become the scene of one of the most hard-fought battles of the Anglo-Zulu War. Nor could he know that, more than a century later, it would gain international repute for its beautiful and unique Zulu handicrafts.

The best-known drift through the Buffalo River, Rorke's Drift was named after James Rorke, a ferryman who drowned in its waters and whose remains lie buried at the foot of a nearby hillside. Looking at the unspoilt, majestic beauty of the surrounding countryside today, it's hard to imagine the bloody battles that once raged in the area.

The mission station was established by the Reverend Otto Witt of the Swedish Missionary Society, who built a small church, mission house and cattle kraal at the foot of a rocky mountain 1 km west of Rorke's Drift. In honour of the King of Sweden, he called it Oscarsberg.

When Lord Chelmsford, the commander-in-chief of British forces in Natal, invaded Zululand at Rorke's Drift on 11 January 1879, he encamped on the other side of the river, 16 km to the east, at Isandhlwana. Being so conveniently located close by, the Swedish mission was promptly converted into a supply depot and hospital. On 22 January, the British were attacked by the Zulu chief, Cetshwayo – and were shocked by the extent of the Zulu resis-

tance. They lost at least 850 of their own men and 470 black allies. The Zulus lost 1 000 soldiers.

After the battle, two regiments commanded by Dabulamanzi were sent to pursue men fleeing from Isandhlwana who crossed the river at what would later become known as Fugitive's Drift. The Zulu impis had received no order to attack Rorke's Drift. Cetshwayo had apparently warned them that any attack into Natal would be futile. A force of impi swam the river, however, and were so heady with victory that they attacked the mission. Their king's warning, which they failed to heed, came terribly true.

At Rorke's Drift, a small force of just over 100 men – a mixed bag of flotsam and jetsam from the Victorian army – had been left under the command of Lt John Chard. Earlier, a column on its way to fight at Isandhlwana had left behind 300 Basuto troops to aid Lt Chard. When the Zulu attack on the mission station began, however, the Basuto and their European leader fled.

Seeing the impi coming, Lt Chard prepared for battle as best he could. A makeshift fortress was made out of things such as sacks of mielies and biscuit boxes. The hospital bore the brunt of the attack, with most of the patients losing their lives. The others escaped to a central courtyard. The engagement raged until the following day, when finally an armed detachment under Lt-Col Russell arrived to relieve the defenders.

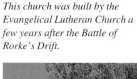

This church was built by the Evangelical Lutheran Church a few years after the Battle of Rorke's Drift.

It turned out that the British had lost only 17 men in what became known as the battle of the 'Heroic Hundred', while the Zulus had lost 300. Both sides showed incredible valour. Eleven Victoria Crosses were awarded, and the bravery of Lt Chard is still commemorated by the SA Army with the John Chard Medal for bravery.

The main attractions at the Rorke's Drift Battle Museum are the magnificent model and audio-visual depictions of the battles that were fought in the region. In fact, the museum has attracted worldwide attention for its outstanding displays of the Anglo-Zulu War.

The countryside around Rorke's Drift is unspoilt and tranquil. You can see the natural grandeur that so many military artists have tried to capture on canvas, and which Gillian Rattray described in her best-selling book, 'The Springing of the Year'.

This is where you can savour the true majesty of a frontier landscape. In the surrounding countryside, you can almost sense what it was like when the Dutch ivory hunters used to carry their loads through here, struggling over Knostrope Pass. You climb the Biggarsberg, go through Helpmekaar, and descend to the meandering Buffalo River and the lovely cascades of the Isibundi Valley. You reach the quaint German mission village of Elandskraal.

Rorke's Drift at a glance (map page 132)

How to get there: Leave Dundee southward on the R33 to Greytown. After 24 km turn left at the signposted crossroads and carry on for about 19 km to reach the battlesite.
Weather: While cool up on the escarpment, it gets hot in the Buffalo Valley. The best months are in autumn and winter.
What to do: There are trails, by foot or horse, from Fugitive's Drift Lodge and Valhalla guest farms.
More information: ELC Art and Craft Centre, PO Rorke's Drift 3016; tel (03425) 627. Talana Museum, Private Bag 2024, Dundee 3000; tel (0341) 22654.
Visiting times: The museum is open from 9 am to 4 pm daily, except on Christmas Day, Good Friday, Easter Sunday and Family Day. The ELC centre is open from 8 am to 4.30 pm on weekdays and from 10 am to 3 pm on Saturdays.

And from the top of the Pomeroy escarpment, the panoramic views take your breath away.

After the war, in 1882, the Swedish missionaries re-established themselves. The Evangelical Lutheran Church (ELC) of Southern Africa built a church partly on the site of the commissariat store at Rorke's Drift. The thatched house, which had been used as a hospital and had been burnt down, was rebuilt and at present makes up part of the mission station. A historical display can be viewed inside.

In the last 30 years, the fame of Rorke's Drift as a battlefield has almost been matched by the fame of an arts and crafts centre run by the Evangelical Lutheran Church. In what started as a tiny workshop in 1962, black artists were initially trained by Swedish art teachers. Those who received their start here include Azaria Mbatha, lino-cut artist John Muafangejo and sculptor Zuminkosi Zulu. Many students of the centre from around the country have later won national and international acclaim, with their work being exhibited in galleries in Europe and North and South America. Many tapestries have been commissioned by well-known institutions, and hang in churches, offices and homes around the world.

The centre, which employs about 80 people, specialises in handwoven tapestries, pottery and silkscreen fabrics. The largest activity is weaving. The rugs and tapestries are made from pure karakul wool, which is handspun, dyed and woven into figurative or non-figurative designs. The weavers are more like artists than factory workers. The designs have a wonderful clarity of colour and balance and, more importantly, not one of them is ever repeated – every work is unique.

The pottery consists of coiled and thrown pieces, ranging from the simplest to the most beautiful works of art. The potters use metal oxides for painting designs on the pots, which then receive a kaolin glaze. Designs are also sculpted or incised on the pots to give them their unique African pattern. The potters, like the weavers and textile printers, are encouraged to develop their own originality.

Where to stay

Fugitive's Drift Lodge, which overlooks the battlefield of Isandhlwana and the Buffalo River, is owned by an expert on the area, David Rattray, PO Rorke's Drift 3016; tel (03425) 843. *Valhalla*, at Helpmekaar, is run by the Italian Pedrelli family, PO Box 790, Dundee 3000; tel (03425) 790. There are numerous other farms and lodges, including *Excelsior Farm*, PO Box 932, Dundee 3000; tel (03425) 741, and *Kalwerfontein*, PO Box 1358, Dundee 3000; tel (03425) 925, which offers bed and breakfast. There are also camping sites and caravan sites in the vicinity.

A rugged terrain of charm and uncertainty

Like a siren song, the Msinga district of northeastern Natal has always had a forbidding, sometimes dangerous allure

THERE CAN BE FEW PLACES as steeped in the blood of fallen soldiers and warriors as Msinga. To put it into its historical context, this district lies within a network of northern Natal battlefields that stretch back in time to 1838 – from Blood River to Keate's Drift; from the Voortrekkers' epic battle with the Zulus at Blood River through to the confrontations of the Anglo-Zulu War; and to cap the turning of the century, the various Anglo-Boer battles from 1899 to 1902.

Today, the Zulu factions of the Msinga district continue to fight their battles over disputed tribal boundaries, and it is not always entirely safe to venture into the area.

The 123-km R33 from Greytown in the south to Dundee in the north will take you through the heart of the Msinga district. After leaving the mountain mist belt of Greytown – itself a garden of Eden groaning with avocados, kiwi fruit, pecan and macadamia nuts – you will drive through timber plantations and canefields typical of the lush Natal Midlands. But, suddenly, as you descend into the Mpanza Valley, the scenery changes to thorn scrub and euphorbias, and in winter the aloes in full blazing colour seem to set the slopes alight. Among them the thatched huts blend with the countryside as naturally as if they, too, had grown there.

The landscape, when the aloes are not flaming, is dramatically stark. Msinga means 'mountainous', a Zulu word referring to a high lookout place used for searching the surrounding countryside for lost cattle. Regrettably, much of the area is riven by erosion. In places no grass remains and dongas look like gaping wounds on the hillsides. All in all, it is terribly harsh terrain, with the inhabitants barely eking out a living. It is for this reason, perhaps, that the area has acquired the dubious reputation of being one of the country's principal dagga-growing areas – the dagga plant being hardy enough to survive in the badly denuded soil.

And yet, despite the rigours of the area, enchantment thrives. All the way from Greytown to Dundee, like bright beads on a string, there are places of interest. Greytown has a fine little museum, and on a farm just outside the town is the last resting place of the legendary Sarie Marais. About 17 km outside Greytown, on the left, is the Bambata Rock, commemorating the Battle of Bambata in 1906 in which a chief by this name, along with some of his men, killed four policemen during what became known as the 'Bambata Rebellion' against taxes.

On the road to Keate's Drift 13 km further on, the hills on the left are home to strange rock formations – one known as Botha's Castle. Keate's Drift itself has a lively market with traditional Zulu handwork for sale. If you take a detour left from Keate's Drift to nearby Muden, you'll find the Mhlopeni Nature Reserve. Here you can walk among aloes, euphorbias and white stinkwood, probably passing a few antelope or zebra along the way.

A further 18 km on from Keate's Drift is Tugela Ferry, the main centre of the Msinga district. It

A series of gentle, rolling hills near Tugela Ferry stretch into the distance – a scene typical of rural Natal.

The countryside between Pomeroy and Tugela Ferry – where the favourite mode of transport is still the trusty horse.

takes its name from the ferry that used to cross the Tugela, but the vessel seems to have vanished without trace and has been replaced by an iron bridge over this turbulent river. In Zulu, the river's name is Thukela, which means 'the startling one' and may be a reference to its vigour in times of flood. There is a lively produce market in the village, sheltered from rain and sun by gravity-defying sheets of plastic and a tangle of sticks and poles. Clothing vendors usually display their bright wares by spreading them over fences.

From Tugela Ferry it's a 27-km drive to Pomeroy. The sturdy stone buildings of this little village lie within a circle of hills, and you can select an iron pot or other indigenous crafts from the wares displayed on the shady veranda of a frontier-style trading post. On Thursdays, local pottery is sold from street stalls.

Fifteen kilometres from Pomeroy is Helpmekaar. If you want to visit the battlesite of Rorke's Drift (see separate entry), take a detour here to the right. Your journey through Msinga comes to an end after a final 54-km drive to Dundee.

A Zulu woman of the Msinga district strikes a majestic pose in her tribal dress.

Msinga district at a glance (map page 132)

How to get there: From Pietermaritzburg, travel 75 km north to Greytown, take the Stanger road for 1 km, then turn left onto the R33 to Dundee. If you wish to visit the Rorke's Drift battlefield, take the Rorke's Drift turn-off at Helpmekaar and travel for 15 km down the Knostrope Pass. Turn right at the T-junction. The battlefield is 5 km from this point. From Dundee, simply reverse the procedure, taking the R33 to Greytown.

Weather: The climate in Msinga is mild to hot in summer, but it can get very cold in winter.

What to do: Tour the historic battlefields, buy ethnic art, and enjoy the spectacular scenery of the region and take advantage of the phenomenal photo opportunities.

Special attractions: Guided tours of the historic battlefields. Contact the publicity associations on the Battlefields Route. See the interpretive display on the Battle of Rorke's Drift and visit the art centre there. Visit the Talana Museum in

Dundee with its simulated coalmine tunnel and recreation of the Victorian farmstead. Also to be seen is a display of the businesses which formed the centre of Dundee in 1912. Do a walk-and-talk tape tour – an audio tape on Rorke's Drift and Isandhlwana is available for sale, or to hire, from the Talana Museum.

Visiting times: The Rorke's Drift interpretive display is open daily to the public.

More information: For details of battlefield tours contact the SA Tourism Board, Suite 520, Southern Life Centre, 320 West St, Durban, 4001; tel (031) 3047144; or the Publicity Association at Dundee, Private Bag X2024, Dundee 3000; tel (0341) 22654 or 22121. For information on the Ladysmith Siege Museum, write to PO Box 29, Ladysmith 3370; tel (0361) 22231. For museum information, contact the Talana Museum, Private Bag X2024, Dundee 3000; tel (0341) 22654.

Where to stay

At Greytown there are comfortable rondavels and a caravan park on the shores of Lake Merthley outside the town – write to PO Box 71, Greytown 3500; tel (0334) 31171.
At Muden try the thatched huts and rondavels at the *Mhlopeni Nature Reserve*, PO Box 381, Greytown 3500; tel (03346) 722.
At Dundee there is the *King Edward Caravan Park*, PO Box 76, 3000; tel (0341) 22121 or 22607. Information about bed-and-breakfast accommodation is available from the Talana Museum .

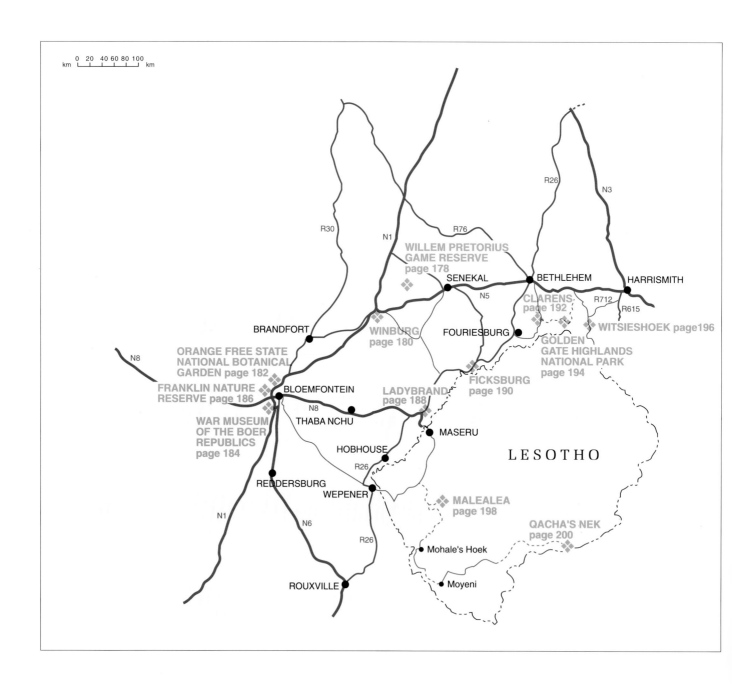

ORANGE FREE STATE/LESOTHO

A scenic reserve with wildlife in abundance

Situated in the central grassveld of the Orange Free State, between Winburg and Kroonstad, the Willem Pretorius Game Reserve is a rich repository of plant and animal life, and even some ruins

T O MOST PEOPLE, the ubiquitous Free State grasslands, broken here and there by distinctive flat-topped hills, are fairly unremarkable. Yet hidden in this terrain are the riches of the wilderness, and a visit to the Willem Pretorius Game Reserve comes as something of a revelation.

This is the province's main game reserve, named in honour of Senator Willem Pretorius of the Orange Free State Executive Committee, who was instrumental in its development. The reserve took over from the Sommerville Game Reserve near Bultfontein which was established in 1924 but which failed because of various factors, such as repeated droughts and isolation from the main tourist routes. Highveld game – such as black wildebeest, blesbok, springbok, eland, impala and zebra – were fast disappearing from these plains and some sort of conservation was urgently needed.

The Willem Pretorius Game Reserve was proclaimed in 1962 and the surviving game from Sommerville were relocated, including a growing herd of black wildebeest. Other animal species which were indigenous to the area back in earlier times were reintroduced from around the country – such as buffalo from the Addo National Park and reedbuck from Natal.

Situated on the shores of the Allemanskraal Dam, the open plains and grasslands of the reserve are green and well-watered. The sweeping expanse is broken in the north by the Doringberg range with scenic cliffs, ridges, overgrown ravines and hills. This lush section of the reserve is dense with trees which range along the kloofs and waterways and at the foot of steep slopes. To assist visitors, many trees in this wooded area have been identified. White stinkwood, wild currant, karee, buffalo-thorn, wild olive, highveld cabbage, star apple, wild pomegranate, camphor and sweet thorn are just some of the species that can be seen.

As for the grassland, there is not merely one species, but a fascinating variety, including red grass, turpentine grass, weeping love grass, wire grass, pincushion grass, finger grass, creeping bristle grass and white stick grass. With this knowledge, that huge expanse of uninterrupted veld will never again look the same to the visitor!

Apart from the animals already mentioned, the reserve has a large variety of mammals, from white rhino and giraffe to bats and rodents, and the rocky heights have been colonised by baboons. The nature conservationists of the reserve pursue a progressive policy with their surplus game. Every year, the surplus is captured and sold, preference being given to Free State farmers to ensure the maximum re-establishment of game within the province. The results are self-evident – once-dwindling populations roam the plains in their hundreds again.

The Allemanskraal Dam, covering 3 000 ha, is responsible for the rich variety of bird life that is attracted to the area. Over 200 species have made their home here, including spoonbills, herons, Egyptian geese, owls, cranes, ibises and cormorants. Ostriches and secretary birds can be seen on the plains, and a regular sight are the martial and fish eagles that breed here.

The dam is popular with anglers, and among the fish to be landed are carp and barbel (both of which can reach an impressive 30 kg), and yellowfish. Certain areas of the dam have been demarcated with red buoys, and it is within these that fishing is allowed. Also, an angling licence, obtainable from the resort office, is required.

This rather unusual stone hut on the Bekkersberg was built by the Ghoya, the early black inhabitants of the area.

When the attractions of the wilderness begin to pall, holiday-makers head for the western side of the reserve, where a sophisticated resort offers a number of pleasant distractions. These include swimming in a spectacularly sited pool overlooking the dam, a supertube and a trampoline for children, a golf course, a putt-putt course, bowling greens and tennis courts. A variety of accommodation is available and, if all this does not suffice, there is also a licensed restaurant, a supermarket and a large education and conference centre.

A particularly interesting feature of the Doring-berg are the ruins of large stone settlements which were occupied by black people during the Iron Age. On Bekkersberg within the reserve, one of their kraals has been restored and there is a site museum.

The Ghoya, the first black settlers in this part of the subcontinent, reputedly arrived during the 15th century and settled on the flat hilltops along the Vals, Renoster and Sand rivers. This locality provided security for the cattle and the fertile soil near the rivers, offering good grazing and arable land. Each kraal complex represented a family unit with several huts. A *lelapa* (courtyard) in front of each hut was used as a cooking area and for social gatherings. Being a polygamous people, every wife had her own hut. The settlement layout included several cattle kraals with associated stone huts in the central area. Domed huts made from reed and grass, arranged in a rough circle on the periphery, supplied housing for adults and young children.

The beehive-shaped corbelled huts found in the kraals were constructed from sandstone or dolorite blocks without mortar. The stones were packed in a sequence of overlapping layers, tapering inwards to an apex that was closed with a single slab of stone. The entrances to these huts were so small that, to enter, a person had to wriggle in on his stomach.

These kraals were occupied during the 18th century, when their inhabitants lived in relative peace. However, at the beginning of the 19th century they were conquered by the Amandebele of Mzilikazi, then absorbed by the Taung, a Tswana group. The ruins have been declared a national monument.

Among the many indigenous trees found within the reserve are white stinkwoods, seen growing alongside this pathway.

Where to stay

Accommodation includes rondavels, family huts and luxury flats, all with living/dining areas and either fully equipped kitchens or refrigerators and two-plate stoves. There is also a large caravan and camping site with braai facilities. To book, contact the resort manager (see panel below for address).

Willem Pretorius Game Reserve at a glance (map page 176)

How to get there: From the N1 take the turn-off to the east 32 km north of Winburg. The reserve is 9 km along the road.
Weather: Hot in summer with storms, mild to very cold and frosty in winter.
What to do: Game and bird-spotting, launch trips on the dam, and, apart from the sporting facilities already mentioned, there is also an entertainment complex with badminton, table tennis, billiards and snooker.
Special attractions: The Ghoya settlement.
More information: The Resort Manager, PO Willem Pretorius Game Reserve via Ventersburg 9451; tel (01734) 4229.

Accommodation includes these attractive rondavels which command an excellent view of the nearby Allemanskraal Dam.

A town imbued with the spirit of the Voortrekkers

Lovers of history will find plenty of interesting venues to explore at Winburg – a town having memorable links with the pioneering days of yesteryear

LOCALS PROUDLY CLAIM that the town of Winburg is set at the core of Voortrekker territory, in the centre of the Free State and at the heart of South Africa. A place of great significance for many Afrikaners, Winburg represents the time of the greatest unity for the Voortrekkers. It was here, in 1837, that the five Great Trek communities under Louis Trichardt, Andries Hendrik Potgieter, Gert Maritz, Piet Retief and Pieter Uys united in the biggest gathering of the Great Trek. Not at any other time was there so much concord between the parties.

The alliance, however, was short-lived. The Trekkers originated from different places and were independent and egocentric. Disunity was inevitable. One point of dissension was the destination of the trek. Potgieter favoured a Voortrekker state in the north, away from British influence, but the other leaders preferred Natal. They decided to trek in both directions and eventually the wagons rolled and the Trekkers were on the move again. But even after they had disappeared beyond the horizon towards Natal and the Transvaal, Winburg maintained a large Voortrekker population.

The first capital of Trans-Oranje and the Orange Free State's second oldest town, Winburg was founded in 1842 – it was originally called Wenburg to mark the victory over a dispute about where to site the town.

Although it's a typical Free State farming town today, with a little bit of help from its various museums, monuments and old buildings, Winburg still retains an almost tangible aura of history. The centre of the town is a large square dominated by the Dutch Reformed *klipkerk*. Adjacent to the church is the large town hall, where tourist information is available. The plan of the town hall is based on the outline of a trek-wagon, although this can only really be appreciated from the air. Inside, the walls are covered with murals depicting traditional African scenes. Further down the road from the town hall is the oldest existing Voortrekker cemetery. Winburg also has a military cemetery and a camp cemetery from the Anglo-Boer War.

Just out of town is the Voortrekker Museum Complex and the Voortrekker Monument. Part of the complex is the farm *Rietfontein*, where the last president of the Orange Free State, Marthinus Steyn, was born. The original homestead has been restored and is well worth a visit. This modest, almost crude, stone house originally had only three rooms: a bedroom, a sitting room and a kitchen. In

Where to stay

The *Winburg Hotel* in Brand Street in the town centre offers rooms at reasonable rates. Write to Box 116, Winburg 9420; tel (05242) 160.

White, cast-iron crosses mark the graves of British soldiers buried in the town's military cemetery.

later years stables and kraals were added. Sensitively restored to its former condition by the Provincial Administration, the house is simply furnished with domestic pieces from the period.

Architects consider the house particularly significant because it marks an important phase in the development of South African vernacular architecture. Only locally available materials were used: the outer walls were constructed of stone from a nearby hill, the unbaked bricks of the inner walls were made from the red earth of the valley, and the clay on the floors and on the fireproof ceiling came from the vlei, which also provided the reeds used to thatch the roof.

Winburg narrowly missed claiming another monument to Trekker fame when a 1936 vote on the siting of the Voortrekker Monument was won by Pretoria. However, it was decided that the Orange Free State and Natal would also have smaller monuments: the Blood River battlefield memorial in Natal and the Winburg monument in the Free State. In 1964 a countrywide competition was held to design the Winburg monument. One of the criteria was that it had to be rich in symbolism – which it is, the design featuring five interlinked sails which symbolise the five great trekker communities united at Winburg.

On a less elevated note is the Voortrekker Museum nearby which depicts the everyday lives of the Trekkers using life-sized, life-like models. There are also fascinating original relics on display, such as the cannon outside the museum which was used at the Battle of Blood River.

South of Winburg, at the foot of Bell's Pass, is a stone cairn and bronze plaque from where you can trace the routes of the five main Voortrekker parties. There is even a line of trees which marks the route taken by Potgieter to the north.

Another stone cairn and bronze plaque sit on a small hill almost hidden by thorn trees about 30 km north of Winburg just off the N1. This cairn commemorates an event of great historical significance for South Africa. It was here on 17 January 1852 that two British commissioners met with Andries Pretorius and a delegation of Voortrekkers on the farm *Sand River*, and signed the Sand River Convention whereby Britain gave official recognition to the independent Voortrekker state situated north of the Vaal River.

The Convention attracted considerable interest and about 50 wagons carrying 500 Boers came from all over to witness the proceedings. Eighteen years after the beginning of the Great Trek, one of its main objectives had been achieved.

Winburg at a glance (map page 176)

How to get there: Winburg is easily accessible, situated just off the N1 about halfway between Kroonstad and Bloemfontein.
Weather: Winburg has a typical highveld climate with summer storms and winter frosts. Generally sunny, it can be very hot in summer and very cold in winter.
What to do: Explore the town's history. The Rietfontein Dam offers anglers an opportunity to hone their fishing skills.
Special attractions: The Voortrekker Museum Complex.
More information: The Winburg Library, PO Box 26, Winburg 9420; tel (05242) 361.

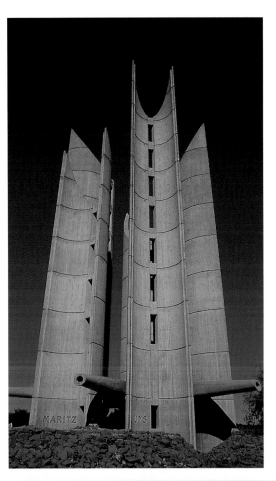

The five soaring columns of the Voortrekker Monument at Winburg honour the five Afrikaner communities which comprised the Great Trek.

The solid, imposing lines of the town's Dutch Reformed church which was built from locally quarried stone.

A beautiful garden between the koppies

The Orange Free State National Botanical Garden, situated some 10 km north of Bloemfontein, is rich in both indigenous plants and wildlife

ANYONE WHO HAS DRIVEN along the highways and byways of South Africa has seen them. They stand there in their thousands, solid, unmoving, and overlooked. They are, of course, the koppies. These dry, rocky hills typify the national landscape perhaps better than anything else. When people reminisce about the countryside, it is often these harshly beautiful geological outcrops that they remember. Whether bathed in a Karoo sunset or glistening with early morning dew, they symbolise South Africa.

The Orange Free State National Botanical Garden pays unintentional tribute to the koppie. Though small – at 46 ha, it is the smallest national botanical garden in the country – it contains within its limited space the unusual attraction of two very different kinds of koppie.

On the southwest side of the garden lies Monk's Head, a naturally wooded koppie typical of the province. And on the northwest side, just a few hundred metres away, lies Karoo Koppie, which, as its name suggests, supports semi-Karoo type vegetation. So special is the location of this dolerite hill and its Karoo vegetation, that it has has been declared a national monument.

The garden is a synthesis not only of geological formations but also of flora of the Orange Free State, the northern Cape and Lesotho. It has truly lived up to the intentions mapped out for it more than 30 years ago. It was the fifth of South Africa's eight national botanical gardens to be established,

having been started in 1963, the Jubilee Year of Kirstenbosch. The National Botanical Institute, with its head office at Kirstenbosch, is responsible for administering all the national botanical gardens in South Africa.

The site that was chosen, Winter's Valley, consists of koppies, kloofs and a series of dams, all of which combine to provide a unique setting. The main aim was to collect, cultivate and display flowers, bulbous plants, succulents, shrubs and trees indigenous to the arid areas of southern Africa. It was officially opened in 1969.

The site itself has a history that can be traced right back to the Iron Age, when Sotho people lived here. Remains of their pottery have been found and are now housed in the herbarium and at the Bloemfontein Museum. During the Anglo-Boer War a patrol path and stone wall were built on Monk's Head and a dam created for watering the horses.

Even though only about seven of the garden's 46 ha have been developed, with the rest left wild intentionally, keeping it in shape hasn't been easy. The area suffers from extreme climatic changes, from drought to floods which break the dam walls and cause severe damage to the vegetation.

The garden contains three distinct types of vegetation. On the wooded slopes of Monk's Head there are species of false olive, karee, wild olive, bush gwarri, mountain cabbage tree and yellow pomegranate. The valley and kloofs, with their deeper and richer soils, support larger trees, such as

(Left) A bird hide artfully concealed amongst the trees. (Right) The impressive karee seen here is just one of many different species of this tree found within the garden.

The view out across the OFS National Botanical Garden from one of the koppies.

the sweet thorn and white stinkwood. And to the east of the koppies there is grassland – a remnant of the vegetation which once covered the area when a different climate prevailed. A study of pollen grain deposits has revealed the past climates which have led to the natural development of these three different vegetations.

At least 110 different kinds of Free State grasses are grouped in the garden, in particular the dry *Cymbopogon/Themeda* grassveld so characteristic of the central region. Grasses feature prominently here because they play such a signficant role in the lives of local farmers and indigenous people, be it for grazing, providing shelter, weaving, or making jewellery and brooms.

Karoo Koppie, as part of the third vegetation type, derives from the later warm, dry conditions which led to semi-Karoo vegetation. The koppie has been used extensively for scientific research by the University of the Orange Free State, and on its flanks you can find many plants from the Cape which have adapted themselves to survival here.

On wandering through the garden entrance, the first thing you will see is a magnificently gnarled wild olive, thought to be over 200 years old. The curator's office, a bit further on, was built by Italian prisoners of war during the Second World War. The herbarium houses a collection of dried and mounted specimens of the flora of the OFS, particularly those occurring in the garden. It is, however, only accessible by prior arrangement. There is also a fossilised tree trunk from the Harrismith district on display, which is estimated to be between 150 and 300 million years old.

While the garden offers a wealth of shrub and tree life, you should, however, look out for examples of the blue daisy, the kanniedood, the towerbossie, wild lucerne and the vermeerbossie. Perennials and annuals from the OFS include the forget-me-not, the Free State daisy, the wild aster, the cancer bush and pink sage. Pride of place in the bulb garden goes to the Orange River lily. The most attractive trees include the wildegranaat, vaalbos, besembos and false olive.

As an added bonsella, there is a wonderful assortment of wildlife present in the garden, including 94 species of birds, 54 species of reptiles and 32 species of mammals.

Where to stay

Bloemfontein has a wide selection of hotels, as well as caravan parks and camping sites. For further information, contact the Tourist Information Bureau; PO Box 639, Bloemfontein 9300; tel (051) 4058489.

OFS Botanical Garden at a glance (map page 176)

How to get there: Take Rayton Road, just off General Dan Pienaar Drive, and drive north out of the city, following the signs to the garden.
Weather: Winter temperatures can fall below freezing point, while in summer they can reach 38°C. The best time to visit the garden is between November and March, when plants are in full leaf. But winter can also be an eyeful, especially when the aloes are in flower.
What to do: Enjoy looking at the plants and the wildlife.
Special attractions: Bulbs are sold during working hours, with more than 300 species available from the nursery. Special plant sales are held annually, usually in late August. The

herbarium has some 5 000 species on view, but entry is possible only by prior arrangement. Moonlight walks are organised by the Botanical Society.
More information: The Curator, Orange Free State National Botanical Garden, PO Box 29036, Danhof 9310; tel (051) 313530; or The Chief Director, National Botanical Institute, Private Bag X7, Claremont 7735; tel (021) 7621166. Brochures and other information can be obtained from the garden's main office from Monday to Friday.
Visiting times: The park is open from 8 am to 6 pm daily throughout the year, including public holidays, Christmas Day, New Year's Day and the Easter weekend.

A stirring tribute to 'die Boer en sy roer'

The War Museum of the Boer Republics in Bloemfontein is a tragic reminder of the full-scale war between Englishman and Afrikaner – a conflict whose shots still echo down to the present

ALTHOUGH IT ALL HAPPENED nearly a century ago, the Anglo-Boer War still resonates like a drum within the collective consciousness of the nation. Books about it continue to pour regularly off publishing presses, memorabilia associated with it are eagerly sought by hordes of avid collectors, and famous battlesites – such as Magersfontein, Colenso and Paardeberg – are visited by thousands of people each year.

What was life in this period of cataclysmic upheaval really like? For thousands of Afrikaners the war was a period of adventure, valour and camaraderie on the one hand, and suffering, tragedy and bitterness on the other. It is this multifaceted experience that you will find reflected within the walls of the War Museum of the Boer Republics in Bloemfontein.

The site of the museum is that of the National Women's Memorial, which was unveiled in 1913. The memorial itself is in close proximity to the museum, as are the evocative sculptures of the Burgher Memorial in the grounds. But perhaps it's better to start inside the museum, among the glass cases, displays and dioramas, to get an idea of exactly what this apparent abundance of memorials commemorates.

The emphasis is frankly partisan. This is, after all, the museum of the republics – Oranje Vrij-Staat and Zuid-Afrikaansche Republiek (ZAR or Transvaal) – so it is their side of the story that dominates.

As the gold-rich and *Uitlander*-overrun Transvaal slid towards war with Great Britain in the closing years of the 19th century, so her burghers methodically armed themselves. Here in the museum you'll find rifles (or *roers*) in abundance: Mausers and Martinis, Enfields and Metfords, and other less known ones like the Krag and Guedes, and the Westley Richards that the Boers dubbed Wessel Riekert. Although some are more than a century old, they are deadly reminders of the comparatively advanced military technology of the day.

And yet, despite the accuracy and proficiency of the guns, when Boer and Brit took to the battlefield, it was no faster than at the pace of the horse. The diorama of the Boer in the veld, situated in the Christiaan de Wet Hall, hints at the loneliness and vulnerability of the individual civilian-soldier caught up in the vastness and anonymity of war.

A particularly interesting exhibit is a collection of tiles, dating from 1900, that depict battles and personalities of the war. They were discovered as recently as 1969 in a cinema in Holland that was undergoing demolition. Paintings and other works of art occupy the Kestell and Hobhouse galleries, the best-known sculptures probably being those by Anton van Wouw. His works on display here include designs for the Women's Memorial and the wartime group entitled 'Bad News'.

Exhibits in the C F Beyers Hall tell the tragic story of the concentration camps, which achieved

Off to war. Several statues depicting scenes from the Anglo-Transvaal War (1880-1) and the Anglo-Boer War (1899-1902) are in the grounds of the War Museum of the Boer Republics.

notoriety for their high loss of life, especially among women and children. By the end of the war some 26 000 Afrikaners had perished in these camps. The British army was neither prepared for, nor able to deal with, the enormous number of people displaced into the camps by the war – and cholera, typhus and other infections soon broke out. It's worth recalling that more than 14 000 blacks died in British concentration camps during the war, but a memorial to them is yet to be erected.

Bermuda, St Helena, India and Ceylon seem far removed from a war in South Africa, yet it was their very remoteness that involved them. It was to these places beyond the sea that Britain sent into exile those burghers who had been taken as prisoners of war. Their lives as exiles are vividly depicted in the C F Beyers Hall.

The J H de la Rey Hall shows aspects of the domestic life of the republican Boer both in peace and in war. Included here are depictions of the 1914 Rebellion, launched by Afrikaner republicans in the hope of regaining their political and national independence lost in 1902. The rebellion was unsuccessful, but cost many lives, including those of important leaders such as generals J H de la Rey and C F Beyers.

Outside, against its background of sky and hill, the Women's Memorial doesn't dominate until you're close to it. You look up into the face of the mother holding her dead child, and the face of the woman whose gaze goes above you and beyond, perhaps into the distant future. Whatever the sculptor intended, you may interpret his work as you will. See the figures as they are, or create, if you like, your own allegory of the land and its people, and war.

There are phases of war – all war – represented in the bronze groups that make up the Burgher Memorial. 'Farewell' shows a burgher riding off to war, strong and strongly mounted on a fiery horse, leaving behind wife and child. Among some trees is another group, called 'The Exile'. Two desolate figures stand by a ship's rail, one a man too old to fight and the other a young boy. Both are defenceless and despairing, contemplating the ordeal of exile and the end of life as they have known it.

For others the end came on the field of battle, or in surrender after the signing of the Treaty of Vereeniging. It was General de la Rey who said that he would fight to the bitter end and, when that bitter end came, tasted its gall. There is an evocative statue of the 'Bitter-ender'. He is raggedly Quixotic and defiant in the inevitability of ultimate defeat. He sits on his gaunt horse, his eyes staring far, far away into the distance.

(Above) The spartan existence of Boer prisoners-of-war is evocatively portrayed in this replica of the corrugated iron dwellings that they occupied on the island of St Helena.
(Left) A mother holding her dead child is the focal point of the Women's Memorial.

Where to stay

There is a wide selection of hotels in Bloemfontein, as well as caravan parks and camping sites. For further information, contact the Tourist Information Bureau, PO Box 639, Bloemfontein 9300; tel (051) 473447.

War Museum of the Boer Republics at a glance (map page 176)

How to get there: The Women's Memorial and the War Museum of the Boer Republics are situated in Memoriam Road, south of central Bloemfontein and west of the extension of Church Street that becomes the R30 leading to Reddersburg. It is signposted from south of the city centre. From the N1 western bypass, take the Curie Avenue interchange, turn right into General De la Rey Avenue and left into Memoriam Road.
What to do: Take in the wealth of exhibits and other interesting sights in and around the museum.

Special attractions: The beautiful surroundings of the museum and the evocative sculptures.
More information: Write to The Director, War Museum of the Boer Republics, PO Box 704, Bloemfontein 9300; tel (051) 473447. An extensive reference library constitutes part of the museum.
Visiting times: The museum is open from 9 am to 5 pm from Monday to Saturday, and from 2 pm to 5 pm on Sunday. A small admission fee is payable on entering the museum, but admission to the grounds is free.

An enticing koppie at the heart of a city

The Franklin Nature Reserve in the middle of Bloemfontein is a must for visitors to the Orange Free State capital

NAVAL QUARTERS, observatories and game reserves are familiar sights to many of us – but to find evidence of all three at the very heart of Bloemfontein is not what one would expect at all. To realise how this disparate trio of elements came together is to know the fascinating origins of the Franklin Nature Reserve.

The navy, it so happened, came to Bloemfontein not to sail boats (a somewhat difficult prospect!) but as part of Lord Roberts' force during the Anglo-Boer War. The sailors were quartered on a flat-topped koppie that now overlooks what has become the city centre.

During the 19th century, this particular hill was known by various names: Bloemfontein Hill, Bloemfontein Mountain and Tafelkop. When the Wiltshire Regiment of the British Navy used the hill as a depot for fresh horses – Bloemfontein was apparently the only place in the region free of horse diseases at the time – the hill, with its various guns and cannons set up to discourage Boer troops, started resembling a coastguard post. In May 1900, the first reference to 'Naval Hill' was made – and the name stuck.

Besides the legacy of the hill's name, the sailors also left behind a monument to commemorate their stay. On the eastern slopes of Naval Hill, and visible from various parts of the city, is the shape of a horse, built from white-washed stones. Near it were inscribed the words 'For Remounts', thus commemorating the reason the regiment came out here. The horse is meant to be a replica of a similar one on a hillside in the regiment's home county of Wiltshire.

Known as the White Horse, the monument has often been the victim of vandals, pranksters and political activists. In 1943 swastikas were painted on its flanks in tar by members of the pro-Nazi Ossewa Brandwag; in 1947 someone added a foal to the monument; and in 1987 it was reported in a local paper that five youngsters had painted it to resemble a quagga – to serve as a memorial to this extinct animal!

Over the decades, Naval Hill passed through many hands and served many needs. Several of the buildings which were used by the British during the Anglo-Boer War and First World War later became the homes of game wardens and are now the offices of the Franklin Nature Reserve.

The reserve itself was established in 1928 and run by the municipality in conjunction with the Bloemfontein Zoo. It was named after Stuart Franklin, who was mayor at the time. The reserve has the distinction of being one of only two in the world situated in the middle of a city. The other is in Heidelberg, Germany.

Where to stay

There is a wide variety of accommodation in Bloemfontein. For details, contact the Tourist Information Bureau, PO Box 639, Bloemfontein 9300; tel (051) 4058489.

The open grassland of the Franklin Nature Reserve provides an ideal home for the fleet-footed blesbok.

But for a few minor additions, the 251-ha reserve has been kept in its original wild state. The road which encircles the summit of the hill gives fine panoramas of the city and its surroundings, while a network of other roads allows visitors the comfort of driving past the animals. These include numerous types of buck, wildebeest and giraffe, and 79 species of birds. If you want to leave your car and walk around, you are free to do so. However, stay on the roads – visitors are not allowed into the grazing areas (most of which are marked).

For such a unique game reserve, it is perhaps fitting that the Franklin should also host a unique event, an annual fun-run – the only one of its kind in the country that takes its course through a nature reserve.

At the summit of Naval Hill stands an old astronomical observatory, built and run until the Seventies by the University of Michigan. This was the Lamont-Hussey Observatory, built in 1927 for the observation of binary stars – or double star systems, as they are also called – of which this observatory discovered more than 7 000. Its principal instrument was a 68,5-cm refracting telescope. Once the biggest of its kind in the Southern Hemisphere, this telescope was used on three separate occasions to photograph Mars during its close approaches to Earth.

Because the Orange Free State offers such clear skies for star-gazing, a second observatory was built by Harvard University, also in 1927, on the outskirts of Bloemfontein, at Maselspoort. For the astronomers who were stationed here, it was a pleasant change from their previous residence: Arequipa, in the mountainous South American state of Peru. The Lamont-Hussey Observatory completed its work in 1972 and the old building now houses a theatre and cultural centre.

Whether you go onto Naval Hill to see the animals, the now-empty observatory or reminders of a naval presence, it's the excellent views of the city that leave the most lasting impression. Looking out over Bloemfontein from the hill, you realise why the famous 19th-century English writer, Anthony Trollope, wrote the following about a still-to-be-named hill during his visit to Bloemfontein in the 1870s:

'There is a hill to the west which I used to mount when the sun was setting because from the top I could look down upon the place and see the whole of it. The town is so quiet and seems to be so happy and contented, removed so far away from strife and want and disorder, that the beholder as he looks down upon it is tempted to think that the peace of such an abode is better than the excitement of Paris, London or New York.'

(Above) One of Bloemfontein's most famous landmarks, the old Lamont-Hussey Observatory now serves as a theatre and cultural centre.
(Left) Almost within sight of the Bloemfontein city centre, a giraffe ambles through the Franklin Nature Reserve.

Franklin Nature Reserve at a glance (map page 176)

How to get there: Drive north along West Burger Street, straight into Union Avenue, then right into the reserve at the bottom of Naval Hill.
What to do: The reserve is worth visiting by day in order to walk or drive the 8 km of road and view the animals; or by night in order to enjoy the sight of the lights of Bloemfontein twinkling below.
Special attractions: There is an annual fun-run through the reserve, usually held in October. Though the reserve doesn't

have a museum of its own, the National Museum in Bloemfontein houses artefacts stretching from the Anglo-Boer War period of Naval Hill, right back to the Triassic period. Notable items on display are the fossilised bones of a dinosaur and the head and horns of an extinct giant buffalo from the Stone Age.
Visiting times: The reserve is open 24 hours a day.
More information: The Department of Parks and Recreation, PO Box 3704, Bloemfontein 9300; tel (051) 4058786/304070.

Frontier charm in the foothills of the Maluti's

Ladybrand, situated in the eastern Orange Free State, is a platteland town that was originally built from sandstone quarried from the hills in which it nestles

Many of the town's houses and buildings are constructed from the attractive sandstone that is quarried nearby.

ONE OF THE PLEASURES of exploring little-known areas of any country, apart from the absence of hordes of tourists, is the warm welcome a traveller receives from the locals.

Such is the case in Ladybrand, an agricultural town in the wheat-and-sunflower belt of the eastern Free State. Though not very famous, the town is charming and its people so friendly that it's hard to believe that having a gun and several rounds of ammunition was once a condition for owning land in Ladybrand.

The town has its origins in the third of the Basuto wars of the 19th century. It was established in 1867 in conquered territory west of today's Lesotho, for defence against further Basuto attacks. Plots were allocated to burghers who had served on commando, on condition that at all times they possessed a rifle, 200 rounds of ammunition, five pounds of gunpowder, and emergency rations for 10 days. A further condition was that they each built a house surrounded by a stone or sod wall as a barricade against attack.

The burghers did not have to look very far for stone to build their walls. Ladybrand nestles, after all, in the sandstone foothills of the Maluti Mountains, on the fertile Caledon River plain. Sandstone characterises most of the town's historical buildings, of which the most outstanding is the Dutch Reformed Church. Of historical interest is the

Children's Home, built in 1904 to house war orphans, while the Ladybrand Secondary School has both considerable aesthetic value and, on its premises, a quirky memorial to an unusual Voortrekker heroine.

A member of the Trichardt trek, Antjie Scheepers was by all accounts 'a woman of great moral strength' but not above using strong language when the occasion seemed to call for it. She raised nine children single-handedly and spent only her last years in Ladybrand, where she came to live with one of her sons. That the people of Ladybrand were moved to erect a memorial based on such a brief acquaintance and such a tenuous claim to heroism testifies to the fact that Antjie Scheepers was indeed a formidable woman, one of several associated with the town.

Ladybrand was named after Lady Catharina Frederika Brand, mother of President Jan Brand. You'll also find the Catharina Brand Museum in the old post office (built of the ubiquitous sandstone, of course) outside of which an old imperial post box catches the eye.

The Catharina Brand is a theme museum – it is divided into various sections relevant to the town's history, and includes displays of rock art, the wheat industry, the local printing industry, the railways, the police force, the town's churches, art and culture and, perhaps the most fascinating of all, the inside of the old Norwood Coaker Pharmacy.

Norwood Coaker established his pharmacy in Ladybrand in 1880. A factory was added later by his son Horace in an effort to satisfy the growing need for medicine. Of the patent medicines concocted here, most were based on tried-and-tested traditional remedies. On display in the museum you'll find recipes for such *boererate* (remedies) as mustard plaster (good for a weak heart), a chest remedy made from goat fat, turmeric and castor oil, and a potent cure-all made from two bottles of brandy, sugar, dried figs and a variety of herbs that could probably relieve just about any symptom temporarily, but was said to be particularly effective against asthma.

Farm implements and machinery of an almost primitive nature are displayed in the grounds. The museum also reveals that Ladybrand is the birthplace of *tiekiedraai* (a type of dance) – the very first Afrikaans *volkspele* (folk dancing) songs were composed here during a visit by Dr S H Pellisier in the summer of 1913-14. It's no mystery what moved Dr Pellisier to such musical creativity during his holiday: the lush countryside that surrounds Ladybrand is still inspiring today and the Leliehoek

Ladybrand is situated in a natural basin surrounded by the Platberg – a sandstone ridge containing many caves and rock shelters.

Pleasure Resort, in the southwestern corner of the town, is a paradise for the outdoor enthusiast.

The attractions of Leliehoek include the two-day, 18-km Steve Visser Hiking Trail, which consists of two loops, 10 and 8 km long. Each loop begins and ends at an overnight hut at Mauershoek, the farm on which Ladybrand was founded. And each ascends a different section of the Platberg, the mountain against which Ladybrand lies.

The trail offers superb views of the Maluti's and of Lesotho, whose border is just 19 km away. And about 2 km outside the resort it takes you past the 'Stables' – a rock fissure entirely hidden from the outside, where the Boers stabled their horses during the First Basuto War in 1858.

In Leliehoek itself the remains of an old swimming pool tell an interesting tale of another formidable woman who made an impression on Ladybrand. She was the wife of James Knight, a Johannesburg resident who drowned in the pool in 1916. The widow lodged a claim against the municipality for her husband's death and won a settlement that so depleted the municipality's coffers that the town's planned introduction of electricity was delayed for several years.

There are many reasons to visit Ladybrand. Catholic pilgrims come here to worship at a unique cave chapel, 10 km to the north at Modderpoort, which missionaries of the Society of the Sacred Mission founded in the 1880s. Horse lovers come for the Saddle Horse and Agricultural Show held in February, and gambling men stop over en route to Lesotho, where a casino is the drawcard for them. (Remember to pack your passport if you're feeling lucky.)

The Cathcart Drift Dam is nearby, and so are the Bushman paintings in the Tandjesberg.

You may need more than just one visit to discover all of Ladybrand – a tiny spot on the map that rates as one of the jewels of the Free State.

Ladybrand at a glance (map page 176)

How to get there: From Johannesburg, take the N1 to Winburg. Turn left onto the N5 and, after about 3 km, right onto the R708 to Marquard and Clocolan. Three kilometres after Clocolan turn right at the T-junction with the R26. Ladybrand is 35 km away. From Cape Town, take the N1 to Bloemfontein, turning right onto the N8. After 64 km you reach Thaba Nchu and after another 58 km the T-junction with the R26. Turn left; Ladybrand is 16 km further on.

Weather: Ladybrand is in a summer rainfall area. During the winter the days are usually pleasant, but the nights are freezing, and nippy even in summer, when the days are hot and dry.

What to do: Explore Ladybrand's legacy of stately sandstone buildings and visit the Catharina Brand Museum, or explore the history and scenery in the countryside beyond.

Special attractions: The Steve Visser Hiking Trail is a two-day trail consisting of two loops that each end at the overnight hut, making backpacking unnecessary. There are some steep inclines, but generally the walking is comfortable and the views beautiful, with historical sites en route. Book through the Leliehoek Pleasure Resort.

Visiting times: The Catharina Brand Museum is open Tuesdays to Fridays, 10 am to noon, and 2 pm to 4 pm, and Saturdays from 9 am to noon. Contact the Ladybrand Municipality, PO Box 64, Ladybrand 9745; tel (05191) 40654 or 40659.

An old 'frontier town' set in a spectacular landscape

Embedded like a jewel below the majestic Maluti Mountains is Ficksburg, an historic farming town that lies at the gateway to Lesotho

FICKSBURG HAS THE HONOUR of being the venue for the country's oldest and largest harvest festival. As South Africa's chief cherry producer, the town's annual highlight is the Cherry Festival, which attracts thousands of visitors during November. From far and wide they come to celebrate the crop with processions through the streets, concerts, parties, food and drink, and the crowning of a Cherry Queen.

For some of South Africa's early pioneers, the fertile, well-watered mountains and plains of the eastern Free State seemed to be the promised land. To secure this chosen place, they drove back rival Basuto settlers in a series of wars, and the area, known as the Conquered Territory, was ceded to the Orange Free State. In 1867 the Volksraad established three towns in the Conquered Territory west of the Caledon River – Ficksburg, Ladybrand and Wepener – to hold and defend the territory from Basuto raiders.

Ficksburg was named after Commandant-General Johan Fick and was laid out on four farms. Residents were given six months to build a house and the property had to be surrounded by a stone or sod wall as a barrier against attack – and the remains of some of these walls can still be seen today. Each household was also required to have on hand, at all times, a rifle, 200 bullets, 5 pounds of gunpowder and 10 days' emergency rations.

Picturesquely poised in a particularly fertile spot, Ficksburg lies to the west of the Caledon River with the Maluti Mountains providing a spectacular backdrop to the east. Before the town was established, a Wesleyan mission station occupied the area, and the missionaries planted willow cuttings taken from the trees shading Napoleon's grave on St Helena. Today, most of the many willows in and around the town are the progeny of those original cuttings.

Apart from this being an area of outstanding natural beauty, many people consider Ficksburg to have the perfect climate: sunny, healthy and comfortable, with clearly defined seasons. In autumn, the countryside turns to gold and the days become crisp – prefacing the cold but sunny winter when the snow-capped Maluti's sparkle behind the town. In spring, the air is heavily perfumed with blossom from Ficksburg's extensive orchards. The colourful spectacle, viewed against the vast African terrain and the snowy backdrop, is breathtaking.

Summers are warm, and in the late afternoon thunderclouds mount up dramatically on the horizon. Local farmers don't always greet the refreshing storms with enthusiasm, as often they are accompanied by hail. (These short but destructive interludes led to the establishment of the Farmers' Hail Insurance Co-operative – now Sentraoes – which has more than 10 000 members.) Yet, despite the fickleness of nature, the area is considered to be

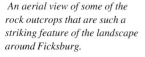

An aerial view of some of the rock outcrops that are such a striking feature of the landscape around Ficksburg.

Like so many buildings in Ficksburg, the town hall is built of local sandstone. Over the decades, stonecutting – one of the town's traditional crafts – has not been allowed to die.

model farming territory and produces a cornucopia of fresh produce – wheat, maize and other grains, apples, peaches, plums, apricots, pears, potatoes, asparagus and, of course, cherries. Visitors are welcome to visit cherry and asparagus farms, some of them experimental.

A feature of the open plains in this area are the magnificent sandstone formations and, as a result, many of Ficksburg's buildings have a warm, mellow appeal not normally found in South African towns. In the early days, the excellent quality sandstone was a popular building material and many of the town's historic buildings were constructed from it: the NG church and church hall, the town hall, the museum, the old post office, the Methodist Church and the old gaol. Stonecutting is one of the local traditional crafts and, as a result, even some contemporary buildings have been made from sandstone. Ficksburg sandstone was also used in the construction of the Union Buildings in Pretoria and of the Raadsaal and the main post office in Bloemfontein.

Ficksburg is easily explored on foot; the streets are tree-lined and the town is renowned for its beautiful parks and gardens. The old magistrate's court houses the General Fick Museum, which reflects the area's history and resources – the Basuto wars, the Conquered Territory, General Fick (the town's founder), the development of the sandstone industry and the cherry industry are all covered. At the high school you'll find the Pelissier Art Gallery, featuring a frieze painted in 1922 by

the headmaster's friend, Pierneef. The collection includes works by Pierneef, Tinus de Jongh and other South African artists. Original sketches of Ficksburg's historical sandstone buildings can be seen hanging in the local library. Also worth a visit is the old graveyard in the heart of the town which has recently been restored and contains many graves dating back to the Anglo-Boer war.

Some of the most interesting attractions are out of town. The Hoekfontein Game Ranch claims to be the largest private game farm in South Africa and, among other animals, stocks rhino, hippo and eland. About 15 km out of Ficksburg on the farm *Dunoon* there is an intriguing collection of carefully restored and maintained carriages. Viewing these fascinating relics can be arranged by contacting the owner.

Anyone would be hard-pressed to find a more beautiful setting than the Meulspruit Dam and Resort. Ringed by high mountains and surrounded by a botanic nature reserve with indigenous plants and sandstone formations, the dam wanders for about 10 km up the willow-fringed Imparani Kloof. Angling and watersport enthusiasts come here, and use the ample camping facilities. The dam is also the starting and finishing point for the Imparani Hike. It's possible to do this hike in seven hours, but it is better appreciated over two days, with a stopover at the overnight hut. Passing through scrubland and forest, the trail skirts the sandstone buttresses of the Imparani Mountain. Along the way, Bushman paintings testify to the good life enjoyed by the early inhabitants of the region.

Where to stay

Ficksburg has two excellent hotels, the *New Ficksburg Hotel*, PO Box 93, Ficksburg 9730; tel (05192) 2214, and the *Rustlers Valley Mountain Lodge*, PO Box 373, Ficksburg 9730; tel (05192) 3939. The *Thorn Caravan Park* is situated in the centre of town – write to The Municipality, PO Box 116, Ficksburg 9730; tel (05192) 2122. The *Meulspruit Dam and Resort* offers campers and caravanners fresh water and electricity – contact the municipality for more details.

Ficksburg at a glance (map page 176)

How to get there: From Johannesburg take the N3 to Villiers. Travel south west on the R51 and the R26 to Bethlehem. From Durban travel west along the N3 to Harrismith and take the N5 to Bethlehem, and from here continue along the R26 to Ficksburg.
Weather: Sunny and warm to hot in summer, sunny and mild to very cold in winter.
What to do: The town has excellent sporting facilities, including an 18-hole golf course, tennis and squash courts, polo, rugby and cricket fields,

bowling greens and even a shooting range. There's plenty to see in town, and watersports and angling can be enjoyed on the Meulspruit Dam. The area also offers excellent climbing, hiking, mountain-biking and pony-trekking.
Special attractions: The Cherry Festival held in the third week of November every year.
Visiting times: The Marschal Library is open from 8 am to 5 pm on weekdays (but closed for lunch between 12.30 pm and 2 pm). The museum can be

visited from Monday to Friday between 10 am and noon, 2 pm to 4 pm, and Saturdays from 10 am to noon. The Pelissier Art Gallery is open only during school hours, unless prior arrangements are made with the Ficksburg High School, PO Box 204, Ficksburg 9730; tel (05192) 2261.
More information: Contact the Town Clerk, PO Box 116, Ficksburg 9730; tel (05192) 2122. Hoekfontein Game Ranch, PO Box 354, Ficksburg 9730; tel (05192) 3915 or 3919.

During autumn, the Lombardy poplars in and around Clarens provide a spectacular splash of gold across the landscape.

Hillside haven for artists and aesthetes

To find out why so many artists have chosen a Free State town as their home, visit picturesque Clarens, a hillside haven near the Maluti Mountains

THIS MOUNTAIN VILLAGE at the gateway to the Golden Gate Highlands National Park has become something of a mecca for scores of artists and photographers who flock here every year during autumn to capture the moment when the early morning sunlight turns the Lombardy poplars into torches of gold. Nowhere in the world, they claim, does autumn create a more spectacular landscape than in this tranquil town in the Rooiberge. Nowhere in the world, others say, is a town more beautiful in spring, when the fruit trees erupt in a haze of pink blossoms.

No wonder, then, that many musicians, potters, painters, actors and sculptors have made Clarens their home. Given that the town's permanent residents number fewer than 300, the presence of this informal artists' community contributes significantly to the character of Clarens. Its first school building, an antique reedroofed *waenhuis* (coach house), is used by some of the artists as an annual exhibition hall. And there is even a stage set in a cave where young musicians are encouraged to perform.

But Clarens has a mixed and often whimsical charm. Beyond its entrance, guarded by a huge rock in the shape of a ship which locals have dubbed the Titanic, visitors find galleries filled with interesting *objets d'art*; fine homes and beautiful churches; the warm hospitality of farmers; the best-tasting tap water in the country; guest farms dotting the countryside; and hiking trails leading to breathtaking views of the Rooiberge and the Maluti Mountains. And, of course, its proximity to the Golden Gate Highlands National Park, the only national park in South Africa that focuses its efforts on protecting scenery rather than biological habitat or endangered species.

It is the majestic Golden Gate and the construction of the Lesotho Highlands Water Scheme, destined to take water from the Maluti Mountains through rivers and tunnels to the Witwatersrand, that are primarily responsible for Clarens's present renaissance. In 1993 it also earned a place in the record books for being the only South African town run entirely by women. From mayor to schoolmistress, bottle-store owner to postmistress, women were running the show, while the men (said with tongue in cheek) concerned themselves with weightier matters – such as golf.

Clarens also prides itself on its association with President Paul Kruger, who, as commandant during the Basuto War of 1865-6, led a punitive expedition into the northeastern Orange Free State and took part in the decisive Battle of Naauwpoortnek. Half a century later, when local farmers founded a village on the farms *Leliehoek* and *Naauwpoort* in 1912, they honoured Kruger by naming it Clarens – after the Swiss village where he died in exile.

Clarens's best-known 'building' is a rather unusual one – a small castle constructed of more than 50 000 beer bottles. Situated in Naauw Street and called Cinderella Castle, it features a collection of precious stones guarded by knights in armour, as well as soapstone ornaments, tableaux of fairytales and a playground for children.

The town has several national monuments, including its two churches, the library, the primary school and the Dutch Reformed parsonage. A ramble up and down its streets will therefore offer much that is of historical interest, but the views of the Maluti Mountains and those beautiful Lombardy poplars are likely to prove a distraction.

Just as Clarens is a town best known for its natural assets, the Golden Gate Highlands National Park, situated 21 km to the east, is most famous for its wonderful scenery. Wildlife takes a back seat to wildflowers, and although hikers may come upon eland, black wildebeest, blesbok and other highveld species, as well as a wide variety of birds, it's the freak formations that the Little Caledon River has carved into the rocks of the Maluti foothills that they've come to see.

The natural beauty of Clarens is complemented by the attractive decorative patterns seen on many of the homes in the area.

The Golden Gate itself consists of two massive bluffs that face one another across the public road that follows the valley. Each stands about 100 m high, with sandstone faces highlighted by gold and purple tints. The Golden Gate is a spectacular sight, but an even more striking natural formation is the massive Brandwag, a giant sandstone rampart with the shape of an ocean liner's bow that juts out from the valley wall.

Opposite the Brandwag is a luxury rest camp named after it, and around the corner is Glen Reenen, offering accommodation for those who prefer to enjoy nature without the intrusion of anything but the most basic mod cons. There is a riverside camping site nearby.

Glen Reenen is the departure point for several excellent trails, including the well-known Rhebuck Trail, a strenuous two-day hike with overnight hut en route. Shorter trails lead to landmarks such as Wodehouse Kop, Mushroom Rocks, Boskloof, Echo Ravine and the top of Brandwag, which overlooks much of the park. A trail leading to Holkrans starts at Brandwag rest camp.

At certain times during the year, those with green instincts can participate in one of the Golden Gate 'Enviro' courses, a unique opportunity to consolidate their acquaintance with nature. These courses are aimed at increasing awareness of human impact on the environment. They're a lot of fun, too, with abseiling, canoeing and overnight expeditions to caves to appeal to your sense of adventure. Contact your regional office of the National Parks Board for more details of these.

Where to stay

Hotel and chalet accommodation is available at *Maluti Lodge*, PO Box 21, Clarens 9707; tel (0143) 2561422/3/4. Famous for its good food is *Sunnyside Guest Farm*, PO Box 24, Clarens 9707; tel (0143) 2561099. The *Country Lodge*, PO Box 191, Clarens 9707; tel (0143) 2561354, offers accommodation in mountain chalets.

At the Golden Gate Highlands National Park there are two rest camps – *Brandwag Camp* and the more basic *Glen Reenen Rest Camp* – and a camping site. Book at one of the two National Parks Board regional offices: Cape Town: PO Box 7400, Roggebaai 8012; tel (021) 222810. Pretoria: PO Box 787, Pretoria 0001; tel (012) 3431991.

Clarens at a glance (map page 176)

How to get there: From Harrismith travel west along the N5 towards Bethlehem; 7,5 km before Bethlehem, turn south onto the R711. Clarens is 28 km away.
Weather: Winters are cold: temperatures can plummet to 12°C and there is often snow on the mountains. Summer nights can also be cool.
What to do: Soak up the old-world atmosphere in Clarens itself. The Golden Gate Highlands National Park offers excellent hiking trails, including the famous Rhebuck Trail.
Special attractions: Autumn is high season in Clarens, which is particularly beautiful at this time of year. Book your accommodation *months* in advance.
Other information: Write to Clarens Municipality, PO Box 16, Clarens 9707; tel (0143) 2561411 or 2561032. For information about the Golden Gate Highlands National Park, contact your regional office of the National Parks Board.

Multicoloured mountains to delight the eye

Majestic vistas are the principal attraction at Golden Gate in the Orange Free State, the location of one of the country's finest national parks

SOME OF SOUTH AFRICA'S most memorable spectacles are to be found within the Golden Gate National Park which hugs the valley of the Little Caledon River. The extraordinary sights to be witnessed here are a direct result of the area's unique geology: Drakensberg lava, Clarens sandstone, red and purple rock of the Elliot formation, flecked mudstone and blue and grey shale of the Molteno formation – all of these unite in an incredible rainbow of strata visible in mountains, cliffs and rockfaces all over the park.

The name Golden Gate derives from two magnificent sandstone buttresses that flank the main road. Jan van Reenen, a farmer who lived in the region in the 19th century, christened the area after witnessing the spectacular effect of the illumination of setting sun on these sandstone bluffs.

The first human beings to occupy the area were the Bushmen, drawn here by the vast herds of game. Eventually driven out by the Sotho and white settlers, they left behind a rich legacy of artefacts such as bone and stone tools and paintings which can still be found in the park's various caves and overhangs. In the early 1800s, *trekboer* hunters decimated the animal population, and the combination of drought and wars thereafter compounded the damage. After the park was officially proclaimed in 1963, animals were systematically reintroduced in an attempt to recreate the large game populations that had once existed.

The Golden Gate region did not escape the Anglo-Boer War. Farms here were torched in pursuit of the notorious 'scorched earth' policy, and Boer women and children were rounded up and taken to concentration camps in Harrismith. One of the exceptions was Ouma Cilliers of *Noord Brabant*. For weeks she and her daughters took refuge in a cave near their homestead and evaded the British soldiers. Hikers sometimes discover evidence of those far-off days in the form of old bullets and cartridge cases dating back to the occasion when British forces blew up Boer ammunition wagons, scattering the contents far and wide.

Although the scenic splendour is Golden Gate's main attraction, visitors are also drawn by the invigorating highlands climate and the wide variety of plants and wild animals. The sour grasses, herbs and bulbs are typical highland vegetation, and the high annual rainfall results in a glorious floral display: arum lilies, fire lilies, watsonias, red-hot pokers and many other flowers thrive on the mountain slopes, which remain lush and green for most of the year.

The park has also re-established a healthy stock of indigenous game which can be viewed from two game drives that meander through the park. Among the animals you could encounter are buffalo, wildebeest, zebra, eland, springbok, blesbok, grey rhebok, mountain reedbuck, oribi, baboon, dassie, genet, porcupine, wildcat, jackal, polecat, mongoose and otter. There are hundreds of different bird species, including various raptors – such as the black eagle, the rare lammergeyer (bearded vulture) and the Cape vulture.

The absence of the big cats means that much of the area can be explored on foot, but never take safety for granted. Don't provoke baboons, and steer clear of black wildebeest and solitary eland bulls, no matter how docile they may appear.

Where to stay

The park's original rest camp is *Glen Reenen*, which is well situated on the banks of the river. The camp has braai and picnic facilities and it provides rustic pleasures including a wonderful natural rock pool for summer swimming. There are pleasant self-catering rondavels as well as a caravan and camping site, complete with an ablution block, electric plugs, scullery and braai facilities. The local shop will probably cater for most of your needs – such as firewood, fresh meat, groceries and alcohol. There's also a filling station with petrol and diesel.

Brandwag Rest Camp is more luxurious with its chalets or single and double en suite rooms, complete with television, radio and telephones. There are also a restaurant, ladies' bar, coffee shop and sports facilities. Both Glen Reenen and Brandwag camps may be contacted by writing to Golden Gate Highlands National Park, Private Bag X03, Clarens 9207; tel (0143) 2561471.

The Golden Gate valley in all its autumn splendour. On the far left can be seen the rocky outcrop called Gladstone's Nose.

The park's principal hike is the 30-km Rhebok Trail, a two-day route which starts at Glen Reenen Rest Camp and passes through some of the finest highland scenery. On the first day you cover about 13 km in seven hours on the way to the overnight hut called Ribbokhut. Beds, a kitchen, and a cold water shower and toilet facilities are provided, and the stream makes a pleasant bathing alternative in summer.

The next day the trail leads past a waterfall and up to the top of Generaalskop, which, at a height of 2 757 m above sea level, is the highest point in the park. You return to Glen Reenen after about five and a half hours.

Glen Reenen is also the starting point for other walks which can be easily completed in a couple of hours. A trail leads to the Mushroom Rocks – sandstone formations in the shape of giant mushrooms. Yet another leads through a small canyon and steep ravine known as Echo Ravine. On the Brandwag route a steep path winds through indigenous forest to the top of the Brandwag Buttress, one of the park's natural wonders that resembles an ocean liner.

Those who enjoy a more arduous physical challenge can continue from here right up to the top of Wodehouse Kop. A tranquil route favoured by bird-watchers leads south from Glen Reenen through a secluded grassveld valley to Langtoon Dam. From here Buffalo Cave is easily accessible – it's a rock overhang which has offered refuge for many and diverse people down through countless centuries.

Other walks lead from Brandwag Camp nearby, and to the west, emanating from the Gladstone administrative centre, there are even more routes. From Gladstone it takes only 20 minutes to reach a fine collection of Bushman paintings; and a lovely rock formation known as Cathedral Cave is a two-hour there-and-back hike.

But explorers are not confined to walking – various guided horseback trails are available from the stables at Gladstone. Visitors can request the special two-day trail which includes a night in Buffalo Cave, otherwise the longest trail is two hours. The Rhebokspruit Trail sets off at two every afternoon and heads south into the mountains. The trail follows the bridle path in the Rhebokspruit Valley and includes the historic Cilliers homestead *Noord Brabant*, a sandstone structure built in the early vernacular style.

All horseback trails are headed by an experienced groom and, as the horses are well trained, no particular riding skills are necessary. However, if you feel that two hours is pushing your limits a bit, hour-long rides set off at 9 am, 10 am and 11 am. During the school holidays, horses are also available at Glen Reenen.

Brandwag Buttress – one of Golden Gate's most spectacular sandstone formations.

Golden Gate at a glance (map page 176)

How to get there: From Durban or Johannesburg, take the N3 to Harrismith. From there, take the N5 and just before Bethlehem turn left onto the R711 to Clarens.

Weather: A typical highveld climate with summer rainfall. The days are pleasantly mild to warm but the nights tend to be cool. Winters can be very cold with frost or snow.

What to do: Hiking, swimming, riding, bird- and game-spotting.

Special attractions: Rock formations such as Brandwag and Mushroom Rocks, and Bushman art.

More information: For reservations or enquiries contact the National Parks Board, PO Box 787, Pretoria 0001; tel (012) 3431991; or PO Box 7400, Roggebaai 8012; tel (021) 222810.

A world of extremes on South Africa's rooftop

An alpine wonderland in the Drakensberg Mountains is waiting to be explored a mere three hours' drive from Johannesburg or Durban

ONE OF THE FIRST THINGS you notice about Witsieshoek – apart from the stunning views – is the weather. Perched at an altitude of 2 600 m, southern Africa's highest resort area boasts some of the most dramatic weather extremes in the subcontinent.

The summer thunderstorms are violent and spectacular – an adrenaline-pumping experience for any visitor. In winter, heavy snowfalls turn the resort into a Mecca for snow-starved local skiers – although the absence of ski-lifts means they have to footslog to the summits before enjoying the downhill run. Above all, Witsieshoek is a magical mountain retreat where walkers, nature lovers and those in search of simply nothing to do, will be able to recharge their minds and bodies.

The resort itself, built in 1972, has chalets, luxury rooms and a licensed restaurant. Stretching away on every side is the most dramatic mountain scenery in Africa: Witsieshoek is within striking distance of the Drakensberg's most beautiful sights. Easily accessible from here are Mont-aux-Sources (the source of five of South Africa's major rivers), the stunning basalt buttress known as the Sentinel, and the magnificent 4 km-wide Amphitheatre.

Numerous trails and bridle paths radiate out into the surrounding wilderness, taking visitors through unsurpassed scenery to beauty spots such as Mahai Falls and Broome Hill. Guides are available to show you the best spots, and you can hire a pony to rock you gently along the lovely bridle paths. A few kilometres away is a 90-minute hike that takes you to the chain ladders from where the intrepid can climb to the summit of Mont-aux-Sources. This area is also rich in Bushman rock art which can be appreciated in the many caves and overhangs.

The drive from Witsieshoek to the car park at the bottom of the Sentinel has attained almost legendary status for its beauty. From this spot there is a two-hour trail leading to the plateau at the top of the Amphitheatre, opening up to even more incredible vistas. The mighty Tugela originates here in the form of a modest stream which then plunges 2 000 m in a series of rapids and cascades.

For a longer walk, the Metsi Matsho Hiking Trail takes about four hours to complete and runs through magnificent scenery along a basalt and sandstone ridge studded with rocks and caves. The trail ends at the Swartwater Dam where trout fishermen can try their luck. There are two overnight huts with accommodation for up to 20 people for anyone who fancies staying on.

Owing to the altitude and climate, the area consists of short grassland and some protea species which thrive on the cool, moist conditions. In spring and summer the grasslands are spangled with hundreds of different wildflowers. Lovely patches of forest occur in more sheltered spots and tree ferns frame the mountain streams.

The high peaks are home to some large birds of prey such as the endangered lammergeyer (or bearded vulture), Cape vulture, jackal buzzard and black eagle, and it's not unusual to see them hovering near the rock-faces or plunging into valleys and ravines.

Other birds you might spot include the rock kestrel, whitenecked raven, black crow, black harrier, bald ibis and wattled crane. There is not a great variety of game here, but grey rhebuck, baboon and dassie are fairly common.

Where to stay

Witsieshoek Mountain Resort is a small hotel offering luxury and standard accommodation. Write to Private Bag 828, Witsieshoek 9870; tel (01438) 5.

QwaQwa Hotel, PO Box 5581, Phuthaditjhaba 9866; tel (01438) 30903.

The *Fika Patso Mountain Resort and Conference Centre* has self-catering chalets and a restaurant. Write to PO Box 17673, Witsieshoek 9870; tel (01438) 891733 or (011) 8882341.

Panoramas to take your breath away. The view down to Witsieshoek, as seen from the hiking trail at the back of the Amphitheatre.

Witsieshoek at a glance (map page 176)

How to get there: From Durban or Johannesburg take the N3 to Harrismith. From there take the R712 and after about 10 minutes, turn left onto the R615. Beyond the Oliviershoek Pass take the road to the right and follow it to the resort.
Weather: Summers are mild and comfortable with rain and fog; the winter is cold with snow. The wettest months are January to March and it can snow at any time between April and September.
What to do: Climbing, hiking, angling, horse-riding and exploring.
Special attractions: The drive to the car park at the base of the Sentinel.
More information: QwaQwa Tourism and Nature Conservation Corporation, Private Bag X826, Witsieshoek 9870; tel (01438) 34444 or 30576.

The Witsieshoek Mountain Resort is set among the green foothills of some of the Drakensberg's highest peaks.

A trading post of yesteryear where the horse is king

Most of the magic of the mountain kingdom of Lesotho is encapsulated in the Malealea Valley, situated about 90 km from Zastron in the Orange Free State

Where to stay

Malealea Lodge has nine rooms, some with en suite facilities and their own kitchens. It also has six rondavels and a dormitory with ablution facilities and a communal kitchen. There is a large dining room or recreation room available for group catering. Write to PO Makhakhe, 922 Lesotho or PO Box 119, Wepener 9944, South Africa; tel (09266) 785336 or 785727 or (051) 473200.

Semongkong Lodge has 10 rooms and a restaurant. *Qaba Lodge* offers four rooms. Reservations: contact the Fraser Lodge System, PO Box 243, Ficksburg 9730; tel (05192) 2730.

FOR THE BEST that the idyllic mountain kingdom of Lesotho has to offer, visitors need go no further than Malealea. At the hub of this small village is the place that in fact brought this settlement to birth – the ever-bustling Malealea Trading Store, founded by Mervyn Bosworth Smith at the beginning of the century.

Today, as ever, the trading store is the nucleus of the village. Riders from smaller, outlying villages meet here to trade hides, baskets, beads and agricultural produce for batteries, sugar, blankets and so on. There is also a mill where farmers from the district bring their wheat and maize to be ground.

The surrounding area from which these horsemen come is well watered by numerous rivers that wind their way through the valley – the largest being the Makhaleng, which is fed by hundreds of smaller streams. These give rise to three spectacular waterfalls: the Ketane, Botsoela and Ribaneng falls. Here there are various marked hikes and rides that are unrestricted by fences or boundaries. Should you

wish to test your equestrian skills on a Basotho pony, approach a local farmer who keeps horses and rents one or more out for trails.

Guides are readily available for taking you through the wilder parts of the terrain, and they always seem eager to share their knowledge of the area. A great source of pride to Malealea's inhabitants are the local Bushman paintings. The hike to this site is in itself a spectacular journey, with the final treat being the sight of a series of wonderful old paintings of animals, people and hunting scenes, mostly well preserved under overhanging rocks and boulders.

Another attraction – located a two-day pony ride from Malealea – are the huge Maletsunyane Falls in the Semongkong Valley. Winds rushing up through the Maletsunyane Gorge provide an aerial playground for flocks of bearded vultures (also known as lammergeyers). These large birds soar up and glide down the currents, providing visitors with spectacular aerobatic displays.

In a scene typical of rural Lesotho, Basotho in colourful traditional dress gather around an animal enclosure.

Malealea also has spectacular sandstone formations – especially at Qaba, where the river has worn through the rocks, producing enjoyable water slides and deep pools for swimming. In winter the waters freeze, creating a magical ice-palace wonderland.

No matter what the time of the year, Malealea is an excellent holiday destination. In summer, at this high altitude, the days are warm and sunny without ever being overpoweringly hot; and because it's a summer rainfall area, the rivers and pools are always full. Summer, too, is the season of the *Aloe algave*, the third largest flower in the world and one of the big scenic attractions of the valley. This attractive aloe was imported from America in the 19th century and has become a particular feature of the Lesotho landscape. The Basotho use the aloe to build kraals – they plant them in a circular formation and the thick, spiky leaves provide a natural barrier that no animal wishes to tangle with.

As autumn moves in, the evenings become slightly cooler, yet the days are still pleasantly warm. This is also the time for enjoying the famous cosmos season and a myriad flowers of pink, magenta and white can be seen covering the fields. Apparently pony trekkers travelling through the mountains from Natal to Lesotho were responsible for the spread of cosmos – the seeds were caught in the pony hooves and blown this way and that as they plodded through the passes.

Winter in the midlands of Lesotho usually brings snow, which creates a magical alpine feel – something of a novelty right in the middle of southern Africa. The days are sunny and clear – ideal for long hikes and rides – and the evenings are cold, perfect for roaring log fires. In spring, as the snow melts, the valley bursts into colourful life again with blossoms appearing on even the most weather-beaten trees.

Among the highlights of the local calendar are the horse-races that Malealea hosts twice a year. Horse-owners from around the country converge on the village, and the events are held in a festive atmosphere, with heavy betting and much socialising being the order of the day.

Ever since Moshoeshoe, founder of the Basotho nation, mounted his first horse in 1830, the Basotho have been proud and able horsemen, and horses and saddlery are among the most valued possessions of any family. Nearly all celebrations include a horse-race – in Maseru, valuable thoroughbreds are raced by experienced jockeys, while in the remote villages herdboys and ponies generate just as much excitement.

In the Semongkong Valley, the mighty Maletsunyane Falls tumble 193 m down a ravine into the Maletsunyane River.

Malealea at a glance (map page 176)

How to get there: The Malealea Valley lies in the western part of Lesotho adjacent to the Thaba Putsoa Mountain Range. It is accessible by car, providing you follow the road entering the valley through the Gates of Paradise pass. From Maseru, follow the southern access road in the direction of Mafeteng; after about 58 km the road crosses the Tsoaing River and, at the Golden Rose restaurant (which can't be missed), turn left. Here the road changes from tar to gravel, but is reasonably well maintained. After 10 km the road forks – bear right and after another 15 km you reach another fork. Keep left and after 3 km the road passes the Gates of Paradise. (Malealea Lodge is 7 km further on.)

Coming from Wepener, you pass through Van Rooyen's border post and follow the road through Mafeteng until the Golden Rose Restaurant. Carry on as above.
Weather: Summers are mild to warm with intermittent showers. Winters are mild and sunny during the day, but at night the temperature often plunges below zero.
What to do: Malealea is hiking and pony-trekking terrain – the valley offers many marked trails and guides and horses are readily available. Bird-watching and angling are also popular pastimes.
More information: Contact the Lesotho Tourist Board, PO Box 1378, Maseru; tel (09266) 323760 or 312896.

Mountain scenery to take your breath away

Discover the rustic charms of the remote little hamlet of Qacha's Nek, situated near the southeastern border of Lesotho

A horseman picks his way through the mountain slopes near Qacha's Nek. Horses are the main means of transport in the high country.

GETTING TO QACHA'S NEK is as much of an adventure as actually being there. The roads snaking through the Maluti Mountains of southern Lesotho, while not the best in the world, traverse some of the most stunning scenery on the continent. If the 'Mile-High Kingdom' has a region which makes you feel a 'mile high' in spirits too, then this is it.

Qacha's Nek is distinctive not only because it is the meeting place of Natal, Lesotho and the Transkei, but also because it is situated on a pass virtually at the top of southern Africa's continental divide. More than a mile high, it is the second highest district in Lesotho after Mokhotlong. To the south, the rivers flow to the Indian Ocean via the Umzimvubu River, while to the north and west they reach the Atlantic by way of the Orange. It is here, in fact, that the Senqu River (which later becomes the Orange) makes a huge bend, changing the direction of its flow from south to west.

The cool misty weather, created by warm air sweeping in from the Indian Ocean, helps keep the mountains green, even when the rest of the country is suffering from drought. Qacha's Nek is one of the few places in Lesotho that has trees, these reputed to have been planted by two Europeans who were convicted of cattle rustling and sentenced to do time at Qacha's Nek.

So remote are the mountain districts of Qacha's Nek and Mokhotlong, which lies to the east, that they were the last to be settled by the Basotho. For centuries this was the home of small groups of Bushmen who survived by hunting eland, hartebeest and other buck. They eventually came into conflict with Basotho and Natal farmers and the last organised band was wiped out in 1871.

The Basotho discovered that they could bring their cattle here to graze in summer and could grow crops in the valleys. The town was named after a son of Chief Moorosi, Ncatya, who settled in the area in the mid-19th century. Ncatya was known as Nqasha in Sephuti – from which is derived the name Qacha's Nek.

The actual town of Qacha's Nek began in 1888 with the establishment of a small station to facilitate the paying of taxes to, and issuing of passes by, the colonial authorities. Today it is a small, pleasantly wooded town of about 1 200 inhabitants, 2 km from the Transkei border and 34 km from Matatiele. Many of the buildings are made from sandstone which comes from the nearby ridges and mountains. Perhaps the most striking of these buildings is the Catholic Church of the Most Holy Redeemer, to the northeast of the town, with its majestic silver spire. Completed in 1967, it has a simple interior interspersed with geometric designs in stained glass.

Other points of interest at Qacha's Nek are the district administrator's office which has a foundation stone laid in 1906, and St Barnabas' Anglican Church. A store further down the main road, on the right, has a veranda paved with sandstone blocks bearing fossilised ripples made by water on sand some 200 million years ago. There is a furniture store called Thupa, thus named because the first owner, who died in 1938, was well-known for his use of a stick, a *thupa*.

You can get a good view of the town from the sandstone ridge known as Letloepe, which rises up behind the hospital and the old Residency. Letloepe, sometimes used as an alternative name for the town, refers to the ridge's resemblance to the hood of a cobra.

The scenic beauty of the Qacha's Nek district generally is why most people take the trouble to come to this hard-to-get-to region and it is best appreciated by car. Leaving the town, the road west takes you to Sekake's. At the first T-junction you can turn right to Tsoelike, and this road loops around hills, then passes beneath three sides of the mountain called Souru (2 645 m). At the village of Tsoelike Bridge, a suspension bridge built in 1930 crosses the river.

Further to the east is Sehlabathebe National Park, established in 1970 in a remote and beautiful part of the area east of Qacha's Nek. Some 65 sq km in size, it is the only national park in Lesotho and makes up one per cent of the country. It features natural sandstone arches and a series of small lakes on a high plateau. From here you can get dramatic

Being one of the highest areas of southern Africa, Qacha's Nek is often blanketed in snow during the winter months.

views, both along the Drakensberg and down into Natal. It is inadvisable to drive through the park in any vehicle other than a four-wheel drive.

Qacha's Nek has always been an important missionary stronghold and you'll find numerous Christian outposts, schools and training stations in the area. On the road towards Tsoelike and Sekake's, you'll reach Our Lady of the Hermitage Mission after about 7 km. Founded in 1922, it consists of a small church with a sandstone tower. About a kilometre beyond the Hermitage, you can see the Sejabatho River to your right. This is a perfect place to hike, the river having plenty of pools suitable for swimming – if you can bear the freezing waters.

Sekake's is reached by turning left at the T-junction, instead of right to Tsoelike. From this road you can enjoy good views of the Orange River and you pass several villages – such as the ominously named Malimong ('place of cannibals'), which is dominated by Maqhaba Mountain. Be sure to stop in at some of the stores that have been carrying on business here for decades – such as White Hill Store and Nutting's Store.

Qacha's Nek at a glance (map page 176)

How to get there: From the south, drive from Kokstad to Matatiele (where the tarred road ends) and traverse about 30 km up the Drakensberg escarpment across the Transkei corridor. Qacha's Nek lies 2,5 km from the Transkei border. The border post is open from 6.45 am to 4 pm daily. From the southeast, follow the national road to Mohale's Hoek or Moyeni. From here road conditions are generally poor; the scenery becomes spectacular as you pass Mount Moorosi, Devil's Staircase and Mphaki's. This drive is about 200 km long and requires an entire day. It can be done in a sedan car, but a four-wheel-drive vehicle is advisable if the journey is undertaken in rainy weather.

Weather: Summer temperatures are cool, with regular mists and an average temperature of about 17°C in January. Winters can be very cold, often with snow.
What to do: Hiking and scenic drives. The nearby Sehlabathebe National Park is well worth visiting. To get there, take the road via the Transkei, drive towards Matatiele and then turn left 19 km beyond the border. A four-wheel-drive vehicle is essential inside the park. Hikes can be organised from the hotels.
More information: The Park Administrator, Sehlabathebe National Park, PO Sehlabathebe, via Qacha's Nek, Lesotho; tel (09266) 323600.

Where to stay

The visitor has two options: the recently-built, 20-room *Nthatua Hotel,* PO Box 167, Qacha's Nek, Lesotho; tel (09266) 950260; and the *Sehlabathebe Lodge,* c/o Conservation and Forestry Division, Department of Agriculture, PO Box 92, Maseru; tel (09266) 323600. Situated in the Sehlabathebe National Park, the Sehlabathebe Lodge boasts some spectacular scenery. Most of its rooms have private bathrooms and there is a fully equipped modern kitchen. Bring your own provisions, however.

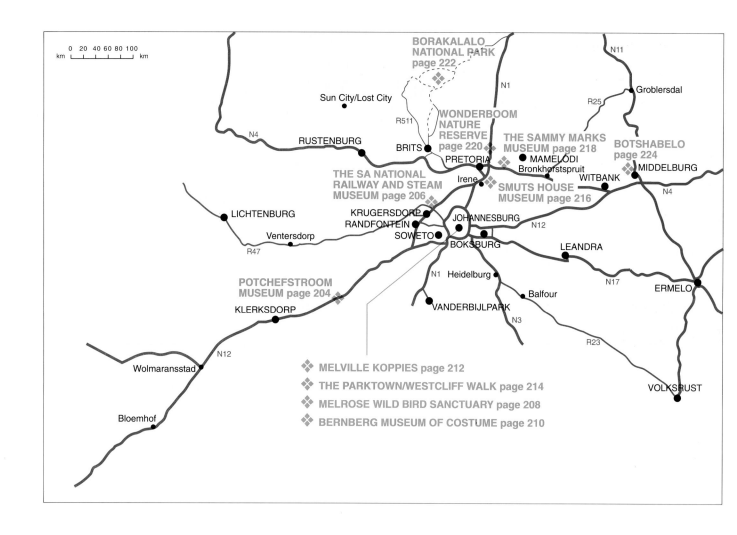

BORAKALALO
NATIONAL PARK
page 222

N11

Sun City/Lost City

Groblersdal

R25

N1

R511

WONDERBOOM
NATURE
RESERVE
page 220

THE SAMMY MARKS
MUSEUM page 218

BOTSHABELO
page 224

N4

RUSTENBURG

BRITS

PRETORIA

MAMELODI

MIDDELBURG

Bronkhorstspruit

THE SA NATIONAL
RAILWAY AND STEAM
MUSEUM page 206

Irene

WITBANK

SMUTS HOUSE
MUSEUM page 216

N4

LICHTENBURG

KRUGERSDORP

JOHANNESBURG

Ventersdorp

RANDFONTEIN

N12

R47

SOWETO

BOKSBURG

LEANDRA

POTCHEFSTROOM
MUSEUM page 204

N1

Heidelburg

Balfour

N17

ERMELO

KLERKSDORP

VANDERBIJLPARK

N3

R23

N12

Wolmaransstad

❖ MELVILLE KOPPIES page 212

VOLKSRUST

❖ THE PARKTOWN/WESTCLIFF WALK page 214

Bloemhof

❖ MELROSE WILD BIRD SANCTUARY page 208

❖ BERNBERG MUSEUM OF COSTUME page 210

SOUTHERN TRANSVAAL

A celebration of great Afrikaner achievements

The Potchefstroom Museum forms a fascinating link with the historical and cultural past of the Transvaal

Totius House was the home of one of Afrikanerdom's greatest literary figures, J D du Toit (Totius), during his tenure as principal of the Dutch Reformed Church's Theological Seminary.

A VOORTREKKER LEADER, a president, an artist and a poet – memories of these four diverse characters linger on in the picturesque highveld town of Potchefstroom.

First there was Andries Hendrik Potgieter, the Bible-toting Voortrekker who founded the town in 1838. Then came Marthinus Wessel Pretorius, president of the South African Republic, who also made his home here. Years later came the artist Otto Landsberg – not in person, but through the many paintings on permanent exhibition in the town. The last of the four was Potchefstroom's greatest man of letters, known by the pen name, Totius, whose lasting legacy was the translation of the Bible into Afrikaans.

Potgieter's arrival followed his victory against the Matabele in the Nine Day War of November 1837. Tempted by the lush vegetation growing alongside the *'stroom'* (stream), he decided to establish a town in the region. Two years later he and his followers discovered why the spot they'd chosen was so lush and green: the wet season of 1840 revealed that the settlement, later to be known as Oudedorp, had been laid out in a marsh! To prevent the settlement from vanishing into the mud, Potgieter decided to relocate on firmer ground 11 km downstream.

The new town was elegantly laid out, with broad streets aligned along the points of the compass – a fitting capital for the South African Republic of which Marthinus Wessel Pretorius would become the first president in 1857.

What is not clear, however, is how the town got its name. The more convincing explanation is derived from old Dutch documents that refer to the town as Potscherfstroom (literally, 'pot fragment stream'), suggesting that the earliest arrivals found fragments of indigenous pottery near the stream they called the Mooi River. But this version is rejected by those who insist that Potchefstroom was named after its founder – in other words that it was somewhat tortuously derived from the phrase 'stream of chief Potgieter'.

Potchefstroom remained a place of political and cultural importance even after Pretoria succeeded it as state capital in 1860. In 1881, the first shot of the Transvaal War of Independence was fired here and during the South African gold rush it earned worldwide fame as the gateway to a new El Dorado.

This colourful past is meticulously recorded in four buildings that together constitute the Potchefstroom Museum. The main museum is in Gouws Street and the Great Trek, the South African Republic and the two wars of independence are its main historical themes.

The museum's art gallery contains a large collection of works by the representational artist, Otto Landsberg, whose grandson Auguste d'Astre was a

resident of Potchefstroom. German-born, Cape-based Landsberg was a multi-talented man. He was highly regarded as a merchant (the same tobacco shop still thrives in Cape Town's Shortmarket Street today), a musician (he co-founded the Cape Musical Society and played first violin in its orchestra) and, of course, as a painter, watercolourist and sculptor. His life spanned virtually the whole 19th century and he died a wealthy man in 1905 at the age of 102. The Landsberg works, donated by d'Astre, form the nucleus of the museum's art collection. It also includes the works of other renowned South African artists such as Maud Sumner, Walter Battiss and Bettie Cilliers-Barnard.

Next door to the main building, on the corner of Gouws and Potgieter streets, you'll find the Goetz/-Fleischack Museum in the former home of Andreas Marthinus Goetz, Potchefstroom's landdrost (magistrate) between 1870 and 1881. It is the only remaining example of the townhouses that were erected around the New Market Square between 1850 and 1885, and has been furnished in opulent Victorian style.

From this museum, it's a short drive (or a long walk) to the next one – the President Pretorius Museum situated where Esselen Street joins Van der Hoff Road, itself an extension of Kerk Street. It is believed that President M W Pretorius built this old Cape-style dwelling with its coach house, stable and smithy in 1868. The homestead with its tranquil farmyard recalls an urban Boer culture which has long since disappeared.

Now cross Van der Hoff into Esselen Street and turn left into Molen Street. You'll see Totius House Museum on your left. Jacob Daniel du Toit was Potchefstroom's most famous resident (although he was born in Paarl in the Cape). Professor du Toit was a theologian of note, as well as a poet who published nine volumes of poetry under the *nom de plume* Totius and a staunch advocate of the Afrikaans language.

The museum is located in the home he occupied as principal of the Theological Seminary of the Dutch Reformed Church. It contains much of the furniture and many of the utensils, pictures and books owned by him and his family. The charming house, with its decorative veranda typical of the early part of this century, also has a number of paintings by Pierneef – testimony to the close friendship between poet and artist.

The Reformed Church, the oldest in the Transvaal, is another of Potchefstroom's gems, while other assets of historical interest include the remains of the Old Fort, in which a British garrison

Totius's stark study is almost totally dominated by books – appropriate, perhaps, for a man of letters.

was besieged for 95 days during the First War of Independence (1880-1), the Gunners' Memorial in honour of the Potchefstroom gunners who died in the Second World War, the Centenary Monument sculpted by Coert Steynberg, and the Anglican Church with its magnificent stained glass windows. Potchefstroom also boasts its own living national monument – an oak avenue of more than 700 trees spanning 7 km.

There are many modern-day treasures in the Potchefstroom University Art Gallery, which you'll find on the campus itself, on the third floor of the Ferdinand Postma Library Building. If you get lost, ask any Puk (as Potchefstroom University students are known). The Anthropological Museum, also on the campus, contains a comprehensive collection of Tswana artefacts.

Potchefstroom Museum at a glance (map page 202)

How to get there: Potchefstroom lies on the N12 about 105 km southwest of Johannesburg. The Potchefstroom Museum is scattered in four buildings near the centre of town.
Weather: Hot summers with late-afternoon thunderstorms; crisp, dry winters.
What to do: Explore the four buildings that together constitute the Potchefstroom Museum.
Special attractions: Potchefstroom offers much to art-lovers. The museum features a large collection of works by renowned South African artists of the 19th and 20th century,

and the contemporary art collection in the Potchefstroom University Art Gallery is an impressive one.
More information: Write to the Potchefstroom Town Council, PO Box 113, Potchefstroom 2520; tel (0148) 995111.
Visiting times: The main museum and art gallery are open from 9 am to 5 pm on weekdays, from 9 am to 1 pm on Saturday, and from 2.30 pm to 5 pm on Sunday. The three house museums are open from 9 am to 1 pm and 1.45 pm to 4.30 pm on weekdays. Visiting hours during weekends are the same as those of the main museum. The museums are closed on Christmas Day and the Day of the Vow.

Recapturing the timeless romance of the railways

*Some of the country's grand old steam locomotives
have found their final resting place in an open-air museum
at Randfontein Estates Gold Mine outside Krugersdorp*

FOR THE PAST FEW DECADES, South Africa has been a favoured destination for railway enthusiasts from all over the world due to its status as one of the last major outposts of steam power. In recent years, however, the number of steam locomotives in active service has dwindled to a mere handful, and it is becoming increasingly hard to find a railway on which these hissing, smoking giants go through their paces.

The era of steam in South Africa may be in the process of passing into the history books, but fortunately for future generations, a group of dedicated enthusiasts has ensured that some of the sturdy old workhorses of this romantic age will remain with us forever.

At the South African National Railway and Steam Museum outside Krugersdorp, dozens of vintage locomotives, together with old passenger coaches, have been collected and are on permanent

A little boy gets down to the fun-filled business of exploring an old steam locomotive at the museum.

display. Many have been painstakingly restored and some even returned to working order. What is so special about the museum is that it ensures that the public will be able to have joyrides on steam passenger trains for many years into the future. At the museum you have the opportunity to examine the old steam trains at close quarters; in fact, you are welcome to scramble all over the locomotives (provided they are not working) and to explore the coaches at your leisure.

The steam enthusiasts who run and maintain the museum's exhibits regard 'their' locomotives with great nostalgia and affection, as do the many other devotees who visit the museum to admire these great mechanical beasts of burden and to enjoy free rides. On monthly open days, the excitement of the men steaming up (preparing) the locomotives is contagious, as is the obvious pleasure of the three qualified steam-train drivers employed by the museum, who look so at home standing on the footplates of their great iron workhorses. The locomotives are paraded in all their splendour, brasswork glittering in the sun, hissing noisily and spewing out great clouds of steam, and when the whistle blows and the train pulls away, you'll often hear the passengers cheering.

The museum owes its existence and success to the Railway Preservation Group, a branch of the Railway Society. The group was founded in 1982 by a number of railway enthusiasts who were determined to find a way to preserve items of historical interest, particularly steam locomotives. The donation of three steam locomotives by the South African Railways marked the starting point (they subsequently donated another five), and since then other donations from various mines have helped build up an impressive collection.

The items on view at the museum now include 60 steam locomotives (of which five are in working order and regularly used), two steam cranes, two steamrollers, a diesel electric locomotive, a petrol locomotive and an underground electric locomotive. There are over 50 vintage passenger coaches, two wood-and-iron-ore wagons, eight coal hoppers and various other pieces of rolling stock.

The collection includes the largest assortment of Natal Government Railways and industrial locomotives in South Africa. Notable among these are the only surviving locomotive from the Jersey Island Railway and the only existing example of a Table Bay Harbour Board locomotive.

A recent important acquisition is the Kitson locomotive (affectionately known as 'Kitty'), which was handed over to the museum for preservation by

Eskom in 1993. Built by Kitson of Leeds in 1879, 'Kitty' is a true veteran of the steam age, being South Africa's oldest working locomotive. In 1979 she became the first steam locomotive in South Africa (and possibly the world) to have completed a century of continuous service. In 1983 she was declared a national monument. 'Kitty' is used for rides on rare occasions, but is too old and precious to steam up on a regular basis.

Another locomotive on permanent loan from Eskom is the Hunslet 2-6-0T. Built in 1902, this handsome locomotive is believed to have worked for a decade in the Newcastle coalfields. In 1912 it was sold to the forerunner of Eskom, the Victoria Falls and Transvaal Power Company. This steam engine has been kept in full working order by

The South African Railway and Steam Museum at a glance (map page 202)

How to get there: The museum is situated on a site at Randfontein Estates Gold Mine outside Krugersdorp, about 40 minutes' drive from Johannesburg. From Krugersdorp, take the R28 to Randfontein. About 5 km outside Krugersdorp you will see a turn-off to the right signposted 'Millsite Siding'. Follow the museum's signs along this road for about 3 km, until you see the gates of the site on your right.
More information: The Railway Preservation Group, PO Box 1419, Roosevelt Park 2129; tel (011) 8881154/5/6.
Visiting hours: The museum is open Monday to Saturday for viewing, from 9 am to 1 pm. Open days are held on the first Sunday of every month (with the exception of January), from 11 am to 4 pm. A small entrance fee is charged but all train rides are free.

Eskom and is one of the five locomotives used by the museum for giving passenger rides.

A fascinating item in the collection is a Cape Government Railways locomotive, built in 1897, which is still in working order. Photographs exist of this locomotive, under armed guard, pulling a train during the Anglo-Boer War.

There are several interesting passenger coaches on display. The museum operates the oldest working passenger coach and dining car in the country, built in 1897 and 1911 respectively. A treasured exhibit is the only known surviving remnants of a NZASM (President Kruger's Railway) coach.

Another notable aspect of the collection is that it includes the oldest diesel electric and articulated (Garratt) steam locomotives in South Africa. There is also a 1924 steam crane which was used by the South African Railways until it was acquired by Heat Exchangers Ltd in 1975 and later donated to the museum.

It is only on the museum's open days, held once each month, that rides are offered on the trains. However, if you would like simply to wander around and explore, the museum is open daily. Plans are afoot to move the museum to a location at Chamdor, on the West Rand close to Krugersdorp, in the near future.

In addition to running the museum, the Railway Preservation Group regularly operates steam-hauled trains to various destinations, including Cullinan and the Magaliesberg. The trains are available for filming and promotional purposes and may also be hired out for private functions.

(Above) An old Hunslet 2-6-0T is in regular use at the museum for passenger rides.
(Below) The gleaming identification plates of 'Kitty', one of the museum's most treasured possessions.

A haven for wild birds in the heart of the suburbs

Thousands of birds thrive in Melrose, 10 minutes outside central Johannesburg, where the Melrose Wild Bird Sanctuary offers a respite from city living

NOTHING PLEASES the dedicated traveller more than finding treasures in unexpected places. It is this sense of discovery and surprise that makes the Melrose Wild Bird Sanctuary such a delightful place to visit.

Melrose Estate is one of Johannesburg's northern suburbs and it seems no different in essence from its well-heeled neighbours. But of the residents of Melrose, a large number could quite literally be described as birds of a different feather. There are more than 120 wild bird species that nest in the reedbeds and indigenous trees around a lake created by the Sandspruit.

The Melrose Wild Bird Sanctuary lies a mere stone's throw away from Johannesburg's M1 freeway, on 10 ha adjoining the James and Ethel Gray Park. To get to the sanctuary, leave your car off Melrose Avenue and walk along a path for a few hundred metres to reach the edge of the lake. On your left there is a deep stormwater culvert beyond which is undeveloped parkland with some large stands of trees. Enter this area at a gate situated just in front of the lake. You will find the sanctuary on your right.

From here you can walk northwards along the banks of the lake, and at a fence marking the sanctuary's northern boundary, continue into the James and Ethel Gray Park; or you can take a path that leads into the reedbeds and turns back south more or less parallel to the path that brought you to the entrance.

Along either route, you'll find the birdlife plentiful and in summer you'll enjoy the rare (in this urban setting) and lovely spectacle of weavers and bishop birds in the reeds, and moorhens and Egyptian geese on the lake.

The sanctuary is of great interest to bird-watchers, and, in a quarterly bulletin mailed to its members, the Witwatersrand Bird Club includes information about all new sightings here. But if you are a newcomer to bird-watching, here are some clues on how to identify some of Melrose's most celebrated residents.

Looking hard among the reeds, you may spot the red bishop or its smaller cousin, the golden bishop. The red bishop breeding male is brilliant orange-scarlet, except for its black face and belly, and brown wings and tail. Females and non-breeding males are less spectacular, with bold streaks of buff and brown above, and white, buff and brown below. Red bishops are a gregarious bunch who like company (usually each other's, not yours!), and attach their nests to upright reeds or thin vertical branches of trees. They call out to each other with sharp *chiz chiz* notes and sing a wheezy, swizzling song that goes *chssss zeeeee tsarippy-tsarippy ts-ts-ts-ts-ts zwipswaay*, for those who want to try imitating the red bishop chorus!

(Left) The yellow-billed duck, usually found in pairs, is a common resident of the sanctuary.
(Right) The distinctive black and scarlet colours of the red bishop – often spotted amongst the sanctuary's waterside reeds.

The golden bishop's song is slightly more straightforward – a simple *zzzzz zzit zzit zzzz* suggests the presence of a preening male to practised ears. As with their cousins, the breeding male has all the glory – it is brilliant yellow, with small accents of black, and brown wings and tail.

The female and non-breeding male are streaked black and grey above, and white, buff and light brown below. This is another gregarious bird that nests in small colonies and prefers to make the upright stems of rushes its home during the breeding season.

The moorhen is a medium-sized bird with black feathers, except for a white undertail and white streaks on the flanks, and a red shield and bill with a yellow tip. Moorhens usually spend most of the day swimming, wading or walking over wet grasslands and nest in a neat bowl of rushes and reeds, carefully concealed well above the water level, but their distinctive high-pitched *krrruk*, staccato *killik* or rapid *kik-kik-kik* may reveal their presence.

The Egyptian goose is another noisy bird. But you don't need to eavesdrop on its conversations – the hoarse *haaa* of the male, the hissing of his partner – to identify this large gooselike bird. A dark brown patch around the eye and another on the breast – earning it the name kolgans (spotted goose) in Afrikaans – make it instantly recognisable. White wings veined with black and edged with green identify the kolgans in flight. But though they fly early morning and evening to grasslands to graze, you're likely to spot the Egyptian goose swimming high in the water or loafing on the shore, where it spends most of the day.

Egyptian geese typically nest in dense vegetation, in grass-lined hollows in the ground, but some prefer heights and are not above converting nests abandoned in high trees and cliffs by crows and hamerkops to suit their lifestyle.

Another prominent Melrose family are the weavers, whose females are usually so dully attired that they're almost impossible to spot in a field. Breeding males are mostly yellow, with distinctive faces – orange in the case of the Cape weaver, black in the case of the masked weaver. But what the female lacks in outright glamour, she makes up for in skill. She is the nest-builder, responsible for those fascinating oval chambers woven of strips of grass and leaves, and attached to drooping branches of trees.

Though their calls are harsh, weavers are year-round singers – keep your ears tuned to the Cape weaver's swizzling song and its cousin's more rasping *zzzzrrrr chik chik chik chik zzzrrr zweee*.

Willow trees and reedbeds surround the sanctuary's lake, providing nesting places for many of its feathered residents.

A symphony of birdsong in a Johannesburg suburb – that is the charm of the Melrose Wild Bird Sanctuary. It's just a 10-minute drive from the central business district but it's capable of transporting city dwellers to the heart of a feathered realm. A visit to the sanctuary is usually most rewarding in the early mornings or evenings, when visitors are few and far between, and the birds seem more confiding.

Melrose Wild Bird Sanctuary at a glance (map page 202)

How to get there: From central Johannesburg take the M1 north and turn off at the Glenhove off-ramp. Turn left for Rosebank and take the first road to the right, which is Somerville Avenue. Turn right into Melrose Avenue and follow it for about 1 km past the intersection with Tyrwhitt Avenue and alongside a golf course on the right-hand side of the road. The sanctuary is signposted on the left-hand side just before the road goes into a dip.
What to do: Stroll through the sanctuary keeping a close watch for birds and, if you have time, include the adjoining

James and Ethel Gray Park on your walk.
Special attractions: The red and golden bishop, the moorhen, the Egyptian goose and members of the weaver family are among the more than 120 bird species which make their home here.
More information: Contact the Johannesburg City Council's Culture and Recreation Department, PO Box 2824, Johannesburg 2000; tel (011) 4076824.
Visiting times: The summer months are best for bird-watching; the sanctuary is open between sunrise and sunset.

Fashion and frippery from a more gracious age

The tiny Bernberg Museum in Forest Town, Johannesburg, is dedicated to the finery of yesteryear, offering visitors a fascinating glimpse into the history of women's costume over the last two centuries

NOT MANY PEOPLE tend to notice the rather modest building that houses the Bernberg Museum, even though it is situated just a stone's throw from busy Jan Smuts Avenue, not far from the Johannesburg Zoological Gardens. Even fewer people actually visit the museum, as a glance at the visitors' book will reveal. This is a pity, because – tiny though it is – the Bernberg Museum has a rather special charm.

The rooms of this little old suburban house are crammed with a wide variety of period costumes, jewellery and accessories, a collection that reveals much about the way women dressed before the advent of cheaper mass-produced goods; about an age where clothes were made by hand, stitch by perfect stitch, and where fine workmanship mattered a great deal.

Women's dresses, dating from the Victorian and Edwardian periods, comprise the greater part of the collection, although there are a few men's and children's garments on display, along with a small collection of hats, fans, shoes, purses and the

A display that will warm the heart of every mother is one featuring a charming assortment of children's clothing.

numerous other small objects that any well-dressed lady once carried on her person.

The museum owes its existence almost entirely to the generosity of the Bernberg sisters, Anna and Theresa, avid collectors of antiques who were also devoted patrons of the arts. They bequeathed the little house and its contents to the Africana Museum in 1960, and by 1973 the house had been refurbished and had opened its doors as the Bernberg Museum. Several of the rooms were furnished in period style using furniture and ornaments from the Bernberg bequest; other items were drawn from the Africana Museum's collection or were donated by the public.

Lovers of trinkets and other frippery will be delighted by the collection of jewellery and accessories exhibited in the foyer area of the museum. To your right as you enter is a display case containing a comical collection of disembodied legs, each of which wears a single shoe. Exhibits include a Victorian button-up leather boot, made to fit an impossibly dainty foot, and – the oldest item in the display – a very elegant cream-coloured satin shoe, circa 1740, complete with embroidered stocking and gilt buckle.

The jewellery display case nearby contains some very fine pieces of Victorian craftsmanship, but it is the collection of 'hair' jewellery that is particularly intriguing to visitors. These pieces are made from, or contain, human hair – this form of jewellery having been quite popular in the late 19th century. There is something rather grisly about the intricately plaited hair 'necklaces' and the lockets containing the fair curls of infants and lovers, perhaps because the original owners of the hair they preserve are so long dead.

In this display case you will also notice some formidable pieces of filigreed steel jewellery. During the Napoleonic Wars, English women who presented their gold jewellery to the state were given items of steel jewellery such as these in exchange; any lady who felt a pang of regret at parting with her precious jewels was no doubt consoled by the knowledge of her patriotism.

Further into the foyer is a very charming collection of babies' dresses and bonnets, each one delicately pin-tucked and exquisitely embroidered. The fact that these fragile garments have lasted for more than a century is testimony to the artistry and skill of the women who laboured for so many hours to make them.

Nearby is the museum's valuable collection of fans – some jewel-bright and gaudy, others delicate and subtly coloured. A particularly beautiful item is

Many of the costume displays are given an added authenticity by the presence of art and furniture from the Victorian and Edwardian eras.

a French fan, circa 1760, on which is painted a romantic garden scene and which has mother-of-pearl sticks that are carved, lattice-pierced and decorated with gold pigment.

The first garment that will catch your eye as you wander towards the back of the museum is a Voortrekker dress, plainly made from serviceable sprigged cotton. This is one of the museum's most valued exhibits, as Voortrekker dresses are extremely rare. In the next display case is another precious exhibit, a delicate wisp of a dress worn in 1919 by Princes Alice, Queen Victoria's granddaughter. It is made from ivory-coloured Brussels appliqué, with a tiered skirt and elegantly dropped shoulders.

Further down the passage to the left is a large case displaying a variety of period dresses arranged in chronological order, the most recent being Edwardian dresses, dating to 1910, with their curious

hobble skirts (these being cut so narrow at the ankles that ladies were forced to take small, mincing steps). The next case houses displays which are changed every few months, and here the various fashions of later, more modern periods are generally shown.

A bit further along the corridor is the first of the period rooms, furnished in the Edwardian style. It shows a group of ladies enjoying a dainty tea-party, all dressed in the elegant fashion of the era, with its extravagant feathered hats and slimmed-down silhouettes. Some intimate ladies apparel, including corsets and bloomers, is exhibited for all to see in the next room, furnished in the style of a lady's boudoir.

An unusual item in this display is the turquoise maternity gown, a garment not often seen in public at the turn of the century. Nearby is a case that is the museum's only real concession to masculine fashion – a variety of pipes on display, along with several tasselled velvet smoking caps.

Three very beautiful old wedding dresses are grouped a little further down the corridor, including one that looks as if it were made for a child. Further along, on your right, you will come to the last period room, a Victorian kitchen containing a mannequin in a kitchen-maid's uniform and another wearing the formidable attire of a cook.

A rather amusing and unusual item to be found in this room is a 'moustache cup' made with a little china bridge just inside the rim, the purpose of which is to prevent the large moustache of a gentleman from dangling unbecomingly into his tea and getting wet – thus causing the moustache's blacking to run.

You can easily make your way through the museum in 20 minutes or so, but if you would like to learn more about the history of the exhibits, and the various stories relating to them, guided tours are offered by arrangement.

Bernberg Museum of Costume at a glance (map page 202)

How to get there: From central Johannesburg follow the M1 north to Forest Town and Oxford Road. Turn left onto Sherwood Road and right at Jan Smuts Avenue. The Bernberg Museum is situated on the corner of Jan Smuts Avenue and Duncombe Road on your right.

Special attractions: The museum is so full of unique items that it is difficult to single out anything more special than the rest. However, the wide variety of voluptuous Victorian and Edwardian dresses which make up most of the collection are particularly impressive.

More information: Write to the above address or telephone (011) 6460716. To arrange a guided tour, or for further information about the exhibits, contact The Curator, Hampo House, 28 De Korte St, Braamfontein 2001; tel (011) 3397170.

Visiting times: Monday to Saturday, from 9 am to 1 pm; 2 pm to 5 pm. Sundays and public holidays, from 2 pm to 5.30 pm. The museum is closed on Christmas Day and Good Friday. Entrance is free.

A sanctuary of peace in the heart of the suburbs

Lying along a 5-km stretch of ridge just northwest of Johannesburg, Melville Koppies is an evocative reminder of how the area must have looked to the prehistoric people who once lived here

THE RESERVE IS TINY by African standards, it is open to the public for only a handful of days a year, and the scenery isn't particularly dramatic. But what makes Melville Koppies Nature Reserve so extraordinary is that this tiny patch of wilderness has been preserved intact, even though it is hemmed in on all sides by busy roads and suburbs, and is a mere 10 minutes' drive from the concrete canyons of central Johannesburg.

It's as if time has stood still on these rocky quartzite ridges, where the breeze is scented with pungent indigenous herbs and the air reverberates with the whistling and twittering of the many species of birds that have taken refuge in the reserve. Imagine, if you can, how generation after generation of ancient hunters must have squatted on these very ridges, painstakingly fashioning their tools, from quartz and, later, iron, while surveying the surrounding grasslands that teamed with abundant game and fresh water.

Today the views from this vantage point are those of Johannesburg's northern suburbs, sprawling to the horizon. It's unsettling to realise that the prehistoric people who inhabited these koppies for so many thousands of years left the landscape without a blemish, while it has taken only a century or so for the city of Johannesburg to spread its tentacles as far as the eye can see.

Melville Koppies originally formed part of the farm *Braamfontein*, which also incorporated the present-day suburb of Emmarentia. The area was proclaimed a nature reserve in 1959 and a natural historical monument in 1968. It owes its pristine state to the energetic efforts of the Johannesburg City Council and the Johannesburg Council for Natural History. So fragile is the ecological balance in the reserve that access by the public is very strictly controlled.

Despite its several attractions, Melville Koppies Nature Reserve still draws surprisingly few visitors – perhaps a hundred or so on an average open day. Of those who do come, many are nature enthusiasts who are fascinated by the richly diverse flora. Among the hundreds of species found here, there are more than 30 edible plants and 112 medicinal ones, 34 being common ingredients in ritual magic.

Probably the best way to learn more about the flora is to buy a copy of the reserve's excellent guide book (available for a few rand at the gate), and to follow the nature trail, a well-marked circular walk that begins at the main entrance in Judith Road. Numbers painted on trees, stones and stakes correspond to numbered paragraphs in the guide book, which also gives details of the vegetation, bird life, archaeology and geology of the reserve. It's a short and easy walk that will take you about an hour, but a good part of it is uphill and across rocky, uneven ground, so wear walking shoes and remember to take along your own supply of water.

Initially, the trail leads you up an open, grassy slope, dotted here and there with mounds made by snouted harvester termites. Soon the path winds

The reserve abounds with indigenous plants, such as this Diospyrus *shrub with its distinctive red and yellow fruits.*

A glimpse across the landscape from Melville Koppies reminds one exactly how close this tranquil reserve is to the suburbs and city of Johannesburg.

through a pleasant shady area of woodland, where enkeldoring (*Acacia robusta*) is the dominant tree species, providing shade in which a variety of weeds and bushy herbs flourish.

This is a good place to stop, catch your breath and do some bird watching. It's remarkable, considering the inner-city location of the reserve, just how many birds you are likely to see. More than 175 species have been recorded in the reserve, including crimson-breasted shrikes, spotted eagle owls, cardinal woodpeckers and red-throated wrynecks. Other birds commonly seen in the reserve are francolin, guineafowl, barbets, swallows, thrushes, and wagtails. The reserve is an official ringing station of the Witwatersrand Bird Club, and on open days members of the club are often present to give lectures and demonstrations.

The path forks after you pass Marker 10. The right-hand fork will take you on a slightly longer trail, leading you to the arboretum, a collection of indigenous trees. The trees in the arboretum – and elsewhere in the reserve – are labelled with numbers that correspond to the National List of Trees. Some of the more common trees occurring in the reserve include mountain silver oak, white stinkwood, firethorn, Cape lilac, wild apricot, cat thorn and wild pear.

The left-hand fork will lead you to the first of the natural terraces, one of the several archaeological sites in the reserve. The archaeology of Melville Koppies is particularly fascinating because this area, small though it is, reflects much of the ancient history of the Witwatersrand. All they left behind them, those generations of prehistoric people, were a scattering of stone implements, fragments of pottery and the sunbaked ruins of stone-walled huts, yet these few artefacts have provided researchers with vital clues to the identity and everyday life of the early hunters, farmers and miners who made these koppies their home.

On the upper terrace, close to where the open-sided lecture hut stands, excavations revealed three prehistoric living floors. At the very lowest and oldest level, hand-axes of the Earlier Stone Age, which may be 100 000 years old, were discovered. At the next level up, a metre beneath the present soil level, is a Middle Stone Age camp, possibly 40 000 years old. And at about 30 cm below the surface lie the remains of an Iron Age settlement, estimated to be 1 000 years old.

Near the lecture hut you will come across the remains of an ancient smelting furnace – now protected from the elements by a sturdy glass case –

Rock pathways take the visitor on a journey through a wide variety of indigenous plants, bushes and trees.

which is one of two furnaces excavated in the reserve. The Iron Age people of Melville were descendants of armed warriors from the north who swept down into the Transvaal sometime around the beginning of the first millennium AD. The invaders spread throughout the Transvaal over the next few centuries, building villages, farming and mining for tin, copper and iron.

Melville's Iron Age people collected iron ore lumps from nearby shale exposures, mixed the ore with charcoal inside the furnaces and fired the mixture to provide iron ingots to be forged into blades, axes, hoes and spears. Other clues about the life of these Iron Age workers come in the form of decorated pottery shards and the remains of stone-walled settlements, which you can see a few metres away from the lecture hut, at the base of the north-facing rocky ridge.

It's a fast two-minute walk back down the slope to the main gate, but you may want to pause for while at the top of the ridge in order to enjoy the views over northern Johannesburg. If the weather is clear, you will be able to see the distant blue-grey smudge of the Magaliesberg. Also visible are the Northcliff and Bryanston ridges and, immediately below the reserve, Emmarentia Dam and the Botanic Garden.

Melville Koppies Nature Reserve at a glance (map page 202)

How to get there: The main entrance is opposite Marks Park Sports Grounds in Judith Road, Emmarentia. It is recommended that you park in Orange Road, which intersects with Judith Road to the west of the main entrance.
What to do: Walking, bird-watching, botanising and examining the ancient traces of the early inhabitants.
Special attractions: A wilderness area close to the heart of the city, and interesting archaeological diggings.
More information: Contact the Johannesburg Botanic Garden, Culture and Recreation Division, Johannesburg City Council, Civic Centre, PO Box 2824, Johannesburg 2000; tel (011) 7827064 or 4076824. If you wish to organise a group

visit to the reserve for educational purposes, also contact the above address.
Visiting times: A good time to visit the Melville Koppies Nature Reserve is after good summer rains, when the veld is lush and green and scattered with summer flowers. The reserve has 'open days' on the third Sunday of every month between September and April, from 3 pm to 6 pm, and guides are available to lead tours. You are also free to wander around at your leisure at other times – provided that you book in advance and obtain a key from the Johannesburg Botanic Garden, PO Box 2824, Johannesburg 2000; tel (011) 7827064.

A stroll past the famous mansions of yesteryear

Some of the most splendid homes built by Johannesburg's early mining magnates are linked together by five circular walks which meander through the old suburbs of Parktown and Westcliff

MANY PEOPLE ASSOCIATE early Johannesburg not with mansions, but with a hot dusty miners' camp, where tents and tin shacks provided cramped accommodation for the thousands of prospectors who flocked to the Reef in their feverish search for gold.

Though tent town it certainly was to begin with, the town of Johannesburg grew with astonishing speed, and within a few years several of the city's magnates – or 'randlords', as they came to be known – had amassed fortunes considerable enough to build imposing mansions on the ridges north of the town. Many of these grand old dowagers are still standing, and are still in daily use as offices, institutions and even private homes. The five routes of the Parktown and Westcliff Urban Walk were designed to introduce visitors to the history and romance of the old houses, at the same time guiding them through one of the city's most historically significant areas.

One of the first magnates to make his home in the area that became Parktown was Lionel Phillips. His wife Florrie discovered the rocky, sun-baked ridge during one of her daily rides out of town, and saw at once that it was the perfect site on which to build a country house. One can easily understand her eagerness to forsake the hurly-burly of the miners' camp, which was all too often a dismal place: dusty, hot, fly-infested and incessantly noisy. Here on the Parktown ridge, the air was sweet and filled with

birdsong, and the views were nothing short of spectacular, stretching right to the Magaliesberg, 50 km to the north. Their house, Hohenheim, meaning 'home on high', was built in 1892.

A year later, the suburb of Parktown was laid out by the Braamfontein Estate and Gold Mining Company, which wanted to develop it and other outlying suburbs as exclusive residential enclaves. To ensure this exclusivity and to attract the right sort of residents, various restrictions were imposed on land usage and the entire suburb was fenced in.

Added attractions of the new suburb were its one-acre stands, which could not be subdivided, its mule-drawn sanitary service and its electric street lighting. With its rocky ridges, abundant trees lining the winding streets and sweeping views, this garden suburb quickly became the fashionable place for the elite to build their homes, and within a few years the number of residents had swelled.

Many famous personalities in South African history owned houses or lived here, among them Sir Percy Fitzpatrick, the Oppenheimers, Sir Thomas Cullinan, Lord Milner and Sir Herbert Baker. Soon several schools were established, including St John's School, Roedean and Parktown Convent.

The mansions built by Johannesburg's magnates were generally built on a grand scale, some of them having up to twenty rooms. Most were expensively fitted and furnished, with extensive solid wooden panelling, deep carpets, massive staircases, imported tiles and crystal chandeliers. They were embellished, inside and out, with all the extravagant detailing so cherished by builders and architects at the turn of the century. The mass production of building materials in the late Victorian period made it possible to order materials through catalogues; many items were imported from England. The park-like gardens, laid out in the English style, were often every bit as splendid as the mansions they surrounded, planted with a variety of exotic trees such as cypresses, oaks and corks, many of which can still be seen.

With the eclectism typical of late Victorian architecture, many of the early mansions incorporated several styles, which collectively came to be known as the Parktown Baronial style. In 1902, the architect Herbert Baker arrived from the Cape, and for the first time a vernacular architecture began to emerge. He experimented with the use of indigenous building materials, such as local sandstone and quartzite quarried from the ridges, producing houses that blended harmoniously with the rocky terrain of the Parktown ridges and soon came to characterise the suburb.

Hazeldene Hall is reminiscent of the grand homes found in the American 'Deep South'. This impressive mansion is now used as business premises.

Parktown was laid out in 1895, and Westcliff seven years later. As Johannesburg grew, the surrounding suburbs of Greenside, Saxonwold, Forest Town, Parkwood and Parkview sprang up with remarkable speed. Several of these suburbs derive their names from the Sachsenwald Forest, a vast plantation of over a million eucalyptus trees, grown for the purpose of supplying much-needed timber for the mines. By 1925, the forest was gone.

The Parktown and Westcliff Urban Walk offers visitors a fascinating insight into the development of these old suburbs. The walk, which forms part of the larger Braamfontein Spruit Trail, actually consists of five short circular routes, three through Parktown and two through Westcliff. All the walks, and their landmarks, are described in detail in the trail's official brochure, which also includes a map. The brochure may be obtained from the Parktown Westcliff Heritage Trust (see side-panel).

The most popular of these routes is the Jubilee Walk through Parktown, which takes about 50 minutes to complete and starts at Pieter Roos Park in St Andrews Road. It's the most interesting route, because it takes visitors through the oldest part of the suburb and past some of the city's most splendid mansions. The View, at 18 Ridge Road, is a large, rather opulent red-brick mansion, built in the Neo-Queen Anne style, with twin timbered gables and lacy woodwork verandas. It was built by Sir Thomas Cullinan in 1896 and later extended to house his family of 11 children. One of the oldest mansions in the city, The View now serves as the headquarters of the Transvaal Scottish Regiment. Further along Ridge Road, at number 20, is a more gracious example of Victorian architecture, Hazeldene Hall, an elegant double-storeyed mansion as ornate as a wedding cake, with a beautiful lacy cast-iron veranda that was imported from the Saracen Foundries of Walter MacFarlane in Glasgow, Scotland. This typically colonial house was built in 1902 for stockbroker Charles Jerome.

Sunnyside, at 32 Princess of Wales Terrace, is now a hotel and one of the city's favourite watering holes, but this huge red-brick mansion once served a loftier purpose, being the headquarters of the British High Commissioner, Lord Milner, during the Anglo-Boer War. Built in the style of a villa or English country house, Sunnyside boasts a turret above the manager's office which once served as his study.

No expense was spared to build Emoyeni, which you will find at 15 Jubilee Road. Built, like several other Parktown mansions, in the Neo-Queen Anne style, Emoyeni is a magnificent example of colonial architecture, a grand and imposing red-brick structure that blended various historical styles. Dolobran, at 1 Jubilee Road, is another well-known landmark in Johannesburg, a delightfully fanciful mansion built of warm stone. With its varied gables, red-tiled roof, intricate roof-line, ornate turret and assortment of windows, Dolobran is considered a classic example of the Parktown Baronial style. The house is a national monument and also a private home.

Other important landmarks on the Jubilee Walk include North Lodge (17 Victoria Avenue), Gable Ends (3 Jubilee Road), Savernake (13 Jubilee Road) and several others, all of which are described in the brochure.

Those who are interested in architecture will find the other four circular walks equally fascinating; of particular interest is the hour-long Baker Walk, which concentrates on the area between Oxford Road and Jan Smuts Avenue, where many of Sir Herbert Baker's famous houses are clustered.

(Left) Now used as a Wits University students' hostel, North Lodge has been caustically described as being a 'scrapbook of architectural details'. (Right) A walk around this house, and a glimpse of the view that it commands, makes it easy to understand why it was named Emoyeni – the Zulu word for 'in the air'.

The Parktown and Westcliff Walk at a glance (map page 202)

How to get there: The five circular walks all begin at different places in the suburbs of Parktown and Westcliff; consult the official brochure, which contains a detailed map and directions.
More information: Johannesburg Publicity Association, PO Box 4580, Johannesburg 2000; tel (011) 3376650. The official brochure is available from the Parktown Westcliff Heritage Trust, Northwards, 21 Rockridge Road, Parktown; tel (011) 4823349 (the office is open weekdays, 9 am to 1 pm).
What to do: Be selective about which routes you will walk; it's probably advisable to do just one or two in a day. Please note that all the houses described in the brochure are private property, and that the privacy of the owners should be respected at all times.

Humble dwelling of a great statesman

Home to General Jan Smuts for over 40 years, Doornkloof, in Irene, southeast of Pretoria, is a unique museum that reveals much about the life and the spirit of this great statesman

SOLDIER, SCHOLAR, STATESMAN and philosopher, General Jan Christiaan Smuts was one of South Africa's most remarkable leaders, an enigmatic and multifaceted person who was never fully understood by his countrymen.

But despite his fame and many talents, Smuts was at heart a simple man who yearned for peace and simplicity. It was at Doornkloof, a modest wood-and-iron farmhouse in the veld outside the village of Irene, that he found the tranquillity he craved; a place where, surrounded by his many children and grandchildren, he could indulge his passionate interest in botany. Doornkloof, now called Smuts House Museum, has been preserved for future generations as a living memorial to the man known to everyone as 'Oubaas', housing many relics and mementos that offer fascinating insights into his extraordinary career.

The museum owes its existence entirely to Guy Brathwaite, a Pretoria attorney and ex-serviceman who, determined to preserve the house as a memorial to Smuts, purchased the property in 1960, narrowly saving it from being converted into a sanatorium. At a congress of ex-servicemen's associations, the General Smuts War Veterans' Foundation was founded, which assumed ownership of the property and which continues to administer the house and its surroundings.

Doornkloof occupied a special place in General Smuts's affections. He regarded it as his true home and, as a lover of nature, he derived great pleasure from the beauty of the surrounding veld. It was here that his seven children were brought up; they, and everyone else, knew it as 'the Big House.'

It's easy to see, even more than 80 years after General Smuts bought the farm, why he chose Irene as a place to establish his family home. This picturesque village, with its deep green meadows and hay-scented air, slumbers in its own little time capsule, a peaceful haven that seems oddly out of place on the industrialised highveld. The road out of the village to Doornkloof winds through deep-shaded avenues of plane trees, poplars and old oaks; after about 2 km, you come to the gates of Doornkloof, where you will catch a glimpse of the old house through the trees.

Although the farmhouse looks as if it has always been there, it actually began its life in Middelburg, where it was the Officers' Mess, erected at the behest of Lord Kitchener. This was the Edwardian equivalent of prefabricated housing, manufactured in sections and assembled on site — the wood-and-corrugated-iron portions were bolted together, piece by piece, to form simple but sturdy structures. General Smuts bought the house from the British in 1909 and had it transported to Doornkloof, a 4 000-acre farm in Irene which he had bought the year before. Although he paid only £300 for the structure, he had to pay another £1 000 to have it re-erected at Doornkloof.

Over the years, a pantry and kitchen were added and portions of the veranda, which runs all the way round the house, were enclosed. Although the house looks modest, there are in fact eleven bedrooms. The design is simple, but there are several decorative elements that give the building great charm, such as the high gables, which are topped by elegant finials and embellished with lacy wooden fretwork bargeboarding.

The first thing that strikes you as you walk up the steps into the high-ceilinged rooms is the simplicity of the furnishings. The unpretentiousness of the interior aptly illustrates General Smuts's utter disregard for luxury: his tastes were simple, verging on the austere. His bedroom, for example, is a narrow, dim room, furnished only with a plain iron bed, a few functional pieces of furniture and framed photographs of his many children and grandchildren.

The interior now appears more spartan than it was when Doornkloof was a happy family home, because, many books, mementos and other objects are now scattered in museums throughout South Africa. The contents of Smuts's study, for example, were removed after his death to the University of the Witwatersrand, where the room, with its thousands of books on philosophy, science and international affairs, has been faithfully recreated.

Nevertheless, many interesting objects still remain. One of them is an unusual gong that sits on a table in the museum's foyer; made from elephant tusks and cartridge cases, this was presented to Smuts by his Imperial Staff in the East African Campaign (1916-17). The bamboo curtain rods in

Where to stay

There is a very pleasant camp site on the property at Doornkloof. Individual sites may be reserved by telephoning the museum at (012) 6671176. Some 5 km west of Irene at Verwoerdburgstad is the *Centurion Lake Hotel*, PO Box 7331, Hennopsmeer 0046; tel (011) 6631825.

The front veranda of Doornkloof, around which much of the social life of the Smuts family revolved.

Simplicity is the keynote of Smuts's home, but particular features – such as the ornate front gable – help to give Doornkloof its unique charm.

this room also have a fascinating story to tell. They come from a house in Bourke Street, Pretoria, the Smuts residence during the time that he was State Attorney in President Paul Kruger's Zuid-Afrikaansche Republiek. When the British forces entered the city in 1900, during the Anglo-Boer War, Smuts's wife Isie rolled up important state documents and hid them in the bamboo rods. Although the house was searched, the papers were never discovered.

In the living room stands one of the few valuable pieces of furniture in the house, a Cape stinkwood armoire made in 1840 by Smuts's grandfather. Also in this room is a display cabinet filled with objects belonging to Isie (known to everyone as 'Ouma Smuts'), who was a gifted scholar in her own right. Exhibits include embroidered linen, medals won for cooking, and an autograph book containing the signatures of a host of famous people, among them General Louis Botha and Olive Schreiner. Her bedroom, a narrow cubbyhole just as frugally fur-

nished as her husband's, is down the passage to the right. This wing of the house was known to the family as 'The Harem', since Oubaas and the boys occupied the other wing of the house, which leads off to the left of the foyer.

One of the bedrooms in the men's wing is rumoured to be haunted. It was used as a spare room and known as the *donker kamer* (dark room), as it is lit by only one small window. Smuts's bedroom is the next one along the passage on the right, but he rarely slept inside, preferring instead the narrow iron bed that stands on the gauze-enclosed veranda outside.

When you have finished touring the house, take a few minutes to stroll around the garden, a natural park where the thousands of indigenous trees and shrubs planted by Smuts are still to be seen. A patch of lawn is the only concession to his stipulation that the veld should 'come right up to the front door'.

Botany, and particularly the study of grasses, was Smuts's favourite hobby, and he spent many of his happiest hours in the garden and surrounding veld, enthralled by the diversity of nature. The administrators of the museum have erected a resting place in the garden, a stone shelter set among the trees, known as the 'Place of Quiet'. There is also a very pleasant tea-garden, where tables are set in the shade of tall trees.

A footpath leads from the garden to Smuts Koppie, the rocky hill behind the house where the ashes of Oubaas and Ouma Smuts are scattered; a granite obelisk has been erected here. It's an enjoyable walk to the top of the koppie, but for the less energetic there is also the option of driving there; ask at the museum's front desk for directions.

Out in the garden, a bronze statue of the 'Oubaas' gazes out across the veld where he spent so much of his leisure time.

Doornkloof at a glance (map page 202)

How to get there: Doornkloof is situated 2 km outside the village of Irene and is well signposted. If you are coming from Pretoria or Johannesburg along the N1, take the Botha Avenue (M18) turn-off and follow the signposts; the museum is 4,5 km further along.
More information: The Curator, Smuts House Museum, PO Box 36, Irene 1675; tel (012) 6671176.
Visiting time: Monday to Friday, 9.30 am to 1 pm; 1.30 pm to 4.30 pm. The museum closes at 5 pm on Saturdays, Sundays and public holidays. It is closed on December 24-25 and on Good Fridays. There is a charge per car to enter the picnic area, and a small entrance fee is charged at the museum.

The house that Sammy built

One of South Africa's grandest colonial mansions, Zwartkoppies Hall, 23 km outside Pretoria, is now a fascinating museum that pays tribute to the genius of its original owner

SET SOMEWHAT INCONGRUOUSLY in acres of rolling veld outside Pretoria, Zwartkoppies Hall epitomises all the ornate elegance of prosperous colonial households during the latter decades of the last century. Its 48 graciously proportioned rooms are filled with all the trappings of refined Victorian living – exquisite furniture, paintings, silver, porcelain – making Zwartkoppies Hall a home truly worthy of Sammy Marks's status as one of the leading industrialists of his day.

What is unique about this museum is that it is the only Victorian mansion in the country whose interior is wholly authentic and preserved intact. This is thanks largely to the foresight of Sammy Marks, who declared in his will that the house and its contents were to be preserved for four generations after his death.

But what is even more appealing about Zwartkoppies Hall is that it has somehow retained some of the well-worn and relaxed ambience of a family home. It's a gorgeous period piece, soaked in atmosphere and appealingly frayed at the edges,

The stately mansion, Zwartkoppies Hall, with the recently re-established rose garden in the foreground.

which is hardly surprising when you consider that the descendants of Sammy Marks occupied the mansion for the best part of a century.

The high-ceilinged rooms may stand silent now, but there was a time when the whole house hummed with activity. This was a grand Victorian household in every sense, run by a small army of servants and occupied by eight children and Sammy and his wife Bertha. It's easy to imagine, as you wander from room to room, how the house once echoed with the happy laughter of children, with the clumping of little boots up and down the Burmese teak staircase, the crunch of coach wheels on the gravel driveway, and the invisible scurryings of parlourmaids as they scrubbed and polished, lugged coal and fetched water. Now you will detect only a faint lingering scent of furniture polish and old wood, but a century ago the air in the old house was heavy with the perfume of roses brought in from the garden, mingled with the aroma of roasting beef drifting from the kitchen, and cigar smoke from the billiard room....

An impressive home, indeed, for a man whose origins were so humble. Born in Lithuania, the son of an itinerant tailor, Sammy Marks was blessed with courage, integrity, astonishing business acumen and the capacity for sheer hard work, all qualities that helped him rise, in the period of a few decades, from being a pedlar of cheap jewellery to one of the old Transvaal Republic's leading industrialists. He came to South Africa in 1868, at the age of 24. After his stint as a *smous* (pedlar) in the western Cape, he teamed up with his cousin Isaac Lewis, who was to become his life-long business partner, and set off for Kimberley, where they made a modest living selling supplies to diggers and mines, and later branched into diamond trading.

After a time they decided to diversify their interests and turned their attention to the Transvaal, buying concessions and starting a variety of businesses, including a distillery, a glass factory, a canning factory, a brick and tile works, a maize mill and, later, an iron-and-steel works that was to be one of the direct precursors of the steel industry in the Transvaal. They mined coal on the banks of the Vaal River, where Vereeniging is now, and gained partial control of the fabulously rich Sheba mine in Barberton. By the last years of the 19th century the Lewis and Marks company had emerged as one of the top ten on the Rand, and both men were millionaires.

'If you want something done properly, you have to do it yourself,' was one of Sammy Marks's favourite maxims, and, true to his word, when the time came to build his own home, he became clerk of works, personally supervising the ordering of materials, which were transported directly from Durban by ox-wagon.

The house was fairly modest to begin with, but as the Marks family and their fortune grew, so too did the house. Eventually there were 48 rooms and numerous outbuildings, including stabling for 14 horses, a coach house, a wine cellar and two cooling rooms, one for meat and another for vegetables. Partly double-storeyed, the house does not look particularly distinguished from the outside, but nevertheless has great charm, with its long trellised veranda, its shuttered French windows, grand porticos and steeply pitched tin roof, embellished with air vents, finials, looped bargeboarding and several chimneys.

The fact that the original part of the house predates the discovery of gold on the Witwatersrand by a year gives an indication of just how remote its location was at the time that it was built. Bertha Marks, the daughter of a respectable middle-class Sheffield family, was no doubt a little dismayed when she first discovered that she would be living so far from civilisation. But, as new mistress of Zwartkoppies Hall, she quickly rose to the challenge, seeing to it that her family did not lack any of the refinements of gracious living.

Endowed with the same unflagging energy that had made her husband so successful in business, Bertha managed the house and its staff with great aplomb, still finding time to raise her eight children, indulge her hobbies of gardening and keeping chickens, and entertaining on a lavish scale.

Dinners, luncheons, croquet on the lawn and tennis and billiards parties were all regular events, and there were seldom fewer than 30 guests at a time. Of course, she was helped along by her staff of 14,

The cool veranda area of the house where visitors can conclude their visit with a cup of tea and scones.

most of whom (the indoor staff, at least) were engaged through an agency in London.

There were kitchenmaids, parlourmaids, laundrymaids and gardeners, as well as a cook and a governess. Then there was the estate carpenter, Mr Potts (fondly known as Daddy Potts), and MacCracken, the English butler whose task it was to sound the great gong in the hallway half an hour before dinner. The massive stove in the kitchen, with 10 hotplates and five ovens, is testimony to the scale on which the Marks's entertained.

Bertha was a passionate gardener and her formal rose garden, with its symmetrical layout and gravel paths, was her pride and joy. In 1950 the garden was destroyed and a kikuyu lawn laid on top of it, but recent excavations revealed the original foundations, with the paths still intact. Using old photographs and books as guides, the restorers reconstructed the garden, replacing the graceful wrought-iron arches that had vanished and planting dozens of varieties of old-fashioned garden roses.

Inside the house, the rooms are grand in scale, with high ceilings and the elaborate architectural detailing so typical of the period. The billiard room, an important Victorian status symbol, is particularly splendid, with its hand-painted domed ceiling and huge mahogany billiard table.

When you have completed your tour, why not relax for a while over tea and scones. Tables are set out under the trees and also on the wide trellised veranda that runs the length of the house, affording splendid views of Bertha's rose garden.

Dolly and Phil, the youngest of the Marks children, photographed in 1905 in the rose garden of Zwartkoppies Hall.

The Sammy Marks Museum at a glance (map page 202)

How to get there: From Pretoria, take the N4 (Witbank highway) and turn off at the Verwoerdburg off-ramp (exit 11). From this point, signposts clearly indicate the way to the museum: turn left at the top of the off-ramp and continue until you reach a T-junction where the road joins the old Bronkhorstspruit Road (R104). Turn right, cross a small bridge and you will see the turn-off to the museum a little further along on your left.

More information: The Sammy Marks Museum, c/o National Cultural History Museum, PO Box 28088, Sunnyside 0132; tel (012) 8036158.

Visiting times: Open Tuesday to Friday, 9 am to 4 pm; weekends and public holidays, 10 am to 4 pm. Because of the value of the house's contents, visitors are admitted to the house only as part of a guided tour. The tours begin every hour on the hour (on the half-hour on Sundays and public holidays) and the last tour begins one hour before closing time every day. A small admission fee is charged.

A miracle tree with shade for a thousand

The Wonderboom Nature Reserve, 10 km north of central Pretoria, was created to protect one of the world's most unusual trees

To LOCAL PEOPLE, it was sacred ground; to the Voortrekkers, a landmark spot where they paused for a brief while before continuing on their journey north. Fortune-hunters dreamed that the Kruger millions would turn up here but found only the Stone Age tools of the prehistoric hunters who ambushed their prey in the *poort* (entrance) nearby. And, indeed, it has been an excavation site where archaeologists have exposed the largest single accumulation of stone artefacts ever discovered in Africa.

But what brought all these people to this plain on the northern outskirts of Pretoria, is a tree unlike any other – a wild fig known all over the world as the Wonderboom (literally, miracle tree).

A 5,5 m diameter trunk at the heart of the Wonderboom is all that remains of the original wild fig that began growing here more than 1 000 years ago. Branches of this trunk first spread out radially but gradually drooped towards the ground, where they sent out roots from which sprang a circle of new trunks. In time, two of the offspring produced a third generation. Today the Wonderboom has 13 distinct trunks that cover an area of 1,5 ha. Its branches spread over an area of 50 m, and can provide enough shade for more than 1 000 people. A typical example of the species *Ficus salicifolia*? Not so, say the experts.

The wild fig is a hardy tree that flourishes in open woodlands, on rocky hills and outcrops, and near rivers and streams. The bark of young trees is smooth and pale grey, while the bark of older trees is rougher and darker. The leaves are thick and leathery, and the tiny white fruits, only about 5 mm in diameter, become yellowish-pink when they ripen between August and May. But while the *Ficus salicifolia* seldom grows higher than 9 m, the Wonderboom stands over 23 m tall. In addition to its great height, the way in which it has extended itself makes it an extremely rare natural phenomenon whose protection against the ravages of man is of great importance.

The tree was probably safest during that period when only local people knew of its existence. They were animists, adherents to a primitive world view that attached spiritual significance to natural objects and phenomena. Because the tree was so unusual, they considered it sacred and allowed it to flourish unhindered.

In Western terms, the tree was 'discovered' in 1836 by the Voortrekkers under Hendrik Potgieter who named it the Wonderboom. (The name Wonderboom has subsequently been given – as the names of landmarks often are – to a *poort* nearby, to a farm surrounding it, a nature reserve proclaimed around it, the ridge in whose shelter the tree stands, and a neighbouring suburb of Pretoria). After Potgieter, several other groups of Voortrekkers paused at this tree, and the site continues to have a special significance for South Africans who identify with Voortrekker history.

In the 1920s, rumours that the legendary Kruger millions were buried among the roots of the Wonderboom brought an influx of fortune-hunters to this site. They dug holes up to 3 m deep but were forced to conclude either that the Kruger millions were no more than a legend or, if they existed, had been buried elsewhere.

As acts of vandalism began to take their toll on the tree, the Pretoria City Council stepped in with a strategy to proclaim the area around it a reserve – modern man's closest approximation to sacred ground. Between 1937 and 1957 the Council negotiated to buy up various parts of what was then Wonderboom Farm. The tree was proclaimed a national monument and a 450-ha reserve created around it which is known as the Wonderboom Nature Reserve.

The reserve is home to several small antelope species as well as monkeys, dassies and a wide variety of birds. (Visitors should note that feeding the vervet monkeys is discouraged in order to maintain cordial relations between human beings and animals.) Besides small game and the Wonderboom itself, the reserve also protects several historical sites, some recent, some ancient.

Vervet monkeys abound in the branches of the Wonderboom – but on no account should you give them food.

The Wonderboom is made up of no less than 13 individual trunks and the whole tree is spread out over an area of about 1,5 ha.

Bulldozers scraping a road through the Wonderboompoort, the narrow pass that opens out on the plain on which the Wonderboom grows, first exposed one of the biggest archaeological finds ever recorded in Africa. The large number of stone artefacts, including stone knives, axes and choppers, convinced archaeologists that they'd come across the 'restaurant' of a prehistoric people who hunted here more than 50 000 years ago. These prehistoric hunters, they concluded, had discovered that it was far easier to trap and kill animals passing through the Wonderboompoort than to chase them around the plains.

The site of the find was probably the working place where animals were cut up and skinned and the bones crushed to obtain the marrow. Reasoning that the hunters would choose to live near their 'restaurant', the archaeologists decided that the small cave halfway up the koppie was more than likely to have been their home. And this in fact turned out to be the case.

Access to the cave is from the Wonderboom Nature Reserve: a stone path leads from the western side of the tree, taking you all the way to the entrance of the cave. If you happen to take the wrong path, you may end up not finding the cave, but you will certainly enjoy a pleasant, peaceful walk all the same. And if the path you took was the one south of the Wonderboom tree, then you're about to discover the recently restored remains of Fort Wonderboompoort.

It's a steep walk and that is as it should be, for where do you build a fort if not on a hill? This hill is a koppie in the Magaliesberg range, and the view is well worth the climb.

Fort Wonderboompoort was one of four erected at strategic locations during the Anglo-Boer War to defend Pretoria against invasions. It was a relatively sophisticated structure, equipped with electrical lamps and searchlights that ran off a paraffin engine connected to a dynamo, and a reservoir that received water from the Apies River via a steam-driven pump.

What glory resides in Fort Wonderboompoort stems almost entirely from the presence of four 'Long Toms' – popular French guns that were transferred here at the end of the war after winning fame on battlefields elsewhere.

Where to stay

The *Joos Bekker Caravan Park* is situated just north of Pretoria, close to Paul Kruger Street and about 5,5 km from Church Square. Included in the daily rate are showers and baths, laundry facilities, playground, swimming pool, braai areas and public telephones. Electricity is available at a small extra cost. No bookings are necessary. For further details contact the Parks and Recreation Department, Pretoria Municipality; PO Box 1454, Pretoria 0001; tel (012) 3352887.

Wonderboom Nature Reserve at a glance (map page 202)

How to get there: From central Pretoria, drive north on Paul Kruger Street through the Wonderboompoort and follow the signs to Warmbaths. The reserve is on the right, within 1 km of the turn-off beyond the entrance to the *poort*.
Weather: Pretoria has dry winters and hot summers; during summer, electric storms are common in the late afternoon.
What to do: After a picnic in the shade of the Wonderboom, explore the reserve on foot. There are picnic and braai facilities, and ablution blocks, on the premises.
Special attractions: From the Wonderboom, a stone path leads to a cave of archaeological interest; another climbs

towards Fort Wonderboompoort, and there are several scenic rambles.
Visiting times: The reserve is open every day from sunrise to sunset. There is a small admission fee but adults over 65 who can supply proof of their age are admitted free of charge.
More information: Drop in at the Parks and Recreation Department, Valforum Building, corner of Van der Walt and Proes Streets, Pretoria, or contact them at PO Box 1454, Pretoria 0001; tel (012) 213411 or 3137583. Alternatively, contact the Pretoria Information Bureau, PO Box 440, Pretoria 0001; tel (012) 3137694 or 3137980.

A true taste of Africa just beyond the Reef suburbs

Just 90 minutes' drive north of Johannesburg is the Borakalalo National Park, a little-known wildlife sanctuary situated well off the tourist track

THE LURE OF THE BUSHVELD is often irresistible, especially for city dwellers who yearn to escape the pressures of urban existence and to experience the 'real Africa'. But to hear the haunting call of the African fish eagle and the chatter of vervet monkeys usually means travelling to the Kruger National Park – too far afield for a weekend stay and booked out for months in advance – or to the exclusive and often prohibitively expensive game lodges of the lowveld.

But have you ever considered the Borakalalo National Park, situated 90 km north of Brits? It's a peaceful and unspoiled nature reserve where you can experience the African bush in all its majesty – and without having to spend a small fortune on accommodation or travelling. Its out-of-the-way location and limited facilities ensure that you are unlikely to encounter crowds, yet it is only an hour and a half's drive away from both Pretoria and Johannesburg, making it an ideal weekend or day-trip destination.

Borakalalo, meaning in Setswana 'the place where people relax', is situated about 70 km north-east of the glittering Sun City complex with which most people identify the region's tourist industry. The huge Klipvoor Dam, which bisects the reserve, literally teems with fish, making the resort a paradise for anglers, while its rich diversity of bird-life has earned Borakalalo a reputation as one of the finest bird-watching spots to be found in the southern Transvaal.

Covering 16 000 ha, Borakalalo is, by African standards, comparatively small. Its entire eastern half is set aside as a wilderness area which has no man-made structures and is not open to the public. The reserve is watered by the Moretele River, which provides about 8 km of dense riverine bush and scrub. The remainder of the terrain comprises

gently rolling sandveld with mixed bushveld, marshland and grassland. The game-viewing roads through the park cover a total distance of about 60 km, looping and twisting through the southern part of the reserve, meandering along the banks of the Klipvoor Dam and skirting the base of the rocky Mogoshane hills, which occupy the western arm of the park.

Borakalalo is stocked with a wide variety of game, including elephant, giraffe, zebra, white rhino, leopard, sable, warthog, antelope, waterbuck, tsessebe, kudu and many smaller mammals, such as brown hyaena, aardwolf, Cape fox, Cape clawless otter and seven species of mongoose. Although at certain times in the year there seems to be game everywhere you look, at other times – depending on the height of the grass and the amount of rain the park has received – it takes more patience and skill to spot the animals. The best viewing times are in the summer months in the early morning and late afternoon. Generally, the animals of Borakalalo seem rather skittish; certainly they are more wary of the human presence than are their relations in the Kruger National Park.

You may get out of your car only at designated spots, but there is a self-guided walking trail along the lower reaches of the Moretele River. This is a fascinating walk for keen naturalists who want to observe the teeming life of the bush at close quarters, but do be aware that you walk at your own risk and that there is a chance that you may encounter hippo, elephant, rhino or even leopard during your rambles.

The accommodation facilities are generally unpretentious, although spotlessly clean and well maintained. There are no manicured lawns or restaurants, but the camps are delightfully rustic, offering visitors a chance to get as close as possible to nature. You can book a camp site and bring along your own tent or camper, or – for a true 'Out-of-Africa' experience – hire one of the reserve's safari-style tents, each equipped with two beds, a stretcher and linen.

There are no fences separating the camps from the reserve's wildlife: at Moretele Camp, for example, where camp sites are dotted among the trees along the shady lower reaches of the river, you are likely to have to share your stretch of water with bushbuck, warthogs, otters, leguaans and, if you're lucky, perhaps even a few elephants. In the morning, campers are woken by the outraged screech of francolin and the soft 'tok-tok-tok' of hornbills in the trees above. Once the sun has set, the air is filled with the nocturnal sounds of the bushveld: the

A family of warthogs quench their thirst at one of the park's waterholes.

A central focus of the Borakalalo National Park is the Klipvoor Dam, a paradise for both anglers and bird-watchers.

soft, faintly ominous crashing of an animal moving through the bush, or the splash of an otter in the river, just a stone's throw from the tents.

The ablution facilities in the camps may look alarmingly rustic at first glance, but those reed-walled enclosures conceal flush toilets and hot-water showers. The camp sites are supplied with taps and braai places.

The most exclusive camp is Phudufudu, to the west of the main entrance, a secluded oasis of greenery concealed in a patch of thick woodland. This is a private camp which may be hired through a commercial safari company (see panel). Four spacious safari tents provide accommodation, and other facilities include a small swimming pool, a rustic *boma* (enclosure) constructed from dry tree trunks, a fully equipped kitchen and ablution blocks that are somewhat more sophisticated than those found elsewhere in the camp. Utensils and linen are provided, but guests must do their own cooking.

The Pitjane Camp, situated along the shore of the dam at the base of Pitjane Koppie, is a more barren affair. There are about 20 camp sites, a few pleasantly shaded, but most of the people who choose to stay here are ardent anglers who camp right at the very water's edge so that they don't have to waste any time getting down to the serious business of catching fish. Because of the good fishing, the camp site is fairly busy at weekends. Reed-walled enclosures, similar to those at Moretele Camp, provide ablution facilities.

Carp, barbel and kurper (bream) are the main angling fishes. At one time the dam was particularly well known for its good-sized kurper catches, but in recent years, with the dropping of water levels and the resultant dying-off of kurper throughout the Transvaal, catches have been less satisfactory. If you would like to fish, be sure to obtain a licence and a permit from the main gate. The river below the dam wall is also teeming with fish, but angling is not permitted there.

Over 300 species of birds have been identified at Borakalalo, making it a very popular destination for bird-watchers, who are sometimes able to identify as many as 200 species in a single weekend. The wide stretches of water support an abundance of waterfowl, including marabou and yellow-billed storks, great crested grebe and African finfoot. The thick scrub fringing the river also attracts many birds; look out for half-collared kingfisher and green-backed heron. In the shaded areas – a mixture of broadleafed and acacia woodland – you may see white helmet shrike, southern black tit, crimson-breasted shrike and red-crested korhaan. A recommended bird-watching spot is the Sefudi Dam, especially during dry spells.

Day visitors are welcome to spend some time at Borakalalo. There is a well-grassed picnic spot close to the dam. A small shop at the gate sells fishing tackle, firewood, cold drinks, beer and curios. The park also has a conference room which seats about 30 people.

Where to stay

It is essential to book for the *Moretele Camp* at all times and for the *Pitjane Camp* over weekends. A deposit is usually required. Bookings can be done through Central Reservations, Bophuthatswana National Parks Board, PO Box 937, Lonehill 2062; tel (011) 4655423. *Phudufudu Camp* may be reserved on either a self-catering or a fully catered basis through a private company, Kgama Safaris, PO Box 2799, Rustenburg 0300; tel (01466) 55587 or 54283.

Borakalalo National Park at a glance (map page 202)

How to get there: From Brits (about 60 km west of Pretoria), take the R511 to Thabazimbi. Drive for about 60 km until you see a turning to the right signposted 'Leeupoort' and 'Assen Police Station'. Travel for 6 km along this road. Turn right at the turning signposted 'Klipvoordam'. Travel for about 22 km along this untarred road until you come to a T-junction that is signposted 'Borakalalo'. Turn left onto a tarred road; about 3 km further along are the main gates to the reserve.

Weather: Very high temperatures in summer, and summer rainfall. Probably the best time to visit Borakalalo is between March and September.
More information: Write to the Bophuthatswana National Parks Board, Private Bag X2078, Mafikeng 8670; tel (01465) 55356/7.
Visiting times: The reserve may be visited during March to September, from 5 am to 8 pm; and during April to August, from 5.30 am to 7 pm.

A mission village rebuilt from its ruins

On the banks of the Klein Olifants River, 12 km from Middelburg, the mission station at Botshabelo lives and thrives again

A FORT FIRST, a church second. These were the priorities of the two young German missionaries who founded the Berlin Mission Station near Middelburg in 1865.

And they had good reason for thinking of protection first. For, ever since their arrival from Germany in 1858, Alexander Merensky and Heinrich Grützner had run the gauntlet of local chiefs. The fort they built on Botshabelo ('sanctuary') was intended as protection for themselves and 113 followers from the wrath of Chief Sekhukhuni. The missionaries had thoroughly alienated the chief by converting two of his wives to Christianity, and he persecuted them with all the vengeance of a Nero.

Only when the fort was complete did the missionaries start building a church, but the mission grew so fast that, within seven years, two more churches were built – the second alongside the first, the third and largest over the second.

By 1878 there were school buildings and a seminary for training black missionaries; by 1898 more than 4 000 people lived at Botshabelo and it was acclaimed as a model mission station; but by 1980 it was a ruin. In 80 years, war, politics and neglect had all but destroyed Botshabelo. Today, however, Botshabelo thrives again as a multifaceted museum that offers a glimpse into life on a 19th-century mission station.

Start your walking tour of Botshabelo at Fort Wilhelm, or Fort Merensky as it is popularly known. It is situated on a ridge above the village and its tower offers a magnificent 360° view of the valley and the rolling hills beyond. Its position indicates just how seriously the missionaries took Sekhukhuni's threat – the angry chief would have been hard-pressed to attack without being noticed. From here stroll down through the lush forest to the church complex which forms the core of the Botshabelo site museum. Like the fort, the churches of Botshabelo have recently been immaculately restored by the Simon van der Stel Foundation, and a fascinating museum established in the old rectory next door.

The large church, built in 1873 from locally baked red bricks and with the help of women and children, is an imposing building with several Gothic features such as arched windows and doors. It has a thatched roof, a dung floor, and rather plain stained-glass windows that offset the splendour of the yellowwood ceilings and pews and the elaborate gallery.

Displayed inside the church is the magnificent church bell which, when it cracked during a service in the early 1950s, was seen by the dwindling congregation as an omen of the final demise of the mission settlement.

(Left) Visitors wanting to purchase traditional Ndebele crafts should drop in at The Trading Post. (Right) The cool, tranquil interior of the mission's church, which has stood for more than 120 years.

Fortunately, however, the Middelburg Town Council – which bought a part of the farm for the purposes of an airfield in 1978 – recognised its historical significance and resolved to restore it to its former state. Funds for the project did not become available until the late 1980s, though, and Botshabelo remains a work in progress.

One of the first buildings to enjoy the attention of the restorers was the Ou Pastorie (old rectory), which has been furnished and finished authentically to represent the era during which Botshabelo thrived. From the coal stove in the kitchen to a brass bed in the governess's room, from the finely ingrained patterns in the yellowwood doors to the sturdy Oregon ceiling beams, everything looks exactly as it might have when Merensky and Grützner lived here.

Of particular interest in the kitchen is a trapdoor that reveals an underfloor rainwater reservoir, a detail that confounded the restorers until a German immigrant among the workers recognised its remains as those of a similar feature he'd seen in Germany as a child.

Back in the 'village' you'll find the beautifully restored Pakendorf House, now The Trading Post with traditional handwork and souvenirs for sale, and opposite it, the Old Seminary, which now serves as office and administrative centre while retaining its educational function in the form of informative maps and displays.

An agricultural museum is soon to be established in the former high school nearby and other yet-to-be-restored buildings include a printing and book-binding centre, the cartwright's shop and house, two training schools and some of the missionary and teachers' houses.

But it is not just the legacy of Merensky and Grützner that thrives at Botshabelo. Indigenous culture flourishes, too, at the Botshabelo Open Air Museum. This colourful village – which constitutes a living museum – was constructed in three phases that illustrate the architectural development of the tribe from the earliest huts to the rondavel-type hut and the rectangular and square constructions that are prevalent now.

Outside these huts, especially in the dry winter months, visitors may find colourfully dressed Ndebele women at work, doing beadwork or applying the elaborate wall decorations that are such a

A Botshabelo woman in traditional dress does beadwork against a backdrop of the wall paintings for which the Ndebele have become renowned.

prominent feature of Ndebele culture. On closer inspection the paintings reveal Western influences both in materials used (synthetic paints have largely replaced natural substances) and in subject-matter (aeroplanes, lampposts, gates and individual letters have been incorporated into the traditional geometric designs).

People live in these huts but residents will sometimes allow visitors to admire the interior, a privilege that should not be merely assumed, nor abused. Wait for an invitation and, once inside, behave like a guest.

For energetic holiday-makers, three hiking trails traverse the farm. The Aasvoëlkrans Trail is a day trail of approximately eight hours' hiking through the Klein Olifants Gorge. It's a wonderful opportunity to study numerous bird species, observe small game and identify prehistoric cycads among the indigenous trees and shrubs. Resist the temptation to swim in, or drink from, the Klein Olifants River – it is *not* bilharzia-free.

The Bobbejaanstert Trail follows the same route but it does not cross the river and takes just six hours to complete, while the three-hour Botshabelo Trail takes you to the top of the surrounding escarpment and offers magnificent views of the farm.

A game park exists at Botshabelo but has yet to be developed to its full potential. When you're there, enquire about guided game drives to see such elusive small animals as the klipspringer, steenbok, grey rhebok, otter, dassie and duiker.

Botshabelo at a glance (map page 202)

How to get there: From Johannesburg take the N4 and N11 to Middelburg. Turn left 12 km from Middelburg at the Botshabelo sign.
Weather: Botshabelo lies on the highveld and on summer days afternoon thunderstorms bring a respite from the heat. During the winter it is warm and dry, but cold at night.
What to do: Explore Botshabelo's museums by yourself, or enquire at the open-air museum about guided tours. Game drives can be arranged, and there are three-day hikes across the farm.
Special attractions: The colourful Ndebele village is a living museum depicting the traditional life style of the South Ndebele.
Visiting hours: The gates to Botshabelo open at 6 am and close at 6 pm every day. There is an entrance fee.
More information: Contact the Curator, Botshabelo Open-Air Museum, PO Box 14, Middelburg 1050; tel (0132) 23897.

Where to stay

Accommodation in Botshabelo requires a certain community spirit. Large groups are catered for and sharing is the order of the day. No linen, blankets, crockery, cutlery or kitchen utensils are supplied. Bring everything you'll need, except firewood.

The youth hostel sleeps 106 people in three separate dormitories, and offers an ablution block, kitchen, dining hall and braai facilities. The *Beuster Rondavel* sleeps 12 and includes a bathroom, hot-plate and fridge. The *Grützner Hotel* sleeps 33 people in six bedrooms and has a kitchen and braai facilities.

The caravan park is situated on the banks of the Klein Olifants River. It has ablution facilities, but no power points.

Booking for all the accommodation is through the Curator, Botshabelo Open-Air Museum, PO Box 14, Middelburg 1050; tel (0132) 23897.

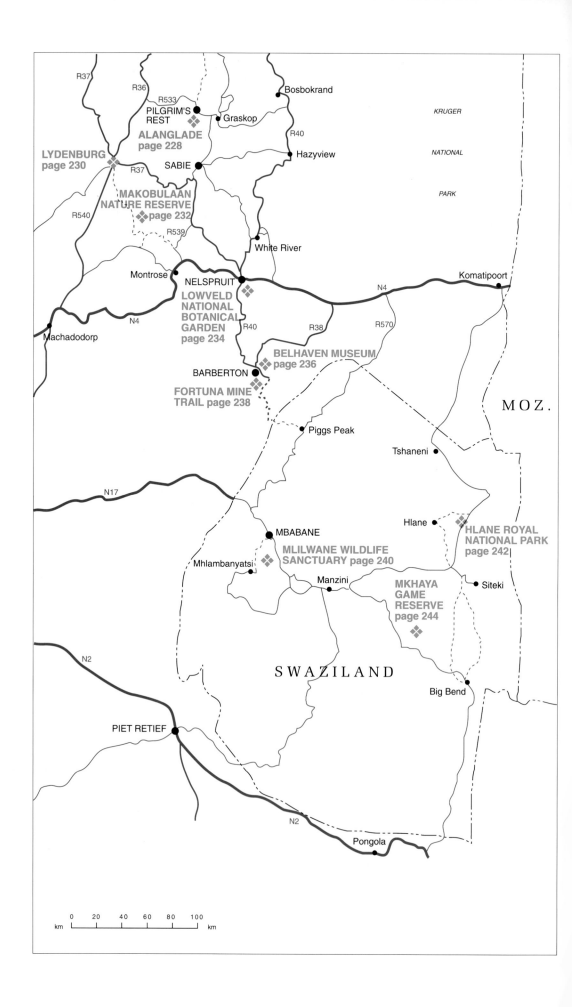

EASTERN TRANSVAAL/SWAZILAND

A domestic monument to mining days past

A counterpoint to the rough and ready shacks of Pilgrim's Rest, the architectural gem of Alanglade adds a note of sophistication to a landscape already rich in contrasts

THE ONLY MEMORIALS that miners tend to leave behind them are empty, echoing underground shafts. An exception to this is Alanglade, the one-time home of Dick Barry, general manager of Transvaal Gold Mining Estates until 1930.

The great house in its gleaming white grandeur seems transplanted from some opulent Edwardian suburb, an illusion complemented by the transformation of scrubby bushveld into tennis court and croquet lawn, and a large and informal garden of old-fashioned roses and flowers that found favour with an earlier generation. Although Alanglade is now a museum, it still retains a distinct feeling of a home. As you walk around this gracious old estate, you half expect to see a vintage limousine making its way sedately along the driveway, past the trout pond and up to the steps leading to the cool, enclosed veranda.

Completed in 1916, the house has a suggestion of the influence of Sir Herbert Baker in the spacious layout; however, the identity of Alanglade's architect has not been definitely established.

Grand though it is, Alanglade entirely lacks the frills and clutter often associated with earlier 'period' houses. The period that it echoes was characterised by a steady opposition to the increasing acceptance of machine-made and mass-produced goods and a return to an appreciation of the virtues of simple articles, hand-made by craftsmen. This was the time of the Arts and Crafts Movement, founded in England in the 1860s by William Morris, artist and writer, socialist, manufacturer and craftsman.

From this phase grew the more widely known Art Nouveau and Art Deco movements, both strongly represented in the fittings and furnishings of Alanglade. The languid, curving symmetry of Art Nouveau – seen in figured glassware bearing exalted names such as Lalique, or in the silver-plated vases that grace a mantelshelf – evolved naturally into the functional lines of Art Deco, which often uses the small-skirted female form as a central motif. Upholstery fabrics reflect patterns created by Morris himself for his own firm of Morris & Company, and crockery by Clarice Cliff and many of her contemporaries graces shelves and elegant tables. And the tables themselves, like all the fittings, are made of excellent materials, soundly made despite the shortages occasioned by the First World War.

Life at Alanglade for Dick Barry, his wife Gladys, and their seven children, was a pleasant round of duties – both social and commercial – and leisure. Mr Barry went daily to his office at the mine, leaving his wife to manage the affairs of their large house. Important guests were entertained and 'shown the countryside', while the higher officials of Transvaal Gold Mining Estates might have joined the family for tennis or croquet, although the

Where to stay

The only hotel in Pilgrim's Rest is the *Royal Hotel*. It has 25 rooms, seven of which have baths. The hotel also has a number of cottages available. Book at PO Box 59, Pilgrim's Rest 1290; tel (01315) 81221.

Mount Sheba, about 9 km from Pilgrim's Rest, is situated in a magnificent upland setting enclosed by primeval forests. It has 25 rooms, all with baths; 10 of these are duplex, 14 are double, and one is the executive/honeymoon suite. There are also 20 cottages, but most of these are taken on time-share. Contact the *Mount Sheba Hotel* at PO Box 100, Pilgrim's Rest 1290; tel (01315) 81241.

Jacarandas in bloom in Pilgrim's Rest. Alanglade stands in imposing contrast to these more modest dwellings found in the area.

The solid, imposing lines of the Alanglade residence are offset and softened by the profusion of colours in the surrounding garden.

pleasures of the swimming pool – probably one of the first heated outdoor pools in the country – tended to be confined to the family.

There was great emphasis on outdoor life. Mr Barry, for instance, was passionate about hunting, and kept a string of greatly loved dogs. Touchingly, a corner of the vast garden, near a huge jacaranda tree, is still kept as the pets' cemetery, where simply carved headstones peep through the grass. One stone commemorates Jock, perhaps named after Percy Fitzpatrick's famous dog.

How secure the house seems, like a time capsule from the past with its now archaic smoking room, drawing room, day nursery and school room, its kitchen with two pantries, dairy room, larder and scullery. Up the dark wooden stairs are the bedrooms.

There's a tinge of sadness to the children's rooms, as though life here was but a fleeting idyll. The youngest girl died at the age of only fourteen and all three boys died young. One lost his life in a climbing accident, and the other two died during the Second World War – one at sea, the other in a blazing Hurricane fighter over southern England in 1940 (one of the nine South African pilots to die in the Battle of Britain). But the old home that housed them all lives on and, for as long as it remains the museum it is, will always transport visitors back into an era gentler and more gracious than our own.

Dick Barry's study, with its austere, masculine atmosphere, is preserved almost exactly as it was when he lived at Alanglade.

Alanglade at a glance (map page 226)

How to get there: Take the R36 north from Lydenburg, then turn right onto the R533, which leads down into the valley of Pilgrim's Rest. Alternatively, you can approach from the opposite direction, from the rim of the escarpment at Graskop. At the Joubert Bridge, turn north up the lovely valley of the Blyde River, dotted with peach trees, on its way to the Blyde River Canyon. A few hundred metres on will bring you to the house museum of Alanglade.

Weather: The weather patterns around Pilgrim's Rest are broadly the same as the upland area of Lydenburg, with warm, dry winters and hot, humid summers. Day-to-day

conditions, though, tend to be considerably more tempestuous. A speciality of the region are the sudden mists, which, while limiting visibility, add a note of mystery to the landscape. Rainfall also tends to be dramatic, though not many years match the historic record of 1915, with 1,7 m!

Special facilities: Guided tours are conducted around Alanglade from Monday to Saturday, at 10.30 am and 2 pm. Each tour, for which there is a small fee, lasts about an hour.

More information: Contact the Transvaal Provincial Administration office at Private Bag X516, Pilgrim's Rest 1290; tel (01315) 81261.

Whispers of history in the 'Place of the Long Grass'

The echoes of a tumultuous past linger on in the quiet eastern Transvaal town of Lydenburg, set in a wide, fertile valley against a backdrop of rolling hills and great planted forests

SEVEN CERAMIC MASKS stare back at you from the shadows – silent, mysterious, a little chilling. Six are of human faces, the seventh of an animal. Their eyes and mouths are slits in the dry clay, their hair is stylised, and their faces are carefully decorated with ritual scars and small animal figures.

These ritual masks are located in the Ethnological Section of the Lydenburg Museum – an ideal place to begin your exploration of this charming, old-world town. It's hard to tell that these masks are in fact copies of the originals (currently housed at the University of Cape Town) which have been carbon dated to about AD 500. These masks are relics of the first Bantu-speaking people who settled in this region about 1 600 years ago.

Move on around the museum, forward in time, and you encounter lovingly created displays of the founding fathers of the town, the sturdy, bearded Voortrekkers. Equally bearded were the swarms of miners who followed them, and who are also celebrated in the museum. Boer and Briton clashed twice in this area, as is recorded in faded photographs of the Lydenburg Commando and of the 'Tommies' of the British Army.

Lydenburg's pride in its heritage is seen, too, in the careful preservation of its old buildings. From the museum, situated on the outskirts of the town in the Gustav Klingbiel Reserve, it is a short drive into Lydenburg, to the corner of Church and Kantoor streets. There you will find the simple thatched and whitewashed Voortrekker School built in 1851 and today the oldest existing school in the Transvaal. Across the road from it stands the Voortrekker Church which also doubled as a classroom after the construction of the larger and more imposing present church, consecrated in 1894.

In sharp contrast is a surviving fragment of the British legacy, in Viljoen Street. This is the old powder magazine, built with bricks taken from the British fort after the siege of 1881 and still bearing the graffiti inscribed by the English soldiers.

To piece all these fragments into a living story, one must go back a century and a half. The valley was then Masiseng, as the local Pedi called it, which means 'Place of the Long Grass'. Here, in September 1849, a weary group of trekkers drew their wagons to a halt. They were the survivors of the fever which had decimated the settlement of Ohrigstad, 50 km to the north. At Masiseng, on higher ground, well watered by the Sterkspruit and Spekboom rivers, they hoped to build a new capital. Their hardships still vivid in memory, they called their new settlement Lydenburg, the 'Town of Suffering'.

Once established, Lydenburg soon developed a spirit of its own. This was reflected in its declaration of independence in March 1857. However, 'De Republiek Lijdenburg in Zuid-Afrika', with its brave new flag, lasted only three years before the burghers were persuaded to rejoin the South African Republic.

Where to stay

Morgan's Hotel, the town's only hotel, has 29 rooms, 15 with baths. PO Box 11, Lydenburg 1120; tel (01323) 2165. Other available accommodation: *Uitspan Caravan Park*, which includes eight rondavels. PO Box 391, Lydenburg 1120; tel (01323) 2914. *Siesta Holiday Resort*, 2 km out of town on the Dullstroom Road, has 16 fully equipped chalets, and four rooms. PO Box 950, Lydenburg 1120; tel (01323) 2886.

Gently flowing trout-filled rivers such as this one make Lydenburg a popular destination for freshwater anglers.

Belying its gloomy name, the 'Town of Suffering' was to prosper. But the outside world had not been left behind. Indeed, within a few years, it arrived on their doorstep, in the form of prospectors clutching picks and shovels. In September 1873, payable quantities of gold were found in the valleys of the nearby escarpment. As the rush got under way, a new town, Pilgrim's Rest, sprang up. The sale of digging implements boomed, and Lydenburg experienced a new prosperity.

It was not long, however, before the Boer desire for independence clashed with British territorial ambition. In December 1880, the Boers redeclared the Transvaal a republic, as a result of which the British immediately mobilised their forces.

In Lydenburg, the Boers laid siege to the British post of 'Fort Mary' – named after the plucky wife of the local garrison commander, Lieutenant Long. This fort consisted of a makeshift square of huts linked by walls, using cement made from pulverised ant-heaps. It held out for 85 days, despite having its thatched roof set on fire, till the news of Majuba and peace negotiations finally rescued the weary garrison. (The fort itself survived for a few years more.)

But the shadows of war had not been dispelled. With the second Anglo-Boer War breaking out in 1899, the British returned to Lydenburg. This time,

under General Buller, they had little difficulty in capturing the town, marching in on 7 September 1900. There was a sting in the tail, however, for as the troops dug in, the Boer forces withdrew to the pass to the east and proceeded to lob shells from two of their Creusot siege-guns, the famous 'Long Toms'. Buller and his men were forced to deal with this piece of insolence, gradually driving the Boers and their guns down into the lowveld over what is now the Long Tom Pass.

As the last echoes of gunfire died away, peace and quiet finally descended on the town of Lydenburg, which has been contentedly sleeping in the sun ever since. New wealth was brought with the planting of large forests, while the heritage of wildlife has been preserved in the Gustav Klingbiel Reserve. It is all very quiet and tranquil. Listen carefully, though, and you can still hear the whispers of the past, endlessly blowing through the long grass....

(Left) Once a convent, this attractive old Lydenburg building now provides facilities for sheltered employment. (Right) The old Voortrekker Church seen against the imposing backdrop of the newer church which was consecrated in 1894.

Lydenburg at a glance (map page 226)

How to get there: Take the N4 east from the Witwatersrand and finally turn left onto the R36 – or left onto the R37 further on, following the dramatic twists and turns of the Long Tom Pass. Each of these approaches brings you through majestic vistas, particularly on the precipitous edge of the escarpment itself, to the town of Lydenburg, situated between the Drakensberg range to the east, and the long sweep of the Steenkampsberge situated to the northwest.

Weather: The winter months around Lydenburg, between May and September, are idyllic, with dry, sunny days tempered by the crystalline mountain

air. The summer, from October to March, is somewhat less bracing, being generally hot and wet.

What to do: Exploring the escarpment, trout fishing, walks in the nature reserve, exploring the town, visiting the fish hatcheries and the collection of animal statues 11 km from the town on the Ohrigstad road.

Special attractions: Outstanding features are the cluster of two Voortrekker churches and the Voortrekker School, the old powder magazine and the Lydenburg Museum. This museum was situated for many years in the town, but is now housed in a

fine new building in the Gustav Klingbiel Reserve on the outskirts of the town.

More information: Tourist Bureau, Lydenburg Municipality, PO Box 61, Lydenburg 1120; tel (01323) 2121. Lydenburg Fishing Institute, Private Bag X1088, Lydenburg 1120; tel (01323) 2121.

Visiting times: The opening times for the museum are weekdays from 9 am to 1 pm and from 2 pm to 4.30 pm; and weekends and public holidays from 10 am to 4 pm. The original Voortrekker School and the powder magazine can be opened on request by the curator of the Lydenburg Museum. The second church is not open to the public.

Timeless trails through an ancient landscape

A day walk in the little-known Makobulaan Nature Reserve near Nelspruit unveils the haunting beauty of the Drakensberg escarpment's foothills, taking hikers past mist-shrouded waterfalls and ancient riverine forests

EVERY YEAR, thousands of hikers walk the numerous trails that criss-cross the nature reserves of the Transvaal Drakensberg escarpment, drawn not only by the majesty of the mountains and the spectacular scenery but also by the atmosphere of mystery and romance that pervades the entire region.

A reserve that many hikers have yet to discover is Makobulaan, a recently declared 1 000-ha sanctuary in the foothills at the southern end of the escarpment, between Lydenberg and the Sudwala Caves.

Although Makobulaan may lack the drama and the dizzy heights of some of the region's better-known reserves – such as the Blyde River Canyon – it has the advantage of being situated well off the tourist track. The reserve's remote location has ensured that its wilderness areas have been preserved in a pristine state, offering hikers a privileged

A misty waterfall hidden in the depths of one of the reserve's many pockets of dense indigenous forest.

glimpse of how this wild territory must have looked before the arrival of the pioneers who tamed it.

The great wall of mountains that makes up the Drakensberg escarpment runs south to north for about 300 km, dividing the cool undulating grasslands of the highveld from the flat, thorny savanna of the lowveld, which stretches eastwards to the Indian Ocean. Along the length of this formidable barrier are steep crags and towering cliffs where strange rock formations, secret caves and pockets of dense forest create some dramatic scenery. Rivers have eroded the slopes over millions of years, carving deep gorges and kloofs, and tumbling over cliff edges to create what are surely among the most beautiful waterfalls in Africa.

If the sheer scale of the escarpment isn't enough to take a visitor's breath away, then the fascinating history of the region certainly will. Man has inhabited these mountains for only a short time – a mere twinkling of the eye in the grand scale of things – and yet he has left behind a rich and colourful legacy that creates an irresistible atmosphere. These hills and valleys have witnessed the triumphs and tragedies of a most colourful parade of characters – pioneers, hunters, prospectors and fortune-seekers, safari traders, transport riders and raiding warrior bands.

Although man's stay has been short, he has certainly not wasted any time in leaving his mark on the landscape. Extensive areas in the foothills of the Drakensberg escarpment are now farmed and afforested. Once there were vast tracts of unspoiled territory, where the water ran clear and the air was sweet; now there are massive plantations of exotic trees, grown to meet the country's insatiable timber needs. But, thanks to the foresight of the Department of Water Affairs and Forestry, whose policy it is to make multiple use of state forest land, extensive pockets of natural wilderness have been left untouched.

Makobulaan is an excellent example of the Department's conservation efforts. Declared a reserve in 1992, Makobulaan comprises northeastern mountain sourveld in the higher elevations, gradually changing to lowveld sour bushveld on the lower slopes. The reserve is one of three in the enormous Uitsoek State Forest. (The other two are the Wonderkloof Nature Reserve and the Flora Reserve; the latter was set aside for the protection of the endangered dwarf cycad *Encephalartos humilis*).

The three trails that pass through Makobulaan together comprise the Uitsoek Trail, which was established in a co-operative effort by various parties, including the National Hiking Way Board and the Forestry Branch. The Houtbosloop Route, a 30-km walk that takes two days and climbs through the foothills to the plateau, is a scenic but strenuous trail, probably best left to serious hikers. The second, the 11-km Bakkrans Route, is a fascinating day walk that passes through plantations above the Houtbosloop River and through patches of indigenous scrub forest in the gorges. The main attraction on this route is the beautiful Bakkrans Waterfall.

The 11-km Beestekraalspruit Route is a relatively new trail that has been planned with great care and attention to detail, with the special involvement of members of the Roodepoort Hiking Club, who were keen to 'adopt' a trail of their own and to assist with its development and upkeep.

Like the two other trails, the route begins at the hikers' hut at the Uitsoek State Forest and then climbs gently through pine plantations, indigenous scrub forest and grassland. Eventually the path reaches a steep cliff, which is the edge of the gorge carved by the Beestekraalspruit. From here, the path winds gradually down into the welcome coolness of the gorge's riverine forest. The route then follows the course of the Beestekraalspruit for about 4 km.

What makes these walks particularly special is that they cross the rivers 20 times by means of sturdy wooden footbridges. The cool and leafy depths of the forest are extraordinarily refreshing to the senses, especially after a hot uphill walk to the gorge. This is a place which seems enchanted, where the air is scented with the ancient aroma of cool mossy rock and damp leaf-mould, where mushrooms push up through the loamy earth and where delicate ferns fringe the pathway. Even when the river is hidden by trees, you can hear its gentle gurgling, and in the summer months, after heavy rains, the Bakkrans Waterfall is a breathtaking sight, roaring as it crashes over the cliff edge, throwing up swirling veils of silvery mist that can drench you to the skin.

The day walks offer many treats for naturalists. The abundance of indigenous trees makes it well worth taking along a guidebook or a tree list; many

Hikers walking through the Makobulaan sanctuary are treated to spectacular views of mountains, valleys and forests.

species are numbered for reference. Species you are likely to see along the rivers include many examples of the rare forest lavender (*Heteropyxis canescens*) – which is found only in indigenous forest in the eastern Transvaal – boekenhout, lemonwood, knobwood, Cape ash, wild plum and several wild figs.

Although a detailed survey of the reserve's fauna has not been undertaken, there are many species to be seen if you have the necessary patience or luck. Thickets and forest patches are home to red duiker, common duiker, bushbuck and bushpig, while on the higher grassy plains you may see grey rhebuck, mountain reedbuck and even the rare oribi.

Numerous small mammals, including mongoose, caracal, genet, vervet monkey and baboon, inhabit the reserve. Along the streams the Cape clawless otter is sometimes observed. Bird-watchers, too, will be enchanted by the abundance of birds to be seen in the reserve.

Another interesting feature of the reserve are the archaeological remains. Terracing dating from the Iron Age is to be seen on the Beestekraalspruit and the Bakkrans trails, evidence of the crop-growing activities of the Nguni people who once inhabited these slopes; there are also the remains of kraals used for stock-keeping.

If you would like to do both day walks, overnight accommodation is available at the hikers' hut at the Uitsoek Forest Station, but note that it is essential to book well in advance and to obtain the necessary permits to enter the reserve.

Makobulaan at a glance (map page 226)

How to get there: Travelling along the N4, take the R539 turn-off to Sabie (about 25 km before Nelspruit). About 18 km further along this road, turn right at the turn-off signposted 'Uitsoek State Forest'. Continue along this road for about another 9 km until you reach the forest station. Park at the hikers' hut, which is where both day walks and the two-day trail begin and end.
Weather: Most rain falls between November and January; thunderstorms may be severe. The hottest months are from September to April. Probably the best time to visit the reserve is in the dry, cooler winter months.
What to do: Take time to observe the abundant bird life and to identify trees along the route. Although the day walks take about five hours each, it's wise to allow a full day.
Special attractions: The Sudwala Caves and Dinosaur Park nearby are both popular tourist destinations.
More information: Reservations to enter the reserve must be made well in advance. To obtain a permit, contact the Regional Director, National Hiking Way Board, Private Bag X11201, Nelspruit 1200; tel (01311) 52169.

Where to stay

Two comfortable hotels nearby are the *Crocodile Country Inn*, PO Box 496, Nelspruit; tel (01311) 63040; and the *Sudwala Lodge*, PO Box 30, Schagen 1207; tel (01311) 63073. The *Come Together Guest Farm*, some 16 km west of Nelspruit, offers self-catering accommodation and stands for caravans. Contact them at PO Alkmaar 1206; tel (01311) 63052.

A patch of paradise where two rivers meet

Nestling amid spectacular scenery at the junction of two rivers, just outside Nelspruit, is one of South Africa's most magnificent botanical gardens – a lush, subtropical haven featuring many rare lowveld species

IN THEIR HASTE to reach the gates of the Kruger National Park before they close for the night, tourists tend to roar at high speed through the thriving lowveld town of Nelspruit – few of them noticing the modest signboard that shows the way to the Lowveld National Botanical Garden. What a pity, because this is a garden of rare splendour, rivalling even Kirstenbosch in Cape Town for beauty, and it certainly warrants a special detour.

What better place to interrupt your car journey for a leisurely picnic than this secluded paradise, with its luxuriant subtropical vegetation, its majestic bushveld trees and rolling emerald-green lawns. Even those who aren't interested in gardening or botany will be impressed by the beauty and diversity of the indigenous plant life, and particularly by the collection of rare cycads for which the garden is famous.

The wide, paved path that meanders through the developed section of the garden will lead you, in less than an hour, through the most extraordinary assortment of habitats. There are shady forest areas where delicate ferns, mosses and orchids thrive in the moist atmosphere, and where clouds of brilliant butterflies flutter through secret sun-filled glades. There are marshy places with their distinctive reeds, ferns and ground orchids; and, not far away, hot, arid patches of ground where aloes and figs and other drought-adapted plants cling to the dry soil.

The garden is particularly glorious in the late afternoon, when shafts of honey-gold sunlight slant through the trees, and the warm, humid air is heavy with the scent of damp earth and pungent in-

digenous herbs. You can hear, through the trees, the soft rushing of the river, overlaid with the non-stop chatter of birds and the hum of millions of insects. There is an abundance of wildlife in the garden, including various small mammals and over 245 species of birds. Not all the animal life is harmless – as befits an Eden like this one, there are a number of species of poisonous snakes, together with many lizards and leguaans. Hippos, too, occasionally find their way into the developed area.

The garden was first laid out in 1969 on land granted by the Nelspruit Town Council and a local citrus producer. Today it is administered by the National Botanical Institute, whose aim it is to use the garden not only as a means of introducing tourists to the summer rainfall flora of southern Africa but also to further the ideals of conservation. Of the 159-ha area of this botanical garden, only 25 ha has been developed; the remainder has been preserved in its natural state.

The garden's developed area is cradled between the two rivers that meet on its northern side. The Crocodile River flows through the garden from west to east, joining the Nels River at the scenic Nels River Falls. There are many other rapids, cascades and waterfalls to be seen along the rivers, including the Nelspruit Cascades, the Funnel and the Black Falls. After heavy summer rains, when the rivers are in flood, the larger waterfalls are a breathtaking sight, their churning waters throwing up a sparkling haze of tiny droplets.

Although there is no public access to the greater part of the undeveloped area, a self-guided trail

Where to stay

Nelspruit and its neighbouring town, White River, offer plenty of accommodation options for the visitor, ranging from luxury hotels to caravan parks. Hotels include: *Drum Rock Hotel*, PO Box 622, Nelspruit 1200; tel (01311) 581217; *Crocodile Country Inn*, PO Box 496, Nelspruit 1200; tel (01311) 63040; *Paragon Hotel*, PO Box 81, Nelspruit 1200; tel (01311) 53205. Caravan parks: *Polka Dot Caravan Park*, PO Box 837, Nelspruit 1200; tel (01311) 25088; *Montrose Falls Hotel and Caravan Park*, PO Box 20, Elandshoek 1208; tel (01311) 63060.

A special platform gives visitors an excellent view out over the Nelspruit Cascades, which are situated on the Crocodile River.

along the Crocodile River offers visitors a privileged glimpse of one 'wild' portion of the garden. This 1,5-km walk meanders along the cliff face on the south bank, through the dense riverine forest.

Plants are grouped in the developed section of the garden according to their habitat needs or their family relationships. The sheer variety of species can be quite bewildering – over 1 500 species have been planted – but you will be able to make better sense of the layout of the garden if you obtain a brochure and map, sold for a nominal fee at the entrance gate. All the major plantings in the garden have been numbered and these are shown on the map; the brochure also provides valuable information on the various groups of plants.

Immediately adjacent to the entrance of the garden is an area planted with monocotyledons (plants with a single seed-leaf) and their various relations. With its lush subtropical palms, wild bananas, dragon trees and amaryllis, this is one of the most beautiful sections of the garden, so don't hurry through; the picnic tables provided nearby will enable you to admire the plantings at your leisure. Flowering plants in this section include arums, lilies, irises and, most spectacular of all, the clivias or forest lilies, which flower in early spring, creating a blaze of orange-red in the shade of the trees.

If you turn sharp left, you will come to the forest area, where a cool, moist habitat for tender herbs and shrubs has been created by planting trees and installing irrigation pipes. Trees you will find here include yellowwoods, stinkwoods, wild banana, common tree fern and the beautiful Cape chestnut, which produces masses of showy pink flowers in spring. The collection of indigenous ferns planted in the forest area is the best in South Africa, and the garden is justifiably proud of it. Many birds, butterflies and reptiles are to be seen here.

Walk back to the main paved pathway and you will find yourself in the cycad section. The garden is world famous for these remarkable plants, which are treasured because they are the living relics of a primeval plant group, the Cycadales, which existed more than 150 million years ago. A complete collection of South Africa's cycads is to be seen here.

Perhaps the most delightful 'residents' of the garden are the bushveld trees, which are planted in great numbers throughout the garden, casting wel-

The garden is world famous for its superb collection of cycads from South Africa and beyond.

come pools of shade on the immaculate lawns. The shapes of the trees are almost artistic in their graceful beauty, while there seems to be endless variety in the texture and colour of the barks – flaky, smooth, papery, knobby and thorned; yellow, silver, fawn and brown.

Five hundred species of trees are found in the park, a number which represents over half the total number of tree species found in South Africa. Related groups of trees have been collected together in various parts of the garden. Important bushveld genera represented include jackal-berries, spikethorns, baobabs, star chestnuts, bush willows (*Combretums*), acacias, coral trees, cabbage trees and the spectacular wild figs.

Many visitors leave the garden with reluctance, but there is one last surprise waiting for them at the entrance gate: a nursery selling a variety of indigenous plants. The garden has a policy of encouraging the use of indigenous plants by making them available at competitive prices, and certainly the cost of these plants is a fraction of what you would pay at a commercial nursery.

The Lowveld National Botanical Garden at a glance (map page 226)

How to get there: The turn-off to the garden is situated on the R40 to White River, about 3 km outside the centre of Nelspruit, and is clearly signposted.
Weather: Nelspruit has a subtropical climate, with hot, humid summers and mild winters. The best time to visit the garden is during the rainy summer months.
What to do: Enjoy the wonderful variety of plants.
Special attractions: A world-famous collection of cycads; also South Africa's best collection of indigenous ferns.
More information: The Curator, Lowveld National Botanical Garden, PO Box 1024, Nelspruit 1200; tel (01311) 25531. South African Tourism Board, Trading Post, Kaapschehoop Road, Nelspruit 1200; tel (01311) 44406.
Visiting times: The garden opens at 8 am every day of the year. Closing time is 6 pm in summer (October to April) and 5.15 pm in winter (May to September). A small entrance fee is charged.

Water lilies add a welcome splash of colour to the various ponds found within the garden.

Grand old homestead in a modest mining town

Belhaven, one of Barberton's most elegant old homesteads, is now a museum furnished with all the elaborate trappings of a wealthy Edwardian family home

BELHAVEN STANDS half-hidden by trees, tucked up a small side street not far from Rimer's Creek, a shady kloof on the outskirts of the former goldmining town of Barberton. Large and graciously proportioned, this wood-and-iron structure is definitely worth a visit for anyone who is interested in history and interior design.

But before we explore Belhaven, it is necessary – for a better appreciation of this historic home – to make a quick historical detour into Barberton itself. It is difficult to believe, strolling along these peaceful streets with their avenues of flamboyant trees and well-tended gardens, that this town was once notorious for its hectic night life. At the height of the gold boom in the area, Barberton was a vibrant and bawdy place, populated by the thousands of eager fortune-seekers who had flocked to the valley from all over the world in the wake of the discovery of the Sheba Reef.

The mood was one of feverish excitement and reckless abandon, fed by frequent gold strikes and the promise of untold riches. In order to entertain the masses, dozens of canteens, bars and gambling halls mushroomed virtually overnight, with prospectors engaging in bouts of competitive drinking

and bidding for the favours of the town's reigning beauties, such as the incomparable 'Cockney Liz'.

But Barberton, like many other boom towns during the gold rush, was built on optimistic dreams which quickly evaporated like mist. By 1888, the boom was over, and there was a mass exodus of disillusioned fortune-seekers. Barberton was left with only a handful of residents, who set about transforming it into a sober and moderately prosperous little town, earning a respectable living from the minerals with which the De Kaap Valley is so richly endowed.

Robert Nisbet was one of the men who helped lay the foundations of the town. In 1892 he took over the lease of the Barberton Club and made such a success of running it that by 1902 he had made enough money to purchase the property. Within two years he was wealthy enough to build his own home, which he named Belhaven. But Robert Nisbet, alas, was not to enjoy the trappings of his new-found wealth, for in 1906 he died, leaving his wife, Kathleen, and children alone in the house, where they lived until 1914.

Members of the Duncan family lived in the house over the years and in 1978 it was bought by the Transvaal Provincial Administration so that it could be preserved as a museum. It has been furnished in the late Victorian style (with many Victorian pieces also on display) but, unfortunately, not a single item belonging to the Nisbet family has been located.

The house is similar in structure to dwellings in mining towns throughout South Africa. At the time of the gold rush, the burgeoning populations of mining settlements in remote locations created an urgent demand for inexpensive, quick-to-erect housing. The obvious materials were wood and corrugated iron, which, apart from being relatively cheap, were also light enough to be transported across long distances by ox-wagon. This was the Edwardian equivalent of prefabricated housing, as it was manufactured in sections and then bolted together, piece by piece, on site.

The houses were simple but sturdy structures, made by constructing a wooden framework and covering it with a skin of corrugated iron on the outside, and wooden panelling (or iron) on the inside. Most houses had simple facades shaded by wooden verandas, often with decorative fretwork. What makes Belhaven particularly interesting is that it is thought to be the only remaining wood-and-iron house in South Africa, that is panelled inside with pressed steel rather than with wood.

Pressed steel was a highly favoured building material at the turn of the century because it was

The long veranda of the Belhaven Museum is decorated with intricately-patterned wooden fretwork.

Belhaven House, now a museum, is a typical example of the 19th century house of a well-to-do family living in a gold mining village.

durable, lightweight and fireproof; it was most often used for ceilings. In Belhaven, extensive use has been made of it on the walls of the dining room, study, passage, drawing room and bedrooms. The panels were always highly decorative, and in Belhaven you will be able to pick out at least 18 different designs, as well as borders, cornices and rosettes.

One of the house's most attractive features is its wide, shaded veranda, where the floorboards, posts and the decorative fretwork are made from Baltic pine. It is easy to imagine the endless golden afternoons that were spent here, the female members of the Nisbet family dressed in their long Edwardian frocks and wide hats, lazing in their wicker chairs as they sipped their tea from delicate china cups. Although by modern standards Belhaven is over-furnished, its interior decor is in fact relatively light compared to the plush and sometimes oppressive furnishings that would have characterised a house built a decade earlier. Dark colours, heavy fabrics and complicated patterns slowly disappeared during the Edwardian era, to be replaced by lighter floral designs; unnecessary furniture was banished and lace curtains were drawn back to allow the sun to enter the rooms.

The drawing room, on the right as you enter the house, is a dainty, rather cluttered room. Chairs and delicate little tables are scattered everywhere; this was where the ladies of the house sewed, read, sketched, drank tea and gossiped. By contrast, the dining room is a rather dark and sombre room, typical of many Victorian dining rooms. The study, with its heavy desk, chair, bookshelf and its Turkish rug, is clearly a gentleman's territory.

A magnificent brass four-poster bed is a feature of the main bedroom, an elegant room hung with heavy velvet curtains. The daughter's bedroom and the guest bedroom are furnished in equally grand style, while the nursery contains some delightful pieces of children's furniture, including a high chair and a brass rocking cradle.

By comparison with the rest of the house, the kitchen and bathroom are rather spartan. The house had no running water, so it had to be fetched in buckets from Rimer's Creek nearby and then heated before being used for bathing or washing dishes or clothes. (Robert Nisbet's original bathroom has now been converted into an office and is not open to the public.)

While you're in the area, it's a good idea to visit Fernlea, another of Barberton's old wood-and-iron houses. This tiny museum is just a minute's walk away along Lee Road and contains an interesting display of photographs showing the rebuilding and restoration of the original home.

Where to stay

There are two hotels in Barberton – the *Impala Hotel* in De Villiers Street, PO Box 83, Barberton 1300; tel (01314) 22108; and the *Phoenix Hotel* in Pilgrim Street, PO Box 77, Barberton 1300; tel (01314) 24211.

Fully serviced chalets and shaded caravan sites may be rented at the town's caravan park, which is set in attractive surroundings in Fitzpatrick Park. Write to PO Box 780, Barberton 1300; tel (01314) 23323.

Fountain Baths Holiday Cottages offer self-catering accommodation. Contact them at 48 Pilgrim Street, Barberton 1300; tel (01314) 22707. Some 14 km from Barberton, on the scenic R38 to Kaapmuiden, is the *Bougainvillea Hotel*, PO Box 9, Noordkaap 1304; tel (01314) 9681.

In Nelspruit, *Bundu Beds* lists an extensive number of homes and farms offering bed and breakfast. Contact them at PO Box 4019, Nelspruit 1200; tel (01311) 22709.

Belhaven Museum at a glance (map page 226)

How to get there: The museum is situated in Lee Road, Barberton. Ask for directions at the Information Bureau (see address in next column).
Weather: Barberton lies in a summer rainfall region, experiencing hot summers and mild winters.
What to do: Other museums depicting the early life and architecture in Barberton are Fernlea House in Lee Road and Stopforth House in Bowness Street.

More information: Barberton Information Bureau, PO Box 33, Barberton 1300; tel (01314) 22121.
Visiting times: Tours of Belhaven are conducted from Tuesday to Friday at 10 am, 11 am, noon, 2 pm and 3 pm; and on Saturdays and public holidays at 10 am, 11 am and noon. The maximum number of people allowed on each tour is 10 and there is a small admission fee. The museum is closed on Sunday, Monday and religious holidays.

Venture into the 'Valley of Death'

The fascinating Fortuna Mine Trail in the hills above Barberton plunges you into the dark depths of a mountain, enabling you to imagine the many hardships suffered by prospectors in their search for gold

The attractive petals of the 'Pride of De Kaap' – an indigenous shrub found in profusion along the Fortuna Mine Trail during summer.

THE BEAUTIFUL De Kaap valley in which Barberton nestles was christened the 'Valley of Death' by early prospectors – on account of the clouds of mosquitoes that infested its lonely stretches of veld.

But neither the threat of malaria nor the harshness of the terrain was enough to deter the scores of prospectors and fortune-seekers who swarmed to the valley in their feverish search for gold. The town sprang up virtually overnight to accommodate and entertain the crowds, and at the height of the gold rush it was an exciting boom town where prospectors thrived on a diet of rumour, speculation, alcohol and a frenetic night-life. Today Barberton is an atmospheric little place, although the sober charm of its well-tended streets and houses reveals little about its flamboyant history.

There is probably no better or quicker way to experience the erstwhile spirit of Barberton than to walk the Fortuna Mine Trail, a route that not only offers visitors a brief and tantalising taste of the town's history of gold prospecting but also brings them closer to the interesting flora of this wild and lovely valley.

The trail begins at Kellar Park in Crown Street, where you will see the path leading up the hill, running almost directly underneath an enormous overhead cableway. Supported by 52 pylons, this extraordinary structure stretches for 20 km across the mountains into Swaziland, carrying asbestos

Scary but safe – a view down the tunnel from its final exit point. The walk through the tunnel takes about seven minutes.

fibre and freight between the Havelock Asbestos Mine and Barberton's railway line. The 2-km walk, which is marked by red arrows, is a circular one. Although steep in places, it is certainly not too strenuous for people of average fitness, while children should manage easily. Allow at least one hour – longer if you intend to stop along the way for a picnic.

There's an initial short, steep climb, after which the trail levels out, following a contour path that winds round the hill through the greater part of the Barberton Indigenous Tree Park. The variety of trees found here is enormous: over 100 different species may be observed, all of which are indigenous to the Barberton area and the lowveld. Many trees are marked with plates that display the National Tree List number, the botanical name and the various common names; a list of the trees is obtainable from the Barberton Information Bureau.

After 15 minutes or so you will emerge from the dappled shade of the trees into open sunlight. The path leads up a short, steep incline, and at the top you will be rewarded with sweeping views of Barberton and the surrounding mountains. From here onwards, the trail becomes wilder; the air is pungently scented with indigenous herbs, and the shrill sound of cicadas competes with the soft chatter of birds concealed in the trees. If you are walking during the summer, you will notice that everywhere you look there seem to be shrubs bearing masses of star-shaped, reddish-orange flowers: *Bauhinia galpinii*, indigenous to the area, is one of the most spectacular of all South Africa's indigenous shrubs and derives its common name, 'Pride of De Kaap', from the valley in which Barberton lies.

The path swings to the east, intersecting a rough track leading up the mountain. Continue to follow the red arrows. This is a fairly steep section, but soon the path leads into a cool, shaded area. Just a little further on you will find the entrance to the tunnel, a square hole in the hillside, propped up by sturdy posts and reached by means of a wooden footbridge.

Contrary to popular belief, this is not an old mine, but a tunnel that was cut into the rock in 1907 for the purpose of transporting gold-bearing ore from the Fortuna Mine to the mill where the ore was crushed. No payable deposits of gold were unearthed in the tunnel. You may notice, to the right of the opening, the sealed entrance to another tunnel; this was also used for transporting ore but is not considered safe enough for the public to enter.

It is absolutely essential to take a torch with you – several torches if your party is large – because the

A panoramic view over the town of Barberton can be enjoyed during the first part of the Fortuna Mine Trail.

tunnel is over half a kilometre long and takes at least seven minutes to walk through. You cannot rely on the proverbial light at the end of the tunnel to guide you on your way, as there is a slight curve to the right. It's important to wear sturdy non-slip shoes too, because in the summer months the floor may be slippery or even filled with shallow pools of water. As the tunnel is long and very dark, it is definitely not recommended for children who are afraid of the dark nor for people who have claustrophobic tendencies.

Walking from bright sunshine into the chill, damp air inside the tunnel can be quite an unnerving experience. Inside, the atmosphere is slightly dank, scented with wet clay and cold rock, and the silence seems to press down on you like an icy blanket. Dwelling on the thought of the millions of tons of mountain poised above you will probably be enough to make you break out in a cold sweat.

The rock through which this tunnel was excavated is probably the most ancient on earth – it's estimated to be at least 3 400 million years old. Palaeontologists have discovered that the rocks of the Barberton region (of the Primitive System) contain the earliest signs of life ever discovered, in the form of blue-green algae fossils and bacteria.

As you venture further into the mountain, the entrance to the tunnel behind you dwindles into a misty semi-circle of bright white light, then a pinprick, and finally disappears as you walk around a gentle bend. Now you are alone in the dark and forbidding heart of the mountain, with only the sound of your beating heart and the slow drip-drip of water for company. Although the tunnel was never mined for gold, it's easy to imagine the discomfort and fear of the early prospectors who spent so many cold cramped hours scrabbling for gold in tunnels similar to this one.

The tunnel seems never to end, but persevere, because after 600 m you will see the exit hole, fringed with greenery, spilling its comforting light into the mountain's dark and lonely recesses. The area around the exit is particularly pretty, with its redcurrant and wild mulberry trees. It's a good place to stop for a picnic. Be sure to take your own water as there is no fresh water along the trail.

The return route takes you through what is probably the most scenic part of the trail. First the path passes through a creek where beautiful specimens of red ivory grow, and then it climbs gradually up a hot and stony hillside, shaded in patches by wild olives and bastard Cape ironwood trees. When you reach the top of the hill, stop for a while to admire the magnificent panoramic views, or perhaps to take photographs: from here, there is a fine view of the entire De Kaap valley and of the surrounding mountains.

It's a fairly steep and uneven walk back down to the starting point of the route. When you reach the immaculately lawned park at the bottom of the hill, flop down in the shade of one of the huge jacarandas and take a few minutes to survey your route and to marvel at the fact that you've just walked straight through a mountain.

The Fortuna Mine Trail at a glance (map page 226)

How to get there: The route begins at Kellar Park in Crown Street, Barberton. Ask for directions at the Information Bureau (see address below).
Weather: Barberton lies in a summer rainfall region. Temperatures can soar in the summer months, so be sure to take a hat.
What to do: Other places well worth visiting in Barberton are Belhaven Museum (see separate entry), Fernlea House, Stopforth House, the Anglo-Boer War Block House, Jock's Statue, the Garden of Remembrance, The Globe, Lewis and Marks Building, the Victorian Tea Garden and the old Stock Exchange.
Special attractions: Indigenous trees and abundant bird life.
Special precautions: Barberton is not a malaria area but it is advisable to take a course of anti-malarial medication before entering the region.
More information: A useful brochure with a detailed map of the trail is available at the Barberton Information Bureau, Market Square, PO Box 33, Barberton 1300; tel (01314) 22121.

Where to stay

There are two hotels in Barberton – the *Impala Hotel* in De Villiers Street, PO Box 83, Barberton 1300; tel (01314) 22108; and the *Phoenix Hotel* in Pilgrim Street, PO Box 77, Barberton 1300; tel (01314) 24211. Fully serviced chalets and shaded caravan sites may be rented at the town's caravan park, which is set in attractive surroundings in Fitzpatrick Park. Write to PO Box 780, Barberton 1300; tel (01314) 23323.

Fountain Baths Holiday Cottages offer self-catering accommodation. Their address is 48 Pilgrim Street, Barberton 1300; tel (01314) 22707. Some 14 km from Barberton, on the scenic R38 to Kaapmuiden, is the *Bougainvillea Hotel*, PO Box 9, Noordkaap 1304; tel (01314) 9681. In Nelspruit, Bundu Beds lists an extensive number of bed-and-breakfast facilities in the area. Contact them at PO Box 4019, Nelspruit 1200; tel (01311) 22709.

Wildlife paradise in the 'Valley of Heaven'

*South of Mbabane in the glorious Ezulwini Valley is the
Mlilwane Wildlife Sanctuary, a 5 000-ha reserve encompassing
some of the finest of Swaziland's numerous attractions*

IF YOU'RE WANTING A TASTE of the romantic Africa of yesteryear, then you may well find it at Mlilwane – where forest-covered mountains provide a stunning backdrop to a lush, warm valley watered by four rivers. Towards the north a pair of rounded, peaked hills create a distinctive landmark – the famous Sheba's Breasts from Rider Haggard's *King Solomon's Mines*. Adding to the mystic African appeal is the notorious Execution Rock, last used by King Bhunu, father and predecessor of the kingdom's long-reigning monarch, King Sobuza II, who died in 1983.

Mlilwane means 'little fire' – a reference to the numerous fires started by lightning strikes on Mlilwane Hill. More than 100 km of gravel road leads through this slice of romantic Africa, taking visitors to some memorable beauty spots. Four-wheel-drive guided tours operate from the rest camp, giving visitors a chance to see the bush through more experienced eyes.

By far the most enjoyable way to explore Mlilwane is on horseback. Numerous bridle trails thread through the most scenic routes, offering excellent game viewing. The more energetic can stretch their legs – and get a taste of Swaziland's famous champagne air – by taking one of the self-guided mountain trails. You'll be treated to some really unforgettable mountain scenery and possibly even spot a black eagle, one of several raptors that make their home here.

Mlilwane is particularly noted for its abundant bird life, which centres on the various dams in the reserve. Hides have been constructed overlooking the waters to give visitors clear views of the roughly 240 bird species, including blue crane, egret and white-faced whistling duck. Hippo and crocodile also find the dam waters congenial, while other game includes wildebeest, impala, eland, buffalo, kudu, giraffe, blesbok, zebra, warthog and jackal, and smaller game like porcupine, otter and the cute thick-tailed bushbaby, which can sometimes be seen peeping shyly from tree holes.

Many of these also make their way into Mlilwane's rest camp – and various tame wild animals and birds roam freely within the camp – proving especially irresistible to children. And after a morning of game viewing there's a lovely, natural river pool that offers bilharzia- and crocodile-free waters safe for swimming, or a regular pool for those who prefer it.

A twofold treat awaits you at the Hippo Haunt Restaurant which overlooks the camp lake: you can view the lake's occupants in supreme comfort while enjoying a good meal. On the subject of food, venison braais around the campfire at night are always popular.

Since Mlilwane is only 6 km from one of Swaziland's famous hotels, visitors can enjoy the best of contrasting worlds, and a special 'night gate' operates from dusk to dawn for revellers returning from an evening at the casino.

On a trail or game drive through this African paradise, it's very hard to believe that only 30 years ago the region was considered to be all but ruined.

Where to stay

Mlilwane Rest Camp offers a variety of accommodation. There are five-bed thatched huts, traditional beehive huts, a timberlog dormitory, one self-contained cottage, and a caravan and camping site. Some of the accommodation offers bedding, towels and a bathroom, and the ablution blocks have hot and cold water. A restaurant and lounge overlook the lake, a camp shop provides groceries, and a filling station and a field kitchen (bring your own food and cooking and eating utensils) complete the picture. A large swimming pool is available to everyone who doesn't fancy the river.

A group of warthogs sun themselves across the water from the Hippo Haunt – a restaurant situated within the Mlilwane Rest Camp.

Seen in the background are Sheba's Breasts, the famous pair of hills found within the Mlilwane Wildlife Sanctuary.

The mountain slopes had been mined for tin and were deeply scarred and badly eroded. Large areas had been destroyed and wildlife was seriously endangered, not only in the valley but in the entire kingdom.

Fortunately, help was at hand. This sanctuary, the first of its kind in Swaziland, owes its existence to the efforts of Terence Reilly, who farmed in the area. In the late Fifties, concerned with the steep decline in wildlife and the destruction of the natural beauty, the Reilly family and some supporters began lobbying the then British Administration to create a climate of conservation by protecting certain areas. However, no one seemed to consider the issue seriously, and some farmers were actively hostile to the proposal.

Undaunted, the Reilly family converted their own farm *Mlilwane* into the proposed sanctuary. But new problems arose, one of the most severe being poachers who regarded the newly introduced and flourishing wildlife as an unexpected windfall. Today, one of the more fascinating but grisly exhibits at the rest camp is the collection of over 200 000 wire snares collected over a period of 30 years. At a rough average of over 6 500 snares

found each year, it gives some indication of the ongoing vigilance required to contain the problem.

The sanctuary really took off after King Sobhuza II threw his weight behind the project, providing animals from his own private hunting stocks. Mlilwane opened to the public in 1964 and attracted a lot of interest and support. The Reilly family turned it into a trust in 1969 with the support of the Anglo-American Corporation, the South African Wildlife Foundation, Dr Anton Rupert, and many more. Since it opened, the sanctuary has increased its size tenfold.

The success of the Mlilwane Game Reserve spawned a conservation movement in Swaziland and led to the formation of the Swaziland National Trust Commission in 1972, which has the brief of creating and maintaining more wildlife areas. In 1978 the National Trust inaugurated the National Environmental Education Centre at Mlilwane; a lecture theatre was built and every year parties of schoolchildren camped here to experience the environment first hand. Although this programme has now been moved to Malolotja Nature Reserve, many parties of schoolchildren still come to Mlilwane for guided day tours.

Mlilwane Wildlife Sanctuary at a glance (map page 226)

How to get there: From Mbabane, take the road towards Manzini. After about 15 km there is a signposted turn-off to Mlilwane.
Weather: Summers are mild to hot with rain, although the temperature rarely rises above 32°C. Winter days are crisp, sunny and mild, but it can get very cold at night. June and July are the coldest months.
What to do: Game-spotting, bird-watching, exploring, hiking, horseriding, swimming.

Special attractions: The scenery and the tame wildlife. The reserve is within easy reach of many centres where visitors can buy Swaziland's excellent crafts and curios.
Visiting times: Mlilwane is open throughout the year, with the sanctuary's main gate operating from sunrise to sunset. The 'night gate' is open when the other routes are closed.
More information: Mlilwane Wildlife Sanctuary, PO Box 234, Mbabane, Swaziland; tel (09268) 45006. After hours calls can be made to (09268) 61591/2/3.

A royal reserve in big-game country

At Hlane Royal National Park in the northeast of Swaziland, the largest herds of game in the kingdom are held in trust for his people by King Mswati III

THE IMAGE OF A LION that graces the emblem of the Hlane Royal National Park does so for a very good reason. The lion is the symbol of the Swazi monarch, and it was King Sobhuza II of Swaziland who, inspired by the success of the Mlilwane Wildlife Sanctuary near the capital Mbabane, in 1967, appointed pioneer conservationist Ted Reilly to restore and protect the dwindling game herds of Hlane.

Today, the affairs of Hlane are personally overseen by King Mswati III, and once a year the *Butimba* (national hunt) rewards hunters with surplus stock from the regenerated herds of zebra, kudu, wildebeest, nyala and impala.

Consisting of 30 000 ha of big-game country, Hlane's low shrubland and large tracts of dense bush make this a natural sanctuary for the endangered white rhino (all of those in the park have been dehorned to discourage poachers) as well as a small herd of elephant which, undeterred by human presence, are frequently seen close to Ndlovu Camp. The flock of ostriches is even more socially inclined, often strolling into the camp for an impromptu display.

Hlane is a bird-watcher's paradise, host to the most southerly nesting colony of marabou storks and the densest population of vultures and other birds of prey in Swaziland. But not all its inhabitants are famous or rare – large numbers of glossy starlings and colourful kingfishers have made Hlane their home, and jackals and hyaenas play a significant role in the ecology of the reserve.

There are two small camps in the park, and because each is set in different terrain and offers a chance to view a diversity of habitat, fauna and flora, it is recommended that you visit both.

Ndlovu Camp – also open to day visitors – offers accommodation in two fully furnished huts that sleep three and eight respectively. Bedding and towels are provided as well as crockery, cutlery and cooking utensils, and candles and paraffin lamps – Ndlovu has no electricity, but each hut has a gas fridge to keep fresh produce cold. There is also a large camping ground for those who like to sleep under the stars. Cooking is done on one of several open fireplaces, and toilets and showers are located in a central ablution block.

Ndlovu is well shaded and tranquil, with abundant bird life. Its proximity to a waterhole provides excellent game-viewing opportunities, especially in the dry season, and after sunset, nearby warthogs, elephants and hyaenas bid you a memorable African 'goodnight'.

Eighteen kilometres away is the Bhubesi Camp on the banks of the Mbuluzana River, which offers captivating views of a riverine expanse of giant hardwood trees, gently flowing water and sand. The three cottages, built of Hlane stone, each nestle in their own secluded area, so you feel as if you alone have discovered this part of the world.

Your veranda has an open fireplace, a view of the river and a footpath leading down to where crocodiles cool off and vultures bathe. But inside your cottage there is every modern convenience, in-

Where to stay

There are two camps offering self-catering accommodation in Hlane Royal National Park. At *Ndlovu Camp,* two furnished huts sleep three and eight respectively, and there is a large camping ground. The three cottages at *Bhubesi Camp* are fitted with modern conveniences and each sleeps four. (See other panel for reservations office number.)

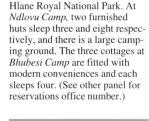

Ndlovu Camp in the Hlane Royal National Park has a rustic atmosphere reminiscent of yesteryear.

A herd of elephant charge across open ground at the Hlane Royal National Park.

cluding a stove, a fridge, a fireplace for chilly winter nights and a natural air-conditioning system for sweltering summers. Bedding, towels and cooking and eating utensils are provided, and each cottage has a bathroom and sleeping accommodation for four. As at Ndlovu, the cottages at Bhubesi are furnished in solid wood. For all their luxury, there's nothing to disturb the sense of being in an unspoilt wilderness.

The camps at Hlane are self-catering and the nearest shop is 10 km from the main gate, outside the park. So stock up on everything you need, and don't forget insect repellent, torch, sunblock and hat. Bring binoculars to spot the birds and a camera to record your encounters with them. Comfortable walking shoes are another important requirement, since the best way to explore Hlane is on foot.

The rangers at Hlane are courteous and well informed and will accompany your walkabout for a small additional fee. You will not regret engaging their services. They will patiently point out game that initially seems invisible in the dense bush, and they will light your campfire too. Self-guided game drives are another way of enjoying Hlane's wildlife – there are about 100 km of game-viewing roads, but some are impassable after heavy rains. Before you head into the wilderness, enquire if it is safe to do so.

Hlane is not Swaziland's only reserve. The Mlilwane Wildlife Sanctuary in the west is the Kingdom's pioneer conservation area, and in the south there is the privately owned Mkhaya Game Reserve (see separate entry). But Hlane has a special place in the hearts of the Swazi nation. In this part of a kingdom unrivalled for its scenic beauty and abundant wildlife, Ngwenyama ('the Lion') of Swaziland has restored to his people, and holds in trust, their natural heritage.

Hlane Royal National Park at a glance (map page 226)

How to get there: Drive to Manzini. Take the main tarred road east from here to Simunye – the route to Hlane is well signposted from here. Your journey will cover approximately 67 km.

Weather: Warm winter days turn into icy nights, and warm clothes are essential. During the hot summers, temperatures can exceed 40°C.

What to do: Game-viewing walks, with or without a ranger, and self-guided game drives take you close to Hlane's abundant wildlife.

Special attractions: At Ndlovu Camp enjoy the proximity of elephant and ostrich, and at Bhubesi look out for the marabou storks.

Special precautions: Hlane is situated in a malarial area and visitors must take appropriate precautions before entering it.

More information: Contact the Mbabane Central Reservations Office, PO Box 234, Mbabane; tel (09268) 44541/45006, or (09268) 61591/2/3 after hours.

Visiting times: The African waterhole experience is most rewarding during the dry winter season. In the rainy season, some roads may become impassable and dense vegetation tends to obscure the game.

Experience the call of the wild in cattle country

A tent in a forest, a shower under the stars, the possibility of walking in the bush past a rare black rhino – these are just some of the natural treats that await you at Mkhaya, a unique game reserve in the southeastern part of Swaziland

ORIGINALLY ESTABLISHED as a sanctuary for Swaziland's Nguni cattle, Mkhaya Game Reserve – situated in a remote corner of Swaziland – has evolved into a last refuge for a variety of endangered species.

Mkhaya represents the most recent and ambitious project of world-renowned conservationist Ted Reilly. To date he has stocked Mkhaya with elephant and giraffe, black and white rhino, buffalo and hippo, roan and sable antelope and tsessebe, eland, ostrich, warthog and impala. Furthermore, he has established visitor facilities that make a trip to Mkhaya a truly unforgettable experience.

Your adventure begins at the Mkhaya 'homestead', located a short distance from the entrance gate, and it is from here that rangers escort your vehicle into the reserve. After arriving at the rangers' base, you transfer to a ranger-driven, open Land Rover – your sole means of transport during your stay. (Don't worry about leaving your car behind, it will be guarded around the clock.)

The company of an experienced Swazi guide is something that even die-hard adventurers are likely to welcome. Here at Mkhaya there is always a very real sense of the ever-present dangers of the wild. This adds to the excitement of an experience that is designed to bring you as close to nature as it is pos-

sible to be without actually clashing with it. But once you have become acclimatised to your surroundings and have placed your trust in your guides, the sudden appearance of a python in the nearby undergrowth or the discovery of a scorpion under your bed is something you will soon be taking in your stride. Along the way, your Mkhaya ranger will probably tell you that the ostrich is the most dangerous species in the reserve, but he'll warn you to be wary around the black rhino and to keep a careful eye on the movements of nearby elephant, buffalo and crocodile.

In addition to the above species, game-viewing in Mkhaya also brings you close to the red duiker and grey duiker, steenbuck, both black-backed and side-striped jackal, honey badger, serval cat, African lynx, spotted hyaena, and various mongooses and genets. For bird-lovers, the visual feast includes the vulnerable bateleur eagle, various other eagles (martial, tawny, Walberg's, booted and crowned), vultures (white-headed, lappet-faced, white-backed, southern hooded and Cape) as well as various goshawks, hornbills, parrots and francolins.

It may be easy, in the excitement at spotting a black rhino, for instance, to forget all about the Nguni cattle for whom this paradise was initially set aside. This colourful animal, which is believed to have inhabited the southeastern seaboard of Africa for no less than 1 200 years, plays an integral part in the culture and traditions of the Swazi people. But for various reasons, its existence as a pure breed had become extremely precarious by the mid-1970s. Ted Reilly's early attempts to resurrect and protect the breed were initially ridiculed, but with the assistance of His Majesty King Sobhuza II of Swaziland, Reilly's efforts won state and, eventually, international support.

To accommodate the needs of this increasingly successful and important project, an area of land in prime Nguni habitat was sought. Ted Reilly acquired Mkhaya and developed it according to the principle of multiple land use. It is now an internationally acclaimed model for balancing the concerns of economic viability and survival. The remarkable thing about Mkhaya is that the money earned from the Nguni cattle, themselves snatched from the threshold of extinction as recently as 1976, is now almost wholly responsible for financing the preservation of rhinos and elephants that, along with other endangered species, have found refuge at Mkhaya.

The other species that makes a significant contribution to the fortunes of Mkhaya and its diverse

The bateleur, listed in the Red Data Book as 'vulnerable', is one of the birds of prey that can be seen in the Mkhaya Game Reserve.

population is, of course, *Homo sapiens* – visitors bring important revenue to the reserve, and for that they are amply rewarded with what it has to offer.

Within the reserve, Stone Camp offers accommodation to approximately 30 visitors – safari-style. Situated on the sandy bed of the Little Crocodile River, deep in a primeval riverine forest, it consists of a central summer house and kitchen built of dolerite boulders under cool thatch, surrounded by discreetly located canvas tents under a canopy of indigenous hardwood trees.

Another unique form of accommodation offered is a stone-and-thatch cottage in which the outer walls separating the bedrooms and bathroom from the bush are only knee high! This suite is recommended only for the very daring.

There's even a honeymoon tent with a king-size bed, tucked away deep in the forest. (Advice to newly weds: experiencing 'the earth move' during the night may turn out to have been the effect of a herd of elephant passing nearby!)

Ablution facilities are allocated to each tent and located nearby. There's always hot and cold water as well as flush toilets, though for those who yearn for times gone by, the notorious 'long drops' can still be found. Unusual and authentic African dishes are prepared on an open campfire, and drinks on sale include excellent South African wines.

New at Mkhaya, and popular with day-trippers and overnight visitors alike, are the day-long white-water rafting trips conducted by qualified and experienced river rafters along the Usutu River and the Bulungu Gorge. For this adventure, no experience is necessary and equipment – and lunch – are laid on. You bring nothing but your courage.

Participants choose between oar-boating (the guide does the rowing, all you do is hang on) and paddle-boating, a team effort that is both a physical and an emotional challenge. Rafting is conducted only from December to May and during this period also depends on the prevailing weather conditions and the water level.

Unique in almost every sense, Mhkaya offers an authentic 'Into Africa' experience – it's a remarkable achievement for a project inspired by a colourful cow. As a testimony to its special qualities, Mkhaya rangers like to quote a woman from Mbabane who on her first visit said: 'If you return to the doctor many times and he fails to cure you, then you must come to this place, and it will make you better.'

They think you'll agree.

A black rhino surveys its territory from a ridge in the reserve. At Mkhaya, visitors have a better chance of seeing black rhino than anywhere else in Africa.

Mkhaya Game Reserve at a glance (map page 226)

How to get there: Follow the tarred road east from Manzini, past Siphofaneni to Phuzumoya on the Big Bend road. Immediately after you cross the road-over-rail bridge at Phuzumoya, turn left off the tar and your Mkhaya guide will meet you right there at the Mkhaya sign next to the little shop at the side of the road. Do not attempt to drive to the reserve yourself – the gates are kept locked and you will not be allowed to enter.
Weather: Warm winter days and cold nights, with summer temperatures that soar to 40°C.
What to do: Hit the trails through Mkhaya, keeping a lookout for thorns overhead and snakes in the undergrowth. Guided game rides in open Land Rovers are available.

Special attractions: White-water rafting is a very exhilarating way of enjoying breathtaking scenery along the length of the Usutu River.
Visiting times: All visits are by prior arrangement; overnight visitors are met outside the entrance at 10 am or 4 pm, and returned 24 hours later. Day tours run from 10 am to 4 pm. Alternative times are possible on request.
More information: Contact Mbabane Central Reservations Office, PO Box 234, Mbabane; tel (09268) 44541/45006, or 61591/2/3 after hours.

Bear in mind that Mkhaya is situated in a malarial area, and visitors should take appropriate precautions before entering the game reserve.

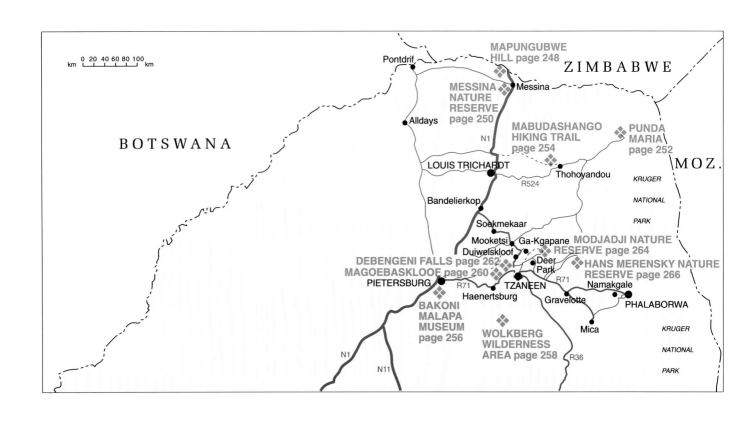

NORTHERN TRANSVAAL

An ancient treasure trove on the banks of the Limpopo

*In the far northern Transvaal, 77 km west
of Messina, is Mapungubwe Hill, the former
capital of a flourishing Iron Age settlement*

Where to stay

Visitors can stay overnight in a
bungalow or in tents at Mapungubwe Hill. Prior arrangements
can be made by contacting the
South African Defence Force,
Messina 0900; tel (01553) 2122
ext 2505.

The *Impala Lily Motel*
provides accommodation at
reasonable rates. Write to PO
Box 392, Messina 0900; tel
(01553) 2197 or 2300. Campers
and caravanners can try the
shady and grassy *Messina
Caravan Park*, Private Bag
X611, Messina 0900; tel (01553)
40211.

ROAD TRAVELLERS to and from Zimbabwe pass
through Messina, the last town on the Great
North Road before the Zimbabwe border.
This is truly African territory – broad mopane
savanna distinguished by ancient baobabs and
studded with rocky hills. Yet few motorists linger
longer than it takes to fill the car with petrol and, inevitably, most miss out on the area's extraordinary
attractions.

About 70 km west of the town, the Shashi River
merges with the Limpopo – this being the place
where the borders of Zimbabwe, South Africa and
Botswana meet at a single point. Here, close to the
southern bank of the Limpopo, a mammoth rock
rises regally from the grassland, stark against an
azure sky and guarded by a battalion of baobabs.
This extraordinary flat-topped sandstone hill is
Mapungubwe, 'Hill of Jackals', one of the
country's most exciting archaeological discoveries.

In the early 1900s an eccentric white vagrant, a
former guide of David Livingstone's by the name of
Wild Lotrie, made his home close to the hill. After
his death in 1917 there were rumours among the
local people that he had discovered treasure on the
summit of Mapungubwe. However, no one dared
test the truth of these stories as the hill was a source
of fear and superstition.

The rumours eventually percolated through to the
local farmers and kindled the interest of one of
them, E van Graan, who decided to investigate. On
New Year's Eve 1932, accompanied by his son and
three friends, Van Graan set off to explore the hill.
On the summit their wildest hopes were realised.
They found the ruins of dry-stone dwellings and

walls, earthenware pots buried up to their necks and
still intact, iron tools, glass beads, copper wire,
heaps of boulders for defence, and numerous other
artefacts – all evidence of a sophisticated settlement
in the same cultural tradition as Great Zimbabwe.

The party were beside themselves with excitement at their discovery, all the more so when their
searching revealed remnants of gold. Fortunately,
they had the good sense to realise that news of their
discovery would bring hordes of treasure-hunters
and vandals who would strip the site bare. They immediately reported their discovery to Dr Leo
Fouché, Professor of History at the University of
Pretoria, and the government stepped in promptly to
protect the hill and purchased the farm on which the
site was situated. Soon after, archaeologists from
the University of Pretoria moved onto the site and
began to piece together the history of Mapungubwe.

However, it was only years later, with the advent
of radiocarbon dating (a technique for determining
the age of organic materials such as wood), that the
significance of the site became known. Tests
revealed Mapungubwe to have been the forerunner
of Great Zimbabwe and occupied from around A.D.
1050 to 1200 – about two and a half centuries
before Great Zimbabwe. The earliest known site of
the Great Zimbabwe Tradition, Mapungubwe had
been the capital of a large Shona state with a complex hierarchy, a marked difference from the simple
social structure which had previously characterised
Iron Age communities on the subcontinent.

The settlement comprised a prestigious hilltop
area and a lower area on the south terrace, with dry
stone walls demarcating more elite areas and chan-

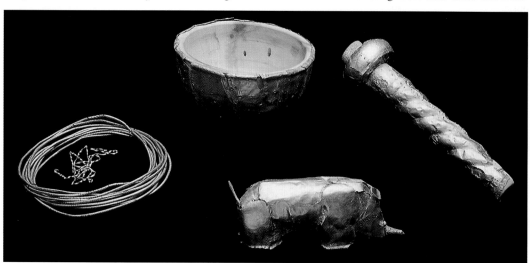

*Some of the famous gold relics –
including a model of a rhinoceros – found by archaeologists
on the top of Mapungubwe Hill.*

The vertical cliffs that surround Mapungubwe Hill made it a perfect natural fortress for its early inhabitants.

nelling pedestrian traffic around the summit. Several huts were found to have had elaborate verandas. The skeletal remains of eleven people were unearthed, and some extraordinary gold treasures discovered in the graves. The gold-working techniques included gold-plating – using gold sheeting to cover carved wooden items and securing it with gold tacks. One of the skeletons was so lavishly adorned with gold jewellery that when it was all removed from the arms, legs and neck, the total weight of pure gold was over two kilograms.

According to the experts, this was the earliest site where gold-working took place and appears to have heralded the era of gold-mining and trade with the east African coast. Early Islamic records state that, after the 10th century, gold from 'the country of Sofala' became the most important trading commodity, usurping ivory.

The most famous objects found on the site – a gold rhinoceros and a gold bowl – date from around AD 1200. Among the relics testifying to the antiquity of the site and evidencing foreign trade are fragments of Chinese ceramics and various imported beads. A black-and-white bead fragment bears a resemblance to those made in Egypt from about 200 BC; there are also red beads from India, yellow ones from Egypt or Mesopotamia, and pink beads thought to be Roman or Abyssinian.

Today, as then, the hill remains a natural fortress. The only access is along a concealed narrow cleft and the approach is assisted by a rope ladder. Apart from the archaeological attractions, the area is also home to a variety of game, including leopard, lion, elephant and many species of buck. Mapungubwe was declared a national monument in 1984, and the area is now administered by the South African Defence Force.

Once you've had your fill of ancient civilization, the attractive copper town of Messina is well worth exploring. The streets are vibrant with colour all year round as bougainvilleas, poinsettias, flamboyant and coral trees all compete for attention. Try to visit the Impala Lily Park in the centre of town in spring when it is particularly spectacular, with many trees in flower. Baobab trees flourish in the town (some thousands of years old) and many have been declared national monuments.

Driving around the town is an experience as, in deference to these venerable trees, the roads skirt respectfully around them. The Messina Nature Reserve just outside town was established specifically for the protection of baobabs. There are at least 100 mature trees here (also all national monuments) as well as a variety of other plants and various birds and animals.

Pride of the town is the railway station which, for many years, won awards for South Africa's best-kept and most beautiful station. An open-air museum alongside the station has as one of its more interesting exhibits the well-restored Zeederberg mail coach, the original mail coach that used to run between Pretoria and Zimbabwe. Also on display is an old steam locomotive and an exhibition of historic photographs.

Mapungubwe Hill at a glance (map page 246)

How to get there: Head northwards out of the town of Messina on the N1 for about 2 km, then turn left at the Pontdrif turn-off. Mapungubwe Hill is situated about 77 km along this road.

Weather: Summers are hot, often extremely so, with thunderstorms; the winters are mild.

What to do: Climb, explore and marvel. Messina has many recreational facilities, including a unique golf course set among the mopanes and baobabs, swimming, tennis, squash, badminton and bowls.

Special attractions: The wonderful baobab territory of the northern Transvaal.

More information: The Town Clerk, 1 Flax Avenue, PO Box 611, Messina 0900; tel (01553) 2210. Tourist Information Bureau, Municipal Library, Main Street, Messina 0900; tel (01553) 40211.

The extraordinary trees that fell from the sky

Towering like an ancient, multi-masted sailing ship above the surrounding mopane and corkwood trees, the baobab dominates the African veld north of the Soutspansberg

THE TALL, TAPERING TRUNK of the baobab tree, topped by a canopy of twisted, root-like branches, is one of nature's most freakish sights. The appearance of the baobab is so decidedly odd that the early inhabitants of what is now the northern Transvaal believed that it grew upside down – after having been dropped from the sky by some supernatural hand.

These lordly wonders of the veld can be spotted at various locations alongside the national road between Pietersburg and the Zimbabwe border – but nowhere is there a better collection than at the Messina Nature Reserve 6 km south of Messina. It is a unique parkland established primarily for the baobab's preservation and protection.

Part of the reserve was originally the Baobab Forest Reserve which was proclaimed back in 1926 in an attempt to stop the exploitation of the trees. But that step proved inadequate and baobabs were eventually declared national monuments to ensure their continued existence. Today a strict conservation policy is enforced which has given every surviving specimen a number. The remains of a pulp factory from the bad old days can still be seen on the banks of the Sand River.

The reserve is home to a forest of around 12 000 baobabs, including one giant that is 25 m high and has a trunk circumference of 16 m. But baobabs are not the only attraction in this 5 000-ha reserve. Keen botanists will delight in more than 350 species of trees and shrubs. Classified as mopane veld, the vegetation naturally includes mopane trees (don't forget to look out for red, white and yellow-striped mopane worms on the branches: a favourite African delicacy), kudu lily, impala lily, white seringa, corkwood and red bushwood.

Besides its botanical bounty, the Messina Nature Reserve also has a variety of wildlife, including indigenous species such as nyala, impala, duiker, steenbok, Sharpe's grysbok and kudu, as well as those indigenous animals that have been brought back to the area, such as blue wildebeest, giraffe, ostrich and sable antelope. Several varieties of cat live in the reserve, such as leopard, civet, caracal and the African wild cat. Bird-watchers may be treated to glimpses of 143 possible species, including rare birds such as the martial eagle, black eagle and crested guineafowl.

Another unique feature of this reserve are the world's oldest rock formations, found in the Sand River. Known appropriately as the Sand River gneiss, the rock is estimated by geologists to be about 3 800 million years old.

Game viewing is allowed in private cars and an interesting circular drive has been laid out in the reserve that passes many of the more spectacular baobabs. There is a small picnic area near the main gate, equipped with toilets and running water.

Of all Africa's many botanical symbols, the baobab tree is perhaps the most potent, its strange appearance and massive proportions interwoven with African myth and legend.

Travelling north through the veld, you can't miss this freak of nature, its enormous swollen trunk contrasting sharply with a light upper structure of short, tapering branches that bear a thick canopy of glossy leaves in summer. The white flowers can grow up to 20 cm in diameter, have an unpleasant smell and are apparently pollinated by bats and bushbabies.

The botanical name for the baobab is *Adonsonia digitata*, this being the African cousin of a species also found in Madagascar and Australia. Its favourite habitat is the undulating plains of southern Zimbabwe and the far northern Transvaal, particularly the Messina Nature Reserve, which boasts a forest of these massive trees, some of whose branches spread to a width of nearly 40 m across.

Size is not the only superlative of this floral natural wonder. It is also superbly useful to man: the leaves can be boiled and eaten as a vegetable;

Where to stay

There is no accommodation in the reserve. In Messina there is the *Impala Lily Motel*, PO Box 392, Messina 0900; tel (01553) 2197 or 2300. Campers and caravanners could try the picturesque *Messina Caravan Park,* Private Bag X611, Messina 0900; tel (01553) 40211.

The baobab tree must rank as one of the most unusual natural sights on the African landscape.

Baobab trees of all shapes and sizes line the stretch of road leading into the town of Messina.

the seeds can be ground and roasted to make a drink not unlike coffee; the pollen can be used to make glue; the giant fruit pod – up to 20 cm long – contains tartaric acid, used in the making of sherbet; and the soft, fibrous bark makes excellent rope and floor mats, and even paper. In addition, there is a cavity among the branches that often holds water, even in the driest months. So if you're ever thirsty in the veld, you know where to look for moisture.

The early pioneers used the fruit to make cream of tartar, which gave the tree its nickname of 'cream of tartar tree' (called *kremetartboom* in Afrikaans). Their predecessors, the local Venda and Sotho, also used the fruit to make a refreshing cordial. These early plains dwellers believed that the baobab did not grow at all, but was deposited from the sky upside down during the winter, with its treeless branches reaching skywards like roots. Their belief was prompted by the fact that the young baobab, a long-stemmed sapling, looks nothing like its parent and they apparently failed to connect the two.

The tree is still the object of much superstition and folklore that has endured down the years. It is believed that drinking water in which boabab seeds have soaked will provide protection from crocodiles; that drinking an infusion of the bark will make a man strong and powerful; and picking a baobab blossom (where spirits are believed to dwell) means certain death in the jaws of a lion. After a severe frost in Zimbabwe in 1968 had killed many baobabs, there were authenticated reports of the fibrous remains of these dead trees bursting into flame by spontaneous combustion, and there is a persistent belief that all the old baobabs create their own funeral pyres in this manner.

Experts have examined samples from the cores of several baobabs and radiocarbon-dating suggests that the largest trees are probably over 3 000 years old. They attain this great age through their extraordinary resilience and vitality – even when their centres have been burnt out, they still thrive. There are stories of hollow trunks being used for such diverse purposes as shops, storage space, hiding places from marauding tribes and wild animals, houses and even prisons.

Yet the extraordinary shape of the baobab, together with its soft, wet, pulpy wood, has given it one weakness – a liability to sudden collapse, particularly during heavy rains when it absorbs too much water. When this happens, the entire tree implodes in an untidy heap of white flakes. Insects and the elements then attack the remains, and in little more than a year there is hardly a trace of the tree that took so long to grow.

Messina Nature Reserve at a glance (map page 246)

How to get there: The main entrance to the Messina Nature Reserve is on the national road 6 km south of the town.
Weather: Summers are usually hot to sweltering with thunderstorms, winters are mild to warm but it can get cold at night.
What to do: Inspect the fauna and flora, and hike.
Special attractions: The diverse botanical heritage and the baobabs themselves.

Opening times: The gate opens at 7.30 am and closes again at 4 pm all year round.
More information: Write to The Subsection Head, Messina Nature Reserve, PO Box 78, Messina 0900; tel (01553) 3235/2307. You can also contact The Regional Representative, Directorate of Nature and Environmental Conservation, PO Box 217, Pietersburg 0700; tel (01521) 74948/9.

The 'crooks corner' that became a wilderness paradise

The game population of the eastern Transvaal lowveld is at its most varied, and the landscapes at their wildest, in the northern section of the Kruger National Park – the focus of which is the charmingly old-fashioned Punda Maria rest camp

Where to stay

Punda Maria Rest Camp offers self-contained three-bed huts and four-bed family cottages (all with kitchenette, shower/bath and toilet) and ordinary huts, which have no cooking facilities. There is also a caravan/camping area with communal kitchens and ablution blocks. The camp has a licensed à la carte restaurant and a shop; fuel is available near the entrance gate.

For a taste of contrasting worlds, consider an overnight stop at the lively *Venda Sun Hotel and Casino* in Thohoyandou, just off the R524 to the east. The hotel has sophisticated amenities; the small territory of Venda is beautiful, has a rich cultural heritage, and is well worth exploring. Bookings and information: PO Box 766, Sibasa, Venda; tel (015881) 21011/2; or Sun International Central Reservations, PO Box 784487, Sandton 2146; tel (011) 7807800.

IN THE EARLY DECADES of the century, the far northern parts of what is today the Kruger National Park were the haunt of a disreputable fraternity, a motley collection of poachers, renegades and adventurers. Many of these hid themselves in the wild country around the confluence of the Limpopo and Luvuvhu rivers, and their presence went virtually unchallenged until three police posts were established in the region.

The first to make its appearance was Punda Maria, built in 1919 and said to have been christened by Capt J J Coetzer, an early ranger whose wife habitually wore striped dresses ('punda' means striped in Swahili), although another version holds that the name derives from the area's profusion of zebra. Later, when the great spaces north of the Letaba River were opened to the public, the post became a tourist rest camp.

Punda Maria is one of the most charming of the Kruger National Park's 20 or so public venues, a small, unassuming, rather old-fashioned cluster of thatched huts and chalets built in terraces on the rocky hillside and shaded by indigenous evergreen trees. Unlike many of the park's various other camps, Punda Maria has a pronounced wilderness feel about it: here one has a sense of seclusion, of remoteness even.

Nor is the impression all that illusory. The Kruger's northern section is the least developed, its landscapes the wildest and most varied. Here, fully nine of the continent's major ecosystems come together to create a magnificent mélange of different vegetation types.

No less remarkable is the diversity of animals and birds, trees, bushes and grasses. Many of the species are rare, some are unique to this particular corner of Africa; especially impressive are the giant sycamore figs and the Lebombo ironwoods, the handsome jackalberries, the ebonies, the Natal mahoganies, the ancient baobabs of the Mashikiri plateau and the ghostly, yellow-green fever trees of the Luvuvhu's riverine forests.

The river and its many sandbanks are home to hippo and crocodile (unusually large specimens of the latter), its jungle-like fringes occupied by vervet monkey and baboon, and an array of rare and beautiful sub-tropical birds. Elephant and buffalo, zebra, shy bushbuck, sable, eland, impala and nyala antelope wander at will through the thickets and over the open grasslands; elusive leopard stalk their prey among the outcrops. The game is especially prolific on the plains of Hlamalala, the 'Serengeti of South Africa'.

Visitors are served by a network of good game-viewing roads, and the short Mahogany loop route provides a superb introduction to the area. Especially rewarding among the longer drives is the one leading north through mopane and then baobab country to the border post of Pafuri, 42 km from Punda Maria.

On the way you pass Gumbandevu, a hill that was sacred to the local peoples long before the region was set aside for the animals and the tourists. This was the domain of Khama, the renowned rainmaker, who made sacrificial offerings and wove magic spells to induce the heavens to open. By all

Thatched accommodation set amidst avenues of shady indigenous trees combines to create a mood of rustic charm at the Punda Maria camp.

The Luvuvhu River near Punda Maria is an important source of water for game in the area.

accounts she was highly successful – people came from afar, bringing with them gifts of livestock and implements, to seek her intercession.

At Pafuri there is a picnic site, an enchantingly embowered spot whose giant fig trees are the resting place of trumpeter hornbills, and the river waters are home to hippopotamus – and, at times, also to that most handsome of wetland birds, the African fish eagle, whose loud and plaintive call is, for many, the authentic voice of wild Africa. Eagle and hippo can often best be seen from the bridge that straddles the Luvuvhu.

At Pafuri, visitors have the use of toilets and hot water, but there are no shopping facilities, so bring a prepared lunch.

A worthwhile excursion, too, is along the road southeastwards towards the Shingwedzi rest camp, 73 km from Punda Maria and close to the Mozambiquan border. The route takes you across flattish savanna and green-mantled mopane countryside with, here and there, the jagged protrusion of a rocky outcrop. Roughly halfway along the journey you'll come to the Babalala resting place, an attractive clearing hemmed in by densely vegetated marshland.

From here, you can either carry on to Shingwedzi – a charming venue of rectangular bungalows shaded by lovely indigenous trees and brightened by spectacular shows of pink and white impala lilies – or turn west onto the 30-km gravelled loop that follows the courses of the Shisha and Mphongolo streams.

The digression leads through woodlands of tall jackalberry, apple leaf and nyala trees into and past a country rich in wildlife: elephant, buffalo, antelope and lion abound; the riverine forests and the flanking thickets are sanctuary for many of the park's more than 700 leopard.

For visitors with time and energy to spare, the Kruger National Park offers a number of wilderness trails – foot safaris led by rangers who are willing to share their knowledge and their deep love of the bush with members of the group. The walks are by no means strenuous. Indeed, they tend to be the gentlest of strolls, designed to stimulate the senses, to inform the mind, to provide an insight into the ways of the wild.

Route and pace are dictated by the mood, interests and preferences of the group, and there are frequent halts – to observe and discuss a particular bird, perhaps, a herd of antelope, a wildflower, a tree. The ranger will talk about each, expertly and with enthusiasm. At dusk you return to base camp, a fairly spartan affair of thatched huts, to shower and change and then to gather around the fire for a companionable meal.

Punda Maria at a glance (map page 246)

How to get there: Punda Maria is the northernmost of the Kruger's rest camps. By road from Johannesburg/Pretoria, take the N1 highway north to Louis Trichardt, a distance of 440 km (from Johannesburg), and then follow the fully tarred R524 east to the Punda Maria gate. Thohoyandou, the Venda capital, is about halfway between Louis Trichardt and the northern Kruger. Once through the gate, follow the road for 5 km and you'll see the Punda Maria turn-off on your left.

An alternative route – one which will allow you to see much more of the park along the journey – is via the N4 east to Nelspruit (358 km from Johannesburg) and beyond, either to the Malelane gate (in the extreme south of the park) or to the Numbi or Paul Kruger gates, which are farther north. You then drive up through the park, which has an excellent network of tarred and gravel roads.

Weather: Sub-tropical, with tropical characteristics. Summers are hot and often uncomfortably humid, with thunderstorms usually building up during the afternoon to discharge torrential downpours in the early evening. Winter days are clear-skied and warm, the nights chilly and occasionally cold.

Special precautions: Take a course of anti-malaria tablets before leaving home. Avoid contact with open water: the bilharzia snail is a hazard.

What to do: Game viewing, by means of self-guided drives, is the principal activity in the Kruger National Park area around Punda Maria. Also bird-spotting and tree identification.

Special attractions: The two-day, three-night Nyalaland Trail.

More information: Bookings for accommodation at Punda Maria and for a place on the Nyalaland Trail must be made through (and information may be obtained from): The Chief Director, National Parks Board, PO Box 787, Pretoria 0001; tel (012) 3431991; or The Chief Director, National Parks Board, PO Box 7400, Roggebaai 8012; tel (021) 222810.

A wonderful walk through a land of legend

Old Africa is alive and well, as hikers can discover on a trail of mystery and imagination in the Soutpansberg highlands

IN THE FAR NORTHERN TRANSVAAL, a tiny mountainous region is the ancestral home of the Venda, whose ancient culture, beliefs and rituals have survived the relentless onslaught of the 20th century. Composed of a number of clans, the majority of these people are thought to have originated alongside the Great Lakes of East Africa and moved southwards through the Congo (now Zaire) and then to Zimbabwe. They crossed the Limpopo River from the 12th century onwards, and brought the traditions of Great Zimbabwe to their new home.

Although small in number, they're a fiercely independent group who successfully resisted, then routed, the Boers when Transvaal President, Paul Kruger tried to impose taxes on them. They were equally successful in repulsing the unfriendly attentions of the Pedi, Tsonga and Swazi. An intensely spiritual and superstitious people, their landscape abounds in sacred sites, so visitors are advised to show respect for ancient rites and customs.

Possibly the most sacred spot of all is Lake Fundudzi, a supposedly enchanted body of water formed by a massive landslide which blocked the valley of the Mutale River. The name refers to the ritual which must be performed by newcomers to the lake: they turn their backs to the lake and view the waters between their legs. Such is the influence of this lake that it has percolated through to Venda rituals and customs.

This is most clearly demonstrated by that most erotic of African dances, the *domba*, which is the proud heritage of the Venda, although several filmmakers have hijacked it for their own inaccurate generalisations on Africa. The distinctive sacred python dance is performed by young women initiates in preparation for marriage. At the signal for the *domba* to begin, the girls – numbering anything from 20 to 200 – join up behind each other, each clasping the elbows of the one in front, and sway around a fire to the rhythmic throb of ritual drums. The dance emulates the sinuous wave motion of a snake, and often continues until dawn.

As most people are forbidden to trespass on such sites, the best way to experience the mysticism and scenic splendour of the region is by walking the Mabudashango Hiking Trail which includes legendary spots and passes within sight of the hallowed Lake Fundudzi. The tropical splendour of these highlands is characterised by an extraordinary richness of colour and texture: red earth, lush, vibrant vegetation, luminous, purple mountains, limpid lakes and pure, silver streams and waterfalls. Each detail, from the leafy tapestry of the forest canopy to the soft mountain folds, is enriched by a rare clarity and quality of light.

The indigenous woodland that characterises the area boasts a lavish variety of plants such as wild fig, wild loquat, wild banana, tree fuchsia, orchids, wild peppers and many, many more. Although the wildlife in the region is plentiful, it is also shy and therefore elusive. But the possibility of a sighting always exists and you could see leopard, red duiker, bushbuck, mountain reedbuck, bushpig and samango monkey. You are, however, far more likely to spot baboons on the rocky ledges and vervet monkeys on the forest fringes.

In contrast, the birdlife is more diverse, with over 400 species that have been recorded in the area, including emerald cuckoo, the ubiquitous guineafowl, shrike, loerie, wagtail, crowned hornbill, rock kestrel and black eagle. Consider yourself blessed if you happen to see a rare Transvaal mountain lizard – only six have ever been recorded. It is black with white bands and was first described in 1933. Most of these sightings have been in the Fundudzi area.

The starting and finishing point of the circular trail is the Thathe Vondo Forest Station, and the first day of the trail covers just over 15 km. Shortly after the start, the trail plunges into verdant indigenous forest and climbs through sumptuous vegetation before emerging onto a plateau. Here there is a viewsite at which hikers can take their first break and view the surrounding tea plantations, the Vondo Dam and a mountain known as Lwamondo Kop. According to legend, the baboons living on its slopes would warn the inhabitants in the village below of an impending attack, giving the villagers ample time to climb the mountain and roll rocks onto their unwary aggressors. Needless to say, the Lwamondo baboons are never killed.

From this lookout point the trail moves along the Nzhelele River catchment area, through more indigenous forest, pine plantations and forestry roads to the Fundudzi camp, which is picturesquely set in a forest clearing alongside a crystal-clear pool formed by the Mutale River. The camp is fairly basic, comprising an open, thatched shelter; bins,

One of the most exotic sights that Africa has to offer is undoubtedly the domba – *the sacred python dance performed by Venda maidens prior to marriage.*

firewood, cold water and a toilet are provided, with a rustic table and benches constructed from thin branches.

On the second day the trail traverses the river to a firebreak, from where there is a stunning view of Fundudzi, the secret lake, cupped in a circle of mountains. From this viewsite the lake's many sacred areas can be seen: the southwestern bank of the lake is where the legendary spirit gardens lie, where the spirits still tend their crops; at the western end of the lake there are several large rocks in the shape of Venda drums where spirits gather for celebrations; and each year, at harvest time, offerings are placed on the rocks on the eastern shores that stretch into the lake so that the spirits can sample the harvest bounty.

There is an almost oppressive air of mystery on entering the Thathe Sacred Forest, the traditional burial ground for Venda chiefs. The forest's holy status has ensured that it has remained untouched over the centuries. The wild quince is the most common tree here; its fruit is used by the people who roast it, grind it down and use the oil to smear on their bodies or leather clothes.

From this sacred ground the trail leads through the Tshamanyatsha indigenous garden, a spectacular, natural Eden where scattered sandstone boulders are softened with moss and ferns, and exquisite exotic flowers (including orchids) tumble in profusion.

Vhulambangwe is the highest point on the trail. From here there are panoramic views across forest and pine plantations, down to Mukumbani Dam, where the hikers spend the following two nights. The trail then dips steeply into the forest and hikers will be relieved to see ladders provided to assist them down this precarious section of the trail.

Day three of the hike is a detour to the Tshatshingo potholes and passes through more lush indigenous forest. It bypasses the Mohovhohovho waterfall and crosses the Tshirovha River twice (beware during the rainy season). Hiking through dry bushveld gives you a glimpse of scattered, rural African settlements. The Tshatshingo potholes have been gouged into the rock over the ages by the swirling waters of the Tshirovha River, which drops several metres into the boiling cauldron of the first pothole, and reappears about 20 m downstream in a smaller one. During winter, when the volume of water is less, it's possible to cross the river and

One of the highlights of the Mabudashango Hiking Trail is this view of Fundudzi, the sacred lake of the Venda people.

climb down to explore the potholes and ravine, but not without extreme caution.

The fourth and final leg of the trail is the shortest. The path leads across the dam wall and climbs towards a spectacular view of the area from the Murangoni lookout, and further on, at Ndoumuhulu, hikers are rewarded with the sight of traditional Venda settlements, superficially unchanged for hundreds of years.

The circular Mabudashango Hiking Trail culminates at the Thathe Vondo Forest Station 10 km from the previous night's camp, and can easily be completed before noon.

Mabudashango at a glance (map page 246)

How to get there: From Johannesburg, take the N1 north as far as Louis Trichardt, where you turn eastwards onto the R524. Continue along this road for nearly 70 km until you reach a turn-off left for the Venda Sun Hotel. Carry on through Thohoyandou to the first traffic light in Sibasa, where you will turn left into Mphephu Street. Follow this road for 20 km until you reach a Department of Forestry sign, where you again turn left. A gravel road leads to the Thathe Vondo Forest Station.

Weather: Hot and humid in summer, with a high summer rainfall, mild in winter; although virtually frost-free, it can get cold at night.

What to do: Along the trail there will be numerous opportunities to swim in the inviting pools, which you may do without fear – the fast-flowing highlands water is bilharzia-free. Apart from the hiking and wildlife-spotting, there are

many other forms of recreation , from gambling at the Venda Sun Hotel to angling in the dams.

Special attractions: The extraordinary diversity of the scenery; the range of ancient African customs and rituals; high-quality arts and crafts such as ethnic painting and sculpture, geometrically patterned traditional clay pots, mats and basketware of every description and woodcarving (including walking sticks, knobkieries, spoons, bowls and trays).

More information: Write to The Director-General, Department of Commerce, Industry and Tourism, Private Bag X2239, Sibasa, Venda; tel (0159) 21031; or The Director-General, Department of Agriculture and Forestry, Private Bag X2247, Sibasa, Venda; tel (0159) 31001, ext 2167 or 2290. Permits for hiking can be obtained from the Director-General of Agriculture and Forestry, Private Bag X2247, Sibasa, Venda.

Where to stay

Before and after the trail, hikers can stay at the old forester's house at the Thathe Vondo Forest Station. There are 12 bunk beds, hot water, and toilet and kitchen facilities.

At Thohoyandou, the *Venda Sun Hotel* offers en-suite accommodation, a pool area and a small casino. Contact the hotel at PO Box 766, Sibasa, Venda; tel (0159) 21011/5; or contact Sun International Central Reservations in Johannesburg at PO Box 784487, Sandton 2146; tel (011) 7838660.

A fascinating insight into traditional Sotho life

*The lives of a Northern Sotho 'captain'
and his wives have been meticulously recreated
at the Bakoni Malapa Museum, outside Pietersburg*

NOT EVERY MUSEUM is an old building where documents and objects of historical interest are displayed behind glass. Such museums are interesting, of course, but for a really vivid picture of the way things were, nothing can compare with a 'living' museum – one in which visitors can observe the practice of traditional skills and not merely their products.

At the Bakoni Malapa Museum outside Pietersburg, the lifestyle of the Bakoni of Matlala, one of three groups constituting the Northern Sotho, has been recreated in a living open-air museum. The 12 structures erected here, reflecting the life style of a man with three wives, are occupied by men and women engaged in such activities as manufacturing grain baskets and clay pots, making furniture and utensils from wood, preparing hides for skin-rugs and clothing, and household tasks such as beer-brewing and grinding maize.

The museum consists of a traditional unit and a modern unit, the latter reflecting the influence of Western civilisation on the architecture, life style and material culture of the Northern Sotho. It was built in the early 1980s, with the enthusiastic assistance of the Matlala people, whose members acted tirelessly as interpreters, guides and advisors during the period of research and construction.

The central feature of the complex is the *kgôrô* – the gathering place of the men. This consists of a large circular area surrounded by a fence of thorntree branches. To the left of its entrance,

another enclosure is set aside as a cattle kraal: to the right there is a simple shelter where the men gather when it rains.

This traditional complex consists of four clusters of dwellings (*malapa*), one for each of the three wives and one for the household of the first-born son. The 'captain' has no *lapa* of his own – according to Northern Sotho tradition, a man is at home in the house of each of his wives.

The wives of the multiple family unit represented at the museum are not equal in status, and the buildings explicitly reflect this. The home of the first wife and her children is larger than the others and situated directly behind the exit of the *kgôrô*. It consists of her sleeping hut, a cooking hut, an initiation hut, separate huts for her sons and daughters, a hut for the witchdoctor and the hut of the support wife (a woman whose purpose it was to bear children for a barren wife).

The *lapa* of the second wife, to the left of the first, also has, apart from a sleeping hut, a cooking hut and potter's hut. The third wife lives on the right side (which is viewed by the Northern Sotho as the weaker side). Her accommodation, too, reflects her inferior status: it consists of only two huts – one for sleeping and one for cooking. The *lapa* of the first-born son, to the left of that of the second wife, is similarly modest.

The huts found at the museum are the rondavel type, supported by poles of indigenous wood tied with bark and ropes of grass and clad with thatch.

Traditional Northern Sotho huts are made out of wood, thatch, ant-hill clay and cattle dung.

Bakoni Malapa Museum as seen from a nearby koppie. The small, circular enclosure next to the cattle kraal is the kgôrô, *a meeting place for men.*

Sleeping huts and cooking huts are easy to tell apart – the sleeping hut typically has a conical shape, while the cooking hut consists of a loose thatched roof placed on top of a hut construction.

The basic construction is the work of the men; afterwards the women soften ant-hill clay with water and knead it to a paste which they press between poles and laths. A second coat of ant-hill clay is followed by a red soil-ash mixture plastered onto the inner and outer walls. Then a layer of red soil is applied over the floor area.

Finally, a mixture of red soil and cattle dung is smeared over the walls and floors of the hut, as well as over the *lapa* surface, and is buffed with a smooth riverstone. The dung may be coloured by adding, for example, wood-ash for grey, charcoal for black, quicklime for white and very dark red soil for maroon. By drawing their fingers through the dung, the women create geometrical patterns such as circles, triangles, half-moons and squares.

The elaborate application of cattle dung to the floors of a dwelling is a feature retained in the modern unit, as is the concept of building separate structures for different purposes, rather than many rooms under a single roof. But in many other ways the modern unit reflects the impact of contact with Western civilisation.

It consists of three structures: a sleeping hut, a kitchen and a living room or 'showhouse'. For the sleeping and cooking huts, stones were used as building material, though they were still plastered with ant-hill clay and roofed with thatch. The living room has no roof structure. It was built with home-made clay bricks and has a flat corrugated-iron roof. Though the addition of bought windows and furniture of Western origin lends an element of grandeur to the showhouse, to Western eyes it is a rather lifeless structure, compared to that of its traditional neighbours.

Other structures on the museum premises are of more practical concern to visitors. These include the entrance building, where orientation exhibitions are arranged and handmade objects are offered for sale, and an ablution block, braai facilities and a tea-garden. A hiking trail has been laid out across the koppie behind the museum, where hikers can view no fewer than 17 species of indigenous trees as well as several archaeological relics recalling the presence of inhabitants thousands of years before the arrival of the Northern Sotho.

The Bakoni Malapa Museum at a glance (map page 246)

How to get there: The museum lies at the foot of a koppie, about 9 km outside Pietersburg on the Chuniespoort/Burgersfort Road.
Weather: Hot in summer, though the evenings can be chilly; icy in winter, though pleasant during the day. The rainfall is moderate.
What to do: Gain an insight into the lives of a Northern Sotho 'captain' and his wives, meticulously depicted in the position, construction and content of their *malapa*.
Special attractions: Traditional skills are practised here for the benefit of visitors.
Visiting times: The museum is open daily from 8.30 am to 12.30 pm, and 1.30 pm to 3.30 pm. There are guided tours from 8.30 am until 3.30 pm. There is a small entrance fee.
More information: The Pietersburg Town Council, PO Box 111, Pietersburg, 0700; tel (01521) 952011.

The dramatic contours of the Wolkberg – an enchanting realm that has been declared one of the country's official wilderness areas.

Peaks and valleys shrouded in myths and mysteries

A natural wonderland of mountains, rain forests, deep ravines and valleys constitute the Wolkberg Wilderness Area situated 80 km from both Pietersburg and Tzaneen in the northern Transvaal

THE MYSTERY AND ROMANCE of the Transvaal lowveld are encapsulated within the Wolkberg Wilderness Area, a scenic 22 000 ha domain embracing high mountain peaks, wide valleys, deep ravines, indigenous tropical rainforests, grasslands, crystal rivers and waterfalls.

In the afternoons huge thunderclouds tower up and blacken the sky, and often mist envelops the peaks, chiffon-like wraiths clinging to the slopes and shrouding the landscape in mystery. Here, visitors can get lost in a primeval landscape untouched by the modern world.

These magical surroundings have inspired many authors and poets down through the years. After visiting the area, the English writer John Buchan penned his classic adventure story *Prester John*, and a lesser-known writer, Harry Klein, wrote two books eulogising the region: *Valley of the Silver Mist* and *Valley of the Mists*.

In the late Seventies, the Wolkberg was proclaimed South Africa's seventh official wilderness area. It lies in a cusp where the northern Drakensberg meets the Strydpoort mountains, creating a wilderness of drama, variety and glorious vegetation that includes both bushveld and grassveld. Patches of tropical rainforest occur in the valleys, with trees such as beech, kiaat, bushwillow, wild teak, tree fuchsias, yellowwoods, lemonwood and marula. In the mist belts on the mountains are unique floral ecosystems, and in the spring sugarbush explode into a riot of vibrant pink flowers.

The clean fragrances of a variety of wildflowers, grasses and shrubs are carried around the slopes on the breezes, often dominated by the distinctive spiciness of the curry bush. At the western end of Devil's Knuckles is Cycad Valley, a steep valley where thousands of South Africa's largest cycad, the Modjadji cycad, are concentrated. In fact, this wilderness area is not far from the legendary Modjadji forest (see separate entry).

Animal inhabitants of the area prefer to keep out of sight, but the varied habitats of the Wolkberg Wilderness Area support a wide variety of wildlife. Bushpigs live in the forests, leopards roam the rocky crags; and other predators include caracal, African wild cat, civet, black-backed jackal, red jackal, hyena, Cape clawless otter, honey badger, hare, dassie, porcupine and genet. Out on the grasslands you can see reedbuck, klipspringer, rhebok, duiker and bushbuck; vervet and samango monkeys, baboons and the exquisite nocturnal lesser bushbaby. A total of 157 species of birds have been recorded here – such as the secretary bird, the black and martial eagles, the black-shouldered kite, the forest buzzard, the fork-tailed drongo, the hamerkop, the Goliath heron, various guineafowl, the black-fronted bush shrike and more.

People have roamed the Wolkberg for centuries: remains of dry-stone walls are evidence of Sotho settlements and archaeologists have found artefacts of early Iron Age people (ancestors of the Sotho) who lived in the area as far back as the fourth century AD. In fact, South Africa's oldest Iron Age site was found not far away, 16 km east of Tzaneen.

For hikers there is no formal trail to follow, but there is a large selection of management paths and jeep tracks to choose from. The public are obliged to use the Serala Forest Station entrance, which is a good place to set off from. A jeep track runs alongside the Klipdraai River, bypassing beautiful waterfalls that are well worth exploring.

The track reaches the Mohlapitse River where the turbulent waters have scoured amazing potholes into the rock. It is this river and its tributaries that, down the centuries, clawed deep gorges and valleys into the mountains, separating the Strydpoort from the northern Drakensberg and resulting in a landscape characterised by dramatic peaks and beautiful rock formations, spectacular waterfalls, deep ravines and valleys.

Wolkberg Wilderness Area at a glance (map page 246)

How to get there: From Johannesburg, take the N1 north to Pietersburg and from here take the R71 east for about 35 km, when you will turn right onto a gravel road. Continue on for about 9 km, until you finally come to a four-way intersection where you carry on straight ahead. After 14 km the road forks again, the right fork leading to Serala Forest Station 6 km along the road.

Weather: Warm to hot in summer with rain; mild to crisp in winter although frost appears overnight and snow could fall on the high peaks. Mist occurs all year round in the higher altitudes and strong, dry winds are common between July and October.

What to do: This is more a case of what you *can't* do: you may not hunt, fish, light fires or use soap or detergents in the rivers. However, visitors to the area are usually after a valid wilderness experience and hiking through the dramatic, unspoilt landscape, exploring the rivers, waterfalls, ravines and forests, more than compensates for the rules.

Special attractions: The potholes on the Mohlapitse River, Wonderwoud and the views from Serala Peak.

More information: Write to The Officer-in-Charge, Wolkberg Wilderness Area, Private Bag X102, Haenertsburg 0730; tel (0152222) 1303.

The Mohlapitse River is a tributary of the Letaba, and geologists have pronounced this an excellent example of river piracy: the Letaba cut through its own bank and intercepted the Mohlapitse River, stealing the headwaters and depriving the upper reaches of running water.

From the potholes hikers can follow the jeep track (which crosses the river several times) to the lowest point of the Wolkberg Wilderness Area and then continue up to Mampa's Kloof, where there is a choice of paths to Thabina Falls, Wonderwoud and Serala Peak.

Mampa's Kloof takes its name from a Sotho chief who lived in the area: a clump of bluegums marks the spot of a homestead that once belonged to a farmer called Van der Gryp, who settled in the area after he had lost everything in the Anglo-Boer War. Continue up Mampa's Kloof to the falls, where the Thabina River dives spectacularly over the edge of the escarpment and continues its journey far below until it is captured in a dam in Lebowa.

An alternative route from the potholes is to walk upstream along the Mohlapitse to the Shobwe River and follow a footpath to Wonderwoud. Inexperienced hikers should think twice before attempting the route over Devil's Knuckles (a row of quartzite cliffs also known as Tandberg or Ararat), which involves a fair amount of rock-climbing, preferably with the aid of a rope.

The Wonderwoud, also known as The Lost Forest, is about 500 ha of secluded forest blanketing the Shobwe catchment area. Pristine and untouched, a protective green canopy hides cool depths of lush vegetation including massive yellowwood trees, some with a circumference of more than 5 m.

From the forest there is a steep climb over Kruger's Nose to the Serala Plateau, through ravines bright with waterfalls and greenery. At just over 2 000 m above sea level, Serala Peak is the highest point in the Wolkberg Wilderness Area and offers incredible views back over Wonderwoud and Devil's Knuckles.

You can pick out Krugerskop, where Paul Kruger's face is seemingly etched in a mountain profile, the Wonderwoud forming his beard. Serala Peak is also the source of the Letsitele, a young river which impetuously plunges down a steep ravine between two peaks. From this point, hikers can either retrace their steps to the office at Serala or explore the network of footpaths that radiate outwards from Devil's Knuckles.

Where to stay

At the entry gate there is a small camp site with ablution facilities; otherwise, for hikers, accommodation is out in the open and a tent and a camping stove are essential.

A kloof of mists and secret enchantments

Situated 35 km directly south of Tzaneen is Magoebaskloof – a majestic realm of towering pine forests, deep gorges, cascading waterfalls and tranquil lakes

MAGOEBASKLOOF provides some of the most spectacularly verdant scenery to be found in the Transvaal. There is much for the traveller to see and do – with hikes and rambles through the glorious mountain terrain being a natural choice. Some of the dams are well stocked with fish, making this an attractive destination for anglers, while the rich vegetation of the area makes it a must for botanists, gardeners and other plant enthusiasts.

A veritable garden of Eden, this seemingly enchanted land produces crops of subtropical fruits, vegetables and flowers in amazing abundance. The lush vegetation of this area is really quite spectacular and reaches a colourful peak in September and October, when the kloof is ablaze with the hot hues of azalea blooms. This riot of colour is still in its full glory when the gentle pastels of the cherry blossom burst forth, creating a decidedly Impressionistic landscape.

The tiny hamlet of Haenertsburg is the main settlement of the Magoebaskloof area. It is named after C F Haenert, who discovered gold in the surrounding hills. Haenertsburg became a gold-rush village in 1887, but all is quiet there today, this little village seemingly having escaped the turmoil of the 20th century.

Although hiking is the best way to enjoy the splendours of Magoebaskloof, motoring through it enables you to cover a greater area – and you pass through rich farmlands with evocative names such as *Grey Mists, Cloudlands, Clear Waters* and *Whispering Winds.*

Most of these farms lie among the pine and indigenous state forests where yellowwood, wild peach, forest elder, ironwood, red stinkwood, cabbage tree, broom, cluster fig and the beautiful rooihart grow in a tangle of wild and often impenetrable undergrowth – so dense that only the sounds of the forest can be heard.

Further down, in the lower regions of the Magoebaskloof and the adjacent slopes of the escarpment, are the tea plantations which carpet the land in their rich green foliage. Tea growing began in Magoebaskloof in the 1960s, when Douglas Penhill, a Kenyan tea planter, settled in the area. With the help of the government, he started the Sapekoe Tea Estates ('pekoe' is Chinese for tea) and the area has been producing excellent quality tea ever since. During the picking season (September to May) the air is filled with the pungent scent of tea.

Motoring through Magoebaskloof is made especially interesting by the wide choice of routes that are available. Among the most scenic is the 12-km gravel drive that passes the Debengeni Falls (see separate entry) and the De Hoek Forestry Station, a route that takes you through cool forests and pine plantations, waterfalls and mountain streams, and one which affords unforgettable views of the lowveld below.

The winding road through Magoebaskloof affords the motorist some spectacular vistas of mountain and forest.

During September and October, flowering azalea bushes and blossoming cherry trees transform Magoebaskloof into a spectacular riot of spring colour.

The road takes you up to the top of the escarpment and past the Woodbush Forest, which boasts a spectacular variety of trees. Returning slowly, the traveller can meander via detours to the main Pietersburg-Magoebaskloof road, or past the trading station of Houtbosdorp to Duiwelskloof.

South of the main road at the summit of Magoebaskloof, two roads branch off and pass the Ebenezer Dam, built to stabilise the flow of the Letaba River. Here, amid glorious scenery dominated by the Wolkberg range, the road winds down to Tzaneen through George's Valley. This valley, which is an alternative route between Haenertsburg and Tzaneen, was named after a road builder, George Deneys, who took great pains to route his roads, with many a detour, lay-by and picnic spot, so that the traveller could appreciate fully the magnificent scenery.

Although motoring enables the visitor to cover the most ground, there is no better way of immersing yourself in the cool magic of the Magoebaskloof than to walk its slopes – possibly by way of the Dokolewa or Grootbosch hiking trails which involve three days of walking through the De Hoek and Woodbush state forests and dense mountain valleys. Groups of up to 20 hikers sleep in huts along the way, these being equipped with essentials such as firewood, cooking pots, lamps, bunks, mattresses, toilets and water. Hikers must provide their own food and sleeping bags.

The easier of the two trails is Dokolewa, which is 36 km long. The Grootbosch trail is hardier, covering 50 km and having an overnight hut only on the first night. On the remaining two nights, hikers sleep under the stars or in simple overnight shelters with no facilities at all. A maximum number of 12 hikers is allowed on this trail and hikers must provide their own food, lighting, first-aid equipment and sleeping bags.

Where to stay

The traveller may choose from a variety of hotels. The *Magoebaskloof Hotel* is set high in the misty hills to the west of Tzaneen, and offers 58 en-suite rooms. The vista across the wooded kloof to the lowveld plain beyond is stunning. Bookings and information: PO Magoebaskloof 0731; tel (0152222), ask for 82/83.

The *Troutwaters Inn* is a pleasant hotel overlooking its own lake (swimming, canoeing, boardsailing and, of course, trout fishing) in the forested Magoebaskloof area. Accommodation is in attractively decorated suites; some way along the hillside are chalets and a caravan/camping ground. Bookings and information: PO Magoebaskloof 0731; tel (0152222), ask for 53 or 80.

The *Coach House Inn* is regularly adjudged South Africa's best country hotel. The inn, overlooking the lovely New Agatha Forest, has 35 rooms, all with superb views, and prides itself on its personalised service. The cuisine is cordon bleu. Bookings and information: PO Box 544, Tzaneen 0850; tel (0152) 3073641.

Self-catering accommodation is available at the *Makutsi Spa* holiday resort near Tzaneen. Bookings and information: PO Box 598, Tzaneen 0850; tel (0152302), ask for 2402.

Magoebaskloof at a glance (map page 246)

How to get there: From Johannesburg and Pretoria take the N1 north to Pietersburg and the R71 east to Haenertsburg. The pass through the Magoebaskloof lies on the R71 between Haenertsburg and Tzaneen to the north east. The 97-km drive down the escarpment to Tzaneen is quite spectacular, dropping 600 m in just one 6-km stretch.
Weather: The Magoebaskloof area has hot summers, cold winters and high rainfall throughout the year.
What to do: Hiking, picnicking, fishing and swimming.
Special attractions: Cherry Blossom Time, a feature of the Magoebaskloof area's annual spring festival, takes place during the month of September at *Cheerio Halt*, a farm situated close to the town of Haenertsburg. The festival is also celebrated at the Magoebaskloof Hotel. Sapekoe Tea Estates offer conducted tours of their facilities from Tuesday to Friday – bear in mind that booking for the tours is essential. For information regarding the tours, contact Sapekoe, PO Box 576, Tzaneen 0850; tel (01523) 53241.
More information: For further information on the various hiking trails, write to: The Regional Director, Northern Transvaal Forest Region, Private Bag X2413, Louis Trichardt 0920; tel (01315) 41051.

Appealing, yet dangerous. The gentle gradient of the falls is deceptive and a number of people have lost their lives trying to slide down its slope.

A treacherous paradise at the 'place of the big pot'

Situated about 25 km west of Tzaneen, Debengeni Falls is set like a glittering jewel at the heart of a misty, primeval forest of indigenous trees

I F THERE ARE REALLY such things as water spirits, they must surely delight in inhabiting the Debengeni Falls, a cascade of slithery silver that glows magically through the swirling, early-morning mists of the surrounding forest.

When lovely Magoebaskloof was home to ba-Tsanene ('the people who live in small villages'), many lived close to the banks of this sometimes tranquil, sometimes angry river they called Rama-dipa, itself a tributary of the Great Letaba River that still carries its waters far to the east – to a coast and sea that existed then only in legend.

Ramadipa is also thought to have been the name of the chief, but, at first sight anyway, there seems to be no doubt about the origin of the name Debengeni – meaning 'place of the big pot'. Look at the big pool at the base of the falls: here, minute fragments of stone borne by the swirling waters have scoured away the rock, eventually forming a smooth natural basin that's ideal for a cooling swim. Incidentally, it's the only part of the falls that is safe to enter.

This pool could certainly be a 'big pot', but there's another story, one of votive offerings that used to be placed at night at the bottom of the falls. One of these – and nobody ever found out what it was – was placed in an enormous pot, on the very rim of the pool. When, eventually, a flood carried it away and smashed the rocks, the mystery – and the name – endured. (It's worth noting that, even today, such votive offerings to the spirits of the dead are left beside pools below waterfalls – the Phiphidi Falls on the Mutshindudi River in nearby Venda being an example.)

Sad to relate, there came to this lovely gorge the clang and cry of battle, as new settlers sought to displace others who were reluctant to move on and leave behind the graves of their fathers and grandfathers. And the greater gorge, in which the cutting made by the Ramadipa River is one of many such shady slashes in the rock, has been named after the loser, Makgoba (Magoeba).

The tranquillity for which he fought has returned and is perhaps at its most profound at Debengeni – for this is not a fall that thunders; rather, it slides sinuously down a sloping channel that has been polished smooth over the millennia. Here and there a small outcrop of some harder rock splits the channel and little rivulets, like fingers feeling their way, twist and writhe briefly before joining again on their downward course. The channel descends over a rocky distance of some 800 m, before the waters stir within the great pot at the bottom.

There's a temptation to ride the river by sitting firmly in the smooth channel and letting the water carry you on its cool course to the bottom. But the gentle ripples are deceptive, and the lazy flow is a great deal faster than it looks. Worse, the rock is hard and unforgiving of the slightest error, be it of balance or of judgement. Many people have died trying to ride the Debengeni Falls, or to climb their slippery cascade. But the greatest pleasure it offers is not reckless adventure – it's simply the joy of resting by its side.

Here are remnants of the great indigenous forests that once covered the deeper sands on the slopes of the Drakensberg Escarpment, and they cast a welcome shade over places ideal for picnics and for play. Here, too, are the exotics that settlers brought with them and planted, perhaps too rashly.

Massed ranks of exotic trees, such as the Indian mahogany, have assumed respectability in plantations, and the gentle green of tea, although strictly another alien, provides the eye with a wonderfully soothing hue. The indigenous tangle of trees, shrubs and creepers is close to impenetrable in parts, and gave the area the name of Woodbush, also rendered as Houtbos. The Debengeni Falls themselves lie within the De Hoek State Forest, and a very pleasant and scenic drive – when you leave the vicinity of the falls – is to continue along the road to the De Hoek Forestry Station.

Much of the forest area around Debengeni Falls consists of an impenetrable tangle of indigenous trees, bushes and creepers.

The road threads its way through plantations of pine and great stands of indigenous trees, including yellowwood, cabbage tree or kiepersol, ironwood and the red stinkwood that is related only by smell to the stinkwood of the southern Cape. Some wear beards of moss or tangles of creeper and, for sheer glamour and colour, are outshone by the exotics that thrive so well in sub-tropical Magoebaskloof.

Azaleas, frangipani and a variety of fruit trees – all of these grow well here and sport their flowers in spring, among the most breathtaking perhaps being the cherry trees. And apart from the trees and flowers, there are views far and wide over the lowveld, with here and there the shining ribbon of a river winding its course to the distant sea, sped on its way by the great slide and gently whirling pool of Debengeni Falls.

Debengeni Falls at a glance (map page 246)

How to get there: From Johannesburg take the N1 to Pietersburg. Turn east onto the R71 for Tzaneen. After some 85 km on the R71, turn left at the intersection with the R36. Four kilometres later turn left into the Magoebaskloof. A good gravel road leads upwards through plantations of Indian mahogany to the well-signposted entrance gate. The falls form part of the De Hoek State Forest which is administered by the Forestry Branch of the Department of Water Affairs. A small admission fee is charged.
Weather: Hot summers, often with high humidity, and mild winters. Rain falls and thunderstorms in summer.
What to do: Bird-watching, tree identification, picnicking, swimming in specified areas.
Facilities: Picnic spots, provided with stone braai places, wooden tables and benches. Toilets.
More information: The State Forester, De Hoek State Forest, Private Bag 4008, Tzaneen 0850; tel (01523) 53001.
Visiting times: The gates are open from 7 am to 6 pm.

Where to stay

There are several hotels to choose from in the Magoebaskloof area. These include: the *Magoebaskloof Hotel*, PO Magoebaskloof 0731; tel (0152222) 82/83/91; *Troutwaters Inn*, PO Magoebaskloof 0731; tel (0152222) 53; and the *Magoebaskloof Holiday Resort*, consisting of thatched, self-contained huts offering accommodation for up to six people. There is an à la carte restaurant. Contact the resort at PO Box 838, Tzaneen 0850; tel (01523) 53142/53147.

Camping is not permitted at the falls.

Mysterious domain of the Rain Queen

Near Tzaneen, in the northeastern Transvaal,
is the Modjadji Nature Reserve, a sub-tropical
paradise that is richly endowed with history and legend

BENEATH THE DRAKENSBERG escarpment in the northeastern Transvaal the countryside is distinguished by its lush picturesqueness. To many people, this is the real Africa, the dense, subtropical air heavy with the scents of exotic blooms and splintered with the tremor of cicadas and crickets. But there is more. For four centuries the area north of Duiwelskloof has been the habitat of the Modjadji, or Rain Queen.

It's over 100 years since the publication of Rider Haggard's famous novel *She,* which he based on the Modjadji, the legendary rain queen of the Lobedu, but time has done little to diminish her mystic reputation. Her mysterious history can be traced right back to the kingdom of Monomotapa in Zimbabwe 400 years ago, where a princess had to escape her father's wrath after having fallen pregnant by her half-brother. Blessed with her family's magical rain-making powers, she and some of her followers fled south and eventually settled in a forest of cycads.

There the Modjadji (as she was called) practised her art and as her power became increasingly evident, her influence began to spread. Other groups thought twice before tangling with the Rain Queen, and as a result, the Lobedu were unaffected by the wars that ripped through the Transvaal. In fact, so keen were neighbouring peoples to ingratiate themselves with the Modjadji, that they sent her a regular supply of gifts.

Although her people believed she was immortal, as the Modjadji aged it became increasingly obvious that she was not. Eventually she chose a successor to whom she passed on her rain-making secrets. Legend has it that, once this task was fulfilled, the old Modjadji had to commit suicide by drinking poison. A piece of the late queen's skin was considered vital to the success of the new Modjadji's rain-making ritual, and the use of this grisly component has persisted down through the generations.

The Lobedu have the distinction of being the only people in Africa with a female line of succession. Stories are rife that, in days gone by, once a man had done his duty of impregnating the queen, he would mysteriously vanish, as would any of the queen's male offspring.

Today the reigning Modjadji lives the same secluded life among her people; her sacred kraal in the hilly country near Duiwelskloof is surrounded by carved totems. She does not get involved in administrative matters and has appointed someone to act on her behalf. According to ancient custom, she is hardly ever seen, even by her own people. It might be possible, however, to engage a guide and try to get permission to observe the sacred kraal.

The kraal of the Modjadji. On the right is a tree that's considered by her people to be sacred. It's old and gnarled but continues to bear fresh, green leaves.

A row of cycads in the Modjadji Nature Reserve. These plants, sometimes referred to as 'living fossils', date right back to the age of the dinosaurs.

Above the kraal is a unique 305-ha forest of cycads which has been stringently protected by generations of Rain Queens. It was largely their vigilance which eventually led to the area being declared a national monument in 1936 and proclaimed a nature reserve in 1985.

This dense, primeval forest forms the world's largest plantation of a single cycad species, *Encephalartos transvenosus*. It is the most famous and largest of the cycads, usually reaching a height of about 5-8 m, but sometimes even exceeding the 13 m mark. With their bare trunks topped with 2 m-long lush, deep green leaves, these cycads are often mistaken for palms, although they are not even remotely related. Experts call them 'living fossils': they date back to the age of the dinosaurs, the Mezazoic Age some 50 or 60 million years ago, when they were particulary prolific all over the earth and probably formed a substantial part of the dinosaurian diet.

Another name for this plant is the *Modjadji-broodboom*, as the flesh in the trunks is a rich source of starch, and it has traditionally been used by the Lobedu and others to make a type of bread. Today, you can appreciate the cycads from close quarters on one of the many hiking trails that meander through the forest. None of the trails takes more than about two hours; along the way you can admire the colourful bird life and try to spot impala, blue wildebeest, nyala and kudu. There is also an attractive picnic and braai area with toilet facilities, curio shop, kiosk and information centre. About 5 km from the reserve is a nursery where you can buy cycads with the requisite permit.

Duiwelskloof is the town closest to the Modjadji's capital, and (coincidentally?) it enjoys a high annual rainfall. Set in an emerald green valley surrounded by dense forests, it is a rewarding area for the adventurous traveller, offering a superb variety of walks and drives.

A centre for the timber industry, the region is also known for the luscious tropical fruit it produces – mangoes, litchis, bananas, avocados, pawpaws, citrus fruit and tomatoes – the choicest examples of which are sold at very reasonable prices from roadside stalls. The town is renowned for its beautiful gardens and the streets are flamboyant with exotic flowering trees and shrubs. Bougainvilleas, potato trees, white and pink frangipanis, red coral trees, poinsettias, jacarandas, cassias, acacias and bauhinias turn this sub-tropical town into an ever-changing kaleidoscope all year round.

Where to stay

The *Imp Inn* is situated in Botha Street in Duiwelskloof. Write to PO Box 17, Duiwelskloof 0835; tel (01523) 9253.

The *Duiwelskloof Holiday Resort* is well situated in lush greenery near a lovely waterfall. It is a well-equipped caravan park and there are also rondavels for hire. There is a swimming pool and a large playground for children. Write to PO Box 36, Duiwelskloof 0835; tel (01523) 9651.

Modjadji Nature Reserve at a glance (map page 246)

How to get there: From Johannesburg, take the N1 north to Pietersburg, where you turn off onto the R71. This road eventually leads to Tzaneen, from where you head north on the R36 to Duiwelskloof. The Modjadji Nature Reserve is well signposted from here.

Weather: It can get very hot here in summer, with welcome thunderstorms. Winters are mild to cold and dry, but with frost overnight.

What to do: In the town of Duiwelskloof there are facilities for bowls, tennis, swimming, golf (18 holes), squash and badminton. Anglers can try for barbel, bass and blue kurper in the nearby Merensky, Fanie Botha and Ebenezer dams.

Special attractions: The primeval forest – the world's largest plantation of a single cycad species.

More information: SA Tourism Board, cnr Vorster and Landdros Maré streets, Pietersburg 0699; tel (01521) 3025. Duiwelskloof Municipality, PO Box 36, Duiwelskloof 0835; tel (01523) 9246; Department of Agriculture and Environmental Conservation, Private Bag X27, Chuenespoort 0745; tel (0156) 24145.

Scenic hot springs deep in the bushveld

Perennial springs, an evocative Tsonga 'living museum' and bushveld where the antelope roam – these are just some of the attractions of the Hans Merensky Nature Reserve, 66 km northeast of Tzaneen

THE HANS MERENSKY NATURE RESERVE is a 5 200-ha expanse of bushveld that is a sanctuary for a range of wildlife that, if not as prolific and spectacular as you'll find in the world-famous Kruger National Park, nevertheless has its own fascination. The best time to visit the reserve is during the dry winter months, when ground cover dies back, trees thin out and the animals gather around the dams and waterholes.

Situated within the reserve is Aventura Eiland, a well-organised, popular resort on the banks of the Great Letaba River, across the way from a 35-ha island in the middle of the river. It comprises a hundred or so comfortable, self-contained rondavels scattered around tree-shaded lawns, a caravan park, a restaurant, an entertainment hall, shops, tennis

The reserve is well stocked with giraffe – in fact it was originally established for the breeding and conservation of these animals.

courts, riding stables – and swimming pools whose mineral-rich waters heal the body (or so it's said) and calm the nerves. There are four pools in all – one indoors, built over the spring itself, and three outdoors (warm, cold and children's) – together with saunas and bubble-jet baths.

One of the highlights of Aventura Eiland is a visit to the nearby Tsonga kraal open-air museum, a reconstruction of a typical settlement consisting of headman's quarters, sleeping huts, cooking shelter, grain store, a sacrificial site and areas specially set aside for cattle, goats and poultry. The residents, dressed in traditional garb, give demonstrations of pottery, woodcraft, basketry, hut-building and the ancient arts of music and dance.

The resort and the nature reserve are run as separate entities, the latter by the Chief Directorate of Nature and Environmental Conservation. Visitors are permitted to drive within the conservation area, and there are bus tours and sunset drives at set times (a special programme is laid on during the Transvaal school holidays). Displays at the visitor centre, close to Aventura Eiland, will introduce you to the reserve, its animals, birds and plants.

The nature reserve was proclaimed in 1954 and is named after Dr Hans Merensky, a one-time local farmer and philanthropist. One of his many endowments and donations was the gift of a fully equipped borehole system to the new conservation area abutting the Great Letaba River.

The countryside within the Hans Merensky reserve is flattish, covered by typical lowveld bush – a mixture of grassland and mopane and combretum woodland, with scatters of red bushwillow and marula, knobthorn, jackalberry, tamboti, rock fig and Transvaal candelabra tree. Here and there you find the tree orchid *Ansella gigantea*, an epiphytic species (it uses the host tree only for support) that is rigorously protected in the Transvaal.

Towards the east, the skyline is broken by a series of low ridges known as the Black Hills because of their darkish colour – a product of their relatively high iron, calcium and magnesium content. Leopard stalk these outcrops, though they are few in number and seldom seen.

Far more numerous and visible are the reserve's game: the area was originally set aside to conserve and breed giraffe and the rare and handsome sable antelope, and these animals still roam the veld, together with Burchell's zebra, blue wildebeest, waterbuck and bushbuck in the riverine areas, impala, kudu, steenbok and duiker, baboon and warthog. Among the nocturnal species are spotted

The Aventura Eiland resort, situated within the reserve, is well-known for its therapeutic mineral pools.

hyaena and black-backed jackal, civet, caracal, serval, genet, antbear, porcupine, honey-badger and the endearing little bushbaby, or night-ape, an animal that can sometimes be seen in the dense stands of trees during the day, sleeping cuddled together in family groups.

Nearly 300 different kinds of birds have been identified within the Hans Merensky Reserve, among them the martial eagle, the magnificent bateleur and other raptors and, along the riverine reaches, African fish eagle, cormorant, heron and stork, jacana, sandpiper and colourful kingfisher. One of the rarer local species is Arnot's chat.

Perhaps the best way of exploring the reserve, though, is on foot, along one of the four walking trails that have been laid out. Among these is the gentle circular Mopane Interpretive Route, named after one of the lowveld's most common trees. This is the shortest walk – the 1,2 km takes a leisurely hour – and some of the tree species you'll see on the way along it are described in an informative booklet.

The Letaba Nature Trail, also short, offers a stroll through the dense riverine bush of the reserve's northern section (but keep a cautious eye open for hippo and croc). Rather more demanding is the Waterbuck Route, a 4-hour, 11-km hike that embraces a dam and its attendant game-viewing hide. A permit must be obtained from the Nature Conservation office before commencing the trail. Among the animals you can expect to see is the bulky (270-kg), shaggy-coated antelope (*Kobus ellipsiprymnus*) from which the walk takes its name.

The longest of the trails is the Giraffe, a 32-km route through the extensive southern portion of the reserve. This takes three days to complete, though if you're feeling energetic you can cover the ground in two days – or alternatively, if time is short, tackle only two of the three sections. There are good views of the Black Hills en route. The camp in which trailists spend their nights is set beside a dam and comprises three thatched huts all equipped with mattresses, a braai area, a cold-water shower and a flush toilet.

Where to stay

Accommodation within the reserve is available at the *Aventura Eiland* resort, which offers one- and two-bedroomed air-conditioned rondavels, all with fully equipped kitchens, many with full bathrooms. All have verandas (some enclosed) and braai areas. There is also a well-served caravan/camping ground (450 sites). Visitor amenities include mineral pools, restaurant, shops, entertainment hall, sporting facilities. Bookings and information: Overvaal Eiland, Central Reservations, PO Box 3046, Pretoria 0001; tel (012) 3462277; or contact The Resort Manager, Aventura Eiland, Private Bag 527, Letsitele 0855; tel (0152) 38667 or 38759.

Hans Merensky Nature Reserve at a glance (map page 246)

How to get there: By road from Johannesburg/Pretoria: take the N1 highway north to Pietersburg (distance from Pretoria: 277 km), east on the R71 to Tzaneen (91 km) and on to the junction with the R529 (27 km), which leads northeast to the Hans Merensky Nature Reserve (38 km) – a total distance of 433 km.
Weather: The region's climate is sub-tropical, with the rains falling during the summer months (November to March). Summer days are hot and humid, with daytime temperatures averaging 36˚C; nights are cooler. Winter days are dry and sunny, with nights tending to be chilly and occasionally downright cold.
What to do: Game viewing, bird-watching, tree identification, walks and hikes and drives farther afield.
Special attractions: Within the Hans Merensky Nature

Reserve is the Tsonga kraal open-air museum; the Aventura Eiland resort offers mineral pools, sport and entertainment.
Special precautions: Prudent visitors will take a course of anti-malaria tablets before setting out. The bilharzia snail is a hazard of the rivers and dams. Beware of crocodile and hippo in the waters of the Great Letaba River.
More information: For further details of the reserve, and to book a place on the Giraffe Hiking Trail, contact The Officer-in-Charge, Hans Merensky Nature Reserve, Private Bag X502, Letsitele 0885; tel (0152) 38632/3/4/5. Reservations for the bus tours and the Tsonga kraal open-air museum may be made in situ, at the visitors' centre or telephone (0152) 38727. For information on the Aventura Eiland resort, contact the Resort Manager or Overvaal Central Reservations (see 'Where to stay' panel).

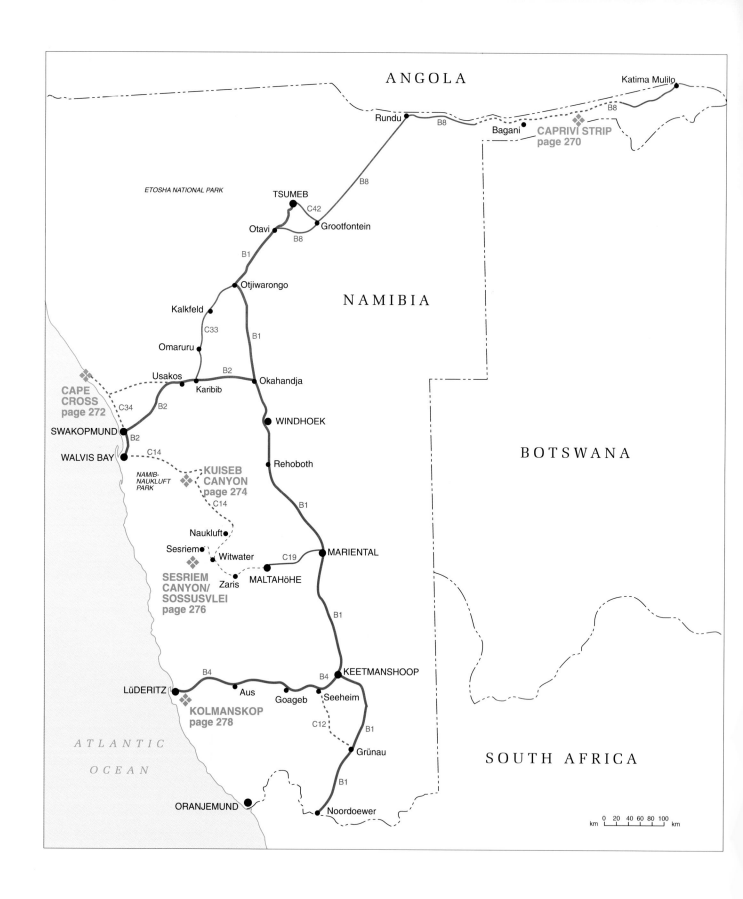

ANGOLA

Katima Mulilo

Rundu · B8 · Bagani · B8 · CAPRIVI STRIP page 270

ETOSHA NATIONAL PARK

TSUMEB · C42
Otavi · Grootfontein
B8
B1

NAMIBIA

Otjiwarongo

Kalkfeld
C33 · B1
Omaruru

Usakos · B2 · Okahandja
CAPE CROSS page 272 · C34 · B2 · Karibib
SWAKOPMUND · B2
WALVIS BAY · C14

WINDHOEK

BOTSWANA

Rehoboth

NAMIB-NAUKLUFT PARK · KUISEB CANYON page 274
C14

Naukluft
Sesriem · Witwater · C19 · MARIENTAL
SESRIEM CANYON/ SOSSUSVLEI page 276 · Zaris · MALTAHöHE

B1

B1

B4 · B4 · KEETMANSHOOP
LüDERITZ · Aus · Goageb · Seeheim
KOLMANSKOP page 278 · C12 · B1

ATLANTIC

OCEAN

Grünau

SOUTH AFRICA

B1

ORANJEMUND · Noordoewer

0 20 40 60 80 100
km   km

NAMIBIA

A land of mighty rivers and big game

Discover one of the world's last unspoilt animal kingdoms in the Caprivi Strip, a sliver of land between northeast Namibia and northwest Zimbabwe

Where to stay

The *Zambezi Lodge* (PO Box 98, Katima Mulilo 9000, Namibia, tel (067352) 203) has modern accommodation and limited facilities for camping. Kalizo Safaris has three lodges – one near Katima Mulilo and two on the Kwando River. Contact their office in Johannesburg, PO Box 343, Randburg 2125; tel (011) 8864067. For reservations at *Lianshulo Lodge* in the Mudumu Game Reserve, contact Wilderness Safaris, PO Box 651171, Benmore 2010; tel (011) 8841458. Bungalows and camping facilities are available in Rundu at *Kaisosi Safari Lodge*, PO Box 599, Rundu 9000; tel (067372) 265.

Caprivi is a developing area for tourism. For an update on accommodation available in game parks and nature reserves, contact the Director of Tourism, Reservations, Private Bag 13267, Windhoek 9000; tel (061) 36975.

NOTHING HIDES the natural beauty of a stretch of land as effectively as a war. For almost two decades the Caprivi Strip was a battleground in the bush war that preceded Namibia's independence. However, when peace came to the region in 1989, this strategic sliver of land began to offer up its secrets and surprises again to those who sought them.

The Caprivi Strip is, first of all, a land of rivers – and thus represents an enormous contrast with that part of Namibia situated between the Namib and Kalahari deserts. Caprivi shares the Zambezi River with Zambia and the Kwando, Linyati and Chobe rivers with Botswana. And though it is politically part of Namibia, it belongs geographically in the tropics of central Africa, where the vegetation grows lush and green.

The unusual name is not of African derivation, but honours General Count Georg von Caprivi di Caprara di Montecuccoli, who succeeded Otto von Bismarck as Chancellor of Germany in 1890, and during whose term of office this area was ceded to Germany as Caprivi-Zipfel.

Much as it was Britain's imperial ambition to possess territory stretching across Africa from the Cape to Cairo, so Germany hoped to link its southwest African colony with its possessions in East

Flat flood plains are the dominant geographical characteristic of most of the Caprivi Strip area.

Africa. The narrow strip of Caprivi was the closest they came to fulfilling that vision.

Geographically, the Caprivi Strip is like an arm with its outstretched hand reaching to the African interior. In the west, between the Kavango and Kwando rivers, is the Caprivi Game Park, proclaimed in 1966 and currently undergoing rehabilitation following the war and a large-scale settlement of refugees. In the east, though, the palm of the hand lies open to reveal a vast wonderland of woodland and flood plain.

Travelling from the west, along the tarred road known as the Golden Highway, you encounter thick woodland, with mopane, silver terminalia, red syringa and Rhodesian teak as the dominant trees, their spreading crowns carried high. To the north of the road, vast areas have been proclaimed a forestry reserve. However, by far the greater part of eastern Caprivi consists of flood plain. Each year the great Zambezi River swells and spreads its waters to cover up to 250 000 ha of the grassy plains, with small, temporary islands here and there occupied by groups of nomadic farmers. At times of greater floods, when even these hillock islands disappear, these subsistence workers of both the land and the water trek out to the edge of the flood waters, in which fish – up to 92 species – breed prolifically.

Most of the inhabitants of Caprivi, such as the Masubia, Mbukushu and Matotela peoples, have their roots elsewhere. Their common language is Lozi (this being a mixture of Sotho, Tswana and various Zambian languages), but English is also widely spoken.

It is in eastern Caprivi that, recently, two national parks have been proclaimed. These are Mudumu National Park, which borders on the Kwando River, and Mamili National Park, between the Kwando and Linyati rivers.

Mudumu is mainly representative of the woodland region and provides a safe haven for growing numbers and species of animals that include elephant, lion, roan and sable antelope, Chapman's zebra, tsessebe and reedbuck.

Mamili, in its lush riverine setting, consists of densely vegetated islands surrrounded by reed swamps and the waving grasslands of the flood plain. Elusive but ever present are lion and leopard, and the shy sitatunga. Here roam great herds of buffalo and lechwe, while elephant, hippo, reedbuck and kudu are also seen. Crocodile lurk here too, as they do in almost all the waters – swimming in the rivers of Caprivi is extremely inadvisable.

The area is a birdwatchers' paradise and the species you may see include Narina trogon, African

Clouds blaze with colour as the sun sets behind the Kavango River near Popa Falls.

finfoot, osprey, western banded snake eagle, brightly coloured bee-eater and kingfisher, heron, crane, and hosts of other waterfowl. Angling, too, is a major attraction in Caprivi and, while sportsmen are divided over the fighting qualities of bream and tigerfish, and the patient skills needed to land them, at least it can be said that bream is the more palatable.

The principal town of Caprivi is Katima Mulilo, which means, 'I extinguish the light'. This name derives from its situation on the banks of the Zambezi, and the funnel-like wind effects created by the night-time cooling of land and water that are said to be strong enough to blow out fires. Accommodation here ranges from the sophisticated 'international' to the distinctly 'African'.

A novel feature of one of the lodges is a floating bar that allows patrons to sip their sundowners while trailing their toes in the Zambezi.

Most places offer camping facilities as well as more conventional accommodation, and this choice is also available in the national parks themselves. At Nakatwa in Mudumu, and at Liadura and Sishika in Mamili, though, facilities are charmingly described as 'basic'. They have no infrastructure other than what nature provides – shade and running water. Not even the hardiest can hope to get much closer to nature than that!

It was its strategic position that once brought Caprivi its wartime prominence. One can only hope that any future prominence will be associated with peace and tranquillity.

Caprivi Strip at a glance (map page 268)

How to get there: To travel to the Caprivi Game Park, take the B8 east from Rundu. The park is situated along the B8 between Bagani (206 km east of Rundu) and Kongola (117 km west of Katima Mulilo). The B8 continues from Kongola to the main town of Katima Mulilo – which is also accessible by road from Francistown in Botswana and from Victoria Falls in Zimbabwe.
Weather: Summers are hot and humid and are accompanied by most of the annual rainfall, in the form of thundershowers, between October and April. The milder winters are pleasantly warm but the nights are chilly.
What to do: View the prolific wildlife in the area.
Special attractions: At Katima Mulilo the Zambezi River offers many opportunities for recreation, such as fishing and bird-watching.
More information: Contact the Ministry of Wildlife, Conservation and Tourism, Private Bag 13306, Windhoek 9000, Namibia; tel (061) 63131.

Cape Cross took its name from the half-ton stone cross that was erected here by the Portuguese explorer, Diego Cao. It has since been replaced with a granite replica, and another commemorative cross.

Historic landing point of the early Portuguese explorers

Seals and other creatures find a home amid the elemental beauty of Cape Cross, situated at the southernmost end of Namibia's infamous Skeleton Coast

Where to stay

Cape Cross has drinking water and toilets but no accommodation. Try camping at Mile 108 (north of Cape Cross) or Mile 72 (10 km south) – these are basic sites with toilets and hot showers. Each has a filling station, firewood and an airstrip.

Henties Bay has the *Hotel De Duine,* which has 10 rooms, three with en-suite bathrooms. Write to PO Box 1, Henties Bay 9000; tel (06442) 1. Also in Henties Bay is *Die Oord Rest Camp* which has 15 bungalows for hire. Write to PO Box 82, Henties Bay 9000; tel (06442) 239.

IN 1486 – more than half a millennium ago – a party of Portuguese sailors paddled ashore from their caravel at a rocky outcrop on the southwest coast of Africa. The leader of the fleet, explorer Diego Cao, was able to congratulate himself on having travelled further south than any other European before him.

As evidence of how far his fleet had come, his men erected a *padrao* here, a huge stone cross standing 3 m high and weighing half a ton. However, despite this triumphant gesture, this point – which became known as Cape Cross – marked the end of Cao's dream of finding a sea-route around Africa. Soon after setting sail again, he died and the fleet returned home.

The *padrao* stood in lonely isolation in this deserted spot for centuries until it was spotted in 1846, 1848 and, more than thirty years later, in 1879 by various captains plying these waters in search of guano deposits. In 1893, when Germany was in the process of annexing *Deutsch-Südwestafrika*, Captain Becker of the *Falke* came to Cape Cross and found the *padrao*. Mindful of its historic significance, he took it on board his ship and in its place erected a wooden cross 5 m high. This was eventually replaced with a granite replica of the original *padrao*, which today stands in the *Museum für Deutsche Geschichte* in Berlin.

This isolated cape is best known for its large breeding colonies of Cape fur seals. Every November and December roughly 200 000 seals converge here to mate. Preparations begin in October when the bulls begin establishing their territories and harems, though not without several vicious fights. After the mating season, the bulls once more head off to the ocean, while the cows remain in the colony, looking after the pups. Despite this being a reserve, these seals are culled annually for their

The large colony of seals at Cape Cross has to be continually on its guard against predators, such as jackals and roving packs of hyaenas.

pelts, and the carcasses are turned into meat, fat, bone meal and liver oil.

A delicate marine eco-system exists in this area, with seals, cormorants, brown hyaenas and black-backed jackals being an integral part of this system. Cape Cross is a breeding ground for a small sea bird, the Damara tern, which is considered to be an important part of this eco-system. Unfortunately the increase in offroad driving near the nesting areas disturbs the terns' breeding and, if this continues, they could become extinct within the next decade.

This part of the central Namib Coast is one of the foggiest places on earth and, although the desert appears to be dry and lifeless, the fog sustains a unique variety of flora and fauna which includes species that are not found anywhere else on earth. Cape Cross and its surrounds fall within a region, stretching from Swakopmund to Terrace Bay, that has the most extensive fields of lichen in the world. Again, however, offroad vehicles have been something of a scourge in this area – being largely responsible for damaging these exquisite lichens which flourish on the gravel plains, casting a wonderful greenish sheen over them during the early mornings. Once damaged, these lichens may never fully recover. Consequently, anyone using an offroad vehicle in this area must stay on established tracks to minimise destruction of the lichen.

Although completely colonised by seals and birds, the region bears some evidence of human industry. Rock salt is mined at Cape Cross, which is renowned for its large saltpans: in some places, solid rock salt reaches down as far as 25 m. Guano is another regional 'crop' and is harvested annually from man-made guano platforms. These have a surface area of about 70 000 sq m and attract huge flocks of sea birds, especially Cape cormorants. The Damaraland Guano Company was formed here in 1895 and a locomotive and railway were needed to work the guano deposits. As a result, Cape Cross became the first point in Namibia to have a railway line, this having been built nearly 100 years ago. The railway operated for 11 years until the company folded, and was simply abandoned. Ghostly outlines of the railway track and sleepers can still be seen marching out across the saltpans.

The desolation of this coastline is echoed in the stark, functional names of angling spots along the way. Heading north from Cape Cross, you'll come to Mile 87, Horingbaai and Mile 108. More hospitable is Henties Bay – a small village resort comprising some shops, garages, tearooms, bungalows and a hotel – situated about 50 km south of Cape Cross. It claims to be one of Namibia's finest fishing areas, with crayfish, kabeljou, steenbras and galjoen found in abundance here. There are also seasonal shoals of pilchards and anchovies.

Cape Cross at a glance (map page 268)

How to get there: From Swakopmund there is only one coastal road, the C34, heading north. Cape Cross is about 129 km from Swakopmund along this road.

Weather: The coastline has a moderate climate, influenced by the cold Benguela current. Fogs roll inland for up to 50 km but usually disperse by noon. Nights can be very cold, so take warm clothes, even in summer.

What to do: Most people who visit these shores are keen anglers, but others come just to experience the incredible stark beauty of the Namib Coast, with the seal colony being a bonus. Beachcombing can be a rewarding pursuit, with semiprecious stones among the rocks and a variety of flotsam from passing ships washed up on the sand.

Special attractions: The wilderness and wide open spaces.

More information: Write to The Director of Tourism, Ministry of Wildlife, Conservation and Tourism, Private Bag 13267, Windhoek 9000; tel (061) 36975/6/7/8.

Visiting times: The seal reserve is open between 10 am and 5 pm all year, every day except Fridays.

Elongated oasis in the world's oldest desert

The Namib Desert is not lacking in unusual natural attractions; indeed, the Kuiseb Canyon in the northern Namib is a unique geological phenomenon

FOR MILLENNIA, the waters of the Kuiseb River relentlessly gouged down through the soft surface rock of the Namib, shaping a canyon that is dramatic in its beauty and isolation. Steep-sided and precarious, the most striking feature of this canyon is the apparent *absence* of the river that created it.

Today the Kuiseb is in fact a subterranean river, surfacing only in a very few places. However, a narrow band of green vegetation tracks the river's passage beneath the ground and a surprising variety of plants and animals flourish along this oasis-like corridor. There are camel-thorn acacias, whose roots can penetrate the ground for more than 15 m in search of water, and wild figs, tamarisk and ebony trees, which provide food for various animals and birds such as springbok, gemsbok, zebra, jackal, hyaena, baboon and ostrich. The sharp-eyed observer will also spot the fascinating microcosm of smaller life, including beetles and other insects. At sunset, listen for the tick-ticking sound of the barking gecko.

Living side by side with the wildlife, Topnaar Khoikhoi have made this desolate canyon their home for generations, and today a group of approximately 200 still live here. They dig wells for their water, herd goats and some cattle, and harvest the indigenous nara melon, a nutritious fruit that has a reputation for being an aphrodisiac. The nara ripens in summer and the pulp is cooked, dried and then stored for later usage. The dried seeds have a pleasant nutty flavour. Each family guards its nara melon clumps jealously, although they do not actively cultivate them.

Geologists consider the Kuiseb River to be one of nature's unique spectacles: so much so that it was clearly visible from space to astronauts of the American space capsule *Gemini V* when they orbited Earth in the Sixties. Photographs taken on that mission show the narrow band of the Kuiseb as a clear division between the Namib's southern sands and the northern gravel plains.

This narrow, subterranean river is alone responsible for holding back the world's highest dunes, which prevailing winds are driving ever northwards. Year after year the sands push relentlessly forward, fighting for a foothold in the gorge, from where they could colonise the gravel plains and advance towards Angola. But this onslaught is perpetually thwarted: the sand that mounts up in the gorge is inevitably washed to the sea by the flash floods that sweep down from the highlands.

The Kuiseb Canyon is part of Namibia's largest reserve, the Namib-Naukluft Park. Precious water from the Kuiseb supplies mining areas such as Rössing, Walvis Bay and Swakopmund. In fact, one of the functions of scientists at the Namib Desert Research Station at Gobabeb is to keep a careful check on its subterranean flow. Were the river to

Kuiseb Canyon at a glance (map page 268)

How to get there: From Walvis Bay, take the C14 in an easterly direction. After nearly 200 km there is a turn-off to the Kuiseb Canyon. The C26 from Windhoek also leads to the canyon. There are good gravel roads all over the Namib-Naukluft Park.
Weather: Fairly typical of the desert, dry and very hot in summer but cool at night. Winters are mild and sunny but it can get very cold after dark and drop to freezing just before dawn.
What to do: Explore the canyon, and watch birds and game. Angling is possible at Sandvis, except between January and April.
Special attractions: The uniqueness of the surroundings.
More information: The Director of Tourism, Ministry of Wildlife Conservation and Tourism, Private Bag 13267, Windhoek, Namibia; tel (061) 3-6975/6/7/8. Windhoek Publicity Association, PO Box 1868, Windhoek; tel (061) 228160.

A clump of trees provides a striking contrast to the brown, domed hills of the Namib Desert's Kuiseb Canyon.

This rock formation in desolate Kuiseb Canyon stretches far into the distance.

dry up, there would be an ecological disaster – the green belt in the river valley would vanish along with the animals and birds, and the dunes would at last cross the great divide.

Near the Atlantic coast, the Kuiseb dissolves into a sandy delta, allowing the dunes to break ranks and head north. But water continues to flow beneath the surface and percolates through the sand, only emerging at the huge lagoon at Sandvis. The Sandvis area used to be known as Sandwich Harbour, and a legend persists that the lagoon conceals a fortune. Two hundred years ago the bay was a refuge from the wild Atlantic where ships anchored to ride out a storm or carry out repairs. Apparently a sailing ship carrying a large amount of treasure was abandoned here after becoming stranded in the sands of the lagoon in 1770. But legend this must remain, because, despite strenuous efforts to find some evidence, the lagoon refuses to yield even a hint of the ship or its precious cargo.

Today, the lagoon is an isolated reserve in an area accessible only by four-wheel-drive vehicles. The river water from the Kuiseb dilutes the lagoon, and the low level of salinity results in a unique ecosystem. Reeds and grasses proliferate around the lagoon edges, and a huge variety of both coastal and freshwater birds (more than 100 species) flourish in the shallow waters and feast on fish left behind by the retreating tide. And yet, despite the depredation by the birds, the lagoon is a major breeding area for a variety of fish.

Anyone wanting to visit this habitat requires a permit – contact the Director of Tourism (see address in other panel). As no vehicles are allowed within the reserve, visitors may enter only on foot.

Where to stay

There is a rudimentary camp at Kuiseb Canyon, but as it offers no facilities except 'long drop' toilets, you should arrive well equipped. However, anyone should try to experience at least one night in the magical stillness and purity of this section of the Namib.

Visitors to Sandvis can easily find accommodation at Walvis Bay, where there are four hotels: *Casa Mia Hotel,* PO Box 1786, Walvis Bay; tel (0642) 5975; *Mermaid Hotel*, PO Box 1763, Walvis Bay: tel (0642) 6212; *Flamingo Hotel*, PO Box 30, Walvis Bay; tel (0642) 3011; and the *Atlantic Hotel*, PO Box 46, Walvis Bay; tel (0642) 2811.

The *Golden Fish Guest House* offers homely accommodation. Contact them at PO Box 577, Walvis Bay; tel (0642) 2775. There are two municipal caravan parks in the Walvis Bay area, one in the town and another, *Langstrand*, some 20 km north of Walvis Bay. For more information contact the Municipality, PO Box 86, Walvis Bay; tel (0642) 5981. *Esplanade Park*, with its luxury bungalows and limited number of caravan sites, can be reached at Private Bag 5017, Walvis Bay; tel (0642) 6145.

Copper-coloured dunes at Sossusvlei set against the blue-grey backdrop of the Naukluft Mountains.

Where the dunes have more colours than a rainbow

Follow the course of the Tsauchab River from Sesriem Canyon to Sossusvlei in the Namib-Naukluft Park

IT IS CHARACTERISTIC of the harsh Namibian landscape that Sossusvlei will reveal its dramatic beauty only to visitors prepared to make a considerable effort in exchange. This wild and singularly beautiful part of the Namib-Naukluft Park is surrounded by the highest sanddunes in the world, so unless you have access to a four-wheel-drive vehicle, a 4-km walk through soft dune sand is the only way to get there.

The park is the largest of Namibia's nature conservation areas and the fourth-largest national park in the world; its vast size means that several different geological features and eco-systems exist within its confines. Sossusvlei lies more or less dead-centre, west of the Naukluft Mountains, about 380 km southwest of Windhoek and 60 km beyond the Sesriem Canyon.

Sesriem is a deep, narrow canyon scoured into the rock over the centuries by the Tsauchab River. The river rises south of the Naukluft and, when in flood, used to reach the Atlantic Ocean – but now reaches a final dead end in the desert dunefield of Sossusvlei.

No one knows where the vlei got its strangely melodious name, but Sesriem owes *its* unusual name to the survival skills of the early settlers. The word Sesriem means 'six thongs' and refers to the fact that in the early days it took six ox-wagon thongs joined together to make enough line from the rim of the gorge to the river bed below in order to scoop up a bucket of water.

No such ingenuity is required of the modern visitor. Sesriem Canyon has a beautiful rest camp with 10 sites and full ablution facilities. Limited numbers per site means that you are assured of the

In contrast to the predominantly bare desert landscape above, the floor of the Sesriem Canyon is a long, extended oasis.

tranquillity necessary truly to enjoy this area. As it is the only rest camp within easy reach of Sossusvlei, you should plan to spend at least two nights here, so that you have time to explore both of these spectacular features of the Tsauchab River fully.

The canyon is easily accessible from the camp, with strategically placed steps chiselled into the natural rock. The canyon itself is at first hardly visible in the calcrete plain – until you look down into its depths at the river that lies far below. An oasis has evolved in the river bed: because of the shade and shelter of the canyon, many plants – and even a few quite large trees – grow there, and these and the pools of water on its gravel bed attract numerous species of birds and small animals.

The canyon is 1,5 km long and varies in width at the top from 1,75 to 2,5 m. In places it is so narrow that a grown man can stand astride it, but this is a feat only the most sure-footed should attempt – it's a 30-m plunge to the bottom of the gorge.

From its abrupt beginning near the mountain, the canyon becomes increasingly wider and shallower until it once again merges with the sandy flats beyond. At Sossusvlei the river runs dry.

From Sesriem the vlei is a 59-km drive and a 4-km march away. The gravel road takes you through breathtaking dune scenery – the blue of mountains, yellow of grasslands and red of sand-dunes preparing you for the visual pleasures ahead.

It's a hard climb to the top of the highest dunes in the world, but it's an effort that is richly rewarded by views that stretch all the way to the ocean. The pan is surrounded by star dunes, monumental piles of sand with four or five crests, rising to a height of more than 350 m. Although the vegetation is sparse, it nevertheless attracts gemsbok, springbok and ostrich, and – when a good rainy season results in the Tsauchab River flowing into the pan – a variety of aquatic birds.

Sossusvlei is most dramatic at sunrise and sunset: in the early morning or late afternoon light the dunes change their colour from light sand to deep brick and even purple. Indeed, Sossusvlei transforms itself almost hourly, as Namibian photographer Amy Schoeman describes it, 'from ivory, yellow-gold and ochre to rose, maroon and deep brick-red, paling and deepening as the day progresses'.

Although no camping is allowed here, the times of entry to and exit from the Sesriem rest camp have been adjusted to allow visitors to Sossusvlei to take advantage of its complete spectrum of light and colour and to take home some truly spectacular photographs.

Many first-time visitors to Namibia find that this arid landscape is an acquired taste. But what seems at first inhospitable and desolate soon reveals itself as a fascinating dialogue of space and light, plants and people, sandy dunes and ocean breakers, animals and birds. After Sesriem and Sossusvlei have initiated you, why not explore the rest of the Namib-Naukluft Park? It covers no less than 4,9 million hectares, of which you have only just seen a strip 60 km long!

Where to stay

At Sesriem Canyon there is a rest camp with full ablution facilities but no bungalows, and only motor fuel and wood are available. There are only 10 camping sites and no more than eight people may occupy one site. Reservations should therefore be made well in advance, especially during school holidays, by writing to the Director of Tourism, Reservations, Private Bag 13267, Windhoek 9000, Namibia; tel (061) 36975. If you are in Windhoek, you'll find the reservation office in the Oude Voorpost building on the corner of John Meinert and Moltke streets.

Sesriem Canyon and Sossusvlei at a glance (map page 268)

How to get there: From Windhoek travel south towards Keetmanshoop, turning west towards Maltahöhe at Mariental. After Maltehöhe the road to Sesriem traverses the Zarishoogte Pass. From Sesriem, Sossusvlei lies a further 63 km to the west.
Weather: Be sure to pack lots of suntan lotion and a nice warm sleeping bag. The winter days are temperate and summer days are very hot, but nights can be cold throughout the year.

What to do: From your base at Sesriem Canyon, make a day excursion to Sossusvlei.
Special attractions: Breathtaking changes in colour and light account for the beauty of Sossusvlei, so don't be in a hurry – this drama takes time to unfold.
Visiting hours: Sesriem restricts entry between sunset and sunrise but bends the rules for visitors to Sossusvlei.
Further information: Contact Namibia Tourism, Private Bag 13346, Windhoek 9000; tel (061) 220241.

An eerie ghost town embraced by sand

*The abandoned settlement of Kolmanskop,
10 km east of Lüderitz, is one of the strangest,
most surrealistic scenes you're ever likely to encounter*

IT HAS ALL THE HALLMARKS of an enigmatic dream: a once vibrant town now devoid of life, its sumptuous homes making their last stand as relentless sanddunes march imperiously through the deserted buildings. This is the legendary settlement of Kolmanskop, a favourite haunt of photographers and artists who come here to try to capture on film and canvas the eerie fascination of this bizarre and derelict place.

'Derelict' may not be quite the right word to describe the actual buildings of Kolmanskop. 'Windswept' is better. Over the past four decades, the wind has almost blown the town to bits. The sands of the Namib sweep through the desolate streets and buildings for almost 10 months of the year, measuring speeds of up to 120 km/h. Nature has torn off roofs, eroded bricks, and filled doorless, windowless rooms with banks of sand.

Some of the buildings have, however, been restored by Consolidated Diamond Mines. The centrepiece of the restoration, Kolmanskop Museum, is housed in what was once a shop and contains photographs of the old days and artefacts found in Kolmanskop. There is old medical equipment from the hospital and even records of mine employees who once came here to try to make a fortune. Next door is a storeroom that has been converted into a tearoom and souvenir shop. Further along is the storekeeper's house, which has been renovated in the style of the period in which Kolmanskop enjoyed its heyday.

Of all the buildings that have been restored in Kolmanskop, the one which perhaps best captures the spirit of the olden days is the recreation hall, or *Kasino*. It is in such good condition that it is still used for functions several times a year. The hall contains painted pillars and a hardboard curtain you can imagine being raised for nightly performances of some jovial theatrical act. Below the hall is the *Kegelbahn*, an operational nine-pin skittle alley that once used to be a prime source of entertainment for residents no doubt tired of listening to the incessantly whistling sand.

The question that begins to form in your mind as you walk through Kolmanskop is how such a prosperous little town came to be built in this forlorn spot, and why it was then abandoned.

It all started in 1908, when the foreman of a maintenance unit working on the railway between Lüderitz and Keetmanshoop, Mr August Stauch, started taking a particular interest in the area. He instructed his workers to bring him anything unusual that they discovered. Subsequently, one of them produced a 'pretty stone' – which turned out to be a diamond. There were no flies on Mr Stauch – and in no time he had obtained a prospecting licence from the government.

From that moment Kolmanskop – named after a transport rider whose ox-wagon broke down at a nearby hill – became a mecca for fortune-hunters. The gem deposits turned out to be so rich that you could literally pick diamonds off the sand in some places. So prolific were diamonds that they were gambled in bars and even used as a form of currency in the early days.

But this free-for-all in the desert wasn't destined to last for very long. In 1908, the German Government decided to place firm controls on the flow of diamonds and declared Kolmanskop and its surrounding area the *Sperrgebiet* ('prohibited area'). Rules were enforced and prospectors had to obtain licences.

Diamond sales, it was also decided, had to be carried out by one body. In 1909 the *Diamant Regie* was formed, and during the next six years, before the outbreak of the First World War, five million

(Left) Strong afternoon winds at Kolmanskop cause the sanddunes around the derelict homes endlessly to change their shape and position.
(Right) Kolmanskop's well-preserved skittle alley. Along with the theatre housed in the same building, this venue was one of the town's main sources of entertainment.

Their gardens smothered by the endlessly shifting sands, these long abandoned homes stand in mute testimony to a once vibrant and bustling town.

carats, weighing 1 000 kg, were recovered. That made up one-fifth of the world's production!

Around Kolmanskop, a substantial and very comfortable town was built for the people who worked at the nearby mine. In its heyday – during the Twenties – some 300 people, including children, lived here – a fact hard to imagine when one wanders the ghostly streets of sand today.

While the natural elements have always threatened Kolmanskop, the inhabitants did all in their power to hold off the inevitable. Sand that collected in drifts was removed every day by Owambos and dumped outside town. Culturally, they lacked almost nothing. Everything from the latest fashions to food was imported regularly from Europe. Lavish dances were held, with no expense spared, either on the clothes that locals wore or on the food spread on the vast tables.

To keep the townsfolk entertained, opera companies, theatrical groups and orchestras were brought over from Europe. Even so, the town had its own orchestral ensemble which was so good that people came from Lüderitz to attend performances.

Despite the acute shortage of water here, even a swimming pool was devised in the form of a salt-water header tank which stood on a hill above the town. The water for the pool was pumped 35 km from Elizabeth Bay.

A combination of factors finally led to the demise of Kolmanskop: the economic consequences of the First World War, a slump in the price of diamonds, and the discovery of rich diamond deposits – with stones six times the size of those found at Kolmanskop – at the mouth of the Orange River. Production at Kolmanskop was phased out after 1938 and Consolidated Diamond Mines moved its headquarters to Oranjemund, which had been established two years earlier to take over as the new centre of diamond mining in the *Sperrgebiet*. A road was subsequently built between Kolmanskop and Oranjemund, stretching 288 km over the Namib gravel plain.

A programme to restore Kolmanskop into a museum town began in 1980, and progress to date gives visitors a chance to relive the dream that once was. Who knows – perhaps the dream will flower once more. In 1986 Consolidated Diamond Mines began prospecting in the area once again, and at a cost of R134 million they built a mine at Elizabeth Bay, 30 km south of Kolmanskop, because they believe, like the prospectors of old, that there are still a great many diamonds to be found in these sanddunes of the Namib.

Where to stay

The closest accommodation to Kolmanskop is situated at Lüderitz. There is the *Bay View Hotel*, PO Box 100, Lüderitz; tel (06331) 2288; the *Strand Motel/Lüderitz Rest Camp*, PO Box 377, Lüderitz; tel (06331) 2398; and *Pension Zum Sperrgebiet*, Bismarck St, Lüderitz; tel (06331) 2856.

Kolmanskop at a glance (map page 268)

How to get there: Take the road from Lüderitz towards Keetmanshoop for 9 km. Permits have to be obtained at the Lüderitz Foundation Office before entering the *Sperrgebiet* to reach Kolmanskop. It is forbidden to enter otherwise. Tours are run every morning from Monday to Saturday. Those wishing to visit Kolmanskop at other hours must make prior arrangements and be prepared to pay more.

Weather: The area has a generally mild climate due to the cooling effect of on-shore winds. The hottest months are the winter months of June, July and August, when berg winds prevail. The most agreeable time to visit Kolmanskop is during April and May. During the other ten months, strong winds usually blow in the afternoon.
What to do: Explore the byways and buildings of this unique town.

Special attractions: The haunting atmosphere of the abandoned houses, the Kolmanskop Museum and the recreation hall.
More information: Get in touch with the Kolmanskop Tour Company, PO Box 45, Lüderitz; tel (06331) 2445; Lüderitz Foundation and Tourist Information, PO Box 233, Lüderitz; tel (06331) 2532; Lüderitz Safaris, PO Box 76, Lüderitz; tel (06331) 2719.

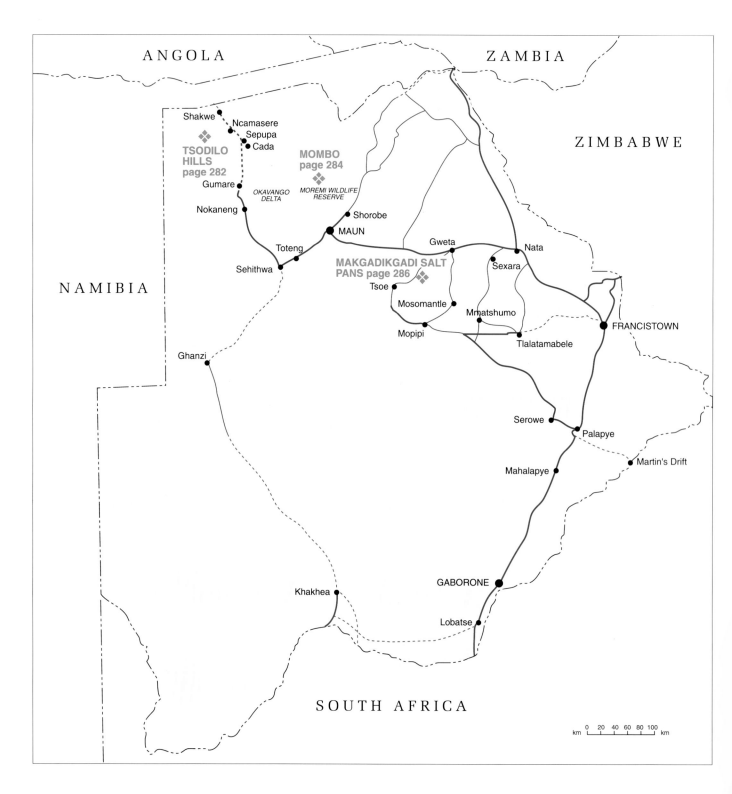

ANGOLA

ZAMBIA

ZIMBABWE

NAMIBIA

Shakwe
Ncamasere
Sepupa
Cada

TSODILO
HILLS
page 282

MOMBO
page 284

Gumare

OKAVANGO
DELTA

MOREMI WILDLIFE
RESERVE

Nokaneng

Shorobe

Toteng

MAUN

Sehithwa

Gweta

Nata

MAKGADIKGADI SALT
PANS page 286

Sexara

Tsoe

Mosomantle

Mmatshumo

Mopipi

FRANCISTOWN

Tlalatamabele

Ghanzi

Serowe

Palapye

Mahalapye

Martin's Drift

GABORONE

Khakhea

Lobatse

SOUTH AFRICA

km 0 20 40 60 80 100 km

BOTSWANA

Magical outcrops on the Kalahari plains

In Botswana's farthest corner, 70 km northwest of the Okavango Delta, is Tsodilo, an enigmatic cluster of hills which has attracted people for thousands of years

AFTER THE RELENTLESS PLAINS of the Kalahari, the first sighting of the Tsodilo hills quickens the pulse: unusual, brooding rock outcrops rising like an island out of the undulating desert sea. This compelling, remote group of hills is part of a landscape, unchanged for centuries, the exploration of which is described by Lourens van der Post in his classic book, *Lost World of the Kalahari*.

The approach to Tsodilo Hills from Maun is a gruelling journey of about 10 hours, 45 km of it being over sand, making a four-wheel-drive vehicle absolutely essential. In some places, the tracks are obscured by deep sand, while in others it's firm but cramped, with dry scrub clawing at the vehicle from both sides.

The rocky outcrops that make up the Tsodilo Hills have a powerful mythical significance for the Bushmen and Mbukushu who live in the area.

About halfway between Maun and Tsodilo you enter an endless ocean of ancient sanddunes that resemble waves marching relentlessly shoreward. Regularly spaced about a kilometre and a half apart, the dunes stand no higher than 20 m. Their crests are wooded with spreading trees that provide welcome shade and, in the valleys between, grass grows chin-high during the rainy season.

The track follows a diagonal course through the inter-dune valleys, making for something of an extended roller-coaster ride over the dunes. Eventually, cresting a peak, weary travellers are rejuvenated by their first spine-tingling sight of Tsodilo, which emerges suddenly on the horizon. The hills loom ever closer for the next hour, mesmerising and enticing the traveller.

The four hills of Tsodilo are known collectively in the Bushman language as 'copper bracelet of the evening' – come sunset, this term becomes self-explanatory as the fading rays throw liquid metallic reflections off the rocks.

The largest of the hills presents a sheer 300-m solid rock-face. The Bushmen thought of this hill as 'The Male', while on the other side of the bush track is 'The Female' – a smaller, but more extensive hill. Behind these lies an even smaller hill, 'The Child'. Like a newborn baby, the fourth and smallest hill has no name at all.

The Bushmen are the oldest residents of this part of the world, and a group of around 40 from the Zhu group have settled close to The Male hill – the ever-increasing numbers of visitors to the area having induced these traditional hunter-gatherers to settle here in order to trade curios for provisions such as salt and tobacco.

Visitors are well advised to hire a !Kung guide, who can point out places of interest as well as medicinal or poisonous plants. You may be able to watch traditional craftsmanship in the village – such as fashioning tiny beads from ostrich-egg shells or making bows and arrows.

But the Bushmen are not the area's only inhabitants. In another village near The Male hill are a group of Mbukushu who farm cattle and grow cereal crops. They believe that they were placed in these hills by their god Nyambi, and a guide can take you to the legendary spot where he will point out evidence in the form of footprints and hoofmarks clearly visible in the solid rock. Historians, however, believe that the Mbukushu migrated from the Zambezi in western Zambia to the Okavango region in the middle of the 18th century. On arrival at the Tsodilo Hills you must report to the Mbukushu village and sign the visitor's book.

The Bushmen construct very rudimentary dwellings out of sticks and grass. These are usually laid out around a central tree which serves as a meeting place for the men.

This area is rich in the relics of these groups' ancestors. Various excavations over the years have unearthed sites from both Stone Age Bushman settlements and Iron Age African settlements. Artefacts uncovered include stone tools and blades, ostrich-egg beads, shells, typical African pottery and fragments of copper and iron.

Van der Post called Tsodilo the 'Louvre of the desert' and The Female hill, particularly, is a wonderful repository of rock art that is comparable with the finest anywhere in southern Africa. There are nearly 3 000 paintings, these being found at over 200 different sites – such as boulders, caves and overhangs – and covering a broad variety of styles and subjects.

The most common paintings are those of animals, including unidentified (probably extinct) antelope as well as zebra, giraffe, eland, gemsbok and cattle. Rhinos also feature quite prominently, and rhino horns which date back to about AD 850 have been discovered here. Apparently rhino horns were prized even then. Witchdoctors stored medicines in them and they were bartered with east-coast traders for beads and shells.

Tsodilo Hills at a glance (map page 280)

How to get there: It is possible to fly in to Tsodilo as there is a landing strip, but if you're driving, a four-by-four vehicle is essential. From Maun the main road west offers two turn-offs – the first one is about 13 km before Sepopa (the zebra logo of the Botswana Museum is a marker on the old road); and the other is near the Shakawe Fishing Camp about 8 km before Shakawe.
Weather: Summers are extremely hot and dry; winters are far more bearable, being warm and sunny.
What to do: Explore, climb, walk.
Special attractions: The atmosphere, views, paintings.
More information: Write to the National Museum, Private Bag 00114, Gaborone, Botswana; tel Gaborone 374616.

Many of the paintings are distinguished by the artists' handprints, these being no larger than a child's. No absolute dates have been established for the paintings at Tsodilo, but some archaeologists speculate that they could date back as far as 20 000 years ago.

In the rainy season, a number of springs form in the hills, a notable one forming a crystal pool in a grotto. Brightly coloured lichen decorates the rock-faces of Tsodilo, and other vegetation is surprisingly prolific in so harsh an environment. Trees include grewia bush, shepherd trees, acacias and fruit-bearing trees such as marula and the prized mongogo, which are found in shaded groves. The mongogo produces fruit with edible flesh and an almond-like nut which is the staple food of the !Kung, who burn the hard shell in order to crack it open and remove the nut.

Tsodilo is remarkable for some unusual creatures that live in these hills, the most remarkable being a species of gecko which is found nowhere else on earth. The various rock pools contain small aquatic fairy shrimps – tiny, tenacious creatures that manage to exist despite the environmental extremes. Sometimes these rock pools are dry for months or even years, but the shrimps have adapted so that the eggs hatch only after having been exposed to air and then soaked in water. These eggs can survive for at least six years in the mud of a dried-up pool and are able to endure great extremes of heat and cold.

Given the remoteness of Tsodilo as well as the area's particular magic, it's worth spending at least a few days exploring the many places of interest that it has to offer. From these hills the grandeur and mysticism of the Kalahari are almost tangible. Virtually any lookout point rewards you with 360° panoramic views stretching towards the endless horizon.

Where to stay

Camping is allowed in certain parts of the hills, but, since there are no facilities, be sure to stock up with everything you think you may need – especially water, food and petrol. Be sure to remove every trace of your presence when you leave and do not tamper with the paintings.

Relatively near to Tsodilo is the *Xaro Lodge*. Here, accommodation consists of luxury double tents, each with a bathroom with hot and cold running water and a flush toilet nearby. Write to PO Box 8523, Edenglen 1613; tel (011) 6092464.
Shakawe Fishing Camp has 10 double tents, with showers and toilets in separate chalets. Write to PO Box 12, Shakawe, Botswana; tel Shakawe 260493.

An aerial view of part of the seemingly endless maze of interleading waterways that surrounds Mombo Island.

Idyllic island wilderness in Africa's largest oasis

Mombo is an island deep in the Okavango Delta which encapsulates everything that the African wildlife experience has to offer – and more

MOMBO HAS BEEN DESCRIBED as Botswana's best-kept secret, where visitors are virtually guaranteed spectacular game viewing, including sightings of less common species.

Lying in the heart of the 15 000 sq km that comprise the Okavango Delta, and about 100 km northwest of Maun, Mombo Island is situated on the northern tip of Chief's Island and borders the Moremi Wildlife Reserve.

Game-spotting begins on the flight from Maun to Mombo as the plane skims the tree tops and visitors are afforded a fish eagle's view of the Okavango Delta – Africa's largest oasis. The whole area is a primeval paradise of tree-covered islands, beautiful channels, clumps of wild date and lala palms, water lilies, reeds – a green wilderness seemingly stretching to infinity.

The spacious camp is picturesquely sited under shady trees overlooking the wide, lush flood plain. Up to 16 people can be accommodated in the large, comfortable tents. Thoughtfully, a reed-and-thatch bungalow, commonly known as the honeymoon suite, has also been provided! Each tent has its own ablution facilites with a shower, basin and toilet, and there is solar-powered electricity and hot water. Reed-and-thatch buildings comprise the dining room, curio shop and pub where, with its wide view over the flood plain, you can relax and watch game in comfort.

There is nothing spectacular about the annual flooding of the plain; in fact it's an almost imperceptible process. After the rains, the waters run down from the Angolan highlands and take about six months to seep through the innumerable channels, lagoons and waterways of the delta. The floods reach their highest level in February and March and then gradually subside. Most of the water then evaporates, leaving lush, nourishing green grass.

Wildebeest, impala, warthog, zebra, red lechwe and buffalo are attracted by the grazing, and the large predators are drawn by the excellent hunting prospects, hence the opportunity for unrivalled game viewing.

A list of the animals found in Mombo reads like a 'who's who' of African wildlife: this is where you're most likely to spot the big cats – lion, leopard and cheetah – as well as elephant, crocodile, buffalo, zebra, giraffe, tsessebe, impala, wildebeest, warthog, side-striped jackal, spotted hyaena, wild dog. There are also relatively rare mammals such as the aardvark, aardwolf, honey badger, lechwe and civet, as well as innumerable insects, amphibians and reptiles. And, of course, birds in abundance.

Mombo, in common with the rest of the delta, is a treat for birdwatchers. Keen ornithologists should pack their cameras, binoculars and bird diaries, and even if you're not bird-minded, the sight of hooded vultures, fish eagles, owls, parrots, jewel-like malachite kingfishers and blue waxbills will certainly enrich your stay.

You can explore the Mombo area either on foot or by four-wheel-drive vehicle – each has its own special appeal. The camp is entirely unfenced, and it's not unheard of to have animals wandering through the middle; certainly they're often spotted on the perimeter.

The day always starts before sunrise when visitors are fortified with tea, coffee and rusks before setting out on an early-morning game drive in an open vehicle. The African bush is at its best in the early morning and evening, and the many scents and sounds seem to have more clarity in the fresh, cool air. The bracing morning air would also have sharpened your appetite, and on your return to camp you'll find that a sumptuous brunch has been laid out. A guided nature walk is on offer after you've had brunch, during which your experienced ranger can point out things at close quarters that you may have missed.

After your walk you'll probably welcome a siesta when you can relax, write up your log book, or simply sleep away the heat of the day. Tea and cake are served before the late afternoon game drive. You'll be given a chance to freshen up and relax with a drink before dinner.

At the main meal, everyone gathers round a huge table and compares notes, and coffee is served around the campfire. If you're lucky you'll find Joseph Tekanyetso at Mombo. As a survivor of a lion attack, Joseph has gained almost legendary status in this area, and has entertained successive guests around the campfire with his recounting of his experience in the lion's jaws.

There are hurricane lamps to light you to bed, but as snakes can be a hazard, make sure you wear shoes and carry a torch. If you'd like to be escorted to your tent, a guide will happily oblige. When you finally bed down for the night, the canvas walls of the tent mean that you can enjoy being lulled to sleep by the sounds of the African night. Some of the sounds, such as a herd of elephant crashing

Mombo at a glance (map page 280)

How to get there: Although it is possible to make your own way to Maun and then fly to Mombo, it's probably easier and cheaper to select a package trip from Johannesburg.
Weather: The Okavango Delta has a subtropical climate with hot summer days (the temperature can reach an uncomfortable 40˚C) relieved by summer storms. In winter the days are sunny and mild to warm (about 25˚C), but cold at night, so don't forget to take a jersey.
What to do: You will have come to this part of Botswana exclusively to see wildlife in one of the world's unique and most beautiful wilderness areas.

Special attractions: The rarer species of game that visitors are most likely to spot here. These include honey badger, civet and aardvark. There is also quite a large population of elephant.
Special precautions: Remember to take anti-malaria tablets (bear in mind that some types require that you start taking them well before your arrival in a malaria area, and for a few weeks after returning). Swimming is not allowed at Mombo – too many crocodiles!
More information: Contact Wilderness Safaris, PO Box 651171, Benmore 2010; tel (011) 8841458 or 8844633.

though the trees or the grunting of a prowling lion, may add to the thrill of the wilderness experience.

Night game drives are a popular feature of Mombo and this is when some of the most dramatic moments are to be experienced. It is at night that the large predators come out to hunt and the rarer, nocturnal species make their appearance. Aardwolf, bushbaby, honey badger and genet are among those to look out for. No supernatural sight is required – the ranger uses a spotlight to locate the animals in the darkness.

You can personally contribute to the success of your game-spotting simply by giving thought to the clothes you wear. When you pack, bear in mind that neutral-coloured clothes are best: khaki, beige, muddy greens and so on, although army-type camouflage outfits are forbidden. Avoid white and bright colours which will announce your arrival to the animals.

Where to stay

The main camp at Mombo offers comfortable accommodation for 16 (see main text for details). Nearby there is also Mombo Trails Camp, a smaller, slightly more rustic set-up for anyone who prefers a more 'authentic' bush experience. Accommodation here is provided in dome tents with groundsheets, and there are camp beds with duvets, pillows and mosquito nets. There is an excellent ablution facility with basins, showers and a flush toilet and plenty of hot and cold water. Meals are enjoyed out in the open, underneath a huge spreading fig tree. The staff in the Trails Camp consists of a ranger and a chef, and there is also a four-wheel-drive vehicle for game drives.

A reed cormorant – one of the scores of bird species found in the Okavango Delta – sits poised among the bulrushes.

Shimmering testimony to an ancient lake

Situated in the central area of Botswana, the Makgadikgadi saltpans beckon to those who want to test their mettle against the harsh African elements

Where to stay

Makgadikgadi Game Reserve and *Nxai Pan National Park* each offer two public camp sites with limited facilities. For more information contact the Department of Wildlife and National Parks, PO Box 131, Gaborone; tel (09267) 371405.

At Nata, on the northern rim of the pan, is *Sua Pan Lodge* which has thatched cottages and a restaurant. Write to Private Bag 10, Francistown; tel (09267) 611220.

Some 100 km west of Nata is the *Gweta Rest Camp*, PO Box 124, Gweta; tel (09267) 612220. It consists of a motel and a camping area with a restaurant and a shop. Game drives into the pans are available.

Francistown offers a variety of accommodation. The *Marang Motel* has wood-and-thatch chalets, air-conditioned rooms and rondavels. Write to PO Box 807, Francistown; tel (09267) 213991/2/3. Hotels include: the *Grand Hotel*, PO Box 30, Francistown; tel (09267) 212300; the *Tati Hotel*, PO Box 666, Francistown; tel (09267) 212255; and *Thapama Lodge*, Private Bag 31, Francistown; tel (09267) 213872.

THE RIDDLE MIGHT GO something like this: when are you in the middle of a sea, but still remain hundreds of kilometres away from the nearest large expanse of water? The answer: when you're in the 'sea' of the Makgadikgadi saltpans in central Botswana.

To the human eye, the Makgadikgadi can truly resemble a sea at times. For several hours a day, when the relentless African sun beats down on this vast area of white salt and clay, optical illusions appear. The pans shimmer like water and the riddle described above suddenly doesn't seem so far from the truth any more.

Once the site of an ancient lake, the Makgadikgadi are the largest saltpans in the world and are the home of a surprising number and variety of animals, such as hyaena, jackal, gemsbok, wildebeest and springbok. As you drive across this vast expanse, meerkats might appear from nowhere, stand on their hind legs and watch you curiously until you disappear.

But mostly one sees nothing except the clear sweep of the horizon, which brings red sunsets you'll never forget and a sky full of the brightest stars, as if etched onto a huge dark canvas. Whirlwinds (or dust-devils as they are more appropriately known here) race across the pan, whip-

The occasional cluster of ivory palms is a welcome sight as you make your way across the seemingly endless expanse of blinding-white saltpan.

ping up columns of white powdery dust. Standing in the middle of the seemingly endless Makgadikgadi is an experience you will not easily forget.

Situated in the centre of Botswana, mostly south of the road from Nata to Maun, the Makgadikgadi consists of two major pans, Ntwetwe in the west and Sowa in the east, and numerous smaller ones. Sowa itself is the Bushman word for salt, while the word 'makgadikgadi' stems from the Setswana verb 'go kgala', which means 'to dry up'. In size, the pans measure some 12 000 sq km, which constitutes much more than half the size of a country such as Swaziland.

It is hard to imagine that the pans were once a vast expanse of water, but there are still remnants of those abundantly watery days. There are still shorelines; beaches of rolled quartz pebbles that marked the perimeter of the ancient lake; peninsulas of grasslands that separate Ntwetwe and Sowa, as well as cliffs. In places north of Ntwetwe, there are even clumps of hyphaene palms, much as you would find at an oasis in the desert. But water itself is scarce.

Perhaps the most outstanding remnant of all is an island called Kubu, which can be found on the southeastern side of Sowa. Rising about 20 m out of the pans, Kubu provides, on all sides, a rare and magnificent view that seems to stretch to infinity.

While Kubu's origin is a mystery, excavations have proved that the island was inhabited as much as two millennia ago. Pottery shards, Stone Age tools and a crescent-shaped wall have been found by archaeologists within this small area. Kubu being the Setswana word for hippopotamus, the island could once have been home to the larger mammals. Or perhaps the rock shapes were reminiscent of the water-loving animals? Or was it because, when the rains came down, the island submerged like a hippo? These riddles only add to the mystery of the Makgadikgadi.

The pans don't always stay dry. During the months of November to April, the rains come and so do the birds. Flamingos and pelicans arrive in their thousands to breed on Sowa, while the grasslands of Ntwetwe fill with zebra and wildebeest. The pans come to sudden new life. Flamingos forage for aquatic shrimps and algae, and if it weren't for their long-legged bodies to give you some perspective, the reflection of the sky in the water would make the horizon disappear.

Although desolate and dry most of the year, the pans are edged by more fertile ground to the west and northwest of Ntwetwe Pan, sometimes including parts of it. The Makgadikgadi Game Reserve,

A solitary baobab tree dominates a tiny peninsula jutting into the dry patchwork of the Makgadikgadi pans.

which runs all the way to the Boteti River south of Maun, intersperses undulating grassy plains with bleached pans.

The Nxai Pan National Park, which lies between the two dry fossilised lake beds of Nxai and Kamakama, has extensive grasslands and islands of trees. Game viewing is best during the rainy season when natural pans fill with rain water, attracting large herds of zebra and wildebeest that migrate from adjoining areas.

When exploring the pans, keep to the roads – because of the fragility of their surface, driving on the pans is forbidden. (This is because vehicle tyres break the seal of a pan's surface, inhibiting its ability to retain moisture.) Furthermore, the pans can be extremely dangerous: the surface may look hard and safe to drive on, but it can just as easily become treacherous. Vehicles can break the surface and suddenly find themselves up to their axles in sand with nothing on which to fix a winch, trees and rocks being so scarce.

During the rains, many of the roads turn to mud, making certain areas impassable for weeks. Visitors are warned to enter the pans in no vehicle other than a four-wheel drive, and even then, no fewer than two vehicles at a time. And don't forget the spades, winches and jacks. The chances are slim indeed that you won't need them during your visit.

Because of its vastness, the Makgadikgadi pans are also an easy place to get lost. Maps and compasses are indispensable. Often there are no landmarks, save a baobab in the distance. One of the most famous of these baobabs, Green's Tree, lies south of Gweta in the Ntwetwe Pan. It is named after the Green brothers, Frederick and Charles, who carved the words 'Green Expedition' into its bark on their way to the Chobe River in 1852. The tree, which became famous as a landmark to people crossing the pans, has since been inscribed with countless other names, many of them stretched and swollen with the growth of the baobab.

Trees occur so infrequently that they become something of a cause for celebration when they do appear. For example, on Kudiakau Pan, on the way to the Nxai Pan National Park, there's a virtual island of trees. Together they are called the Baines Baobabs, after the artist-explorer Thomas Baines. On the edges of the pans, you'll also notice a tree with a whitish bark. It's called the African star chestnut or the tick tree.

Makgadikgadi at a glance (map page 280)

How to get there: There are various routes. You can take the main road north from Gaborone to Nata, which is tarred all the way, although once you reach the pans a four-wheel-drive vehicle is essential, or you can take the road from Francistown to Orapa and Mopipi. From the north, you take the road from Nata to Gweta and then continue on one of several tracks south into the pans.

Weather: The pans being part of the Kalahari system, desert conditions prevail: hot in the day and close to freezing at night. Dust storms can blow up. Rains fall mostly from January to April. The best time for a visit is during the winter months of May to August.

What to do: The reserves are open throughout the year and safaris into the pans are run from Nata Lodge and Gweta Rest Camp. By going into the Makgadikgadi Game Reserve and the Nxai Pan National Park – the one south of the road to Maun, the other to the north – you can drive through grasslands that are rich in game and still see large parts of the pans. However, the reserves are quite expensive.

More information: Write to the Nata Lodge, Private Bag 10, Francistown; tel (09267) 611220; Destination Africa, PO Box 78823, Sandton 2146; (011) 8842504; the Botswana Tourism Development Unit, Private Bag 0047, Gaborone; tel (09267) 353024; the Department of Wildlife and National Parks, PO Box 131, Gaborone; tel (09267) 371405.

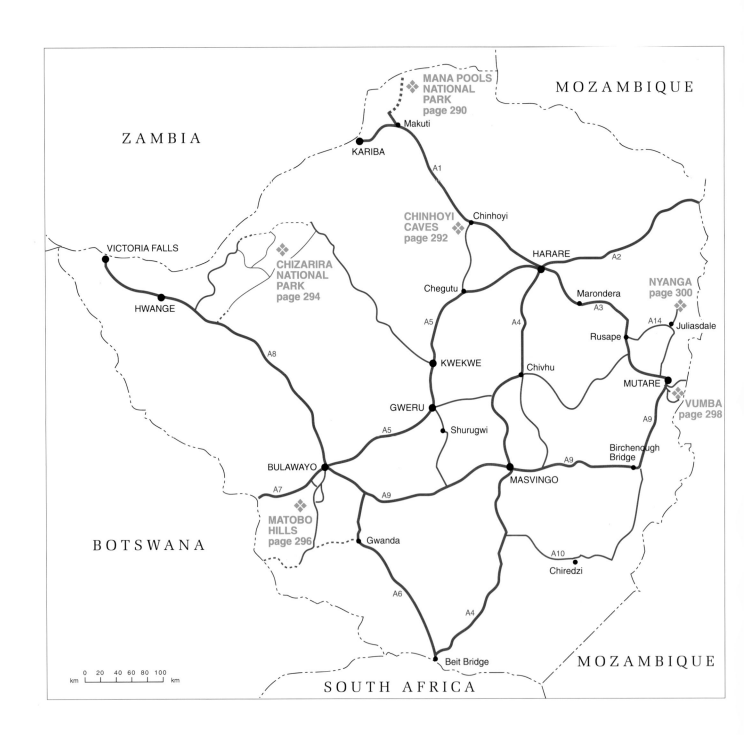

ZAMBIA

MOZAMBIQUE

MANA POOLS
NATIONAL
PARK
page 290

Makuti

KARIBA

A1

Chinhoyi

CHINHOYI
CAVES
page 292

HARARE

A2

VICTORIA FALLS

CHIZARIRA
NATIONAL
PARK
page 294

Chegutu

Marondera

NYANGA
page 300

A3

HWANGE

A5

A4

A14

Juliasdale

Rusape

A8

KWEKWE

Chivhu

MUTARE

GWERU

Shurugwi

A5

VUMBA
page 298

Birchenough
Bridge

A9

BULAWAYO

A9

MASVINGO

A9

A7

MATOBO
HILLS
page 296

Gwanda

A10

Chiredzi

BOTSWANA

A6

A4

Beit Bridge

MOZAMBIQUE

SOUTH AFRICA

0 20 40 60 80 100
km ┣━┻━┻━┻━┻━┫ km

ZIMBABWE

A fertile flood plain teeming with wildlife

Downstream from Lake Kariba, the mighty Zambezi flows alongside Mana Pools – a national park that those who've been lucky enough to visit call the most beautiful in Zimbabwe

IN TERMS OF what serious nature lovers are looking for, Mana has virtually everything: languorously flowing waters, shaded parklands, almost every type of wild animal you'd want to see, a wealth of fish life, and a plethora of birds that would constitute any ornithologist's dreamland. Of the 13 World Heritage Sites, Zimbabwe has two. And Mana, of course, is one of them.

Mana is as unspoilt as it is remote. Extending for close on 2 200 sq km, it boasts a unique ecosystem that has been created over centuries by the strong currents of the Zambezi.

The persistent action of one of Africa's greatest rivers has gradually removed sandstone that once made up what is now the Zambezi Valley, leaving behind an unusually flat floor. This area is often referred to as 'the flood plains', and it is these flood plains which give Mana Pools its particularly lush character, with the old river channels forming small seasonal ponds and pools.

The word 'mana', which means four, is said to refer to the number of main pools in the park, although others maintain that it could also refer to the families who once lived in the area.

While there might be a discrepancy about the origin of its name, there's no doubting what Mana has become. The abundance of water in the flood plains has created an incredibly fertile area, rich not only in animal life but also in plants. The huge, slow-growing *Acacia albida*, with its highly nutritious fruit, grows alongside mahoganies and woodlands full of mopane trees. The sausage tree also abounds, its fruit favoured by baboon as much as by rhino.

As for wildlife, Mana is teeming with animals, both large and small. Especially in the dry season, stretching from August to October, herds of animals are drawn by the abundant water and by the lush grazing on the riverbanks and in the flood plains. Mana plays host to some of the biggest concentrations of game in the country. You can also expect to see here the second largest assembly of elephant in Zimbabwe (after Hwange).

With large stretches of water being such a feature of Mana Pools, the reserve's abundance of hippo comes as little surprise.

Elephant watching on the Zambezi's 'flood plain'. One of the novelties of Mana Pools is that visitors are allowed to wander around the reserve on foot.

Birdwatchers too, take note. Mana attracts both woodland and water birds, a total of no fewer than 380 species, including everything from carmine bee-eaters and Egyptian geese to kingfishers, Nyasa lovebirds, yellow-spotted nicators and banded snake-eagles. At Long Pool, not only birds can be seen but also large numbers of crocodile lazing on the banks or skulking just beneath the surface, waiting for an unsuspecting impala to come to the water's edge for what might turn out to be its very last sip.

There are, however, certain animals you will definitely not see. For some curious reason, Mana has no giraffe, wildebeest or hartebeest. Neighbouring game parks to the south and the east, as well as Luangwa in next-door Zambia, have plenty of all three species. Why Mana doesn't, nobody knows. And it will surely remain one of its secrets.

More sadly, though, you will also see hardly any black rhino: what was once one of Zimbabwe's largest herds of black rhino has virtually been wiped out by poachers.

With its existence so dependent on the floodwaters of the Zambezi, it was obvious that Mana's future would be affected by the construction of Lake Kariba. Some scientists predicted that the alteration of flooding seasons, the reduction of silt and the unnaturally rapid changes in the river's levels would adversely affect Mana. But, so far, the signs of deterioration haven't been too pronounced.

There is still constant talk, though, of a hydro-electric scheme at Mupata Gorge, which would create an 850 sq km lake, putting most of Mana underwater. Other people talk about drilling for oil. And yet others suggest that the land may be taken over for human settlement.

Yet Mana is still there. And while it is, make sure you get there and enjoy one of the only game parks where you can leave your car and walk around. It's a feature few game parks are brave enough to offer, but be careful that you don't abuse this privilege. Another bonus in Mana is that the park authorities have wisely limited to 50 a day the number of vehicles that can enter its gates. So the experience you have will be a rare one indeed.

Once inside, don't expect to see any fences, even around the few camping sites. Animals have unrestricted movement, so don't be surprised if, after nightfall, you hear something munching the bushes next to your sleeping bag. It will probably be an elephant. It's hard to find anything closer to a real African wildlife experience.

Besides walking, one can canoe or fish in waters that hold the promise of tigerfish, barbel, vundu and bream, tilapia, and lungfish. While lazing on the water's edge, you can look across to the Zambian escarpment and the mountainous northern wall of the valley. It's a sight you won't soon forget.

Perhaps the only negative aspect of Mana is the climate. Subtropical, with temperatures that have been known to hit 46°C, Mana's waters also bring the tsetse fly, bilharzia and malaria. But anyone who takes precautions will greatly reduce the risks.

Note: Mana Pools is open only seven months of the year, from 15 April to 15 November, depending on the duration of the summer rains.

Mana Pools at a glance (map page 288)

How to get there: Air Zimbabwe and South African Airways offer regular flights from Johannesburg to Harare. Mana Pools is situated some 400 km north-west of Harare on the road to Chirundu. Turn right onto a gravel road 6 km north of Marongora (where Mana Pools permits must be obtained), drive 30 km to Nyakasikana Gate, and then 42 km to Nyamepi Camp.

Weather: Summer temperatures are extremely hot and humidity is high. Winters are temperate.

What to do: Game viewing, fishing, canoeing and walking.

Special attractions: Mana Pools is one of the few game reserves in the world in which you can wander around on foot.

More information: Get in touch with the Zimbabwe Tourist Office, PO Box 9398, Johannesburg 2000; tel (011) 3313137 or 3313155/8. Local travel companies, such as United Touring Company, offer safari tours to Mana Pools. Contact them at PO Box 2914, Harare, Zimbabwe; tel (09263-4) 793701.

Where to stay

Mana Pools has 43 camping and caravan sites and two luxury lodges. Contact the Central Booking Office, Department of National Parks and Wildlife Management, PO Box 8151, Causeway, Harare; tel (09-263-4) 703376, 792782/9 or 792731.

Chikwenya Camp, consisting of six luxurious thatched chalets, is situated to the east of the Mana Pools National Park. Write to African Savanna Touring (PVT) Ltd, PO Box UA471, Harare, Zimbabwe; tel (09-263-4) 707438/9.

Measureless caverns on the road to Kariba

The rolling plain 120 km north west of Harare gives no clue to the presence of Zimbabwe's famous Chinhoyi Caves, a subterranean maze still largely unexplored

Where to stay

There is a camping and caravanning site right next to the caves; write to the National Parks address provided in the other panel, or telephone Harare 706077.

The *Caves Motel* is situated very close to the caves; write to PO Box 230, Chinhoyi; tel 2340. In Chinhoyi itself you'll find the *Orange Grove Motel*, which has a caravan park as well as a restaurant and a swimming pool. Write to PO Box 436, Chinhoyi; tel 2785/6. Another alternative is the *Chinhoyi Hotel*, PO Box 22, Chinhoyi; tel 2313.

APPROACHING THE CAVES from ground level, the unsuspecting first-time visitor is rewarded with an unforgettable sight. Fifty metres down a sheer drop lies a seemingly bottomless pool of the most vibrant, vivid azure, startling in its contrast against the ochre African earth: this is the legendary Sleeping Pool. It is probably at its most breathtaking at noon, when the sun strikes the water and transforms the surface into a glittering spectacle. Many locals aptly refer to the Chinhoyi Caves as *Tshirodziva*, 'the fallen pool', as it was a huge sinkhole that created the magnificent Sleeping Pool far below ground level.

The water is crystal clear, and the submerged rock formations and flourishing population of goldfish (released by some mischievous person) can be seen with amazing clarity below the surface. The water temperature remains a constant 22°C throughout the year.

From the top, a natural sloping tunnel leads to the edge of the Sleeping Pool, and the surrounding dolomite is shot through with numerous caverns, galleries and passages. A steep flight of steps (illuminated with electric lights) leads you to the viewing platform in Dark Cave, which offers a stunning view of Sleeping Pool – complete with stalactites and a mosaic of blue reflections, ever changing during the course of the day. From Dark Cave galleries and passages lead off into the darkness for more adventurous visitors to explore.

In the 1830s a Nguni outlaw named Nyamakwere settled here. He carried out a reign of terror in the area, robbing people and performing executions by hurling his victims into the Sleeping Pool. Many locals believe that the caves are haunted by the spirits of Nyamakwere's victims. According to another legend, the caves are also home to a huge serpent which fortunately, seems to keep a low profile (rather like the Loch Ness Monster!).

Many years after Nyamakwere's time, this subterranean maze served as a sanctuary to the Shona chief after whom the caves were named. Chief Chinhoyi stored provisions here and fortified the entrances. When the going got tough he would retreat into the caves, safe from marauding Ndebele warriors. It was he who controlled the area when the first white man to visit the caves, hunter and explorer Frederick Selous, arrived in 1887. In May of the following year, Selous, who was considered to be the 'discoverer' of the caves, presented a dissertation on the subject to the Royal Geographical Society in London.

Although there is much to delight the casual visitor, the subterranean labyrinth of chambers and tunnels that comprise Chinhoyi are more suited to professional cavers who have the experience and equipment for serious exploration. Much still remains to be discovered and some experts believe that the present caves are just a small part of a much more complex system, which probably includes even larger areas of water. Archaeologists have found traces of early human occupation in these caves, some remains having been radiocarbon dated to around AD 650.

A pleasant recreational park with camping and picnic facilities has been created around the caves, which are situated 8 km from the town of Chinhoyi at the foot of a range of hills (see next page).

On either side of the town, lying to the west and east of Chinhoyi, are Alaska and Eldorado respectively, reminders of a more colourful era: the centre of a goldrush scam. In 1904 there was a reported discovery of a gold formation here that was speculated to be of a similar magnitude to the gold reefs on the Witwatersrand. Although the find was unverified, a confidence trickster named the area Eldorado and pegged claims along several kilometres.

News of this 'discovery' spread like wildfire; the trickster manipulated the share market and a goldrush began. He sold claims to hundreds of gullible fortune hunters who arrived in droves, some all the way from Europe, others from South Africa, all of whom eventually discovered their shares to be worthless. However, copper has been mined in this area for hundreds of years, and these days Chinhoyi benefits from copper mined at Alaska and Mangula.

The small town of Chinhoyi was previously known as Sinoia (a European corruption of Chinhoyi) and was renamed, along with many other places, after Zimbabwe became independent. Today, it is a centre for tobacco and maize farming as well as copper and chrome mining. The town is still predominantly white and is fairly typical of Zimbabwean rural centres: quiet, friendly and well kept. However, it differs from other rural towns in yet another claim to fame: a place in Zimbabwe's more recent history.

In the middle of the town stands the memorial to the *Gallant Chinhoyi Seven*, commemorating the day when the Second Chimurenga began. Chimurenga is derived from the Shona *murenga*, which means 'rebel' or 'fighter'. The First Chimurenga refers to the Shona-settler clashes of 1896-7, the Second Chimurenga to the guerrilla war against white minority rule. On 28 April 1966, in the Chinhoyi district, seven Zanla guerrillas were killed in a skirmish with Rhodesian forces. Chimurenga Day is now celebrated on this day every year.

Chinhoyi Caves, once the battleground of warring chiefdoms and the hideout of a notorious robber, has now become a favourite tourist attraction.

Chinhoyi Caves at a glance (map page 288)

How to get there: The caves are situated 8 km north west of the town of Chinhoyi, 120 km from Harare on the main Kariba road.

Weather: Hot in summer and warm in winter, although winter nights can be cold with frost.

What to do: Explore the caves as far as you dare, and stroll around the recreational park afterwards.

Special attractions: The Sleeping Pool.

More information: Write to The National Parks Central Booking Office, PO Box 8151, Causeway, Harare, Zimbabwe; tel Harare 706077. You can also obtain details about the caves by writing to PO Box 193, Chinhoyi; tel Chinhoyi 2550.

Visiting times: Sunrise to sunset.

The northern area of the park affords spectacular views down the precipitous escarpment towards Lake Kariba.

Behind a mountain barrier, a place of primeval splendour

Situated in the northern province of Matabeleland, the Chizarira National Park is the most remote of Zimbabwe's national parks, providing a wonderful glimpse of an Africa that has, for the most part, long since disappeared

ROLL BACK THE CENTURIES in southern Africa and you will arrive at a place not unlike Chizarira National Park – a primordial landscape of floodplains and plateaux watered by perennial streams, dropping in the north down a ravine-slashed escarpment to Lake Kariba. An estimated 12 000 elephants wander across the face of this spectacular corner of Africa, although who keeps count is a mystery, for not many human beings are around to do the job.

Named after the Chizarira Mountains which form the mighty northwestern backbone of the park, this is Zimbabwe's most remote national reserve, and it has always been forbidding territory.

Chizarira is a Batonka word meaning 'barrier'. Dominating the range in the northeast and sealing the isolation of the land that lies in its shadow, is the 1 371-m high Mount Tundazi. Local legend has it that the mountain is home to a giant serpent – a supernatural deterrent to those unmoved by the natural dangers that lurk in the countryside.

For those willing to make the effort, the rewards are rich in equal measure to the rigours of getting to Chizarira – and extremely arduous it is. From

Victoria Falls it is a 6-8 hour journey (about 290 km), climbing down the steep Zambezi Valley escarpment and grinding up again through the Chizarira hills. The last petrol and supply stop is Binga, 90 km away, and from this town the tar road becomes a dust one.

From Harare, the traveller faces 300 km of dirt road after the turn-off near Karoi. From there Siabuwa, behind the Chizarira barricade, is the only place en route for petrol. Four-wheel drive is helpful on both routes, and essential in the park. Those coming from Harare can alternatively take the A5 south to Kwekwe and turn off right to Gokwe. The road is tarred all the way, but between Gokwe and Chizarira it is untarred.

But the further you go, the deeper you penetrate a world unaffected by time and tourist trappings. Here the exquisite Batonka basketware is in use, not for sale – although the people you meet at the roadside are not above parting with their utensils for fair remuneration.

Inside the park, the real battle for Africa plays itself out. The elephant and black rhino within the reserve are in permanent danger from well-armed poachers intent on spoils of ivory and rhino horn. The visitor need not be surprised, then, when gun-slinging rangers, often backed by ZRP policemen, unexpectedly appear at camp. Infinitely polite and enormously brave, they move wraithlike through the bush, the spearhead of the Zambezi Valley anti-poaching units.

But the ever-present threat to the elephant and rhino is the only cloud that hangs over this prince among parks, a realm that is breathtaking in its abundance.

Msasa trees cover the open deciduous woodland; a tree perfect in shape and balance, the flush of its young leaves in spring clothes the earth in a rainbow of reds, from the palest blush to deep claret. The msasa is useful, too: an extract of its bark is used by locals to tan hides; an infusion of the roots is an effective treatment for diarrhoea, and a decoction of the same is used as an eyewash for conjunctivitis. It provides all this and shade, too.

The delightfully named Prince of Wales' feathers, or mufuti tree, also abounds. Its newly opened young leaves are bright red, contributing to the symphony of colour, and its bark, properly treated, makes good rope.

Here, in addition to the elephant and black rhino, are herds of antelope that include the roan and tsessebe, buffalo, lion, leopard, cheetah, zebra and the cocky warthog. A word of warning to those obsessed with big game: the uneven landscape, so ideal for predators, makes game-viewing difficult. The real charm of the Chizarira National Park lies in the sense of the place being rooted in a more ancient, primeval time.

This appeal is exploited to the maximum by the three camps built at varying distances from the park headquarters, Manzituba, which is situated 22 km up the escarpment from the Binga-Siabuwa road. Manzituba is the administrative office of the park – there are no chalets or lodges here.

Six kilometres from Manzituba, on the Lusilu-kulu River, is Kasiwi, the biggest of the camps. Here the thatched accommodation, built on stilts, is quite literally open to the wilds: there are only three

Visitors to Chizarira have the option of walking around the reserve in the company of an armed game scout.

log 'walls'. When you wake in the morning, you can lie on your rudimentary bed and watch a crested barbet or maybe a hoopoe eating its breakfast on the branches of the tree opposite you. At night, only a curtain of stars separates you from the lions below: you can hear them roar, making you wish that the stilts were taller.

There are cooking facilities in a circular dining area below, and a discrete distance away there are hot-water showers and a flush toilet.

The facilities at Mabolo Bush Camp on the Mucheni River below the Manzituba Spring, also 6 km from HQ, are more primitive. Water has to be drawn from the spring and visitors must bring a tent. About 35 km away at the Busi Bush Camp you can experience the different environment of the floodplain and lowveld vegetation. The Parks department has promised to bring this camp up to the standards of Kasiwi – make enquiries on progress before you book.

It is also worth enquiring about professional guides who will take you walking through the park. Based at Victoria Falls, these old bush hands are the key to an entirely new understanding of the wilds, from the number, nature and significance of the grasses to the curious habits of beetles and birds. Everything, including transport, is provided.

A cheaper option is to do a wilderness trail with a National Parks guide. These are run only during the dry season for a maximum of six people per group. This option means taking your own gear and making your own way to the camp. Visitors are not allowed to walk around the park alone, but the services of an armed game scout can be obtained.

Only one party at a time is allowed in each camp. Booking is through the National Parks' Central Reservations office in Harare.

Where to stay

Stay at one of three camps: on the plateau there is *Kasiwi Camp* on stilts or *Mabolo Bush Camp;* and on the floodplains there is the *Busi Bush Camp.* All camps provide cooking facilities, hot and cold water and flush toilets. Bring tents for Mabolo. Book through the Central Booking Office, Department of National Parks and Wildlife Management, PO Box 8151, Causeway, Harare; tel Harare 706077.

The Chizarira National Park at a glance (map page 288)

How to get there: Air Zimbabwe and SAA offer regular flights from Johannesburg to Harare, and Air Zimbabwe offers daily flights to Bulawayo and Victoria Falls. From Victoria Falls/Hwange: turn right 16 km north of the Hwange Park turn-off on the Bulawayo-Victoria Falls road. From Harare: just after Karoi, take the Hostes Nicolle Drive.
Weather: This is a summer rainfall area and temperatures often soar to uncomfortable levels in the Zambezi Valley. The winters are mild and ideal for camping.
What to do: Enjoy spectacular scenery and explore the wilds by vehicle or on foot with an armed ranger.

Special attractions: This is the best place to see the almost extinct black rhino. Victoria Falls-based commercial companies run all-inclusive walking trips through the park and National Parks guides offer wilderness trails during the dry season.
More information: Contact the Zimbabwe Tourist Office, PO Box 8052, Causeway, Harare; tel Harare 793666/7/8/9 or 706511/2/3. Alternatively, contact the Zimbabwe Tourist Office in South Africa, at PO Box 9398, Johannesburg 2000; tel (011) 3313137 or 3313155/8.
Visiting times: The park is open all the year round and the gates are open from sunrise to sunset.

A primordial landscape of 'chaotic grandeur'

The ancient granite formations of the Matobo Hills, situated about 20 minutes by car from Bulawayo, are of great historical and spiritual significance, with art and artefacts dating back thousands of years

The granite outcrops of the Matobos are home to countless lizards, such as this brilliantly coloured agama.

NO-ONE CAN VISIT the Matobo Hills and remain unaffected by their brooding majesty, not least Cecil John Rhodes who described them in the following lyrical fashion: 'The peacefulness of it, the chaotic grandeur of it all! I call this one of the views of the world. It brings home to me how very small we all are.'

Situated in the heart of Matabeleland, the hills have long been the scene of ceremonies and rituals. Mzilikazi, founder of the Ndebele nation, gave the area its name. Apparently the smooth granite boulders reminded him of a gathering of his old *indunas* and he called the area *amaTobo*, 'the bald heads'. Mzilikazi is interred here in a hillside tomb. His possessions, including wagons and furniture, have been sealed for over a century in a cave nearby, and visitors can view this fascinating collection through small openings in the rocks.

It's hard to believe that this area of giant granite domes and precariously balanced boulders was once a flat and featureless landscape. Subsequently, over a period of two thousand million years, rock and sand on the surface were washed away by wind and water, to reveal the hard granite below. The balancing boulders are a result of natural faults along the weakest lines, and weathering and erosion did the rest. The *dwalas* – domed and whaleback formations – get their shape from a self-explanatory type of weathering known as onion-skin peeling. The many smooth-walled caves of the region were also formed by a similar process in which the internal layers gradually peeled and fell off.

Although the granite outcrops are the most outstanding feature of the region, the Matobo National Park – within which the Matobo Hills lie – is an area of immense botanical variety with wooded valleys, grassy marshlands and streams between the hills. Most of it is accessible only on foot or horseback, except the Whovi Wilderness Area Game Park, where you have to stay in your car to view some of the larger mammals such as white and black rhino.

Animals are plentiful throughout the park and include leopard, monkey, baboon, impala, zebra, klipspringer, dassie, porcupine, red hare and many smaller mammals. Visitors may be less pleased to know that 39 species of snakes flourish here, particularly the deadly black mamba. The high cliffs and craggy outcrops are a favourite haunt of various

Throughout the Matobo Hills, precariously balanced boulders create evocative shapes – such as this cluster of rocks which conjures up the image of a child, surrounded by his parents, gazing out towards the distant horizon.

Stark simplicity is the keynote of Rhodes's grave at World's View. It features no ornate marble carvings or eulogies – just a brass plate saying: 'Here lie the remains of Cecil John Rhodes'. In the background is the top of the Wilson Memorial.

raptors which help to keep the snake population in check. In fact, the Matobo National Park boasts the world's largest concentration of black eagles. If you keep your eyes peeled, you will also spot Wahlberg's eagle, tawny eagle, secretary bird, snake eagle, Peregrine falcon and many others. The dams, too, boast a wide variety of denizens – 16 fish species in all, including exotics such as bass, barbel and salmon.

The rock art of the Matobo Hills compares with the best anywhere in southern Africa, and is predominantly the work of the Bushmen who lived in this region for thousands of years. What distinguishes these paintings are their incredible diversity and animation – human beings are depicted playing, running, hunting, dancing, lying down, and sitting. Animals are anatomically correct, making identification easy, while trees, birds, insects and reptiles are all accurately rendered.

A number of these caves are within easy reach of the road. Nswatugi Cave has some excellent paintings, although it does involve a 500-m climb up a steep slope. Pomongwe Cave, which involves a gentle climb of only 100 m, was the recipient of a well-intentioned but disastrous application in the Twenties of glycerine, which was meant to preserve the paintings but had the opposite effect. Nevertheless, it's an impressively large cave and an important archaeological site where thousands of Stone Age artefacts have been discovered. A short climb will take you to White Rhino Shelter, which also

Matobo Hills at a glance (map page 288)

How to get there: From Bulawayo take the A47 leading to the southwest. The hills are reached after driving about 32 km along the well-tarred road.
Weather: Summer rainfall from November to April. Summers are generally hot to very hot, winters mild to cold.
What to do: Angling and boating on Maleme Dam, otherwise, exploring, game-spotting, bird-watching, hiking and riding.
Special attractions: World's View, the caves, the rock art and the feeding of the lizards.
More information: Write to The Warden, Matobo National Park, Private Bag K5142, Bulawayo; tel Matobo 0-1900.

has some good paintings, as does Gulubakwe Cave, which is the nearest to the road.

Of course, there are numerous other excellent examples of prehistoric art, but these are not accessible to anyone who isn't prepared to do some serious footslogging. If you are, the reward far outweighs the effort and, after all, the Matobo Hills offer some of the best hiking in the country. Inange Cave lies 8 km up a steep *dwala*, but follow the green arrows and eventually you'll be confronted with a gallery of some of the finest prehistoric paintings in the world, with the added bonus of breathtaking scenery to take your mind off your physical labours both there and back.

The hill where Rhodes is buried is known to the Ndebele as *Malindidzimu*, 'the place of the benevolent spirits', but most people know it as World's View. The massive granite *dwala* dominates the area, and the surrounding boulders are softened and decorated by lacy patterns of red and gold lichen.

When Rhodes died in his little cottage overlooking the sea at Muizenberg, Cape Town, his body was transported by train and then by ox-wagon for more than 2 000 km, and was eventually laid to rest in his beloved World's View on 10 April 1902. As Rhodes was lowered into his grave, the assembled Ndebele chiefs gave him the traditional Ndebele salute, '*Hayete*' – the first and only time that a white man has ever been accorded this honour.

In his will, Rhodes made the Matobo National Park a gift to the people of Bulawayo, and his burial place has become a place of pilgrimage for thousands of people since his death. At the foot of the hill is a car park with pleasant braai sites and a display of old photographs covering Rhodes's fascinating life.

One of the most bizarre attractions of the Matobo Hills is the lizard feeding that takes place here at World's View. A ranger, holding out a small piece of *sadza* (cooked maize meal), calls out to the rocks, whereupon scores of rainbow-hued lizards appear from underneath various boulders, race across the rocks and even clamber over the ranger to claim their share. This spectacle occurs three times a day and is not to be missed.

Where to stay

Maleme Dam is the park headquarters and has picnic sites, nine fully equipped lodges and 12 chalets, as well as caravan and camping facilities. For reservations, write to the National Parks Booking Agency, PO Box 2283, Bulawayo; tel (092639) 63646. Take your own crockery and cutlery if you stay in the chalets. The approach to the caravan site is very steep and may be tricky for caravanners, so there is a tow service available on request during office hours. Guided horseback trails are also available from here. Although the waters of the dam may look inviting, don't risk a swim. Apart from the fact that there is a good chance of your contracting bilharzia, the waters are apparently home to a few crocodiles. Fryer's store, which stocks basic groceries and curios, can be found about halfway between Maleme Dam and World's View.

Mtshelele Dam and the Arboretum also have camping and caravan sites with ablution facilities.

Spectacular scenery in the 'mountains of the mist'

Situated in Zimbabwe's Eastern Highlands, a few kilometres southeast of Mutare, are the majestic Vumba Mountains, offering wonderful views and some of the best hiking trails in southern Africa

EUROPEAN SETTLERS named the area Vumba, an adaption of 'mubvumbi', the name used by the local Nyika people, meaning 'mountains of the mist' – an apt description of these rocky outcrops. Every day, as the early morning sun warms the mountain slopes, moisture from the forests changes to steam and, as the day's heat builds up, these soaring mountain peaks become shrouded in mist and billowing clouds.

Vumba ranks as one of the most beautiful areas of Zimbabwe's Eastern Highlands – consisting of a towering terrain of mountainous rainforest overlooking the Mozambique plain. The area is one of dense forests, festooned with ferns through which the samango monkeys swing. The trees tower above crystal-clear, fish-filled streams that are fringed with flowers of every hue. High in the trees, the chatter of a myriad birds – bronze sunbird, augur buzzard, forest weaver and wood owl – gradually gives way to the silence of moist, leafy glades where the orange ground thrush, shy duiker and bushbuck make their home.

The main attractions of Vumba are the wonderful sanctuaries situated here, namely the Bunga Forest Botanical Reserve and the Vumba Botanical Gardens. Situated 27 km from Mutare, the Bunga Forest Botanical Reserve is an area of dense indigenous forest which thrives on the area's high rainfall. Wander along the rambling, well-kept footpaths and revel in the primeval beauty of this luxuriant, unspoilt wonderland. It is home to a multitude of different species of butterfly and moth, and also to a varied animal population that includes monkey, leopard, duiker and bushbuck.

A few kilometres beyond Bunga, on the eastern lee of Castle Beacon, is the entrance to the other sanctuary, the Vumba Botanical Gardens, which in contrast to Bunga, is a landscaped garden created around a series of small streams where flowering plants from all over the world flourish. It is an area of leafy glades and sparkling pools surrounded by moss and ferns. It glows with the riotous hues of fuchsias, cycads, orchids, hydrangeas, proteas, begonias, lilies and aloes. The park is one of the showpieces of Zimbabwe and boasts many species of fauna and flora which are seldom seen – hence the name of the Seldomseen Naturalist Centre, which is situated in the Vumba Botanical Gardens!

Another famous landmark situated a short distance from the Vumba Botanical Gardens is Leopard Rock, so named after the many leopards that frequented the area. Beneath the rock bluff is the Leopard Rock Hotel, which was built after the Second World War and subsequently had the honour of hosting the Royal Family in the 1950s. It was closed in the Seventies after repeated guerrilla attacks, but is now open again after having been extensively refurbished and expanded.

For motorists, one of the best ways of exploring Vumba is by means of the splendid circular scenic

Kilometres of well-maintained footpaths take the visitor through the cool, quiet depths of the Bunga Forest Reserve.

A crystal clear lake lies at the heart of the Vumba Botanical Gardens – one of the highlights of the Vumba area.

route from Mutare which winds through steep mountains and rolling farmland. This road affords the traveller wonderful views of the terrain from viewpoints strategically sited to give spectacular panoramas of the Vumba Mountains and the Mozambique plain far below. From the Cloudlands junction, this scenic drive zigzags some 67 km through and around the Vumba Mountains to the Prince of Wales Viewpoint. After Lion Rock, it soon becomes a gravel road climbing up and down through eucalyptus forests into the coffee plantations of the Essex Valley. After another 25 km, the road winds down along the Mozambiquan border and rejoins the tar road into Burma Valley, travelling through banana and tobacco plantations until it finally passes through the Zimunya communal lands and Chitakatira town back to the Prince of Wales Viewpoint.

Where to stay

The best-known hotel in the Vumba area is the luxurious *Leopard Rock Hotel*, PO Box 1297, Harare; tel (4) 728597. Others hotels in the area include the two-star *Impala Arms Hotel,* PO Box 524, Mutare, tel (20) 60722; the three-star *Manica Hotel,* PO Box 27, Mutare; tel (20) 64431; the elegantly rustic two-star *White Horse Inn*, PO Box 3193, Paulington, Mutare; tel (20) 60325; and the recently completed *Eden Lodge,* PO Box 881, Mutare; tel (20) 210717. Other possibilities are the *Christmas Pass Hotel*, PO Box 841, Mutare; tel (20) 64412; and the *Wise Owl Motel*, PO Box 588, Mutare; tel (20) 64643.

You can also camp at the Mutare municipal caravan park in Christmas Pass, just outside Mutare on the Mutare-Harare road (PO Box 910, Mutare; tel (20) 64412) and at the Vumba Botanical Gardens. Contact the Central Booking Office, Department of National Parks and Wildlife Management, PO Box 8151, Causeway, Harare; tel (4) 706077.

Vumba at a glance (map page 288)

How to get there: Drive from Beit Bridge to Masvingo and then east along the paved Masvingo-Mutare road to the Chimanimani turn-off. Continue north on the main road to Mutare, turn onto the Vumba Road which is the second turning east out of Mutare off the south-bound road to Birchenough Bridge. Bear in mind that the Vumba Road is a dead end – the traveller has to backtrack some kilometres to return to the Cloudlands junction and the start of the circular scenic route. The main paved road to Vumba, a 60-km gravel road, branches to the right into the Burma Valley and encircles the Vumba Mountain. Both Air Zimbabwe and South African Airways fly daily between Harare and Johannesburg.

Weather: Summers in the Eastern Highlands area are warm, and winters are cool to cold. However, even in summer it can turn quite cold after rain, so sweaters are advisable at all times. Summer showers can be sudden and heavy, and these are frequently accompanied by lightning.

What to do: Hiking and nature-watching of all kinds – especially wildflowers, reptiles, birds and insects. It is a wonderful environment for artists and photographers, but remember to take your own photographic and art supplies as these are sometimes in scarce supply in Zimbabwe.

A number of tour operators offer minibus trips from Harare into the Eastern Highlands, including Vumba, Nyanga and Chimanimani. Contact United Touring Company, PO Box 2914, Harare; tel (4) 793701, or Africa Savanna Touring, PO Box UA471, Harare; tel (4) 734817/707438/9/0.

Special attractions: The Bunga Forest Botanical Reserve and the Vumba Botanical Gardens.

More information: Write to the Zimbabwe Tourist Office, PO Box 9398, Johannesburg 2000; tel (011) 3313137. The office is in the Carlton Centre in Commissioner Street.

A mountain paradise for hikers and fishermen

The lofty and mysterious mountainous region of Nyanga on Zimbabwe's northeastern border with Mozambique is a natural paradise offering spectacular scenery, plunging waterfalls and some of the best trout fishing in Africa

NYANGA TAKES ITS NAME from Zimbabwe's highest mountain, Inyangani, which soars up to 2 592 m in height from a giant plateau of granite outcrops. The mountain was named after a powerful *sangoma* (witchdoctor) called Sanyanga who lived in this mountainous region during the early part of the 19th century.

The founder of the original country of Rhodesia, Cecil John Rhodes, first visited Nyanga in 1897. Captivated by the unspoilt beauty of the area, he immediately purchased a parcel of farms totalling 40 000 ha and then proceeded to import cattle from Mozambique and develop extensive plantations of apple and fruit trees.

When he died in 1902, Rhodes bequeathed most of the estate to the nation, and this now forms the Rhodes Nyanga National Park. Rhodes's original farmhouse has been meticulously preserved, and is now the Rhodes Inyanga Hotel. Housed in the original stables is a fascinating museum that focuses on Rhodes's life and his achievements.

Nyanga is essentially a scenic area with excellent trails and walks. The steep slopes of Inyangani can be reached only on foot and it is advisable to plan carefully as venturing onto the mountain when there is a mist is not only dangerous but also forbidden. The slopes are prone to sudden, torrential downpours, dense mists and attendant dangers which have cost a number of mountaineers their lives.

Inyangani and the surrounding mountain peaks of Nyanga are the birthplace of several great rivers – such as the Pungwe, Odzi, Gairezi, Nyangombe and Mtarazi – which cascade down the precipitous mountain gorges (sometimes via spectacular waterfalls) on their journey down to the Indian Ocean.

The natural vegetation of the area has been largely replaced by exotic species of trees such as pine, eucalyptus and wattle. What natural vegetation remains – stunted woodlands, lowland forest and heath – bears many similarities to that of the southern Cape. Regrettably, the remaining indigenous growth is rapidly being eroded by frequent fires and the incursion of various species of alien vegetation. This in turn is threatening many of the birds and animals that migrate seasonally between the mountains and the park.

Many of the rivers flowing through this area have been dammed and stocked with a variety of trout. Rainbow, brown and brook trout provide fly fishermen with some of the best trout fishing in Africa.

The region is indebted to Colonel MacIlwaine, who was the driving force behind the development of the trout industry, and the building of Troutbeck Inn, one of the country's oldest hotels. About 2 km before the Troutbeck Inn is a gravel road leading to World's View, whose name is self-explanatory!

White water cascades down the Nyangombe Falls, situated within the Nyanga National Park.

Where to stay

Two of the oldest established hotels in the area are the *Troutbeck Inn*, PO Box 1, Troutbeck; tel (298) 305/6; and the *Rhodes Nyanga Hotel*, Cecil Rhodes's original homestead in the area – write to Private Bag 8024N, Rusape; tel (298) 377. Other hotels include the *Montclair Casino Hotel*, PO Box 10 Juliasdale; tel (29) 441/6; the *Nyanga Holiday Hotel*, PO Box 19, Nyanga; tel (298) 336 or 339; and the *Pine Tree Inn*, PO Box 1, Juliasdale; tel (29) 25916.

Private holiday cottages can be rented in Nyanga. National Parks offer fully equipped and serviced lodges at the Rhodes, Mare and Udu dams. There is a caravan site at the Mare River, and a camping and caravan site at Nyangombe River on the Vyanga village road, 2 km past the Rhodes Dam turnoff. Contact the Central Booking Office, Department of National Parks and Wildlife Management, PO Box 8151, Causeway, Harare; tel (4) 706077.

From this particular vantage point, hundreds of metres above the surrounding plains, you can – on a clear day – 'see forever'.

Nyanga is a region which has been inhabited by man since the Stone Age and is rich in ruins of fascinating and as yet unidentified origin. Controversy still surrounds the remnants of stone walls, enclosures, irrigation furrows and terraces that are spread out over an area of 80 sq km. Who the builders were remains a mystery.

One theory is that the builders were ancestors of the Karango people who today live in the warmer lowlands. Other theories suggest that the level of sophistication evident in the structure of the ruins ties them to Great Zimbabwe. The real story may never be known, and herein lies the mystery and the fascination of any abandoned settlement – a place full of whispers, shadows and imaginings!

(Above) Although much of the natural vegetation of Nyanga has been replaced by exotic species, there are still many pockets of indigenous forest remaining. (Left) A lone fisherman tries his luck in one of Nyanga's many lakes.

Nyanga at a glance (map page 288)

How to get there: Air Zimbabwe and South African Airways offer regular flights between Johannesburg and Harare, and Zimbabwe and South Africa are connected by excellent roads. Situated in Zimbabwe's Eastern Highlands, Nyanga can be reached from Mutare (105 km), Harare (268 km) or from Bulawayo (682 km).

Weather: Summer days can be extremely hot, though the nights are generally cool. Nyanga can be bitterly cold during the short winter months.

What to do: Walking, climbing, exploring, fishing, swimming, nature-watching and boating.

A number of tour operators, such as United Touring Company, offer minibus trips from Harare into the Eastern Highlands, including Nyanga. For more information, contact UTC at PO Box 2914, Harare; tel (4) 793701.

Special attractions: Nyanga is renowned for its fishing. Year-round fishing is allowed with a permit (obtainable from the office at the camping ground) at Mare, Udu and Rhodes dams. *Troutbeck Inn* has an excellent golf course. Tours of the tea and coffee plantations can be arranged.

More information: Write to the Zimbabwe Tourist Board, PO Box 9398, Johannesburg 2000; tel (011) 3313137.

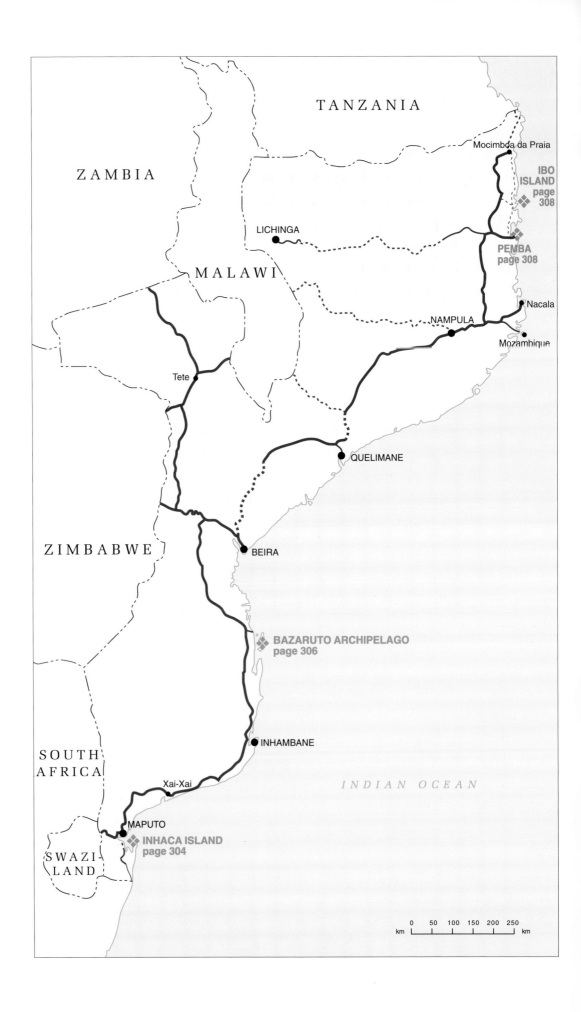

MOZAMBIQUE

Island delights aplenty for the scuba diver and fisherman

Just across the bay from the port of Maputo is Inhaca Island, an attractive holiday destination for anyone who wants to savour the laid-back rhythms of a small, semitropical, Indian Ocean island

POSITIONED AT THE ENTRANCE to Delagoa Bay, Inhaca Island has much to recommend it: it is easily accessible by boat or ferry from the capital of Mozambique, Maputo; it offers some of the best scuba diving and big-game fishing in the world; and it has some excellent two- to three-day hiking trails for the avid walker.

All told, Inhaca has some 100 km of coastline, much of it having some of the best coral reefs in the Mozambique Channel. Snorkelling conditions in the inshore bay areas are excellent for novices and, while visibility may not be as good as it is on the offshore reefs, marine life is plentiful.

The best time to dive here is when the water level is at its highest: you can then catch the tide on its ebb and drift a kilometre or more along the reef. Spearfishing is permitted on the offshore reefs, but is prohibited in the immediate vicinity of Inhaca, which has been declared a national park. Be warned that the park staff are very active, and dedicated to their appointed task of ensuring that the regulations are not broken.

A fascinating experience for scuba divers is exploring the many shipwrecks in the area. One of the most well known of these, a ship torpedoed during the Second World War, is situated on the Bassas Denae, a large reef about 12 km out to sea from Inhaca and easily accessible by boat. The ship is totally broken up, covering an area equivalent to three or four rugby fields. Its jagged remains attract a wide variety of reef fish, including rock cod, grouper, the occasional shoal of barracuda, shark, moray and moorish idol.

Deep-sea fishermen will find themselves well catered for on Inhaca by Gone Fishin' Safaris, which has an office at the Inhaca Protea Hotel. They have several large ocean-going boats with experienced crews, and all the necessary fishing equipment is provided. Catches in the vicinity of Inhaca are often outstanding, with the island holding several world records for various game fish and shark. Game fish in the area include marlin, sailfish, tuna, dorado, kingfish and barracuda. Game fishing costs are roughly comparable to those in South African waters.

A series of two- or three-day hiking trails forms an important adjunct to aquatic activities on Inhaca. A highlight of the trails are the mangrove swamps

When the tide is out, the locals go down to the beach in search of the succulent white clams that can be dug up from just below the sand's surface.

which cover much of the interior of the island and provide a fascinating array of aquatic life, both above and below water.

The tidal flats at the northern and southern ends of Inhaca are especially interesting due to their fascinating array of shell life. Another drawcard is the abundant wealth of bird life, especially the flocks of flamingos.

Sanddunes provide another dimension of enjoyment. In keeping with the general topography of the East African coast, the seaward east coast of Inhaca Island forms huge rolling dunes abutting the sea. Some of them make for excellent sand surfing and you won't have to dodge a single beach buggy or motorcycle!

Situated just to the northwest of Inhaca Island is another smaller island called Portuguese Island. You can amble across the narrow strait when the tide is low, snorkel in the enclosed lagoon, or be even more adventurous and venture out further towards the reef with flippers, snorkel and mask. However, only do so if the water is clear, since there are sharks in the deeper waters off both of these islands.

Be sure to plan your return carefully since it is too far to swim all the way and, with an incoming tide, the currents can be treacherous in the narrows between the two islands. There are usually many small boats about and you can easily hail one of them from the shore and pay a small fee to be returned to Inhaca.

Other possible activities on the island include water-skiing and windsurfing, and there are also hobie cats available for hire. As is the case along most of the Mozambiquan coastline, the seafood dishes are superb, especially preparations of the famous 'LM' prawn.

Inhaca is a wonderful place to live for virtually no cost at all. You can camp on the beach of your choice, and if you have fishing or scuba diving skills, the sea will provide for most of your eating needs. You can always arrange for a passing canoe to bring you a few additional beers or a carafe of cheap Portuguese *vinho tinto*, paraffin for your lamps, a basketful of *camaroes* (prawns) or a clutch of the delicious white clams that so many of the island women spend their time searching for on the mud flats at low tide.

(Above) The distinctly Arabian lines of lateen-sail boats off the coast of Inhaca.
(Left) A scuba diver has a close encounter with a brilliantly coloured lion fish.

Inhaca Island at a glance (map page 302)

How to get there: From South Africa to Maputo: There are flights every day of the week, except Saturday, between Johannesburg and Maputo with South African Airways and Linhas Aereas de Moçambique being the two carriers serving this route. Good excursion rates are available for short visits. By road you can enter Mozambique through Swaziland (Namaacha) or the more direct route through Ressano Garcia, via Nelspruit and Komatipoort. Avoid driving through Mozambique after dark and check at the border post whether there have been any recent 'incidents'. It is better to travel in convoy, at least as far as Boane. The Mozambique National Touring Company can offer useful advice on how safe it is to drive (see address below). By boat from Maputo to Inhaca Island: There is a fairly inexpensive ferry service from Maputo to Inhaca Island which runs intermittently on Saturday, Sunday, Tuesday and Thursday. The ferry is old and in need of constant repair – but the captain is insistent that it is thoroughly seaworthy! It is also possible to hire a ski-boat

for the trip, but this can be expensive. A number of private ferry services have been launched. They cost more, but are very reliable and do the crossing in one hour instead of three. You can make your bookings through the Mozambique National Touring Company.

Weather: Hot in summer with the rains setting in from November through to April and sometimes even May. July and August are usually windy and unpleasant. Cyclones are sometimes experienced during the early part of the year.

What to do: Snorkelling, scuba diving, big-game fishing, hiking, bird-watching, canoeing, sailing and walking.

Special attractions: The diving and deep-sea fishing.

More information: Contact Gone Fishin' for information on tours and accommodation: PO Box 46122, Orange Grove 2119; tel (011) 4851420. For general information, contact the Mozambique National Touring Company, PO Box 31991, Braamfontein 2017; tel (011) 3397275/3397281 or 3394900.

Where to stay

On Inhaca Island there is only one hotel, the *Inhaca Protea,* which offers excursion rates if these are arranged (and preferably paid for) prior to arrival. Write to Inhaca Protea, Inhaca Island, Maputo, Mozambique; tel (092581) 490551.

Alternatively, you can camp on one of the dozens of beaches which encircle the island – most campers prefer the secluded west coast of the island. You may also camp on Portuguese Island. There is a charge for camping on the beach, and permission must be obtained at the local museum or from the maritime authorities. The Mozambique National Touring Company can assist you with the details (see other panel).

If you camp, be sure to take every item you'll be using since there are no shops to speak of. Local restaurants on the island offer cheap, basic fare. Liquor is available at the hotel, but is very expensive – so take your own.

A string of idyllic islands in the tropical sun

The Bazaruto Archipelago, situated just off the coast of Mozambique is one of the world's great fishing spots – and who knows, you might even catch a coelacanth

Where to stay

The hotels and lodges mentioned here offer rates at full board, including tea and coffee. Tariffs usually include all laundry and non-powered water sports, but do not include drinks, boat and tackle hire or hire of diving equipment or diving tuition.

Visitors to Bazaruto Island can enjoy the novelty of staying in an A-frame thatched dwelling situated right on the edge of a palm-lined beach.

Now that the crippling civil war in Mozambique has ended, tourists are again savouring this country's special holiday magic. Arguably the most beautiful area of this country is the Bazaruto Archipelago, an island chain 24 km off the African coast which has remained almost untouched by the war.

For years before the Mozambiquan civil war broke out, these islands were a paradise for big-game fishermen who flocked here from all over the world. The aquamarine sea teems with large fighting fish such as swordfish, shark, barracuda, giant marlin, sailfish, kingfish, queenfish, wahoo, tuna, bonito, dorado and dolphin.

Experts believe that these waters may also be home to the coelacanth – the strange prehistoric fish discovered in the Thirties that was thought to have been extinct for 70 million years. There have been numerous descriptions of fish that match the characteristics of a coelacanth from local fishermen.

The archipelago stretches southwards from the largest island Bazaruto, which gives the chain its name, with the once popular Paradise Island (or Santa Carolina) lying to its west; below the southern tip of Bazaruto is Benguerra, followed by Magaruque (off the coast of Vilanculos), and the tiny island of Bangue, just north of Cabo San Sebastian on the mainland, bringing up the rear.

Accommodation on all the islands (except, of course, Bangue) is provided by rival but nevertheless similar resorts, all pleasantly set out and offering similar facilities and attractions. One thing you'll find common to all is the wonderful array of seafood on offer, as well as old-style Mozambique favourites such as peri-peri chicken. The food provided includes such delicacies as giant prawns (of course), cockles, oysters, crabs, calamari, gamefish steaks and so on.

Flying to your island destination over the archipelago is a wondrous experience: the depth of the sea is reflected in magical shades of aquamarine, turquoise and azure; an occasional dhow adds oriental spice, and the islands themselves lie strung out like jewels, rivalling each other in tropical beauty.

Paradise Island used to be a favourite playground for South Africans, and many have fond memories of sun-filled holidays spent lazing on its beautiful beaches. Accommodation is still provided in the hotel and, although it might not be the same as some remember, Paradise Island itself remains unchanged. It's small, being only 3 km long and just over 0,5 km wide; like the other islands, it is surrounded by clean white sand and fringed with lala and coconut palms and casuarinas. The beaches are safe for swimming and protected from sharks by stunning coral reefs which provide hours of snorkelling.

Dwarfing Paradise Island to the east is Bazaruto, largest of the islands and the most northerly in the archipelago. Long and narrow (about 45 km long and up to 7 km wide in places), it is surrounded by magnificent stretches of beach and in the interior has freshwater lakes that contain crocodile.

Long before the arrival of the Portuguese, Bazaruto was used by Phoenician and Arab traders as a base for expeditions into the hinterland, and lucky beachcombers sometimes find small blue glass trade beads left behind centuries ago. The locals are prepared to trade pearls and small shells; there is even a legend that the Queen of Sheba's pearls were found in these waters, and in the early 19th century a pearling company operated here.

As on the other islands, life revolves around the lodge. It is situated on the northern tip behind a sand spit that reaches several kilometres out to sea. Accommodation is in attractive thatched bungalows with showers, and there is a large thatched communal area close to the beach where food, drink and conversation are plentiful.

Game fishing is still the main attraction and a variety of boats (with skippers) can be hired from the lodge. As it's a large island, there are plenty of walks. These lead through a wide variety of scenery: huge sanddunes, inland lakes (crocodiles

Daily life has changed little over the centuries and a common sight on the islands is that of fishermen hauling in the day's catch.

Bazaruto Island, with its distinctive white sanddunes, is clearly visible from the shore of nearby Benguerra Island.

notwithstanding), light forest and marshy grassland. Several hiking trails have been laid out for visitors, incorporating overnight stops in beach huts.

A narrow channel divides Bazaruto from its neighbour, Benguerra, the second largest island of the group and only recently developed. The Benguela Island Lodge is where everyone stays. The lodge consists of comfortable reed-and-thatch bungalows set in a grove of milkwood trees.

Most visitors come to Benguerra for the big-game fishing and first-timers are welcomed with enthusiasm as well as being encouraged and assisted all the way. Diving and snorkelling are also popular around the island and just off Benguerra is Two-Mile Reef, a submerged Eden which attracts divers from the three main islands of the archipelago. On the landward side are shallow waters that are ideal for snorkelling, and the seaward side provides more of a challenge for scuba divers.

When the tide recedes around Benguerra, many sandbanks and small islands are exposed and it is a pleasure to explore these in the shallow aquamarine water. Beachcombing is particularly rewarding, there being a good chance of finding beautiful, fragile pansy shells, cowries and cone shells. Old porcelain shards from shipwrecks have also been discovered. A bonus for wildlife enthusiasts are the flocks of flamingos, the white-chinned petrel, osprey and redshank.

South of Benguerra is Magaruque. In contrast to Benguerra, which mainly caters for anglers, Ilha de Magaruque is primarily a diving resort. Nevertheless, anglers are also well provided for, and there are boats and tackle for hire. For divers, numerous stunning coral reefs lie beneath the warm tropical waters, from House Reef right in front of the hotel to excursions to Two-Mile Reef and San Sebastian. Apparently some unknown coral reefs are still waiting to be discovered in this area.

From Magaruque, you can arrange to explore the southernmost island in the archipelago, the uninhabited island of Bangue, comprising luminous sandy flats and sparkling dunes surrounded by an azure sea and some remarkable reefs of its own.

The Bazaruto Archipelago at a glance (map page 302)

How to get there: Although it may be possible for intrepid adventurers to reach the archipelago by road (in convoy) to the coast and then to try to hire a dhow, it is far better to choose an established tour company (see information below). Those with time and money to spare can take advantage of island-hopping yacht charters around the archipelago; however, before you do so, be sure to examine the charter company's credentials carefully.

Weather: The Bazaruto Archipelago falls within the tropics and can be very hot in summer. It never gets cold, but at night in winter you might need a jersey. Tropical storms are always a possibility.

What to do: If swimming, beachcombing,

game fishing and diving are not enough for you, the various resorts in the archipelago offer numerous other water sports – such as sailing, parasailing, boardsailing, tubing and water-skiing.

Special attractions: The tropical waters and everything in them.

More information: Mozambique National Touring Company, PO Box 31991, Braamfontein 2017; tel (011) 3397275/3397281/3394900.

Benguela Island Holidays, PO Box 87416, Houghton 2041; tel (011) 4832734/5.

Bonaventure Tour Operators, PO Box 84540, Greenside 2034; tel (011) 7870219.

Saltwater Anglers, PO Box 38359, Point, Durban 4069; tel (031) 328982.

A dream destination for fishermen and divers

Lying just south of the Tanzanian border in northern Mozambique, the coastal town of Pemba – and the nearby island of Ibo – epitomise the Africa that some people can only dream about

PEMBA – known as Porto Amelia during the colonial period – was once regarded by Portuguese civil servants as being the most sought-after posting in Portuguese East Africa – or Mozambique, as it is known nowadays.

Today, the greatest attraction of Pemba is the big-game fishing. Marine bounty includes dorado, blue marlin, sailfish, tunny (by the boatload), kingfish, barracuda and as many varieties of sharks and rays as you care to mention. In fact, the fishing and the diving at Pemba are reputed to be so good that it is beyond comparison with most other southern African resorts.

One of the great joys of Pemba is the opportunity of chartering a dhow-like boat (complete with skipper) for a mere few rands a day, and sailing northwards to Ibo or any one of the other 20 or so outer islands, many of them uninhabited. It takes a week or so to get to Ibo and back, so allow for a leisurely pace, fishing or diving along the way.

Pemba itself is a town of about 20 000 people. Many of them are refugees from the bush and almost all live on the beautiful isthmus jutting into the entrance to Pemba Bay. Nowadays, many of the buildings are covered with moss and in a poor state. Running water and adequate toilet facilites are found only at the Complexa Nautilus Hotel.

However, despite the dilapidated condition of the town, it still retains something of its elegant, old colonial flavour, especially in buildings such as the open-air café, the once splendidly Iberian-tiled esplanade along the bay, and the one-time house of the Portuguese regional commander (today used by the chief political commissar of the region).

The pristine beaches of Pemba are backed by the remains of tropical palm plantations that – because of the vagaries of two decades of civil war – are now mostly overrun by the encroaching jungle. Some really outstanding coves, beaches, shallows and tropical hideaways are to be found among the islands and reefs to the north of Pemba. These stretch for several hundred kilometres and can be visited at any time as there are few security problems this far north.

This stretch of coast compares with any other group of coral atolls in the Indian Ocean – in places

Who needs suburbia? With the sea right at their doorstep, the fishermen of Pemba have an idyllic place in the sun that must make many a city dweller green with envy.

it's just like the Great Barrier Reef. Diving in these shallow crystalline waters is outstanding, with a plentiful population of skates, rays, porpoises, moray eels and game fish. Out in deeper waters the diver may encounter large shoals of marlin, tunny, black- and white-tip reef sharks and, occasionally, swordfish. There are also whales some months of the year, and whale sharks gather here during the southern summer. It has been suggested that they migrate all the way across the Indian Ocean from Australasia, where they produce their young.

If you like ancient Portuguese castles, mildewed 17th- and 18th-century mosques and cathedrals, and palaces and colonial buildings that are mouldering to ruin, you'll love Ibo Island. As already mentioned, you can sail here or, alternatively, catch the daily half-hour flight from Pemba.

Be warned, though, that Ibo is very basic. Many of the buildings are sorely in need of attention and there is only one vehicle on the island – a tractor. On arrival by air, the pilot usually circles the administration block to warn officials that he intends to land. The tractor is then sent (pulling a trailer fitted with two loose wooden benches) to fetch the passengers. When it's not on tourism duty, the tractor collects garbage around the island. If it is not functioning for some reason, visitors have to undertake a 10-minute walk to or from the airstrip – a journey that can be exhausting in the humid heat that prevails.

Apart from the harbour, which at the turn of the tide swarms with Arab dhows and other sailing craft (many of them from Tanzania), the most interesting spectacle on Ibo Island is the old Portuguese castle that dates from the 16th century. Until a year or two ago, it was used as a high-security institution for political prisoners. Word has it that the inmates were usually bundled off in chains into the jungle when visitors or representatives of the International Red Cross arrived.

The castle is now, however, the centre of a burgeoning industry in silver filigree jewellery, and real bargains can be had. The silver used in these

A Portuguese cannon lies in pieces in the grounds of the Ibo Fort. A number of other cannons are, however, still in 'battle-ready' position on the ramparts.

delicately crafted pieces comes mostly from molten Maria Theresa dollars taken from an unidentified East Indiaman that went down on this shoreline a few centuries ago. None of the locals will reveal the wreck's location, but everyone knows that it continues to yield its bounty to those in the know.

The island reflects a way of life that has changed little down the centuries. The water, drawn from the local well, is slightly brackish but is said to be safe to drink. However, it would probably be best to take water purification tablets, and to boil water before drinking or using for cooking. Palm wine is the only alcoholic drink that is tolerated on this very Islamic island. The island hierarchy – apart from the local commissar – is still structured in accordance with local custom, and that includes palm wine on all ceremonial occasions!

Pemba and Ibo Island at a glance (map page 302)

How to get there: There are regular flights from Johannesburg to the capital of Maputo, and two flights per week to Pemba from Maputo Airport on new Boeing 737 300s recently acquired by Linhas Aereas de Moçambique (the national airline). Driving is possible – a four-wheel-drive vehicle is not essential. If you want to go from Pemba to Ibo Island, either hire someone to sail you there in a dhow or take one of the daily flights.

If you are travelling in a large party, discounts on Linhas Aereas de Moçambique flights from Johannesburg can be negotiated, as well as discounts at the hotel at Pemba.
Weather: Hot, humid, tropical climate for most of the year.
What to do: Fish, swim, enjoy all the delights of a tropical paradise (albeit a slightly primitive one).
Special attractions: Game-fishing and scuba diving. At Pemba and Ibo, fishing boats can be hired by the hour, day, week or month. They are rented along with their owners, who know the reefs well.
Special precautions: Malaria is endemic to the area and you need to take precautionary drugs before entering it. At night, a mosquito net is essential.

Because of the poor state of Mozambique's health services, it is advisable to take a fairly comprehensive medical kit with you – especially if there are children in your party.

This should include antibiotics for various stomach ailments (such as diarrhoea and amoebic problems), as well as an antibiotic suitable for treating burns or infection from coral cuts. (You may need a doctor's prescription for these.) Take adequate supplies of electrolyte (such as Electrona) in case of dehydration (over-depletion of body fluids, for instance, as a result of chronic diarrhoea). If you anticipate travelling by road, include saline drips, needles, bandages and dressings (in case of a serious accident). A medical insurance policy is advisable to cover the contingency of a seriously injured person needing to be airlifted back to South Africa. There is a constant risk of sunburn, so remember to pack a sunhat and a protective sunscreen cream.

Try to avoid drinking untreated local water. Bottled water and South African and local beer are available at a reasonable cost. Ensure that the seal of the bottled water is opened in your presence.

Be circumspect about the local palm wine – it can be a very 'heady' experience. Also worth noting is that palm wine containers seem rarely to be washed. Spirits are very expensive, so take your own.
More information: Mozambique National Touring Company, PO Box 31991, Braamfontein 2017; tel (011) 3397275/ 3397281/3394900.

Where to stay

The *Complexa Nautilus Hotel* is the only holiday resort in Pemba. It offers bungalow accommodation. Bookings should be made through the Mozambique National Touring Company (see other panel for address). Local private houses are available for hire in Pemba, but lengthy negotiations are often necessary to achieve a reasonable rental. Many of these homes have spectacular sea views.

On Ibo Island, houses are occasionally available for rent, but negotiations can take place only after you arrive. Be sure to take water-purifying tablets and the basic toilet necessities – such as soap and toilet paper. Local food is of good quality and all seafood is fresh, being brought in daily by the local fishermen. There is an abundance of cheap fresh fruit.

Finding a secret place to cater for your interests

This easy-to-use chart links the places in this book to a variety of specific interests, such as natural wonders, museums, bird-watching, hiking, and watersports. In order to find a place that caters for your particular interest, look along the top section of the chart. For example, if you are fascinated by battlefields, look for the column headed 'Battlefields and military interest' and then down the relevant column until you find a symbol. Once you have located the symbol, look across to the left hand or right hand column for the name and page number of the place.

	Page number	Battlefields and military interest	Bird-watching	Camping	Churches, missions and religious buildings	Country towns and villages	Diving	Ethnic interest	Fishing	Flora and gardens	Hiking, walking and climbing
NORTHERN/WESTERN CAPE	8										
Kalahari Gemsbok National Park	10		✤	✤							
Kuruman	12			✤	✤	✤					✤
Augrabies Falls National Park	14		✤	✤							✤
The Orange River	16		✤								
Calvinia	18		✤	✤	✤	✤				✤	✤
Lambert's Bay	20		✤				✤		✤	✤	
Elands Bay	22		✤				✤		✤		✤
Wuppertal	24			✤	✤	✤		✤			
Algeria	26		✤	✤					✤	✤	✤
Citrusdal	28					✤			✤		✤
Rolfontein Nature Reserve	30		✤							✤	✤
Karoo National Park	32		✤	✤						✤	✤
SOUTHWESTERN CAPE	34										
Grootwinterhoek Wilderness Area	36		✤							✤	✤
Bain's Kloof	38		✤	✤						✤	✤
Du Toitskloof	40		✤							✤	✤
Robben Island	42	✤	✤		✤						
Bertram House	44									✤	
Groote Schuur Residence	46									✤	
Rondevlei Nature Reserve	48		✤								
Police Cultural History Museum	50	✤									
The Manganese Mine	52		✤								✤
Sandy Bay	54		✤				✤		✤	✤	✤
The Village Museum	56					✤		✤			
Genadendal	58		✤	✤	✤	✤		✤		✤	✤
McGregor	60		✤			✤			✤	✤	✤
Elim	62			✤		✤		✤		✤	✤
Cape Agulhas	64		✤	✤			✤		✤		✤
Shipwreck Museum	66			✤	✤	✤					
Drostdy Museum	68	✤				✤		✤		✤	✤
Lover's Walk	70		✤			✤				✤	✤
Tradouw Pass	72		✤		✤					✤	✤
Boosmansbos Wilderness Area	74		✤							✤	✤
SOUTHERN CAPE	76										
Seweweekspoort	78		✤							✤	✤
Calitzdorp	80		✤	✤	✤	✤				✤	✤
Prince Albert	82				✤	✤					
Swartberg Pass	84		✤							✤	✤
Bartolomeu Dias Museum	86		✤							✤	
Montagu Pass	88		✤							✤	✤
Millwood	90		✤	✤						✤	✤
Baviaanskloof	92		✤	✤	✤	✤		✤		✤	✤

	Page number	Battlefields and military interest	Bird-watching	Camping	Churches, missions and religious buildings	Country towns and villages	Diving	Ethnic interest	Fishing	Flora and gardens	Hiking, walking and climbing
EASTERN CAPE/TRANSKEI	94										
Burgersdorp	96	✤	✤	✤	✤	✤		✤	✤	✤	✤
Mountain Zebra National Park	98		✤	✤						✤	✤
Somerset East	100		✤		✤	✤		✤		✤	✤
Adelaide	102	✤			✤	✤		✤		✤	✤
Uitenhage	104	✤	✤	✤	✤	✤		✤		✤	✤
Apple Express	106		✤			✤				✤	✤
The Observatory Museum	108										
Forts Route	110	✤									
Bathurst	112	✤		✤	✤	✤		✤			✤
Water's Meeting Nature Reserve	114		✤						✤	✤	✤
Hogsback	116	✤	✤		✤			✤	✤	✤	✤
Keiskammahoek	118	✤			✤	✤		✤	✤	✤	✤
Amatola Hiking Trail	120		✤					✤	✤	✤	✤
Kaffrarian Museum	122	✤			✤	✤		✤			
Mazeppa Bay	124		✤	✤		✤	✤	✤	✤	✤	✤
Coffee Bay	126	✤	✤			✤	✤	✤	✤	✤	✤
Port Grosvenor	128						✤	✤	✤	✤	✤
Naudésnek/Rhodes	130		✤	✤		✤				✤	✤
NATAL	132										
Spioenkop	134	✤	✤	✤				✤	✤		✤
Giant's Castle Game Reserve	136		✤	✤				✤	✤	✤	✤
Sani Pass	138		✤					✤			✤
Himeville	140	✤	✤	✤		✤		✤	✤	✤	✤
Banana Express	142					✤		✤			✤
Hare Krishna Temple of Understanding	144				✤					✤	
Old Fort	146	✤			✤					✤	✤
Muckleneuk	148							✤		✤	
Karkloof Falls	150		✤	✤					✤	✤	✤
Harold Johnson Nature Reserve	152	✤	✤					✤		✤	✤
Mgungundlovu/Dingaanstat	154	✤						✤			
Lake Sibaya	156		✤				✤	✤	✤	✤	
Kosi Bay Nature Reserve	158		✤	✤			✤	✤	✤	✤	✤
Ndumo Game Reserve	160		✤							✤	
Itala Nature Reserve	162		✤	✤				✤		✤	✤
Ntendeka Wilderness Area	164		✤	✤				✤			✤
Blood River	166	✤						✤			
Talana Museum	168	✤				✤		✤			
Maria Ratschitz Mission	170				✤			✤			
Rorke's Drift	172	✤		✤	✤	✤		✤			✤
Msinga District	174	✤				✤		✤		✤	
ORANGE FREE STATE/LESOTHO	176										
Willem Pretorius Game Reserve	178		✤	✤				✤	✤	✤	✤
Winburg	180	✤			✤	✤			✤		
Orange Free State National Botanical Garden	182	✤	✤	✤				✤		✤	✤
War Museum of the Boer Republics	184	✤						✤			
Franklin Nature Reserve	186	✤	✤							✤	✤
Ladybrand	188	✤	✤	✤	✤	✤		✤		✤	✤
Ficksburg	190	✤	✤		✤	✤			✤	✤	✤
Clarens	192	✤	✤	✤		✤		✤		✤	✤
Golden Gate Highlands National Park	194	✤	✤	✤				✤		✤	✤
Witsieshoek	196		✤			✤		✤	✤	✤	✤
Malealea	198		✤			✤		✤	✤	✤	✤
Qacha's Nek	200		✤		✤	✤		✤	✤	✤	✤

Historic buildings and places	Islands	Mountain locations	Museums	Natural wonders	Roads, routes and passes	Rock art and archaeological interest	Seaside locations	Watersports	Wildlife and game parks	Page number	
										94	EASTERN CAPE/TRANSKEI
❖		❖	❖			❖		❖	❖	96	Burgersdorp
❖		❖		❖		❖		❖	❖	98	Mountain Zebra National Park
❖		❖	❖	❖	❖					100	Somerset East
			❖							102	Adelaide
❖			❖	❖				❖	❖	104	Uitenhage
		❖		❖	❖					106	Apple Express
❖			❖							108	The Observatory Museum
❖			❖	❖	❖					110	Forts Route
❖			❖							112	Bathurst
			❖	❖				❖	❖	114	Water's Meeting Nature Reserve
❖		❖		❖	❖				❖	116	Hogsback
❖		❖								118	Keiskammahoek
				❖					❖	120	Amatola Hiking Trail
❖			❖						❖	122	Kaffrarian Museum
				❖			❖	❖	❖	124	Mazeppa Bay
❖	❖			❖			❖	❖	❖	126	Coffee Bay
❖				❖			❖	❖		128	Port Grosvenor
❖		❖		❖	❖					130	Naudésnek/Rhodes
										132	NATAL
❖			❖					❖	❖	134	Spioenkop
		❖		❖		❖		❖	❖	136	Giant's Castle Game Reserve
❖		❖		❖	❖	❖				138	Sani Pass
❖		❖	❖		❖	❖		❖	❖	140	Himeville
			❖		❖		❖			142	Banana Express
										144	Hare Krishna Temple of Understanding
❖			❖							146	Old Fort
❖			❖							148	Muckleneuk
				❖				❖	❖	150	Karkloof Falls
❖									❖	152	Harold Johnson Nature Reserve
❖			❖							154	Mgungundlovu/Dingaanstat
				❖			❖	❖	❖	156	Lake Sibaya
				❖			❖	❖	❖	158	Kosi Bay Nature Reserve
				❖					❖	160	Ndumo Game Reserve
				❖				❖	❖	162	Itala Nature Reserve
		❖		❖				❖	❖	164	Ntendeka Wilderness Area
❖			❖		❖					166	Blood River
❖			❖	❖						168	Talana Museum
❖		❖	❖		❖					170	Maria Ratschitz Mission
❖		❖	❖		❖					172	Rorke's Drift
❖		❖	❖		❖					174	Msinga District
										176	ORANGE FREE STATE/LESOTHO
❖			❖			❖		❖	❖	178	Willem Pretorius Game Reserve
❖										180	Winburg
❖		❖		❖	❖				❖	182	Orange Free State National Botanical Garden
❖			❖							184	War Museum of the Boer Republics
❖					❖				❖	186	Franklin Nature Reserve
❖		❖	❖	❖		❖		❖		188	Ladybrand
❖		❖	❖	❖		❖		❖	❖	190	Ficksburg
❖		❖		❖		❖			❖	192	Clarens
❖		❖		❖		❖		❖	❖	194	Golden Gate Highlands National Park
		❖		❖	❖	❖			❖	196	Witsieshoek
		❖		❖		❖		❖		198	Malealea
❖		❖		❖	❖	❖		❖	❖	200	Qacha's Nek

	Page number	Battlefields and military interest	Bird-watching	Camping	Churches, missions and religious buildings	Country towns and villages	Diving	Ethnic interest	Fishing	Flora and gardens	Hiking, walking and climbing
SOUTHERN TRANSVAAL	202										
Potchefstroom Museum	204	✦			✦			✦	✦		
The SA National Railway and Steam Museum	206	✦									
Melrose Wild Bird Sanctuary	208		✦							✦	✦
Bernberg Museum of Costume	210										
Melville Koppies	212		✦					✦		✦	✦
The Parktown/Westcliff Walk	214									✦	✦
Smuts House Museum	216	✦	✦							✦	✦
The Sammy Marks Museum	218									✦	
Wonderboom Nature Reserve	220	✦	✦					✦		✦	✦
Borakalalo National Park	222		✦	✦					✦	✦	✦
Botshabelo	224	✦	✦	✦	✦			✦		✦	✦
EASTERN TRANSVAAL/SWAZILAND	226										
Alanglade	228									✦	
Lydenburg	230	✦	✦	✦	✦	✦		✦	✦	✦	✦
Makobulaan Nature Reserve	232		✦	✦						✦	✦
Lowveld National Botanical Garden	234		✦							✦	✦
Belhaven Museum	236									✦	
Fortuna Mine Trail	238		✦							✦	✦
Mlilwane Wildlife Sanctuary	240		✦	✦				✦		✦	✦
Hlane Royal National Park	242		✦	✦						✦	✦
Mkhaya Nature Reserve	244		✦	✦						✦	✦
NORTHERN TRANSVAAL	246										
Mapungubwe Hill	248							✦		✦	✦
Messina Nature Reserve	250		✦	✦						✦	✦
Punda Maria	252		✦	✦				✦		✦	✦
Mabudashango Hiking Trail	254		✦					✦		✦	✦
Bakoni Malapa Museum	256							✦		✦	✦
Wolkberg Wilderness Area	258		✦	✦				✦		✦	✦
Magoebaskloof	260		✦	✦				✦	✦	✦	✦
Debengeni Falls	262		✦					✦		✦	✦
Modjadji	264		✦		✦			✦		✦	✦
Hans Merensky Nature Reserve	266		✦	✦				✦		✦	✦
NAMIBIA	268										
Caprivi Strip	270										
Cape Cross	272		✦						✦		✦
Kuiseb Canyon	274		✦	✦				✦	✦		✦
Sesriem Canyon/Sossusvlei	276		✦	✦							✦
Kolmanskop	278										✦
BOTSWANA	280										
Tsodilo Hills	282			✦				✦		✦	✦
Mombo, Okavango Delta	284		✦	✦				✦		✦	✦
Makgadikgadi Salt Pans	286		✦	✦				✦		✦	
ZIMBABWE	288										
Mana Pools National Park	290		✦	✦					✦	✦	✦
Chinhoyi Caves	292	✦		✦				✦			
Chizarira National Park	294		✦	✦				✦		✦	✦
Matobo Hills	296		✦	✦				✦	✦	✦	✦
Vumba	298		✦	✦				✦		✦	✦
Nyanga	300		✦	✦				✦	✦	✦	✦
MOZAMBIQUE	302										
Inhaca Island	304		✦	✦			✦		✦		✦
Bazaruto Archipelago	306		✦	✦			✦	✦	✦	✦	✦
Pemba / Ibo Island	308			✦	✦	✦	✦	✦	✦	✦	✦

Historic buildings and places	Islands	Mountain locations	Museums	Natural wonders	Roads, routes and passes	Rock art and archaeological interest	Seaside locations	Watersports	Wildlife and game parks	Page number	
										202	**SOUTHERN TRANSVAAL**
❖			❖			❖				204	Potchefstroom Museum
			❖							206	The SA National Railway and Steam Museum
										208	Melrose Wild Bird Sanctuary
			❖							210	Bernberg Museum of Costume
						❖				212	Melville Koppies
❖										214	The Parktown/Westcliff Walk
❖			❖							216	Smuts House Museum
❖			❖							218	The Sammy Marks Museum
❖				❖		❖			❖	220	Wonderboom Nature Reserve
					❖				❖	222	Borakalalo National Park
❖			❖						❖	224	Botshabelo
										226	**EASTERN TRANSVAAL/SWAZILAND**
❖			❖							228	Alanglade
❖			❖			❖			❖	230	Lydenburg
❖		❖		❖		❖			❖	232	Makobulaan Nature Reserve
										234	Lowveld National Botanical Garden
❖			❖							236	Belhaven Museum
❖		❖				❖				238	Fortuna Mine Trail
		❖							❖	240	Mlilwane Wildlife Sanctuary
					❖				❖	242	Hlane Royal National Park
					❖			❖	❖	244	Mkhaya Nature Reserve
										246	**NORTHERN TRANSVAAL**
❖		❖		❖		❖				248	Mapungubwe Hill
			❖		❖	❖			❖	250	Messina Nature Reserve
					❖	❖			❖	252	Punda Maria
❖		❖		❖				❖	❖	254	Mabudashango Hiking Trail
			❖			❖				256	Bakoni Malapa Museum
		❖		❖		❖			❖	258	Wolkberg Wilderness Area
		❖		❖	❖			❖		260	Magoebaskloof
		❖		❖				❖		262	Debengeni Falls
❖				❖		❖			❖	264	Modjadji
	❖		❖		❖			❖	❖	266	Hans Merensky Nature Reserve
										268	**NAMIBIA**
										270	Caprivi Strip
							❖		❖	272	Cape Cross
				❖	❖		❖		❖	274	Kuiseb Canyon
				❖	❖				❖	276	Sesriem Canyon/Sossusvlei
❖			❖							278	Kolmanskop
										280	**BOTSWANA**
❖				❖		❖			❖	282	Tsodilo Hills
	❖			❖	❖				❖	284	Mombo, Okavango Delta
	❖			❖	❖	❖			❖	286	Makgadikgadi Salt Pans
										288	**ZIMBABWE**
				❖				❖	❖	290	Mana Pools National Park
				❖		❖				292	Chinhoyi Caves
		❖		❖	❖				❖	294	Chizarira National Park
❖		❖		❖		❖			❖	296	Matobo Hills
		❖		❖	❖				❖	298	Vumba
❖		❖	❖	❖		❖		❖	❖	300	Nyanga
										302	**MOZAMBIQUE**
	❖						❖	❖		304	Inhaca Island
❖	❖			❖			❖	❖	❖	306	Bazaruto Archipelago
❖				❖			❖	❖		308	Pemba / Ibo Island

INDEX

PICTURE CREDITS

Picture credits for each page read from top to bottom, using the top as the reference point. Where the tops of two or more pictures are on the same level, credits read from left to right.

Abbreviations:
AAI Anka Agency International
ABPL Anthony Bannister Photo Library
AI African Images
PA Photo Access

Opposite title page: Trevor Barrett

Northern/Western Cape
10 Shawn Benjamin, Gerald Cubitt, Lex Hes. 11 A J Stevens/PA. 12 David Bristow. 13 Both CL Gittens/PA. 14 Gerald Cubitt. 15 Mark van Aardt. 16 Anthony Bannister/ABPL, Shawn Benjamin. 17 Patzer/Felix Unite. 18 Di Paice. 19 Gerald Cubitt. 20 Walter Knirr. 21 Peter Pickford. 22 Steve Morton, David Bristow. 23 Ken Gerhardt/PA, Peter Pickford. 24 Gerald Cubitt. 25 John Yeld/PA, Jean Morris. 26 T V Bulpin. 27 Both David Bristow. 28 Shawn Benjamin, Jean Morris. 29 Mark van Aardt. 30 Gerald Cubitt. 31 Gerald Cubitt. 32 Walter Knirr. 33 Walter Knirr.

Southwestern Cape
36 Colin Paterson-Jones, Mark van Aardt. 37 Mark van Aardt. 38 Mark van Aardt. 39 Mark van Aardt. 40 Jean Morris. 41 Mark van Aardt, Walter Knirr. 42 Owen Coetzer. 43 Mark van Aardt. 44 Jeannie Mackinnon. 45 Jeannie Mackinnon, Keith Young. 46 Groote Schuur. 47 Both Groote Schuur. 48 Keith Young. 49 Peter Pickford. 50 Shawn Benjamin. 51 Both Shawn Benjamin. 52 Denoon Sieg. 53 Marianne Alexander, Hout Bay Museum. 54 Peter Ribton. 55 Shawn Benjamin. 56 Jean Morris, David Bristow. 57 David Bristow. 58 Keith Young. 59 Keith Young. 60 Reader's Digest. 61 Reader's Digest, David Steele/PA. 62 J Paisley/PA. 63 David Steele/PA, Gerald Cubitt. 64 Walter Knirr. 65 Walter Knirr. 66 P Wagner/PA. 67 Keith Young. 68 Keith Young. 69 Keith Young. 70 Cloete Breytenbach. 71 Cloete Breytenbach. 72 David Steele/PA. 73 Mark van Aardt. 74 Marianne Alexander. 75 Marianne Alexander.

Southern Cape
78 Walter Knirr. 79 T V Bulpin, Walter Knirr. 80 Mark van Aardt. 81 Walter Knirr/PA. 82 Both David Steele/PA. 83 David Steele/PA. 84 Mark van Aardt. 85 Herman Potgieter/ABPL, Walter Knirr. 86 Colin Paterson-Jones. 87 Colin Paterson-Jones. 88 Mark van Aardt. 89 Peter Ribton. 90 Marianne Alexander. 91 Both Marianne Alexander. 92 Colin Paterson-Jones. 93 Walter Knirr.

Eastern Cape/Transkei
96 Keith Young, Brian Johnson Barker. 97 Don Briscoe. 98 Lorna Stanton/ABPL. 99 Anthony Bannister/ABPL. 100 Somerset East Publicity Association. 101 Somerset East Publicity Association, Colin Urquhart. 102 Dr A J G Black. 103 Brian Johnson Barker, Dr A J G Black. 104 Cape Archives, J Alves/PA. 105 Brian Johnson Barker/Reader's Digest. 106 Larsson/Landmarks. 107 Bob Binnell. 108 Duncan Greaves/Albany Museum. 109 Both Duncan Greaves/Albany Museum. 110 Brian Johnson Barker. 111 Both Brian Johnson Barker. 112 Brian Johnson Barker. 113 Gerald Cubitt, Brian Johnson Barker. 114 Mike Cooke. 115 Mike Cooke. 116 David Bristow. 117 David Bristow. 118 Denver Webb/Ciskei Dept of Education. 119 David Bristow, Frescura/Landmarks. 120 Contour (Ciskei National Nature Conservation & Tourism Board). 121 David Bristow. 122 Gerald Cubitt. 123 Cape Dept of Nature Conservation. 124 David Rogers. 125 Owen Coetzer, David Bristow. 126 Kathryn Costello. 127 Owen Coetzer. 128 T V Bulpin, Owen Coetzer. 129 Owen Coetzer. 130 Walter Knirr. 131 Duncan Butchart/AI.

Natal
134 Walter Knirr. 135 Roger de la Harpe/PA. 136 Walter Knirr. 137 Colin Paterson-Jones. 138 Jean Morris. 139 Walter Knirr. 140 Roger de la Harpe, Walter Knirr. 142 Mark van Aardt, Hennie Mattheus/AAI. 143 A A Jorgensen. 144 Mark van Aardt. 145 Mark van Aardt. 146 Both Keith Young. 147 Keith Young. 148 Trevor Barrett. 149 Trevor Barrett. 150 Keith Young, Walter Knirr. 151 Walter Knirr. 152 Gerald Cubitt. 153 Both Gerald Cubitt. 154 Owen Coetzer. 155 Owen Coetzer, Africana

Museum. 156 Nigel Dennis/ABPL. 157 Herman Potgieter/ABPL. 158 Both Trevor Barrett. 159 Trevor Barrett. 160 Malcolm Funston/ABPL. 161 All Trevor Barrett. 162 Trevor Barrett. 163 Keith Young. 164 Michael Peter. 165 Michael Peter. 166 Walter Knirr/PA. 167 Voortrekker Museum, Pietermaritzburg. 168 Talana Museum. 169 Owen Coetzer, Talana Museum. 170 Talana Museum. 171 Talana Museum. 172 Walter Knirr/PA. 173 Roger de la Harpe. 174 Roger de la Harpe/Natal Parks Board. 175 Talana Museum, Jean Morris.

Orange Free State/Lesotho
178 T V Bulpin. 179 Both Gertie Joubert/OFS Provincial Admin. Directorate of Nature & Environmental Conservation. 180 Brian Johnson Barker. 181 Roger de la Harpe/ABPL, Brian Johnson Barker. 182 Both Susan Imrie Ross. 183 Susan Imrie Ross. 184 Lanz van Hörsten. 185 War Museum of the Boer Republics, Brian Johnson Barker. 186 Cape Dept of Nature & Environmental Conservation. 187 Both Keith Young. 188 David Bristow. 189 Mark van Aardt. 190 Herman Potgieter/ABPL. 191 Walter Knirr. 192 Walter Knirr. 193 Keith Young. 194 Walter Knirr. 195 Walter Knirr/PA. 196 Mark van Aardt. 197 Mark van Aardt. 198 Dirk Schwager. 199 Dirk Schwager. 200 Dirk Schwager. 201 Dirk Schwager.

Southern Transvaal
204 Potchefstroom Museum. 205 Potchefstroom Museum. 206 Jane-Anne Hobbs. 207 Both Jane-Anne Hobbs. 208 Ken Newman, Peter Steyn. 209 Jeannie Mackinnon. 210 Africana Museum. 211 Africana Museum. 212 Gerald Cubitt, Jane-Anne Hobbs. 213 Jane-Anne Hobbs. 214 Beth Peterson/AI. 215 Both Beth Peterson/AI. 216 Jane-Anne Hobbs. 217 Both Jane-Anne Hobbs. 218 Jane-Anne Hobbs. 219 Jane-Anne Hobbs, Sammy Marks Museum. 220 Anthony Bannister/ABPL. 221 Gerald Cubitt. 222 David Steele/PA. 223 H Rayner. 224 Both Jeannie Mackinnon. 225 Walter Knirr.

Eastern Transvaal/Swaziland
228 John Paisley/PA. 229 Both Brian Johnson Barker. 230 Peter Pickford.

231 Both Jeannie Mackinnon. 232 Jane-Anne Hobbs. 233 Jane-Anne Hobbs. 234 Jane-Anne Hobbs. 235 Both Jane-Anne Hobbs. 236 Mark van Aardt. 237 Mark van Aardt. 238 Both Jane-Anne Hobbs. 239 Jane-Anne Hobbs. 240 Ted Reilly/Big Game Parks. 241 T V Bulpin. 242 Big Game Parks. 243 Big Game Parks. 244 Peter Pickford. 245 Lex Hes/Big Game Parks.

Northern Transvaal
248 University of Pretoria. 249 University of Pretoria. 250 Mark van Aardt. 251 Lanz van Horsten. 252 David Steele/PA. 253 Malcolm Funston/ABPL. 254 Jean Morris. 255 Walter Knirr. 256 Pietersburg Museum. 257 Pietersburg Museum. 258 Walter Knirr. 260 Walter Knirr. 261 Walter Knirr. 262 Walter Knirr. 263 David Bristow. 264 Jean Morris. 265 Mark van Aardt. 266 Gerald Cubitt. 267 Gerald Cubitt.

Namibia
270 Colin Bell/Wilderness Safaris. 271 Mark van Aardt. 272 Roger de la Harpe. 273 Roger de la Harpe. 274 T V Bulpin. 275 Mark van Aardt. 276 Mark van Aardt, Walter Knirr. 278 Anthony Bannister/ABPL, Marianne Alexander. 279 Mark van Aardt.

Botswana
282 Duncan Butchart/AI. 283 Colin Bell/Wilderness Safaris. 284 Mark van Aardt. 285 Peter Pickford. 286 Gerald Cubitt. 287 Tim Liversedge/ABPL.

Zimbabwe
290 Mark van Aardt. 291 B & L Worsley/PA. 293 Mark van Aardt. 294 Lanz van Hörsten. 295 P Wagner/PA. 296 Both Gerald Cubitt. 297 Gerald Cubitt. 298 Mark Tennant/AI. 299 Mark van Aardt. 300 S J Vincent/PA. 301 Both Peter Pickford.

Mozambique
304 Al Venter. 305 Both Al Venter. 306 Duncan Butchart/AI. 307 Duncan Butchart/AI, Colin Bell/Wilderness Safaris. 308 Al Venter. 309 Al Venter.

Front cover: David Steele/PA
Back cover: Colin Bell/Wilderness Safaris

Reproduction by Hirt & Carter Repro, Cape Town. Printed and bound by C & C Offset Printing Co, Hong Kong.